The Retreat of the Elephants

Other books by Mark Elvin

The Pattern of the Chinese Past. Stanford University Press: Stanford, California. 1973.

Cultural Atlas of China. Facts on File: New York. With Caroline Blunden. 1983 and 1998. (The revised edition is under the 'Checkmark' imprint.)

Another History: Essays on China from a European Perspective. Wild Peony Press and Hawaii University Press: Sydney and Honolulu. 1996.

Changing Stories in the Chinese World. Stanford University Press: Stanford, California. 1997.

Sediments of Time: Environment and Society in Chinese History. Cambridge University Press: New York. Edited with Liu Ts'ui-jung. 1998.

As 'John Dutton' (fiction)

St Giles's Fair. Samara Press: Tarago, NSW, London, and Portola Valley, California. 2000.

Tiger's Island. Samara Press: Tarago, NSW, London, and Portola Valley, California. 2000.

The Retreat of the Elephants

An Environmental History of China

Mark Elvin

Yale University Press *New Haven and London*

For information about this and other Yale University Press publications, please contact:

U.S. Office: sales.press@yale.edu   yalebooks.com
Europe Office: sales@yaleup.co.uk   www.yalebooks.co.uk

Set in Minion by Northern Phototypesetting Co. Ltd, Bolton
Printed in Great Britain by St Edmundsbury Press Ltd, Bury St Edmunds

Library of Congress Cataloging-in-Publication Data

Elvin, Mark
The retreat of the elephants: an environmental history of China / by Mark Elvin.   1st ed.
   p. cm.
Includes bibliographical references and index.
ISBN 0-300-10111-2 (cloth: alk. paper)
1. Human ecology—China—History. 2. Elephants—China—Migration.
3. Deforestation—China—History. 4. Environmental degradation— China—History.
5. China—Environmental conditions. I. Title.
GF656.E48 2004   304.2′0951—dc22   2003017378

A catalogue record for this book is available from the British Library.

10 9 8 7 6 5 4 3 2 1

Dedicated to Dian Montgomerie,
Richard Grove, and Kay Oldfield,

each of whom helped me to see things differently

The straight tree is first to be felled;
First drained dry, the well of sweet water.

"Trees on the Mountains," third century BCE, *Zhuangzi*

Contents

Illustrations

Maps

Figure

Tables

Acknowledgments

Many other authors, friends, and colleagues have helped with the making of this book, either consciously or perhaps unconsciously. Maybe even one or two critics, opponents, and enemies. There is no way for me to be sure of recalling all of them, nor maybe even to be aware of all of them. But I would like to offer my gratitude, sometimes—sadly—only in memory, to those who, I think, have been the most important.

First, to the late Kay Oldfield, of the Soil Association, who taught me while still a boy how to make a compost heap. Also to Rachel Carson's writings, beginning with *The Sea Around Us*; to the *Whole Earth Catalog*, and to the *Ecologist* magazine, founded by Teddy Goldsmith, for all of them provoking me into thinking differently—in what now seems an era long past. If I have gone my own way since, that is where it started.

Second, to those who taught me to read classical Chinese after I graduated in history from Cambridge: Ted Pulleyblank, Denis Twitchett, and Piet van der Loon. The translations in this book are based on their teaching, though they should in no way be held responsible for the idiosyncrasies and imperfections.

Third, to the late Joseph Needham. His inspiration as the founding father of the history of Chinese science and technology—and a personal friend—was crucial, even if—even from the start—my historical vision differed from his. This last was shaped first and foremost by the late Philip Whitting, the Byzantine scholar, who taught me history at St Paul's School, London. A debt never adequately repayable.

Fourth, to the libraries, bookshops, dealers in books, and generous fellow scholars who have provided the bedrock information for research. My thanks therefore in particular to Andrew Gosling (now retired) and his staff at the

East Asian collection of the National Library of Australia, to Susan Prentice, formerly of the Menzies Library of the Australian National University, and other members of the East Asian staff there, mostly now departed to other employment, to John Moffett, the Librarian of the Needham Research Institute in Cambridge, a nonpareil of generosity, to Charles Aylmer, who presides over the Chinese collection in Cambridge University Library, to the Harvard-Yenching Library in Cambridge, Massachusetts, and the library of Columbia University in New York for procuring copies of rare items vital for the study of Guiyang and Zunhua, and to friends who gave me some key books: Professor Liu Shuren of the Huadong Normal University in Shanghai, Professor C. S. Juju C. S. Wang of the National Tsing Hua University in Taiwan, Professor Shiba Yoshinobu now at the Tōyō Bunko and the International Christian University in Tokyo, my Australian colleague Professor Warren Wan-kuo Sun, and my former co-author and continuing friend Dr Su Ninghu, who has now moved back to Australia after working for the government in New Zealand. I cannot any longer recall even the names of all the bookshops in the Kanda in Tokyo and in Kyoto where I have bought books in Japanese, but they have been an irreplaceable resource. I would also like, however blurred the focus may have become with the passage of time, to record my gratitude to them, and likewise to Heffers of Cambridge (now taken over by Blackwells) for English-language items.

Fifth, I owe a permanent debt for the intellectual stimulation provided by academic colleagues too numerous to mention individually, but most commonly at research conferences. I would like therefore at least to express my appreciation to those who organized the most important of these meetings, sometimes in times now long past. To Bill Skinner, whose conference more than thirty years ago on the Chinese city in late-imperial China helped crystallize my interest in the study of historical hydraulics. To Dwight Perkins, whose conference on China's modern economy in historical perspective stimulated my re-examination of late-traditional Chinese technology. To Itō Shuntarō and Yasuda Yoshinori, and the Nichibunken Center, for the great international conference at Kyoto in 1992 on "Nature and Humankind in the Age of Environmental Crisis." To Hsiung Ping-chen of the Academia Sinica in Taipei for suggesting that Professor Liu Ts'ui-jung and I organize a conference on China's environmental history, and to Dr Li Yih-yuan and the Chiang Ching-kuo Foundation for paying for most of it. To Alan Macfarlane of King's College, Cambridge, whose workshops on the history of science and technology in comparative perspective have been a source of many fruitful insights. To Rick Edmonds, the then editor of the *China Quarterly*, for the conference early in 1998 on China's environmental problems. To Kaoru Sugihara for the environmental history panel at the 1999 conference on economic history in Kyoto, and visits to other Japanese universities; and, finally, to Jack Goldstone of the University of California at Davis for his multifaceted conference in the fall of 1999 on almost every conceivable topic of interest to economic and environmental historians, with a particularly strong emphasis on China. I garnered a wealth of ideas and details from friends, and others, who participated in these gatherings, and hope they will excuse my not mentioning them one by one. They provided many seeds and grafts for the garden of intellect.

Sixth, I think it proper to express gratitude to those institutions that have kept me financially alive and helped me pay my family's bills. My thanks, then, to the universities of Cambridge and Glasgow, where in earlier days I taught Chinese history and economic history. To Harvard, where I enjoyed a total of three valuable years as a visiting fellow thanks to the Harkness-Commonwealth Foundation and the support of the late John Fairbank; and to the University of Oxford, and St Antony's College, where I taught from 1973 to 1989. More especially, though, to the École Normale Supérieure, in the rue d'Ulm, Paris, where I was invited by Marianne Bastid-Brugière, and gave my first course on the environmental history of China, as the first holder of the Chaire Européenne, in 1993; and to the Research School of Pacific and Asian Studies in the Australian National University in Canberra, where I was able to set up the Project on the Environmental History of China and Japan during the Directorship of Professor R. Gerard Ward.

Finally, there are a handful of special individuals from whom I have learned more than casually over the years. Among these are those with whom I have collaborated on papers, notably Su Ninghu, hydrologist extraordinary, and Zhang Yixia, the microbiologist and expert in public health. Richard Grove, for five years at the Australian National University's Research School of Social Sciences, and founding editor of the journal *Environment and History*, proved a constant source of new contacts and perspectives. Basia Zaba, of the London School of Hygiene and Tropical Medicine, and Griff Feeney, then at the East–West Center in Hawaii, were indispensable guides through technical demography, though most of this has proved too complex to include in the present book. Doug Whaite, formerly of the Coombs Computing Unit, gave crucial assistance with the computing as I taught myself how to write programs again. Professor Liu Ts'un-yan and Chiang Yang-ming (Sam Rivers) gave irreplaceable assistance with difficulties in translation. Help with particular technical details in this book was also kindly provided by Georges Métailié of the Laboratory of Ethno-Botany in Paris, and by Ian Williams of the Research School of Chemistry, Australian National University. Indispensable generosities.

My wife, Dian Montgomerie, artist, ceramist, photographer, and lifelong amateur naturalist, has constantly helped train my eye as an observer, brought serious amateur expertise to problems in the identification of Chinese plant-names, and done her valiant best to absorb the strains endured by her husband working in a still-great but threatened institution that was for a long time in a state of both government-imposed and internal managerial stress. To her no thanks can ever be enough.

Gratitude, too, to my elder son, Dr John Elvin of Cambridge Antibody Technologies, for reminding me, whenever I seemed to be in danger of forgetting it, that micro-organisms are the foundation of everything. And to Charles, my younger son, for his acute insights into the realities of power.

The last fine-tuning of this work was done at the Sinologisches Seminar of Heidelberg University, under the kindly auspices of Professor Rudolf Wagner, where I gave a course of lectures based on the draft chapters, and reaped many small but critical corrections. My warmest thanks to him and Cathie, and to all who came and listened.

Finally, I should like to express my warm appreciation of the way in which Robert Baldock and Diana Yeh and their colleagues at Yale University Press have looked after the editing and production of this book with a combination of high speed and painstaking attention, and Barry Howarth, formerly of the Australian National University, has taken care of the complex index.

Mark Elvin
Tarago, New South Wales and Heidelberg, 2003

Permissions

Parts of the following chapters have either appeared in previous publications or have drawn substantially from the material in them:

Chapter 5: M. Elvin, "The environmental legacy of imperial China." *China Quarterly* 156. (Dec.), 1998. Also in book form in R. L. Edmonds, ed., *Managing the Chinese Environment*. Oxford University Press: Oxford, 2000.

Chapter 6: M. Elvin and N. Su, "Man against the sea: Natural and anthropogenic factors in the changing morphology of Harngzhou Bay, circa 1000–1800." *Environment and History* 1.1 (Feb.), 1995; and id., "Engineering the sea: Hydraulic systems and pre-modern technological lock-in in the Harngzhou Bay area circa 1000–1800." In Itō Suntarō and Yoshida Yoshinori, eds., *Nature and Humankind in the Age of Environmental Crisis*. International Research Center for Japanese Studies: Kyoto, 1995.

Chapter 6: M. Elvin and N. Su, "Action at a distance: The influence of the Yellow River on Hangzhou Bay since AD 1000." In M. Elvin and T.-J. Liu, eds., *Sediments of Time: Environment and Society in Chinese History*. Cambridge University Press: New York, 1998.

Part of chapters 7, 8, and 9: M. Elvin, "Blood and statistics: Reconstructing the population dynamics of late imperial China from the biographies of virtuous women in local gazetteers." In H. Zurndorfer, ed., *Chinese Women in the Imperial Past: New Perspectives*. Brill: Leiden, 1999.

Chapter 10 was presented to the conference at Rheine in March 2000 on "Das Naturverständnis in China und Europa vom 6. Jh. v.u.Z. bis zum 17 Jh." organized by Professor Günter Dux and Professor Hans Ulrich Vogel.

Chapter 11: M. Elvin, "The man who saw dragons: Science and styles of thinking in Xie Zhaozhe's *Fivefold Miscellany*." *Journal of the Oriental Society of Australia* 25 and 26, 1993–4.

Chapter 12: M. Elvin, "Who was responsible for the weather? Moral meteorology in late-imperial China." *Osiris* 13 (1998), issue entitled "Beyond Joseph Needham," ed. Morris Low. Published by the University of Chicago Press.

Chapter 12: M. Elvin, "*The bell of poesy*: Thoughts on poems as information on late-imperial Chinese environmental history." In S. Carletti, M. Sacchetti, and P. Santangelo, eds., *Studi in Onore di Lionello Lanciotti*. Istituto Universitario Orientale: Napoli, 1996.

Permission to use this material is gratefully acknowledged.

Special thanks, too, to Dr Wen Rongsheng, son and literary executor of the late Dr Wen Huanran, and the Chongqing Publishing House for their kind permission to use materials from the latter's *Studies on Changes in Plants and Animals in China during Historical Times* (1995) on which the map of 'The Retreat of the Elephants' in Chapter 2 is to a great extent based.

Conventions

Double quotation marks are normally only used in the main text to indicate direct quotation from an identified source, the emphasis being on the fact of citation. Single quotation marks are used for all other purposes, notably for picking out a term or phrase that is the topic of discussion, either semantically or in a literal sense, or else is being used with an unusual meaning.

Other uses of double quotes include the demarcation of the titles of individual poems in the main text, and of journal articles in the bibliography, as well as the indication of direct speech in dialog. As usual, embedded use of multiple quotation marks requires an alternation of the two types for clarity.

Single quotes are used to demarcate the titles of chapters within a book and of sections within an article, written by a single author. For collections of chapters by different hands, the chapters are treated as 'articles', and demarcated by double quotes.

All *italics* in passages translated from Chinese sources have been added for emphasis by the present author, and this fact is not noted in individual cases.

The omission of lines or verses in translated poems is marked by '...' following the final word and stop of the extract presented, and is sometimes on the same line, to save space.

Introductory Remarks

This book is an overview of the environmental history of China. The span covered is about four thousand years, but weighted toward the last thousand. The main reason for this is the greater availability of relevant materials for the more recent period.[1] It is based on the findings of other scholars, Chinese, Japanese, and Western, and on my own researches. These include historical geography, local histories, poetry touching the environment, systems of belief about and representations of nature, local demography, and water-control systems.

The first aim is to sketch the factual record, so far as we know it at present. The second is to try to resolve a problem. Why did human beings here interact with the rest of the natural world in the way that they did? And, more tentatively, to what extent was it distinctive?

There are three main sections. *Patterns* gives the general picture, including the retreat of the elephants that contributes the title. Broadly speaking, their long retreat, from the northeast to the southwest, was the reversed image in space and time of that of the economic development and environmental transformation of premodern China. The central story, long-term deforestation and the removal of the original vegetation cover, is outlined in the two chapters that follow, more descriptively than analytically. But a core contention is documented, that classical Chinese culture was as hostile to forests as it was fond of individual trees.

The next two chapters look at two key questions. What were the original social driving forces and then the economic forces, behind the long-term environmental transformations of China, both constructive and destructive? Conversely, how did these environmental transformations, especially water-control engineering on an often immense scale, interact with economic growth, and with social and political institutions? I argue that the foundation of the answer to the first lies in a form of cultural social darwinism: cultures that actively exploited nature tended to gain a military and political *competitive advantage* over those that did not. I hypothesize that much later, once premodern economic growth had reached the point where money could be securely invested at interest, natural resources then came under a further pressure: a resource, such as a tree, that was not utilized economically appeared as income foregone. This is labeled 'the cash-in imperative'.

A chapter on water control then follows up the story of the state-driven aspect of growth through the imperial period. Hydraulic enterprise moved from a mix of impressive early successes and some massive failures, along a curve of steadily improving technology, toward an eventual form of environmentally constrained premodern technological lock-in. That is, once a large system had been established, it became the foundation of a local optimum that could not be easily abandoned because of the threat to livelihood and even lives. It was incapable of being much further developed after a certain point, and its hydrological instability incurred a perpetual burden of maintenance that made heavy social and economic demands. The long-term opportunity cost of this achievement was high when seen in a wider perspective.

The second main section, *Particularities*, presents the environmental histories of three contrasting regions. It focuses on the impact of development by smaller-scale units, communities, family farms, manors, and religious institutions, all of them increasingly oriented economically by the magnetic-like fields of the multicentered competitive market system. One region, Jiaxing on the central east coast, illustrates what is perhaps the major pattern of premodern Chinese economic growth from a profusion of ecological riches to a resource-strained complex of ultra-intensive garden-farming and handicrafts that placed an all-but intolerable workload on working people. The second, Guizhou in the southwestern interior, shows Chinese colonialism and imperialism at work on a Han/non-Han environmental frontier. The last, Zunhua on the old northeastern border, explores a still relatively resource-rich underdeveloped area and the *negative* correlation between premodern economic growth and some indices of well-being, such as the expectation of life, which was longer here than in the more 'advanced' regions.

Each had different population dynamics. People, or at least adults, lived longer in northern backward Zunhua than in subtropical colonial Guiyang, the capital of Guizhou, and longer in Guiyang than in advanced east-coast Jiaxing. Technical difficulties make presenting new results in population history unattractive in a general book like this. It is critical, though, for the reader to be aware of the trend of recent findings on fertility, including those of James Lee and his collaborators, of Zhao Zhongwei, and of my own team, still partly unpublished. The key point on which we broadly agree, though with nuanced differences, is that at least by late-imperial times *the pace of childbearing within marriage was slowed down by a spacing of births*. In our view this was first and foremost the consequence of a longish infertile period following the live birth of a child. The reasons, in our view, were principally a mix of post-birth amenorrhea, prolonged lactation, *coitus interruptus*, and social restraints on intercourse imposed by convention. Female infanticide must also have played a part, though how big a one is still open to serious debate. Methods of contraception and abortion were likewise known but are rather unlikely to have had a decisive quantitative impact. Life expectancy, though it varied from place to place, was too high—sometimes reaching over forty—for the death rate alone to have kept population growth within envi-ronmentally sustainable bounds. There was virtually universal marriage among women, and the majority of them married at close to the age of seven-teen, prior to the peak period of natural fertility, which occurs at about twenty. Restraint within marriage *must* have existed; the direct evidence strongly suggests that it did; its pattern over the years of marriage, especially with rela-tion to the effects of parity (the number of children born) and parental gender-preferences, and with regard to its mechanisms, awaits further clarification though a beginning has been made. Overall, there was indeed, as is commonly thought, population pressure on resources, especially during the later empire as easily exploitable space filled up. But it was moderated by long evolved customs, and a measure of conscious awareness and appropriate action. As Lee has stressed, China was *not* 'Malthusian', in any usual sense of this overused, often hazy, but still evocative word. Chinese environmental history was not just driven by a helpless subservience to the excessive replica-tion of human beings.[2]

Subtler, more fugitive, patterns are also sketched in these pages. How indi-vidual landscapes were brought under conceptual, religious, and aesthetic control. Cartography, shrines and temples, myths, legends, and landscape poetry. How communications consolidated communities, as by the millennial proliferation of new bridges. They detail local interactions with microfauna—epidemics and diseases like malaria. With macrofauna such as tigers, both the eaters of men and increasingly their prey. The use of raptors for hunting. And local plants, whether domesticated or wild, or imported from the New World and elsewhere. The differing degrees to which the ancient environmental buffers against natural disasters disappeared, diminished, or endured. Even how patterns of war and criminal activity were shaped by the natural environment and its man-made transformations. Overall they combine to define the envelope of possible variations in relationships between humans and their habitat that were recognizably 'Chinese'.

Perceptions follows. How did the Chinese understand, and value the natural world in which they lived? This section consists of three essays that illuminate different aspects of this immense subject. The first asks, how did 'Nature' become a theme for art in and of itself,[3] even the focus of what I call an 'unavowed religion'? The second, how did Chinese protoscientific ideas condition their observation of the natural world? Sober, sharp-witted and educated people saw dragons in this age, sometimes collectively. Why? The third explores how Chinese understanding of the environment interacted with orthodox morality, and why favorable or unfavorable weather was seen as a message of Heaven's approval or disapproval. It then goes on to ask, what was the spectrum of personal emotional attitudes toward Nature that had developed toward the end of the imperial era? The case is argued that there was by this time no such thing as a single 'Chinese' view of nature.

The original conception of this book was that it would conclude by looking at the development of environmental practice and policy under the Nationalist Republic and in the People's Republic of China. Reluctantly, I have come to the view that this has to be a separate enterprise. The stage is no longer China but the world, and modern science has transformed the technology, both for good and for ill. The short final chapter, 'Concluding Remarks', therefore only offers some speculations on the nature of economic pressure on an environment and on how to compare late-imperial China with northwestern Europe on the eve of 'modernity'.

Given this prospectus, two questions require answers at once. What is environmental history? And, why China in particular?

'Environmental history' in the sense used here is limited to the period for which documentary evidence exists to give us access to how men and women were thinking. Its theme is the changing relationship between people and the biological, chemical, and geological systems that both supported them and threatened them in complex ways. In specific terms: climates, rocks and minerals, soils, water, trees and plants, animals and birds, insects, and, at the foundation of almost everything, microbes. All of these are in various ways both vital friends and, at times, lethal enemies. Technologies, economies, social and political institutions, as well as beliefs, perceptions, knowledge, and representations interacted continually with this natural context. Human systems had their own dynamics to some extent, but they cannot be fully understood over time without reference to their environment. The history of disease is a major, and regrettable, lacuna in this book. China suffered from some huge epidemics,[4] but reliable knowledge of what was happening is extremely patchy before the last two hundred years or so,[5] and I have not had the time to give the subject the attention it deserves.

China is an important historical case for three reasons. First, it has an unusually long record which allows tentative answers to many questions that are hard to answer for other areas. Second, it complements, and contrasts with, the environmental histories of other major countries and peoples.[6] It often provides a critical analytical challenge when testing any general theory mostly formulated in some other context. And, last, it provides a perspective in which to examine the developing environmental crisis in the People's Republic of China today, the origins of which predate modern times.

Nonetheless, some comments and a word of warning on specific comparisons. The Chinese environmental story is a rich source of apparent parallels and divergences with its Western and other counterparts. Differences in the sequences and the prima facie connections of approximately similar elements raise important questions about the commonly assumed causalities. Thus the Chinese from early times, if not the earliest, found a religious and philosophical exaltation in the ascent of mountains and their contemplation, whereas these were only occasionally explored and admired in the classical West, and mostly abhorred or ignored during the Western Middle Ages. Thus the association of a kind of growing secular religious absorption in the Alps and other mountains with the Enlightenment and the burgeoning of the mentality that we think of as 'modern' in the West may be correct in chronological terms; it cannot be adequate in the kind of causation that it implies.[7] In at least approximative terms the phenomenon existed *without* these correlates in premodern China. Speaking with more finesse we may say that issues like this reveal the decisive analytical importance of how we choose to define an adequate 'approximation' to similarity.

Mountains in early medieval China were the home of beneficent magic and of beings who transcended ordinary humanity. Thus Cao Zhi, who flourished at the beginning of the third century CE wrote of Mount Tai:[8]

> I roamed the Mountain in the dawn,
> Secluded in its misty depths,
> When suddenly I met two boys
> With faces that were fair and fresh.
>
> They gave me herbs of the immortals
> The Numinous Supreme had made,

> Medicaments that when absorbed
> Revive the seminal essence and brain,
>
> So life, like a rock's or metal ore's,
> Passes through eons, *but does not age.*

Du Fu in the eighth century, having climbed the same mountain, experienced in a more abstract and philosophical way the especial gift of mountains, 'the unity of Heaven and mankind', as the conventional phrase had it:[9]

> What, then, is this — the greatest of mountains' — nature?
> Greens, far below, over Qi and Lu, reach endlessly away,
> Up here are daemonic beauties, gathered by the Reshaper,
> Where the Two Forces — dark, bright — split apart sunlight and shade.

This second poem expresses a mood that has something in common with the modern Western impulse to search for a kind of immanent transcendence in the contemplation of high mountains, but if we survey the full range of Chinese beliefs and feelings, we also find much that is different. An example is the search for immortals who possessed, and might bestow, the magical keys to physical longevity. The 'Reshaper' mentioned in the second poem, it should be noted, is not a creator but a continuous transforming power.[10] The 'Two Forces' are the yin and the yang, negative and positive, female and male, soft and hard. 'Daemonic'—Chinese *shen*—suggests forces neither intrinsically favorable or unfavorable to human beings, simply supernatural. The metaphysics underlying perception is thus quite different from that in the West.

So the question remains: how far are we justified in seeing the medieval Chinese passion for mountains and the early modern European passion as sufficiently comparable to justify more than casual comparison? Our sense of the possible difference is heightened when we recall that the first ascent of Le Mont Blanc, by Horace Bénédict de Saussure, was primarily motivated by scientific inquiry and a need to make measurements.[11] The destiny of the Alps was however soon to become, in Nicolas Giudici's words, "a theater of fabulous exploits,"[12] that fostered the sport of pitting oneself against extremes, and a cult of records and Promethean supermen. As recounted in the chapter on 'Science and Superfauna' in *Perceptions*, there may have been the faintest echoes of some of this in China: Xie Zhaozhe at the end of the sixteenth century seems to have made a kind of mental catalog of the most dangerous places that he had experienced in a lifetime of traveling in the mountains, but felt no sense of embarrassment in mentioning that his fear had inhibited him from proceeding through the most dangerous of them all—even though there was still a path of sorts. The young serf who did make it across, trembling, though thought worth a brief mention, was not seen as the prototype of future heroes. In cases like this, the complexities of analysis rapidly become hard to disentangle.

Even so, much of what appears in the chapters that follow has been written with the shadowy presence of possible Western analogies and differences at the back of my mind. This is especially true of those relating to perceptions. The obvious Western counterpart—though it is a much richer tapestry—to the story I outline is Clarence Glacken's *Traces on the Rhodian Shore: Nature and Culture in Western Thought from Ancient Times to the End of the Eighteenth Century.*[13] Perhaps the most overpowering contrast is the virtual absence in premodern China of the idea of a transcendent creator God who is distinct from Nature in a fundamental qualitative sense. The Chinese had notions of a supreme god in various guises (that is, 'hypatotheism'),[14] and also, as we have seen, of a somewhat demiurge-like 'transformer' constantly reshaping the cosmos.[15] They also conceived of abstract forms, either moral-material principles inhering in different types of entities[16] or dynamic patterns that both embodied and directed the sequences of situations.[17] But none of these set up the Western question of the divine design of the universe that is the first of Glacken's three major themes, nor, broadly speaking, any of the nagging Western problems of cosmic purpose, final causes, or teleology. Whether this immense difference in perception led to any major differences between the human transformations of the environment—such as long-term deforestation—is an interesting issue. My provisional answer, for what it is worth, is 'no' or, at least, 'in no immediately obvious way'.

One of the persistent themes of this book is in fact that the relationships between how the environment was perceived and represented, as well as the approach to it that was proclaimed as appropriate, on the one hand, and what was actually happening, on the other, were always to some degree problematic. The second can never be simply inferred from the first. Sometimes it may even have been approximately the opposite, a question looked at in the first chapter in *Perceptions*, in the context of the discussion of the ideas of Heiner Roetz who first flagged this issue in its acute form.

Another key problem that needs resolution is that we are still some way from having a plausible precise conception of the environmental exploitation characteristic of premodern China that both includes its wide internal range of variation and neither blurs, nor ignores, these differences. I think there *was* a distinctively 'Chinese' style to the 'premodern economic growth' that gradually, and with some notable regressions followed by renewed advances, as well as periods of temporary imbalance, took over the transformation of the environment from the original politically and militarily driven onslaught described in the chapter 'The Logic of Short-term Advantage'. But a fully satisfactory definition remains to be determined. For the time being we might formulate it roughly as follows: Structurally the Chinese style was based on a capacity to operate through highly disaggregated units (like the peasant family farm) that could be coordinated either administratively (as for middle-sized and large water-control operations) or commercially (mostly through networks of markets that were, with some important qualifications, free of monopolistic control) to form, where needed, enormous *modular aggregates* that were inherently transient, existing only while immediately required. It is my suspicion that this combination of small-unit initiative and all but unlimited facultative aggregation (either administratively or commercially based) produced a thoroughness of environmental exploitation that was distinctive in the premodern world.[18]

One of the objectives of the three chapters in *Particularities* on economic development in a specific environmental context in contrasting areas is to show how elusive the formal definition of a coherent 'Chinese' premodern style still is. It is in fact even possible to demonstrate a significant degree of microvariation in economic relations with the environment within the catchment of a single large lake. My colleagues and I have recently shown that this was the case for the northern and western shores of Lake Erhai in western Yunnan province.[19] From about the middle of the eighteenth century, once the clearance of hillslope surface vegetation for farming had got under way in the upper reaches of the Miju River at the northern end of the lake, the lower river was burdened with so heavy a load of sediment that a massive mobilization of labor was needed each year to contain it by dredging and diking, and a huge protective deflection barrage had to be created at the terminus of the upper river, where the flow was concentrated into a gorge. By the end of the eighteenth century, the river dikes rose several meters above the roofs of the houses outside them. The system was perilous and only sustainable at a substantial cost, and by maximal coordination. In contrast, on the west side, irrigation water was drawn from eighteen small streams flowing down over often overlapping alluvial fans at the foot of an abrupt range of mountains. They were tapped by a network of small channels that anastomatosed and were even made to run across each other in places. The courses of these could be changed or allowed to change whenever they became filled up with sediments, and little damage was done by this to life or livelihood. No large-scale organization was required, and the system was sustainable without great effort. It would be a mistake to regard either of these systems as more 'Chinese' than the other. Both, and many other types, need to be catered for in any analytical formulation. In summary, before we go deeply into comparisons of 'China' with other parts of the world in terms of its premodern transformation of its environment, interesting though these can be, we need to have a much surer hold on what 'China' itself was.

For these reasons, external comparisons are not a major concern of this book.

A few words on my own attitude to the subject may help readers allow for bias on my part:

I am a historian by training, but with enough knowledge of some areas of science to have collaborated with professional scientists. I believe that sufficient objectivity in historical work is possible to make it reasonable to try to distinguish between more plausible and less plausible reconstructions of the past. I am aware that people in different times and cultures have lived, and live, in different conceptual worlds. I have even written a book on this subject.[20] The barriers between these worlds are not absolute, however, but semipermeable. With effort and care one can learn to move between them. This is not fundamentally different from the 'bootstrapping' process by which a child learns his or her own culture as he or she grows up. Only the multiple perspectives in the mind of the outsider create an element of unavoidable dissimilarity.

More importantly, it can be demonstrated that there is no necessity for evidence from another time or culture to be flawed by this otherness to the point of being unusable by us. Medieval Chinese maps of coastlines long ago vanished can be shown on occasion to match well with modern remote-sensing images where differences in reflectance can pick out a similar pattern.[21] Ages at death of 'virtuous' women recorded in premodern Chinese local histories, in random sequence over the centuries, fall, when reassembled, into the smooth curves of age-specific mortality familiar to modern demography but unknown to those doing the recording.[22] Historical sources may be disconcertingly partial in coverage. They may offer a view that seems to us distorted. But they are not *just* apologias for the power of those who compiled them. Nor are they *just* mirrors that reflect *only* our own faces, and *nothing* but our own prejudices, back at ourselves.

Immersing oneself in another mental world can also provide a vantage point from which to look at one's own mental world from the outside. The influences are not all one-way.

Following a personal preference, I have quoted more from original sources than is usual in an introductory survey. There are two purposes in this, apart from the fact that premodern Chinese is on the whole hard to translate, and a reliable translation in itself a service. The first is to illustrate the kind of evidence on which the story told here, and my analyses, are based. It is thin by the standards of the present day, even if abundant compared to that for our own Western medieval and ancient history. Quotation of sources also allows the reader some opportunity to conceptualize the evidence differently. The second purpose is to make it possible for him or her to enter, even if only for a moment or two, into the mental world of those who made the history examined in these pages. To acquire, as it were, a second, and imaginary, self.

My own environmental values are probably close to those expressed by Aldo Leopold in his *Sand County Almanac* half a century ago:[23]

> Wild things, I admit, had little human value until mechanization assured us of a good breakfast, and until science disclosed the drama of where they came from and how they live. The whole conflict thus boils down to a question of degree. We of the minority see a law of diminishing returns in progress; our opponents do not.

I would be happy to be able to maintain this type of balance and to combine practicality and poetry in the way that he did. Readers who find themselves at odds with these views, from whichever side, catastrophist or cornucopian, should make allowances as appropriate.

This can be put another way. While patterned catastrophe rules sand piles and stock markets,[24] I am inclined to believe that, at a historical level, life is mostly logistic. That is, from time to time a near-equilibrium state springs into an accelerating growth, but after a time this acceleration slows down and vanishes, the system returning to a new near-equilibrium.[25] This puts me philosophically closer to biologists and demographers than to orthodox economists, but it is always possible to argue about which part of the curve one is on. The initial section of a logistic *looks* exponential.

Literate Chinese wrote poems constantly, and on a wider variety of themes than educated Westerners, often very mundane themes. Poems are as a consequence used more frequently in the chapters that follow than is common in Western historical writing. They often contain information not available elsewhere. This is why they are included, not for their impact on the heart. It is nonetheless necessary to remember that they are literature. They have a character that is partly defined by the particular genre they are written in, by particular conventions of imagery and symbolism, and by a framework of reference to other literary works familiar to their readers. They are not simply—indeed, not at all simply—reflections of the human and natural environments of their time. Even compared to depending on more ordinary historical texts, which have their own conventions, too, and are rarely only what they purport to be on the surface, the use of poems is hazardous; but it is unavoidable.

Most of the originals rhymed. Premodern Chinese poems generally do, apart from those—with a few exceptions—in the genre of rhapsodic 'prose-poems' or *fu*. This feature is hinted at in the translations given here by *vowel-rhymes* on the final stressed syllable of each line. Older Chinese poems also have a crystalline regularity of syllabic structure, usually with a break of some sort in, or near, the middle of each line. This regularity is not reproducible as a rule in polysyllabic English, but I have tried to suggest the breaks, at times marking the dividing caesura with a '—' dash. The free-floating unrhymed English lines pioneered by Arthur Waley, and more or less imitated by most translators ever since, however good (or bad) in their own right, misrepresent the sonic and metrical nature of historical Chinese mainstream poetry almost as totally as it is possible to do so.

Here, as an illustration of the conventions I have adopted, are the opening lines of Ji Qiguang's "Farming Women," probably written in the later seventeenth century.[26] The rhyming vowels are in **bold**, and all the midline breaks shown by a '—', which normally only needs to be done when the pause is not obvious:

On a road beside the Huai River — I met with some farming w**o**men.
They stood barefoot, with unkempt hair — on the rising slope of a r**i**dge.
Pointing to where the sun was setting — they told me, a stranger, their
   h**i**story:
"Up there, in the western Huai valley — land and climate have always
   brought b**i**tterness.

"Only here and there are there farmable patches. — It's an arid waste,
   short of str**ea**ms,
Even if it produced Han Xin long ago — who helped found the Han in
   their gl**o**ry.
The wind there howls for three hundred miles. — Rice in the fields is
   infr**e**quent,
Though on the vein-like upland ridges — grows many a plot of s**o**rghum."

This is a powerful evocation of one of the most degraded landscapes of late-imperial times. It is material like this that, more than any other, enables one to build up, fragment by fragment, a picture of particular places at particular times.

The most difficult practical obstacle to assimilating Chinese history for those who are not Chinese speakers is one that is, paradoxically, both trivial and all but insurmountable. This is remembering Chinese names of people and places.

Much of the difficulty is the result of the transcription into identical roman letters of Chinese syllables that have different pitch-tones when spoken, and different ideographs when written, and of course different meanings. Where necessary, I have put in accents to indicate the different tones. Thus Zhòu (in the falling tone) was the 'evil' last ruler of the Shang dynasty, and the Zhou (in the unmarked level tone) the dynasty that overthrew the Shang. The acute accent shows the rising tone, and the inverted circumflex the dipping-rising tone.

The most commonly used transcription, and the one adopted in this book, pinyin, also seems to put mental barbed wire in the way of most English-speaking readers. The worst letters are the 'q' pronounced as 'ch' and the 'c' pronounced as 'ts' as in the English 'cheats', and the 'x' pronounced as 'sh' as in 'she', and the 'zh' pronounced like the 'j' in 'Joe'. Ignoring for a moment that Chinese does not have a final 'c', we could say that, with pinyin vowels, 'she cheats Joe' would be written as 'xi qic zhou'. The noninitiated may be forgiven for finding this grotesque. I have therefore tried to put nonessential Chinese names in the notes or leave them out where possible.

The plain inverted comma is used when the break between two transcribed vowels or syllables is not unambiguous. 'Xian' (one syllable) means 'a county', but 'Xi'an' (two syllables) is the city. The province names 'Hu'nan' and 'He'nan' are therefore properly written with the inverted comma, as 'hun'an' and 'hen'an' are both permissible pinyin readings.

Converting historical Chinese measures of length, capacity, and weight is more a problem for the author than for readers. In general, where a precise equivalent is important, I have relied mainly on Qiu Guangming's *Researches on Measures of Length, Capacity, and Weight in Successive Dynasties in China*[27] which is based on modern measurements of actual surviving measuring devices. These vary significantly among themselves, even for the same epoch, but in most cases a reasonable central value can be established. Normally I use the metric system, but a partial exception has been to allow myself 'miles' rather than the equivalent in 'kilometers' where a precise distance is of no great concern, and the old word comes more easily off the tongue. Likewise, and in the same sort of contexts, I sometimes use 'feet' and 'inches' which are close to their Chinese counterparts.

I have tried to reduce scholarly clutter to a minimum. Thus square brackets have been removed from obvious and necessary interpolations in translations. Additional information about locations, dates, peoples, technical terms, and commentaries on problems, has mostly been put in endnotes.

Bon voyage!

Patterns

1

🐘 *Landmarks and Time-marks*

The environmental history of China covers a varied space. The core is about 1,000 miles east to west and 1,200 miles north to south. Readers not already familiar with Chinese geography need points of reference if they are to place stories and analyses in a context.

A first approximation is given in the accompanying schematic map. This shows present-day China's ten main regions simplified almost, but not quite, to the point of caricature. Readers who know China well should glance at it just long enough to note the definitions of the regions adopted here, as every important place-name is followed by a regional label when it first appears. Thus 'Beijing (Northeast)' and 'Shanghai (East)' show that these two cities are in the Northeast and East regions respectively. The table appended to Map 1 on p. 4 shows the major provinces assigned to each region. For a more detailed treatment of the historical geography, it is useful to have to hand an atlas such as C. Blunden and M. Elvin, *A Cultural Atlas of China*.[1]

The basic social story of 'China' is the four-thousand-year expansion of 'Han' or 'Chinese' population, political power, and culture from their birth-place in the Northwest and Northeast, with secondary centers in the West and Center, into all the other areas shown, and indeed beyond them.[2] There were times when Han culture temporarily retreated. This was the case for the Northwest and Northeast from the third to the sixth centuries CE.[3] The temperature was colder in these years, as may be seen from Table 1 on p. 6, and non-Han, or, in Han terms, 'barbarian', peoples swept in from the north, and the frontier between pasturage and farmed land moved south. During such times, which included the Mongol conquest, Chinese culture was in considerable measure assimilated by the conquerors, and when Han political

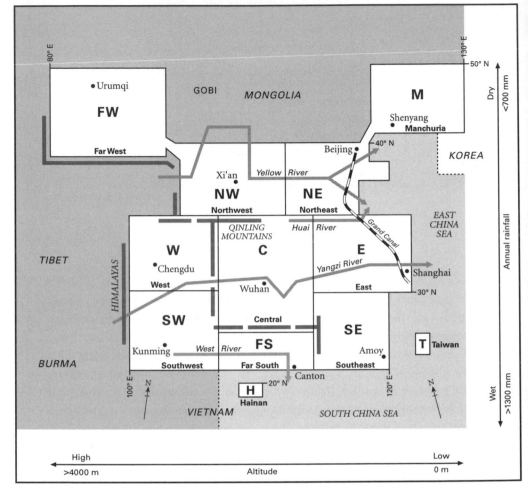

Major provinces in each zone

FW	Xinjiang (E. Turkestan)	C	Hubei, Hunan, Jiangxi
M	Liaoning, Jilin, Heilongjiang	E	Anhui, Jiangsu, N. Zhejiang
NW	Shaanxi, Shanxi, Gansu	SW	Yunnan, Guizhou, Guangxi
NE	Henan, Hebei, Shandong	FS	Guangdong, Hainan
W	Sichuan	SE	S. Zhejiang, Fujian, Taiwan

Notes

This diagram is for the purposes of quick reference only and carries no political implications.

The lower Yellow River at some times exited north of the Shandong peninsula, and at others south of it, in both cases by a variety of routes.

The northern section of the Grand Canal shown here is that used under the Ming and Qing dynasties from the early fifteenth to the early twentieth century.

Mean annual rainfall starts to increase again with more northerly latitudes in eastern Manchuria.

'Canton' is 'Guangzhou' and 'Amoy' is 'Xiamen' in current PRC usage.

—— indicates topographical barriers to easy movement in historical times.

Map 1 Schematic model of China for rapid reference (not to scale)

power re-emerged the end result was frequently an expansion of the Han socio-political domain. In some marginal areas, like Korea and Vietnam, Chinese culture was also absorbed, though never entirely, while Chinese political power was to a large degree successfully resisted, in part because of these acquired cultural skills. The Manchu dynasty, which ruled during the final part of the late-imperial period, from the mid-seventeenth century to the early twentieth, was in many respects a sino-'barbarian' condominium, and its immense periphery to the north and west was only partially sinified by the time it fell. Overall, though, the picture is one of Han Chinese expansion up to natural limits—coasts, steppes, deserts, mountains, and jungles. It was a multi-millennial transformation of a variety of habitats by some version of the Chinese style of settlement: cutting down most of the trees for clearance, buildings, and fuel, an ever-intensifying garden type of farming and arbori-culture, water-control systems both large and small, commercialization, and cities and villages located as near the water's edge as possible.

Map 1 also shows the main gradients in space of yearly rainfall and height above sea level. China on the whole gets wetter as one goes south, and higher as one goes west. These are only approximations. For example, the lowest point in the People's Republic, the Turfan Depression at 154 meters below sea level, lies in the Far West toward the high end of the rising east-to-west altitude gradient.

Thick grey lines pick out mountain barriers that made communication difficult in historical times. As can be seen, Chinese space was to some degree compartmentalized. This was, and is, particularly true of the West, a basin ringed by mountains and with the Yangzi gorges its only outlet to the sea.

Table 1 likewise provides time-marks for the basic chronological patterns of Chinese history: millennia, periods, dynasties, and key economic and environ-mental developments. A minimal set of the most important time-marks is printed in bold-face type. If they can be remembered, almost everything else falls into place around them.

Mean annual temperatures as compared to those of the present day are indicated, as climatic changes seem to have been associated with some of the major political and cultural turning points. A colder climate accompanied the end of the archaic world in the later Western Zhou dynasty almost three thou-sand years BP.[4] Colder weather was the accompaniment of the break-up of the Early Empire in the first centuries of the first millennium CE. A colder and often unstable climate was likewise the background to the destruction of the Middle Empire after the twelfth century CE by the Jürchen and the Mongols, both non-Han peoples from the north. Conversely, the Middle Empire rose during the middle of the first millennium CE, when the temperature was warmer than it is today.

The most likely mechanisms were simple. A shift toward cold and dry climatic conditions in north China and the grasslands to its north was associated with attempted or successful southward migrations and invasions by nomadic pastoralists. A shift to warmer and wetter periods was linked with agricultural Han Chinese re-expansion northward, and sometimes westward. Pastoralists came south when lowered farm output reduced Chinese logistical capacity and ability to resist, and drier colder conditions simultaneously put pressure on them to move by reducing the availability of forage grass north of the frontier. It is likely that the *change* of climate was the critical factor: pastoralists would probably not have had the means to invade successfully if they had not previously enjoyed reasonably good conditions. For the second

Table 1 Time-marks in Chinese environmental history

Millennia	Periods	Major dynasties	Economy*	Climate
2nd BCE	Archaic	Xia/Shang	**Settled farming**	Much warmer
		W. Zhou	**Cities/Bronze**	than today
	Fragmented	E. Zhou	**Iron**	
1st BCE		Springs and Autumns†		Colder than
		Warring States		today
	Early Empire	Qin/W. Han	**Large hydraulic**	Same as
			works	today
1st CE	Early Empire	E.Han		Same as today
		Three Kingdoms/W. Jin		
	Fragmented	Northern and Southern	Some environ-	Colder (Bohai
		Dynasties	mental recovery	Gulf freezes)
	Middle	Sui/Tang	**Grand Canal**	Warmer than
	Empire	Five Dynasties/N. Song	**Rice-farming**	today
			MEDIEVAL ECONOMIC	
			REVOLUTION	
2nd CE	Jürchen/	N. and S. Song	**Tea**	Cold/variable
	Mongols	Jin/Yuan	**Cotton**	(L. Tai freezes)
			Population decline	
			in NE and NW	
	Late	Ming	**New World crops**	Cold but
	Empire	Manchu/Qing	**Rapid population**	warming
			growth	
			Final-phase PMEG	
			Environmental degradation	
	Republic		Some MEG	As today
	People's Republic		**Spreading MEG**	
3rd CE		ACCELERATING ENVIRONMENTAL DEGRADATION		

* PMEG, premodern economic growth; MEG, modern economic growth.
† For reasons I have never understood, English language writers prefer the singular 'Spring and Autumn'. The rational French prefer the plural 'Printemps et Automnes'. See, for example, J. Gernet, *Le Monde chinois* (Colin: Paris, 1972). The Chinese term permits either translation.

and third of the colder periods shown in Table 1, these correlations can be documented in some detail.[5] Clearly, though, we are talking here of pressures operating in contexts that, overall, were much more causally complex.

The 'medieval economic revolution' referred to in the column on the 'Economy' is associated with a southward shift in the center of China's economic gravity from the Northeast to the East. It was distinguished by more productive farming, especially of rice, by better transport, especially on water, by extensive commercialization, and by the widespread use of money and written contracts. The populations of its cities at times reached more than a million. It used woodblock printing, and hence enjoyed increased literacy. It pioneered the first elements of mass production by making millions of cast-iron arrowheads for its armies, and mechanization, as in the water-powered spinning of hemp yarn. Although this 'revolution', whose impetus later faded away, was responsible for some environmental degradation, the worst premodern destruction of habitats, and of forests and soils, actually took place during the population explosion in the eighteenth and nineteenth centuries, on the eve of the modern era in China.[6]

The term 'final-phase PMEG' refers to the extremely intensive form of premodern economic growth that developed in the more technically advanced parts of China toward the end of the imperial age. It was characterized by an exceptionally high productivity of cereal per hectare (far in excess of that in Europe before the nineteenth century), and long hours of work almost round the clock and the year. Ordinary people bore a health-sapping workload and endured virtually unremitting stress, especially women. Local handicrafts could often only make a profit if interprovincial market networks functioned properly; and forest clearances and the eventual complete coverage of the surface by private property rights removed any significant environmental buffer when society was threatened by extreme events, notably drought. With the proviso that the other criteria of advanced premodern technology are also met, it seems that the routine sale of children during economic crises can be taken as a marker of the onset of this final paradoxical stage, one that may be summarized as 'productive but precarious'.[7] When Shao Changheng in the later seventeenth century wanted to convey the extreme horror of a famine near Nanjing, he wrote:[8]

From Sichuan, and the middle Yangzi, come the rolls of the drums of war.
Downstream, the lower Yangzi is cruelly scarred in its plight.
In previous years, when people were poor, they could sell their sons and daughters.
This *year, if a child's for sale, there's* nowhere *to find a buyer.*

In premodern terms, this was one of the most advanced areas in China.

This completes the preliminaries. The map and table are oversimplified, and will need fine-tuning in the course of our journey across four millennia. They are nonetheless needed to hold in place frameworks of space and time during a discussion that unavoidably moves back and forth across both in what can be a disconcerting fashion.

2

🐘 *Humans v. Elephants: The Three Thousand Years War*

Four thousand years ago there were elephants in the area that was later to become Beijing (in the Northeast), and in most of the rest of what was later to be China. Today, the only wild elephants in the People's Republic are those in a few protected enclaves in the Southwest, up against the border with Burma. The stages of this long retreat south and west are shown in Map 2, 'The Retreat of the Elephants', which is based on the research of the late Wen Huanran.[1]

That elephants were abundant in the Northeast, Northwest, and West during the archaic age is clear from the elephant bones found in Shang and Shu archaeological sites,[2] from the cast bronze elephants of this time, and from records on oracle bones[3] that mention elephants being sacrificed to the ancestors. Not long after the start of the first millennium BCE, however, they were rarely overwintering north of the Huai River on the Northeast/East boundary. By the beginning of the second millennium CE they were confined to the South, and during the second half of this last millennium increasingly to the Southwest.

What were the causes of this disaster (seen from the elephants' point of view)? In part it was likely to have been the cooling of the climate, as referring back to the last column in Table 1 in the previous chapter will suggest. Elephants do not resist cold well. But since the elephant population did not recover to more than a small degree in somewhat warmer periods (such as 700 BCE to 200 BCE, when it seems to have moved back north from the Yangzi valley to the line of the Huai River), and mostly not at all, some other force was at work. The most obvious explanation is that it was the result of a protracted war with human beings which the elephants lost. The pattern of their withdrawal in time and in space was, so to speak, the reverse image of the expansion and intensification of Chinese settlement. Chinese farmers and elephants do not mix.

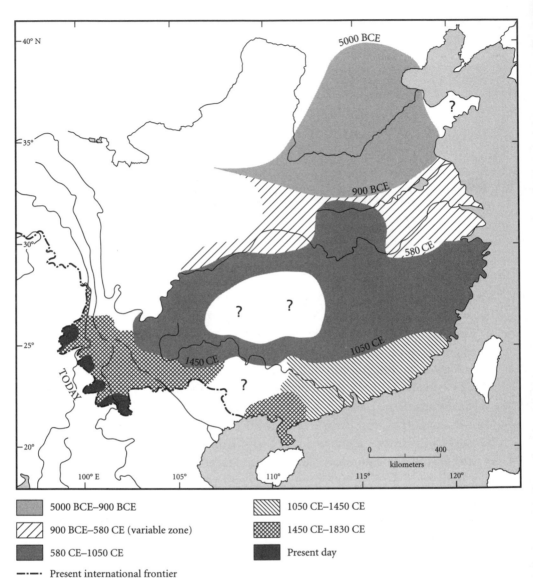

Legend:

5000 BCE–900 BCE	1050 CE–1450 CE
900 BCE–580 CE (variable zone)	1450 CE–1830 CE
580 CE–1050 CE	Present day

—·—·— Present international frontier

Note: Apart from the variable zone, earlier dates include later dates. Modern coastlines.

Map 2 The Retreat of the Elephants (after Wen Huanran)

It is necessary to say 'Chinese' here as some non-Han cultures in the Far South seem to have had a less confrontational relationship. One writer in Tang times observed of the Manshi 'barbarians', who are of Tai stock, that "peacocks nest in the trees by people's houses, and the elephants are the size of water buffalo, the local custom being to rear them to plow the fields, and, even now, to burn their dung as fuel."[4]

The war against wild animals generally was a defining characteristic of the early Zhou-dynasty culture from which classical China later emerged. This can be seen from the *Mencius*, the book that describes the ideas of Mencius, the second important thinker in the Confucian tradition. The philosopher lived in the fourth century BCE, and was therefore speaking about events more than three-quarters of a millennium before his time. What he has to say about the Duke of Zhou is nonetheless revealing:[5]

> After the sage–rulers Yao and Shun had passed away, the way of the sages fell into decay. Oppressive monarchs . . . abandoned the farmland to make it into gardens and hunting enclosures, and as a result the people could not get clothes or food . . . . As the gardens and hunting enclosures, ponds, lakes, thickets, and swamps became numerous, the birds and the beasts moved in. By the reign of Zhòu [the 'evil' last sovereign of the Shang dynasty], the world was once again in great disorder. The Duke of Zhou assisted King Wu of the Zhou dynasty to destroy Zhòu . . . . He drove the tigers, leopards, rhinoceroses, *and elephants* far away, and the world was greatly delighted.

Presumably this applied to the middle and lower valley of the Yellow River toward the end of the second millennium BCE. We do not have to believe the details, but can take it as expressing a continuing social memory of an attitude of mind reflecting the struggle to consolidate a farming culture.

The 'war' was fought on three fronts. The first front was the destruction of the elephants' forest habitat by clearing land for farming. One reason we hear of their intrusions, from time to time even into walled cities, is probably that they were under pressure from the shrinking of the resources available to them. The second front was the farmers' defense of their crops against elephant trampling and plundering, based on their belief that the security of the fields demanded the extermination or capture of the thieves. The third front was the hunting of elephants for their ivory and their trunks, which were a gourmet's delicacy, or their trapping to be trained for war, transport, or ceremonial. These three fronts can be looked at separately, but in all cases habitat destruction was the key.

Chinese elephants need a warm and moist environment, without steep slopes, in which they can avoid direct sunlight and move around easily. The ideal is open forest near water or wetlands. They may weigh up to five tons, and consume a large quantity of food every day, typically leaves, wild bananas, and tender bamboo tips. Water is needed not just for drinking but also for washing in and cooling down. The *Book of the Prince of Huainan*, a compendium on natural history put together around 120 BCE, and infused with a sense of the power of natural environments to engender specific living things and shape them in particular ways, described the southern regions at this time as "places where the bright–positive aethers[6] accumulate, being warm and moist . . . with land well suited to rice, and having numerous rhinoceroses and elephants."[7]

Elephants reproduce slowly, the gestation of the usual single calf taking about 1.8 years. It is therefore difficult for them to make good in a short time losses from slaughter inflicted by humans. Nor, in spite of their exceptional intelligence and memory, do they adapt easily to altered environments. But they are mobile. It seems unlikely that any other quadruped mammal of the present day can easily ford or swim rivers the size of the middle reaches of the Yangzi. Mobility has been a partial substitute for adaptability.

Elephants live in small groups and, in this state, are not normally dangerous to humans who do not provoke them. The rogue male who has left his group, or been pushed out of it, is however a serious threat. As one writer observed in the eleventh century: "There were formerly numerous elephants in the territory of Zhangzhou [in the Southeast], which is next door to Chaoyang [in the Far South]. They commonly formed herds of somewhat more than ten, but caused no harm. Only if a solitary elephant met someone would he pursue him, and trample on him till his bones and flesh were pulverized, before making off."[8]

The crux was that elephants could not survive without tree cover, and its destruction implied their departure. This can be illustrated from two accounts of the so-called 'elephants' hideouts' in Wuping, on the border of the Southeast with the Far South. The first is from a Song-dynasty writer. "Elephants' hideouts [he says] were found between Chaozhou [in the Far South] and Meizhou [on the Far South border with the Southeast] in an area that is at present under the jurisdiction of Wuping county. In times past, when it had not yet been opened up for farming, herds of elephants would stop in them . . . . These days, the land is fertile and harvests abundant."[9] The second is from a late fourteenth-century local gazetteer for Linding, on the border of the Southeast with the Far South:

> The forest provided a screen overhead and there is an old tradition that elephants would emerge from the hideouts, hence their name. Later on,

people gradually felled the trees and removed the couch grass. If they found a place that wrapped around them like a spiral coil [a sort of small sheltered valley], they would make it into a settlement. Ninety-nine times out of a hundred these places were once elephants' hideouts.[10]

Farmers and elephants were in direct competition for habitat.

Villagers also killed elephants by forcing them to be exposed to direct sunlight. A Ming-dynasty author describes this for the county of Hepu, in the Southwest, on the coast:

> In 1547 a mob of elephants trampled down the common people's harvests at Mount Dalian. When chased, they refused to move off. The prefect . . . induced the most prominent people in the rural district to lead the inhabitants in catching them. Before they began, they fashioned connected tree trunks into portable barricades. Each of these was ten feet in length and needed several men to lift. They then waited until the herd of elephants was hidden behind a small hill, and at once surrounded them on all sides with the barricades, this being done in the twinkling of an eye. Outside the barricades they made a deep ditch, and encircled it with people holding bows, arrows, and long spears. The order was given not to let the elephants smash through the barricades and get away. People were also told to wait for a moment when they could cut down the trees that grew within the barricades, so the herd could be attacked by the heat of the midday sun. Elephants are afraid of heat; and in three or four days all of them were dead.[11]

The devastating effects of an increasingly treeless environment on elephants could not be brought home more brutally.

Crops were the second point of conflict. According to the *Song History*, elephants appeared in 962 CE in Huangpo county, which is in the Center, north of the Yangzi. Here they "hid in the woods and ate the common people's grain sprouts and harvests."[12] They did the same in some other areas including Tangzhou (in the Northeast), which was 140 miles away. This suggests the sort of distances they moved. The same source says of Chaozhou in 1171 that "several hundred wild elephants devoured the harvest. The farmers put pit traps in their fields. Since the elephants were unable to eat, they led their herd to encircle carts and horses traveling on the roads. Grain was collected to feed them, after which they went away."[13]

In 991 an auxiliary academician in the Bureau of Military Affairs sent up a memorial in which he observed that in Leizhou (in the Far South), and other areas nearby that were on or near the western end of the south coast, "there are elephants in herds" in "the mountains and forests." The common people were banned from marketing any tusks they obtained, and he proposed that the local officials should pay them half the price. His objective, it seems fair to guess, was to limit what he called "concealment and illicit dealings with others."[14] The most likely reason, though, that the peasants made the effort to get their hands on tusks from time to time was that the returns from the *combination* of crop protection and ivory trading made the substantial risks seem acceptable. This is explicitly spelled out in another report from Zhangzhou (on the southeast coast), late in the twelfth century CE:

> Many of the common folk who won their living among the mountain gorges had their crops trampled on or eaten by elephants. Some were capable of snaring pits with crossbows and arrows, and were happy to have thus rid themselves of the damage; but when the officials demanded that they pay in the feet and the tusks as a tax, this was too much for them. The common people thereafter preferred to endure damage from the elephants and did not venture to kill them.
>
> Just recently, when some of them have presented tusks, the prefect has returned them. He has moreover given orders that families who kill elephants in the future can keep the tusks for themselves. Since the people know how to put an end to the harm caused by elephants, changes will be seen in the deep forests and the spreading footslopes of the hills, and the crops will flourish.[15]

It would be interesting to know why tax policy was the decisive factor in tilting the balance of advantage for farmers here either against, or for, trapping elephants. Seeing that it is said that they were able, though unhappily, to coexist with elephants who ravaged their fields, one suspects that the crucial factor was the cash from the sale of ivory, not just stopping the loss of harvests.

This brings us to the third front: the economic, military, and ceremonial uses of elephants. Elephants may have been domesticated in the Northeast in Shang times, though the evidence is thin.[16] They were certainly hunted, though the numbers seem to have already been low. In the state of Chu, however, in the middle Yangzi valley, ivory was regarded as a routine product during the seventh century BCE.[17] A century later there is a brief account stating that the ruler of Chu "had torches lashed to elephants to make them rush upon the army of the state of Wu."[18] In 548 BCE, in the course of a rhetorical attack on the extortion of excessive presents by the ruler of the state of Jin, it was argued by Zichan, a statesman celebrated for his wisdom and skill, that "Elephants have tusks that are the cause of their death, since they are offered as presents,"[19] though he says nothing about where the ivory comes from. In the West, much later, in the third century CE, the inhabitants were said to "extract the tusks of elephants, and do violence to the horns of rhinoceroses."[20] The tusks were turned into ivory artifacts, like the tablets on which officials placed their papers for writing during imperial audiences; and the rhinoceros horns were used, ground up, for various medical purposes, especially as an antidote to poisons. At times the private sale of the tusks was forbidden—for instance, in the Far South in the late tenth century CE—but there was a black market in them all the same.[21]

The trunk was eaten. In Xunzhou and Leizhou (both in the Far South) around the beginning of the fifth century CE the flavor was said to resemble that of a piglet. Slightly later, a Tang writer, after noting that there were "numerous wild elephants" in the Far South, went on to observe that people "competed to eat their trunks, the taste of which is said to be fatty and crisp, and to be particularly well suited to being roasted."[22]

In most of China the use of elephants in warfare died out in the course of the first millennium BCE. The exceptions were the West and Southwest, where it continued, perhaps intermittently, for almost another two thousand years. In the early 1370s, the defenders of the city of Chengdu (in the West) used elephants carrying men in armor against the forces of the founder of the Ming dynasty, but were routed by the use of firearms.[23] In the Southwest the anti-Ming resistance did likewise. According to the Ming *Veritable Records*:

> In the third month of 1388[24] the rebel Si Lunfa mobilized his entire forces of 300,000 men and more than a hundred elephants. He went back to ravage Dingbian [in the Southwest]. Mu Ying, the Ming general, selected 30,000 brave horsemen to oppose them. The entire horde of 'bandits' sallied forth from their encampment and formed into ranks to await the conflict. Their leaders and senior officers all rode on elephants, and the elephants all wore armor. On their backs they carried fighting towers that resembled screens, and bamboo tubes hung down both sides, with short spears in them to prevent thrusts from the side. When the two lines met, the throng of elephants smashed their way through and continued on forward . . . . The 'bandit' horde was heavily defeated. More than half of the elephants perished and thirty-seven were captured alive.[25]

Over two hundred years later, the Southwestern resistance to the Manchus made use of elephants commandeered from the non-Han locals, partly for military transport. After 1662, however, the curtain falls, and we hear no more about war-elephants in China.

On the economic uses of elephants in late-imperial times, we can draw—with cautious care—on Xie Zhaozhe's *Fivefold Miscellany*, published in 1608. This is a collection of reports about natural phenomena and human affairs assembled by a connoisseur who was always playing in teasing fashion with his own and his readers' sense of what was plausible. He was an official in the Ministry of Works, becoming an expert in water control, and also served in Guangxi province (in the Southwest). He is therefore likely to have had some direct knowledge of what he was writing about in the items that follow.[26]

> The people of Yunnan rear elephants the way those in the heartland of China rear cattle and horses. They ride them on journeys. They load them up with grain, and the animals have an exceptionally docile nature. On occasion they erect frameworks on their backs in which two people can sit face to face when feasting and drinking. When elephants meet with ceremonial arches, they invariably pass through them on their knees. When they are going up a hill they kneel on their forelegs, and going downhill they kneel on their hindlegs, maintaining stability to a greater degree than one can express.
>
> When, at times, people have been forcibly pillaged by bandits, they have cried out in desperation to their elephant. This has caused the elephant to grasp a large tree with the end of his trunk forthwith and to sally out to battle, at once putting the bandits to flight in disorder.
>
> There are times, though, when rogue elephants kill people. These rogues are trapped in pits and put to death.

Xie then shifts to the use of trained elephants at the Ming-dynasty Court to maintain a sort of honor guard outside the audience chamber, and to carry the imperial insignia. The Chinese Court met, it should be remembered, at a very early hour in the morning. It was believed that people thought more clearly at this time of day.

> They are used for these purposes not only because of their imposing appearance, but also because they are mild-mannered and intelligent in a way that other animals are not. The elephants observe an order of precedence, each one having his designated position and category of fodder to consume.
>
> Every morning they stand on either side of the Palace gate. Before His Majesty's carriage has set out, they wander about at random, munching hay; but once the bell has sounded and the whips cracked, they line up on each side with a reverent demeanor. Once all the officials have gone in, they stand with their trunks crossed, and no one ventures to enter by going past them. When the Court is concluded, they once again resume their normal behavior.
>
> If one of them is ill and cannot take his place in the honor guard, a mahout will lead him to visit another elephant, and ask the latter to take the

sick one's place. After this, the other elephant will be willing to do so. If this procedure is not followed, the second elephant will not go.

If an elephant commits an offense, or injures a human, the imperial command will be issued for him to be beaten. Two other elephants will twine their trunks around his feet until the offender topples onto the ground. Only when the beating has been concluded will he rise to his feet to give thanks for the favor received, with an attitude just like that of a human being.

If one of them is demoted in rank, he always takes the position in the honor guard to which he has been demoted. He will not dare to stand where he was previously accustomed. This is much to be marveled at.

In the sixth lunar month they are bathed and mated. The coupling takes place in the water with a female who floats with her face upward, in all respects like a human being . . . .

Although these beasts are bulky and awkward in nature, and do not have an elegant shape, they nonetheless possess uncanny intelligence. Thus it is that many humans are not the equal of animals.

The reader is at liberty to believe as much, or as little, of the details of this account of bureaucratized pachyderms as he or she feels inclined; but the underlying point holds good. By late-imperial times, the elephant only survived in China in what amounted to a ritual circus at the capital, and on the southwest frontier.[27]

This sketch is the preliminary approximation of a description of the long-term human impact on the environment in China since the agricultural revolution and the early Bronze Age. The retreat of the elephants maps *in reverse*, both in space and time, the growth of the Chinese farm economy. More rigorously, the space dominated by elephants in China was the *complement* of the space dominated by humans. It also symbolizes the transition, slow at first but then accelerating, from an environmental richness counterbalanced by perpetual dangers from wildlife, to a sedentarized human dominance accompanied by a relative security from wild animals, but also—at least from the perspective of an Australian who has lived many years in the bush—an impoverished life of the senses,[28] and a scarcity or disappearance of many of the natural resources on which humankind had previously existed.

There is another necessary perspective. In some areas the human struggle against wild animals was a matter of life and death. In the early first millennium CE, though the exact period is cloudy, in the lands of the Bai people around Lake Erhai in western Yunnan there were large pythons—known in Chinese as *mang*—that daily devoured not only livestock but also people.

Surviving accounts have become mythologized, but it is clear that a heroic and at times desperate struggle was needed to destroy them.[29] Only when this had been done was it safe to farm the fertile lakeshore marshland. One of many such battles over habitat. The descendants of these pythons survive today on the eastern side of the Erhai, but much diminished in size and, so far as one can tell without a special inquiry, in danger.

It is important to balance the awareness of what has been lost by victories like this against our predators with a robust realization of how much has been won. Philosophical regrets, inspired by an understanding of our inseparability from the rest of nature are not mere folly or romanticism. But in cases such as this they encompass less than half the story.

3

The Great Deforestation: An Overview

The following poem was written by Liu Zongyuan, a philosopher and essayist who lived around the turn of the eighth and ninth centuries CE. It symbolizes the longest story in China's environmental history:[1]

> The official guardians' axes have spread through a thousand hills,
> At the Works Department's order hacking rafter-beams and billets.
> Of ten trunks cut in the woodlands' depths, only one gets hauled away.
> Ox-teams strain at their traces — till the paired yoke-shafts break.
>
> Great-girthed trees of towering height lie blocking the forest tracks,
> A tumbled confusion of lumber, as flames on the hillside crackle.
> Not even the last remaining shrubs are safeguarded from destruction;
> Where once the mountain torrents leapt — nothing but rutted gullies.
>
> Timbers, not yet seasoned or used, left immature to rot;
> Proud summits and deep-sunk gorges now — brief hummocks of naked rock.

The destruction of the old-growth forests that once covered the greater part of China.

Some comment is necessary. The poem is a political one. The felling of the trees alludes to the destruction of men of talent at Court. The ecological reality was familiar enough, however, for the image to carry a powerful symbolic impact. 'Official guardians' is a title that had in archaic times referred to those whose task it was to protect natural resources, including animals. Now, more than a thousand years later it had been transformed, by a twist of bureaucratic spin-doctoring, into meaning almost the opposite: officials responsible for providing the Court with timber for its new buildings.

Another way the story may be encapsulated is by juxtaposing two facts. In east-central China two thousand years ago, it was still common to cut down a whole tree to make a single coffin.[2] In 1983 the People's Republic of China placed a ban on using wood for floors, staircases, electricity poles, mine-props, railroad ties, bridges, and—vain hope?—coffins.[3] China's reserves of wood per person today, at approximately ten cubic meters for each inhabitant, are only about one-eighth of the world average.[4] The roots of this disaster go back to antiquity.

The causes of deforestation, and the stripping of other original vegetation cover, were threefold. The most common was clearance for farming and settlement, including safety from wild animals and fire. The second most common was probably the provision of fuel for heating, cooking, and industrial processes, like the firing of kilns and smelters. The third was the supply of timbers for building: for houses, boats, ships, and bridges, as well as for other forms of construction such as the pine pilings that were rammed into the coastal mud flats as the foundation for stone seawalls.

There was already a shortage of wood for fuel in the central eastern area by the eleventh century. In 1087, the poet Su Dongpo wrote of the elation caused by the discovery of coal in what is today the northern part of the province of Jiangsu.[5] The mineralogy in the fourth couplet is interpretative, by the way, not scientifically based:

> When, the year before last, rainstorms and snowfalls had blocked off
>   land-based travel,
> The people of Peng were afflicted — by their shinbones splitting and
>   cracking.
>
> For half a bundle of sodden firewood they picked up their quilts in their
>   arms
> And hammered on doors from dawn till dusk, but nobody wanted to
>   barter.
>
> That a rich inheritance lay in their hills was something they did not know:
> Lovely black rock in abundance, ten thousands of cartloads of coal.
>
> No one had noticed the spatters of tar, nor the bitumen, where it oozed
>   leaking,
> While, puff after puff, the strong-smelling vapors — drifted off on their
>   own with the breezes.
>
> Once the leads to the seam were unearthed, it was found to be huge and
>   unlimited.

> People danced in throngs in their jubilation. Large numbers went off to
> visit it. . . .

> In the southern hills, rest, and return to life, await the forests of chestnuts,
> Yet iron, stubborn ore from the hills to the north, will be no trouble to
> smelt.

Already an awareness of the dangers of deforestation. And concern for the fuel
supplies of premodern industry.

The Chinese also grew trees and bamboos for use, sale, or amenity,[6] but this
never compensated for the losses. Regrowth of course occurred in some places
and at some times, after fire and ax had had their way. At the local level it is
over-simple to think solely in terms of unilinear removal.[7]

As a counterbalancing image to that of destruction we can call to mind the
groves of cultivated bamboo in the Boai region, which is near the western edge
of the Northeast.[8] Here irrigation turned part of a barren land into a miniature paradise. According to a late-Ming description:[9]

> In the eighty-three cantons of Henei county,[10] the region of the districts of
> Wanbei and Lixia has channels for water alongside the cultivated land. The
> richness of the fruit trees and the bamboo gardens here is manifest, but they
> represent a mere tenth of the area. The remainder . . . are empty wastes as
> far as the eye can see. A hundred *mou* of their gravels, saline soils, and
> barren lands, with their countless mountain boulders, are not worth one
> *mou* elsewhere.

The *mou* was at this time just under seven per cent of a hectare.[11]

Boai drew its supplies from two rivers. It is not clear when the system was
started, but renovations had to be undertaken in the eighth century CE and
again in the sixteenth, to remove the silt blocking the channels. The network was
thus slightly unstable hydrologically. It could also be disrupted by warfare, as
during the fighting between the Jürchen and the Mongols in the twelfth century,
and by overexploitation, as when too many bamboos were cut down by
officials early in the Mongol dynasty. Irrigation—that is, human intervention—
was necessary because of intermittent drought, which made the bamboos flower
and then die. Damage was also done to the groves during the drought of 1690,
when the Manchu government diverted water from the two rivers to help the
transportation of tax-grain by making it easier to float the boats.

When all was going well, the place was celebrated for its beauty around the
seasons, and for the 'freshness and seclusion' provided by the bamboo gardens
among which the inhabitants built their houses. A late-seventeenth-century
poet wrote of the speckled bamboos said by legend to have been stained by the

tears of the two wives of an ancient sage–emperor when they lamented his passing:[12]

> By multiple branching, the sweet-tasting waters flow down through as
>   many hamlets,
> In numberless acres of high-yielding fields, fine edible sprouts are swelling.
> They cultivate, too, the speckled bamboos, till, mature, they're as stout as
>   beams,
> And, everywhere swaying like dangling splint screens, show the remnants
>   of widows' tears.

Clearly, by no means all development was environmentally damaging. But good or bad, it needed continual maintenance.

Why then do forests matter? One reason is that they reduce the erosion by which wind and water remove topsoil.[13] Vivid descriptions from the late-imperial period reveal the damage done by their destruction when population pressure drove migrants to clear the uplands for short-term planting with crops like maize and sweet potatoes. Mei Boyan, who lived from 1786 to 1856, wrote a classical account of how this was done by wandering groups of squatters called 'shed people' who farmed in the hills south of the Yangzi.[14] Parallels can be found in many other areas, and it epitomizes one aspect of the late-imperial environmental crisis.

> When the late Dong Wenke was governor of Anhui province [in the East] he wrote a memorial ... on the opening up of the mountains by the shed people. The thrust of his argument was that all those who had attacked the shed people were so steeped in geomantic theories[15] that they had let the riches in several hundred *mou* or so of mountains run to waste ... just in order to safeguard land harboring a single coffin.[16]
>
> The shed people were, on the contrary, capable of confronting difficulties and being content with insipid food in the high mountains and places that but rarely saw traces of human beings. They knew how to open up and sow dry-field cereals in such a way as to supplement rice and sorghum, and the land gave forth all its benefits to them. It was an appropriate policy to encourage them, and wrong to put obstacles in their way with prohibitions that gave rise to quarrels.
>
> When I had read what he had to say, I thought he was right, but when I went to Xuancheng [in the East], in Anhui, and asked the country people about it, they all of them said that when the mountains had *not* been developed the soil had held firmly in place, and the stones had not budged. The

covering of plants and trees had been thick and abundant, and after the rotting leaves had been heaped up for a few years they might reach a depth of two or three inches. Every day the rain passed from the trees to these leaves, and from these leaves into the soil and rocks. It passed through the cracks in the rocks, and drop by drop turned into springs. Downstream, the rivers flowed slowly. What was more, the water came down without bringing the soil along with it. When the rivers flowed slowly, the low-lying fields received their water without suffering from disaster. Furthermore, even after half a month without rain, the fields lying high up still obtained an influx of water.

These days, people have used their axes to deforest the mountains. They have employed hoes and plows to destroy the coherence of the soils. Even before a shower of rain has come to an end, the sands and gravels will be coming down in its wake. The swift currents fill up the depressions. The narrow gorges are full to the brim, and cannot retain the mud-filled water, which does not stop until it reaches the lowest-lying fields, where it is then stagnant. These low-lying fields become completely filled, but the water does not continue to flow in the fields up in the mountains. This is opening sterile soils for farming, damaging the other fields where the cereals do grow, and profiting squatters who do not pay taxes, besides impoverishing registered households who do pay them.

I also listened to what they had to say, and found it to be correct. It has—alas!—always been impossible for benefit or harm, either one of them, to be unmixed.

Thus the litter created and held below the trees created a sort of filter for the rainwater.[17] This filter also prevented the soil being washed down into the irrigation systems below, and clogging them. Since the soils below the surface layer were largely sterile, which is why hill-farmers had to move on every three years or so, the washdown once the trees had gone could make further difficulties for the settled agriculturalists downstream.

In the end a proportion of eroded soil became sediment deposited either on the bed of a river, its flood plains, or its delta. Thus upstream deforestation almost certainly lay behind the rapid filling of the Canton Delta in late-imperial times.[18] The growth of the deltas of the Yellow River, on its various north and south courses, and of the Yangzi, must both have depended to some degree on the same effect, mostly at earlier periods. The action of waves and tides then removed, reworked, and redeposited these sediments, especially once a river mouth had ceased to be active. This was what happened with the old south-course mouths of the Yellow River, on the boundary between the East and the

Northeast, after 1855. The total *vertical* accretion at the mouth of the south course between 1194 and 1855 has been estimated at *almost ten meters*. The horizontal extension seaward in this period was about ninety kilometers.[19] In the extraordinary thirteen years from 1579 to 1591 during which the hydraulic engineer Pan Jixun's system of scouring silt out of a single consolidated channel was in full operation, the delta grew seaward at the rate of 1.54 kilometers *a year*.[20] One way or the other, deforestation also *created* potentially cultivable land, and in doing so inscribed a visible record on the coasts of China.

Delta land could be separated from the sea by seawalls, then washed free of salt, and made into rice-fields enclosed within polders. A 'polder', technically, is an area surrounded by defensive dikes, and below the level of the surrounding water at some time in the year. This reclamation is what created much of the Jiangnan region, on the south side of the lower course of the Yangzi. The site of what is now its greatest city, Shanghai, only emerged from the sea in about the thirteenth century CE.[21] Jiangnan is thus, in a sense, a 'Chinese Netherlands'.

The formation of new coastal farmland was on balance economically advantageous, even if it tied up other resources for its protection and maintenance. The problem was what happened along the middle and lower courses of the major rivers, especially the Yellow.

The Yellow River, though, was not called 'Yellow' until about two thousand years ago, but simply 'The River'. Toward the end of the first millennium BCE the *History of the Han Dynasty* declared that sixty per cent of its water was mud.[22] This was certainly an exaggeration. Today, for example, just offshore from the mouth, the average solid content ranges from 0.4 to 3.75 kilograms per cubic meter of water (which weighs a metric tonne).[23] The most likely reason for the change in color was the promotion of farming in the Northwest by the Qin and Han dynasties. The grasslands that covered much of the land along the middle reaches were stripped for agriculture; the temperate-zone forests in the southeast of the Northwest were felled to meet the need for timber created by the capital cities.[24] Erosion, followed by the deposition of suspended sediment, made the bed of the Yellow River rise above the surrounding plain, only kept in its place by man-made levees. In the absence of levees the banks would have overflowed from time to time and, as the overflow slowed down and its carrying power fell, have dumped its load on the flood plain. The result, until in the end the river broke out anyway and picked itself a new course, was a perpetual hydraulic headache.

The technology required for building these huge embankments, involving the mobilization of vast amounts of labor, was in part a product of earlier military practices. During the period of the Warring States that had preceded the unification of the Early Empire, several of the combatants had built massive walls along state frontiers and also used them to direct floodwaters across the territories of their enemies.[25] This theme, namely the push given by military pressures to economic technology and early economic growth, is one to which we shall return in the later chapter on short-term advantage.

During the Warring States period levees were set back about ten kilometers from the river bank, in order to provide space for flood waters. The *History of the Han Dynasty* tells us that eventually the sediments within the levees were "so rich that the common people cultivated them. It would happen that [for a time] they would suffer no evil consequences, so they would build houses there, and later these would form villages. When there were large floods, these villages would be drowned; but they would again construct new dikes to defend them."[26]

The varying frequency of serious breaks in the levees of the Yellow River over the next two thousand years provides a proxy index of the intensity of farming and logging in the Northwest and Northeast. The figures are approximate, and subject to possible distortions arising from variability in recording. They most likely also reflect to some degree long-term climatic change. Nonetheless the differences are clear enough to be fairly unambiguous.

During most of the Han, from 186 BCE to 153 CE, one disastrous break in the levees occurred about every sixteen years. The highest concentration was between 66 BCE and 34 CE, when the frequency rose to one every nine years.[27] In around 6 BCE Jia Yi estimated the cost of annual repairs falling on the ten commanderies (approximately, prefectures) along the river as "ten thousand ten thousands" of copper cash, that is hundreds of millions if the figure is taken at face value rather than as rhetoric.[28]

During the next four centuries, the transfer of populations to the Northwest, and agricultural colonization, came to an end. The weather grew colder. The frontier between farmers and pastoralists moved south. Grass and forests regrew. The frequency of serious breaks in the levees fell to one in every fifty years or less.[29] Barbarians were good for the environment.

Toward the end of the Northern Wei dynasty, around 500 CE, the conversion of parts of the middle reaches of the Yellow River to arable began again. An example is Hetao on the northwest corner of the great bend. The capital at Chang'an,[30] one of the largest cities in the world at this time, and possibly *the* largest, also generated a heavy demand for wood and fuel. After the middle of the eighth century CE the transformation of the Northwest's grazing lands to cereal-growing accelerated.[31] In 788 CE, the military governor of a circuit on the southeastern edge of the Far West, in modern Gansu province, restored a ruined city there:[32]

He led his soldiers in person, sharing with them both hard toil and leisure moments. They felled the forests, mowed the grasses, and cut down the thickets, waiting until they had dried, then burning them all. Over an area several tens of square *li* all was farmland, beautiful to behold. He urged his soldiers to plant trees and crops; and their yearly harvest of millets and vegetables came to several hundred thousand *hu*.[33]

Here, as so often, the military appear as developers of marginal lands.

In the last hundred and sixty years of the Tang, from 746 to 905 CE, breaches in the Yellow River levees occurred about once in every ten years. During the following period of the Five Dynasties, this rose to one in every 3.6 years.[34] In the first phase of the medieval economic revolution under the Northern Song, from 960 to 1126 CE, the frequency was one every 3.3 years.[35] This is an underestimate. Only breaches explicitly mentioned have been included but not severe floods. The most catastrophic of these dike-breaks occurred in 1117 CE, when more than a million people are said to have been killed.[36] The way this figure stands out like a pinnacle among the records of the death toll in much smaller disasters gives it, curiously, a certain measure of authenticity. Whatever the discount applicable for exaggeration, it is clear that a mismanaged ecosystem can kill on a colossal scale.

The course of the Yellow River began moving about in the later twelfth century,[37] often taking multiple courses, and comparative statistics are not meaningful again until after the end of the sixteenth century. The south course of the Yellow River during most of the Qing period, that is from 1645 to 1855 CE, a time when population pressure meant a renewed effort to open up the fragile loess[38] lands through which the middle course of the river runs, had one disaster every 1.89 years.[39] Abnormality had become the norm.

A second environmental function of forests is safeguarding the regularity and the quality of the supply of water.[40] An unusual example of this is provided by Suninga's account,[41] written in 1802, of the water supply of Ganzhou, which lies north of the Babao mountains in the Far West:[42]

The livelihood of the people of Ganzhou relies entirely on the water from the Hei River.[43] As spring turns to summer, the first melting occurs of the snow piled up in its pine forests, and it flows into fifty-two channels to irrigate the fields. The second melting of the snow takes place as summer gives way to fall, and only when it has flowed into the fifty-two channels is their harvest assured. Without the pine trees in the Babao mountains, when the end of spring comes, the winter snows would all melt in a single surge, the Hei River would overflow, the fifty-two channels could not contain it, and a disastrous flood would break through them. As a result of the feebleness of the second snowmelt at the transition from summer to the fall, the water in the Hei River would be in short supply and low, hence unable to make its way into the channels to irrigate the fields, which would cause fear that there would be a severe drought. The livelihood of the inhabitants of Ganzhou depends wholly on there being numerous pine forests and on the snow that accumulates among them. Were they to be cut down it would not be possible for the snow to pile up among them, which would be a great catastrophe for the populace. It goes without saying that they should be protected in perpetuity.[44]

By a twist of fortune, this disaster was exactly what happened toward the end of the century. According to an account of a journey made in 1891:[45]

When they installed electric telegraph lines, a certain high official was in charge of the poles, and he despatched soldiers to cut [the pines]. They caused immense destruction, since without the snow being kept in the shade it melted immediately there was the slightest warmth, and thus caused fear of flooding. There was no rain when summer began, which gave further concern that there would be drought. The sounds of reports of resentment were heard in all quarters.[46]

Many travelers' accounts associate the presence of trees with good-quality water, though without drawing an explicit connection between the two. Tulishen, a Manchu diplomat who visited the Tsarist Russian empire and the Torguts of the lower Volga early in the eighteenth century, quotes the description of his northern homeland given by his associate Gajartu to the ruler of the Torguts: "The mountains there are lofty and forbidding, the forests and wetland thickets deep and dense, and the rivers numerous," adding that "the water in all the rivers is sweet and fine. Even in the low-lying places where flood water has accumulated it is also excellent and in no way different."[47]

The Helan or 'Piebald' Mountains in the northwest of the Northwest, to the west of the loop of the Yellow River,[48] may be a case where the long-term degradation of the once-abundant forest cover was associated with a partial drying-up of watercourses. Yuanhao, the founder of the Xixia, or Minyak, a non-Chinese state that flourished from the late tenth to the early thirteenth century, had a palace here where he could escape from the summer heat. This and the later building of a city put heavy demands on timber for construction. It was said that long after the state had perished woodcutters could still "find nails a foot or two in length among the ruined trees." Some time before the beginning of the seventeenth century, the lesser peaks had been "destroyed up hill and down dale by logging; woodcutters and hunters had trampled about, and gradually made tracks through them." In the higher mountains, though, there were still "deep woods that gave protection from the sunlight." The gazetteer for the prefecture of Ningxia (in the Northwest) reported in 1780 that "there is little soil in the mountains, but numerous stones. The trees all grow in crevices in the rocks." This suggests erosion, though it also seems that there was still some good cover on the western-facing slopes. Furthermore, the gazetteer continued:

> It is cold in the heights, with snow normally remaining on the peaks until the fifth or sixth month in high summer. The springs of water are sweet to the taste and transparent, with a color as white as milk.[49] This is so in every valley with a stream. Lower down, the sands and gravels form a barrier, so the streams reach the feet of the mountains and there stop. It is not possible to use them to irrigate places far away.[50]

Without more evidence it is hard to know whether or not the water supply had been damaged. One suspects so, but the climate may have become more arid, or it may have behaved like this even before deforestation. Late-imperial deforestation is not in doubt, but it is necessary to retain an element of caution with regard to its effects in particular cases such as this. Future, more detailed, research may cast doubts on the representative nature over time and space of individual case-histories like this, or interpret the evidence differently.[51]

Forests also affect microclimates.[52] In temperate zones they usually cool the temperature, both by evapotranspiration and by providing shadow cover.[53] Humidity also increases. Under certain circumstances, they may tend to increase local rainfall, though the reverse can also occur.[54] Some historical evidence suggests that clearing the woods in tropical and subtropical areas has in fact reduced rainfall, and that under some circumstances this has even been helpful to human beings.

An example is the Lianzhou[55] area on the south coast near the boundary between the Far South and the Southwest.[56] According to the national gazetteer for the early nineteenth century,

> they cut channels in the sides of the hills and drew in water from springs. They constructed dikes and built dams to hold the water. Near the rivers they made square-pallet chain-pumps to drive the water into the irrigation system. Thus, when the weather turned to drought, they had water to provide for irrigation. They repaired ditches between the fields, and cut channels, so that when there was flooding they could remove it. They separated out

rice-shoots for transplanting, adding manure and clearing weeds from the seeds. . . . All the waste land among the forests was fully developed.[57]

This transformation of the landscape reduced 'disease due to pestilential vapors', which probably refers to one of the forms of malaria.[58] Some species of *Anopheles* mosquito found in this region, such as *A. dirus*, do best under heavy forest cover. The same account continues.

> The commandery of Lian used *long ago* to be described as a place of disease due to pestilential vapors, on account of its deep valleys and dense woods. The population was sparse, and the aethers[59] of the Bright and Dark Forces[60] not healthy. There were in addition the influences of poisonous snakes, venomous insects, strange birds, and unusual animals spreading through the forests and valleys. It was always overcast with rain, and there were floods in its streams and torrents. The exhalations off the mountains and the savage aethers, when added to the foregoing, gave rise to diseases due to pestilential vapors. . . .
>
> *At the present time*, the forests are sparse and the torrents widened out. The light from the sky above shines down; the population is dense, and the secluded forests every day more opened up. It is a long time now since Lian and Lingshan [also in the Far South] were afflicted by disease due to pestilential vapors. Qinzhou [in the Far South] has in like manner had but little. Only in Wangguang, Shiwan, and Sidong next to the border with Jiaozhi,[61] *where the mountains and streams have not yet been developed*, does it still sometimes exist. Even so, it has not been reported that those who are skilled in looking after their health and who have traveled there have been smitten by it.

Liu Ts'ui-jung has found a similar process of change in the microclimate caused by clearing forests for wet-field rice-farming in Taiwan after the later seventeenth century as Han migrants from the mainland settled and transformed the nonmountainous areas of the island. One mid-nineteenth-century commentator wrote: "When Gemalan was first opened up, there were more rainy days than sunny ones; now, however, cold and warm are both the same as in the interior, and there is no more poisonous 'miasma.'"[62] She also identifies the disease here described as being caused by pestilential vapors as malaria.

The mechanism by which clearing forests for rice-farming to some extent controlled malaria must remain a matter for speculation at present. Depending on the region concerned, one of the several species of the *Plasmodium* protozoans that cause the disease are carried by a member of one or other of certain species of *Anopheles* mosquitoes, whose preferred habitats are not identical. The mosquito acquires the protozoans as the result of a blood-meal on an infected human. It passes them, in its saliva, back into the bloodstream of another human victim in the same way. The female *Anopheles* lays her eggs on the surface of water in the spring, and the full process of development after this takes about three weeks.[63] The theory that the control of water by the rice-farmers, which involves the flooding of fields prior to transplanting the shoots, followed by the drainage of the fields as the harvest ripens, in some way reduces the opportunities for the successful reproduction of the mosquitoes is questionable, given the range of breeding habits of different species, and the preference of some for moving water.[64] The most likely cause of the reduction of the incidence of malaria seems to be the increased exposure of shade-loving species of mosquitoes, such as *A. dirus* mentioned above, to direct sunlight as the result of clearance.[65] Otherwise an increased density of human settlement would simply have provided more infected humans to pass on the protozoans to local mosquitoes, and more accessible potential new victims for them to bite. Some degree of immunity of course may also have been selected for in the population as the generations passed.[66]

Dense tree cover thus has disadvantages as well as advantages.

Forests provide habitats for birds and animals and plants.[67] Often these are a source of foods and medicines, as well as other materials. For a farming community they can serve as a reserve to fall back on if the harvests fail. Their diminution or loss impairs security through the removal of an *environmental buffer*—a theme to which we will often return. The disappearance of forests is like depriving a population of an environmental insurance policy. They can—to the contrary—also be a source of danger, both to people and crops. This dual character creates an ambiguity in their relationship to humankind.

Hunting animals and birds provided part of the diet of ordinary people in archaic times. The *Ordinances for the Months*, a work with a degree of scriptural authority, probably compiled in the third quarter of the first millennium BCE, has a number of prohibitions that make this clear. For example, in the last month of spring, "the nets for snaring animals and birds, and those mounted on long handles for birds, the concealment shelters for those shooting game, and the toxins used to poison animals should not be taken through the nine gates of the palaces, cities, suburbs, and barriers outside."[68] In other words, they were to be kept in storage at this time of year, but could be used later. It is not clear to what period this text refers, though it was presumably considerably earlier than the date of compilation.

A famous moral tale from the second quarter of the first millennium BCE relates how a leading official upbraided the duke of Lu for his "insatiable greed" in fishing with nets at a time when the young fish were only just beginning to grow up.[69] In the golden days of yore, he said, "when birds and beasts were pregnant with young . . . the official guardian of animals would forbid . . . the use of nets to catch four-legged beasts or birds." Likewise, "where deer were concerned, fawns were to be permitted to grow up." The use of the beasts was said to be "both for presentation as sacrifices and practical use."[70] It seems likely that these bans reflected a growing awareness of the approaching exhaustion of many forest resources in northeast and northwest China by this time, and were an attempt to prevent it.

The great royal hunts of the Shang, which occurred earlier, in the second millennium BCE, were probably *not* mainly to obtain food, but to secure sacrificial animals, train troops in the maneuvers used in war, protect crops, and possibly even engage in sport.[71] In the world of the early farmers, surrounded by forests, deer could be such a threat to growing grain that tigers were seen as beneficial animals on account of the part they played in keeping the numbers of deer down.[72] The Shang however did not tackle only such modest game as deer, foxes, wolves, and badgers, but also the aristocrats of the forests like elephants, tigers, and rhinoceroses. The dynasty maintained a vast hunting-ground to the west and south of Mount Tai in what is today the province of Shandong. Such large-scale hunting within China Proper seems not to have continued under the succeeding Zhou, though the unabashedly exaggerated Han-dynasty rhapsody on the states of Qi and Chu, *Master Emptiness*, partially translated in chapter 4 below (pp. 50–1), to some extent hints otherwise. I suspect that the excesses it describes were felt to be exciting precisely because they surpassed reality. But, equally, the phenomena depicted cannot have been entirely unfamiliar if readers were to be gripped, or amused.

Rhinoceroses were almost as widespread as elephants in archaic times and were regularly hunted by shooting with arrows, or with traps and fires. Their hides made the standard protective armor for Chinese soldiers for more than a millennium in archaic times. Their horns were used as drinking cups, or, later, in powdered form, as an antitoxin.[73] The two commonest species in historical times were the little single-horn and the double-horn. Both are forest-dwellers, needing access to water for a daily bath to fend off mosquitoes, and are sensitive to cold. Cold winters killed rhinoceroses in the Tang imperial menagerie in Chang'an (in the Northwest) in the late eighth century CE. In the Far South, at about 23° S, in early Song times, they are reported to have kept themselves warm in the winter months by digging themselves into the ground.

Rhinoceroses had gone from the lower Yangzi valley by the early empire. By the middle empire they were becoming something of a rarity in the West. The Tang emperor Xuanzong, who ruled in the middle of the ninth century, ordered that one found in Quzhou (in the West), after having been brought to

Court to be looked at, be "returned and set free in the wilds of Quzhou," as he "felt anxiety about harming the nature of an animal." Iron armor had long replaced hides by this time, and rhinoceroses had changed from being the source of a military necessity to exotic curiosities. The Tang poet–monk Qiji, seeing a friend off on a trip to the Far South, romantically envisaged him

Where, among southern-barbarian blooms, lie peacocks hid,
And the rhinoceros rage through stone-strewn wilderness.

All of which is literary imagining regarding a relatively timid and mostly nocturnal herbivore, and suggests a lack of direct experience of the animal in the wild.[74]

Rhinoceroses hung on in the Southwest until the end of the nineteenth century, but are now extinct in China. Climatic change must have been a factor in their long and eventually fatal southward retreat, and the desire of the Court for tribute in the form of horns from particular localities must also have kept up the pressure for hunting an animal that only reproduces slowly, with a gestation period of between 400 to 550 days for a single offspring.[75] But habitat destruction was probably, as usual, the crux.

Along the outer northern margins of the historical Chinese world, the large-scale hunting of animals took another form, spectacular but intermittent compared to that driven by commercial pressures or regular levies by bureaucrats and the military. In 423, the advisers of the ruler of the non-Chinese Northern Wei dynasty, which at that time still ruled mainly over the largely nomadic Toba people, told him that if he was unable to destroy a small state as a source of booty with which to sate his followers, "we should engage in a hunt within a constructed enclosure on the Yin Mountains[76] and slaughter a vast number of birds and animals. Their skins, flesh, tendons, and horns may be used to meet the needs of the army."[77] A few years later, in 431, "several tens of thousands of horsemen" from three of the northern tribes under Toba rule "drove several million deer to this place where the emperor then proceeded to hold a great hunt, whose spoils he presented to his followers. He had a stone engraved south of the desert to record his capacity for achievement." We are not told what sort of landscape these hunts took place in, but it seems likely that they were at least partly forested, perhaps in a fairly open fashion.

At the less dramatic everyday level, and across the empire as a whole, supplementary hunting continued over the centuries until, region by region, the forests had shrunk or vanished to the point where this was often difficult or even no longer possible. In later chapters on Guizhou (in the Southwest) and Zunhua (in the Northeast) we shall see how emergency hunting and gathering could even so provide an ecological buffer against inadequate harvests for some people into late-imperial times.

The opening of an international market could be still deadlier than the megalomania of barbarian monarchs. Liu Ts'ui-jung has described how up to the start of the seventeenth century the aborigines in Taiwan hunted deer on a sustainable basis, even with the exportation of some deerskins and dried venison to Fujian province across the straits. With the coming of the Dutch East India Company, and an annual export of sometimes over 100,000 skins a year to Japan, the herds went into decline. Deer were largely extinct in southern Taiwan by the end of this century, and the reclamation of grasslands by Chinese farmers in the century that followed came close to making them extinct in the island as a whole.[78]

Parrots, who are in the main woodland birds, likewise grew scarcer as the trees disappeared. They symbolized the ambivalent character of the forests as reserves of biological resources. The Chinese appreciated parrots. In Qing times, a poet[79] wrote of Lintao in the Northwest:[80]

> Lintao's beauties come to mind —
>   The ample light in springtime on
> Its peonies open a full foot wide,
>   Its parrots flying past in throngs.

They were admired for their skill in avoiding nets, their taste for cleanliness, sometimes (it was said) even pulling out a feather that had been stained with oil, and for their ability to copy and respond to human speech. But parrots were a menace. In the Qing dynasty, one observer[81] wrote of the region of the Greater and Lesser Jin rivers in the West:[82]

> Every year, just as the harvest of naked oats is ripening, parrots come flying in hundreds and thousands, darkening the sky as they descend. Their green wings are resplendent, their voices a squawking babble. The farmers grasp hold of staves to defend the crops. Some of them are crafty and lay traps among the ears. Once the birds have gathered, the mechanism releases a concealed catch that grabs their feet, so that it is possible to capture them alive.

The *Treatise on the Strange Beasts of the South* mentions that there were numerous parrots in various parts of the Far South, including what is today the Canton area. If one of the flocks of several hundred birds chanced on fruit in the mountains that was coming to maturity, the fruit would vanish in an instant. The so-called 'stone chestnut' that grew between rocky crevices in the mountains in the Far South, and tasted like a walnut, was particularly prized by local people because it was so difficult to get a ripe one before the local parrots did.[83] Rearing parrots in captivity was also known to be dangerous. Folklore had it that if one touched their backs too often one would catch 'parrot malaria', presumably some form of psittacosis, and die.[84]

Nature may be beautiful, at times stunningly beautiful, but beauty is no guarantee that it is healthy for humankind. Take peacocks. They like sparse woods and thickets rather than dense forests, and were once common in the Far South, not just the Southwest which is their refuge today. Humans reduced their numbers, not only through habitat destruction, but also because they are tasty to eat, particularly when fried in oil. Their feathers were also in demand as tribute to the imperial court. But peacocks poison the environment. According to one writer[85] in Qing times,[86]

> That the water in the rivers in the region of Laibin,[87] Nanning, and Xunzhou [all in the Far South][88] is foul-smelling and turbid is connected with the excrement of peacocks. The color of the water is sometimes jade-green and at others a dirty red, and so unpleasant that one cannot go near it. Boats have to travel for fifty kilometers without coming to a well. This leaves them no option but to use alum to settle and clear the water, and then add flowers of sulfur to remove the poison. After this it is fit to drink. Eighty to ninety per cent of those affected by the poison either have diarrhea or are over-come by depression.

The dense woods of South and Central China also harbored tigers, which were responsible for the deaths of many travelers and others.[89] On occasion this prompted human counterattacks. One unusual instance, using gunpowder, was recounted by Shi Dakai in the middle of the nineteenth century. Shi was one of the leaders of the anti-Manchu Heavenly Kingdom of Great Peace. After falling out with his fellow rebels he took his troops off on a long march into western China which lasted from 1857 to 1863 and ended in his destruction by the Manchu government. At a town near Nanshi,[90] where his scouts were mauled by tigers, Shi found that the inhabitants often kept the south gate of their town closed in the summer for fear of these animals which lived in the dense forests on a hill just outside. He therefore had one of his explosives experts, a certain Wang, blow up a section experimentally:[91]

> I climbed up onto a stele to watch from a distance, and personally saw thick smoke covering everything. This was followed by a clap of thunder and 'the heavens fell in and the earth split open'. A small section of the mountain had been pulverized and had collapsed. The roots of the trees had been torn out and were flying and dancing about. The wild animals were dashing away in frenzied disorder. I could not make out which were tigers, leopards, jackals,

or wolves. Wang observed that for this he had only made use of a little explosive force. If substantial explosive force were used for half a month the entire sector could be made into a level road running through to the other side of the mountain. The dens of the savage beasts and venomous snakes could be eliminated overnight.

Once again we are forced to confront the ambiguity of forests.

With the passing of the centuries, the environmental buffer provided by trees became more and more degraded. Here, from the later seventeenth century, are the opening lines of "The Song of the Elms" about famine in Jurong, which was in Jiangsu province, southeast of Nanjing:[92]

> Beside the walls of Jurong city, along the verges of ancient roads,
> Rise a thousand — ten thousand — stumps of elms, but all of them are
>   colorless.
> Nothing but withered trunks are left, their bark-cover stripped off totally,
> As the famished inhabitants, loathing it, pestled the chunks into crumbs.

The last remnants of a life-support system.

Across the economy of the late empire the scarcity of wood for fuel and construction was the daily price paid for more than two thousand years of deforestation. For many people in many areas life had become a constant struggle as a result. Typical are some lines written in the Qing dynasty on Shizhou in Shanxi province (in the Northwest):[93]

> Limping through fearsome defiles, the old men return
> With bundles on their shoulders of the wood they need for burning.
> To draw their water the young married women must travel a long way off
> And far down dip their earthenware crocks into the deep-sunk torrents.

It was the same story in the lower Yangzi region. Jiang Tingyi wrote six poems on various kinds of shortages here, among them the following on fuel for cooking:[94]

> Our family's courtyard's filled with grass and weeds.
> Below the steps grow pines, and innumerable bamboos.
> From here, at dawn, we take the fuel to cook our morning meal,
> And, as dusk falls, we gather more to steam our evening gruel.

> It's the easiest of matters to exhaust bamboos and pines,
> And our grasses, and our weeds, can never grow enough.
> So we take a hundred cash in hand when the day is growing light,
> And come back, as it's getting dark, with a market-purchased bundle.

The damp can make the firewood too soggy to really burn,
And rice that's not boiled dry is still not properly cooked.
Emptiness in our stomachs makes us utter plaintive murmurs:
Eight unfilled mouths, and eyes — that swell with hopeful looks.

When we trudged along those ridges not so many months ago,
Like clusters of upright arrows stood the trees upon the hills.
All that we can see today, as we pass through the lands below,
Are those same slopes in the distance, but sharp-edged now, and stripped.

The common folk who farm have nothing left for fuel,
And set the wooden axles of their water-pumps ablaze.
They have no prospects after this. Husbandry is useless.
So they smash their shacks and sell the planks inside the city gates.

Probably rhetorical exaggeration, but other references to this sort of desperation can be found.

Environmental plundering was common. Vagrants who moved round in bands big enough to overawe local people sometimes engaged in this crime:[95]

> They pull rocks from the banks to prop up their stoves
>   And from the walls they wrest out the bricks.
> They scythe brush for fuel, and fell cemetery groves,
>   Till most pines and cypresses lie about — killed.

At the other end of the social scale, the difficulty in finding timbers large enough to build ships led the Qing government to commandeer trees from gardens and even grave sites. According to a poet writing near the end of the seventeenth century:[96]

To build ships in Jiangnan demands they cut huge trees.
So strict warrants go to Zhejiang, and to Hedong and Hexi:[97]
'Fell elms and willows in garden groves that are ten spans around,
And the hundred-foot-tall conifers that stand by burial mounds!'

Whatever great families, and titled clans, have available they begrudge,
Yet how can the quotas be obtained from yokels of little substance?
The county officials mark off trunks, their tallies held in their hands,
Their commands to the Yangzi villages throwing humble folk into panic.

The remotest mountains and boundless marshes are already scattered
    wreckage,
In vain, amid the winding lanes, people cherish their scattered hedges.

And so he goes on, shocked that graveyards, previously spared by imperial decree, are no longer exempt.

Industry was similarly affected. In a poem on the official Yunnan copper mines, probably composed in the middle or later eighteenth century, Wang Dayue expressed a sobering vision of the coming exhaustion of reserves of wood:[98]

> Rarer, too, their timber grew, and rarer still and rarer,
> As the hills resembled heads now shaven clean of hair.
> For the first time, too, moreover, they felt an anxious mood
> That all their daily logging might not furnish them with fuel.

Cutting wood for the market became big business. But as some problems were solved, others intensified. Large-scale operations provided valuable materials, but also caused environmental damage. Lumbering offered much-needed employment, and violent social disruption threatened if it closed down. This could happen if the price of grain rose to the point where it did not pay an employer to hire labor, since supplying workers either with food, or with adequate wages to buy it, was crucial to the system. Or the economically accessible supply of suitable trees in a particular place could run out.

The following prosaic verses from Yan Ruyi's "Song of the Timber Yards" on commercial logging in the Northwest, probably early in the nineteenth century, reflects these anxieties.[99] Several points need a word of explanation. The Zhongnan in the first line are a range of mountains just south of the Wei River, and crowned by Mount Taibai which rises to over three thousand meters.[100] The reference to two capital cities at the end of the second stanza is a literary turn of phrase that comes from earlier dynasties, such as the Han and Tang, when there were in fact two capitals. This was not the case under the Qing. The 'sky-trucks' and 'sky-bridges' are said in an author's note to have been made from wooden frameworks; the first may have been an early form of cable skidder.[101] The invented terms 'water-jacks' and 'timber-monkeys' are my guesses for otherwise untranslatable words that seem respectively to refer to men who took care of the logs floating down the rivers, and those who pulled them out at the end of their journey. Ox Mountain was a famous deforested hill referred to by the philosopher Mencius in the fourth century BCE. He argued that its treeless state was no more natural than the state of the men was in his degenerate times.

> Extending West, the Zhongnan twist and wind
> Until they crosswise meet with Mount Taibai,
> A bluish darkened green, more than three hundred miles
> Of intertwining shrubs against the sky.

Famed as materials, straight firs, *Castanea* trees,[102]
And pines and cypresses, verdant throughout the winter,
Are, when collected, useful — to meet the people's needs,
And shipped and traded in both capital cities.

To serve as beams or rafters is only for logs that are massive,
The destiny of slender lengths is to end in cookhouse flames.
Merchants, since well endowed, can provide investment capital;
And make plans calmly for returns beyond all expectations.

Supervision of the accounts is under the head clerks' direction,
While engineers survey and gauge for the operations in hand,
Bookkeepers enter the records — of payments — into their ledgers,
And labor-contractors organize sworn brethren into gangs.

Several fathoms in girth around are the multitudinous trunks.
And once the axes are laid aside, cables are used to haul them,
Dragged up and down by 'sky-trucks' over the slopes and summits,
And ferried, along 'sky-bridges', across ravines and gorges.

The boards, on the porters' backs, tax their strength with their heavy weight,
Men who are nicknamed 'mules' because of their sturdy endurance.
The accumulated logs will wait, till the river's again in spate,
And 'water-jacks' send them on their way — down the ebullient currents.

'Timber-monkeys' pile up the logs where the river valleys open,
Stacking them up to towering heights like wooden city walls.
A single yard has a numerous force of workers at its disposal:
The largest can bring together a thousand of them, or more.

Opening the forest little by little is how they make their way forward,
Under such disciplined control they seem to be a battalion. . . .

Half of these gangs of workers are wandering, homeless, men.
Great numbers depend upon these jobs to provide them with a life.
Some years ago, when there arose the stirrings of rebellion,
No hesitation held them back from joining in the fighting.

By relying on tough commanders, the insurgency was throttled.
Those who'd originated revolt were all of them put to death.
But how can we impose a ban on what brings people profit?
Compassion is also needed when livelihoods are threatened.

Opening forests and gathering timber depend on the merchants' funds,
And also rely on the weather being, time and again, propitious.

When foodgrain's cheap and their workers find — the cost of living no
    trouble,
They sit at their ease and lick their lips at the thought of the year's-end
    profits.

Returns accrue to the businessmen that are bigger than their investment,
And mobs of workers congregate like the swarms of summer's insects.
But it's not so easy to forecast when flood or drought will occur.
Sudden the alternation between bumper harvest and dearth.

If, for a single year, the cost of food has gone up,
Then, in the year that follows, to continue production is tough.
When eleven liters of millet fetch a price of a thousand coppers,
The merchants' reserves are inadequate. And jobs come to a stop.

Lumberjacks who lived by their muscles will scatter and disperse.
How can they supply themselves? Or themselves direct the work?
Could Ox Mountain again be beautiful, clear-felled so long ago,
When arid, bare, reflection is now the state of its slopes?

True, it is sometimes said, when an old-growth forest's downed,
That one can cultivate the soil by putting it under the plow.
But do those who say this realize, when lumber's taken out,
That for every trunk that's cut, hundreds of men milled about,

And the twisting roots plunge down, ten feet or more in depth?
If you sow grain in such a place, how many stalks will you get?
Still, in that stony tilth, there lingers the chill of the heights.
The usual cereals we eat need other land and dikes.

Late-imperial Chinese premodern economic growth, as we shall see repeatedly
in later chapters, was already close in many respects to its Western counterparts on the eve of the industrial revolution. The market dominated production, including the hiring and firing of a workforce that had no security. There
was a complex, literate and numerate, internally specialized, managerial staff.
The technology used was self-consciously advanced for its time. The state
picked up the tab for the social dislocation caused by business activities. Useful
economic needs were being serviced, but the environment was being mauled
and exploited in an unsustainable way. And with a profit-motivated stamina
that made the 'official guardians' mentioned at the opening of the chapter
appear intermittent and inefficient despoilers in comparison.

4

The Great Deforestation: Regions and Species

Let us be more systematic. At the coarsest focus, there would currently be three main zones of vegetation cover in China if there had been no human interference. The first is that where there is little or no cover, mostly various kinds of deserts in the Far West. The second is the world of grasses, meadows at the higher altitudes and steppes lower down. This covers western Manchuria, inner Mongolia, the western edges of the Northwest, and most of Tibet. The third is what would be mostly a domain of trees and substantial shrubs, had agriculture not become widespread.

Turning up the focus on this last, it is clear that the major divide within the actually or potentially forested region is between a temperate and warm-temperate region to the north characterized by deciduous broadleaf trees, and a subtropical region to the south characterized by evergreen broadleafs. As would be expected, there is a wide zone of transition, which lies mostly between the Huai River and the middle and lower Yangzi, though forests of a mixed type extend well to the south of the Yangzi. Nor is the contrast between the domains dominated by 'deciduous' and 'evergreen' broadleaf trees as sharp as has just been suggested. There are important deciduous broadleafs in the subtropical zone. Natural bamboo forests are also an important marker of the southern zone, though the pattern has been blurred by human plantings. Each zone also has its own distinctive conifers. In the Far South, there is another world again: the trees become a mix of subtropical and tropical species. Hainan Island even has coconut palms.

This pattern has been derived by a selective amalgamation of the information in the detailed map of China's vegetation cover published by Hou Xueyu in 1988. It would be possible to interpret his data in a somewhat different way, putting more stress on east–west differences, or creating more finely graded north-to-south subdivisions in the two main forest zones. Schemes of subdivision along the general lines used here have however been formulated by Wang Chi-wu in 1961, Hou himself in 1988, Menzies in 1996, and Ueda Makoto in 1999, though there are differences in their sense of what is critical.[1] I have opted for the simplest possible system, using the seasonal loss or retention of the foliage as the major marker so far as possible. Strictly, this requires a separate zone in the far north of Manchuria to provide for the deciduous larches, notably *Larix gmelinii*, whose Chinese name means 'the pine that drops its leaves'.[2]

The Western reader will already be familiar with many of the common genera of Chinese trees: oak (*Quercus*), pine (*Pinus*), elm (*Ulmus*), ash (*Fraxinus*), and other old friends.[3] A good number of trees that are East Asian in origin have also been introduced into parks and gardens in the West, and can often be found described with illustrations in handbooks such as *The Reader's Digest Encyclopaedia of Garden Plants and Flowers*. Examples are the Pagoda Tree (*Sophora japonica*) and the Maidenhair Tree (*Gingko biloba*) with its distinctive partly divided leaves. Others can be found in illustrated guides like Roger Phillips's *Trees in Britain, Europe and North America*. Instances are the Japanese Cedar (*Cryptomeria japonica*) and the (conventionally misnamed) 'Chinese Fir' (*Cunninghamia lanceolata*). This last is a quick-growing evergreen conifer that is resistant to decay, and was used in past times for coffins, boats, and pilings. Understandably, it has long been a favorite for commercial exploitation.

Even if books such as these do not contain the exact Chinese species that one wants, they sometimes describe a close relative. An example from the Phillips is the maple-like Oriental Sweet Gum (*Liquidambar orientalis*) which is not too different from the Chinese *L. formosana* that a millennium-and-a-half ago lined the banks of the lower Yangzi.

But identifying many individual species does cause difficulties. It does not help that the constant revision of botanical names means that older works of reference are frequently incorrect. Take the *wutong*. Myth had it that this was the only tree on which a phoenix would alight, but it can nonetheless sometimes be found today lining streets in cities south of the Yangzi. Herbert Giles's *Dictionary*, now more than a century old, gives it as *Sterculia platanifolia*, which hints at the plane-tree-like leaves. The 1947 edition of the widely used Chinese encyclopedia *Cihai* [Sea of Phrases] identifies it as *Firmiana platanifolia*.[4] Today it is *Firmiana simplex*. In the sketches of the individual zones that follow I shall keep unfamiliar botanical names to a minimum.

Let us then take an armchair historical journey around the main regions of China as characterized by their trees. Besides providing an overview of what were very different patterns of deforestation, this tour will also serve as an introduction to the regional geography. The one major omission is the Yangzi delta, which is covered in detail in the later chapter on the prefecture of Jiaxing.

The heartland

The southern part of the temperate and warm-temperate zone of deciduous broadleaved trees was the heartland of archaic China. The mean annual temperature here varies greatly with latitude, and has also varied over time. It is currently around 14.5° Celsius in places like Kaifeng in He'nan and Ji'nan in Shandong. The weather regularly drops below freezing in the winter, yet averages between 26° to 28° in these areas at the height of the summer. Yearly rainfall can reach 1,000 mm on the coast, but sinks below 600 mm as one moves west. Two-thirds or more of this precipitation occurs during the summer, and the amount varies sharply from one year to the next. Dry-land farming here has long been a risky undertaking.

When we turn now to the pattern through time, it is not possible to begin at the beginning, which is inaccessible to historian's history—that is history based on documents that give some direct insight into the human mind. We have to start some way into the story, when windows of evidence have opened through which we can get glimpses of the causes behind human interaction with nature.

The Zhou dynasty that wrested mastery of the Chinese world from the Shang, or Yin, toward the end of the second millennium BCE was a civilization based on deforestation. Self-consciously, passionately, so. The opening lines of an anthem in the *Scripture of Songs*, which claims the divine right of the Zhou house to rule, are unambiguous in their enthusiasm for destruction. It is the basis for development:[5]

Majestic indeed was our Lord God Above
As He gazed down in splendor upon this, our world.
The four quarters lay under His rule, and His judgment,
That the people below should live undisturbed.

But neither Xia's state, nor successor Shang dynasty,
Had proved able to govern the empire correctly.
So He scrutinized deeply, appraised, and considered
All the other realms spreading north, east, south, and west.

This done, His verdict came into effect:
Detesting Shang's style so befouled by excesses,

He shifted to us, in the west, His affection,
And bestowed on our Zhou — a place we could settle.

We uprooted the trees then! Lugged trunks aside
— Those that, dead, still stood upright, and those that had toppled.
We pruned back the branches, or flattened entirely
The stands in long lines and the thick-tangled coppices.

We cut clearings among them. We widened the openings
Through tamarisk forests and knob-jointed cane-trees.
We tore from the soil, or else lopped back, groves
Of wild mulberry bushes and spiny Cudranias. . . .

When our Lord God Above had examined these hillsides,
We ripped out oaks whose leaves fall, and those green the year round,
Clearing spacious expanses amid pine and cypress.
Here God made our state, and our sovereign, His counterpart.

The tale of 'Prince Millet', quasi-mythical founder of the Zhou line, and symbol of farming culture, as recounted in the *Songs*, mentions how as a baby he survived various hardships thanks to the help of animals and birds. And also, more enigmatically:[6]

When he was abandoned — in some woods where land was level,
Chance so had it that these flat-land woods were felled.

Farming meant the removal of the forest. Another of the Zhou anthems begins[7]

After cutting down trees, and scything the grasses,
Their plowing has scattered the soil into fragments.

Another again mentions how Danfu, the historical ancestor of the Zhou state, cleared the Plain of Zhou:[8]

Widespread his hatred — unfailing!
So, too, his renown — never fading!
He tore out both shedding and evergreen oaks
So that the highways for travel lay open.
Headlong the Gunyi barbarians fled.
Then indeed were they breathless!

The conqueror's ecstasy of dispossession and development. The non-Chinese, who lived among the trees, almost defined as non-Chinese by doing so, were sent packing by the destruction of their habitat.

It is not surprising that, somewhat later, when 'barbarians' wished to stress how 'Chinese' they had become, they would point to their having cleared the land for farming. In 557 BCE a prince of the Rong barbarians was being mocked as the descendant of a grandfather who had been driven from his lands wearing a cloak made of reeds and covered with brambles—contemptible garb—and told he was not fit to take part in a meeting of rulers. The prince gave a dignified answer, part of which ran as follows:[9]

> Duke Hui . . . bestowed on us fields on his southern frontier. It was a place inhabited by foxes and where wolves howled. *We Rong cut and cleared the thorny bushes.* We drove away the foxes and wolves. We became subjects of those former rulers, and never invaded them and never rose against them in revolt.

He was accepted.

There is not yet enough evidence even to guess as to whether or not the Zhou attitude to forests differed markedly from that of their predecessors. Was it to some degree more aggressive? Clues are frail and fugitive. Perhaps the most tantalizing is that the Shang-dynasty oracle-bone graph for 'farming' appears to show an activity being carried on in the midst of trees.[10] The account later given by Mencius of the origins of Chinese civilization close to two thousand years after the event probably only reflects the more-than-likely different attitudes of the late archaic or early classical period:[11] "The sage–emperor Shun commissioned the forestry official Bo Yi to manage the fires. Bo Yi set fires in the mountains and marshes, and burnt them clear. The birds and beasts fled away to hide themselves." This is another statement of the policy of environmental clearances attributed by Mencius to the Duke of Zhou, and quoted in the previous chapter.

By the early first millennium BCE, if not considerably earlier, the focus of state economic concern was on farming. The *Commentary of Zuo*, which covers events from early in the eighth century BCE till early in the fifth, has frequent accounts of the organized military theft of the grain reserves of other states and the pillaging of harvests. The disasters normally thought to be worth recording were those that affected an agricultural economy: droughts, floods, granary fires, and plagues of cereal-devouring insects.[12] By the Warring States period, however, it was not uncommon for a besieging army to cut down the trees in the territory of the state it was attacking—seemingly as valuable plunder.[13]

Overall, we can conclude that there was once considerable forest cover in the heartland of late-archaic China. Otherwise we would not have records, such as those cited above, of the efforts spent in removing it. Nevertheless, it is wise to be cautious and not to assume that it was originally widespread everywhere. There are extensive accounts of hunting by rulers and the aristocracy in two-wheeled chariots pulled by four horses. It seems unlikely that, in the absence of some sort of a trackway, it would have been easy to drive such a vehicle through country much more densely wooded than an open savanna. So much at least is suggested by the handful of anecdotes that have survived. In 596 BCE, when Zhao Zhen was being pursued, "he abandoned his chariot and fled into a wood."[14] In 588, when the ruler of the state of Qi was at war with an allied army from a number of other states, "the two outer horses of his foursome became ensnared by a tree, and stopped."[15] Finally, during a skirmish in 549, a certain Luan Le was about to loose off a second arrow against an opponent whom he had missed with his first shot, when "his chariot drove into the trunk of an acacia tree and overturned." This cost him his life.[16] Chariots and heavy woodland don't mix.

Large-scale hunting tended to be done in the 'plain', grassland typically covered with flowers and plants such as thistles, rather than with closely set trees, and inhabited by deer, wild pig, and rhinoceroses.[17] That hunting such animals was regularly done in chariots is at least suggested by a story told of the ruler of Qi when he was hunting in 685 BCE. He saw a large boar, which his attendants said was the incarnation of the murderer of the ruler of the state of Lu. Enraged, the ruler of Qi loosed off an arrow at this 'man–pig', but it only stood up and howled at him. Panicked, the prince "fell over in his chariot and injured his foot." Not long afterwards he was the object of an unsuccessful attempt at assassination.[18]

There are close to no accounts of forests affecting warfare, though sometimes a wood would give its name to a military rendezvous. One of the rare exceptions to this absence relates to events in 518 BCE. After some of the armed forces of the small state of Zhu, located in the south of what is today the province of Shandong, had fortified a stronghold, they found themselves obliged to return home past the hostile city of Wucheng, which belonged to the state of Lu:[19]

> The people of Wucheng blocked them off to the front. To what was to be the Zhu rear they cut trees, but not to the extent that they fell over. Once the army of Zhu had passed this point, they pushed them so they toppled down. They then made the Zhu army their prisoners.

By the sixth century BCE wood had already become a scarce commodity in the region along the northeastern sea coast. In 538, the statesman Yanzi commended the fair dealing of the Chen clan of the state of Qi, observing that "when the trees from *their* hills go to market, they charge no more for them than they do back in the hills."[20] Somewhat later, in 522, he criticized the selfishness of the ruler of the same state, implying that this might have prompted the spirits to make him ill in consequence:[21] "The trees of the mountain forests are watched over by the officials called *henglu*." There was already the beginning of a shortage of natural resources, and the state was extracting profit from it.

The core culture of classical China, located in the central part of the Yellow River valley, the southern part of the deciduous broadleaf zone, thus had no attachment to forests, no commitment to preserve them except—in rather later times—as reserves of useful timber,[22] and certainly no reverence for them. There were regular sacrifices to mountains and rivers, and a sense of the numinous magic in these natural phenomena. There was a belief that deities presided over the winds and the rains. The scriptural *Monthly Ordinances* does forbid the sacrifice of female animals to "mountains, *forests*, rivers, and marshes,"[23] which indicates at least a minimum of forest worship or propitiation, but, so far as I know, there were no distinctive gods or goddesses of the forest in this most ancient of the areas that we recognize as 'Chinese'. In the *Rituals of Zhou*, which is at least partly and probably largely an idealization from early-imperial times, it must be noted that the Guardian of the Mountain Forests[24] is described as being in charge of "sacrificial offerings to [the spirit[s] of] the mountain forests." This involved cleaning the ritual site, which probably had an altar and some image or representation of the spirit(s), and keeping passers-by away from it. We are not told any more.[25] The chapter on religion in Song Zhenhao's *History of Social Life under the Xia and Shang Dynasties* identifies numerous rituals of pre-Zhou times dedicated to natural phenomena, but nothing to forests.[26] A millennium later, in 540 BCE, Zichan, the celebrated prime minister of the state of Zheng, is likewise said to have observed:[27]

> When we are afflicted with floods, or droughts, or epidemic disease, we sacrifice to the gods of the mountains and the rivers to remove them. When we meet with snow or frost or winds and rains that are out of season, we offer sacrifices to the gods of the sun and moon and stars and planets to remove them.

But not forests. Forests seem to have been primarily the lairs of demons. In 605 BCE a certain Wangsun Mang spoke as follows of the nine bronze caldrons reputed to have been cast in an age long gone by the sage–emperor Yu the Great:[28]

> He had the caldrons cast to bear the representations of the various beings. All of them were to be found there. This was how he caused the people to know how to recognize the evil tricks played by supernatural forces. So it

was that when the people went out into the rivers and wetlands, or the mountains *and forests*, they did not meet with any misadventure. None of the demons of the hills or rivers was able to attack them.

The more positive supernatural side possessed by the mountains and rivers seems to have been, with the most minor exceptions, absent from the world of forests.

A forest is a world, a physical and spiritual habitat, whether one loves it or shuns it. A tree is a resource. The Zhou Chinese certainly valued trees that had an economic use, whether for fruit and nuts, for construction timber and firewood, or for feeding silkworms. In 711 BCE, in the course of settling an argument about precedence, the point that it was the host who determined the ranking of his guests was clinched by the remark "The Zhou have a saying: 'When there are trees upon a hill, it is the carpenter who gauges what they are useful for.'"[29] One of the anthems of the state of Lu records the logging of the mountains of what is today Shandong province to build the New Temple:[30]

> From Mount Culai they brought the pines,
> From Mount Xinfu the trunks of cypress,
> Cut them according to the measure,
> In fathoms and feet marked widths and lengths.
>
> Massively thick the raftered pine,
> The chamber imposingly immense.

There arc also many references to chopping down trees for fuel in the *Songs*. Most of them are probably literary devices to score a point by analogy or implication. They should therefore not be taken as necessarily reflecting common practices—at times maybe even the opposite, in the search for increased rhetorical impact—but their frequency confirms the impression that trees were often seen as not much more than firewood waiting to be burnt. For example,[31]

> How densely clustered the oak-tree thickets!
> Fuel for the sacrificial rituals!

In later times, at least, these lines were used to refer to the abundance of political talent surrounding the ruler. Or again, consider this part of a rebuke to a faithless lover:[32]

> Getting my firewood by cutting that mulberry —
> As it burns in the portable stove, I warm up.

This may—perhaps—carry the implication that a mutual affection that could be flourishing and beautiful is being used up in a way that is self-destructive.

Conversely, trees with flourishing foliage often serve as a symbol of well-being.[33] A closely knit family was also likened to the branches and foliage on a central trunk, each assisting the other.[34]

As a political, rather than a personal, lament there are lines like[35]

> Take a look at that forest placed in the middle:
> Fit only for firewood, only for kindling.

This is an indirect way of saying that the ministers at court are worthless. What was probably a protest against the suffering of the innocent is contained in some other verses:[36]

> Fine plant-cover grows on the mountain's flanks,
> Such as chestnut trees and *mume* plums.
> People, perversely, molest them and damage them,
> Yet no one knows what wrong they have done.

Mume plums are the so-called 'Japanese apricot' (*Prunus mume*).

Trees were thus a part of the rich world of rhetoric and allusion in late-archaic and early classical China. But not forests. The two should not be confused.

Useful trees were planted beside buildings and around homesteads. These included hazels, catalpas, chestnuts, lacquer, willows, mulberries, and Chinese dates.[37] In 535 BCE, when Gongzi Qiji of the southern state of Chu passed through the state of Zheng he took pains to make sure his followers behaved themselves:[38]

> He placed prohibitions on the gathering of fodder, putting out animals to graze, and gathering firewood: farmers' fields were not to be entered, *planted trees were not to be taken for fuel*, cultivated plants were not to be gathered, rooves were not to be pulled off, and nothing was to be seized by force.

In other words the opposite of the actions of the usually ill-behaved military.

Last of all, it should be noted that catalpa trees—probably mainly *Catalpa bungei*, which still grows on the foothills round the north China plain—were often planted beside graves.[39]

Especially in the first half of the first millennium BCE, when it was still possible to relocate entire cities—because they were small and there was unused land to move to—the Chinese showed a great sensitivity to the economic, health, and psychological aspects of their environment, including the availability of trees. The following is said to have happened in 584 BCE in what is today the southern part of the province of Shanxi:[40]

The people of the state of Jin planned to abandon their old capital at Jiang. The senior ministers declared, however: "We should stay here in the land of our ancestral clans. . . . The soil is fertile and we are close to a source of salt. The state profits from so doing, and the ruler is content. This must not be forfeited." . . .

The ruler asked Xianzi: "How should we act?"

"It is *not* appropriate to stay here," Xianzi replied. "The soil of this land of our ancestral clans . . . is thin, and its streams are shallow. One can easily catch diseases, and when this is so the people suffer from anxiety. If they suffer from anxiety they feel stressed and cornered. Under such conditions they are afflicted by the internal accumulation of fluid and swollen lower extremities.[41]

"Xintian is better. The soil is thick, and the streams run deep. If one lives there one does not become sick. The Fen and Gui rivers carry illnesses away. People there will also be in a fit state to receive instruction. The benefits will last for ten generations.

"Now mountains, marshes, *forests*, and salterns are the treasures of the state. When the state is affluent, its people grow arrogant and idle. Though such treasures lie near at hand, the ruling house is impoverished. It cannot be said to be content."

The ruler was pleased with this counsel. . . . Jin moved its capital to Xintian.

The rhetoric is slightly opaque. Xianzi's view seems to be that the affluence of the state is of less concern than the health and character of the people. What is worth noting for our present purposes, though, is that wood was scarce enough here for a forest to be a profitable 'treasure'.

The Old South

The middle Yangzi was a different world.[42] Most importantly, it was warmer. At the present day no month in the year has a mean temperature that falls below zero Celsius in the lowlands. The average annual temperature ranges from 13.5° to 16° in its northern section, and from 15° to 20° in the southern part. Due to the influence of the summer monsoon, the yearly rainfall is from 900 to 1,500 mm or more, the quantity increasing as one moves south. In contrast to the more alkaline conditions in the north, the soils are either neutral or acid.[43] From the point of view of its forests it would be appealing to say that this is the region in which evergreen broadleaf trees dominate, those that can be thought of as having leaves mostly glossy on one side, in contrast to the matt finish of most deciduous leaves. This is too simple a formulation: the broadleaf forests are mixed, and stands of bamboos and distinctive conifers, like the *Cunninghamia*, important. But it symbolizes something of the shift from a comparatively austere natural world to a richer one.

It was generally recognized in late-archaic times that the state of Chu, in the central Yangzi valley, had more woods than the states of the Yellow River valley. In 546 BCE, the diplomat Shengzi remarked to the prime minister of Chu that the senior ministers of the state of Jin were more talented than those of Chu, from which—though he did not say this—some of them had fled. He then made his point with a comparison: "It is the same as the way that the evergreen oak and the catalpa,[44] and skins and hides, come from Chu. Although Chu has these materials, it is Jin that makes use of them."[45] A handful of lines in the *Compositions of Chu*, an anthology that took final form in the second century CE but most of whose material is probably several centuries older, stress the darkness of the Chu forests.[46] The richest picture, though, is that in the rhapsody *Master Emptiness* by Sima Xiangru, who lived in the second century BCE.[47]

The intent behind this prose-poem is problematic. That the story it tells is not presented as factual is evident from the names of most of the characters, notably 'Master Emptiness' himself. My sense of the first section translated here, on hunting by the ruler of Qi, is that it is a mockery of the megalomania and obsession of ruling-class hunters, but I may be mistaken in this. The description of the 'Marshes of Clouds and Dreams' that follows clearly has an element of fantasy. It may all the same convey something of the nature of the wetlands that once lay on either side of the central Yangzi, and probably acted as natural sponges, absorbing surplus water during floods and releasing it slowly during dry spells.

'Master Emptiness', so the story goes, was once sent—in preimperial times—on a mission from the mid-Yangzi state of Chu to the state of Qi on the northeast coast. He was taken out hunting by the ruler in the grandest style, both to please him and impress him. He recounts what took place:

> The king traveled forth with ten hundred chariots,
>> Chosen soldiers on foot, and ten thousand horsemen,
>> To go hunting — along the shores of the ocean.
>> The ranks of his infantry filled up the marshlands,
>> His game-nets extended across the hills.
>
> Rabbits were grabbed, stags squelched in the cart ruts,
>> Deer skewered with bowshots, unicorns heel-nabbed.
>> Down to salt-water inlets the huntsmen went rushing,
>> The fresh meat, cut and salted, discolored their wheels.

His shooting on target, the king's bag was immense.
He ascribed himself merit, puffed up with pride.
Then looked over his shoulder and put me the question:
"Does Chu, too, have such plains, such vast wetlands for venery,
   As delightful as this is, and with game as abundant?
   Chu's ruler and me — do *his* hunts measure up?"

I got down from my chariot, gave him this answer:
"I, your servant, from Chu, have but commoner status.
   By luck, ten years and more His Majesty's guardsman,
   I have followed him, oft times, out for amusement.
   I have been to the park at the back of the palace
   And seen what has happened there, also what hasn't,
   But I've not had the chance to see all that there is.
   As to marshlands outside, what could I tell you?"

He replied to me then, "If that's how it is,
Still tell me a little of what you've experienced."

With respect, I responded: "I, your servant, have heard
Seven the marshes Chu's realm encompasses,
   But I've seen only one,
   Not laid eyes on the others.
And the one I have looked on's uniquely minute.
The name that it bears is 'Clouds and Dreams Marshes'.
Clouds and Dreams Marshes are in circumference
   Three hundred miles.
   In their midst there are mountains.
   Labyrinthine their windings,
   Sharp-pointed their peaks.
   Below the irregular summits and pinnacles
   Sun and moon pass occulted in partial eclipse.
   In crisscrossing confusion
   They oppose the dark clouds.
   Stagnant water forms pools, but flows where it slopes,
   To submit at the bottom to rivers and streams. . . .

Dark woods rise to its north. Gigantic their trees:
   Machilus and camphor,
   Pepper, cassia, magnolia,
   Wild pear, cork tree, and poplar,
   Chestnut, sour pear, date-plum,
   Pomelo, and mandarin — spreading sweet fragrance.

And he goes on to describe the animals and birds.

The landscape is essentially imaginary. So if the poem is a benchmark, describing an archaic environmental richness still untouched by premodern economic growth, it is one ornamented by literary art into a baroque splendor, not a dispassionate catalog. But with, it is reasonable to believe, at least a certain memory of a reality.

What happened to this world? Tracking specific localities through long periods of time is a crucial control on generalizations, but difficult. It is attempted later in this book for three small areas. Here we are still sketching, and some general impressions at a forest-regional level, caught by snapshots widely spaced in time, is all that will be undertaken.

Early Chinese imperial civilization made use of many different kinds of timber, and connoisseurs had a keen appreciation of their appeal to the senses. Lu Jia, for example. He was chamberlain to the founder of the Han dynasty at the turn of the third to the second century BCE, and wrote as follows in his *New Discourses* of the trees of his native Chu:[48]

> Things of fine quality have to be widely known if they are to be prized. Talents of excellence have to be brought to light if they are to serve any useful function. What can one use to explain this point?
>
> Well now, the *Machilus* and camphor are trees famous throughout the empire. They are born among the deep hills, and are the offspring of the banks of valleys where the streams flow. When they are standing upright, they are the patriarchs of the multitudes of trees in the great mountains. When they lie prostrate, they are of practical use to countless generations. They are floated down on the currents of the mountain streams, and emerge from the dark depths of the wilderness. They follow the courses of the streams and rivers until they reach one of the capitals.[49] Here they submit to the craftsmanship applied by the ax which brings forth the beauty of their patterns and hues: unflawed and durable, straight-grained, close-packed and delicate, and of the same quality throughout. Gnawing insects and worms cannot penetrate them, and being soaked in water does them no harm. They are flexible when above ground, unyielding when sunk in the earth. They are lustrous without being oiled, and their elegant beauty is perfect without carving or painting.

Didactic trees to adorn a courtier's rhetoric. They are of course a symbol for officials. 'Oiled' is a metaphor for receiving favors, and an 'elegant beauty' that needs no improvement suggests in the original Chinese an effortless literary style. But a certain reality is also evident: the exploitation of the distant southern forests to supply the raw materials for imperial palaces.

Some wood for building may even have come from overseas. In the later second century BCE, Emperor Wu of the Han dynasty had a Cypress Beams Tower constructed out of 'fragrant cypress', and used it for drinking parties and poetry competitions. A later medieval source, often more romantic than reliable, says that the tower was two hundred feet high and that its odor could be smelt about fifteen kilometers away. The species most likely to have been used is thus *Chamaecyparis obtusa*, which is known for the scent of its wood. Today, at least, it is native only to Taiwan and Japan, so it was also probably exotic enough to showcase imperial extravagance, and leave its imprint on the historian's pages.[50] Thus culture exacts its tribute from nature.

Religion, too. Wood was required for every burial. A hermit–scholar wrote about the cult of coffins as follows:[51]

In ancient times, when someone was buried, they would swathe him thickly in firewood and inter him in waste land. No mound would be raised, and no trees planted. Nor was there any fixed time for mourning.

In later generations, the sages changed this to the use of an inner and outer coffin. The *Firmiana simplex* tree was used to make the inner coffin, and the bindings to secure it were *Pueraria* fibers. The corpse did not contaminate the springs of water below it, and the stench did not leak out above.

About halfway from that time till now, people shifted to using *Catalpa bungei*, *Catalpa ovata*, sophora, cypress, *Cedrela sinensis*, and *Ailanthus altissima*, in each case according to local conditions. They used glue and varnish to keep the coffins in shape, to ensure that they were sturdy and trustworthy. This was all that was needed for the latter to perform their function reliably.

These days, families of noble status in the capitals always want to have the wood from an ailanthus, catalpa, or camphor tree *from south of the Yangzi River*. Even on the distant frontiers, and in areas with no great pretensions, people compete in like manner to follow whatever is in fashion.

Now the ailanthus, catalpa, and camphor tree come *from extremely far away*. They are chopped down high in the hills, then dragged through the stripped-bare valleys. They go onto the sea from the mouth of the Yangzi, then ride back up the River Huai. They next make their way against the current of the Yellow River, and travel upstream along the Luo to reach the capital at Luoyang. Carpenters carve and cut them for days and months on end. Multitudes have to be assembled if the timbers are to move. Oxen have to be numerous if they are to reach their destination. Each log may weigh a quarter of a tonne, and the work needs tens of thousands of laborers to complete. . . . Resources are squandered and farming damaged across a vast area.

The long-distance trade in southern wood for de luxe coffins was presumably just the visible top of a more extensive business activity.

Other uses of wood were mostly obvious. It was employed for building houses and boats, bridges, chariots, and carts. It provided the greater part of tables and beds, tools, utensils, and parts of weapons and musical instruments. We have also to remember that in the days before paper was widely used, vertical wooden strips were the commonest medium for writing. The vertical columns of characters in which paper books were later written, and, later still, printed, were the ghosts of these vanished strips. They can still be found in some old-style Chinese books today, especially in Hong Kong and Taiwan.

By the second century of the next millennium, even the Marshes of Clouds and Dreams were beginning to feel the pressures of the expansion of human settlement. A vision of the peaceful coexistence of people and wild animals was still possible, however, though whether it was the survival of an old vision or a new one born of an urban idealism is impossible for the moment to say. According to the *History of the Later Han*, when Fan Xiong took up the post of prefect of Nan commandery in what is now the province of Hubei:[52]

> The commandery was by the banks of the Yangzi and the Mian rivers, and included in addition the Marshes of Clouds and Dreams. During the Yongchu reign-period [107–113 CE] there had been many violent attacks by tigers and wolves. The previous prefect had offered rewards to recruit people to seize them in nets, but contrary to what he intended a very large number [of humans] were killed. Xiong in consequence wrote to the magistrates under his jurisdiction: "For tigers and wolves to be in the hills and forests is like human beings living in cities and towns. In the age that attained the perfection of moral transformation in antiquity the fierce beasts gave us no trouble. This was entirely due to the widespread beneficial influence of our favor and good faith, which was such that our empathetic understanding extended to the birds and beasts. Although I, the prefect, am lacking in charismatic virtue, how could I dare to neglect this public obligation? Let everyone bear firmly in mind that they are to destroy their cages and pit traps, and not irresponsibly to catch animals in the hills and forests." After this, deaths from tigers largely ceased, and people obtained security.

Under the charming story the battle for habitats is apparent.

We move forward to the middle of the fifth century CE, when the Liu Song dynasty ruled a state based on the lower and middle Yangzi valley. By this time, nongovernmental economic development had a taken a firm hold on the more easily opened areas. The attempt of the authorities to maintain a public economic domain to which commoners had only controlled rights of access for a limited exploitation was collapsing, a centrally important story we shall return to later, and which was more complex than it appears here.

We also shift downstream. 'Yangzhou' at this time was a region centered on what is today Nanjing. According to the *History of the Song*:[53]

> The Prefect of Yangzhou ... reported to the Emperor: "Though the prohibitions regarding the mountains and lakes have been established since times past, the common people have become accustomed to ignoring them, each one of them following in this the example of others. *They completely burn off the vegetation on the mountains*, build dams across the rivers, and act so as to keep all the advantages for their families. . . .
>
> Rich and powerful people have taken possession of ranges of hills. *The poor and the feeble have nowhere to gather firewood or hay.* These incursions are serious abuses that damage good government, and to which the administration should put an end. It should be reaffirmed that the old laws that defined what was beneficial and what harmful are still in force."
>
> The authorities examined the edict of 336, which said: "To take possession of the mountains, or to put the marshes under one's personal protection is tantamount to robbery with violence. Those who steal more than ten feet of land are to be beheaded in public."
>
> Yang Xi demurred: "This system of 336 contains prohibitions that are rigorous and severe. Since it has been difficult for the people to obey them, their principles have in practice been eased so as to be in keeping with the spirit of the times. Nonetheless, taking possession of mountains, and blocking rivers with dikes, have become more and more common. Because people copy each others' bad example, these places have, so to speak, become their hereditary property. Were we to take back these properties all of a sudden, this action would provoke anger and resentment.
>
> "We ought now to repeal the old rules and create a system based on the following five provisions: As regards the mountains and the wetlands, we shall not charge with an offense, nor confiscate the lands of those who have become accustomed to *clearing them by burning the vegetation*, and *planting bamboos and all sorts of fruit* in such a fashion that these can renew themselves, and to building dams and lakes, and also barrages to keep captive river and sea fish, . . . which they maintain in good repair.'

And he goes on to lay down maximum holdings for officials of various ranks, and for commoners, and proposes their properties be recorded in land registers.

The popular economic energy that emerges from this passage conveys an impression of considerable social and political strength. Enough to push aside laws of exceptional ferocity in a century or so. Here is a passing glimpse of what was a more-than-millennial irresistible program of unofficial, demotic, clearances, to make space for agriculture, water systems, orchards, and fish-farming. The privatization of the commons.

An important change of gear occurred during the medieval economic revolution in the centuries after about 900 CE. This was the result of the extension of the influence of the market for ordinary wood, from the local level, where it had long existed, to trade over a wider and wider range, with varying patterns in terms of region and time. To give just one example to illustrate where this was eventually to lead, a censor memorialized as follows in 1789, near the end of the late-imperial age, on the traffic traveling north up the Grand Canal:[54]

> The official grain-boats of the Hubei group were late. Investigation revealed that the cause of this was that the entire group was engaged in dragging through the water 1,800 mast timbers belonging to the provincial judge Li Tianpei. . . . If this official has timber for his own use, he ought to have it transported himself. How can he allocate its transport to the tribute-grain ships in the hope of economizing on carriage costs and avoiding the customs duties—so holding up the grain transport?

Good-quality but hardly luxury wood from the middle Yangzi valley was thus being transported several thousand kilometers, down tributaries and the Yangzi and then up the Canal,[55] in response to demand at the capital. By taking such transects at widely separated moments in time it is possible to sense a slow but on the whole cumulative long-term change that must have been invisible to those living through it.

In the remoter parts of the forest region of the middle and lower Yangzi the pressures of the market made themselves felt even later. Here is what seems an illustration of this from 1851. It comes from Tongdao,[56] which is in the south of Hu'nan province. Today it is an autonomous county for the Dong minority people, hence unlikely in the past to have been fully Han in a cultural sense. In a place called Camp Baoshan—and the term 'camp' in a place-name tends to signal a non-Han population—the elders created a system to protect their trees from being overexploited. They left a record of this engraved on a stele:[57]

> Was the vegetation of the forests of these mountains always the way it is today? No, it was not. A phenomenon whose age is of many centuries has met with a disaster.
>
> On the mountain of Houlong in Shangxiang, *we have always had several thousands of trees of vast girth.* The people of the present time are not of a quality comparable to those of more remote ages. They have acted in their

personal interest in *cutting down trees in an unreasonable fashion.* The result has been that the beauty of the mountain trees has undergone a change. The mountains shine as if they had been stripped naked.

This means that we have reached a moment in time when the mountains have been ruined, the arteries of vitality drained dry, and the spirits of human beings become inconstant. Our locality is in a state of decomposition and decline for which there is no remedy. Seeing that this decline is already an accomplished fact, who possesses the power to remedy this situation of rottenness? Or to find the means by which the springtime may return?

All the trees, on all sides of this Camp, must be cared for so that they can return to a good condition, and then surpass the past, becoming flourishing, rich, and of great age, such that our children and grandchildren may pass on their abundance from one to the other without end.

We have now resolved that all the land on Mount Houlong, up to the summit of its slopes and as far down as the reservoirs, gardens, fields, and houses, and toward the interior as far as the crest of Linglou, and toward the exterior as far as the fields and reservoirs of Yanchong, shall become *communal land.* It will not be permitted either to buy it or sell it. *All the trees of this forest are to be conserved* and placed under an interdict. It is forbidden to fell them in an unreasonable fashion. Those who do not obey this resolution approved by public discussion are wicked thieves. They will be held responsible, and punished by collective action. . . .

We have decided that *the trees around the source of the river* at Camp Baoshan provide it with a comprehensive protection, and that *all of them must be cared for* and placed under an interdict. It will not be allowed for them to be felled in an abusive fashion. Those who disobey will be punished.

We have decided that the second circumscription of *Cunninghamia* at Camp Baoshan, and the first of *Cunninghamia* on Mount Maque are to be *communal mountains.* They are not to be sold or bought.

We have come a full circle. Here are a people who seem not just to care for useful trees but to love forests. Who envisage their grandchildren continuing to live surrounded by the forest. The language of the inscription and not a few of the characteristic phrases are conventional literary Chinese. The underlying sentiment comes from somewhere else, from some tradition that was not Han. A tradition that wanted to maintain forests. That felt that the moral and physical well-being of humans and forests were interdependent.

The inscription raises questions, however, that we are not in a position to answer confidently. What entitles us to guess that the forest was declining because of the pressure of commerce?—Mainly the emphasis on stopping buying and selling, though strictly speaking the bans apply to land. But there is also the lament for the recently degraded character of humankind. They now cut down trees for their 'personal interest', which suggests selling the wood rather than using it for building. Also the recent arrival of markets easy to access. But we do not know what felling trees in a 'reasonable' or 'unreasonable' fashion meant to them in practice. We could be cynical, and suspect that under the fine rhetoric of communal interest the elders were establishing their own privileged claim to be the only ones to be permitted to cut down timber, and profit from it.[58] This is possible, but one can detect a note of real affection for the forest that does not seem just rhetoric.

What is unarguable is that it is a symptom of pressure on forest resources even in remote areas as China entered her modern era.

The Old West

The middle-imperial Chinese economy gradually crystallized into three main commercial regions until the fading of the medieval economic revolution in the thirteenth and early fourteenth centuries. These were the north China plain, the lower Yangzi, and the western inland basin of Sichuan.[59] The forest history of the first has already been outlined, and the second touched on tangentially awaiting a fuller treatment in the chapter on Jiaxing. The third had its own style and pattern. Isolated to the west by the Himalayas, with difficult access to the central Yangzi valley in the east via the great river-gorges, and precarious land communications to the old northwest through the man-made 'gallery roads', it was part of Chinese history from almost the earliest period, but at the same time a different world.

At the present day it has a humid and close to subtropical climate, sheltered by the mountains to its north from the cold polar air masses in winter. Its mean annual temperatures lie between 16° and 18° Celsius, depending on location. Winter temperatures do not drop to a monthly mean below between 5° to 8°. Rainfall averages between 1000 and 1300 mm, peaking in the summer, and the runoff from the mountains ensures abundant water.[60]

There were two historic centers. The ancient state of Shu, with its center in the Chengdu plain in the west at a height of 450 to 750 meters above sea level, was the larger and more important of these. The state of Ba in the east, at a height of 300 to 500 meters, was the other, in the region around what is today the city of Chongqing just above the upper entrance to the gorges.

Present-day surveys show the main trees divide as follows into conifers and broadleafs respectively: fir, spruce, pine, 'oil-pine' (*Keteleeria*), larch, hemlock, cunninghamia, metasequoia, and cypress; and camphor, catalpa, *Phoebe* and *Machilus*, oak, lithocarpus, beech, birch, alder, hornbeam, chinquapin, maple, lime, poplar, and paulownia. In the warmer climate following the end of the last ice age, pollen analysis also shows plentiful windmill or fan palms (*Trachycarpus*). To these should be added fruits such as mandarin, orange, pomelo, crab apple, and lichee, as well as the lacquer tree and the tea bush. Sichuan was the first area in the world to cultivate tea systematically. One tea plantation from Tang times is said to have employed 900 workers.[61]

In this section, the focus is on clarifying the nature of the pressures that reduced the forest resources of a region almost totally covered in trees in archaic times, and that did so in spite of unusually strong efforts to cultivate economically useful sources of wood. Some of these effects are unsuspected. One, for example, is books. Sichuan in the late Tang was the first region to produce woodblock printed books on any significant scale. Under the Song, a Daoist compendium was printed of about 130,000 pages in over 5,000 fascicules, as well as the world's first paper money. This created a demand for the paper mulberry tree, the 'silk thorn' (*Cudrania tricuspidata*), and bamboos, for use in the manufacture of paper. Pear and 'mountain pear' were needed for cutting the wooden blocks.[62]

Another distinctive demand came from the bamboo engineering used for the tube-wells introduced in the eleventh century to extract brine and natural gas, to some extent superseding the older broad-diameter wells. Bamboo also found a role in the hawser bridges over rivers too difficult to cross by less heroic means.

More familiar pressures were clearance for farming, fuel for domestic use and proto-industries, and engineering—whether derricks over brine wells, gallery roads, or installations in irrigation systems.

The first chapter of the story may be summarized as follows:

Once iron axes began to be available, some time after the middle of the first millennium BCE, Sichuan became a prodigal user of wood. A recently excavated grave from the Warring States period used about 100 cubic meters of *Machilus*, some of it in the form of beams over 9 meters long.[63] By Han times timber was being floated downstream in rafts.[64] A gazetteer on the area completed in 347 CE reported that: "The Min hills have plenty of catalpas, cypresses, and large bamboos. *Denudation follows the courses of the streams.* The logs are cut and trimmed into timber.[65] The effort required is moderate, and the uses to which it can be put richly rewarding."[66]

A detailed picture can be brushed in by the third century CE, when Zuo Si wrote rhapsodic descriptions of each of the capitals of the Three Kingdoms. That on Chengdu, the capital of the Sichuan region, gives a description of the

Min River basin at the end of the early imperial period.[67] Zuo criticizes some of the earlier examples of this type of poem for making mistakes with trees and animals, and even deities, ascribing them to areas where they were not found. He aimed at a greater realism, he said, and explicitly states that he is modeling his work on the earlier *Rhapsodies on the Two Capitals* by Zhang Heng. In these, he says in his preface, "hills, rivers, and cities can be examined as if they are on a map, and the birds, animals, vegetation, and trees may be verified as if in a local gazetteer."[68] Writers of lyric verses, he asserts, "sing of what their hearts are set upon," but "those who, mounting the heights, can compose descriptive rhapsodies, praise what they observe."[69] In principle, at least, truth was the target.

The main passages of Zuo's poem that touch on vegetation and trees show an environment busily exploited but still not yet spoiled by the process. He begins by noting that the city drew on a wide hinterland:

> Here traffic by water and land converges.
> People crisscross and meet, from all points of the compass.
> Here is rich vegetation — almost a surfeit —
> Thickly thatched every which way, abundantly flourishing.

To the south lay a humid world with a great variety of trees:

> Valleys hug one like arms; gullies close round like mouths.
> Crests, straight-ridged or circling, are tangled and twisting,
> Interposing their rocks and deflecting the clouds,
> The dense forests a haze under bluish-green mists,
> The lone summits imposing, rising uplifted.

Then he turns to the trees that grow here, mostly evergreen broadleafs:

> Sturdy multiply-knotted bamboos climb up the ranges of mountains.
> The cinnamon-cassias gaze — down on the cliffs far below them.
> From rifts traversing the slopes, are dragon's-eye trees, springing out.
> Likewise, from cracks in the banks, there are lichee trees growing.
> Their green foliage masses like clouds, when they thicken.
> Their fruits swell, and hang widely scattered, red-purple.
> Yet when winter's most chill, still their leaves do not wither,
> But shine, splendid as ever, amazingly verdant.

> Peacocks roaming about and kingfishers flitting in multitudes,
> Rhinoceros striving with elephant — to determine who canters more
> swiftly —
> In the dawn, the white pheasant's cry — foretelling ill luck,
> In the darkness of night, lugubrious howling by gibbons.

The 'multiply-knotted bamboos' were Qiong bamboos, often used for walking sticks. What I have called the 'cinnamon-cassia' was a 'cassia' whose bark was said to roll up like a length of bamboo, which suggests the Chinese cinnamon, the bark from whose smaller branches when shaved off will dry into quills or tubes in the sun. The 'dragon's-eye tree' is the long'an (*Nephelium longana*), a fruit tree that often grows where the lichee does.

Looking to the north of Chengdu, Zuo observes:

Up north, in the Valley of Bao, is where one can gather good timber.
Among the trees *here* there are found the magnolia and cinnamon,
Two kinds of catalpa, the narrow-leaved osier, and Fortune's paulownia,[70]
Firs and thorn-bearing junipers, windmill palm trees and coconuts.
Machilus and camphor lie hidden, deep on the valley-floor bottoms,
While magnificent cypress, and pine, flourish up on the mountainous tops,
Their long trunks and their branches uplifted, so high as to be unbelievable,
Fanning the clouds flying by as they brush on the substanceless aethers.

The presence of the windmill or fan palm this far north at this time is surprising but perhaps not impossible. Pollen analysis shows it was common in Sichuan in the warmer climate of 10 000 BP.[71] The presence of the coconut defies credulity, but I have not altered the sense of the text arbitrarily as the dictionaries and Qu Taiyuan's commentary all agree on it. The 'thorn-bearing juniper' is unclear but may be *Juniperus rigida*, one Japanese name for which is 'rat-thorn'.[72] The point of these verses is that, by this period, Chengdu's catchment area for timber extended at least three hundred kilometers north from the city. Bao was on the border with Shaanxi province.

The city itself was still something of an island among settled but non-Han people. Among those trees and shrubs to the east

Are cathartic croton-oil beans, and the antitoxic euphorbia,
And the 'tree of lively old age' for canes, the red-skinned peach-bamboo.
Gardens, where vegetables are grown, ring round their homesteads like
    cordons,
And along their property boundaries are located saline pools.

To the west, although the people had become civilized,

In this waste-land, distant from settlements, darkness lurks under the weeds,
And the forests along the mountains' feet are sunk in the dappled shadows.
Here, alternating life and death, there grow the twin-trunk trees,
While, hidden beneath the earth, swell the roots of the edible taro.

The mythical 'life-and-death-alternating tree' was believed to have two trunks, one of which was alive in any given year and the other dead. The following year the two trunks exchanged roles.

The surroundings of the city were an immense man-made garden. At the heart of the production system was the irrigation network which used gravity to distribute the water diverted from the Min River down a gentle slope to fields, and then to collect it and remove it at the bottom:

> Within the bounds of its domain
> There are banked mounds, rich piedmonts, wetlands, and plains
>   Spreading as far as the eyes can range,
> Made moist by the Qian and the Mei, whose flow is in part subterranean,
> And water supplied by the Mian and the Luo, spilling over in inundations.
>
> Branching off, like a body's arteries, there extend the canals and channels,
> Marking out the fields' limits, like inlaid metal, or openwork silk with
>   patterns.
>
> Bright-shining here, and plentiful, are both the sorghum and millet,
> And the nonglutinous rice — has stalks that are serried, and thick.
>
> They regard their inlets for irrigation as gateways down from the clouds,
> Their reservoirs make provision of water, out of dry land, through
>   distributaries.
> Even the moon in the star-zone Bi, which provokes torrential showers,
> Still cannot yield the equivalent — of this liquid — in bringing fertility.[73]

In complete contradiction to what Max Weber maintained, more than any premodern northwestern Europeans, the Chinese were driven by a desire for *the rational mastery of the world*. Here, freedom from the uncertainties of the weather.
The outer suburbs were filled with fruit trees:

> Looking across at each other, the roof-slopes rise to beamed ridges.
> Homes touch one another, adjacent, under mulberry trees and catalpas.
> Families can draw up their brine — from wells that tap salty springs;
> Households have orchards whose pride is having both grapefruits and
>   mandarins.[74]
>
> Their gardens have loquats, red Hubei crab apples,
> Pears from the mountains, persimmons, and sweet-tasting oranges,
> Mountain peaches as well, planted out in straight ranks,
> And plums, common and *mume*, patterned net-like and orderly.
>
> These diverse kinds of fruit trees, their bud-cases bursting,
> Are alike in their splendor, contrasting in color.
> In springtime the red cherry's blossoms come first;
> White crab-apple flowers are full-blown in summer.

When the seventh-month Firestar inaugurates autumn,
    The cold wind gets an edge,
    While white dews condense,
And miniature crystals of frost begin forming.

Purple pears are awash then with succulent juices.
Fine fissures appear in the hazelnuts' shells.
As bunched grapes, over-ripe, rot to gunge in confusion,
Pomegranates compete to split open their fruits.
Their sweet flavor endures till they gently drop off,
The strength of their perfume oppressing our nostrils.

This passion for cultivating trees has to be put into counterpoint, not contrast, with the passion for clearing untamed forests. Arboriculture is a part of the enterprise of bringing landscapes under horticultural and hydrological control.

Chengdu was also a commercial suction pump that drew in goods from a wide hinterland, with an unavoidable impact on its environment, including trees. At this period, trade in Chinese cities was generally concentrated in specially dedicated centers, to facilitate political supervision and taxation:

We turn to the secondary city next,
Which adjoins the main one to its west.
Here markets, and stores, are concentrated
To form an ocean of countless traders,
Bazaar-filled alleys repeated in hundreds,
Stalls like meshes of nets a thousand-fold multiplied,
Goods and commodities stacked up like hills,
Lovely, subtly made, objects — like stars in their millions.

Men of standing, and ladies, who live in the capital,
Come, tastefully dressed, to observe others' fashions.

And the businessmen who are locally based dispose of their piled-high stocks,
Using the pell-mell confusion as cover — for dealing with buyers improperly.
Weird, little-known, is their merchandise, or else it's unique curiosities,
All eight points of the compass supply them — with heretofore never seen objects.
Thus, among fabrics for clothing on sale, there is cotton from the southwest,
And — among the edible starches — ground-up pith from the palm tree *Arenga.*

Cotton came from a place called Yongchang, which is now in Yunnan but was then outside the Chinese cultural sphere. It was not to be cultivated on any scale in China for another thousand years. The sugar palm *Arenga saccarifera* grows wild in Burma and Assam, but may have already been being planted in south China at this time as it certainly was later.[75] Thus, even at this early date the fate of such trees was being determined by consumers who were at least a thousand kilometers distant.

After this age of prosperity, Sichuan went into an economic decline from the fourth to the sixth centuries, the period of colder temperatures. Recovery came under the Tang and the Song, when what remained of the original forest cover in the basin and the lower hills was cleared for farming. Farmers thus had increasingly to grow their own firewood. Alder saplings were favored, being said to be able to double their size in three years, and the common people were reported to "rely upon using them, substituting them for other firewood."[76] Du Fu, perhaps China's greatest poet, spent time in Chengdu during the 760s, and wrote several couplets that refer to alders. They reveal the Sichuanese people's custom of planting groves of trees and bamboos round their homes. Thus Du wrote to a friend in official life, thanking him for providing him with some alders:[77]

> West of the moat, round my thatched hall, there was missing a grove of
>   trees,
> And who was there, other than you, aware of my deep-hidden feelings?
> I've been happy to hear that alder saplings can reach a good height in
>   three years
> And will make me an acre or so of shade, along the bank, by the creek.

Not long afterward, in a poem called "The hall completed," he wrote:[78]

> My grove of alders blocks off the sun. The breeze sighs through the
>   boscage.
> The huge bamboos blend with the mists, their tips bedewed with droplets.

The commentary to the first of these poems quotes a work on the Shu region that says: "To the east of Mount Yulei there are numerous alder trees. They come easily to maturity and can serve as firewood." Mount Yulei was some way north of the city of Chengdu.

In Song times, some scholars and officials had a passion for planting trees. Su Dongpo, self-inflating and exaggerating, once described himself as the only person who had a taste for pines:[79]

> Others love willows and elms, when they're planting new trees.
> They wait for their acres of shade, and recline at their ease.
> It's my growing of pines and of cypress that makes *me* unique:
> These are trees that protect the integrity — of the heart's feelings.

Pines were something special to him. He estimated that he had in his younger days planted "ten thousand of them by hand."[80] Why? Speaking later of his youth in Sichuan with the wry skepticism of maturity, he wrote a self-mocking poem that gives some hints.[81] They had had for him an association with the Daoist quest for physical immortality. In other words it is important not to think of him—and others of this period—as just environmental rationalists with a touch of romanticism, although as he grew older the rational element seems to have become stronger. Part of his way of thinking about the world was, by our standards, extremely strange.

The humor of the poem depends on a tension: the understanding shared between author and reader that while the unmagical realities of everyday life tend to thwart our fumbling efforts to make our bodies incorruptible, we even so persist, perhaps perversely—who knows?—in loving the dream. Planting large numbers of pines may be classified, from our modern perspective, as reforestation, but pines in his mind were *not just pines*. Once, at least, they were embodiments of a magical world immanent in the mundane one, seemingly ever-present, yet tantalizingly impossible to grasp.

> In times now long gone by, when I was young,
> *I planted the whole of the Eastern Ridge with pines.*
> I re-rooted the saplings, the length of my thumb,
> — As tricky a task as pricking out rice.
>
> In year two they extruded Long Life's yellow sprouts,
> Piercing through, one by one, like awn-spikes on wheat.
> In the third, artemisia from Faery came out
> — Then the hills were invaded by cattle and sheep!
>
> How fondly I hoped, when not ten years had passed,
> Soon to see them extending like dragons or serpents,
> But a night-storm, tempestuous, smashed them to fragments,
> Though the dew-fall at dawn was scented like pearls.
>
> I hacked down, since I wanted to eat my pines' resin,
> Five score mulberry trees, to mix in their cinders.
> But human affairs are contrary and vexed,
> And elusive the elixir potent with spirit![82]

Frustrated in his attempts to concoct the right recipe, he ends by hoping that by refining certain substances associated with pines, he might still attain an imperishable bodily substance:

> Once my Three Corporeal Presences are extinguished, like dead ash,
> The Five Cereals cleansed from my guts, their ancient consistency changed,
> Then a green marrow will congeal, within my bones' bluish-black,
> And my abdomen's Cinnabar Field be shining and subtly radiant.
>
> There's no need to dwell on the fact that the hair on my head will be white,
> And the pupils, in both my eyes, have been caused to become quite square.
> An Immortal, once five hundred years have taken their course and gone by,
> I shall mount on a crane and return — to the homeland whence I once came!

We cannot be certain what his 'real' thoughts were. Perhaps a superposition of belief and disbelief?

He certainly cared about pines. The magistrate of Macheng, northeast of Hankou in Hubei, had, Su said, "planted tens of thousands of pine trees along the roads, surrounding them with shade." In less than a decade, axes and fires had left less than thirty to forty per cent of them alive. He therefore wrote a poem of rebuke about this, being, he said, "painfully concerned that generations to come will not continue to support the magistrate's intentions."[83] But this was clearly a matter of amenity, not the restoration of the forests, nor magical longevity.

Let us return to more mundane activities.

Wood and bamboo were the structural basis of most premodern Chinese engineering. *The Records of the Country South of Mount Hua*, completed in 347 CE, refer to bamboo tubing used to store and transfer the natural gas from wells of the region around present-day Chongqing:[84]

> There are fire wells in Jiang whose light blazes up into the sky at night. When people want to set this fire alight, they apply the fire from their home hearth to it, and before another instant has passed there is a sound like thunder, and flames shoot forth and light up the land for ten miles or so around. Bamboo tubes are used to hold a store of this light, which can be transported by dragging,[85] and will not go out all day long.

In the eleventh century the traditional broad-gauge brine wells of the Sichuanese salt industry, dug with shovels, were mostly replaced by drilled narrow-gauge wells. Su Dongpo left the following account of the technology. I have interpreted his sometimes opaque terminology in a few places:[86]

After the period 1041 to 1053, tube-wells first began to be created in Sichuan. A circular bit is used to drill an opening the size of a bowl. The deepest of them go down several hundred feet. They remove the septs from large bamboos and slot them into each other to form the well. Fresh water is injected from the side into the space between the tube and the wall of the shaft, so that the brine rises of its own accord up the tube in the center.

Furthermore, they use a bamboo slightly smaller in diameter than those of the tube, which is repeatedly extracted from and reinserted into the well as a bucket. It is bottomless and yet blockable. A flap of a few inches of cured leather is attached as a flap-valve. As the tube comes out of and goes into the water, the aether of its own accord blows it shut or sucks it open. One tube can handle several *dou*-measures of water.

All tube-wells use lifting machinery. No one is unaware of where profit is to be found. The *History of the Later Han* mentions a water-driven flap-bellows. This technique is used in the iron-smelteries of Sichuan, and has an overall resemblance to the water-extracting tubular buckets of the Sichuan brine wells.

Su Dongpo's model for explaining the shutting and opening of the valve was thus, it seems, the metallurgical single-flap bellows that used flap-valves to draw air into and then expel it out of a rectangular chamber linked to the furnace by an exit duct.[87] The Song-dynasty *dou* is a tricky measure to evaluate, but 5.85 liters seems the most reasonable.[88]

We move on from the period of the medieval economic revolution to the last phase of the late-imperial age, noting in passing the coverage given by the late-Ming technological survey *Heaven and the Artificer Develop Commodities*. This contains a detailed account of the brine wells and fourteen panels of woodcut illustrations added during the Manchu dynasty.[89] Our last source, *The Classic of the Waterways of Sichuan*, was completed in 1794. It incorporates material from a range of dates, but its descriptions of the salt wells and natural gas wells near the junction of the Min River with the Yangzi, some way south of Chengdu, seem contemporary:[90]

Beside Lion Bridge,[91] east of the Looking-Four-Ways brook, are salt works. Of the several tens of counties in Sichuan that produce salt, only Great Peace, Brine Water, and Cave Source obtain it from a flowing current that never ceases day or night, like a source from a spring. The others all make salt derived from wells.

The two wells at Cloud Peace and Warm Water have circumferences that are, respectively, several tens of feet for the larger and several feet for the smaller. They resemble household wells, and are drawn from every day without becoming exhausted. All that is needed is once a year to clean out the mud that has accumulated.

The salt wells at Bullock's Work, Easy Wealth, and North Of The Stream are all over a hundred feet in depth, and their pierced openings are reached by means of bamboo. The septs have been removed from these bamboo tubes, and on their bottoms is basted a flap of ox-hide that opens and shuts of its own accord. It opens when it enters the water; and when filled with water, it closes, not letting even a drop escape. Up above the well they erect pulleys that are made to operate by oxen and horses pulling on ropes.[92]

These wells are drilled by ingenious craftsmen who have a good knowledge of the subterranean arteries carrying the brine. They do not dig open the ground when drilling, but use a pointed iron bit five feet in length that bores the hole from above. A bamboo cable winds and rewinds the bit, causing it to fall repeatedly. Its strength is like that of an arrow from a bow, and it falls as straight as a plumb line, penetrating both stone and mud. It takes a number of years to drill a well to completion.

They will then, as usual, remove the septs from large bamboos and socket them into each other to make the tube for the well of the same length as the well is deep. They pour fresh water into the transverse gap between the tube and the wall of the well, and the brine rises of its own accord.

Generally, when a well has been in operation for a long time, or when the fresh water has seeped into the brine, they will calk the fissures in the tube. If other unwanted matter blocks or contaminates the brine, they will remove the blockage, even if it is a thousand feet below the ground. . . .

All the wells at North Of The Stream are brine wells. Some of those at Bullock's Work and Easy Wealth are fire wells. In general the nature of a fire well is that of cold pertaining to the Dark Force. If ordinary domestic fire is brought into contact with it, it will make a noise like a roll of thunder, and fire will come forth from it. One extinguishes it by snuffing it out with a piece of cloth, but some of the cold aether will remain inside.

When the base of this sort of fire is only an inch or so above the ground, it is extremely narrow, but as it rises it gradually flares out until it can be as much as several feet across. The tip of the flame is not like that of a normal fire.

It can be used as fuel to boil brine, steam rice, calcine limestone to make lime, or to smother-burn wood to convert it to charcoal. When it is drawn through an opening in a bamboo tube to serve as a substitute for firewood or candles, this aperture is smeared with clay. Thus it burns hotly at the mouth but the bamboo does not catch fire. At other times it is drawn off into the bladder of a pig, the opening sealed, and the bladder placed inside a box or bag that one can take home with one. When night falls, one pierces a hole with a needle, applies an ordinary domestic flame, and fire will come out of the bladder and light up the room.

There are also oil wells. The color of the oil is turbid, but it burns well and one can have a fire anywhere. It will not diminish or go out in wind or rain, or even when plunged into water. If one is traveling at night, and stores oil in a bamboo tube, it is possible to travel for one or two kilometers on a single tube. . . . Such wells are commonplace, and no cause for astonishment.

So parts of this region of late-premodern China not only used gas for industrial processes, but had domestic gas cookers, domestic gas lighting, and a primitive form of mobile illumination using bottled oil. All based on bamboo tubing.

Once again, as with the large-scale logging in the Zhongnan mountains, there is something of the feel of an emerging modern economy about this technical vigor and virtuosity, yet no certain evidence that anything was in fact in the process of happening to make economic modernity a reality.

Sizable structures were fashioned from wood and bamboo. The *Classic of the Waterways of Sichuan* lists three methods used for cable bridges. The precise details of the techniques used are not easy to determine with confidence, but the amounts of timber and bamboo used to make and maintain them is the important point:[93]

(1) Two trees are first set upright in the middle of the river to serve as columns. The bridge is built as a framework on top of them. Bamboos are used to make cables, closely interlaced into the framework and secured to the two banks. Sometimes stones will be dropped into lengths of large bamboo until they are filled, and a rope attached to their tops. A bamboo hawser is plaited into this rope and spans the banks. *Wood is used to make machinery.* When the rope grows slack, this machinery is rotated to wind it in.

In other words there was a winch and a counterweight.

(2) There is also a bridge featuring a spanning-cable and a 'climbing pole'. Where the great river's water speeds as swiftly as an arrow, a bridge is made by attaching a rope to the sides of the two banks. A tree is hollowed out to make the 'pole' through which the rope is threaded. The traveler is lashed on top of it, and uses his hands to pull himself along the rope to the opposite bank, where there are people standing by to release his bonds. It is exceedingly dangerous.

The third type is the only one whose dimensions are given. A sort of suspension bridge, it seems close to being unbelievably enormous:

(3) The rope bridge is 1200 feet in length, and divided into five frames. Its width is made up of twelve ropes running along in parallel but linked like the scales of a fish. A woven bamboo mesh is spread on top of them. *Several tens of large trees* are forced by joint efforts into the river's deposited sediments, and stones dragged up to consolidate them at the base.

Every few trees form a frame. They suspend the bridge in mid-air between them. When a fierce wind blows past it, it swings agitatedly up and down. It broadly resembles the shape of a fisherman's net spread out to dry in the sun, or the multicolored silk from a dyer's household drying away from the light.[94] People have to leave their carrying chairs and hurry across on foot. The slightest dawdling and they will collapse in fright, unable to proceed.

Engineering here was based on forest products.

The Far South

The region south of the southern ranges (that is, the Far South) was conquered by the Qin and Han dynasties from the Yue or Viet people more than two thousand years ago. The part that remains in China today forms the provinces of Guangdong and Guangxi. The present climate is subtropical verging on tropical. The mean annual temperature ranges from about 18° to 24° Celsius. The yearly rainfall for most areas lies between 1500 and 2000 mm. It is thus warm and wet. The east-to-west mountains to its north protect it against cold winter air moving down from the north, and the reservoir of heat in the sea tends to stabilize the weather.

Seasonally, rainfall is concentrated in the summer; the winter being relatively dry, cold, and clear. Regional variations are also important. The winds are stronger along the coast than inland, and it is the coastal zone that bears the brunt of the typhoons that come in off the ocean. About four of these each year move onshore, and of these four only about two are classed as 'major', that is, with wind speeds over 117 kilometers per hour.[95] They are, however, terrifying experiences, as anyone who has been in one knows.

Botanically, the far south of China in historic times had as much in common with the tropical worlds that lay further south as it did with central China. Already by 304 CE, Ji Han had written *The Forms of the Plants and Trees of the South* because, as he said, "the people of the central regions are often unfamiliar with their nature."[96]

In many ways, the Far South was an exotic and bewildering experience for northerners. They found, for example, Chinese spinach[97] being grown on tethered rafts, and fabrics woven from the fibers of banana plants and bamboos.[98] And novel foods and addictions, like the chewing of betel nut.

Betel is the fruit of the betel-nut palm,[99] and the fruit is chewed together with the leaf of the betel-pepper[100] and lime, often ground from oyster shells. It produces a mild intoxication, and is thought to improve the digestion. The saliva of those indulging in it becomes red, and is often spat out. The addiction seems harmless, but, to most tastes, unaesthetic.

The trees can grow over a hundred feet high, with trunks that have an almost constant girth from bottom to top. They have no branches until the fan of leaves shaped like banana leaves that spreads out from the highest point, and the partially enfolding bracts, or spathes, that contain the fruit. Su Dongpo was exiled to the Far South in 1094 to serve as a county magistrate, this being his punishment for some politically incorrect remarks at court. The first part of his poem "Eating Betel" evokes the surprise of the observant outsider confronting this novel world:[101]

> The moon shines down on the branchless trunks of the forest
> Whose nighttime columns rise on tens of thousands of plinths.
> High up among the cloudbanks wave the distant fans of fronds
> Covering us with darkness, in this summer heat just before winter.
>
> From aloft the spathes droop down, enclosing their load of fruits,
> Each fruit-base ringed with red spines, providing for its defense.
> During rain at night one might think one glimpsed the azure dragon's
>   brood,
> Or else imagine them, in the wind, to be purple phoenix eggs.
>
> Once they have dropped to the earth, looking as if they are splitting,
> They continue to ripen on their own, encased within their skins.
> When a visitor from the north arrives he finds them unfamiliar,
> But when urged by local custom to eat, it is hard for him to resist!
>
> One is nervous of letting off gas from one's hollow internal places,
> And as one takes one's first bite, one may well half-want to spit.
> When one sucks upon the juices, one detects a faint sugary taste,
> But when one lets one's teeth sink in, the flavor is also bitter.
>
> If someone's facial demeanor has become too severe and cold,
> The savor no longer conveys its old seductive sweetness.
> For removing assertive arrogance it merits an encomium,
> Yet when it gives one a boost, one's courage deserves esteem.
>
> Often, when stubborn malarial fever sets in and will not vanish,
> Betel is the restorative that leads back to healthy vigor.
> Of the medicines we have in reserve, it may well be one of the handiest,
> And, in the catalog of fruits, are there any more beneficial?

A new landscape, with new flora and foods, and new mood-altering and medical drugs.

For late-imperial times, Qu Dajun's miscellany *New Comments on Guangdong*, completed in 1700, gives descriptions of the more important species of trees.[102] The book is an idiosyncratic mixture of the styles of the sober local gazetteer and the traditional credulity-teasing book of marvels. To be used with caution. Here, though, are parts of his largely unproblematic entry on the banyan, that extraordinary member of the fig family where one tree becomes an entire grove:[103]

> The banyan has luxuriant foliage, and its boughs and branches hang down like vines one after the other. A trunk can reach a size such that three men are needed to encompass it in their arms. The branches sprout rootlets that brush against the ground in unbroken sequence to gain invigoration from the soil and stones. These roots in their turn put forth branches. After this has happened repeatedly, the branches and trunks are so entangled with each other that there is no above or below. Everything interlocks.
>
> To begin with, the rootlets grow like hundreds and thousands of hanging silk threads. After a long time, these hundreds and thousands fuse into one, or perhaps two or three, then one by one descend to the ground like beams and columns that prop each other up. From the distance some of these trees seem like great mansions, with the straight elements becoming doors, and the curved ones windows. They form an openwork lattice through which one can look in all four directions. . . .
>
> One of its names is the 'tree that grows upside down'. Many of the trunks are hollow inside. They lack solidity and cannot be used for anything [structural]. For this reason, wherever people have formed village communities, they let these trees live out their natural span. The largest attain several hundred years of age. Thus, when one sees from far off tall trees clustering thickly around their homesteads, those that rise straight up are the silk-cotton trees (*Ceiba pentandra*),[104] while the huge bushy ones growing crosswise and downward are the banyans. . . .

And he goes on to mention how banyan twigs were used when dried to make kindling that would not go out, even in wind and rain, and how the sap from banyan rootlets could be used like lacquer. Banyans were planted beside roads to provide shade, and around the places where periodic markets met, in the belief that they would make them prosper. Some trees had even been observed to predict a coming disaster by emitting a smoky white vapor. . . .

The silk-cotton or kapok tree was another spectacular sight:[105]

Its branches stick out in pairs, clutching and grasping into space, giving it the aspect of a dragon spreading its wings. Buds appear in the first lunar month, as plump as those of the magnolia, either deep red or golden yellow, the stamens having six stalks. From a distance they look like an innumerable multitude of colored lanterns burning in space and reddening it everywhere. . . .

The fruits are the size of betel nuts, ripening in the fifth and sixth lunar months. When one splits into two, floss flies out from inside it into the air as if it were snow. This floss is brittle, though, rather than tough and flexible, and fit to use as wadding but not for weaving. It can be used to stuff cushions and kneepads, and is better for this purpose than the reed-tufts from between the Yangzi and Huai rivers. Sometimes it is made into a cloth called 'tie' or 'rough cloth' that can keep out the rain. Northerners think highly of it.

Inside the floss there are seeds like those of the *Firmiana*, which are carried with it, whirling hither and thither. When they make contact with the soil, they turn into trees once more. . . .[106]

The oldest trees are the ten or more in front of the shrine in Nanhai. In the second lunar month each year, on the morning of the birthday of the God of Fire, their blossoms are open to the fullest extent, and up to several thousand people will be present to look at them. The energy of the light is overwhelmingly brilliant. It reflects off the spectators' faces as if they had been dyed red-brown.

When the blossoms are out, there are no leaves. They appear once the blossoms have fallen. . . . Before the leaves are out, the trees really look like corals a hundred feet in height. . . . Their wood is of no use, so they are little harmed by axes. They are also the dwellings of demons and spirits, and a medium for geomantic forces. It is for these reasons that the height of most of them matches that of the banyans.

The author of the *New Comments on Guangdong* notes elsewhere that "numerous sugar palms,[107] fan palms,[108] and silk-cotton trees are planted beside shrines, numerous 'rosary limes'[109] by Buddhist temples, numerous banyans by village community altars, and numerous water-pines[110] and lichee trees beside reservoirs formed by dams."[111] In other words, the Cantonese of this period had a number of companion trees, with a special spiritual significance. Some of them were also economically useful. The sugar palm, for example, yielded an edible white flour from the pith inside its bark.

How does this relate to observations made earlier about the apparent lack of any specific Chinese deities for trees, let alone forests? We can only guess, but where trees and forests did have a numinous quality in the Chinese world of late-imperial times, it seems likely to have originated from outside the world of classical Han Chinese culture, at least as narrowly defined. There is a hint of this in a passage from the *Record of Jingzhou*, written back in the fifth century CE.[112] 'Jingzhou' was an old name for the south-central region of China, including the northern part of Guangdong province. The passage refers to a time more than half a millennium earlier when this last-mentioned area was still inhabited mainly by the Nan Yue people, who were of course not Hans:[113]

> There were camphor trees in Yangshan county in Shixing commandery whose diameter could reach twenty feet. *They were designated 'sacred trees.'* At the time of the Qin dynasty, the Qin forces cut down these trees to make cylinders for drums. Once these drum cylinders were finished, they abruptly hurried off north to Guiyang.[114]

Nothing is said about why the camphor trees were sacred, or 'sage-like' to translate the text more pedantically. But it was the troops of the first Chinese emperor who cut them down, untouched by their quasi-divine qualities. Or at least so it would seem. The passage implies that it was the size of the trees that was their attraction, not any mystical properties with which they could endow a musical instrument.

A few true forest peoples still existed in the seventeenth century when the *New Comments* were written, even if only at the environmental margins. Thus the aborigines of Hainan Island ranged through their woods looking for the perfume that developed under certain conditions from the eaglewood tree[115] and has been called by various names such as 'garu wood' and 'lignaloes'. Demand was driven by trade, some of it non-Chinese. Getting this precious commodity out caused a certain amount of forest destruction, and induced a state of economic dependency among the tribes having the ownership of the lands where it could be found. Here is part of Qu Dajun's account:[116]

> Collecting the perfume has always to be done among the tangles of fallen dead trees in the depths of the mountains. They go in groups of several tens of people and may find it in a day or two on some occasions, but on others return with empty hands after half a month. The likely explanation is that some supernatural power is at work.
>
> When the weather is fine and dry at the height of the fall, they look at all the mountain trees that have withered, both large and small, since it is always these that contain the perfume. They search by moonlight for any scented vapor wafting through the woods, and use straw ties to mark its presence.
>
> If there are termite mounds[117] two or three feet high in these places, they are certain to obtain 'oilswift'[118] and *jia'nan*, but lignaloes in greater quantity

still. After the knots of the tree have been slumbering in the soil for a long time, they exude a liquid, and once this has congealed, the strata of perfume will be below it. . . .

Trees like the evergreen *Ilex pedunculosa* vary in size, and perfume is found in less than one or two out of every hundred. Sometimes the perfume congeals in the trunk and branches, but at others in the roots, just as an ulcer grows at some times in the upper half of the human body, and at others in the lower. A person's appearance becomes gaunt and haggard when he or she has been harmed by a disease. When the perfume has brought affliction on a tree, its leaves and branches [likewise] wither and decay. It happens that when the winds and rains have splintered them, and their resinous sap has been splashed onto other trees, like the transmission of infection during an epidemic, the perfume will congeal in the latter as well after much time has passed.

Whenever the aboriginal people see yellowed leaves telling them that perfume has already congealed in a tree, they will cut it down, open a trackway, and remove it as their booty. Those who buy the perfume will first sacrifice to the gods of the mountains, then give presents to the leader of the aboriginals. The mountains will be opened up after this, with vines being used to mark out the circular zones of operations.

The contract with the aboriginals will run from ten days to a month or two. It comes into effect on the day the 'perfume fella' lays his hands on some perfume. This 'perfume fella' is an assimilated aboriginal who is skilled at telling which perfume is which. He points out the trees that have perfume, or the spaces round the trees that do, following which they cut them down and remove them. They give the aboriginals half the yield as payment.

The perfume is mostly in the main trunk as a rule, since the energy in the branches is too feeble for it to congeal there. Perfume that has congealed on a living tree has matured in it during its lifetime. For perfume that has congealed in a dead one, they will have chopped into it as it lies on the ground (hacking into its twisted trunk and slanting branches with their axes to make nicks that will hold the rain and dew[119]). The perfume needs thirty to forty years to mature after this. In the case of trees uprooted while still flowering[120] the essential liquid will have gushed out. Even if, being broken into droplets, it cannot form sheets, the winds and rains cannot strip it away, nor grubs or termites devour it. . . .

Even though the perfume is produced in the mountains, the aboriginals themselves were unaware of it until people from outside wanted to buy it. When these outsiders first had dealings with them they recompensed the aboriginals with wine, cattle, or other commodities, according to what they wanted. Later on, however, the opening up of the mountains has been delegated to in-migrants.[121] Even when a large amount of perfume is obtained, the aboriginals feel no regrets. *Even when the mountains have been stripped so empty that no more exists, the in-migrants cannot demand a price for this from the outside merchants.*

Thus the aborigines pass their lives in the midst of this perfume and it provides them with their food and drink. It can be calculated that their harvests of rice grown by slash-and-burn methods, and of beans grown in the ashes in fields they have cleared by fire, are not enough to fill the stomachs of their wives and children. So long as perfume is available, most of their daily needs can be met by relying on it. It is Heaven's means of providing for the aboriginals.

The familiar tale of faraway markets creating pressures on environments of which the consumers know nothing. The tentacles of Chinese commerce were extraordinarily far-reaching. We should also note the seriousness of the preoccupation of late-imperial Chinese scholars like Qu with natural history and environmental issues, including a sensitivity to the inequity of the extinction of aboriginal assets without compensation.

The Cantonese attitude toward trees in late-imperial times was complex and to some extent distinctive. The colorful follies of folk religion were interwoven with sharp-eyed observations of nature, and with the scholarly pseudo-sciences of the *Book of Changes* and the five-phase theory of matter. Calculating economic exploitation was counterbalanced by aesthetic delight in particular trees. Destruction was complemented by a passionate arboriculture and the loving restoration of damaged stands. The first page from the section on trees in the *New Comments* conveys something of the Far-South flavor of realism mixed with fantasy:[122]

In the Luofu mountains east of Canton there were once, in times past, the pines of the Seven Stars standing below the altar to the Seven Stars of the Northern Dipper.[123] They were extraordinarily uncanny, and since that time have changed into swordsmen and followed the Daoist master Concealed Light Zou to the Court, where they have had an audience with the emperor in the Hall of Immortals of Crystallized Substance. They have been again transformed, now into seven Daoist masters, and come and go to and from the world under the mountains.

Loving care was bestowed by the government on trees thought of as special:

The Plum Tree Ranges between Jiangxi and Guangdong have numerous pines, the largest of which measure more than ten spans around, with branches of immense length that intertwine like vines or convolvulus, many of them hanging upside down and snapped. Their needles are a greenish black and from the distance resemble clouds dark with rain.

Several hundred of them flank the road as it winds back and forth.[124] Most of them were planted by Zhang Qujiang but have suffered from the attacks of axes. Fires have also entered into their tubes[125] so that the seasonal flow of nutrients has been interrupted, and they look like the withered pines described in poems.

Some time ago the policy was proposed that the authorities should make a register of the numbers of the trees and record their girths. Subordinate government personnel complied with this for the red flowering plums by going on tours of inspection. Every month they made an investigation. Trees that had been injured were without fail restored. This was done for all the old plum trees, so they will be able to survive a further few hundred years without rotting. This was really an extraordinarily admirable policy. Alas! People have been aware of the plum trees in the Plum Tree Ranges but not of the pines!

Around 1700, there was still relatively little deforestation. The entry in the *New Comments* on *Cunninghamia*, the 'Chinese fir' that was the commonest commercial plantation species, observes that:[126]

> There is not much *Cunninghamia* in Guangdong. The saplings come mostly from the province of Jiangxi, and the majority of those buying them are landowners who have clear-cut their plantations and are planting replacements. They therefore take as many to plant as equals the number of stumps. *Guangdong and Guangxi have plenty of trees for timber.* Those who use *Cunninghamia* are only forty per cent. For this reason this species is not often planted.[127]

The stripping of the hills mostly took place at the end of the late-imperial period. Robert Marks, a specialist in the environmental history of the Far South, concludes that:[128]

> The accumulated evidence ... indicates the progressive deforestation of Lingnan [the Far South] in the eighteenth century, coincident with peaks in the population and cultivated land area surpassing previous peaks in the Song and Ming, and with official state policy after 1740 encouraging the clearance of the hill country and the periodic—if not annual—burning of grass off the hills. If, as Ling Daxie has estimated, forests in 1700 had covered about half of the land area of Lingnan, decreasing to 5–10 percent by 1937, then most of that deforestation ... occurred during the eighteenth century.

Exceptionally, cereal cultivation might be exchanged for the growing of trees, which could sometimes give higher returns. Here is a fragment from the entry on lichees and long'ans from *New Comments on Guangdong*:[129]

> The diked banks inside the stone-walled polders of Canton are all planted with lichees and long'ans. *In some cases people have abandoned their rice-fields in order to plant these trees.* . . . They use mud deposited as sediment to construct mounds about two feet in height so that the floodwater cannot reach the trees. They make coverings for them of cut grass so that they are not touched by the fierce sun. If they want to make the water rise inside the trunk of a long'an they bind it with rice-stalks. If they want the fruits to be large and numerous, they bury salt beside it. If grubs appear they prick the tree with iron wires dipped in a drug. If this is not done, the tree will become totally worm-eaten.

In contrast to the subtle but passive indigenous knowledge used to find perfume in the eaglewood forests, the cultivation of trees could be a form of premodern high-tech.

The northwestern margins

We have seen that the original core of classical Chinese culture was hostile to forests, and saw their removal as the precondition for the creation of a civilized world. The major later ideological exception to this attitude was Buddhism, which was imported into China from India early in the first millennium CE, and soon acquired extensive influence. Archaic Indian beliefs embodied a deeper respect for trees and forests than their Chinese counterparts,[130] even if, besides being a place of saintly hermitage and royal exile, the forest was also regarded as the refuge of robbers, and the spread of civilization often seen as linked to deforestation,[131] as it was in early China. Buddhism probably brought something of the positive side of Indian sentiment along with it.

The importance of Buddhist institutions in countering the pressures typically at work on forests may be illustrated from the section on woods in the 1909 gazetteer for Dan'ger subprefecture[132] in Xining prefecture in Gansu, near the headwaters of the Huang River.[133] This was basically a pastoral region, on the edge of ethnic Chinese settlement, and was probably never heavily forested, at least in late-imperial times.

The gazetteer section translated here makes plain other aspects of these northwestern margins. These are the sparse distribution of the woods, their restricted extent, the small size of most trees, and the degree to which the preservation of small patches of forests depended on special factors such as public ownership, ownership by monasteries, or the sacred nature of the groves. Silviculturalists experienced constant difficulty in protecting growing trees from theft, timber being an ever more valuable property commercially. The Domesday-Book-style accounting in this section—the listing of woods given here being presented as complete, though it is unlikely to have been—is a reminder of how acutely the need for wood was experienced by the late-imperial economy.[134] As of 1890, the meager reserves of timber other than willow, as listed below, had to meet the needs of a subprefectural population of at least 16,000 Han Chinese people, in addition to a number of Tibetans and Mongols.[135] The key phrases have been italicized:[136]

> *Xiangher wood*　... On the mountain slopes south of the Huang River, from the base to the summit. It occupies about 40 *mou*. The trees range from 10 to over 20 feet in height, with trunk diameters of from 5 to 6 inches up to 8 to 9 inches.[137] These are the largest of the forest trees in the mountain passes, and consist solely of birches. *Little of the material is suitable for making carts or barrows.*
>
> On the slopes to the east there is another wood, of somewhat more than 10 *mou*. Although the trees here are not large, they are dense and of an equal height. It is apparent how well they flourish when the right methods are used to *cultivate and protect them.* Both of these woods are *the public collective property* of the Xiangher village, and are cut *and sold* by the people of the community to provide for public purposes. Private persons are not permitted to take trees from them.
>
> *Ahadiu wood*　... In the curve of the mountains south of Ahadiu village. From the bottom of the mountain to the watershed it occupies more than 200 *mou*. The trees are over 10 feet tall, with trunk diameters from 1 to 2 inches up to 4 to 5 inches, with a sparse and not very flourishing distribution. There are both birches and poplars. To the southeast ... there is another wood of perhaps 40 *mou*, rather more thickly set but with trees of no great height. Both of these woods are owned by farming families in the neighborhood; *but even by making use of the strength of several households to safeguard their growth, it has not proved possible to stop throngs of thieves coming in repeatedly.* In the area near the south mountain the ground is entirely sprouts and stumps on account of *the difficulty of protecting it*, and woods here are particularly few in number.
>
> *Qubutan grove*　... Occupies rather more than 10 *mou*. The wood is very densely set, and the trees likewise fairly large. ... There is a small temple in the middle. The elders of Qubutan village *revere this grove as being of sacred*

trees, and do not dare to collect the branches and twigs. Tradition has it that anyone felling a tree will meet with a supernatural calamity. They therefore keep a respectful watch over it. . . .

Lamole wood . . . Occupies about 200 *mou.* Of intermingling pines and birches. Although there are some large trees, it is not very dense. This wood is *the property of the Buddhist monks of the Dongke Temple, and they have forbidden thieving and unauthorized felling.* For this reason it spreads about in luxuriant growth. . . .

Yaoshui Gorge grove On the shaded slope of the Yaoshui Gorge mountains. . . . Discontinuous and not very dense. In recent years *the temple monks have begun to propose that it be protected,* this being because the timber can be encompassed in the span of one's hands and there are no large pieces. The trees are birch, and it will still be several decades before there is usable timber from a mature stand.

Dongke Temple South Mountain Wood Covers about 200 *mou.* Pines and birches. Numerous large trees, especially pines. Diameters run up to more than 2 feet, with not a single horizontally growing branch broken off from bottom to top. For this reason they are twisted and swollen, coarse and knotted everywhere, so that the timber is, on the contrary, not of good quality. *The monks consider that trees before a temple are a means of showing reverence for the Buddha, and for this reason since the time the temple was built until the present, they have never cut one down.* The luxuriance of the growth is exceptional. *Tibetan monks like cultivating woods,* and since this one is near the temple, it is particularly easy for them to cultivate it.

Zhacang Temple grove . . . Rather more than a thousand pines, both large and small, and birch trees all told. *Gathering fallen branches and felling is likewise forbidden. The property of the Buddhist monks of the Zhacang Temple.* Nearby to the southwest . . . are several tens of small cypresses *with no one to tend them, which makes it hard to hope that they will grow into a mature wood.*

Willows on the Molin River Spontaneously growing trees are very numerous in the flood plain of the Huang River and along its banks. *Once those near the watermills were protected by the people there they have been able to form a mature wood.* They are however only from 8 to 9 feet in height up to a little over 10 feet. The branches and twigs are luxuriant, affording a green shade that covers the ground. . . . They are not much use for timber. Branches are at times gathered from them and woven into large baskets to be filled with stones [as gabions] to serve as defense against floods. . . .

Within the subprefecture over a hundred *mou* of land in all are occupied by watermills, and trees of this sort are owned by the proprietors of the watermills in various places.

Planted willows These are either along the dikes or the sides of the roads, or else beside fields and gardens. . . . *There are plantings every year.* The total of old and new, large and small, is at a casual estimate 400,000 to 500,000 trees. About thirty per cent of newly planted trees will find it difficult to stay alive; and approximately a further fifty per cent which have achieved a reduced span of life will not attain a condition in which they are fit for use as timber. Large trees with trunks whose diameters range from 5 to 6 inches up to a foot and some inches will only amount to twenty per cent. The general explanation for this state of affairs is that it is necessary for the trees planted by well-to-do families to wait until they have grown large before they are fit to be timber. *Those that do not wait to grow large but are cut down and sold to be beams for houses can fetch a mere two or three tenths of an ounce of silver for each one. This has even so caused large trees to be ever fewer in number.* Although replacements are planted year after year, it is hard to have any hope that there will be woods of a flourishing appearance. These trees all belong to the common people.

Officially owned woods . . . The subprefect of Dan'ger . . . contributed funds in 1907 for these to be planted. The two locations concerned have more than 10,000 trees altogether, and they are already emerging as saplings. If it desired, however, that they stay alive and mature, *there will have to be supplementary planting.* There were no official trees in Dan'ger in times past; these have only started in the present day. . . . *If in the future these official trees are not safeguarded in a variety of ways . . . they will gradually become fewer until finally none are left.*

Since the Qing-dynasty *mou*, the unit in which areas were recorded, was 0.067 of a hectare, there were thus on the face of it about 47 hectares of forest, not all of them accessible for use, plus half a million willow trees, some pines, and some saplings. Not counting the trees planted around farmers' fields, which were not included, this was equivalent to about 0.003 of a hectare of trees, basically pines and birches, plus 31 willows, per person. As the area was said to be self-sufficient in timber, the data is therefore likely to be incomplete.

It would seem that the financial attraction of cashing in the market value of immature trees, especially when the risk of losing everything through theft, and the high cost of protection, were taken into account, was hastening the disappearance of mature stands of cultivated trees. And Dan'ger had almost no old-growth forests.

Changing economic pressures were probably at work in creating this situation. The Dan'ger mercantile economy was thought of as fairly conservative in the late nineteenth century, but putting money with merchants on deposit at interest was by this date a standard practice.[138] The time-discount rate may thus have risen compared to earlier times, exponentially increasing the amount that timber cashed in at the present moment was worth relative to the same timber left standing at any given point in the future. It needs to be emphasized that this, like the illustrative calculations that follow, are hypothetical and have the status of an idea still awaiting specific validation (or disproof) from documentary sources.

In rough terms, the tree-grower would have done something like the following calculation each year for each tree:

> What is the likely proportionate increase g in the present value of this tree ($\$T$) from natural growth over this year, minus the cost $\$P$ of caring for it and protecting it against theft effectively for this period? What is the proportion s by which I have to then reduce this amount to allow for probable survival from fires and other hazards over the coming year? Is *not* cutting it down going to yield me more by the end of the year than cutting it right now (even if it is a little smaller in size and so lower in value than it would be next year), selling it for $\$T$, and investing the proceeds at an annual proportionate interest of i per annum during the forthcoming year, discounted by the probability b that the bank will not go bankrupt during this time?

Calculation shows that if it is arbitrarily assumed for illustrative purposes that $T = \$50$, $g = 1.2$, $P = \$5$, $i = 1.1$, $s = 0.95$, and $b = 0.95$ the two courses both yield the same small profit. (Because $[(50 \times 1.2) - 5] \times 0.95 = (50 \times 1.1) \times 0.95 = 52.25$.) Even slight changes in the relationships between the rates g, i, s, and b will tend to alter the best course of action. (Just dropping s to 0.9, for example, makes keeping the tree for another year a loss-making proposition.) Different species of tree also vary greatly in the time it takes them to come to maturity.

The example is of course unrealistic in several ways, most obviously because it ignores possible economies of scale, but it lays bare the mechanism at work. Once a reasonably reliable financial market was in place, when a cultivated or protected tree was felled was basically determined by when its approximately *logistic* rate of physical growth was overtaken by the intrinsically *exponential* rate of growth of a sum of money invested at compound interest.[139] In the limiting case, when growth has stopped entirely, so that $g = 1.0$, retaining the tree for a further year reduces the return to $(50 - 5) \times 0.95 = 42.75$. Another oversimplification is that the foregoing ignores what could be done with the $\$5$

Figure 1. Modeled revenue from cutting and selling a tree, with protection costs, and the option of investing proceeds at interest.

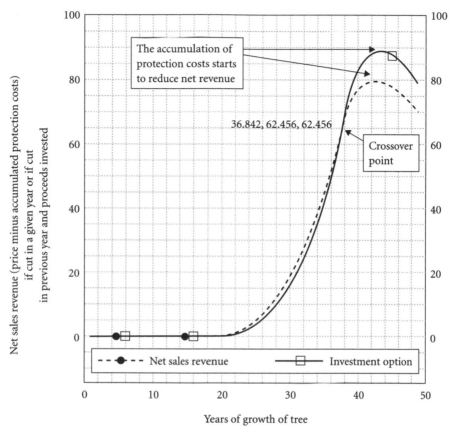

Logistic curve: a =maximum = 100, b = 1,000,000, c = 0.4 (see p. 473 n. 25); tree matures at 50 years; rate of interest per annum, 10 per cent; protection costs per annum, 2 per cent of current market value.

for *P*, protection services, that are released if the tree is sold at once. Invested at *i*, with the same value for *b*, it would yield a further net income of $0.475. Under this scenario cutting down at once would be the better option. Financial institutions thus have a demonstrable impact on the environment. In the hypothetical but plausible scenario suggested here they could have created a *cash-in imperative* pressing on those growing trees.

Figure 1 shows the pattern that emerges when the income from cutting and selling a tree in a given year, after the accumulated costs of protection have been deducted, is contrasted with the income resulting from cutting and selling it the previous year and investing the proceeds (including the protection saved). The age of a tree at maturity has been arbitrarily set at 50 years, its growth pattern over time is represented by a simple logistic curve with an asymptote of 100, the market value has been taken as determined by the age of the tree up to maturity, the protection cost per year has been set at two per cent of the market value in a given year, and the interest rate at ten per cent per year. The risks of the loss of the tree and the failure of the bank are not included. The two points that need to be noted are how the costs of protection virtually compel the sale of a tree before it is fully mature, and how the availability of the investment option lowers the optimal age for cutting and sale.

The three phases

This chapter may be seen, in an abstract sense, as having in a sketchy and approximate fashion combined for the history of forests and woods the pattern through time of the 'economics' column of Table 1 with space–time weightings taken from Map 2. This last, it will be recalled, suggested from figure-and-ground analysis of the retreat of the elephants that over the two-and-a-half thousand years from the ancient down to the late-imperial period there was a general spread of premodern development from the north to the south of China Proper, with a further southwestward shift near the end. In other words, where elephants had retreated, intensive farming had usually arrived.

Equally importantly, some documentation has now been provided in support of this reconstruction. It is patchy because the sources are patchy, and the historian has somehow to combine the few glimpses of detail available into a coherent imagined panorama. The items cited, often at some length, are not an anthology drawn from a much wider reserve of materials, but a substantial proportion of what can at present be identified as relevant.

The history of forests, trees, and wood provides crucial tracers for past economic growth and its environmental impact. In most places trees had to be cut down to make space for fields. Timber was the main material used to make houses, means of transport like boats and carts, and machinery. Logs were the most important premodern source of fuel for cooking, heating, and industrial processing. Forests provided ecological services such as protection against erosion, and a buffer against hard times in the form of game and birds to hunt, and a supply of wild foods. They also of course harbored dangerous animals and pests like the mosquitoes that were the vectors for malaria.

A broad pattern of three phases emerges, reinforced if we also anticipate by implicitly incorporating the findings of the later chapter on Jiaxing in the lower Yangzi delta. The first phase of extensive and enduring human impact on the forests began in the north during the second half of the first millennium BCE. An early feature was the effort by governments to conserve and sometimes monopolize scarce or diminishing forest resources. There later developed a trade in wood that at times covered many hundreds of kilometers in distance, and, toward the end in the more economically developed areas, an increasing de facto privatization (mostly for nonforest uses) of what had once been woodlands open to some measure of public exploitation. By the early centuries of the first millennium CE the area affected had expanded to take in parts of Sichuan in the west and of the lower and central Yangzi valley.

The second phase was associated with the medieval economic revolution of about a thousand years ago. It had its most visible impact in the lower Yangzi valley and parts of the west. In this phase serious shortages or even local disappearances of wood are first reported, though with markedly uneven spatial distribution. It was characterized by the onset of bitter quarrels between communities over the use of forests where these had become scarce, and also by the first efforts to replant large stands of trees.

The third phase started in the seventeenth century but did not become clearly established until the eighteenth and the nineteenth centuries. Only during this period did the shortage of timber for fuel and construction become severe in many areas, including, toward its end, the Far South. Even remote regions were affected, with only a handful of exceptions such as Zunhua, in the far northeast corner of China Proper, which is studied in detail in a later chapter. Communities in economically marginal areas, sometimes of non-Han origin, organized themselves to try to protect remaining reserves as formally constituted communal property. The theft of wood became a widely prevalent scourge, which inhibited production by small producers with inadequate means to defend themselves; and market pressures probably tended to compel not only a concentration on cultivating quick-growing species but also sales of relatively immature trees as soon as a profit could be taken. A handful of large commercial timber operations appeared in the remaining uncut old-growth forests, with organizational features that resembled those of late pre-industrial capitalism in the West.

The basic conclusion is that China's general forest crisis is only about three hundred years old, even if in a few areas, such as the lower Yangzi valley, its roots are considerably deeper in time.

Before the lens zooms in to look at selected areas in *Particularities*, the next task is to determine what it was that first set this multimillennial process of premodern development into motion, and then kept it going. In other words, having established an outline of the kinematics—the motions without the causes—it is now necessary to consider the dynamics—the motions *with* the causes.

5

War and the Logic of Short-term Advantage

There is a problem. The three previous chapters have recounted a story that started after the process of Chinese-style premodern economic development was already under way. What was it, though, that set this process in motion in the first place? Or, at least, *accelerated* it dramatically compared to what had been happening during the five or six thousand years immediately following the ending of the last ice age around ten thousand years ago?

The truthful answer is that, currently, we don't know. Broad perspectives are easier to survey here than detailed historical realities. For these latter, we have to push back too far too often from the oldest well-established facts into the shadowy domain of the 'must have been'. Even so, there is a simple and coherent hypothesis that seems to pull the fragments of our knowledge together into a structured intellectual field. This is that the late-neolithic and early bronze-age acceleration in the process of development was driven by *a competitive struggle* with two related aspects. The first of these aspects was a struggle for increasingly scarce resources between rival groups. The second, implicit in the first, was a competition between warring social and cultural patterns to survive and to achieve supremacy.[1] Particular patterns were embodied for a time in various peoples and—the crucial novelty—*polities*, which conferred superior competitive capacity. The initial transformations of the natural environment chronicled in earlier chapters were, in the last analysis, the by-products of the demands of this struggle. The patterns of action created by the most effective short-term exploiters of human and natural resources won. What might have been more viable long-term patterns counted for little or nothing faced with short-term power, just as, in chess, brilliant tactics can make a nonsense of the most deeply conceived strategy.

This analysis fits in perfectly with—though it was not originally inspired by—Jean Baechler's conclusion about what he terms "the neolithic mutation" that "war is the unique motor of evolution."[2]

It is important at this point to set aside any simple notion of 'progress'. Early 'development' was probably not welcomed by most of those undergoing it. Farming cereals in temperate-zone conditions—though possibly not some early tropical forms of multicrop horticulture[3]—was unattractive for a long time to many farmers. The work was backbreakingly hard. Those who did it were exposed to the extraction of rents and taxes, to conscription for wars and public works, and to the raids of human predators from outside. Farming provided a less varied and healthy diet than hunting and gathering.[4] The increased density of population made possible the so-called 'crowd diseases' that had hardly existed before.[5] Domesticating animals allowed zoonoses (animal diseases) to transfer themselves to human beings as new and often deadly infections.[6] Husbandry, overall, offered a less interesting, sensually rich, and challenging life than the mobile world that had preceded it. And, as Charles Maisels has pointed out, "social . . . stratification is about the majority's loss of control over the resources that sustain life."[7] Extensive evidence, some of which will be quoted later in this chapter, shows how hard the Chinese ruling class had to exert itself in early times to prevent its farmers from moving back to hunting, fishing, and gathering—the original occupations of humanity.

As centuries, then millennia, passed, the areas open for retreat dwindled, and farming culture became ingrained and habitual. The assumption of its 'superiority' has likewise become ingrained in us, its modern inheritors. This is the assumption that we have now to question. Superior it certainly was in most cases as the mode of production at the base of a new competitive complex—the militarized urban–agrarian state. But in terms of the quality of life for the general run of the population at the time of its introduction, as opposed to the elite? It seems doubtful. It must be remembered: fields end freedom. Whatever the astonishing subsequent achievements of civilization, it had a little recognized price: humanity itself became one of its own domesticated species. We enslaved ourselves to conquer.

The central question we confront is not the much-discussed origins of the 'state', the details of which are still too obscure.[8] It is, rather—to repeat—why, once political units with most of the characteristics of rudimentary states had begun to emerge in the area that was to become 'China', this triggered a long-lasting process of 'development' that soon radically altered the surrounding natural world. The two questions are of course to some extent interrelated. Thus a recent multi-author survey of aspects of state formation in various parts of the globe focuses on a number of topics that are also touched on in this chapter.[9] A selective list of these overlaps is interesting: (1) Intensified military conflict and competition between previously relatively peaceful political units;[10] (2) intensified economic production as part of this interstate competition;[11] (3) increased internal discipline and subordination linked with the needs of competitive warfare;[12] (4) increased interaction, often violent, between sedentary and more mobile populations;[13] (5) the displacement or subjection of outside ethnic groups;[14] (6) a shift from minimal internal social violence to a much higher level;[15] (7) the imposition of tribute and labor-services;[16] (8) the inculcation of the belief that the head of the polity, who could range from a 'chief' to a monarch, played a crucial ritual role in ensuring the general prosperity;[17] (9) the mobilization of religious authority to organize political and economic activities;[18] (10) the building of massive defensive structures;[19] (11) advances in bronze metallurgy, especially for weapons;[20] and (12) the development of, or increased use of, writing as a means whereby political and ideological authority could transcend the limitations of space and time for communications, recording, bureaucracy, the preservation of orthodoxy, and public display.[21] There was no single pattern, but a loosely related family of somewhat similar patterns, differentiated by effects due to the environment, to inherited social structures and beliefs, and—very noticeably in the Chinese case—to scale.[22]

Similar echoes can be heard in the general analytical political history developed by Baechler.[23] War, an act of violence between polities, was born about ten thousand years ago.[24] It may originally have been motivated by a quest for glory and booty; but once born, affected societies most consistently through their fear of being attacked by others.[25] Baechler argues that "the intensification of production is a consequence of war rather than its cause."[26] "Once war has been invented, it exerts a powerful pressure for technical innovation."[27] War is a crucial force for the development of a unified, pyramidal—that is, stratified—society.[28] A permanent concentration of power also tends to require that a state rule over ethnic outsiders as well as its own people.[29] Competition in war imposes efficiency, and this leads to a single dominant leader.[30] The need for additional resources impels an autocratic ruler to be forever expanding his empire.[31]

Other comments suggest that the Chinese experience was to some extent part of a broader pattern. Technical progress in the procurement of food reduces the proportion of the land surface that is used for making a living: more than a third is typically exploited for hunting–gathering; perhaps a tenth for extensive farming; and maybe one hundredth for irrigated agriculture.[32] Emigration is only a viable means of escape from unwanted domination so long as there is usable vacant territory not too far away.[33] 'Tribalization' of the original human 'bands' is, correspondingly, in part a response to population saturation.[34] While substantial kin-groups still underpin tribal polities, and, though less strongly, states governed by monarchs and aristocrats, they are later almost obliterated by an imperial structure ruling through a bureaucratic apparatus.[35]

Religion alters in its focus in the Neolithic. Since farming is a chancy business, religion now tries to relieve the resultant anxiety.[36] Since the prevalence of war heightens the danger of being killed or enslaved, fear of these fates strengthens the desire for divine protection.[37] Another perspective is offered by the duality of the new warrior's psychology: in his dealings with his equals he is controlled, even courteous; confronting his enemies in the world outside his polity, he can slaughter, rape, pillage, destroy, and profane with self-satisfied impunity. In the war-oriented society, 'masculine' values likewise relegate 'feminine' values to a secondary position.[38]

How far China was distinctive in late-neolithic and early bronze-age times must be measured against these rough-and-ready benchmarks.

Effective warfare

The cores of the earliest Chinese civilization in the late Neolithic about four thousand years ago were local states based primarily on settled cereal farming, ceramic vessels to store grain safely, walled cities to guard granaries and populations,[39] stone and wood and horn tools, and with bronze metallurgy for weapons and, before long, religious ritual vessels. Their societies were divided into distinct classes, controlled by severe social discipline, and using writing derived from pictographs for recording such information as the ownership and purpose of ritual vessels, the verdict of oracles, major gifts from superiors, and other matters. This complex gave these first archaic states a real if precarious superiority in warfare over the less civilized or uncivilized, but otherwise rather similar, tribes that surrounded them or lived interspersed among them.[40]

The majority of these tribes also practised agriculture. Both groups had domesticated animals: notably dogs, sheep, pigs, cows in the north, and water buffalo mainly but not only in the south. The horse appeared some time probably in the early second millenium BCE, for pulling chariots, not yet for riding, and so belonged for the moment mainly (but not exclusively) to the civilized domain. Divination based on the shoulder blades of large animals, or the undershells of turtles, and interpreting the cracks that appeared when they were pierced with a heated instrument, was found from Shandong (in the Northeast) to Gansu (in the Northwest), and from Inner Mongolia to Anhui (in the East). The technique was most refined along the east coast.[41] There was thus no single key factor that emerged in one privileged place. What was new was a particular *combination* of political, social, economic, and ideological elements that, together, conferred a competitive military advantage.

Let us anchor these comments in some evidence. The last ode in the *Scripture of Songs*[42] describes the campaign led by Wu Ding of the Shang-Yin dynasty some time around 1200 BCE[43] against the 'Tiger Quarter', most of which probably lay south of the central stretch of the Yangzi River. The text as we now have it probably comes from at least some hundreds of years later, after the fall of the Shang-Yin. It may well have been altered to accord with the values of the Zhou dynasty that followed, and should not be assumed to be a fully accurate reflection of the Shang period. Nonetheless, its emphasis on farming, discipline, and fighting seems authentic:

> Swift were the blows of King Wu Ding of Yin
> In his punitive onslaught on Jing and on Chu,
> Thrusting deep past the obstacles these lands opposed to him,
> Till the warrior cohorts of Jing were diminished
> And their settlement-strongholds likewise reduced.
> The descendant of Tang — this was his doing!

> Lands of Jing and of Chu, you were annexed,
> So that you dwelt in our state's southern region,
> In times now long past by King Tang the Achiever.
> From the Di folk and Qiang, who both live to the west,
> None dared not come — to offer their presents,
> None dared not come — to submit to the emperor!
> So it was said, "Our Shang lives forever!"

> Heaven commanded the numerous princes
> To continue Yu's work, establish their capitals,
> And inform the king yearly of what had been happening:
> "Spare us disgrace, and punishment's misery!
> In both sowing and reaping we have no wise been indolent!"

> Heaven told those in charge to control their inferiors,
> So subordinate folk respected strict discipline,
> Free of arrogance, also restrained and obedient,
> Not daring be lazy, nor waste their time wilfully.
> It also instructed subordinate states
> That their enfeoffment was good fortune's basis.

> The City of Shang has a well-ordered pattern,
> The summit supreme of the world's four directions.

> Awe-inspiring in fame, it rises resplendent,
> Its magical influence cleansed and immaculate.

Fighting, farming, cities, discipline. Also the imperial mystique of divine favor. Most of the new complex is explicitly exalted in these lines. Ordinary people had therefore to be held to agriculture by coercion and persuasion. Otherwise rulers and their armies went unfed.

The Zhou tribe first appeared in recorded history during Wu Ding's reign just mentioned. They founded a state in western Shaanxi, northwest of the Shang domain. Over the next two hundred years they had a varying relationship of conflict and cooperation with the Shang, but ended by becoming their allies on a basis of near-equality. Finally, near the end of the first millennium BCE, they combined with the somewhat less civilized tribes to their west—but including the Shu from Sichuan, masters of bronze-working—and defeated the Shang army at the battle of Muye, most probably in 1041 BCE. Their triumph was due partly to these alliances, partly to the charismatic leadership of King Wu and the favorable omens with which he was blessed as the campaign opened, and partly—probably—to the use of four-horse chariots against the Shang's two-horse vehicles.

For the early Zhou, too, success in war was, ultimately, everything. When the founder of their dynasty, King Wen, had annihilated the city–state of Chong on the south side of the middle Wei valley (in the Northwest), he built a new capital nearby at Feng. The closing stanzas of an ode[44] celebrate the early Zhou mastery of siegecraft that made possible this destruction of a rival. The walls whose scaling and breach is described here were probably built of rammed earth.

> To King Wen of Zhou, God conveyed his conception:
> "Consult with the regions now your confederates.
> Link with brothers and cousins, kin of one generation.
> With curved hooks for grappling attached to your ladders,
> With wheeled towers and rams for approaching and battering,
> Smash the ramparts of Chong with righteous attack!"

> The wheeled towers advanced, and rams, steady and serried.
> Chong's walls rose above, unperturbed and immense.
> — Their seized chiefs came in lines, to be put to the question,
> And in calm, awesome, fashion we axed off their heads.
> These we gave God, and the vanquished land's spirits,
> Spoke respects to the dead, to their shades offered gifts.

> In the four-quartered world, none showed him insolence.
> His wheeled towers and rams were as dense-packed as thickets.

Though Chong's walls were massive, soaring uplifted,
He chastised them in battle, and smashed his way in,
Snapped their line of descent, and snuffed out their existence,
So that nobody, anywhere, showed opposition.

Whatever civilization was, or was to become, its bedrock was—and remains—superior skill in human butchery.

The matrix of power

The new factor was *organization*. Both of bodies and of minds. By the late Neolithic, the components that were soon to be combined in the emerging concentrations of power, skills, resources, and articulated action that can only reasonably be defined as 'states' were present in many places across the subcontinent we today call 'China'. Cereal farming of rice could be found as easily along the southern shore of Hangzhou Bay (in the East) as that of millet in the central valley of the Yellow River (in the Northwest and Northeast). Fired earthenware was similarly widespread, as were walled settlements. Sophisticated bronze-casting could be found not just in the traditional northern heartland of early Chinese culture, but in Sichuan in the West and the Gan river valley in Jiangxi to the south. There is an underlying affinity between objects from these centers, and certain shared motifs, that suggest a common origin, but local differences in style and emotional tonality can be striking. Examples are the eerily elongated more-than-life-size bronze human figure and masks from Sanxingdui in Guanghan in Sichuan. They are from the Shang period but have no known Shang counterparts.[45] What seem to be meaningful incised marks, pictographs or even, possibly, traces of proto-scripts can likewise be found long before the mid second millennium along the east coast and in what is today Qinghai in the Northwest, as well as the Shang heartland.[46] What is relevant is how these components, and the others, were put together.

Everything interlocked. Settled farming supported denser concentrations of population than did hunting, fishing, and gathering. This provided the extra manpower and supplies needed for larger armies and more numerous temporary conscripts for public works, whether rammed-earth walls or public buildings. The colossal scale of preimperial warfare in China, especially during the Warring States period from the fifth to the third centuries BCE at its end, is well known, but it is worth recalling that it went back further. The Shang were constantly fighting other states and peoples, mobilizing thousands to some tens of thousands of troops on each occasion for the purpose. Since the population of the Shang at the start of the dynasty has been estimated to have been between 4 and 4.5 million,[47] this would not have been an impossible operation. The Zhou army that defeated the Shang towards the end of the second millennium BCE had close to 50,000 soldiers. By the Springs and Autumns period, the forces raised by the separate individual states were of the same order of magnitude; and by the time of the Warring States armies are frequently mentioned as having exceeded 100,000, sometimes several-fold. There were over 480 recorded wars in the 242 years of the Springs and Autumns period, and 590 in the 248 years of the Warring States period which followed.[48] These figures for the size of armies, huge by the standards of the archaic world, have understandably raised skepticism, but references in the sources are quite numerous and broadly internally consistent.

A large section of the ten-meter-high defensive wall built about 1600 BCE around what is now Zhengzhou (in the Northeast) is still standing, and it is estimated that its total length was about 7 kilometers. The average width at the base was about 20 meters, and at the top about 5 meters.[49] If we (arbitrarily) assume that the inward extension of the base clear of the top was twice as great on the inside as on the enemy side, this gives in round figures a volume of 875,000 cubic meters. Without a good idea of the efficiency of Shang tools it is hard to estimate the workforce that would have been needed for digging up the raw material, transporting it to the site, lifting it, and ramming it, besides constructing the temporary wooden shuttering to hold the earth in place while it was pounded, and other lesser tasks. If it took 8 men a day to handle a cubic meter of finished rammed earth through all these stages, then it would have needed 3,500 men working 200 days a year for 10 years to complete it.

Increased military power made possible tribute and taxes, and obligatory services. All of these intensified the concentration of financial, material, and technical resources. One result was increased specialization among artisans. Certain Shang clans or kin-groups seem to have focused on particular crafts.[50] Shang cities supported workshops that were skilled not only in casting bronze weapons and ritual bronze vessels, with their spectacular animal patterns, but also in other, more mundane, techniques. Bone was made into arrowheads, hairpins, awls, needles, knives, forks, fishhooks, and even incised with tables showing the sixty-unit cycle composed of paired units taken from the ten 'trunks' and twelve 'branches'. These were used for recording the days. There were also rulers for measuring lengths. Stone was shaped into the bases for pillars, grindstones, axes, knives, pestles and mortars, chisels, spinning whorls for yarn, and chiming musical stones. Specialist potters heated kilns to 1000° Celsius, glazed their wares, and imprinted them with patterns cut into molds. Textiles included hemp, *Pueraria* fiber cloth, and silks, some of them already figured and woven on looms of some complexity, probably for the royal house itself.[51]

Exchange and trade have deep roots in human history. There are hints that in China, as elsewhere, they predated civilization. One such hint is the presence of cowry shells—the produce of the South China and East China Seas,[52] and later used as proto-money in China as in other parts of the world[53]—at a site in Qinghai, far inland to the northwest, and dated to 2500 BCE. Plus imitation cowries made of bone.[54] Under the Shang, cowries were to serve as a form of high-status quasi-money, in contrast to their low per-unit value in some other regions. Oracle bones record kings giving quantities such as two and five strings of these shells on special occasions to favored recipients.[55] Early in the first millennium BCE greater quantities were in circulation and they became close to authentic money for a short time. There is, for example, a record of a field being valued at from seven to eight strings.[56]

In similar fashion, an even earlier site in He'nan (in the Northeast) from the sixth millennium BCE has yielded turquoise, at a vast distance from any known geological source.[57] Oracle bone records show that under the Shang dynasty ox-drawn carts were used to transport supplies for the armed forces, a logistical advantage over those without them. Some scholars think that Wang Hai, the first known ancestor of the Shang line, and revered as the original tamer of wild cattle, was killed by the Youyi barbarians in north China when transporting goods in wagons hauled by oxen.[58] The critical point is that the growing demand that early civilization created for both luxury and basic materials *accelerated* the volume and value of tribute, transport, and trade over longer and longer distances.[59] Where strategic goods, like tin ore from south of the Yangzi, were concerned, it further became necessary for the state to safeguard the routes over which they came.[60]

At the core of the new civilization were the cities, often like garrisons in a far from fully subdued countryside. The creation of the city began a crucial decoupling between the dominant, decision-making, part of the human population, now living increasingly in a built environment, and the rest of natural world. In other words, where and when a decision was made less and less coincided with where and when its environmental impact was felt. *Decisional distance* of this sort has the dimensions of space (from the point of decision to the point of impact), time (from present to future generations), and social rank (from decision-makers to the lower classes). Increasing it has progressively lessened the awareness of and sensitivity to the environmental effects of their policies among rulers and their advisers. This still holds today.

The city required the invention of social and material structures to moderate and channel the increased rate of social interactions between different members of the population, and, in parallel, techniques and institutions for controlling a larger compact demographic unit than any known before in human evolution.[61] This interlocked with the development of the stratified society needed for the exercise of power both more intensively and more extensively than ever before.

The city was, and is, the epitome of most of these sorts of separation. Donald Hughes has observed of ancient Mesopotamia that "it is as if the barrier of city walls and the rectilinear pattern of canals had divided human beings from wild nature and substituted an attitude of confrontation for the earlier feeling of cooperation. . . . Literature . . . often use[s] the image of battle to describe the new relationship with nature."[62] In his view most ancient cities in western Eurasia also "placed too great a demand on available resources, depleted them within their sphere, and then went as far as they could to gain access to additional resources, until this effort also failed," leading to their eventual decline.[63]

Chinese settlements first acquired moats in the Yangshao period (commonly identified by its pottery painted in swirling geometric patterns) in the penultimate stage of the Neolithic. These ditches were probably mainly for defense against animals, since storage areas at this time could be outside the moat. Walls followed in the Longshan period, known for its characteristic shiny, thin-walled black ceramic wares. They were presumably for protection against other people.[64] The *Record of the Rituals* says of this period when the "Great Way had already fallen into obscurity" that "inner and outer walled cities and moats provided security; ritual behavior and public-spirited principles provided discipline. . . . Thus whatever was advantageous was put into effect, but from this *warfare came into existence*."[65] Walls were of rammed earth, sometimes multiple, and had substantial areas of nonurban land within them. A fairly standard urban spatial pattern developed under the Shang, with graves and workshops being just outside the defended area. Military control was based on each central city—above all, the principal capital—being surrounded by a network of satellite cities, and on the development of 'secondary capitals'.[66]

The *Scripture of Songs* tells of how in Shang times Gong Liu, progenitor of the Zhou lineage, "mounted the southern ridge, discovering there the site for the Capital," and how "the farmed lands for the military cantonments of the Capital at the appropriate time spread everywhere." Furthermore, "his armies had three divisions, so he measured the wetlands and the uplands, and had the land share-cultivated to provide his tax-revenue in grain."[67] Nine generations later, Gong Tanfu, founder of the Zhou royal house, moved his capital to Zhouyuan, or the 'plain of Zhou', where "a hundred walls all rose up."[68] The driving force behind this agrarian–urban transformation was acknowledged to have been military effectiveness. As the *Scripture of Songs* say of Tanfu's city: "He raised the grand Earth-Altar whence the great armies marched forth."[69]

The multiplicity of walls spoken of by the *Scripture of Songs* probably refers to internal walls around palaces and urban subdivisions. The Chinese city during the first two millennia of its existence was, perhaps with some exceptions, a cellular structure under tight control. Only a few favored mansions of the great opened directly onto the main thoroughfares, ordinary residences being confined within walled enclaves—the quarters—that were dead ends. For details we have to turn to the late-preimperial work on statecraft, the *Master Guan.*

It is easy to criticize such an apparently anachronistic jump forward in time, and the professional conscience of the historian is uncomfortable with such a procedure. Its justification is that it lets us access, in explicit form, what appears to be the logic of a long-term trend, and simple reactive criticism of the attempt to do this is just that—too simple. Nonetheless, the reader has been warned.

The *Master Guan* is one of the most awkward of sources to use. It is a compilation, probably consisting of a core from the third century BCE with later additions. There is a measure of unity of point of view when it is considered in relation to works from other major schools, but the different parts seem to come from different hands, and to some degree reflect somewhat different outlooks on the world.[70] Despite the dangers of anachronism in using so late a work even as a general guide to the likely underlying thrust of earlier ideas and institutions, the kind of political world it purports to describe often seems, at least superficially, like that of the late Springs and Autumns or early Warring States, though harshly simplified and schematic. It is impossible to determine the extent to which the text is an attempt at a description of something that once existed, and the extent to which it is a prescription of an ideal. There would seem to be a mixture. Nonetheless the obsession with control is suggestive.[71]

> The main city wall must be unbroken. The walled suburbs that surround it must not communicate with the outside. The urban quarters must not communicate laterally with each other. The gates to the domestic precincts must be kept shut. The doors closed with bolts in the walls round the mansions should be maintained in good order.
>
> The reason for this is that if the main city wall is not unbroken, rebellious people will start to plot. If the walled suburbs surrounding communicate with the outside, treacherous refugees and transgressors will appear. If the urban quarters communicate laterally with each other, there will be no end to robbery and thieving. If the gates of the domestic precincts are not kept shut, and the domains of the home and the world outside come into

contact, there will be no separation between males and females. If the walls round the mansions are not kept in good repair, and the bolted doors are not secure, those who possess goods of high quality will not be able to safeguard them.

The sense of the city–state being a garrison city is palpable.

Urban dwellers were supposed to live under unremitting surveillance. In an earlier section a hierarchical administrative system is detailed, based on units of five or ten families. The *Master Guan* then continues:[72]

One must build in the separations. One must block up the hiding-places. A single road should provide an ample width for all entering and leaving. One should scrutinize closely the gates of the neighborhood precincts, and pay particular attention to the control of the bolts and the storehouses by the chiefs of the quarters. Wardens should be established at the precinct gates to open and close them at the proper times. The precinct gate-wardens should observe those who leave and enter, so that they can report to the chief of their quarter. All cases of leaving or coming in at the wrong time, or of wearing of abnormal clothing, or of family members and personal followers disobeying moral rules, when noticed by a gate-warden, should be reported at once.

A control system was thus in place well before the imperial age. For the moment there is no way of saying how early. He Xiu, a commentator of the second century CE, noted with reference to 539 BCE, that[73]

In the spring and the summer the people went out to the fields. In the autumn and winter they went in to defend the inner and outer cities. In the seasons of agricultural work, the fathers and elders and chiefs of the urban quarters would open the gates at dawn, and sit at the surveillance posts. Those who left later than the proper time would not be allowed to leave. In the evening, those who did not keep to their [own proper] gate-tower would not be allowed to come back in.[74]

Discipline was at the heart of the new urban-agrarian life.

Looking forward for a moment, even more anachronistically, we can note in passing that during the first part of the imperial age that followed, locational subdivision by status and occupation seems even to have been intensified, and strict urban policing maintained. Life within the walls ran to a time-schedule, including a ban on most movements around the city at night. Market areas had a monopoly of permitted trading, and were walled and officially controlled during the early and middle empires up to the Tang.[75] Unlike that of medieval Europe, the air of the ancient Chinese city did not 'make one free'.[76] Ultimately the medieval economic revolution, and the spread of a multiplicity of largely free markets, were to break these bonds, but not till the eighth and ninth centuries, and, above all, the Song.

How was this all kept together? Let us leave our excursus into later times and go back to the second millennium BCE again. First and foremost the new empire was an empire over the soul. A small part of this invisible dominion was rational, focusing on the numerical subjugation of nature. The Shang prescribed a basic unit of measure (1.7 centimeters), a musical scale, a calendar, and presumably the number of cowries in the standard double 'string' (probably ten).[77] For the most part, though, its pre-eminence was in the realm of the spirits.

The inheritance of a late-neolithic substratum of belief in numinous animal powers constituted the foundation of the religious sense of the world at this time. Its inner nature is now hidden from us, but its existence is palpable not only from the zoomorphic pictographs but above all from the animal motifs that dominate Shang bronzes, their sometimes theriomorphic shapes, and the so-called *taotie* masks that often adorn their sides, composites of the features of a number of different species, and hauntingly indecipherable. The transition at the end of the second millennium BCE from the Shang to the Zhou dynasty, who did not share this concern with the animal world, started a process whereby these bronzes slowly lost their old spiritual power, and became little more than symbols of social rank. If they were still potent to some degree it was because of their link with sacrifices to the ancestors.[78] For the environmental historian this later change prompts a profound but still unanswerable question about the alteration of the relations of human beings with the once circumambient animal world now being subdued and marginalized by civilization.

The Shang seem to have hierarchicalized, rationalized, and syncretized these ancient inherited beliefs, without however acknowledging them directly—at least in the brief oracle-bone texts that have survived, a curious and noteworthy fault line in the records. There is an unexplained gulf between the bronze visual symbols and bone-based writing. Since people in this age of the world believed that everything that happened was the work of a multitude of invisible beings, the Shang ideology—reconstructed from the written records—defined these latter as ultimately ruled by a God Above or Ultimate Ancestor, *Shangdi*. The spirits, God included, could be questioned about their feelings and the future by means of divination—burning cracks in the shoulder blades of large mammals or the undershells of turtles, or casting the stalks of certain plants. These ever-present but invisible entities could also be influenced by sacrifices of animals and human beings. But the intermediaries stated to be qualified to do this questioning were now exclusively *political*. Shang religion presented the king as a spirit in human incarnation, as all-powerful in the tangible, visible world as his ancestor God Above was in the domain of spirits. These spirits, including the departed forebears of both genders of the royal house, inhabited everything and moved everything—stars, winds, rivers, mountains, plants, and dreams. They determined the weather, the harvests, natural disasters, the outcome of battles and illnesses, and the founding or destruction of cities. The ruler's intermediary role had been made indispensable.

As the chief link between God Above and the spirits on the one hand and his human subjects on the other, the Shang king was a privileged channel of communication, as well as the principal patron, and at times practitioner, of divination and sacrifice. Sacrificing was an act that implied political legitimacy: princes could only sacrifice in their own territories and only so long as they possessed authority there. The emperor, or his envoys, everywhere. This amalgam must have drawn most of its elements from the late-neolithic religion, with diviners, sorcerers, and offerers of prayers and sacrifices already in existence, but 'God Above' was a political invention of sinister genius: a deity who was, or became, specifically linked to the Shang without any moral preconditions, and yet endowed with an allegedly universal suzerainty.

Royal life in second-millennium-BCE China consumed hours every day in divination. Results were repetitively rechecked almost in the manner of a scientist duplicating an experiment. Treasure-troves of resources were expended on sacrifices. At times three hundred oxen might be butchered, or a hundred or even three hundred Qiang—western barbarians probably akin to Tibetans, and skilled herders of sheep—sent to the shadows by beheading. Or else by burial in a pit, or cutting in two, or burning alive, or by slicing. It is only possible to guess at the psychological intuition that underpinned this political behavior. Most probably it conveyed to the people the message that society was in a state of perpetual peril from which only the vigilance, and the unique skills and prerogatives of the ruling house, continually exercised, could save it. The seriousness of the blood price repeatedly paid drove home into the consciousness of the subjects of the Shang how much was at stake if the demands of the spirits were not met and their anger not assuaged. Rebellion—which of course happened frequently—was not only presented as a sacrilege, but redefined into being a threat to the security of humankind as a whole.[79]

The other innovation was a *command structure*. In our own bureaucratized, policed, and nannied society it is easy to forget how unnatural it has been throughout most of the human past for adult men to give orders to other adult men.[80]

In the oracle-bone texts from the late second millennium BCE, the graph for 'order' or 'command'[81] is linked to the two powers that issued the ultimate orders: the Ultimate Ancestor or Supreme God[82] in the invisible world of the spirits, and the Emperor[83] in the visible world of nature and humankind. God gave orders for the rain to fall or not, for the winds to blow or not, and for the lightning to flash or not.[84] Often the winds were his envoys who carried out his commands.[85] God it was who ordained the good or bad quality of the harvests, the outcome of battles, and the occurrence or absence of sickness.[86] The ruler had constantly to confirm through divination that what he was doing was in compliance with God's orders.

His own commands were characteristically given to his *zhong*.[87] The meaning of this term is controversial, but most probably indicates a corps of elite warrior–administrators.[88] He might also issue directives to subordinate tribal states such as the Zhou,[89] or to individuals to take some particular action. Government ministers at times gave orders to the *zhong* to perform military duties, construction, or farming, or to other officials in what was still a relatively undifferentiated bureaucracy.[90] There was also a lower command structure consisting of those to whom orders were given and who passed them on.[91] Some farming was done under the supervision of state officials, but may mostly have been for ritual purposes.[92] At the lowest levels of society, existing kin-groups probably formed the basis of Shang political organization, through the services and tribute they owed to the ruler.[93] A later text mentions that in the reign of Emperor Cheng at the start of the Zhou dynasty, the son of the regent, the Duke of Zhou, was given six named kin-groups of the defeated Shang, and one of the Duke's brothers another seven. It speaks of the 'main line of the clan', the 'subdivided family groups', and 'the others of their kind'—the meaning of this last term not being entirely clear. It may possibly point to a group of lower status.[94] Slaves were also found, an example being the captives taken in the wars of the last of the Shang emperors against the 'eastern barbarians'.[95]

Under the early Zhou, inscriptions on bronzes reveal a quasi-feudal landed economy—which we should not assume was the whole of the rural economy— in which the labor force was under tight discipline. Records now tell of 'managers', commoners, retainers, and slaves being given to nobles by the ruler as enfeoffment gifts, along with horses, chariots, weapons, and land. Human beings were used to pay fines for offenses, and sometimes bought and sold. By the end of the early Zhou such gifts were also being made by leading aristocrats to their subordinates.[96] This suggests an expanding farm economy in which labor was in short supply, and kept in place and driven by coercion. At the same time an obscure but important transformation of the kinship system crystallized it into a patriarchal, patrilineal structure that is recognizable as the ancestor of that which existed through imperial times. With its own strict and distinctive discipline over both juniors and women.

Chinese society was becoming regimented.

Clastres has given us the key to understanding these processes. "It is the political break that is decisive, and not the economic transformation. The true revolution in man's protohistory is not the neolithic . . . ; it is the political revolution, that mysterious emergence—irreversible, fatal to primitive societies—of the thing we know by the name of the state."[97] He adds that, in general, "the tribal chief does not prefigure the chief of state."[98] Critically, "the preparation and conduct of a military expedition are the only circumstances in which the chief has the opportunity to exercise a minimum of authority. As soon as things have been concluded . . . the war chief again becomes a chief without power."[99] He suggests that increasing demographic density can disrupt the otherwise tenacious primitive antipolitical order of society, and also that, by unifying thinking, prophets may help to open the way to the state.[100] In archaic China, the modalities were different from those of the tribes Clastres studied in South America. But, with suitable mutations, his analysis offers a new perspective on the revolution started by the semilegendary sage–kings.

The social machinery was now in place to develop, enhance, exploit, degrade, and in the end partially destroy, the natural environment in the same way as the human environment. And the primary purpose of agricultural development was the provision of tougher sinews of war. In the state of Chu in the sixth century BCE, the surveying of fields, pastures, and water channels, as well as fiscal planning, was entrusted to the Minister of War. He, or his staff, calculated "the numbers of chariots to be supplied, and made a register of the horses, and determined the quotas of soldiers mounted in chariots and on foot, the numbers of suits of body-armor and of shields."[101] *Kriegswirtschaft.*[102]

The politically driven economy

The economy of these early Chinese states is best described as having been 'politically driven'. This choice of words allows for stimulation, control, and monitoring in varying measure by political power, both central and local, but avoids implying universal political management, which was not the case. Some of it was of course also driven by religion, in so far as religion can be distinguished from politics during this age. The technology of fermenting wine, the drink that put the imbiber in touch with the gods, and of the first virtuoso casting of richly ornamented sacrificial vessels in bronze, were both the by-products of religious faith.

Over the thousand years that separated the later Shang dynasty from the Qin empire in the third century BCE transformations also took place in the social forms through which power was exercised at the local level. In broad terms this was a shift first from tribal kin-groups to a type of feudalism, and then to a rudimentary bureaucracy. A little, at least, of each was present at all three stages, but their relative weights altered dramatically. In terms of time, the first of these stages covered the late Shang and early Zhou, the second the middle Zhou through the Springs and Autumns period,[103] and the third the later Zhou, that is mainly the Warring States epoch, down to the beginning of the empire.

Detailed descriptions of the politically driven economy exist only for the last of these three periods. They are idealized, that is to say partly imagined, systematizations of selected real components. Though often in essence prescriptions for the future, they present themselves, in order to sound more authoritative, as looking back in time. In some respects they are demonstrably anachronistic, and with little doubt also rosy and hazy. Even so, it is my intuition that they pick up the underlying economic objectives pursued by states over this millennium, even if emphases and circumstances may have changed. The concern for conserving the diminishing base of natural resources, for example, seems to have been a development of the second and third stages. Used with great caution these late materials open a window into a Chinese mental universe of social-darwinian brutality gradually becoming explicitly conscious of what had been implicit since much earlier days.

What was exceptional about it was not that it was exceptionally brutal, but the degree to which it was aware of its own nature. Donald Hughes glimpses something of the same sort of brutality in the ancient west Eurasian classical world, but it seems to have possessed less self-understanding. He writes that a "most damaging aspect of Greek and Roman social organization as it affected the environment was its direction toward war. . . . Ancient cities and empires were warrior-dominated societies, never at peace for very long. . . . Nonrenewable resources were consumed, and renewable resources exploited faster than was sustainable. As a result, the lands where Western civilization received its formative impulse were gradually drained."[104] The point that needs to be added is that in both regions this was due to competitive necessity. Of course, both Europe and China in the fullness of time found new 'resource frontiers' in the Middle Ages: Europe in the north, and later overseas, and China in the south and southwest. This is part of the Chinese story we will look at in later chapters when economic growth had acquired an independent momentum.

Discipline was of the essence. "One controls the people as one controls a flood. One feeds them as one feeds domestic animals. One uses them as one uses plants and trees."[105] Cereals were the lifeline of government. In the realm of an incompetent ruler, "the farmland lies uncultivated and the state capital is empty."[106] In a poorly governed state, "the elite among the commoners will esteem profit and think little of military bravery. The masses will be addicted to quaffing and feasting, *and detest farming*. In a situation like this, the state's coffers will be exhausted, and food, drink, firewood, and vegetables lacking."[107]

Exploitation was a state necessity. "Production comes from expending energy. Energy is produced by exhausting our bodies. For this reason, that the ruler has limitless resources is because the common people exert themselves without respite."[108] A saying quoted with approval in the context of a discussion of the need for rewards to be reliable and appropriate was, "If the good-quality farmland is not in the hands of the military officers, within three years the armed forces will have become feeble."[109] Elsewhere in the book, two questions are listed as needing answers when another state is being evaluated. The first is, "In the families of how many warrior–administrators do they farm in person?" The second, "How many warrior–administrators own farmland but do not farm it in person?"[110] In a properly run polity, access to resources was linked to state service.

The other side of the new dependence on farming was a perpetual terror of famine. "If for five days people do not eat, it is like a year without a harvest. If for seven days they have no food, the state's territory vanishes. If for ten days they are starving, there are no fellow human beings. All of them are dead."[111] Unlike for the Australian aboriginal, who knows—or knew—how to live off the land, lack of food is the ever-present unacknowledged fear shared by all civilized people, and the hidden core of the social discipline on which civilization is built.

Discipline apart, the crucial economic concern in this age was a shortage of labor:[112]

If one walks around the fields of a city–state and its cleared outer zone,[113] and takes a look at their planting and weeding, evaluating their farming on this basis, one can tell if the state is going to suffer from famine or enjoy plenty. If the plowing is not deep, and the weeding not done scrupulously, so the terrain is not in proper order, and if there are numerous weeds in the fields of hay, and if the areas cultivated are not always those of high fertility, nor the ones uncultivated always those of low fertility, one may use the number of inhabitants as the criterion for judging its cleared outer zone.

If the hayfields are numerous and the tilled fields few, then, even in the absence of flood or drought, this is the cleared outer zone of a state that will suffer from hunger. Under such circumstances, if the inhabitants are few in number, there will not be enough of them to defend the territory. If, under these same circumstances, the inhabitants are numerous, the city–state will be impoverished, and its people short of food. If a flood or drought occurs, the multitudes will scatter, and be impossible to retain. In cases where there are not enough people to provide defense, the city walls will not be secure. In cases where the people are short of food, it will be impossible to make them fight. If the multitudes scatter and cannot be retained, the city–state will become a mound of ruins.[114]

The need to stop peasants deserting agriculture became linked to the concern with preventing the depletion of resources:[115]

Even if there are wooded hills nearby, and the plants and trees there are in flourishing condition, limits must be set to the size of the houses, and prohibitions on felling imposed and lifted at the appropriate seasons. Why so?— It is not possible to fell large trees in isolation, nor handle them in isolation, nor transport them in isolation. [Other trees need to be cut to clear routes for access and transport.] . . .

Even if the pools and wetlands spread far and wide, and the fish and the turtles are plentiful, there must be regulations on the use of nets. It is not possible to be successful solely on the basis of skill with boats and nets. This is not the state taking plants and trees to be its private possessions, nor is it grudging the people their fish and turtles. How can the people be allowed to stop producing grain? This is why it is said that the kings of former times put prohibitions on activities in the hills and wetlands *in order to increase the involvement of the people in the production of grain.*

In the same spirit *The Book of the Lord of Shang*, a text of physiocratic Realpolitik, argued that if the state has "the unique power over the mountains and marshes, then *the common people, who detest farming,* are lazy, and want doubled profits, will have nowhere to find something to eat. If they have nowhere to find something to eat, they will be obliged to engage in the cultivation of the fields." A traditional commentary explains that 'unique power' meant state bans on the mountains and marshes, and that the people were "not permitted to gather wood, to hunt, or to fish in an uncontrolled manner."[116]

The lower classes were to be kept working at their inherited tasks by means of separate residential areas:[117]

The common people should not be allowed to live in heterogeneous confusion. If they do live in a heterogeneous confusion, what they say becomes mixed up with ideas not appropriate to their station, and their activities breach good order. For this reason the sage–kings always settled the warrior–administrators in their own secluded dwellings. They settled the farmers in the farmlands and the cleared outer zones. Craftsmen they settled next to the government offices, and merchants adjacent to the marketplaces.

Each succeeding generation was to be schooled in the behavior and values that suited its status.

> Once the farmers have been settled together in groups, they will pay close attention to the four seasons and weigh up the changing circumstances. They will make ready the tools they need to use, plows and plowshares, winnowing flails and large sickles. When the cold weather comes, they will bind up the straw and clear the fields to wait for the time of the year to plow; they will then plow deeply and broadcast the seeds evenly, speedily covering them with soil. Before the rains come, they will weed and hoe, waiting for the 'seasonal rains'.[118]
>
> Once the seasonal rains have arrived, they will take their sickles and hoes under their arms to toil with them from dawn till twilight in the fields and cleared outer zones. They will take off their upper garments to go to their work where they separate the tares from the sprouts of grain, and even up the distances between plants. They will wear hats of China grass or rushes on their heads, their bodies clad in coarse cloth raincoats, their persons soaked, and their feet muddy. Their hair and skins will be exposed to the sun. They will exhaust the energy of their four limbs to pursue unremittingly their work in the fields and the cleared outer zones.
>
> They will have become accustomed to this since they were young, and their hearts will be content with it. They will not be enticed into going off elsewhere by the sight of unfamiliar things.[119]

As always, anxiety over the absconding of the labor force.

It was the responsibility of the minister for agriculture to "open up the grassy lands for farming, appropriate the crop for the cities, extend the territory, stockpile grain, and increase the population."[120] The political supervision of the economy is elaborated in more detail in several places. For example,[121]

> It is the business of the forest wardens to see that the rules about fires are enforced, so respect is shown to the hills, wetlands,[122] forests, and thick vegetation. *This is because these are the sources of materials.* Prohibitions should be imposed and lifted in the appropriate seasons so that the people have materials for their houses and stockpiles of firewood and kindling.
>
> It is the business of the Director of Works to breach dikes to release flood waters, and to ensure throughflow in the irrigation and drainage channels, to repair the levees and embankments, and to have storage reservoirs in

readiness, so that even if the seasonal floods exceed due measure, no harm is done to the cereal crops, and that, even if there is a year of severe drought, there is grain to be sickled for harvest.

It is the business of the Director of Farming to appraise the lie of the land, to judge which soils are more fertile and which less so, to consider what is suited to the terrain, and to issue clear instructions as to the sequence of the periods for each task, so that the timing of the farmers is arranged in a well-adjusted fashion, and so that cereals, mulberry trees, and hemp plants are all located where they can do well.

It is the business of the District Community Supervisors to travel through the districts and cantons, look at the houses, examine how people plant their crops, and grade their six domestic animals, so that their timing is arranged in well-adjusted fashion. Also to urge on the common people so that they labor energetically and do not behave frivolously, are happy in their homesteads, and treat leaving their district or village as a matter of gravity.

It is the business of the Director of Artisans to evaluate craftsmen of every sort, and their activities in each season, so as to distinguish the well-made from the coarse . . . and to ensure that none of them in the five artisans' districts dares to cut overly fancy patterns in stone or metal.

The role of the state was thus seen as covering policing, mobilizing labor for water-control work, giving advice, guidance and cheerleading, monitoring, appraisal, and censorship but—hydraulics apart—not 'management'. Of course in real life Chinese society must time and again have wriggled partly free from the straitjackets imposed on it, but this does not mean that the control system did not have an impact or that we should not take it seriously, any more than we should dismiss Mao's commune system of the late 1950s to the late 1970s as 'simply' unworkable.

The organization of a system for preventing floods proposed later in the book does come close to prescribing political management of economic matters. The translation that follows is precarious with respect to details, but robust as regards the general sense. The fictional simulacrum of the historic Master Guan is presented as speaking to an equally imaginary pasteboard Duke Huan of Qi, the title of a once-real ruler.[123] It contains that element of truth that led Karl Wittfogel to characterize China as a 'hydraulic despotism', a seriously incomplete description, as we shall later see, but not foolish or without perception.

I would request you to establish a Water Office and to order persons experienced in hydraulics to serve as Commissioner and Assistant Commissioner. Under their jurisdiction they will have section leaders and assistant officers, plus various conscripted persons of full age.[124] This done they will select a man from each side of each river to serve as supervisors of river works. These persons will be told to make tours of inspection along the rivers.

Those who are charged with the handling of the repairs to city walls, suburb walls, dikes, rivers, irrigation channels, pools, government offices and residences, and other such matters in their districts, are the assigned subalterns and conscripted persons of full age. They will be told to pass their commoners in review on a regular basis every year in autumn once the harvest is over, and to determine the families and the numbers of persons to be in the groups of ten families and the groups of five, following the criterion that their lands must be adjacent to each other. The registers will distinguish between men and women, and between adults and juveniles. Those not fit for service will be excused from it. Those with deep-seated illnesses, and unable to work, will be given sick leave. Those with a diminished capacity for labor will perform half of the duties. At the same time they will determine the number of military officers liable for active service. . . .

If the ruler becomes aware of some place that has too much or too little of something, he will send an order down to the Water Office. The Water Office will make use of the military officers liable for active service, together with the village elders and officials, plus the head of the five-family groups, to visit each village. Here, through the good offices of the parents in each household, they will systematically pass in review the equipment they have prepared for controlling floods.

The people will make use of the time in winter when work is at a standstill. Every ten persons should have six baskets, shovels, and side-planks and pestles for ramming earth walls, and one barrow for transporting earth, and two carts roofed with mats to keep out the rain. Each individual should have two vessels of his own for eating from. All these items will be securely stored in the village so that they can be used in place of equipment that has become worn out. . . .

During the winter, when there is little work to do, orders will be given to the military officers to go in turn from one staging-point to the next to increase the stacks of cut firewood on the banks of the rivers. The district magistrate will be in charge of them, and see to it that they do not fall behind schedule.

After the spring equinox, the days grow longer and

It is advantageous to make use of this to construct earthworks, since the soil is increasingly firm. Orders will be given to the military officers to raise levees along the banks of the larger rivers. These will be broad at the base and narrow at the top, following the line taken by the water. If there is land in some places in which plants will not grow, it is necessary to convert it into a polder.[125] Dikes are built around the bigger ones, and embankments around the smaller. The water will surround them on all sides, but the harvests will not be damaged. These dikes are enlarged each year, and planted with thorns and brambles to consolidate the earth of which they are made. Junipers and willows are mixed in with them, as a defense against breaches made by the flood waters.

In this vision, society is close to being an army. Or the army, society.

In another passage this last idea is taken to its ultimate conclusion. Everyone lives in units. The men go out to hunt together in the spring and fall, to master military skills. Life is collective. The rituals of good and ill fortune are shared in an atmosphere of emotional solidarity. The objective is a disciplined and fearless fighting society. We are told that this was once put into effect and that, with thirty thousand such indoctrinated troops, the duke of Qi "was able to act without restraint throughout the world."[126]

Last but not least, the *Master Guan* stresses the value of technology. The ruler must pay discriminating attention to the abilities of his craftsmen. They are a key to his success. Here, too, the state was a driving force for development.[127]

Almost nothing in these passages is likely ever to have been fully 'real'. Equally, it is unlikely that anything was entirely 'false', pure imagining. What we can infer from them is the crystallizing of the political logic of state-driven economic development that had, probably originally barely consciously, underlain the more-than-millennial quest for coercion.

In counterpoint to these grim formulas, but *not* in contradiction, was the tradition, elaborated by the Daoists around the beginning of imperial times, that recounted the loss of an original environmental innocence. Of expulsion from a natural Paradise. The *Book of the Prince of Huainan*, compiled in the second century BCE, contains perhaps the most explicit version.[128] It is woven from three strands:

The first is a mythologized folk-memory of a unity that once existed between human beings and the world around them. Cosmic forces and seasons were in harmony. "Winds and rains did not send down their catastrophes." Humans were simple and honest. "Mechanical contriving and deception were not hidden deep in people's hearts." The auspicious phoenix and unicorn, symbolic sovereigns of the bird and animal realms, flew and walked on the earth.

The second strand is the tale of the destruction of this harmony by economic development, the state, social stratification, and war. History and

Daoist–anarchist polemic are intertwined here, but the perception of causal interconnections is at times acute. The primacy of human action is stressed. "The cooperative harmony of Heaven and Earth, the reshaping of the multitude of beings by the Dark Force and Bright Force are both sustained by the vital aethers of humankind."[129] If these last become vitiated, the world is thrown into confusion.

The final strand is what was probably an unconscious collective recollection of the disruption caused by the sudden fall in temperature at the beginning of the first millennium B C E.[130] That inappropriate *human* actions had created the baleful aethers that had disrupted the workings of Heaven and Earth was seen as proven by the catastrophes that had followed.

As elaborated, the story is a romantic fable. Anachronistic, too, at times, as in its reference to iron. This should not conceal the fact that at its core, giving it its power, is an evocation of the most critical shock in human history: the onset of progress.

When the age of decadence arrived, people cut rocks from the mountains, hacking out metals and jades. They extracted the pearls from oysters, and smelted copper and iron ores. After this the multitude of living things multiplied no longer.

They slit open the wombs of wild animals, and butchered their young, after which the unicorn roamed about no more. They tipped over the nests of birds and smashed the eggs, after which the phoenix ceased to soar aloft.

They extracted fire with rotating drills, and structured tree trunks into platforms. They hunted by setting the forests ablaze, and fished by draining dry the pools. Even with less than the full number of people and full amount of equipment, their storehouses still had a surplus. But the multitude of living things did not proliferate. The greater part of them perished as sprouts, or in the egg, or womb.

People heaped up the earth and lived on mounds. They manured the fields and planted cereals. They excavated the ground and drank from wells. They dredged the streams and turned them to advantage. They built walls behind which they could be secure. They seized wild animals and made them into domesticated livestock. After this, the Dark Force and Bright Force became disordered, and the four seasons lost their proper sequence. Thunder and bolts of lightning wrought devastation. Hail and pellets of frozen snow sent down disasters. Fogs, frosts, and snow did not clear away, and the multitude of living things withered.

They removed the thickets and weeds, and grouped together boundary-embankments for their fields. They sickled the rushes in the cleared spaces beyond the settlements, and caused the seeds and swelling ears to grow. Then beyond counting were the plants and trees that perished when they were but curving sprouts, or bearing blossoms or fruits.

Next came the great mansions and the frame-structured palaces, with their lines of flying eave-beams and their upright columns to which the doors were locked. The protruding decorations on the battens borne by the rafters were sculpted and incised. The five colors of the water-chestnut and water-lily flowers vied for primacy, intermingling and various. . . . [The skilled workmen] could still not satisfy the desires of the ruler. This was why the fungi on the roots of the pines and cypresses lay exposed to the air when these [were felled and] turned to dead wood in summer. This was why the Yangzi and the Yellow River, and three other major rivers, stopped flowing . . . and flying locusts filled the countryside. The heavens dried up and the earth split in fissures. The phoenix descended no more, and the wild creatures with talons, fangs, and horns who sought to escape were thus impelled to confused violence. The common people, with only thatched huts to live in, had nowhere to seek refuge. They froze and starved, the dead lying pillowed on each other.

Next came the demarcation of the hills, rivers, and valleys so that there were territorial boundaries. They reckoned the populations by totals and densities, so that they could be subdivided into units of a given number. They built city walls, dug moats, and installed cunning devices at strategic points so as to be ready for emergencies. They conferred a decorative external appearance on those in government service, and established different grades for the clothes that people might wear. They distinguished between noble status and servile, and differentiated between the virtuous and the unworthy by means of praise and censure, bestowing rewards and inflicting punishments. Following this, offensive weapons and defensive armor abounded, and there were divisive conflicts. The destruction of the people, and their affliction by death at an early age . . . arose from this.

The same story. A different point of view.

Imperial times: A brief prospect

We have a provisional answer. The process of development that transformed most of the landscape of the archaic Chinese world began in the requirements for success in the military rivalry between early political entities, whether states, proto-states, or tribes. The process then gradually grew more complicated, as economic forces, first nurtured in good measure by the demands of the state, moved toward an ever-increasing degree of self-propelling independence. This second, more purely economic, aspect will be described in the chapters on Jiaxing (in the East), Guizhou (in the Southwest), and Zunhua (in the Northeast). But the state did not disappear as a promoter of economic and technical development either in times of imperial unity or of fragmentation. This was most visibly so when it needed to enhance its military and other forms of power, and occurred most commonly in frontier zones. Some of these were in the center of what is now China during periods of imperial disunity. Here, by way of illustration, is an example from 243 CE. The state of Wei in the North was planning a campaign through the Huai valley to destroy the rival state of Wu based on the lower Yangzi. A leading statesman reported to the ruler of Wei as follows:[131]

> Though the soil is good, there is not enough water to use to the full its productive power. It will also be necessary to dig canals to provide water for irrigation, so as to stockpile large quantities of military provisions, and to serve as transportation routes for the government. . . . [South of the Huai River] for each large-scale military expedition more than half of the troops have to be used for transport, which is highly expensive. . . . Twenty thousand colonists should be stationed to the north of the Huai, and thirty thousand to the south. At any time, twenty per cent of the men will be off duty, and so there will be a regular force of forty thousand men who function simultaneously as farmers and soldiers. . . . Wu will be conquered.

The linkage between hydraulic schemes and military logistics, both the supply of food and its cheap transport by water, had long become a commonplace in official thinking.

Examples from periods of imperial unity can equally easily be found. When Tian Le was the military commander in charge of the Northwest in the second half of the sixteenth century his achievements in creating an iron industry were recorded there by one of his subordinates.[132]

> Armor, spears, arrowheads, cannons, and swords are the means of attack and defense, but they are all matters that depend on metallurgy. Every year the province of Shaanxi supplied Ganzhou with more than 100,900 catties[133] of wrought iron for military requirements; and every year Fengxiang supplied Xining with more than 7,500 catties of wrought iron. If there was a shortfall, then emissaries were sent to buy more east of the passes in the province of He'nan. This was a journey of more than a thousand kilometers, and took months or even years. Money was wasted on nothing more than travel and transport, and doing this was even so of no use in emergencies.

H.E. Tian therefore prepared plans with his senior subordinates, and had searches conducted everywhere in the mountains and scrublands for ores. He also requisitioned foundry-workers from Shaanxi and Shanxi who were capable of smelting metal and assisting in the planned operation.

I myself . . . had already mobilized some soldiers and they had located ore at the foot of the Northern Mountains. . . . In these mountains the crystal-clear rocks[134] were piled up in countless quantity. Only a little over a kilometer away the mountain trees grew in profusion, providing fuel for burning charcoal.[135] . . .

After this I established a government office of six columns' width below the Northern Mountains, with two furnaces to smelt iron, barracks quarters of fifty units of space in extent, a signal beacon straddling the summit, and a beacon-lodge of four columns' width. I surrounded this last with a wall and a moat in readiness for emergencies.

His Excellency selected four hundred foot soldiers . . . to supply the labor for the task of ramming down the earth walls. . . . As before, personnel were chosen to become practised in this craft, and the order further given that . . . they should draw maps by surveying and make them available. Both those to do the forging and those to gather fuel were chosen. It was a scheme designed to last for a long time.

There are five advantages from this undertaking. The first is that in Hexi, west of the Yellow River, the region where the wars are conducted, iron smelted in the morning can be put to use the same evening, being taken from an inexhaustible source. The second is that, since the toil of transporting iron for more than a thousand kilometers no longer exists, the commoner–civilians have obtained a respite. The third is immediate availability, with no delays of months and years. The fourth is that labor is provided by soldiers who would otherwise be eating in idleness. The charcoal and ore are taken from mountain forests not subject to official prohibitions on felling, so the village communities are not disturbed nor the authorities bothered by demands for funds. The fifth is that the five commanderies supply the materials for their own needs, so the neighboring commanderies can stop supplying their quotas, and requirements for stores and weapons are made ready at a reduced price.

What is more, those barbarians within our frontiers[136] have repeatedly been given a bloody nose in recent times by our forces. . . . When they now further hear that we are smelting iron here, won't they be inclined to behave themselves?

Military power, economic development, and pressure on resources remained interlinked. By this later period, however, when in most of China the premodern economy was highly developed, the state would have almost certainly have preferred to rely on the commercial system for the production of iron and transport. It is only because there was nothing adequate in this remote corner of the empire that the old relationship can be seen still functioning with a paradigmatic clarity.

Falteringly and irregularly during early imperial times, and then more and more clearly by the later Tang and the Song dynasties, a duality became established. Coercive organization, its roots in the archaic past, continued to be the defining feature of some important areas of economic activity. This was notably the case for large-scale water-control systems, whether they were irrigation channels, river levees to stop floods, or seawalls to keep out the salt tides and storm surges. In contrast, relatively small, free, and privately owned units, whether they were farms practising agriculture of a gardening-like intensity, craftsmen's workshops, or businesses built around partnerships and families, characterized much of the rest of the economy, especially in Ming and Qing times. These latter lived in a world of commercialized competition far removed from the imposed monopoly inherent in large hydraulic and other state-run systems, such as the transport of tax-grain from the South to the North under the Ming dynasty. This last employed on the order of 150,000 men and shifted about a quarter of a million tons of rice a year.[137]

What finally emerged was a symbiosis, and any description of the later imperial Chinese economy that focuses only on one of these aspects, falsifies. It was *both* controlled *and* free, *both* pulverized *and* gargantuan. Simultaneously.

The next four chapters take this complex story or, more accurately, major parts of it, through the two millennia of imperial times. The chapter that follows looks at perhaps the most enduringly important aspect of the state side: the world of the colossal water-control undertakings made possible by Chinese administrative virtuosity in planning, organizing, conscripting, taxing, and coercing. These reshaped the Chinese physical environment, and committed a large part of the Chinese economy to a paradoxical relationship with water that was startlingly productive yet relentlessly costly to maintain, protective yet intermittently terrifyingly hazardous, and, above all, one from which it could not, and has not to date been able to, extricate itself. The three chapters after that on water control look at how the pattern of premodern economic growth in China, ever more based, as the centuries passed, on the creation of private initiatives, made its impact on three very different environments.

The two systems of course intertwined. As I have suggested in the 'Introductory Remarks', the mature imperial Chinese style of development was based on a capacity to operate through highly disaggregated units that could, when necessary, be coordinated either administratively or commercially to form, as needed, enormous modular aggregates that were inherently transient, existing only while immediately required. It was this combination of small-unit initiative and all but unlimited facultative aggregation that produced a sustained thoroughness of environmental exploitation that was probably distinctive, at least on any large scale, in the premodern world.

6

🐘 *Water and the Costs of System Sustainability*

Control of water has long been at the heart of farming—especially irrigated rice production—and of bulk transport in the most densely populated parts of China. Hence at the center of its later premodern economic history. Over the long run, and moving up an extended learning curve with many failures, it was by world-historical standards both successful and sustained.[1] The eventual price was high: commitment to a system that required incessant and expensive maintenance and that, after a certain point had been reached, was all but impossible to expand further. The environment imposed limitations on the availability of suitable locations and on quantities of water.

Central to the argument that forms the core of this chapter is the point that man-made systems of water control are to a greater or lesser degree inherently unstable, and constantly in interaction with disruptive external environmental factors. They are affected by rainfall, flooding, drought, the removal or re-establishment of vegetation cover, erosion effecting the transport and deposition of sediments, the drainage of wetlands, irrigation, salinization, and incursions of the sea. Water-control systems are where society and economy meet the environment in a relationship that is more often than not adversarial.

Systems vary. Some are concerned with defense. Levees along the banks of the great rivers protect the farmlands outside. Seawalls keep the surges of the tides and storms at bay, and prevent salt water poisoning the fertility of the land. Others are designed for drainage, as wetlands are converted into paddies. Others again for irrigation, often storing water in lakes and reservoirs, then redirecting it, and distributing it through channels and sluices. Premodern industries often require the motive power provided by streams and rivers. Large cities need engineered systems for the provision of drinking water. Also for the disposal of waste; and who gets the water first, when its quality is still good, can be a matter of social and political status.

An example of this last point was the Li Canal, which was built in 809 CE and provided the modest-sized city of Yuanzhou in Jiangxi (in the Center) with water for drinking, washing, fighting fires, and transport. Upstream the water was also used to drive mills; downstream it ended as an all-purpose sewer. Since the mills slowed the current, they were in due course banned. Encroachment by houses eventually made the waterway in the city too narrow for boats. A permanent organization under canal chiefs was set up to stop people throwing rubbish into the stream, and it was forbidden to build kitchens or privies that abutted onto the water. With limited effect. Where it first entered, and flowed through official gardens, it was clear. Lower down was a different story. Social position was inversely correlated with exposure to pollution.[2]

Canals need to be kept topped up to a level at which boats can proceed along them, no small task when staircases of locks take them up and down the slopes of hills, as was the case with the Ming and Qing Grand Canals. And when water is in short supply, these locks have to be kept closed, with the boats dragged along haulovers around them. It was for this reason—scarcity of water—that, although the Chinese in the Song dynasty invented the pound lock,[3] which fills and flushes, and whose gates open and shut to permit the passage of boats, they made little use of it. Another environmental constraint on economic technology, since haulovers require smaller vessels.

Watermills and hydraulic triphammers and presses, and norias—huge openwork wheels that lift water in containers fixed around their circumference—likewise need strong currents and races to furnish them with power. These different needs—especially irrigation, transport, power, and drinking—are to some extent in competition with each other. Conflicts between rival interests, and between rival areas, such as those upstream and those downstream, and those that are from time to time sacrificed as flood overspill basins versus those that are not, are common to most systems.

An example is Mianyang (in the Center), where the Han River empties into the Yangzi. In the middle of the nineteenth century small-scale battles were fought by armed protesters from the south bank who saw themselves as being victimized by their side of the river being flooded, with government approval, during periods of peak discharge. They favored flooding the north. The rebels were triumphant for a time, and built 'illegal' dikes to protect the south, which thereafter enjoyed improved harvests. According to the provincial government, if the local people "failed even slightly to do as they wished, they would drive off their cattle and smash up their houses."[4] River water meant quarrels. And in an extreme case gang-warfare hydraulics, as here.

It could also mean a sort of proto-democracy. In Shanghai county (in the East) after about 1775, when the county magistrate wanted the creeks dredged, he often summoned an assembly of local notables to provide him with advice and legitimation. In view of the materials quoted from the *Master Guan* in the preceding chapter, and the common but oversimple belief that water control in China was the changeless bedrock of despotism, it is worthwhile quoting— as an explicit proof that this was not so—one of the characteristically tedious and detailed documents that proliferated in late-imperial hydraulic adminis- tration. It concerns the Chaojia Creek in 1870:

> Zhu Fengti, the acting county magistrate, called together *the [gentry] direc- tors and [commoner] wardens* of the county, from both city and countryside. It was concluded *after a discussion* that in 1836 the whole county had provided laborers on the basis of acreage [owned by each landowner], no wages being given for the quantity dredged, and administrative expenses being provided by the officials. In 1858 a payment had been made [to the workers] for the amount dredged and administrative charges had all been met from unallocated levies and fines, no money being taken from the landowners and tenants of the county. In recent years the officials had become poor and the commoners rich; the latter had ample resources since the reduction of taxes. . . . *They requested that . . . a levy on acreage should be imposed.* . . . Where the 'market river' [used for transport] was twisty or turbulent, or encumbered with sand banks, reeds, or irrigation channels, places in the past being designated as tedious or difficult, and such that the normal payment per hundred cubic feet of mud was insufficient, it had been the practice of the [gentry] group directors who were in charge of the dredging to advance the difference. Usually the work had been finished off carelessly, the waterway hardly being dredged before it silted up again. *The gentry directors suggested that* on this occasion the best thing to do would be to make additional payments for the difficult parts. . . . In addition, the miscellaneous expenses for pumps, for embankments, for the salaries of deputies [potential officials on secondment to special duties], for retinues and sedan chairs for the directors, and for the clerks and constables should all be reported to the county magistrate.[5]

By this period this was the routine way of doing things, not despotic but perhaps best described as a 'consultative oligarchy under central legitimation'. In some other areas it approached proto-democracy. An example is the Sangyuan polderland in Guangdong province.[6] Here there were regular annual meetings of publicly selected representatives and systematic public selection of hydraulic managers.[7] When water is a menace the need for collective action against danger may reinforce social bonds. The Qing gazetteer for Sangyuan polder observed:[8]

> If the West River is in spate, and the dikes in danger, the villages concerned at once beat gongs. The neighboring villages pass on the message from one to the other, and come hurrying in response. This is something that concerns the lives of the men of the various wards, and of their families. They never fail to hasten.

The need for this solidarity is explained by the mid-Qing gazetteer for Songjiang prefecture south of the Yangzi estuary:[9]

> An entire polder is interdependent. It is even so exceedingly hard to bring people's feelings into unison, since, if a polder contains a thousand *mou* of land, it will not have fewer than several tens of families. If, however, the wall of the polder for one family's holding has collapsed, then the wall in sound condition in the rest of the polder is useless. Under these circumstances, the poor and rich will give each other mutual support.

Contrast this with the case of Mianyang given above. A difference in the hydraulic environment could change how people behaved toward each other.

Commercialized water systems also existed in north China by the nineteenth century. In East River Village, near Baotou, watered vegetable gardens were funded with money from the pawnbroking business and other trades. Operations were handled by a Gardens Guild, whose ninety or so members held 'water shares' and contributed to costs in proportion to the number held. The post of Garden Head was held by every member in turn, but for a period of time determined by his share-holding. The channels were the common property of the Guild, but the 'water shares' were bought, sold, and borrowed independently from the ownership of land.[10]

As will be shown later, 'hydraulic despotism' is not a total myth,[11] but, as should be apparent from the above, an inadequate description of a more complex situation that also changed over time.

Huge amounts of labor, money, materials such as stones and wood, and administrative skill are usually needed to build and to maintain water-control systems. Consider this description in the gazetteer for Shangyu, on the south side of Hangzhou Bay (in the Southeast), of what was needed to rebuild just under 20,000 feet of seawall in 1347:[12]

> The method is to use, for every 10 feet, 32 pine trees 1 foot in diameter and 8 feet in length. These are set in 4 rows, unevenly and sunk deeply into the ground. After this, stones 5 feet long and a half of this in width are laid at right angles to each other in an interlocking pattern on top of the level

stones [base stones?] in 5 layers, all set into each other like dog's teeth, so they cannot be dislocated. In places where there is a depression in the sands on the seaward side they build 8 layers. The height is over 10 feet. The top is covered with flagstones so as to seal it with their pressure. On the landward side there is a fill of stone rubble to a depth of more than 1 foot, and then earth is banked up next to it. The base is 20 feet wide, and the top diminishes to a quarter of this.

Approximate calculations indicate that this fairly short sector—on the order of 6 kilometers compared to the total south Jiangsu and north Zhejiang seawall's length of over 400 kilometers—would have needed about 63,000 trunks, and close to a million cubic feet of stone. This sort of structure was more durable than the earlier earth-and-brushwood seawalls often found in this region, which had to be rebuilt every three years. It therefore probably economized on labor over the long run. But such hydraulic works devoured forests and the output of quarries.

Also human beings. The gazetteer for Huating county, on the south of the Yangzi estuary, has this to say about the repairs to the seawall in the late nine-teenth century:[13]

> At the present time the wall is always rebuilt in the dog days of the summer. The laborers are boiled and scalded by the scorching heat, suffering sunstroke in the daytime and exposed to the dews at night. I do not know how many in all are suddenly smitten with 'cholera' or heatstroke, and die at the foot of the wall.
>
> This takes place, moreover, in the midst of the busy season for farming. Most of them cannot come to the work as this would require their being in two places at once. The wardens and seawall constables take advantage of this to cheat them. Each *mou* of land incurs three to four hundred cash, this being known as 'purchasing leisure'. If any are obdurate and refuse to pay up, wanting to go and scoop up mud, the constables and wardens will always find some pretext to make them melt or dry out in the ferocious sun, vexing them in many ways until they have no option but to beg for release.

This passage is late enough in date for the 'cholera' to have been true cholera, which first arrived in China from Bengal around 1820, though there is no way of being certain that it was.[14] The concentration at the worksite in the warm part of the year of a large number of workers in close contact with each other, with poor sanitation, improvised accommodation, and a high level of stress, would certainly have facilitated the spread of an infectious disease of this sort: one mainly passed on through infected faeces, contaminated drinking water and food, and flies.

The hydrological instability of almost all systems, due to wear and tear, and to the deposition of sediments that requires either dredging channels or the heightening of dike walls as river beds rise, makes the burden perpetual. Far more is spent over the long run on maintaining a system than is ever expended on its creation. And while hydraulic systems are hydrologically unstable, they are also economically inherently static. There are limits to accessible runoff and rainfall, and to suitable topography. Ground water only replenishes itself at a fixed rate. Once the opportunities that are profitable given a particular level of skill have been used up, trying to go further is a waste of resources. This is what seems to have happened in China by the end of the middle Qing.[15]

To visualize the brake on dynamism created by hydraulic systems after the initial surge of increased production and productivity, imagine trying to double-track the late-imperial Grand Canal that ran north from Hangzhou (in the East) to just outside Beijing (in the Northeast). In other words, to build a second canal parallel to it. It would have been impossible. Not enough usable water flowed off the hills. This was particularly evident in Shandong, where the Canal went over the western spurs of the Mount Tai massif. The summer floods carried so heavy a load of suspended sediment that directing them into the Canal would soon have silted it up, and they had therefore to be diverted into the sea by an alternative channel. The clearer but less abundant winter and spring water was stored at the summit in a reservoir. It was drawn through a feeder-river into the canal when the convoys with grain for Beijing were passing through, after a temporary dike had been built across the mouth of the alternative channel. Once the flotillas had gone by, this dike had to be demolished again, year in year out. Preventing the feeder-river from shifting its course entirely to the alternative channel was also a headache, requiring more engineering.[16] It was thus not normally possible to retain enough water in the Canal for it to be open over this stretch round the year, even as a single track. A railroad is not subject to this sort of limitation.

The long-term survival of Chinese water-control systems was variable. In some the technology reached apparent near-perfection early and endured; in others it crumbled and declined; and in others again it grew ever more refined with the passing of the millennia. Two examples will suggest the complexities of hydraulic histories and show how Chinese hydraulic engineering both changed its environment and was, in turn, constrained by it, and even—sometimes—broken by it.

The state of Qin in the Northwest, which was in due course to unify the empire in the second half of the third century BCE, increased the effectiveness of its preconquest war-machine by taking over one great irrigation scheme and creating another. They were to have different fates. One is still operating. The other declined quite rapidly, and in spite of repeated efforts over the centuries to revive it, proved impossible to restore as a large-scale integrated system.

When Qin absorbed the state of Shu, in present-day Sichuan province (in the West), toward the end of the fourth century BCE, it acquired the Min River irrigation network which had been built where this river leaves the mountains and flows out across a fan-shaped plain that slopes down at an almost ideal angle, between 0.29 per cent and 0.42 per cent.[17] The principles were simple: gravity was the motive force, no pumping was needed, and water was diverted from the main stream into distribution channels, where it was drawn on for irrigation, and the residue returned to the main course over a hundred kilometers downstream. The art lay in the details. Some of these may have been added in later times, so what follows is a composite picture rather than one precisely focused on a particular moment in antiquity. But the basic concept was old.

First, it was necessary to stabilize, in so far as possible, the quantity of water entering the system. At low water the Min flows at about 500 cubic meters per second; but at peak discharge this rises to 5000 or even 6000 cubic meters per second. The second problem was more difficult: keeping the channels from being filled with deposited sediment. The slowing of the current reduced its competence to carry suspended particles. Thus the channels tended to fill up over time.

The solution adopted was twofold. First, regular dredging was carried out in the winter during low water. Fifty-seven per cent of the rainfall today falls between June and September, and the pattern was probably broadly similar two millennia ago. This was in accordance with the advice of the first director of the scheme, Li Bing: "Clear out the deposits of mud to a good depth, and build the dikes low."[18] Second, a bend was engineered upstream of the main diversion intake in such a way that much of the suspended sediment was deposited on its *inner* side, as the result of the slower flow there, and the subsidiary helicoidal current in the plane at right angles to the main current.[19] These deposits were then flushed out periodically by opening another channel that led back directly into the original main course of the Min but was normally closed off, while at the same time shutting the regular diversionary intake on the *outside* of the bend, which was normally left open. The flushing channel was kept shut by a barrage of huge bamboo baskets filled with heavy stones and resting on a fixed stone sill, which also served as a spillway regulating the height of the water in the system. Hence it could be an emergency overflow during heavy floods, or even a sort of safety valve, since the gabions— the stone-filled bamboo baskets—could be swept away. Hard and dangerous labor was required each year to remove and then later replace these baskets. They were three feet in diameter and ten feet long, at least in Tang times, from which these figures come. The productivity of the system could thus only be preserved and the original investment safeguarded by costly maintenance. In fact, the Min irrigation scheme has proved a champion among irrigation schemes for survival. In spite of the repeated destruction of the main diversion head, and of the crescent-shaped dikes that fashion the artificial bend, an expanded and updated version is still working today.[20]

The second example is the Zheng Guo canal, north of the Wei River in what is today Shaanxi province (in the Northwest). It had a different fate. Started a little later than the Min scheme, in 246 BCE, it took heavily silt-laden water from the Jing River along a contour-line to the Luo River. In the first part of its course it released water into the fields below, where, in the words of a Han-dynasty ditty, "it served as both irrigation and fertilizer." This was also an effective way of combating the salinity of much of the land. The average gradient of its two-hundred-kilometer course was 0.64 per mil, which indicates a masterly level of surveying skill. Its critical contribution was to feed the people living 'within the passes', where the Qin dynasty and the Han after it, both had their capitals. The historian Sima Qian attributed Qin's triumph to this hydraulic system. Without adopting any such monocausal explanation, it is reasonable to accept that economic development was an important part of military and political hegemony.[21]

Why didn't it survive?

The story has been masterfully covered by Pierre-Étienne Will.[22] Here we need only review his conclusions and comment on them. The region today has a subarid climate, perhaps more so than two thousand years ago, largely alkaline surface soils, and an unstable topography based on loess, which is in origin a wind-blown, powdered rock. The Jing River, which fed the system, steadily cut down its bed, and this made it harder and harder to continue drawing off enough water without opening new intakes further upstream. Large variations in the summer spate also made stable engineering difficult. The silt in the water, originally described as fertilizing, gradually became more sterile, perhaps because it came from lower soil horizons. The original system became partially defunct quite rapidly, probably between the end of the Han and the beginning of the Tang. An adjunct system, the Bai Canal, opened in 95 BCE, continued to work, however.

During the Tang, water mills took so much water away from farming that the government had repeatedly to order their destruction. Resource shortage prompting the usual conflicts.

By the middle of the tenth century the Bai, too, was in difficulties. A dam across the river was installed each year to raise the level of water intake, but was usually eventually swept away. By the fourteenth century, at its largest, this temporary barrage had to be 850 feet across and 85 feet in depth. It seems to have been made from containers of interwoven vegetation containing earth and stones. When the intake point was later moved higher up, smaller structures were adequate. In the fifteenth century a feeder tunnel was cut in an attempt to revive the system, but silting up and the weariness of the workforce meant that reliance had mostly to be placed after this time on the tapping of local springs, but the amount they could supply was minute compared to the river.

Ingenuity was used to ease the worst natural hazards: damage done by the intermittent flooding of the Jing, and torrents carrying rocks down the gullies that the contour-line feeder canal had to traverse at right angles. Overflow tunnels were excavated; grille-like barriers were erected across the gullies to let water through but block the débris, and the canal was roofed at key points to let gully runoff flow over it.

Finally, the mass mobilization of unpaid labor was not feasible under the Qing to the same degree as it had been under earlier dynasties. Long-term socio-political change thus restricted the options of hydraulic planners dreaming of restoring the grandeur of antiquity. By the eighteenth century, in spite of an extensive survey and more efforts at rehabilitation, it was clear that drilling wells was the most reliable basis for irrigated farming, though only a few well-to-do households could afford the pumps to make the lifting and distribution of water easy. Thus environmental pressures made the technology go, in a sense, backward over time. Until the 1930s that is, when the first use of modern engineering opened the possibility of new Faustian bargains.

In general, the Chinese water-control economy had become caught by the eighteenth and nineteenth centuries in a form of premodern 'technological lock-in'. 'Technological lock-in' is a concept used in economic theory to describe cases where an established but second-best technology continues to dominate because of advantages that derive from its prior establishment. In the words of W. Brian Arthur, "Increasing-returns mechanisms . . . can . . . cause economies . . . to become locked into inferior paths of development. . . . Technological conventions . . . tend to become locked-in by positive feed-back."[23] At the present day these include investment in the training of those using, servicing, and selling the existing system, and the availability of compatible accessories and interfaces.[24]

I have adopted the idea here to describe a premodern situation where the commitment of an economic and social system to a particular technology—Chinese-style hydraulics—had proceeded to the point where (1) its voluntary abandonment would have led to immediate losses in production, and often social stability and physical security, that were unacceptable under normal conditions, and (2) a substantial proportion of the economy's currently available resources (notably money, labor, materials, skills, and political and organizational capacity) were required for the *maintenance* of the system. The effect was that a sizable part of the future was, so to speak, 'mortgaged'. If, as in the case of the Zheng-Bai, it broke down irretrievably, a huge investment was forfeited. Expansion within the available technology had also reached a virtual dead end. An estimate of the true cost of the system should therefore ideally include the loss of the opportunity to use a significant amount of this proportion of output in a different, and possibly ultimately more productive, fashion. Obviously modern technology has now radically altered the possibilities. The magnificent but onerous heritage of the past remains.

Changing patterns

Organization reflected environment. Thus on the west shore of Lake Erhai (in the Southwest) the so-called Eighteen Streams that came down the vertiginous side of an elongated mountain ridge tended to readjust their courses over the alluvial fans at the foot of the ridge whenever they silted up. This caused little lasting damage, and no massive organization for their maintenance was required.[25] In contrast, on the northern side, was the Miju River, so heavily loaded with sediment that it eventually ran above the level of the surrounding fields, like a miniature Yellow River. In late-imperial times it built up a spectacular delta, which was cellularized into diked fields protruding out far into the lake. The Miju came to require the labor of many thousand men each year. This need developed over time as upstream clearance of surface vegetation released more sediment into the water. The shift from a relaxed community-based maintenance system to a tightly bureaucratized one from the fifteenth to the nineteenth century can be followed in the documents.

Repairs under official auspices are first recorded between 1403 and 1424, and three more times down to 1506–1521. At this time military-colony soldiers maintained the dike on the east side, and commoner–civilians that on the west.[26] A bureaucratic system for the regular yearly repair of the dikes is said to have first been put into place by the local government some time between 1436 and 1469, but cannot have worked well, as there was a crisis in the middle of the sixteenth century. The 1563 gazetteer for Dali prefecture says, or quotes someone as saying, without being clear about the exact dates concerned,

> For the last thirty years no one has been paying close attention, and [the dikes] have almost completely fallen in ruin. Those who have debated the issue have decided to order workers to be levied according to the acreage

[owned by the landlords served by the system], and boundaries for sectors to be established and inscribed on stone as a visible record of permanently fixed regulations.

Every year in the first lunar month, on the day following the rural district drinking meeting, *without waiting for anyone to lead him*, each person shall proceed to the work of banking up the earth and planting trees. Anyone who arrives a day late shall be fined according to what is announced by a collective discussion. This is to be done constantly every year.[27]

Community-based maintenance was still the desideratum, though now under government surveillance.

A débâcle of 1552, when the defenses broke, prompted a further response from the officials. The quantitative details of maintenance work were laid down, such as the number of 'dragon caves'—lateral open conduits—to be provided for draining off water. They concluded by remarking "That the soldiers are exhausted at the present time, and the commoner–civilians impoverished, is not due to any lack of fertility in the soil but to inadequacies in the management of water."[28] The cost of repairs in terms of the timber and stone needed, as well as in labor, was likewise becoming high. The 1563 gazetteer describes a society already under pressure:

Those who own land sometimes have to sell it. Those without land are sometimes obliged to perform hard labor-services, their hair becoming grey because of their lack of rest. Nor are the women and children in tranquillity. In emergencies they demolish their fences and walls to block up the breached dikes. When times are calmer they steal the timber used for the engineering work to supply their private cooking.[29] Those who watch over the system are not capable of dealing with these vexations. Those who do the reconstruction are wearied with their sufferings. At the worst it even happens that landlords along the east side dike criminally breach the dike to the west, and landlords along the west dike criminally breach the dike to the east.[30]

In fact, the system proved sustainable. As always, there was a price.

Organization was improved between 1628 and 1643, with more changes shortly after 1736. The responsibility for specific lengths of dike was assigned on the basis of taxes paid by landowners. Workers were sent out in the middle of the first lunar month, and at this period normally worked for a month, their effectiveness being checked on by the officials. Further changes introduced by the department magistrate shortly before 1795 did not yield good results, however; the organization was overhauled once more in 1818, and then again twice more by three different department magistrates. These repeated efforts ensured a period of stability after the disasters of 1815–17. Defensive hydraulic engineering above the main gorge at the head of the river's lower course, designed to reduce the silt it carried, also played a part.

Essentially, what had been happening was that the increased loads of sediments carried by the Miju River, because of land clearance and deforestation upstream, had raised its bed, and made it necessary both to keep dredging it and building the dikes higher and higher. From 1828 to 1843 the river bed in the course immediately below the gorge rose by 10 feet in spite of dredging. Stone columns were then installed as markers to provide a measure of the depth of dredging needed.[31] Despite this, by some time not too far into the Qing dynasty a substantial proportion of the course of the Miju immediately south of the gorge was running above the level of the rooftops of houses on the surrounding land, as it still does today. By the early nineteenth century the clearing and dredging required sixty thousand men during the period from the first lunar month to early in the fourth month, though not continuously, and half again that number to rebuild the embankments.[32]

A general manager of the Miju dikes in the middle Qing period wrote the story in dramatic terms:

> Ordinary rivers travel *through* the land. Only the Miju travels *above* the land. Ordinary rivers all penetrate deeper [with time], but the Miju fills up every year with deposited sediment. These are the major contrasts. . . . In the region of the Mao Family gorge [in the upper catchment above the main gorge] everything is broken peaks, hateful precipices, streams that lose themselves, and fragmented valleys gathered together or scattered about. They unite at Three Rivers' Mouth. Whenever a wind from the northwest arises, mountain soil, whirling dust, and flying stones frequently strike one in the face. With the arrival of summer and fall the continuous heavy rains destroy the ridges and split the valleys open. Stones from the mountains and sediments in the gorges come down in the frenzied current, a flood like a landslide, its breakers roaring with a sound like stones falling. On every side it is blocked off, with no way through. It only drains out by way of Putuo Gorge [the main gorge], but over the years the people of Langqiong [above this gorge] have used huge claws to push the clogging piled-up sediments at the Three Rivers' Mouth downstream. Under these circumstances, water and stones from all directions have treated Dengchuan as their drainage ditch. The origins of the afflictions suffered by the Miju River in fact lie in this.
>
> When it goes south from here there are the mountains of the Black Ants Gorge and Serpent Gorge. All of them are bodies without a full covering of skin [that is, they have no vegetation]. They are inserted in the river's bed,

lofty and vertical. Their sands fly about and their stones shift along, more and more helping the [river's] power to fill up the Erhai Lake. Thus the route of one long river receives the sands and gravels of a hundred courses. To begin with, it is as if bound in the coils of ravines and gorges. When it reaches the Upper Gong Sands [at the bottom of the main gorge]. . . , it suddenly opens out and rushes along rumbling like startled thunder, speeding like a myriad horses almost wishing to take all thirty kilometers of level plain and soil embroidered [with crops and houses] for the pleasure of its swiftly sweeping position-power. In all the spatial structure of the river there is no danger to equal that which is here.

Next, downstream from Wangwu . . . the entire river is as perilous as suspended scaffolding. Wherever there is a bay or bend, one further feels the flying foam and the press of the spray. The shaking is out of the ordinary. It is always here that flooding over happens and that breaches that are naturally caused occur . . . .

In summer and fall the current is turbid. Silts and sands come down together, but the sediment that accumulates in the river has always entered the Erhai, [so,] with the passing of time, the mouth of the Erhai has become obstructed, and the tail end of the river [its entry into the lake] has also grown congested. For this reason, thirty years ago the place where the river entered the Erhai was [just] downstream of the Water Lock Pavilion. Today [*circa* 1854–5] it is about 2.5 to 3 kilometers distant. [A linear extension rate approaching 0.09 kilometers per year.] . . . It is undoubted that there are advantages for the people living in the neighborhood, but harm is caused to the upper reaches. The reason is that greed for the profits from [new] fields formed by the accumulation of silt and [the consequent] lack of dredging it clear, causes the tail end of the river to narrow to the extent that it will not admit boats. If the anus is not wide open, the digestion is incommoded. The disaster of flooding over arises from this. Furthermore the disasters of sediments and stones are endured all the way from the source to the tail . . . .

Dengchuan's disasters are from water, but what provokes these disasters in fact comes from the mountains. In all the mountains the aethers of metal are weighty, and many of them lack vegetation cover. If it has no vegetation cover, the surface of a mountain will be bare and reddish, and it will be easy for it to be stripped and [for material] to fall, and for it to become permeated with water. When the cliffs and valleys are full of holes, heavy rains set the sediments in flight off lines of ridges and contiguous ranges. Shifting rocks and speeding currents form landslides and floods with a tumultuous hubbub, competing for a way through as they come down. This is the reason large rivers flood over and branch streams become choked with alluvium.

> An array of discussions of policies, from both ancient and modern times, to keep rivers in check exists, but I have never heard of keeping *mountains* in check.[33]

In fact the deforestation and clearance were new. Transformation of the environment on the hillslopes above the main gorge, probably due to population pressure, had led to new environmental problems below it, and these prompted the formation of a new and more disciplined type of socio-political organization, with a higher level of direct state involvement. This case is important in that it shows the *changing* chains of cause and effect that could exist between human impact on the environment and resulting adaptations in the structure of human society.

The sections that follow describe two of the largest water-control systems in imperial China, following up the theme outlined in the previous chapter, that of the part played by the state in driving economic development. To keep the picture balanced, it should be remembered that the majority of hydraulic schemes in imperial times were relatively small-scale, and that the state's main role in their regard was only arbitrating disputes between the participants, or re-establishing a local hydraulic organization that had decayed. Supervision rather than hands-on management. A number of these more autonomous operations—not unlike that for the early Miju—will also be described in the three chapters that follow, when the focus shifts to the environmental impacts of small-unit enterprises.

The south-course Yellow River

From 1194 until 1853–5 the final section of the Yellow River ran to the sea south of the Shandong peninsula. For all the period of recorded history previously, though not the longer span of what might be called 'geomorphologist's time', it had run out to the north. This southern chapter of the story forms a cameo that illustrates most of the hydrological problems of imperial times, and the techniques adopted to tackle them. Above all, the unending battle between natural and human forces. Hydrology versus hydraulics.

One talks of a single southern course, but in fact it took a number of different routes downstream of the Kaifeng region. Before 1578 these were usually *multiple* at any given time, interacting in a variety of ways with the Huai River whose mouth the Yellow had captured (see Map 1). The scale of the man-made effects that resulted from the struggles to control the merged flows was probably unequalled anywhere in premodern history. Tables 2 and 3 below summarize the sedimentological data, without attempting to show minor changes, with the crucial exception of distinguishing the periods before and after 1578, when man-made effects become strikingly apparent.

Table 2 shows the long-term pattern of land formation in what is now the abandoned delta compared with the recent pattern of land formation in the gulf of Bohai since the river moved back north. A recent estimate is that the Huai coastal plain was growing at about 2.55 square kilometers per year *before* 1194.[34] The Yellow River's shift to the southern course thus more than doubled this rate.

Table 2 Land formation by the Yellow River on its southern and northern courses, from 1194 to 1983

Course	Period	Duration[†] (years)	Land formed (km²)	Rate of land formation (km²/year)
South	1194–1577	384	2300	5.99
South	1578–1854	277	6700	24.19
North	1855–1908	54	1239	22.94
North	1909–53	45	588	13.07
North	1954–70	17	270	15.88
North	1976–83	8	261	32.63
Total*	1194–1983	785	11 358	
Mean				14.47

* Excluding 1971–5

† The calculations have been adjusted to avoid double counting the years at the boundaries between periods.

Source: Li Yuanfang, "Fei-Huanghe sanjiaozhou-de yanbian" [Changes in the deltas of the abandoned Yellow River], *Dili xuebao* 10.4 (1991), 37.

The first point to be noted is the shift in the scale of delta deposition after the later sixteenth century. Initially, at least, this was a *man-made* effect due to a change in hydraulic technology. Since it was also a long-term phenomenon, and there was some reversion at times to an earlier hydraulic approach, there were probably other contributing causes. The relative unification of the course was not undone, so its carrying power was greater, and under the Qing dynasty there was intensified stripping of the vegetation cover along the middle course of the river.

Table 3 presents estimates for the advance of land in the Yellow River delta and the accretion of sedimentary deposits during the period of the southern course. The effect of the hydraulic engineering by Pan Jixun (on whom more later) is visible in the bold type of row 2. By unifying the course of the river and eliminating multiple channels, and then constricting the channel that remained, he unintentionally raised the level of the bed of the channel at the mouth by more than 2 meters in 13 years. The reason, which he had over-looked, was that it was here that the current, after scouring the lower course at an increased speed, had then to slow down, and so dropped much of its load.

Table 3 The speed of advance, and the rate of accretion, of the Yellow River delta from 1195 to 1854

Period[†]	Duration (years)	Advance (km)	Speed of advance (m/year)	Rate of accretion (cm/year)	Total accretion (m)
1195–1578	384	15.0	39	0.4	1.536
1579–91	**13**	**20.0**	**1538**	**16.6**	**2.158**
1592–1700	109	13.0	119	1.8	1.908
1701–47	47	15.0	319	3.4	1.598
1748–76	29	5.5	190	2.0	0.580
1777–1803	27	3.0	111	1.2	0.324
1804–10	7	3.5	500	5.4	0.378
1811–55	45	14.0	311	3.1	1.395
Total*	661	89.0			9.877
Mean			135	1.5	

[†] The terminal dates of the periods have been adjusted for consistency.

* For slightly different figures, see Wan Yansen, "Subei gu Huanghe sanjiaozhou-de yanbian" [Changes in the old delta of the Yellow River in northern Jiangsu], *Haiyang yu huzhao* 20.1 (1989).

Source: Ye Qingchao, "Shilun Subei fei-Huanghe sanjiaozhou-de fayu" [A provisional discussion of the development of the abandoned Yellow River delta in northern Jiangsu], *Dili xuebao* 41.2 (1986), and Xu Hailiang, "Huanghe xiayou-de duiji lishi he fazhan qushi" [The history and trends of development of the sediments in the lower course of the Yellow River], *Shuili xuebao* 7 (1990).

The shifts in course, and in the hydraulic strategies adopted and discarded, during the south-course period reveal the nature of the continuing battle. They show how maintaining the viability of the Grand Canal, whose convoys had to cross the Yellow River not far upstream from its mouth (see Map 1), committed the Chinese state to a conflict with the river that it could not afford to lose, and could only momentarily win. The Canal was the lifeline that made it possible to maintain supplies to Beijing—the principal capital after 1420 under the Ming. What was intuited as politically and militarily necessary to block non-Han invasions of the central Chinese plain from the north led to a war with water instead. Since the capital was not expendable, this was another form of lock-in.

The crossing required the grain boats to go along a short stretch of the Yellow River between Huai'an and Xuzhou, famous for the dangers of its rock-studded rapids. The cost of keeping the junctions between the Canal and the river functioning here was immense. In 1606, dredging and diking in the Xuzhou area required half a million workers for five months, and the expenditure of 800,000 ounces of silver.[35] The late nineteenth-century gazetteer for Huai'an prefecture explains how the deposition of sediment on the river bed made it harder for the junctions to work properly:[36]

> When the transport route was first opened [early in the fifteenth century], the Canal lay at a *higher* level than the Yellow River and the Huai River. Thus it suffered relatively little damage. As the dikes along the Yellow River and the adjacent lakes rose ever higher, the Canal sank ever *relatively lower*. Since the middle of the Ming dynasty, disasters have been caused by *reverse flow* from the two rivers into the Canal such that there has been no year untroubled by clearing, dredging, building, and blocking off.

The knock-on effects from attempting to stabilize the Canal could destabilize other hydrological systems. An example is the cutting of the Jia River in the middle of the sixteenth century. The object was to allow the northbound boats to cross the Yellow River more or less directly and so avoid the rapids. Here is the president of the Ministry of Public Works surveying the terrain:[37]

> He once again in person led the officials responsible for the Yellow River, climbing the plateaus and descending into the wetlands to calibrate the relative heights. . . . He came upon the place called Hanzhuang, where the terrain becomes more and more marshy and it was possible to clear a way through for the channel. He thereupon sank six well shafts in order to test its 'pulse'. When he had excavated to a depth of several feet there were small stones and gravels, and a soil with a consistency like curds, that crumbled when hoed. . . . "This," he declared, "is suitable for a channel!"

Contrary to common impression, Confucian mandarins sometimes dirtied their hands with practicalities. An official's expertise in water control was a source of respect.[38]

The problem with creating the Jia was the side effects. These are described in the mid-nineteenth-century gazetteer for Peizhou (on the boundary between the East and the Northeast):[39]

> There is no stream greater than the Yellow River, and no flooding greater than that of the River Yi. The Yellow River now flows along the old course of the Si; and since the Si has thus been captured by the Yellow, *the Yi has not emptied out to the south*. After the Jia Canal was opened, the streams of Shandong province were all coerced toward the southeast. The Ying, the old Jia, and the Yi were cut off at one and the same time. There is a multiplicity of embankments and locks, and much troublesome concern with opening

and shutting them. The water is blocked to the east and debarred to the west, the pulses of the streams having been thrown into disorder.

Worse,

> Lake Guan, four kilometers east of the present county capital, . . . and Lake Lianwang near the mouth of the River Yi, as well as Lake Ge and Lake Wan to the northeast, and Lake Zhou and Lake Liu to its east, are *all filled in with sediment as a result of these overflows from the rivers in Shandong*. Furthermore, downstream from the River Zhi there are no banks or channels surviving because of the inflow of silt-laden currents. It is for this reason that the transport canal is a disease of our stomach and heart, while the Yellow River is a robber in our gateyard. With regard to our stomach and heart we are concerned about blockage by constipation, while with respect our gateyard we are afflicted by lawlessness.

This was the environmental payment exacted for the convoys carrying southern rice to the bureaucrats and soldiers in the north.

Why did the river shift south? The main events were as follows.[40] The reader without a historical atlas of China to hand should not be concerned at the cat's cradle of place-names. What matter are the broad patterns. These have been highlighted by italics:

(1) In 1077 the Yellow River temporarily broke into *two branches*. One went south of the Shandong peninsula (in the Northeast) along the so-called Southern Qing River, which was the old course of the Si River, and shared a mouth with the Huai (in the East). The other continued to go north along the Northern Qing River, the old course of the Ji. The full northern course was restored the following year, but this was the shape of events to come.

In 1168, the *History of the Jin* relates that "the River broke out at Li Gu's Ford, its waters invading the city of Caozhou [in the Northeast], and dividing its course to flow through the region of Shanxian [in southwest Shandong]. . . . The Director of Waterways . . . further observed: 'The new river's waters have taken sixty per cent and the old river's waters forty per cent. If we now block off the new river, the two rivers will again join together to form a single one.'"[41] When this was done there was again a single course. Before long, though, the Yellow River's *pressure on the state's resources and manpower intensified* to the point that in 1193 the regional commandant observed: "The Great River in the past had branch streams and debouchments off its southern bank. If it were possible to lead it off in such a way that it *spread out*, this would be enough to drain away the position-power of the water."[42] 'Spreading out' was one of the standard recipes for controlling the river at this time. The chief problem that it created in practice was that if the channels became wider relative to their depth, the current would slow down, and drop a proportion of its sediment load.[43]

(2) In 1194 debates continued in the Jin government as to how best to subdivide the river while avoiding heavy expenses on hydraulic works, or damaging cities and farmland that lay in the path of possible routes both north and south, especially since their actual course could not be exactly determined before the dikes were breached. The objective hoped for was to "nullify the water's position-power by means of subdivision." In the fall of this year the river broke out southward from north of Kaifeng (in the Northeast), and the report of the Department of Affairs of State asserted that the regional commandant and other officials had taken "no care at all, but, since they saw that the water was tending in a southerly direction, made no plans in advance to deal with it."[44] In the event, the river was again *divided* between the same two 'Qing' rivers as before, but also used the Bian River for its southern route after 1351. In other words, its courses were now out of control. This continued during the next phase.

(3) Only after the floods of 1391, did "the Yellow River *in its entirety* enter the old course of the Huai," which it reached via Xiangcheng[45] and Shouzhou[46] along the Ying River, with a lesser branch exiting to the sea via Xuzhou.[47]

(4) Between 1416 and 1448, the now dominant southern course took the bed of the Guo River, but between 1448 and 1455 there was again a substantial *northern course*, via the Northern Qing River, which was eventually closed off by human intervention. A very limited control was momentarily returning.

(5) After the floods in the late 1480s and early 1490s, up to seventy per cent of the water went *north once more*. In 1492 a decree directed an inspection to be made:[48]

> We have heard that the Yellow River, which passes through a wide expanse of land in He'nan, Shandong, and North and South Zhili [modern Jiangsu], moving its course in irregular fashion, has been a menace for a long time past, and has recently grown significantly worse. The general explanation for this is that *previously* it flowed southeast from Kaifeng *into the River Huai*, but today its old course has silted up and become shallow, so that it has gradually shifted north, joining with the Qin River,[49] and its situation is becoming more and more unmanageable.

Proposals were made at Court at this time *to give up the effort to control the Yellow River and to cease maintaining the Grand Canal*, because of the expense in money and manpower. It was argued that it was preferable to transport the state's tax-grain by sea instead.[50] The point to remember is that during this period the greater part of the sediment carried by the Yellow River was still being deposited *on the plain* through which it ran. It was only transported to a limited degree all the way to the sea mouth.[51]

(6) In 1493 Liu Daxia, the first of the river-tamers, rebuilt the system of dikes in such a way that an *exclusive southern course* was assured after this date. This increased the quantity of sediment coming down to the river mouth where it formed 'mounds'.[52] In 1534, according to the then director-general of the Yellow River,[53]

> In times past *the waters of the Huai* flowed into the sea *on their own*, and there were also curved channels at the sea mouth, for the flow upstream and downstream of Andong. There were in addition the Jian River [which flowed past Huai'an and was at one time used for transport to Yancheng], and the Maluo Creek, whereby the waters were divided and so entered the sea.
>
> *Today the Yellow River has joined with the Huai*, and the position-power of the water is not as it was before, with the Jian River, the Maluo Creek, and all the curved channels at the sea mouth having become blocked up, so that they are unable to drain the water swiftly. *The way through downstream is blocked*, and there are floods upstream, *which obstruct the grain transport to the capital.* The creeks should be dredged one after the other, and the sediment in the curved channels dealt with by installing numerous 'dragon-claw boats' as dredgers to go backward and forward so as to scour and scrape, and widen the way to the sea.[54]

In other words, Liu Daxia's success was generating new problems.

(7) During the first three-quarters of the sixteenth century, the Yellow River took a *multiplicity of paths* across the Huai valley, often simultaneously. An illustration of what was happening may be found in a passage quoted by the great historical geographer Gu Zuyu with reference to events in 1558:[55]

> The old south course of the Great River was from Xinji [in Guide prefecture in the Northeast] . . . to Jimenji in Xiao county, from which it came out at Xiaofu Bridge in Xuzhou [on the boundary of the East and Northeast]. This was the old course of the river that was restored [in 1344[56]] . . . , its configuration being like that of an overturned jar flowing easily from above to below.
>
> Later, because the disasters caused by floods in He'nan had become a matter of urgency, a separate lesser river was opened [in the late fifteenth century] with the intention of *destroying the position-power of the water by subdividing it.* The river would not, however, follow two courses. The original main course became ever shallower and more obstructed. Over 125 kilo-

meters of it thus became silted up between Xinji and the Xiaofu Bridge. The river flowed north of the previous line . . . and further split into *six branches* . . . all of which followed the course of the Grand Canal to the rapids at Xuzhou. A further branch separated off from the town of Jiancheng . . . and then split again into *five small branches* . . . and these likewise went from the Xiaofu Bridge to join the Xuzhou rapids. The Yellow River was *divided into eleven streams* and its position-power was weakened. *When its position-power had been weakened it deposited sediment on a vast scale*, and the breaches of dikes, and the floods, thus became even worse.

In 1565 there were said to be sixteen channels.[57] One might almost talk of 'Yellow Rivers' in the plural at this time, at least in the lower reaches, and a river of this sort can hardly be considered hydrologically the same as that which was to emerge after the hydraulic transformation of 1578–9.

(8) After the mid sixteenth century, *the sea mouths* shared by the Yellow River and the Huai *became blocked* by sediment. According to Wu Guifang, then in charge of the imperial grain transport, "the general cause is that for many long years the way through the branching creeks along the coast has been blocked by dams. Entry to the sea relies wholly on the single route via Yunti [the customs station on an island off the main mouth]. When the river reaches the sea it is obstructed in a transverse fashion, and its entire current has become an overflow of mud."[58] By 1578 the width of the central sea mouth had narrowed from the 7 or 7.5 kilometers downstream of Yunti in early Ming to from 3.5 to 4, or at most 5 kilometers.[59]

In 1577 Wu Guifang opposed proposals to divide the Huai and the Yellow rivers and divert them into the Yangzi. He contrasted the *earlier* channel pattern whereby the greater part of the Yellow River had joined the Huai in *mid-course* with that of his own day where the two rivers only joined *close to the sea*:

> The Yellow River is laden with silt to an extreme degree. If the clear Huai is not used to cleanse it, the sea mouth will be nothing but turbid mud. This will inevitably cause a worsening of the blocking of the lower course. Breaches of the dikes along the banks, and irruptions of water, will become an ever more menacing threat . . . .
>
> Since the Song and the Yuan dynasties, and down to the Zhengde reign of our present dynasty [1506–21], a period of almost five hundred years, the Yellow River has entered the sea via the Huai without the sea mouth becoming blocked up. When the Yellow River reached the province of He'nan it joined with the Huai and they proceeded together, passing by Ying, Shou, Feng, and Si to the Southern Qing River, and thus the clear

water cleansed the turbid, and it was made possible for the muddy dregs not to be deposited. So it was that for several hundred years there were no disasters [quite untrue]. The general explanation for this is that during this time seventy per cent of the water of the Yellow River was passing by way of Ying and Shou, and only thirty per cent by way of the branch stream that flowed via the Xiaofu Bridge in Xuzhou.

Recently, though, since some time in the Jiajing reign-period [1522–66], the flow past the Xiaofu Bridge in Xuzhou has become insufficient, and the two sets of rapids, at Xuzhou and at Lü, have often dried up. Those in authority have not set their minds upon the long view, but have struggled to divert the Yellow River so that all of it flows through Xuzhou and Peizhou to the Southern Qing River.

For the first time there has been no [mid-course] juncture with the Huai. Thus the position-power of the Yellow River is now strong, but the flow of the Huai is weak, and its contribution to the cleansing process minimal. Thus it is that *the sea mouth is gradually growing higher*, and every year the threat of floods overflowing becomes more urgent . . . . If the flow of the Huai is now to be permanently cut off, and it is no longer to join with the Yellow River, then only mud will flow down, and day after day the deposition of sediment will increase. 'The ocean will turn into mulberry fields'[60] between Yunti, Cao Bay, Jincheng, and the mouth of the Guan. To an ever increasing extent, *the Yellow River will have nowhere to go.*[61]

Concentrating the Yellow River into its Xuzhou branch, with the intention of helping the imperial tribute-grain transport cross the river there, thus began before the time of Pan Jixun's work. The effects of this concentration were already visible at the sea mouth, and understood as being such.

In fact, the Yellow River also had a number of smaller exits both to the north and the south of the main mouth. Gu Yanwu, the great seventeenth-century chronicler of regional diversities, quotes a source that describes how in recent times the minor mouths on the southern side had become silted up as the result of the tides washing back the sediment flushed by the Yellow River into the sea:[62]

In the old days none of these supplementary sea mouths was silted up. That they have silted up in recent times has been due to the yellow sediment . . . . The general explanation is that the sea water is subject to tides twice a day . . . . The sea water blocks the lake water for two double hours when it comes in, so that the latter cannot flow. This happens for eight hours during every day. How can the yellow sediment fail to be deposited?

The supplementary sea mouths to the north were in the same situation, having been "in recent days" blocked by the yellow sediment, and the main mouth there had shrunk to half its former width. This source is not dated, but is probably from just before Pan Jixun's main period of activity as it advocates the view that "if the position-power of the waters of the Yellow River and the Huai is not divided as they come south, but their strength is joined as they approach the sea, then the new sediment will not remain and the old sediment will automatically be removed."[63] This was to be Pan's mantra.

(9) Pan Jixun (1511–95), the greatest of the river-tamers, put this prescription into practice.[64] He set forth his basic hydrological views as follows:

> When waters divide, then their position-power is weakened; and *when their position-power is weakened, the [suspended, saltating, and bedload] sediments come to a standstill.* When the sediments come to a standstill, then the river becomes as it were bloated with food, with a foot or a few inches of water passing above the surface of the deposited sediments. One only perceives how high the channel bed has become.
>
> When waters join, their position-power is fierce, and *when their position-power is fierce, then the sediments are scoured away.* When the sediments are scoured away, the river becomes deep, with fathoms of water passing above the bed of the channel. One only perceives how low the channel bed has become.
>
> One builds dikes to confine the water, and one uses the water to attack the sediments. If the water does not precipitately overflow the two banks, then it has to scour in a straight line along the bottom of the river. There is here a fixed pattern-principle and a position-power that is inexorable.
>
> This is why joining the river channels surpasses dividing them.[65]

A new orthodoxy had been born. Although Pan's views were not quantified, they approximated to the modern theory whereby the capacity of water to carry sediment is proportional to the *fourth* power of the speed of the current. Sediment-carrying capacity is thus sensitive to small changes in velocity, and velocity is sensitive to changes in the depth of the channel. Hydraulic engineering can make a major difference.

From 1578 to 1579 Pan restructured the lower Yellow River. In round numbers, he built 1,200,000 million feet of earthen embankment, 30,000 feet of stone embankment, stopped 139 breaches, constructed 4 stone spillways of 300 feet each, dredged 115,000 feet of river bed, planted 830,000 willow trees to stabilize the tops of the dikes, drove in a large but unrecorded number of tree trunks as pilings under the embankments, and spent almost 500,000 ounces of silver and nearly 127,000 piculs of rice.[66] He *unified the channel* of the Yellow River and confined it within so-called 'thread dikes' close to the banks, but backed these up in most places with 'set-back dikes' that were a kilometer or a kilometer-and-a-half removed from the river. The purpose of these was to contain any overflow that broke through or came over the top of the thread dikes during the peak discharge period of the late summer and fall.[67]

One difficulty with this strategy was that the more rapid flow of the Yellow River past the junction with the Huai at Qingkou tended to block off the weaker Huai, and even force reverse flow up the latter, so causing siltation at the junction of the two rivers. The traces of this, the so-called 'threshold sediments', are still visible today.[68] The miscalculation was based on Pan's belief that, in the words of the _Ming History_, "if we can bring it about that the Yellow River and the Huai exert their full strength, and that every drop of water goes into the sea, then the force will be immense and concentrated. The accumulated sediments in the lower course will be automatically removed, and the sea mouth will be opened without dredging."[69] More specifically,

> The old sea mouth is all accumulated sediment, but although human power is incapable of dredging it, _the power of the water itself_ is capable of scouring it away by impact. No pattern-principle in nature permits the sea to be dredged. When, however, the river is led to make its way to the sea, then one is using water to control water, in other words a strategy for indeed dredging the sea.
>
> Likewise the Yellow River cannot be led by human power. If, however, we keep the dike defenses in good repair, so that there are no breaches of the banks, then the water will pass through the midst of the land and _the sediment will be removed by being entrained by the water._ In other words, this is indeed a strategy for leading the Yellow River.[70]

Conquering nature by obeying her, as Francis Bacon was to put it in the West not long afterward.[71] The perception was magnificent; the details inadequately thought through. The effect of the new strategy was to increase deposition at the sea mouth, and reduce the gradient of the lower course.

(10) Flooding returned in a decade. In 1591 the capital city of Sizhou (on the East–Northeast boundary) was inundated to a depth of three feet and it was said that "ninety per cent of the inhabitants were drowned."[72] An official observer[73] described the city wall in the floods as being "like a cup floating on the water, the cup itself also being full."[74] He recommended that "clearing the sediment accumulated at the sea mouth be made the first priority."[75] Later he added that "since there is no hope of dredging the sea-mouth sediment, the channel bed grows higher every day; and, since _the Yellow River constantly flows in a reversed direction_, Qingkou becomes more obstructed by the day." He suggested clearing

Qingkou and then dividing the Yellow River there, but rejoining the branches lower down so that the water "strikes the sea with concentrated force."[76] The debate over what to do about the sea mouth "growing ever more obstructed" continued without interruption, some critics of Pan also pointing out that too much constriction had in fact caused the flooding. The majority were inclined to revert to the policy of multiple channels.[77]

In 1593 the emperor put Yang Yikui in charge of hydraulic operations, and during 1595–6 Yang basically implemented this majority view, which he had himself contributed to forming. "The waters of the Yellow River were divided and drained into the sea, in order to repress the power of the Yellow River. Three-and-a-half kilometers of sediments were cleared at Qingkou, ... and the Huai was drained into the sea by three channels, and its branches diverted into the Yangzi."[78] Yang's efforts were moderately successful, but only in the short run. Neither Pan's concentration nor Yang's division was in itself a sufficient fix. The point to be noted, though, is that we now have a man-made hydraulic explanation for the sixteenth-century changes in the pattern of the growth of the Yellow River delta shown in the two tables.

(11) The next surge in the rate of advance of the delta, and of sediment accretion, was from 1701 to 1747 (as shown in Table 3). It was slighter than that associated with Pan Jixun's hydraulic policies, being almost twenty-one per cent of the 1579–91 rate of advance and twenty per cent of the rate of accretion. There is a possible connection here with the shift in hydraulic policies effected by Jin Fu, another celebrated river-tamer who was in charge of the Yellow River almost continuously from 1677 until his death in 1692.[79] Jin broadly agreed with Pan's ideas,[80] and he built an earthen extension to the levees along the lower course of the river downstream of Yunti Guan for about 180,000 feet or 64.5 kilometers,[81] in order to concentrate the flow, and so scour away the accumulated sediment. Thereafter, it was said, "the water was constricted within the levees, being swift all the way, and having the force to scour the sediment. The undesirable accumulation of silt in the sea mouth was removed and a sink for drainage thereupon cleared."[82] The date of this must have been before 1690 by which time the divided lower course had been unified again and was cutting a wider and deeper channel.[83]

The lower course of the Yellow River had silted up rapidly during the third quarter of the seventeenth century.[84] This may have been due to several causes: the alleged cutting of dikes by the rebels in the last years of the Ming dynasty,[85] the Ming government's breaching of dikes to drown the rebels,[86] and what Jin Fu called the "division of drainage" caused by floods such as those of 1676 that were unable to reach the sea.[87] By this latter date "only a thread" of the main course through the sea mouth remained. "In addition," he noted, "coarse grasses and thickets of reeds intertwine there, and are not something to which human strength can usefully be applied."[88] The deposits also hardened with time:[89]

> There is a difference between old and new deposits of sediment. In the case of those newly deposited within the last three years, although their outside is as hard as a board, the sediment inside has not yet dried out and it is easy to scour them by means of the impact of water. Before five years have elapsed, though, the sediment inside will have become dried into a clod of board-like sediment, and scour by impact will have become very difficult.

Besides building constricting earthen levees, Jin Fu increased the height of the barrage and the embankment that retained the Hongze Lake upstream on the Huai and before its confluence with the Yellow River. This was "to assist in the storage of water that may be used to have an impact on the sea mouth when released."[90] He also cut a large *dry* channel in the dried-up sediment of the main course—which latter he described as now being "299 parts out of 300 of the former exit to the sea." This was aligned close enough to the remaining trickle of current so that when the peak discharge was directed into it the boundary layer between the two would collapse, making a single enlarged course.[91] After difficulties with floods that occurred before the planned scouring was complete,[92] the scheme seems to have been successful in achieving this limited objective.

Important events took place in the remaining century and a half of the southern phase. Some of them have been studied, while others still await examination. Jane Leonard has, for example, described the "growing ecological degradation" of the Grand Canal by 1824–6, and linked it with the collapse of the dike that contained the Hongze Lake. Manipulating the lake was critical in getting the grain-transport ships across the Yellow River without an influx of river water carrying a heavy load of sediment impairing the canal. The crisis had to be met in 1825 by the costly use of transshipment into vessels with a shallower draught than that of the standard ships. The following year required the temporary use of *private sea-transport* from Shanghai to Tianjin, made possible by offering generous terms to leading merchants based in the lower Yangzi valley, whose skills and assets were indispensable.[93]

Essentially, though, over the long run, premodern techniques, however good, could not contend with a rise in the level of the mouth of the great river by almost ten meters (Table 3). In 1855 the Yellow River switched back to a northern course.[94]

The Hangzhou Bay seawall

Pan Jixun's concentration of the lower reaches of the southern-course Yellow River in the later sixteenth century may have been the single engineering work that had the greatest environmental impact at any time anywhere in the premodern world. If we turn to a *program* of engineering and maintenance sustained over the centuries, the seawall that protected the coastline south of the Yangzi down to the southern side of Hangzhou Bay (in the East) from at least Tang times onward must outrank it. The shelter it gave made possible the creation of what has been described earlier as a Chinese Netherlands. A world of thinly populated saline marshes and creeks invaded by the sea was turned into a level land of drained polders and canals, where the density of the inhabitants was among the highest anywhere before the twentieth century. Both the 'Chinese Netherlands' and their European counterpart were of roughly the same size, 40,000 square kilometers in the roundest of round figures. If we also include the section of seawall north of the Yangzi, then the Chinese area was considerably bigger.

The challenge and inspiration presented by nature were of course different in the two cases. Thus the wetlands of the original Yangzi delta had no feature comparable to the elongated ridges of sand and grass that guarded, and still guard, most of the coast of the Netherlands west of Amsterdam, a natural defense that has only needed filling in, extension in the north, and strengthening with inner lines as reinsurance. (The mounds of shells mentioned in the next chapter, on page 175, are the nearest parallel.) The two also present many differences in appearance. In particular, the Dutch water-systems, unlike the Chinese, are not primarily designed to provide for irrigated farming.

There is only space to describe a part of the epic battle that was waged here against the East China Sea, so I will focus on the inner part of Hangzhou Bay, where over a millennium or more the coastline was almost totally reshaped, partly by natural forces and partly by the indirect results of human actions. The outline of the story is freeze-framed by Maps 3, 4, and 5.

Map 3 shows the bay as it was a thousand years ago, a funnel-shaped macro-tidal estuary with a celebrated tidal bore that swept in along the south shore from the east and passed below Hangzhou city. Two expanses of pastures and salterns form the northern shore, anchored on Zheshan, the 'ocher-red mountain' which faces Kanshan, 'idol-alcove mountain', across the narrowest part of the strait to its south. A seawall, already some centuries old, guards the southern coast, and a triple arc of dikes linking mounts Hezhuang, Yanmen, Shu, and the Lesser Jianshan, up to more than ten kilometers inland from the sea, provides the reserve lines of defense for the cities and farms.

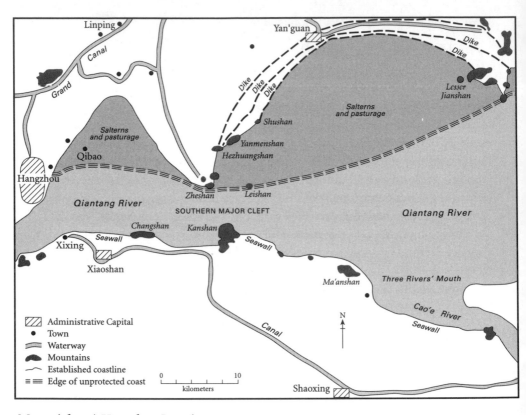

Map 3 (above) Hangzhou Bay, circa 1000

Map 4 (facing page, top) Hangzhou Bay, mid eighteenth century

Map 5 (facing page, below) Hangzhou Bay, 1986

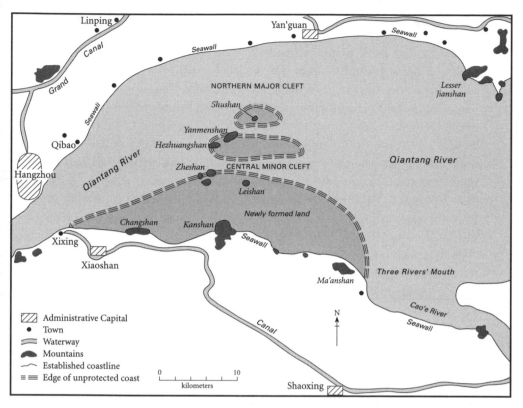

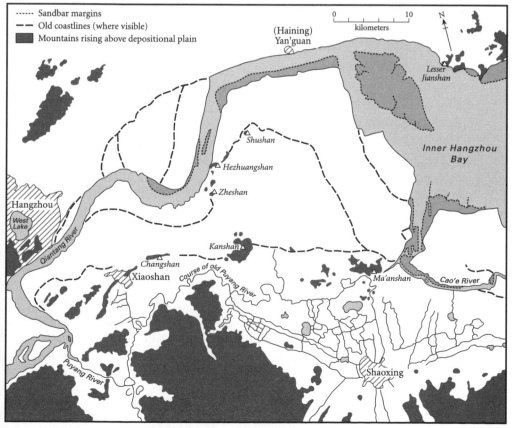

Fast forward more than five hundred years. Map 4 shows the bay in the middle of the eighteenth century. The sea has engulfed the northern pastures and salterns, driving the coast back to a vulnerable line of seawall with no natural anchorage between the Lesser Jianshan and the city of Hangzhou. This defense is vital for the protection of the first leg of the Grand Canal which can be seen on the map going north from the great city. The city of Yan'guan is now on the coast. The tide enters mainly through the northern strait, and the mountains that once studded the tongue of land descending from the north have switched to being eminences in an emerging tongue that is growing up from the south composed of a mass of newly deposited or transported sediments. The southern strait has choked up.

Another two hundred years takes us to Map 5 and the present day. Unlike the two previous maps, this is based on a satellite image, taken in 1986. The southern tongue, known as the 'Southern Sediments', has been consolidated. The western part of the inner bay has been filled in, the river reduced to a channel whose sand bars are in constant motion (though this cannot be shown in a single map). The residues of parts of earlier shorelines show some of the steps in the process of infill. The original southern seawall has been lost to sight inland. The old central cleft has filled in. The channels to the east and west of the city of Shaoxing that spread out like a dragonfly's wings are the remnants of Mirror Lake, a famous source of irrigation water until the early Song, but for almost a millennium now only an anthropogenic scar on the plain. Silted up, like most shallow lakes in this part of the world. Only the familiar mid-bay mountains, up which one can still clamber, and stand and survey the scene around, have survived the passing of the centuries. The water, it should be added, is now gray and polluted with progress, and birds, apart from the egrets and gulls, few and far between.

How did this transformation happen? How far was it man-made? The story told here by way of a response is the most complex in the book, but the complexity is of the essence. The brief answer to the second question is, 'To a significant degree'. The longer (but still incomplete) answer is more difficult.

The dominant pattern of runoff is from the hills on the south side of the bay. This water feeds not only the Qiantang River but also other lesser but still important rivers. These include the Puyang which today flows in a northwest-erly direction into the Qiantang a little distance *upstream* from Hangzhou city (coming in from the other side). Immediately before the mid-fifteenth century it took a more northerly course directly into the Bay, well *downstream* of the city. There was also the Cao'e River, which enters the bay east of the Southern Sediments from the southeast. Smaller streams off the hills fed the elongated man-made Mirror Lake which lay for a millennium from the Later Han on the east and west sides of Shaoxing just south of a slightly later transport canal,[95] that was built because sailing in the inner bay was so dangerous. The patches of the lake that remain today are shallow reaches full of staked-out expanses of cultivated water plants, dotted with fishing nets, and overhung with clusters of willow trees. Five hundred years ago, all three of the major rivers entered the bay where only the mouth of the Cao'e now survives (Maps 3 and 4). The point of confluence was and still is known as 'Three Rivers' Mouth', a name that today only makes sense in the light of its geographical history.

The present coastline is enclosed within seawalls. The traces of parts of earlier seawalls may sometimes be identified lying inland. They have often been built outward sequentially, spreading like the growth rings of a tree. Others have long since sunk out of sight under the waves and tides. Two thousand years ago the coast was mostly salt marshes and tidal flats, probably fringed, as it still is in places, with stands of the club-rush *Scirpus xmarigueter* in the upper part of the intertidal zone, where they damp the waves, and increase the deposition of sediment and the build-up of organic matter. They are succeeded, after a transitional zone, by narrower bands of the reed *Phragmites australis*, a plant that has a number of economic uses, such as material for the manufacture of paper, and has hence to some degree been planted deliberately. The *Phragmites* zone is also used for grazing cattle and sheep, and most likely was so in historical times.

The total influx of seaborne sediments brought down the coast from the mouth of the Yangzi River to the north amounts to about 4.66×10^7—that is, close to forty-seven million—tonnes per year. This massive supply of sediments from the sea is unusual. The Qiantang River, which has a catchment area of 49,000 square kilometers, discharges 6.68×10^6—about six and two-thirds of a million—tonnes per year of sediment as measured at Lucibu, where the tides become insignificant. Total sediment influx into the bay is thus 5.328×10^7 tonnes per year.[96] The tidal bore today forms near the Greater and Lesser Jianshan, and recent measurements indicate a speed of from 4.8 to 9.6 meters per second.[97]

The long-term changes are summarized in the *Complete Documents relating to the Affairs of the Lock at Three Rivers' Mouth* compiled around 1702 by Cheng Mingjiu:[98]

The overall pattern is that the water from the upper reaches of the Qiantang River flows out through one of three clefts. There is a large cleft to the south and to the north, and a small central cleft in the middle between them. When the water makes its exit through one of these clefts, the other two are both silted up. They have opened in sequence, changing around among themselves.[99] The time during which water is passing out through one of them may be several hundreds of years or less than a hundred, but is not to be reckoned in years and months.

If we speak with respect to the Song dynasty, then in 1094 the water went out through the large southern cleft [implying, but not stating, that it had taken a different route previously]. More than five hundred years later, in 1620, it went out via the small central cleft, but in less than a century this was silted up, and the cottages, graves, fields, and gardens of the large northern cleft were all given over to the flow of the river. During 1692 and 1693 the current was still slight, but on 2 August 1695 it broke through in tumultuous fashion and became a large river. The sands in such places as Guali and Jiudun on the border between the counties of Xiaoshan and Shanyin forthwith lay exposed to the air. In the fall of 1693, for no reason, they collapsed totally without trace. Fortunately the sands in such places as Dongtang Bay [seaward of the Lock] were actually extended, and the people could not contain their delight. I have heard, however, from those living along the sea coast that they did not consider this to be a cause for rejoicing, but as something deserving profound anxiety.

The inner bay was unstable.

It may have been even more so in earlier times. Su Dongpo, who served in the eleventh century as the subprefect of Hangzhou, wrote:[100]

> The tide comes in from the east of the sea gate with the force of a thunderstorm, but there are shifting hills rising up in the midst of the river and facing the hills of Fisherman's Inlet [south of Xiaoshan and approximately opposite Hangzhou], and interlocking like dog's teeth. So it is that one sees the waters of the tide swirling in eddies there, and striking against them with redoubled fury. The silt shoals shift around, assuming the forms of demons and spirits, often surging forth from the deep pools to form mounds that run for more than fifty kilometers and then vanish again between sunrise and sunset. Even the captains of boats and fishermen are unable to be certain where the deeps and the shallows are.

In similar fashion, Qian Weishan, a native of Hangzhou, wrote in the middle of the fourteenth century that[101]

> A hilly eyot shifts about in the river, appearing to be a stable rock. When the incoming tide leaves the sea gate behind,[102] it divides in the middle into two branch-streams, the eastern one of which goes along the shores of Shaoxing towards the Qiantang River [above Hangzhou], and the western one of which strikes straight against this eyot with furious onslaught, and then withdraws. It is called the 'tide that turns its head around'.

This feature is not mentioned at later dates. It seems there may have been pressure at this time against the northern bank of the river, which then ran from Hangzhou city to Mount Zhe (Map 3), but across which the river now flows on its way to the bay.

In looking at the possible causes of coastal change, we need to distinguish between long-term changes that were under way *before* the period of extensive building of seawalls and those, rather later, that could have been influenced by human hydraulic activities. We begin by looking at the first of these processes.

The prelude was that the salient on the northeast coast of the outer bay that over 1,500 years ago linked the mainland to the Wangpanshan, today a group of islands about twenty kilometers offshore from Zhapu (off Maps 3 and 4 to the northeast), was scoured away before Song times.[103] This opened the north coast of the inner bay to more direct attack from the tides. Morita Akira's study on the hydraulic organization for seawalls in Jiangsu and Zhejiang provinces[104] also shows that one of the reasons for the building of the seawalls that run down the coast of southern Jiangsu and northern Zhejiang provinces was to protect the inhabitants of these coasts from the incursions of high tides, which appear to have become a more serious problem in the Southern Song dynasty, in the twelfth and thirteenth centuries, for reasons perhaps connected with colder and less stable climatic conditions in the world generally.[105] These were changes outside human control, though the second brought a human response.

It is clear that the northern shore was under attack from at least the early twelfth century. According to an official writing in 1116, "in recent years the hydrological circumstances have changed somewhat. From passing out to the sea by Mount Zhe, the water has turned and gathered at Yanmen and Baishi in the area along the northern bank. The damage done to the commoners' farmland and to the salterns extends fifteen kilometers from east to west and more than ten kilometers from south to north." In 1117 the prefect of Hangzhou observed that "the towns of Tangcun, and Yanmen, and Baishi lie alongside the Qiantang River as it makes its way out to the great sea. Day and night the two tides have little by little gnawed them away and encroached inland."[106] This situation worsened after the end of the fourteenth century:[107]

> On its southern side, Changle district is close to the Qiantang River, and from the closing years of the Hongwu reign-period [about 1390] until 1409 in the Yongle reign-period it was smitten by the river and the tides. The diked banks were broken down.... In the fifth lunar month of 1414 Heaven–Nature unloosed torrential rains and merciless winds. The lightning-swift river and the tides overwhelmed the level land, the deep water reaching more than five kilometers from south to north and over twenty-five kilometers from east to west.... Many of the inhabitants were

drowned. There were countless deaths, and the survivors fled. Dwellings were swept away without trace. Farmland was totally submerged.

The Minor Central Cleft and the approach to the Major Northern Cleft were thus being opened, by a curl-round effect, from the *landward side* at this time.

On the seaward side the low-lying flats along the north coast of the outer bay were the first to be stripped away. A Song-dynasty gazetteer records loss of land southeast of Haiyan (off the maps to the northeast), including irrigation systems, "now all submerged in the sea."[108] This may have further removed the outer defenses of the northern coast of the inner bay. A benchmark for the inner bay is provided by the record that when the seawall for Yan'guan (Haining) was rebuilt in 721 it was at that time *fifteen* kilometers south of the city, which today is *on* the sea coast, and the sea was a further five kilometers south of the seawall.[109] Some erosion was noticed in 1122,[110] but the real assault began early in the thirteenth century:[111]

> In 1219 the sea at Yan'guan forsook its ancient course, and the tides rushed in across more than ten kilometers of level land, reaching in their incursions as far in as the county capital. The creek at Luzhougang, and a number of salterns ... were all destroyed. Mount Shu [Shushan on Map 3] was engulfed in the sea. Almost half of the dwellings and farmlands were lost. The salt water reached four prefectures. The prefects of that time reported that, "Last year the waters of the sea rose suddenly, and rushed in across the sandy shores, each breakthrough carrying them in a few tens of feet further, for day after day. . . . The might of the tides presses in on the inhabitants. If the spring tides should irrupt with angrily bubbling waves, and a typhoon to back them, inspiring a convulsion of nature, it is all but inevitable that for fifty kilometers the common folk will be buried in the guts of fishes."[112]

In 1222, when the tides broke in again, the intendant of Zhexi[113] told the emperor that the threat was to the whole area to the east and south of Lake Tai (off the maps to the northwest), which might be rendered uncultivable by salinization if nothing were done.[114]

The overall pattern during the Yuan and Ming can be summarized by quoting Chen Shan's *Discussion of Seawalls*, written early in the seventeenth century:[115]

> The county capital of Haining [Yan'guan] borders the sea on its southern side. . . . The seawall is only a hundred paces away from the city wall. Eastward it goes as far as Haiyan, and westward to the Qiantang River, stretching north to south for fifty kilometers. To the southwest of this seawall is Mount Zhe, which faces Mount Kan to the south. These mountains [Zheshan and

Kanshan in Maps 3 and 4] enclose the sea gate between them, where the tides enter the river's mouth.

Theorists aver that the sea is clear when out in the vastness of the ocean,[116] but that when it arrives here it is constricted so that it cannot do as it will. It forthwith turns back eastward in anger, reversing its direction of circulation. There is also Mount Shidun [just east of Haining city] to obstruct it, so that it becomes still more enraged and thereupon strikes in unstable fashion both east and west. The damage that this does is concentrated on Haining.

I would observe that, according to the old gazetteer, there were more than ten kilometers of sediment-fields outside the seawall, and that on the land-ward side of these sediment-fields there were more than 1120 to 1190 hectares[117] of farmland, pastures, and orchards of mulberries, silk-thorns, and jujubes. {So long as there was this external protection for the seawall, the tides could not impact on it and wash it away, and there was every assurance that what was on the landward side of the stone seawall could endure.

Today, the sediment-fields and pastures have been entirely swept away by the sea. The protecting sands have totally disappeared. *Life depends solely upon this girdle of newly constructed seawall.*

I shall not record the constructions and destructions of the seawall since Song and Yuan times},[118] but from the Hongwu reign-period [1368–99] to the Wanli reign-period [1573–1619], *the sea has changed on five occasions, and the wall has been rebuilt five times.*

One source suggests that the mouths of the Qiantang were becoming blocked as early as the beginning of the fifteenth century. In 1420 an official from the Memorials Office reported that, "in the past there were seaways at Mount Zhe and Mount Yanmen, but today both are closed by sediment, and so the behavior of the tides has become still fiercer."[119] In spite of this, it does not seem likely that the Northern Major Cleft was already being used by this time. Evidence that it was not is provided by a letter written some time in the seventeenth century by a native of Haining (Yan'guan):[120]

The sea at our county of Haining is no more than an arm of the great ocean, but, when the tides strike and the sands are gnawed away, one at once sees people's fields and their houses being submerged. . . . To the west, mounts Kan and Zhe face each other south and north, enclosing the sea gate between them, the mouth where the sea enters the river. To the east are Mount Shidun and the Greater and Lesser Jian hills rising up unexpectedly in a corner of the sea, and forming the entranceway through which the sea comes into Haining. The tide rises in the east and passes Zhapu and Ganpu, being confined within the 'Eight Mountains of the Nearby Sea'.[121]

The Qiantang River drains out to the west of its confluence with the Puyang River.[122] It passes the Yan Foreshores[123] and so exits into the sea. The Yan Cleft is constricted between the space of the sea gate between mounts Kan and Zhe. *The entrance is exceedingly narrow, and of such a nature as to compel the waves to strike against each other.* Since the waves have come from far away, they inevitably grow tumultuous and angry. For this reason they strike about in swirling fashion, with a dashing noise, and there is the menace of their bursting through the seawall . . . .

The county capital is bounded by a seawall a hundred paces to its south . . . . The section of more than ten kilometers near the city is locked by the two Jian hills at the east, and secured by Mount Zhe at the west, making an embracing arc whose ends protrude out into the sea. The county capital is to the north of these two mountains, the three of them constituting a pattern like a tripod vessel that is struck at an oblique angle by the water. The area outside the city wall has become a headland-enclosed bay for the sea.

When the tide rushes into the Yan Cleft it is held fast by the outflow of the river, which it strikes against and then returns north. These more than ten kilometers are attacked from three sides, and so it is that we constantly see the seawall being broken down here.

The geometry was generating is own destruction.

There was, however, a period of about fifty years in the middle of the seventeenth century during which the pressure on the northern seawall eased. According to the county gazetteer for Haining:[124]

After the seawall of Haining county was rebuilt in 1664, the area outside it was covered with protective sands that piled up for more than ten kilometers. The local people built shacks on them, to the extent of several hundreds of families. This settlement was called 'The Village Without A Name'. Near to the dike the sand gradually became less saline and cotton was cultivated. On the new sands along the sea shore they reduced brine by evaporation and boiled it to make salt. People garnered these profits without any longer being aware of the menace presented by the sea. In this year [1715] the wind-driven tides suddenly irrupted, and the seawall was smashed through.

Then instability returned:

From 1720 to 1721 the protective sands were demolished each day by a hundred feet or more, even by several hundreds. . . . After 1724 the tides struck northward every day. The protective sands were swept away without a remnant left. The dike was repeatedly rebuilt and repeatedly broken.

In 1720 the governor of Zhejiang[125] reported to the emperor that, "recently, on account of the blockage caused by the deposition of silt, the river water and the tides have been made to move entirely to the northern bank."[126] This sounds like a decisive shift, but in fact there followed two decades of efforts to redirect both river and tides back to the Minor Central Cleft, especially by dredging. In 1733, some time after an earlier effort at clearing the central channel started by the governor had been abandoned, the Yongzheng Emperor observed that:[127]

> If we dredge an induction channel in the Minor Central Cleft in addition to the other measures proposed, and thus divide the flow of the Qiantang River into the sea, so as to reduce the force of the water, it would seem that this would also offer advantages.

This personal interest in the hydraulic details was shared by his successor, the Qianlong Emperor. In 1762 the latter wrote that "in recent years the pattern imposed by the tides has been gradually pressing into the Major Northern Cleft,"[128] and it is clear that during the middle of the century there was a period during which the flows moved about considerably. Later in the same year Qianlong wrote a summary history of these changes, much of it based on his own observations:[129]

> After 1745, and prior to 1757, the sea went through the *Central Cleft*. The people of Zhejiang remarked that this was most fortunate and something exceedingly hard to obtain. I made visits on two occasions in 1757 to observe it, and to offer my congratulations on this good fortune to the God of the Sea. I did not dare to be certain, however, that this situation would last.
>
> Not long afterward, in the fall of 1758, there were scars in the sediment[130] piled up on the northern headland of Mount Lei [Leishan];[131] and in the spring of 1759 the tides pressed exclusively through the *Northern Major Cleft*. The protective sands along the northern shore were little by little scoured away. These had been the defense both for the seawall of wooden billets and the stone seawall. At this moment it was no longer possible to delay the conversion of the section of the wall that was made of wooden billets to stone.

The main channel seems to have oscillated between north and south up to 1765, but by 1780 or thereabouts it had settled into essentially the modern pattern.[132]

The present-day course of the lower Qiantang River is thus only a little more than two hundred years old. That its earlier pattern is wrongly shown in almost every published Western historical map, and all but a handful of Chinese ones, is a minor matter. What is important is, that in spite of serious efforts at engineering in the eighteenth century, the changes that have been described above were predominantly the work of natural forces outside human control.

The deposition of sediment was another matter.

As has been already noted above, the massive supply of sediments from the sea into a bay is unusual. Approximate overall equilibrium requires that the discharge from the river should scour away any residual quantity representing the difference between what is brought in by the rising tide and what is taken out by the predominantly slightly less rapidly moving ebb. Otherwise the estuary would fill up and vanish, or the deposited sediments be displaced offshore. Evidence collected since 1915 indicates that, when the riverine flow is below 2000 cubic meters per second, tide-driven deposition dominates, and that when it is greater than 8000 cubic meters per second, river-driven scouring of the channel prevails, with an unstable equilibrium at intermediate values. The reason that the flow of the river is crucial is because, under appropriate conditions, it can reverse the difference between the normally greater sediment-carrying competence of the incoming tide as compared to that of the more slowly moving ebb.

Since the period of heaviest rainfall is between May and August, discharge reaches its maximum in July and August, and falls to its minimum in November and December.[133] At Haining (historically Yan'guan) characteristic values for sediment brought in and sediment removed in one semidaily cycle of the tide (season not specified) have been measured as, respectively, 1.8×10^6 tonnes and 0.85×10^6 tonnes. The sensitivity of the balance of forces between the river and the tide is apparent from Table 4, which shows the values at Qibao Station, which is about thirty-nine kilometers upriver from Haining.

In years of low rainfall the bar of sediment in the bay builds up, while it decreases in height during years of heavy rainfall. Thus, after increasing during the dry period through 1951 and 1952, and the only moderate rains of 1952, it had reached a maximum at Zhakou in 1953 of twenty-six meters. The scouring due to the heavy rains of 1954 reduced its maximum height in the year by almost two meters. For the historical period, rainfall in the Lake Tai area was relatively low in the periods 1504–59 and 1636–1723, and relatively high in the periods 1288–1378 and 1449–1518.[134]

Given this basic understanding of the processes at work, it seems reasonable to suppose that human alteration of the river flow around the bay in historic times had some significant effect on the pattern of sediment deposition. More specifically, closing off the coast with a seawall, and regulating the outflow of major rivers with locks, so that periods of peak discharge disappeared, caused a net deposition of sediments. The timing fits. The south shore of the bay was

Table 4 *Riverine and tidal flows, with related sediment transport, in the Qiantang River measured at Qibao Station*

River discharge*	Direction of tide	Velocity of tide (m/sec)	Volume of tide ($10^6 \times m^3$)	Sediment transported (10^3 tonnes)	Sediment Density (kg/m³)
Low					
232	In	+0.80	106	+582	5.49
	Out	−0.63	105	−203	1.93
High					
6030	In	+0.49	24.7	+47.1	1.95
	Out	−1.11	259	−719	2.78

* Annual mean: 988 m³/sec.
Source: Qian Ning, Xie Hanxiang, Zhou Zhide, and Li Guangbing, "Qiantang-jiang hekou shakan-de jindai guocheng" [Fluvial processes in recent times of the sand bar at the mouth of the Qiantang River {authors' own translation}], *Dili xuebao* 30.2 (June 1964). Last column calculated by M. Elvin and N. Su, "Man against the sea: Natural and anthropogenic factors in the changing morphology of Harngzhou Bay, circa 1000–1800," *Environment and History* 1.1. (Feb. 1995).

already enclosed by a seawall over two hundred and fifty kilometers long in Tang times, and for the period that concerns us, the section of some 61,600 feet protecting the area that is now Shaoxing prefecture was built twenty kilometers north of the prefectural capital in the early thirteenth century, replacing the earlier Tang wall. By Ming times about one-third of it was faced with stone.[135] The purpose of the wall was mainly "to keep the fresh water in and to irrigate the fields."[136]

A small-scale example of the causal mechanism being suggested is given in the Wanli reign-period gazetteer for Shaoxing prefecture:[137]

In 1457 the prefect Peng Yi had the White Horse Mountain Lock built in order to block off the tides at Three Rivers' Mouth.[138] Eastward of the lock [the seaward side] it all silted up and became farmland. After this the river's water was no longer in direct contact with the sea.

White Horse Mountain Lock did not last long, however, being derelict by the seventeenth century.[139] Another illustration of the effect is that the alteration of the course of the Puyang River between 1457 and 1464, so that most of it emptied into the Qiantang upstream of Hangzhou, is said to have increased the scour below Wenjiayan, and thus made the upper end of the bar in the bay retreat seawards.[140] Another passage that may refer to the effects of installing locks or sluices on the rivers emptying into the sea gate off the mountains of the south side is quoted in the Haining county gazetteer as a note to an entry dated 1500:[141]

The streams[142] have all thrown out sand bars like obstructing walls. Thus the river mouth has become constricted and the tides constrained so that they strike when reflected against the concave shore of Yan'guan [Haining].

We can provisionally take this as pointing to the reduction in the sediment-carrying competence of the streams discharging into the southern sea-gate channel, slowed down because of sluice and lock construction. Finally, in more general terms, since the larger rivers that were blocked in this way, above all the Puyang and related streams, were on the south side of the bay, it is here that the effect should have been most pronounced. It was.

When we turn up the focus it becomes clear that the seawall was only the final control mechanism in the irrigation system created for the Shaoxing plain to the south of it. This had been advancing slowly northward from the alluvial fans at the foot of the mountains for more than a millennium as the tidal wetlands below were reclaimed for farming, and reducing peak discharge. A historical overview of this process is given by one Ma Yaoxiang, writing at an unknown date but before the middle of the seventeenth century:[143]

The water sources of Shaoxing flow from the southwest to the northeast. *In ancient times they were in direct communication with the sea.* The inrush and the drainage were not regulated, which harmed the common folk. After Later Han times, when Ma Zhen had built Mirror Lake to receive the water off the mountains, *sluice-gates were installed along the dikes,* being opened and shut at the appropriate seasons. When water was in short supply they drained the lake to irrigate the fields. *When water was plentiful they closed the lake and drained water from the fields into the sea. . . .*

Later they also built the seawall and opened Jade Hill Sluice [the principal control-point for water from the south entering the Qianqing River, about sixteen to seventeen kilometers north of Shaoxing city and Mirror Lake]. *After this the embankments of the lake slowly fell into disrepair.* Though there were proposals in the Song dynasty to restore the lake, it had by this time become unnecessary. The reason for this was that the waters flowing into Shaoxing by diverse channels were several tens in number. . . .

One may say that those fields that lie along the feet of the mountains are watered by their springs, while those that border the sea are supplied by the streams that branch from the former. These latter, having obtained what the former has accumulated for them, are also spared the disasters [i.e., spate flooding] that afflict the former, both of these benefits depending on *the seawall* along Hangzhou Bay, *which both stores the water and discharges it.*

For this reason, when previously, under the Han, there was no seawall, it was essential to build Mirror Lake [as a reservoir for fresh water]. In these later times when, since the Song, there has been no Mirror Lake, keeping the seawall in good repair has been essential.

Hydrological instability then struck in its usual fashion. The loss of Mirror Lake, through the deposition of sediment and the reclamation of its area as fields by powerful local farmers, led to increased flooding in the plain below as the seawall stopped the water easily escaping to the sea. This was intensified by changes in the pattern of flow of the Puyang River, which was also known as the 'Wan' in its upper course, and as both the 'Qianqing' and the 'Xixiao', or 'West Small River', in its lower course. This river came north at this time and then, turning northeast, flowed across the lower plain in an approximately west-to-east alignment. Ma Yaoxiang describes what had happened when the lower Puyang had shifted to this course from an earlier one apparently not greatly different from the northwestern route that it follows, again, today as shown in Map 5, (though it would have had at this time to have circumvented an intervening mountain that was cut through in the fifteenth century):

> There was a further cause for anxiety. All the water of the lakes of the counties of Puyang[144] and Jiyang[145] *used to flow* into the Jiyang [Puyang] River, then turn north*west* and enter the Qiantang. Its configuration was *curvilinear* and it could not go straight to its destination.[146] *Later* it passed through Fisherman's Inlet and entered the Qianqing River [i.e. going *north* and then *east*]. To the north it went out of White Horse Mountain and other locks, and so entered the sea.
>
> Today, however, *these locks have also silted up*. The water has no through passage. Once there are floods, it has to flow eastward and make Shaoxing its sinkhole. Although there is the Jade Hill Sluice [North of Shaoxing, South of Ma'anshan], this is not adequate to discharge water moving westto-east with such force. Every time this happens, *people break open the dikes*. Though some limited relief is thereby obtained from the emergency, they are obliged *at once to repair the dikes* of these inlets so that they are ready to store water again. This, too, is work that is hard to accomplish.

Technological lock-in again, though in this case the problem was eventually solved. Once a community is committed to a system of this sort, it has no easy option—barring a new technological fix—but to allocate labor and resources to maintaining it. If costs start to rise, then tough.

The county gazetteer for Shanyin, the western part of Shaoxing, emphasized this problem, while hinting at the extent to which the rivers had by now been separated from the sea:[147]

After Mirror Lake had been done away with, and made into farmland, whenever the springs in the hills above it overflowed, there was nowhere for the water to be stored. It was joined by the water of the Wan River [i.e., the Puyang], which poured into the West Small River [the 'old Puyang' shown on Map 5]. . . . *Shanyin thus became a vast flood.* Whenever there were heavy rains, the water was so placed that it spread far and wide. With only the single lock at Jade Hill, it was impossible to drain it all off.

This was the price to be paid for irrigated agricuture. The terrain here was said to have had 'the configuration of a water-jar'.

Between 1448 and 1511 at least thirteen new locks were built to drain off the water of the West Small River both to the north and the south, and to drain two 'new rivers'. Both presumably ran north into the sea-gate area.[148] These measures were not adequate, and the temporary breaching of the dikes was still required in emergencies. According to one source:[149] "The mouths of the two locks near Jade Hill are narrow in the extreme. When the water arrives here it overflows almost a hundred square kilometers.[150] When it reaches the seawall it has become a ferocious and turbulent commotion that is a great disaster for the farmland." The Shanyin county gazetteer also commented that, "once the dikes had been broken and the wild torrents had foamed swiftly away, it was inevitable that the channels would rapidly run dry. The weary people were then burdened by having to plug the breaches, yet before this work had been completed they would be suffering from a *shortage* of water."[151]

The solution lay in partially rerouting the Puyang River, using locks at and near the Ma Stream[152] to stop too much water coming north, and building of the Yingxiu or Three Rivers' Lock, whose twenty-eight sluices were each named for one of the twenty-eight stellar mansions, across the mouth of the Puyang at Three Rivers' Mouth. It was constructed between two hills (the southern one of which was a small outlier) that were joined by a natural stone pavement into which the huge stones of the lock's foundation were 'mated' and then calked with a paste made out of boiled millet stalks and lime or mortar.[153] It was flanked to the north by an earth wall four thousand feet long and four hundred feet broad, reinforced by iron and later bamboo, needed because the mud of which this barrier had been made proved "unpredictable at first." The flow of water was regulated by a double layer of wooden planking in each sluice. The construction is said to have been hurried. The threshold on which the lock stood was not perfectly level and tight; the wooden boards leaked and had to be repaired; and some of them had to be replaced every dry season. The initial outlay was six thousand ounces of silver for the lock, and that for the earth dike several times that amount. Both were raised by a levy on acreage in the three counties affected. Labor was mobilized by conscripting local commoners on a rotating basis. "With this, the water no longer behaved violently, and the seawall was no longer deliberately breached and repaired."

The massive lock was completed in 1537. Note the date. The engineered separation of the Shaoxing plain water system from the sea was now total except for the Cao'e River on the eastern edge. The result was the immediate build-up of sediment deposits offshore:[154]

> The tides were blocked by the lock and the earthen dike, and could no longer insinuate themselves upstream. This made it possible to farm more than seven hundred hectares within the seawall. Outside the dike, where hills formed flanking wings, *the sediment became soil* so that little by little close to a further two thousand hectares of farmland could be obtained. The marshy portions could be used for growing reeds. The brine could be drawn off to make salt. The swampy pools could be used for fishing. Mulberry trees could be grown along the edges of its fields, and merchants could travel on its paths.

Given that land formed on its seaward side following the lock's building in 1537, it is likely that the filling in of the Major Southern Cleft and the ensuing shift in the mouth of the Qiantang River in 1620 to the Minor Central Cleft were in part the consequences of the preceding hydraulic closure of the coastal plain along the southern shore of the bay.

It was said in the seventeenth century of the work of Tang Shao'en, the creator of the Three Rivers' Lock, that "with regard to the high and low conditions of the water, he regulated them to proportional quantities."[155] What this means is that the peak discharge was replaced by a *managed* regime. In the words of Cheng Mingjiu:[156]

> *In years past,* both the sea and the river channel were deep. *Today* the sediment accumulates easily, *and needs the flowing river water to scour it clear.* The water of summer and fall is, however, closely linked to farming operations. It is necessary to conserve it with a grudging parsimony. When winter has come, *then* there is no cause not to take the boards in the lock-sluices down, or to desist from calking the fissures in them with mud.... Before the peak discharge is finished [in the early summer], the lock gates are closed, but calking is not necessary. Once the peak discharge is past, it is essential, once the gates have been shut, to calk the cracks....

The lock was like a crude piece of experimental apparatus. Its management had observable effects. As Cheng wrote:[157]

> It is now a hundred and some tens of years since His Honor Tang built the great lock, and renovation has been undertaken twice in the space of this

time. . . . Over these years *the tides have caused difficulties, with sediment blocking it up*, the problem being that there is no strategy for dredging it clear. . . .

If the lowest boards of the deeper sluices are entirely removed, then the state of the water will be swiftly rushing along, and the ferocity of the current redoubled. *The sediment that comes in with the tide will, in the same fashion, be taken out by the tide.* If it is not seen to that the lowest boards are removed, then inevitably the current cannot move swiftly right down at the bottom.

It is, however, entirely the responsibility of the lock-workers to remove or retain these lowermost boards at the times when the lock is vented. In the deep sluices, where opening and closing off are difficult, they either go only halfway, or do not remove the boards completely. For this reason the clear water floats over the top and the current does not reach to the bottom. The sediment accumulates here, and there are no means of expeditiously draining it away. This is one reason why the river is silted up.

The equipment had to be used properly if it was to perform its function, and this was not always the case.

A lack of rain and an overly well-repaired lock could also trigger deposition. The 'Summary of Current Concerns' relating to the lock noted that[158]

Harm caused by silt blockage began in 1671. After this time there were years of hot, dry weather. Although the situation was manageable upstream of the lock, it often happened that *downstream the silt piled up* as far as the East Chan Spit at the mouth, and the water inside would often accumulate for a month or more without draining away. After the repairs done to the lock in 1682, there were not many fissures through which the water could leak out, and the current in the river below the lock repeatedly flowed *in reverse direction*. Under these conditions it was easy for the sediment to block it up.

The current was also slowed down by fishing screens. Cheng noted that:[159]

What is more, curved screens are used to trap fish. According to the old system, this would begin at mid-fall and the screens would then all be withdrawn after the first full moon of the lunar new year. *Today, the number of fishing screens has incessantly increased*, and there is no season at which they are withdrawn. Furthermore, multilayer fishing screens are set up everywhere, cutting off the current and making . . . pools in which the waterweeds start to grow after enough time has passed. This is even more effective in bringing the flow to a stop.[160]

It was a familiar story: efforts to cope with the late-imperial pressure on resources were triggering further awkward consequences.

The destruction of local vegetation cover also accelerated deposition in the channel:[161]

> In 1664 the main provincial army forces pastured their horses along the sea coast by the mouth of the river. By so doing they destroyed all the reeds. The salt-producing households took advantage of this opportunity to develop it all as being 'unvegetated land'.[162] Since the turbid flows were no longer confronted by the reeds, whenever there was a fierce rainstorm, the mud floating on top of the bare land was swept into the river, where it accumulated. . . .
>
> Since the reeds were destroyed by this pasturing of horses, the sand flats in several places have been eroding away for the last twenty years or so. Both upstream and downstream of the lock the channel has been constantly full of sediment. It is from the fact that this has been happening for the last twenty years or so that it is possible to be certain that it is *because of the destruction of the reeds that the river is filling up*, and, perhaps, that the land is eroding. . . .
>
> Although there is no unvarying pattern to erosion and deposition, it is deposition that dominates, and this is an omen that the land surface is in the course of extending. After a few more years the sea mouth will be locked shut.

There is thus a persuasive case that the historical build-up of the Southern Sediments peninsula from the south was in a significant measure the unintended result of human hydraulic engineering. Since the land was cultivable, it was not in itself a disaster. The problem lay on the now vulnerable northern shore where the seawall was under constant threat, and behind which lay the Grand Canal.

In spite of the immensity of the forces at work, the conception of controlling the bay itself therefore emerged in the eighteenth century. In 1723 the Yongzheng Emperor favored dredging one of the blocked mouths of the Qiantang "so that there is a throughflow, causing the tides not to make an obstruction by dropping their load of sediment" and thus safeguarding the Haining (Yan'guan) seawall.[163] The clearest example of this interventionist approach was the plan put forward in 1732 to build a stone barrier across the neck of the sea separating the Lesser Jianshan hill on the mainland east of Haining from Mount Ta about half a kilometer off the coast: "It will divide and overcome the force of the water, so that the tides go south, and we may anticipate the renewed deposition of protective sands along the northern bank."[164] This barrier was to be 1820 Chinese feet in length, and it was estimated that it would have to range from 40 to 130 feet in depth. When the final sector of 810 feet was completed in 1739, however, the greatest depths were reported to be only 18 to 19 feet because of the deposition of 'floating sand', or as we would say 'suspended sediment'. The disparity was commented on, but no further explanation given.

Groins of two sorts were also built to neutralize the impact of the waves on the northern seawall. One type was the 'chicken's-beak bar', a narrow, pointed spit whose purpose was to "deflect the return flow so that the fury of the waves would find it hard to act in mutually reinforcing fashion."[165] The other type was the semicircular 'grass platter', which was described as "a barrier-dike to deflect the water" sticking out into the sea, and thirty or forty feet high. The rationale behind it was that, "in those places where the dike is fundamentally stable, it may happen that when sands have piled up on the shore opposite, or sand bars have accumulated out of sight under the sea, the pattern of force in the water will strike directly against the dike, which being thus assaulted will no longer be safe but in peril. For this reason 'grass platters' are built to deflect the currents."[166] In practice it may have served as a sort of artificial headland refracting the waves around itself in such a way as to reduce the energy impacting on the unprotected stretches of shore.

A third protective measure was the 'water-leveler'. This was a kind of hydraulic glacis sloping downward at the foot of the outer side of the seawall. It was constructed with rubble, topped with stone slabs secured between double rows of timber pilings. The idea may have been to destroy the coherence of waves being reflected from the seawall, and so lessen their capacity for undermining the wall's foundations by interacting with the incoming waves. The *Record of the Seawall* observed that:[167]

> To the east of Haining, however [in contrast to the firm 'iron-board sands' of Haiyan discussed immediately before this], in the district around the Jian hills, there is also water from the river flowing down. The tide and the river strike against each other in conflict, and if the tidal bore then rises high, feeling out the shore at an oblique angle and gnawing at it sideways on, the resulting situation is impossible to resist. Furthermore, when the tide is ebbing, the river water, following the lie of the land, washes and scours the mud away.[168] If the foot of the seawall is not solid, it is hard to be without anxieties. For this reason the seawall at Haining has been repeatedly rebuilt. After the main body of the seawall was doubled in size the hydraulic glacis at its base was also doubled, but since on all previous occasions rubble was used, even though numerous slabs were laid, from three to five layers of them, it was still easily scattered. Thus there have been frequent relayings, and this is in no way a policy that provides a permanent solution.

When that part of the seawall that directly defended Haining city, some 5,052 Chinese feet, was being rebuilt in stone in the early 1730s, it was given a glacis that it was hoped would be massive enough to resist this destruction. Each section of this glacis, some 10 feet long and 12 feet across, contained about 100,800 *jin* of rubble, of the general order of 60 tonnes[169] about 6 feet deep, and had a covering of stone slabs 7 inches thick, and 12 feet by 1.2 feet in size. The size of the undertaking is evident: the weight of the rubble alone in the 505 sections would have been approximately 30,000 tonnes. An indirect cost of the development of rice farming on the other shore.

This was the rationale behind the efforts to clear a central exit for the river in the mid-1730s:[170]

> Although the disasters to the seawalls take place on the northern shore in Haining county, *the causes of the trouble are on the south shore*. This is because on the south shore there are always sandy foreshores rising up by deposition, and deflecting the current so that it goes northward, and the seawalls are in ever more danger. . . .
>
> Grand Secretary Ji Zengyun created the method of 'making use of the water to attack the sand'. He either used metal implements to excavate the sandy islands of the southern shore in a way that followed the lie of the land, or 'cut off the roots' in accordance with the flow of the current,[171] or else dug channels to meet the incoming tide, so causing the water of the river and the tides of the sea to come and go day and night, themselves doing the scouring. The flow of the river moved toward the south shore day by day, while on the north shore the deposited sands grew daily higher. Thus was the great work accomplished.
>
> In 1744, the governor, Chang'an, contrived the means to dredge an induction channel through the Minor Central Cleft; and, in the area around Mount Shu, he used as before the method of cutting the sand. On the inside he dredged and scooped, while on the outside he extracted and cut. In the spring and summer of 1747 the tides little by little swung towards the south, and the deposited sands [on the north side?] appeared wider and wider each day. In 1748 the Minor Central Cleft was flowing through in full, and it is by no means certain that the method of cutting the sands was unconnected with this success.

At the same time as an exit channel was being cut south of Mount Shu, the Qianlong Emperor ordered that bamboo panniers (presumably with stones in them) should be placed along the northern shore of the bay "to deflect the current and suspend the silt."[172] The late-imperial authorities thus believed—for a time—that it was to some extent within their power even to manipulate the coastal sea. But, as the Qianlong Emperor had noted and we have already recorded, it was all over by about 1780. The channel had shifted to the north. But the dikes held.

Comment

Large hydraulic systems were thus one of the key forms of lock-in in pre-modern China. Each successful solution was apt to lead to new problems. It is not for the moment practical to try to quantify the costs in the case just described, but it makes sense to talk of lock-in in terms of the perceptions of the officials and members of the gentry responsible for making decisions.

When the government cut in half the funds for the maintenance of the Three Rivers' Lock in 1678, in order to make money available for military expenditures, the harvests in Shaoxing suffered for year after year in consequence.[173] Likewise, it was said in 1682 on a stele inscribed in memory of 'His Honor Jiang' that if the dike along the West Small River (the 'old Puyang' in Map 5) was breached, "the fields of three counties had no harvest for two years."[174] The compilation of the documents relating to the Three Rivers' Lock, and a two-volume supplement in 1854,[175] was primarily motivated by a concern for continuity in the methods used by those undertaking maintenance and reconstruction. As one of the prefaces observed, "Alas! If there are founders of enterprises in this world, there must be continuators who come after them."[176]

The scale of work needed for a major renovation may be seen from the report on that directed in 1578 by Prefect Xiao Lianggan. It cost about sixty per cent of the original construction only forty-one years earlier:[177]

> They first built crossdikes upstream and downstream of the lock, in order to provide a barrier against floods and tides [while the work was in progress]. The method used for these was that of heaped earth faced with slabs of stone. They also emplaced small 'shuttle mounds' in front of the lock [perhaps raised walkways on which the workmen could walk back and forth to access their work]. They used stones mated in interlocking fashion, built upward from below. Whenever they met with fissures in these stones, they would consolidate them with [molten] cast iron.
>
> On the top of the lock, from head to tail, they ensured that the covering stones were level; and they further added large stones on both sides of each sluice to serve as water-guides, so that each of the twenty-eight sluices was separately fed by a sluice-way cut in these guides.
>
> In places where there were cracks or splits they would pour in [molten] tin to which the ash of glutinous millet[178] had been added. They also attended in comprehensive and scrupulous fashion to the base-boards, the threshold stones, and the banks on both sides, wherever these needed repairing, replacing, or resetting in correct alignment, and wherever mortar or iron were needed. . . .

They spent several thousand ounces of silver, and employed several thousand workers. The project was completed in three months. . . .

The shape of the lock was stronger and thicker. It was on this account really *a second creation.*[179]

The nature of routine maintenance may be seen from the regulations left by Prefect Xiao, and the other officials who also rebuilt the lock over the following century. The following is an example:[180]

Item: There are 1,113 lock boards [used to close off the sluices]. Each one is 8.3 inches across and 4.2 inches thick. The labor cost is 0.3 ounces of silver. On each board is a pair of iron rings, weighing 12 ounces. The labor cost is 0.06 ounces of silver. The selection and procurement of material for these boards shall be entrusted either to honest and capable officials or to the lock officials themselves. They shall be furnished with the money and go in person into the hills to purchase large pine trees at standard prices, and hire artisans to split them into sections. The pieces used should have all four corners square, and be sturdy and without imperfections. Those with flimsy edges are to serve as roofing-boards. . . . Old boards are to be replaced every other year, and the lock-workers are to send them as before to the area in front of the Zuosheng temple for the quantity to be verified. If there is a shortfall, they are to be punished and obliged to make restitution, and the same will apply if there are cases of boards being carried off by the current when the lock has been being opened, or of having rotted when piled up together, or of having been stolen.

This was but a small part of a task that was seen as severely taxing the local inhabitants.

In a stele dated 1630 and commemorating the dredging of the Qianqing River (part of the 'old Puyang') by the prefect of Shaoxing,[181] the burdens of water control are likened to the attacks made on China by the northern barbarians:[182]

The disasters caused by water in the Southeast are like the troubles occasioned by the barbarians under the late Southern Song dynasty. A poison to our people when they entered, and trampled upon our cities. Yet *the affliction of water is worse than they were.* . . .

Though the Yan Brook rushes down vigorously into the southern parts of Shaoxing, and the Qiantang River and the sea have fierce tides that shake its north, disasters such as the present blocking-up have not been heard of before. Among these are the approximately 210 hectares or more of newly emerged sands stretching out from Houguo,[183] which have caused the nature of the water to become unruly, rushing northward and then following a path southward. The fertile soil in the places harmed has been engulfed and cannot pay its taxes. The thread-like length of seawall, struck both head-on and at an angle, has had no means to resist it. When the floodwaters broke in during the spring, there was no wheat harvest. When they broke through in the fall there was no rice harvest. . . .

Though the county magistrates spent their treasure to buy masonry, and led the people to rebuild the seawalls, yet time and again the wild waves flooded in, and the stones did not always adhere firmly together. This was indeed bestowing a fortune on the boundless floods, or like repeatedly sending our wealth each year to the barbarians at the time of the Southern Song, without being able to sate their desires. . . . [Although the prefect has had the river dredged,] the situation resembles that caused by the barbarians after 1126 when the Northern Song capital fell, and the exhaustion of our people is like that following the demographic contraction after the migration south at that time. But for Prefect Liu, though, those of our people who live here would now be fish and turtles.

Hydraulic responsibility could be shirked but not escaped. Unless by luck the pattern of local natural forces changed—and that too had its costs—the past held the present captive.

A paradox has to be confronted. The same skill in water control that had contributed so greatly to the development of the Chinese economy in ancient, medieval, and even in the early part of late-imperial times, slowly fashioned a straitjacket that in the end hindered any easy reinvention of the economic structure. Neither water nor suitable terrain was available for further profitable hydraulic expansion. A remarkable but prescientific technology was approaching the limits of its capacities. Deadliest of all, hydrological systems kept twisting free from the grip of human would-be mastery, drying out, silting up, flooding over, or changing their channels. By doing so they devoured the resources needed to keep them under control or serviceable. And made these resources unavailable for other purposes prior to the coming of modern engineering. No other society reshaped its hydraulic landscape with such sustained energy as did the Chinese, nor on such a scale, but the dialectic of long-term interaction with the environment transformed what had been a one-time strength into a source of weakness.

Particularities

7

Richness to Riches:
The Story of Jiaxing

Jiaxing is to the south of the lower Yangzi delta, on the coast of the east region. In many ways its story over the last two millennia can be taken as a model for most of China. It was far from being one of the earliest areas of traditional Chinese intensive urban–agricultural growth. The major centers of this were in the Northeast, the Northwest, and a part of the West. But because it was something of a latecomer, compared to these cultural heartlands, it had the advantage that we can glean a notion of what it was like *before* it was developed, which is less true of the older north.[1] At the same time, the process of premodern development ran its course here to what can be loosely thought of as its logical completion. Many other areas, especially along the frontiers, had not moved so far by the time the empire ended; or else had gone into decline, as did much of the old Northwest. This makes it a useful region to take as at least a preliminary model, though of course every area—not least Jiaxing—had its own particularities.

The most awkward problem we face is the fragmentation of the sources. Time and again an interesting story starts and is not finished. Too often we sense that something important is going on under the surface, particularly social and political conflicts, but the narrative merely hints at it. It does not pursue it. The interplay of interpretative imagination and a severe factual discipline is constantly needed to create a picture that is both coherent and plausible. It can be a difficult undertaking.

The story in outline

Jiaxing in the early imperial age was a reed-covered marshland where wild rice is said to have grown.[2] Cultivated rice was raised by the rough-and-ready method known as 'plowing by burning, and weeding by flooding'.[3] Other occupations at this time were fishing, hunting, boiling brine from the sea for salt, and cutting timber in the hills.[4] This last does not reappear in medieval times or later, which suggests deforestation. Food, including fruits and shellfish, was so abundant that the poor are said to have lived from day to day without needing to keep reserves. "They have no anxieties about going cold or hungry."[5]

Jiaxing in medieval times was still environmentally rich, though more domesticated and decorated by human art than it had been under the early empire. It had become a domain shaped by water control, by seawalls, canals, and locks and levees, and pinned down by roads and bridges. Its natural visage was now set off, like a face by beauty spots, with inscribed stone steles bestowing their stories, and hence their meanings, on particular places, and by Buddhist and Daoist temples that both enhanced and also spiritually subdued the once wild slopes and summits. Magic still lingered in the landscape, the memories of Daoist immortals and the illustrious dead, of the rain-bringing dragons that haunted the wells and springs, and of local deities with dominion over epidemics, locusts, and other disasters.

Blocking off the sea with seawalls, desalinating the land within them, and creating polders developed slowly under the middle empire. It was by no means yet technically perfected.[6] This can be seen from such comments in the thirteenth-century gazetteer as that certain lakes had "recently . . . all become enclosed fields," but that where more dikes and fields had been built along their edges, "the annual floods are stored in an increasingly constricted space."[7] A familiar recipe for disaster in years of heavy rainfall. The polders, though, were the key to the spread of intensive rice cultivation based on precise control of the input and draining of water, and the backbreaking transplantation of seedlings, which allows the maximal exploitation of the area of each field. Water had to be pumped in at transplanting time, and later pumped out as the harvest ripened. Returns to resources (that is, land) were increased at the cost of what, if we imagine other technology held constant for the purpose of the argument, were diminishing returns to an hour of work. Keeping the channels dredged, and the locks maintained, also proved an unending labor.[8] The sea remained dangerous. Every storm left the corpses of the drowned washed up on the sands.[9]

In Haiyan county there was no natural source of irrigation water, which had to be drawn from official reservoirs. Ten days without rain could set all the pumps working in the fear that the rice-fields would dry out.[10] Reeds had to be cultivated to serve as fuel for brine-boiling, which points to a shortage of wood. Crops newly mentioned as economically important in medieval times include wheat, beans, hemp, and cotton. The resource base of cultivated, as opposed to wild, plants was widening. Silk was now also produced.[11]

At the end of the middle empire and during the later empire, environmental, economic, and social stress is apparent everywhere. In 1838, just before the middle of the nineteenth century, the population was around 2,933,764[12] and possibly more than thirty times what it had been two thousand years before, in the roughest of rough terms. A speculative estimate of the "Han-dynasty" population gives 79,431 inhabitants, which in fact implies a multiplication of about 37 times over almost two millennia.[13] It is hard to be confident of the Tang-dynasty figures as the future 'Jiaxing' area was embedded in the larger Wu (or 'Suzhou') commandery. The data for the two constituent counties of Haiyan and Jiaxing for the 'Tang', without further indication of the period, give 30,254 households, which might have been as many as 151,270 persons, using a round ratio of 5 per household.[14] In other words, population roughly doubled in the first half of the first millennium CE. The most rapid growth took place from the eleventh to the thirteenth centuries, recorded population rising from 693,310 in 1080 CE to almost 2,290,260 in 1290.[15] This is a growth rate of almost 0.6 per cent per year for over 210 years. There were considerable fluctuations in recorded numbers after this date, which were probably a mix of actual changes and changes in the comprehensiveness of statistical coverage.[16] At the "beginning of the Ming" (in the later fourteenth century) there were 1,112,121 recorded inhabitants, and 2,416,105 in 1769.[17] In other words the medieval economic revolution, with an annual growth rate over twice that of the later part of the middle Qing era,[18] seems to have been the distinctive formative experience for the environmental–economic character of Jiaxing, though the pressure eased in the Ming,[19] and presumably again in the widespread troubles of the middle of the seventeenth century, before intensifying again after perhaps some time around 1700.

One symptom of late-imperial-period stress was the degendering of technology, especially in farming. Women were becoming a crucial additional part of the agricultural workforce. While producing silk yarn remained primarily women's work,[20] in areas like Haiyan, where "the land is constricted and the people numerous, to the extent that exerting oneself at farming does not yield a sufficiency," rearing silkworms was an "urgent matter" in which the men also took part, mostly through the cultivation of mulberry trees. When the silkworms were feeding, "the men do not wash and the women do not comb themselves."[21] If the silkworms failed, the sericulturalists might have to sell their children.[22] Seawalls were stronger in this later period, huge constructions faced with stone, and often equipped with the sloping glacis on the seaward side and groins referred to in the preceding chapter.[23] Apart from this last, a millennium and a half of development had left life and livelihood if anything more vulnerable to extreme events than they had been at the beginning, when there had been reserves of natural resources to buffer economic crises.

Late-imperial rice-farming had turned into multicropping with dry-land winter crops. In a good year these could provide half the year's harvest, but there was an extra cost in labor because the paddies had to be drained as dry as possible before the winter planting, just as the polder walls had to be rebuilt each year to stop flooding.[24] An ever more dense network of markets did provide some added resilience in the face of disasters. They made it possible, for example, to buy new rice seedlings if it was necessary to replant after a flood.[25] Given that the cash was in hand to do so, or the credit available.

The intensity of labor is conveyed in the sources by such remarks as that in the busy season "*women and children* work flat out" at planting wheat and beans, caring for mulberry trees, and building threshing floors.[26] Where water was distant from the fields, double pumping was used. The variability of the climate demanded constant small adjustments in the schedules of planting out, and particular varieties of cereals had to be finely matched to local variations in the soil and location to maximize yields. Applying supplementary fertilizer to the crops while they were growing was a late-imperial refinement that improved output, but it could easily be mistimed.[27] Collecting and buying fertilizer, often from some way away, placed further pressure on time and money.

This transition from richness to riches, as it may be epitomized, a paradoxical mix of gains and losses, was accompanied by other transformations and also involved other costs. One such transformation was that much of the 'magic' passed out of nature. At least among the elite, whose records are the basis of our story, the enchantment and miracles of ancient and medieval times seem to have faded from the groves and the streams without however vanishing entirely. They were replaced by a world of increasingly rational and secular calculation, though uncontrollable catastrophes like the frequent epidemics still evoked frenzied religious responses.[28] Above all, though, it locked local society in to a particular style of economic functioning from which escape was difficult. Within the limited possibilities open to the sophisticated, if still premodern, technology that had developed over the millennia, it became all but impossible to move in a different strategic direction if the same numbers of people were to be supported.

The sea

In early-imperial times, the sea infiltrated deeply into Jiaxing, so that it was an environmentally ambiguous world, half saline water and half salt marsh. As the system of seawalls and locks and levees and polders became articulated in the middle empire and the first centuries of the late empire, the sea was excluded, except for the occasional violent storms when it broke in through human defenses. Little by little the water and land inside the defensive perimeters were desalinated and separated.

Storm surges driven by the northeast wind were the most dangerous threat to the fragile lines of defense. Here is a description of the county of Haiyan (whose name means 'sea salt') from the late-nineteenth-century gazetteer:[29]

Only Haiyan confronts the sea face-on. When one looks east, there is no limit visible. To the south the mountains of Ganpu and to the north those of Zhapu offer resistance and support on either side. When one looks from far away, there is no defense at all for the more than twenty-five kilometers within the curve like an ox's horns that lies between them. These can only rely on the single line of the defensive dike, which does daily battle with the water of the tides. The magnitude of the rise and fall of the tides depends, however, on whether or not there is a wind from the northeast helping it to inflict damage. . . .

When the weather is fine and the aethers bright, the wind does not howl. Even the large spring tides during the 'mildew rains' [in June and July][30] and the dog days [in July and August] do no more than surge up along the seawall, where they revolve and fall back. If, however, there is a wild gale riding upon the tides, even during the severe cold of the depths of winter, it is like silver mountains approaching in closely crowded ranks. They press close against the body of the dike. They show their power as they make their impact. Those that strike and leap straight upward seem like countless white dragons rising aloft and scattering into a flying rain that splashes and spills behind the seawall. Those that tug at it from below resemble sharp hills being smashed to pieces. They are destroyed with a roar. The waves' onslaught is unceasing. The noise is like that of a war between a million thunderstorms. Before the tide in front has fallen, the tide behind it is rising up again. For two or three days the wind gives them their rhythm. Sometimes the wind falls but the tide does not go down. The entire sea will be rocking and rolling, in a state in which it cannot swiftly become calm.

Last year[31] there were repeated storm surges and danger such as had not been seen for ten years past. . . . The tiles flew off all the rooftops and great trees were ripped out. All one could hear was the sound of the wind, the sound of the rain, and the sound of the tide coming across through the air and beating down upon us. No official or commoner in the area had the facial expression of a human being. . . .

People who lived under such a threat had to possess social and political discipline. If they were to safeguard their lives, they had to accept, even welcome, a certain degree of state interference, including coercion, in the organization of the necessary public works.

Two lines from a poem on a storm by Zhang Shiya, probably from the Ming, show how easily the lost linkage between land and sea could reassert itself. After speaking of the "unmasterable grief of this storm-tossed watery land" as the "fearful billows" roll in, he observes that

> Waves link together vast wetlands, overflowing the flood-dragon's lair.
> Tides shift the egrets' sand banks, and set trembling the multiple lakes.[32]

It is likely that Zhang regarded the flood-dragon as being as 'real' as the egrets. Rows of these large birds standing in silhouetted lines on distant sand-flats in Hangzhou Bay are among my most vivid memories of this area. As so often, there is a political undertone to this poem. Zhang ends by saying he is shedding tears "for state policies and the hardships faced by the people."

The disasters that could occur when the sea broke in are evoked with brutal images in a poem by Zhang Yongquan on the storm that smashed through the seawalls of Shanghai, Jiading, and Chuansha in 1696. These areas were further north up the coast than Jiaxing, and perhaps more exposed, but they shared the same general environment, and, indeed, the same long seawall. Here are three sections showing how the coastal inhabitants struggled to avoid their fate:[33]

> Some of the people used ropes, to tie themselves together,
> Hoping this way to support each other, or give each other help.
> How were *they* to know that, together, they'd be swept away and drowned?
> Some of them sought to escape, boring holes in the rooves of their houses,
> But their bodies, along with their reed-thatched shacks, were borne off
>   and tossed about.
>
> Some clutched at beams and rafters, and let themselves go where these
>   went,
> But the wind pounded and battered them, and scattered them east and west.
> Some clambered to the tops of trees, where they floated for a time,
> But snakes climbed up to the treetops, driven, too, by fear of dying.
>
> Men, scared the snakes would bite their hands, of themselves released their
>   hold.
> Men and snakes have gone, together, into the other world. . . .

The downpour ceased at dawn, but the storm did not let up.
Those people who had not been drowned congratulated each other.
Then they saw a sand bank far away, among the rolling waves,
Where a thousand others called for help that their lives, too, be saved.
The tide came in, then, with a swirl, and half of them went down.
With the second swirl the bank submerged, and every one was
    drowned. . . .

Their faces, two days later on, were still easy to recognize.
Like mounds, or hillocks, the washed-up corpses had stacked themselves
    in piles.
By the third day, or the fourth, skin and flesh were soggy-rotten.
One could smell the stench some thirty miles. It made one want to vomit.

Zhang goes on to describe how the fish ate the corpses' intestines, and the birds pecked at their livers and brains. He concludes by asking why the people who lived by the seaside should have been so guilty that they deserved this extraordinary punishment. A punishment inflicted, without distinction, on the worthy and the misguided, and the old and the young. This takes us into the world of moral meteorology which is discussed in chapter 12. The poet's answer here is that it was the doing of the God of the Sea, but he offers no deeper reason as to why.

The sea could also be a source of physical and aesthetic excitement, even moments both of release from social inhibitions, and of an initiation into mystical exaltation, to which fear gave an added intensity. Some doggerel verses from Ming times by Shen Yaozhong about a day he spent on the Jiaxing beach touch on all these themes.

The reference to the whale almost certainly alludes to the legend that the Tang-dynasty poet Li Bo ascended to heaven on one of these beasts. The Heavenly Weaving Maid was a star-spirit who lived on one side of the Milky Way, separated by it from her sweetheart, the star-spirit called the Cow Lad. She is said once to have given a magical stone to a band of explorers looking for the source of the Yellow River which, some people believed, ran in the skies as the Milky Way. Commonplace and exalted, as well as wry humor, are mixed in unusual fashion:[34]

Lifting up my lower robes, I go out by the sea's shore,
Where — kicking away my clogs — I feel contact with its pebbles.
For several hundred paces, I stride along through the water
With legs immersed, maybe, some two or three feet in depth.

Among the things I bump against is the stump of an old tree.
Making it serve me as a mat, I sit in a squat upon it;
Calling out to my serving lad, to bring the wine jar to me,
I condemn myself to the forfeit of gulping down a goblet.

Under the soles of my feet I push the corals loose,[35]
Throwing fish, and shrimps, into agitation behind my splashing wrists.[36]
I turn, and I gaze at the sea, its colors all in movement.
— Along the eastern skyline lies a single streak of crimson.

For a fleeting instant, only the top — of the panorama's before me,
Then, for a moment, all of it — rises up into my vision,
Where the pennons leading the cloud-fronts are spread flying, in disorder,
And like glittering spears in clusters are the rays from low-lying mists.

Its whiskers lifting up, the sea gives a long-drawn roar,
The resonance setting shaking the Dragon–Serpent's mansion.
The silver mountains tumble over, on the land, as they roll forward,
While the snowy breakers drain away into nothing as they attack.

The serving-lads are faltering: they walk with shortened steps.
Every one of my friends — my guests — has by now made good his escape!
So it is, as I sit on the rotted stump, and spreading out my legs,
That, doing just whatever I please, I throw off all restraint.

My feet atop his head, I am borne by a mighty whale,
With the Great Boar stars supporting me, from underneath my shoulders.
Now that I desire to travel, along the Milky Way,
I shall ask the Heavenly Weaving Maid to give me her magic stone!

My senses in confusion, I leave with a pounding heart,
Returning, once again, down the old familar paths.
To find my well-tried friends continuing with their party,
Where they calm me with the comfort of a kindly proffered draught. . . .

Few birds are now about. The tide has long since ebbed.
Yanghou — the wave-spirit — 's, traces are no longer to be seen.
Leaving me uncertain if there's any past or present:
It seems as if, all at once, this great Earth had come into being.

Still unable to sleep, at home, when I return,
In every wall beside me are the autumn insects. Chirping.

Chinese landsmen, like Shen, did not see the sea as a kind of chaos gnawing
away evilly, but vainly, at the eternal reliability of the land guaranteed by God,

as was the case to some extent in early-modern northwestern Europe.[37] Earlier, though, under the middle empire, there had been something like a milder version of this European view in the Jiaxing popular belief that the raised fifty-kilometer-long ridges, based on immense quantities of oyster and mussel shells, that ran between the prefectural capital and the sea, were "the means used by Heaven to put a limit to the ocean and preserve the people of Wu."[38] Nor did Shen see the sea as the home of demons, as seems to have been the case to a certain degree with premodern Bali, for example.[39] But it was the dwelling of gods and immortals, as another of his poems makes clear.[40] It frightened most people unaccustomed to it, as we can see by the panicky behavior of Shen's guests and servants. Partly for this reason it was also, for those capable of responding to it, a source of physical excitement and metaphysical visions.

Nor, unlike Europeans before the eighteenth century, did the Chinese regard the shoreline as stable. Experience made it evident the opposite was the case. In some areas of Jiaxing inhabited land had been swept away, as in the case of Wangpan, mentioned in the previous chapter. Once it had been linked with the mainland, but according to Chang Tang, writing in the Song dynasty,[41]

> The Wangpan mountains are far out to sea, though the pillars of the bridge are still standing. In 1241, one could still find such things as old wells, small stone bridges, and stumps of large trees along the shoreline in the tide. If one looked at the characters inscribed on the bricks of these wells, one could learn that a military colony had been stationed here in Eastern Jin times [the fourth century CE].

The late-Ming gazetteer tells us that:[42]

> According to the Song-dynasty gazetteer, there were in those days, some twenty-five kilometers to the south of Haiyan city, the Water-Storage Barrage, and, one-and-a-half kilometers south of this, the Indigo Field Inlet. One-and-a-half kilometers east lay the Transverse Inlet, which was linked to the east with Guyi,[43] and to the south entered the sea. There were also the Thirty-Six Sands, the Nine Mud Flats, the Eighteen Mounds, and the Seven Peaks of Mount Huangpan [Wangpan] spread out in a row along the fore-shore of the sea.
>
> Today the county capital is a mere two hundred and fifty meters from the ocean. The traces of the barrages and dikes of former times have all been engulfed by the sea, and Jinshan [a mountain to the north] is ever further and further away. The tides mount the semi-submerged sand bar between Mount Kan and Mount Zhe,[44] flowing in a rotating manner to strike against the territories of Haining and Huangwan. When they reach the strait between the land and the former Qin-dynasty military station on White

Tower Rocks [today two kilometers offshore], their position-power is doubly agitated. Rogue waves, carried by the wind, destroy people's cottages, damage the rice harvest, and are a grief to all of Wu.[45] Proposals for dikes have become a matter of urgency.

It was a landscape in perpetual transformation. Conversely, the shore built up in other places, like the Nanhui peninsula at the south tip of the mouth of the Yangzi, slightly to the north of Jiaxing.[46]

By late Ming or early Qing times, the battle against the sea was basically won here, as we have seen in the previous chapter.

Polders

In the course of many centuries in the Middle Ages the ambivalent landscape was controlled by the building of polders. The literal translation for the Chinese term is 'surrounded fields'. They had the shape of shallow inverted conical hats. A raised rim—the protective dike—ran around the outside, and channels sloped gently down to a common drainage ditch at the bottom. Draining the polder meant pumping the water out of this ditch with a pedaled pump that dragged it up a square open trough by means of pallets linked together into a continuous wooden chain. Backbreaking work.

During the middle empire and the first half of the later empire, the fields of the better-off were located at the top of the polder, where the farmers both had easier access to the water outside, and could more easily drain them into the ditch below. In the relatively more egalitarian rural society of Qing times, the pattern tended to shift to fields divided like slices of pie, all of them running down from the top to the bottom in the center. The prefectural gazetteer for 1600 has the following account of the first transformation:[47]

> *Polder fields in the prefecture* The streams and creeks crisscross north and south. This is said to be the remnants of the pattern of the well-fields of antiquity [laid out in ticktacktoe grids] but there are no details available.[48] In 763–4 CE, under the Tang, the commissioner for military colonies Zhu Zimian dredged the ditches to reach the sluice-ways, and the sluice-ways to reach the streams, and *for the first time* they were of economic benefit. Later the prefect Yu You repaired the dikes, cleared the river junctions [or 'feeder canals'], *cut down the trees*, and signposted the roads. . . .
>
> At this time the prefecture consisted of the two counties of Jiaxing and Haiyan. The land in Jiaxing has a level character, making it easy to prepare in

advance for droughts and floods. Haiyan faces the sea and runs parallel with a range of hills, being high to the south and sloping down toward the north. If there are ten days without rain, the fields have no recourse. It was therefore a matter of urgency to have locks and embankments. Haiyan as it is today has the three hundred and one old creeks opened in 821–4 CE by Li E, who also created the Ever-Bumper Locks. During 993 to 1003 CE, under the Song, Lu Zongdao redirected the water in Indigo Field Inlet and White Tower Channel over a distance of nine kilometers. In 1056–63 Li Weiji dredged the sluice-ways and drains, installed wooden locks, and put in place thirty district-boundary embankments.[49] In 1131 to 1162 Li Zhiyang repaired eighty district-boundary embankments, and the two Ever-Bumper Locks.[50] He also built twenty-four embankments along branch channels. Later, Zhao Danxi dredged the two dike-side waterways[51] at Black Mound and Summonwealth,[52] and built eighty-one embankments. Such is what was accomplished by the embankments and locks of Haiyan.

Hydraulic domestication thus took about four hundred years. The participation of the state at a subregional level seems often to have been crucial.

Underneath the success story lay social and political conflicts driven by different economic and environmental interests. Something of the way in which state and private interests could clash emerges from a more general account of the Jiangnan region as a whole:[53]

As regards polders, the Qian family [who ruled the state of Wu-Yue during the Five Dynasties period[54]] had instituted four sections of 'battalion-fields troops', totalling eight hundred men, who devoted themselves solely to matters affecting farmland. The Song dynasty abolished the battalion-fields troops, but in 1234 to 1236 the transport commissioner Qiao Weiyue once again excavated the ditches and embankments that they had been in charge of, in order to facilitate transport by water [of tax-grain].

The rich commoners, who were taking the full amount of rents from the farmland, did not repair these polders, and crassly considered that repeatedly altering the farmland was a pointless undertaking. If the fields produced a doubled harvest they only received the same amount of rent. On account of all this, their tenants were able to profit from the seasonal inundations, and in consequence bored holes in the aging dikes so that they could catch fish [who came in through the holes], or grew crops on [top of] them. In some cases the destruction spread to neighboring polders. Thus the dikes around the fields were totally ruined. When the heavy rains came in spring and summer, the fields would be an expanse of water.

In 1022 a commissioner was sent out by imperial decree to take the direction of the troops from the various sectors in clearing out the obstructions [in the waterways]. In 1058 the transport commissioner . . . sent up a report, and an imperial decree ordered the county authorities to command their commoners to make dikes around their fields in such a way that they all joined together continuously, and indicated that inferior or superior administrative performance would be judged according to this criterion. In 1059 another decree instituted 'river-clearance troops' and established the Wu River commander and three other commanders to undertake hydraulic maintenance.

Thus the state was perpetually intervening, using the military if it was thought appropriate.

In this last case, state fiscal interests were presumably involved; but transport versus irrigation was a common conflict. The description of the single reliable transport link between the town and the sea in the gazetteer for Ganpu gives an example of this. Unusually, a private initiative held the upper hand here, for a time at least, over an irritated officialdom:[55]

The Three Kilometer Crossdike[56] lies three kilometers west of the town. It is several fathoms in height[57] from top to bottom. The three villages of Huishang, Ganpu, and Shifan depend on it to protect the *supply of water to their irrigated fields. Ships and boats* come and go; and it is in truth the gateway to the town. For this reason a capstan-turned cable[58] [to haul vessels up or down the ramp at its side] has been installed, and comes at present under the authority of the commandant of the town.

One-And-A-Half Kilometer Crossdike lies one-and-a-half kilometers to the west of the town. Originally this crossdike did not exist, but in July 1249 there was a serious drought, and the common people living along the waterway pounded down a small crossdike here *without having official authorization to do so.* This caused all the other crossdikes that let water pass through them to be put out of operation. Only at this crossdike have the residents installed a capstan-turned cable without official authorization, and intercepted those passing through and inflicted exactions on them. This has long been an established rule.

Moreover, there is no alternative route for the coming and going of military vessels, the transport convoys from the salterns, and the inputs and outputs for the official monopoly wineries,[59] not to mention the escort with documentation of goods from the various tax depots, and the transfer from the coast by long-distance merchants of their overseas goods from the south. The branch streams easily run dry. This is indeed an inconvenience.

What is more, there is already the Three-Kilometer Crossdike in this area, which is adequate to protect the water-control system by closing it off [from the incursion of salt water, and by limiting outflow]. The establishment of this other dike is superfluous, and without question inflicts damage. In 1250 a tea-and-wine monopoly official ... requested the county magistrate to have it removed by digging it out, so as to benefit the area. The control of crossdikes falls, however, under the jurisdiction of the town officials, whose duty it is constantly to keep matters under observation and severely repress the abuse of intercepting traffic and making demands upon it.

The entry stops at this point, but it seems that no action was taken, the town officials in all likelihood being remunerated by the offenders for turning a blind eye.

Water-control structures took a long period to stabilize. After the Song dynasty had moved its capital south to Hangzhou (on the frontier of the East and Southeast) in the second third of the twelfth century, Jiaxing was filled with powerful families who had migrated with the government. Many of them drained lakes and wetlands to make fields. The military also rebuilt some of the lake-shore dikes so that they could profit from the 'barrage fields' created inside. In droughts their needs for water had to be satisfied before others could obtain a share. During periods of flood these barrage fields are said to have "towered like peaks" above everything else. They also blocked the outlets to the channels downstream so making it hard for the common people to drain their fields.

In the period 1297 to 1307, after the Mongol conquest of south China, a supervisory office was set up to take charge of 'battalion fields', including determining the boundaries of lakes and preventing the common people from encroaching any further on them. But, as the gazetteer for the year 1600 comments, "most of those in charge were barbarians and not well versed in water control." The farmlands "increasingly deteriorated." Some time after 1341, efforts were made to remedy matters but as the dynasty came to a close "polders, banks, locks, and sluices were in a state of total dereliction, and provided no means of controlling floods." If the path of the downflow was cleared "the lake water rushed into the fields, provoking severe damage."[60]

Shallow lakes, like those in Jiaxing, tend to silt up relatively quickly, and even more quickly if deforestation in their catchment areas increases the load of sediment in the water. Overall, though, it was human activities that had converted a regularly fluctuating environment into one of artificial equilibrium that needed an attentive government and continual maintenance to keep it under control. Because the ensuing Ming and Qing dynasties came remarkably close to achieving this it is easy to overlook what an effort was involved.

Land as a scarce resource

At some point in the long-term history of most regions in China there came a moment when the economic input in shortest supply was no longer labor-power but land. Clearly this moment is difficult to pinpoint, and it differed in different places, often by many hundreds of years. Moreover, there had probably always been serious competition over the best land. Conversely, even in well-developed regions it is likely that some poor land that could not be profitably improved, given existing technology, was never much used or sought after. Various factors slowed down any convergence to a broadly similar situation across the empire at any one time. There were economic and geographical difficulties in the way of migration, and social and linguistic difficulties inhibiting settlement among strangers. Physical, immunological, and technological adaptations were also needed in any new location with a different terrain, different resources, and different diseases. This general haziness of definition, and the uneven nature of the process involved across space and time, in no way means that the change was unimportant. It is likely that it altered the character of almost every facet of economic and social interaction. Among other things, it probably fostered an intensified preoccupation with landed property.

Undeveloped land was still quite plentiful in Tang-dynasty Jiangnan.[61] In the early part of the dynasty the custom of letting rice-fields lie fallow in alternate years still persisted for some time.[62] Optimizing the use of land by transplanting rice seedlings was not practised before Tang times, and then only came in gradually. Killing weeds by flooding the land was still done in the early years, as was fertilizing the soil by burning the stubble.[63] More efficient farming techniques began to spread at this time, reducing the average amount of land needed to support each family. These better methods included the use of ox-drawn plows and manures, a little double-cropping of rice with winter wheat, more extensive use of water pumps, and intensifying schedules of work round the year for peasants.[64] The population, as suggested above, began to increase.

The transition from labor to land as the key scarce component in the economy seems to have crystallized in Jiaxing in the twelfth and thirteenth centuries. The number of registered inhabitants per square kilometer in 980 CE was 15 (a figure that is fairly certainly substantially too low). Between 1080 and 1102, it was an average of 84. In 1290 it was 294.[65] Thus population density in Jiaxing's 7790 square kilometers apparently increased almost twenty-fold in just over three hundred years, and—much more certainly—by three-and-a-half times over 199 years. These swollen numbers were mainly fed by an expansion of polder land, on which wet-field rice could be grown in intensive cultivation, with increasingly often a dry-land winter crop of wheat or vegetables.

If we turn to qualitative evidence for the nature of the transition, we can at least illustrate it by contrasting the period when there was sufficient land for the government to create military agricultural colonies as development enterprises (like that of Zhu Zimian mentioned above), with the later age in which obsessive legal battles were fought over quite small patches of acreage. The first of these two periods lasted until at least the later part of the Tang. The second was well established by the end of the twelfth century.

In 304–5 CE the Jin dynasty sent three thousand soldiers to Jiaxing as military colonists. "With the passing of time the pacification commissioner had taught two thousand of these soldiers to farm the official fields. Every year they had rich harvests and the public granaries were overflowing."[66] To obtain a clearer impression of what these early colonies may have been like as organizations we have to move on to the Tang dynasty, half a millennium later. After the rebellions in the middle of the eighth century CE, which inflicted fourteen years of warfare on Jiaxing, there were "famines on this account, made worse by sicknesses and premature deaths. Dead bodies lay exposed to the sky. The dispossessed wandered idly about. Less than a third of the registered population remained, and not one person in a hundred returned to agriculture. There were more generals than civilian officials, more soldiers than farmers."[67] In 763 or 764 CE the government ordered a high minister of state[68] to create military colonies:[69]

From the lands of Jiaxing he formed twenty-seven colonies. Their areas twisted this way and that and covered more than 250 square kilometers.[70] He subdivided them into sections demarcated by borders. They were linked with the sea, and he dredged the ditches between their fields so that these were connected with the rivers. He pursued the archaic method of managing areas far removed from an urban center,[71] and put in good order the administration of the planting and reaping used by the officials in charge of rice cultivation in archaic times.[72] The land was cleared by the removal of weeds, and scraped clean *by the extraction of trees*, while *seeds were broadcast* by means of the breezes, and the roots consolidated by means of the rain. He propagandized these methods. In the winter they plowed, in the spring sowed, in the summer weeded, and in the fall harvested. In the mornings he went on a tour of inspection, and in the evenings gave the laborers encouragement. There was an appraisal every day and a meeting every ten days. This was urging them to observe the tasks appropriate to each of the seasons. The diligent were rewarded and the indolent urged on. He helped them to find marriage partners, and assisted them if they moved from farming one field to another. He examined their achievements and reported them to the superior authorities, and transmitted back to his subordinates the emoluments determined by these superiors.

Read in the context of what we know of later times, this description is startling in several respects. After allowing for the fact that these military colony lands were developed as part of a program of recovery from disasters, hence not typical of normality, and being alerted to an element of idealization indicated by references to the forms of administration used in the golden age of antiquity, we can note the following points: Land was still relatively easy to secure. Two hundred and fifty square kilometers was a substantial area in the context of a prefecture. Simple rice technology, involving no seedbeds or transplanting, with weeding but no fertilizing, and only a single crop a year, without winter wheat or vegetables, was enough to obtain the harvests "like clouds covering the skies" referred to in another account of the same system when it was run by Commissioner Zhu Zimian.[73] The basic restructuring of the terrain was still being undertaken.

This other account also speaks of the "groups of laborers spread out like the pieces on a ruled board for the game of *go*, and the ditches and divisions in a decorated fabric of crisscross patterns." Most tellingly, since the use of the phrase in Chinese sources is almost exclusively restricted to accounts from the early days when irrigation was still something of a novelty, "they made the ditches *serve as their weather*."[74] In other words, they had freed themselves from the need to rely on rainfall. The organization of farming activities was also directly bureaucratically managed—they were, after all, *military* colonies—and in this quite unlike the independent activities of the majority of at least those peasants who were not in some form of semiservile status under the middle and later empires.

Society's attitudes toward farmland after the transition to land shortage can be inferred from an account written about Jiaxing in 1219 CE by Qian Fu, a compiler in the Privy Council. It has the title *A Record of the Restoration of the School Fields*, that is, fields whose income was used for supporting Confucian scholars. A preoccupation had developed with even quite small areas of productive real estate. The intensity of lawsuits over land at this time may be taken as an index of this obsession.[75]

> The state [says Qian] has established schools of Confucian learning throughout the empire. The system is different for large ones and for small ones. . . . None of them however lacks farmland which is used to fill the granaries for them. The reason for this is that scholars are taught by instruction, but supported by nourishment. Both of these should be provided, and

neither should be missing. If there are numerous holes in scholars' shoes when they go out of doors, or their supply of grain cannot be maintained by those in charge of the granary, this is also a matter on which those who give instruction should bestow their attention.

After this introduction he tells the story of the Jiaxing education officer, Xiao Qi. Xiao commented that "scholars are made content by a full stomach, and instruction on its own does not allow them to go their own way independently." Since "not many of the old school-fields could be traced," he had had a town-level education official who was "good at checking accounts" "search for what had been concealed and pry out what was lurking hidden."

The most dramatic finding turned up by this inquiry was the farmland "occupied under false pretences by the Buddhist monastery of the Six Harmonies Pagoda."

Some time previously, the monks of this monastery had deluded a Mr Gu, who was an imperial bodyguard, and so obtained twenty-eight-and-a-half hectares of his farmland.[76] They had established a contract of sale at a cheap price that had no foundation in real-life circumstances. What then happened was that a Mr Xia, a commoner, stated to the authorities that one-tenth of this was land that had been '*mortgaged*' by his family, and that the monks had no right to talk of it having been 'sold'.[77] He requested the county magistrate to permit him to redeem it. The magistrate gave his assent to this. It was through this that the conclusion was reached that the land the monks had received from Mr Gu had not been lawfully obtained. This was reported to the prefectural authorities and they, after a fair examination, confiscated it and donated it to the school.

The monks repeatedly went to law over this and repeatedly suffered setbacks. In particular they maintained that those who had redeemed some of the fields were not the descendants of those who had mortgaged them. The authorities however only gave the redemptors these lands; the remainder were to stay without question with the school. They assembled the most learned scholars of the prefecture to effect the transfer. The monks however did a [covert] deal with the government clerks, and made use of internal splits [in local society] to keep possession of these lands that had in principle already been officially confiscated. They kept them in secret this way for twenty years. Almost none of those officials who supervised the Confucian scholars looked into this matter, but grew habituated to the falsehood so that it became as it were the truth.

Only when this concealed state of affairs became entirely obvious was it reported to the prefectural authorities, the censorate, and the grain-transport authorities, for them to act in concert in presiding over the oaths [of the accused]. These latter authorities punished the criminal acts of the clerks, and as before returned the land to the school. The monks then foolishly further sued them before the Ministry, and the Ministry likewise found the monks to be in the wrong. The monks in consequence submitted and returned all the farmlands that they had received, half of which had been the result of covert subversion. . . .

These lands are now rid of Buddhists and returned to Confucians. They are not now used to support vagrants [that is, monks], but commoners of high quality.[78]

The anti-Buddhist bias to Qian Fu's story is patent. Irrespective of this, the seriousness of the conflict over a relatively small acreage (not much more than 0.1 per cent of the area of the colony lands in the preceding example), and the effort put into the struggle by all sides, suggests the extraordinary importance that land had acquired by this date. Twenty-eight hectares were enough for a quarrel eventually to claim the attention of central government officials, including the author of the account just given, who was asked by the locals to write it up.

There were of course moments when political disorder led to a renewed availability of more cultivable land than there was labor to work it. Thus the biography of the recorder of Jiaxing at the beginning of the Ming dynasty[79] notes that "many of the fields had gone to waste and become overgrown; and he put everything into urging those who had the resources [in labor power or funds] to open them up."[80]

As the dynasty progressed the cities also filled up; maybe we should say 'filled up again'. The late-Ming gazetteer describes this process, which became apparent during the sixteenth century:[81]

At the beginning of the Ming dynasty, the dwellings of the commoners in the prefectural capital were still few in number. To the inside of the four water gates everything was a grid of large waterways. Boats could be rowed even along the branch canals. After the early 1520s the population steadily increased. Houses became aggregated on both sides of the city's rivers like the sequences of scales on a fish. By this time domestic refuse had choked up the branch canals, and these little by little turned into dry land. Some of the larger waterways also became clogged with silt, which was a misery for the residents.

In 1547, the prefect . . . formulated proposals to dredge the city waterways, which led to the clearing of canals that had become blocked up or had disappeared. He put a stop to the encroachment of commoners' houses into confined areas. Where the approach ramps to the bridges had caused congestion with muck, he had them cleared. He also ordered the canton districts each to send out a boat to carry away the sediments that had been removed and dump them into the South Lake, so as to build up the base there for a tower.

In fact it seems likely that the city population had risen during the Southern Song and then declined again during the troubles both of the Song-to-Yuan transition and the Yuan-to-Ming transition. For the moment at least, the fragments of evidence that hint at an earlier urban opulence are too slight to allow us to judge with certainty if this was so.[82]

Clashes over real estate also related to wood, which was becoming a scarce resource in some areas during the middle empire. The Song-dynasty gazetteer for the coastal town of Ganpu tells the tale below following an entry on six of the hills to the west and northwest of the town:[83]

> Woods are *not* planted on the six hills just mentioned. They are [unlike other hills] a place where the common people pasture their cows and sheep. Earlier the salt-making households and the commoners fought between themselves over *the hills providing firewood.* Lawsuits occurred from the period of the Five Dynasties until the present Song dynasty, and imperial judgments were repeatedly issued. People used stone containers to conceal their land-entitlement documents for safety in the ground. *From two hundred years ago onward it was not determined what belonged to whom.* Every year there were armed clashes in the hills, and people were continually being killed. In 1184 the granary commissioner . . . examined the details and organized them in comprehensive form. Whenever he was out on a mission to handle official business, he regularly used his leisure moments to collect the opinions of the public. He consulted over what should be given and what taken away, and *defined the boundaries* for each section in a way that he proposed should never thereafter change. He submitted this to the Emperor, who was delighted, and the fighting stopped as a result.

What can be glimpsed here is a part of the process, often marked by environmental wars, through which once generally accessible nonagricultural areas, like woods and hill pastures, were being assigned to particular families and communities. The need in general to *grow* trees for timber and firewood by this time, which is indicated by the term 'plant' at the beginning of this extract, is confirmed by a terse comment in the two lines devoted in this little book to Ganpu's topography: "On the bare hills the people do not plant forest trees."[84]

The situation was worse by Ming times. In the Song era there had been a shipbuilding yard at the foot of Longwall Mountains, sometimes called Sun–Moon Conjunction Mountain, where there was an anchorage known as the Dragon's Eye Basin. Building ships implies a supply of timber. Interestingly, the only drinkable water locally available came from a well halfway up the mountain that had been dug at the initiative of Buddhist monks, and was indispensable for travelers. In the sixteenth century, Dong Gu, a native of Haiyan and the compiler of the continuation of the Ganpu town gazetteer, related a story showing how the shortage of wood had intensified by this date:[85]

> Sun–Moon Conjunction Mountain . . . once provided a pillow at its foot for the Dragon's Eye Basin. Beside this ship's anchorage there is a naval station that is on guard against threats from the open sea outside. There is a temple halfway up the mountain. . . .
>
> In later times the Dragon's Eye Basin became blocked up. In 1552 the island pirates[86] pillaged Huangwan and Yanshan[87] and threw the northern part of Zhejiang province into a state of emergency. In 1553 they next violated Jinshan to the north and invaded as far as Haiyan. The navy kept guard over Ganpu town on the outer [that is, the seaward] side of the mountain. *Some of their soldiers climbed the mountain and cut down a cypress tree that stood in front of the temple, in order to make a tiller for a rudder.* The spirit allowed them to do this, but said: "So you have had the audacity to cut down my cypress! If you sacrifice to me, then I will forgive you!"
>
> They thereupon made plans to renovate the shrine. All of a sudden the tide struck on the sands and gravels blocking the former anchorage. The Dragon's Eye Basin at once became overflowing and as deep as it had been before. When the warships reassembled below the shrine, the winds and the waves caused them no alarm. The pirates passed by repeatedly after this but in the end did us no harm. Such was the manifestation of the power with which this spirit is endowed!

This story implies an absence of good-quality timber in the coastal ranges by this date. In cutting down the cypress that had survived as a sacred tree protected by its location in the temple grounds, the marines were committing what they recognized was an act of sacrilege, though pardonable in a emergency. They were lucky their act of atonement was so generously recompensed.

Bridges

Bridges were essential because fording many waterways was both unpleasant and dangerous. Around the end of the fifteenth century, Shen Lian wrote these lines on Yunweng's Bridge in Pinghu:[88]

> Something as mild as water, how can it so overflow
> That, at a risky ford, a gourd for support is essential,
> Those in the middle of the stream so buffeted that they float
> And, in panic-stricken terror, yell that their plight is desperate!?

There is a reference here to one of the archaic *Odes*,[89] and, as is often the case when a poem is being used as evidence, there is no way of knowing how much the literary reference is affecting the sense of what is being said. It is unlikely that in the mid-Ming people in fact still used gourds in this way.

Unlike embankments, whose tops also served as roads, bridges allowed water to pass in and out beneath them, and so did not interfere with irrigation, drainage, or transport. When the Transverse Bridge in Pinghu collapsed, a walkway was needed over the creek it had spanned, and so "the locals collected earth to make a levee." When a new magistrate arrived two years later he found this had blocked the streams:

> It happened to be hot, dry weather. Every branch stream far and near was parched and waterless. I made inquiries of the old men, and all around they called for it to be opened up again. I had it breached as a matter of urgency, and strictly forbade that it be obstructed. Water was able to come in in large quantities and no fields were dried out into cracks. I established a boat to ferry people across.

A plan to install a lock was later turned down as too expensive, but eventually a flat stone bridge with three channels under it was erected.[90]

Stone bridges of the kind that were cheap to erect were vulnerable. Wooden bridges rotted.[91] When the Neighborhood Bridge in Tongxiang was rebuilt as a flat stone construction, floods due to sudden torrential rains were able to demolish it a few months later. The sponsor then had it rebuilt as a stronger stone-arch bridge, which was much more difficult to put up and much more expensive.[92] By Ming times people were becoming aware that agricultural development could reduce the space available to floodwater, and so increase the pressure on bridges by intensifying the outflow through the remaining channels where they stood. It was observed of the Bridge of a Myriad Tranquillities in Pinghu, for example, that "as the land was increasingly mastered, water accumulated in ever greater quantities outside the polders, and year by year the bridge was gradually destroyed."[93]

Bridges were more often matters for community and individual initiatives than water-control schemes, though at times there might be official prompting. If there were elements of 'civil society' under the middle and later empires to some degree independent of the state the construction of bridges would be a good place to look for evidence for both them, and also their limitations. Compare the following two stories, the first of Goodluck Bridge and the second of Dragonsighting Bridge, both in Jiashan county. The 'dragon' in the second of these names seems to have been an allusion to the chief donor's name, not, as one might suspect, to any belief in the actual sighting of a dragon.[94]

> *Goodluck Bridge*   In 1341–67, under the Yuan, the richest man in the area was a certain Zhang Jushan. He sired a son called Jusen, who remained dumb until the age of eighteen, being unable to speak. A monk, who was collecting funds to build a bridge, passed by his door. "May I ask what I should do about my son?" Jushan inquired of him. When the monk paid a visit to the son to question him, the latter suddenly replied: "Our family should undertake the completion of this bridge on its own!" Jushan was overjoyed and contributed the funds to build the bridge. . . . From this moment Jusen could talk.

A miracle of the morally rational kind favored by most Chinese.

> *Dragonsighting Bridge*   The county city was encircled by water. Every city gate had a wooden bridge by which people came and went, with the exception of the south gate where there was the Dayong Canal. Merchants' sailing vessels gathered here morn and night, thick as the scales on a fish. The boats with cabins of high-ranking officials and visitors of elevated status confronted one another, vying for precedence. If they bumped into each other it was easy for them to be smashed. . . . When Li Shihua became county magistrate of this area [some time in the Ming dynasty], the people of the county suffered from having to ford here, and reported to him that it was an urgent matter. *He thereupon summoned the local residents* [and the money was forthcoming].

Sometimes the 'private' individual would be an official born in the area concerned, and therefore, by the traditional rule of avoidance, not entitled to hold office there. This was the case in the sixteenth century with Feng Rubi, a native of Pinghu county, and the bridge at Fuelgathering Mountain Gate and others. He told the story himself:[95]

> In 1561 . . . I was traveling from Han Dike to the prefectural capital when a storm of rain and wind arose suddenly. I saw the banks on both sides broken

into muddy mire. Those who were fording the river, hauling each other along, were drowned one after the next. I could not bear to watch it. I returned to use bamboos, timbers, bricks, and stones to repair the levees for some twenty-eight kilometers. Over the next somewhat more than ten years they repeatedly collapsed and were as often mended. I became concerned that this plan was not a long-term solution. I therefore gathered together materials and workmen, and rebuilt thirty-two stone and wood bridges, and reconstructed the stone and earth levees in fifteen places. With respect to matters where I was not adequately endowed, I was obliged to look for help to other gentlemen who shared my purpose.

In the early Ming, Buddhist monks were still important fundraisers and organizers for bridges.[96] Sometimes this was in self-interest. Toward the end of the fifteenth century, the late Ming gazetteer tells us of Haiyan:[97]

To the west of the county capital there is a marsh where the water ponds. It is known as 'Bright Lake'. In the middle of the lake there is a small monastery . . . on both sides of which used to be earthen levees along which people walked. They repeatedly collapsed. The monks of this monastery . . . concerted their plans with the leaders of the area to convert the earth to stone, regarding this as a long-term solution. They made bridges through the spaces below which the lake water could drain away or swell in, as a means of removing its position-power.

After the sixteenth century, however, monks seem no longer to have performed any function in building bridges. The last time may have been the case of the Dahui Bridge in Haiyan. This seems to have been repeatedly first in a functional, and then a nonfunctional, state during one observer's lifetime, because of the damage done by the sudden rising of water every year after the spring[98] and summer rainstorms. After an unsuccessful official attempt to have the local water-control leaders mend it, and then the failure of the observer to do it on his own, the official commissioner for water control in 1550 organized the local gentry and a monk to collect funds and assemble workers. This was at last effective.[99]

Bridges were sometimes important markets or linked to them. Here is an account of Springtime Bridge:[100]

All sorts of commodities congregate in our Jiaxing, but nowhere in more abundance than the east corner of the city wall. The peddlers there are shrewd and canny in their exchanges. People from far and near rub shoulders with each other and cross paths. Like a rainbow, the bridge spans the belt of water that cuts the north side off from the south.

When it was rebuilt, "the method used did not copy that used in the past, but was that of suspended steps of brick and stone, which were both stronger and more solid than its predecessor."[101] The wording suggests a stepwise arch.

Three kilometers outside Jiaxing city was the Horseteam Bridge. We are told that "Lü Taichang thought that it was difficult for the country folk to wade across to come to market, so he constructed this bridge."[102]

Whereas only a handful of bridges seem to have been first built under the Tang and the Song, by the mid nineteenth century the number of bridges in the prefecture was almost four hundred.[103]

Environment and crime

A world of waterways was a world in which crime was easy. Criminals could vanish in no time into the maze of creeks. In the late sixteenth century or the early seventeenth, Li Rihua, a mandarin who had been born in the prefecture, therefore proposed that barriers should be put across the junctions of the more important streams, as they had been earlier, though it is not clear when. His proposal conveys the character of a world where water communications shaped human movement more than dry-land routes, and is symptomatic of a common official Chinese attitude to nature, an enduring determination to subject it to tight bureaucratic control. Also the sense of frustration at the way in which institutions and installations alike crumble away if not constantly supervised.[104]

> Consider [wrote Li] that the walls of Jiaxing's prefectural capital are encircled on all sides by water, which . . . thereby provides sustenance and wealth. The water in the larger streams has to be split into many subdivisions and then has to join once more to flow away, again finding its way to the larger streams. These larger streams are removed by the lakes, wetlands, inlets, and broads, which form a vast expanse reaching for innumerable kilometers. *These are the refuges where bandits from every corner come together*, and from which they emerge, and into which they then disappear.
>
> This is why in Jiaxing prefecture it is not appropriate to take defensive measures against bandits on the land. *It has to be done on the water.* Nor is it right to take preventive measures on the bending waterways of the inner areas. They have to be blocked at the mouths of the larger rivers, and where the branch streams hasten to join with these larger rivers. The wider of these may be several hundred feet across, or fifty or sixty feet. Once bandits have entered one of these waterway mouths one can anticipate that they will pillage every homestead within. Once they have made their exit, then the

vast watery expanses are the bandits' home territory where, fully laden with their cargoes and sails bellying in the wind, they can no longer be pursued.

Although the brigands love loot, they must also safeguard their lives. Brigands in earlier years did not dare to enter the inner areas, but only robbed solitary travelers on the paths along the dikes in desolate places without inhabitants. Thus when there are barriers at each river mouth, it is not easy for them to enter a mouth; and, even if they are able to make an entry, it is not easy for them to leave by another mouth. A situation where it is difficult to get out, once one is in, leads to being captured. Are the brigands going to be willing to go lightly to their deaths?

In recent times peace has lasted for so long that *everything has decayed.* Not one of the barriers at the mouths of the rivers still survives. The excuse for this is that establishing barriers and closing off a waterway with chains is only to be done under the bridges in the city. The diameter of the cylindrical wooden crossbar in such cases does not exceed a foot, and it is no more than twenty feet in length. Even if there are chains as well, they are not strong. Furthermore, the authorities have selected some of those in poverty and distress among the lowest category of the registered population, and forcibly assigned them to be barrier-keepers. This is merely obstructing the movement of small boats within a locality, and, as it happens, providing a means for the keepers to make extortionate demands. What advantages are there in this as a plan for defense? If major bandits turn up, then, once their axes have been applied, these barriers are instantly cut to pieces; and one would have done better to rely on a strand of hair!

It would be appropriate at the present time to send out officials to find out in every quarter where the smaller rivers join with the larger ones. Four or five serried rows of pilings should be hammered in on both sides of these mouths. Care should be taken that the trees used are large, rough, and sturdy. Between them a way through should be left, with a gate of one or two sections to permit the passage of boats. The gate should only be opened wide for vessels on which officials are traveling, and for [official] transport boats. For all other vessels space should only be made for one vessel at a time. A massive iron chain should be opened and closed morning and evening. Wealthy people who live in the neighborhood should be assigned the duty of providing for labor and rations of food, according to how well off they are.

As in the past, residences for officials should be installed in the space on either side of the barrier so they can live there and be in charge. This will make it easier to keep watch over it.

Wherever there is a bridge, as in the past a transverse boom will be installed, and be opened and closed according to a timetable. Once this is done, even if major robbers are able to chop down a barrier and get in, and those guarding the barrier lack the strength to resist them, these latter will make speed along the land route to the next line of defense, and call together those who live in the area as a means of resisting the brigands. What is more, a military vessel should be assigned to important river mouths with barriers, and will fire cannon, and go out on patrol. . . .

The end of the story is not given. It is doubtful if anything was in fact done.

Food supplies

Many parts of Jiaxing were not self-sufficient in food supplies under the late middle empire and the late empire. People there earned much of their income from waterborne trade, by boiling brine to make salt, by cultivating mulberry trees and rearing silkworms, or by growing cotton. Extra food in such cases had to be bought from merchants. The pattern was a mosaic of micro-environments and micro-histories. Around Zhapu, which had formed out of a conglomeration of coastal villages in Song and Yuan times, there was, for example, a different situation on each side of the town:[105]

> To its west the people live by making salt. The sound of the salt-boiling caldrons can be heard for more than ten kilometers. *There is quite some quantity of surplus land.* One's gaze is everywhere filled with reeds and rushes. *They do not farm.* To its north, there is a plain whose fields connect with Pinghu county, but only a few of the people who have rice come to Zhapu; all of them go to Pinghu. Only to the south and east are there several hundreds of thousands of *mou* of farmland, and only near to Zhapu are the fields fertile, yielding a *zhong* per *mou* each year. *Its trade is in contact with other places. Zhapu's lifeline depends entirely on it.* In times of peace it is still possible to avoid shortages, but the moment there are alarms, the rice takes up its dwelling far away in the hills.

The *zhong* was not routinely used in later mid-imperial times, and it is impossible for the moment to determine an equivalent in Western measure.[106]

Rural insecurity was linked to the fluctuations in the harvest caused mainly by the weather. Low yields of grain meant high prices, and high yields low ones. This may seem predictable, but it should not be forgotten that when a system of long-distance transport and marketing is well developed, even in premodern times, this can damp down or even remove these fluctuations. Robert Marks has shown that this is what happened in Guangdong province (in the Far South) in the later eighteenth century.[107] Wu Hongji's stele inscription on the 'Ever-Normal Granaries' of Jiaxing describes the situation in the prefecture at the end of the sixteenth century. These granaries were responsible for buying and storing grain in years of plenty and selling it at an affordable price in years of shortage. They constituted a sort of 'bureaucratic buffer'.[108]

> I have observed the [varying] abundance of the harvests in Jiaxing. If grain is plentiful, then everyone hurries to market to sell it. If there are numerous sellers and few buyers, the price drops lower and lower but the people are *obliged to sell because they are suffering from a lack of money.* This harms the farmers. In years of poor harvests the grain is in short supply, so everyone hurries to market to buy it. When buyers are many but sellers few, the price rises higher and higher. If the price rises higher and higher, people are even so *obliged to buy, as they are suffering from a lack of grain.* This harms the people [as consumers].
>
> At times such as these, it is possible to bring it about that damage is done neither to the farmers nor to the people, that in years of glut the farmers are not tossed away as worth no more than shit, but in years of dearth the poor people are not compelled to get their grain as if it were as costly as pearls or jades. [In other words, keeping official reserves of grain.] . . .
>
> On another occasion I heard the elders say: "In 1561, we were oppressed by dark fogs, and frogs perched on the stoves and caldrons. More recently we have seen how in the drought of 1588, as far as the eye could see, the dry-land grain was like scrubland bushes. In these two years, the annual tax obligations were not paid in; *those suffering from famine looked at each other, and sold off their wives and children as if they were pigs or deer.* Even so, the white bones piled up. How about if use had been made of the method of planning in advance and laying in reserve stocks, to give these people a pint or a peck of grain? . . .
>
> In the last five years the authorities have likewise been concerned with this ancient strategy that ensures that low prices do not hurt farmers and high prices do not hurt consumers. The command has been received to establish Ever-Normal Granaries in every prefecture and county, in readiness for years of bad harvest, and to take charge of buying in and selling grain. Hence I have been able to observe, within my limited sphere, the setting up of these granaries within a single county.
>
> Let me go systematically around the towns of the county. Some thirteen or more kilometers to the north is Wangjiang Creek, where the people have to go to Suzhou for their [major] market. There are ten farmers there for every three traders. Ninety per cent of them suffer from floods, but only ten per cent from droughts. Their land is suitable for rice and there is little

wheat. Yields are almost double those of the high-lying land, but floods damage the rice and cause famines. A granary has been established there, in the middle of the market. It faces south and is square in shape. . . . Its size, if one measures the dimensions at right angles to each other, is 300 *xun*.

Rather less than fifteen kilometers to the southwest of the county capital is Newtown, whose people have to go to market at Tiao River. For every ten farmers there are four traders. They suffer to an equal extent from drought and from flooding. Their fields are suited to wheat, rice, and mulberry trees. Compared to those of the level and swampy areas their yields are extremely meager. Both drought and floods damage their wheat and rice, and so cause famine. Their granary is in the middle of the market, close to the official highway, facing south and rectangular in shape.

And so he continues round the rest of the county towns.

The *xun* was a length of 8 Chinese feet. Since the Ming foot used for building purposes averaged 31.9 centimeters,[109] a *xun* was about 2.55 meters. It seems that the floor area was about 766 square meters, which implies that the walls would have been about 28 meters in length. The text also indicates that the building was divided into two halves, with a narrow passageway running between them, and further subdivisions.

The erection of such massive buildings, and the operation of the administration needed to buy, store, and sell grain, were part of the costs of coping with the combination of variable weather and a sophisticated but precarious system of cereal production vulnerable to these variations. The sale of children in times of distress was one of the key markers of the increasing lack of resilience, linked to the disappearance of a natural environmental buffer.

Natural disasters

Famines, and floods, and droughts in early imperial times on the whole affected smaller numbers of people than under the middle or late empire. Some time between 107 and 125 CE, the magistrate of Wuyuan (that is, roughly, Haiyan) opened the granaries when there was a famine and "saved the lives of three hundred households."[110] That means about 1,500 individuals. Compare these numbers with those in the biography of Hong Hao, who was the paymaster of Xiuzhou (approximately, Jiaxing) some time between 1119 and 1125:[111]

There were heavy floods and the common people suffered from famine. In order to relieve the scarcity he took on his own responsibility the decision to open up the official granaries, and reduce prices. He displayed banners in the markets proclaiming that no one was to dare to sell grain at a high price. For those who could not feed themselves he had rice-gruel boiled to feed them. He established rooms in two abandoned temples, one in the east and one in the south of the city, sheltering ten persons per room, and with men and women lodged in separate places. He had their hands marked with a black spot to prevent any of them cheating [to get double rations].

At that moment 40,000 *hu* of grain tribute rice from the southern part of the Liang-Zhe [on the East/Southeast border] were passing through the city [on the Grand Canal], bound for Kaifeng [in the Northeast]. He sent down orders that they were to be intercepted and retained for relief. When permission for this was denied, Hao declared: "I prefer to exchange my own person for ten thousand lives," and actually retained the grain. When the commissioner conducting the inquiry into this came to know the circumstances he submitted a memorial that Hao's crime should be pardoned and more grain sent to the capital. From start to finish Hao saved the lives of more than 95,000 people.

Compared to a thousand years earlier, the scale of disaster relief extensive enough to be thought worth recording had risen by an order of magnitude.[112]

The episode just related was not so extraordinary as to give a misleading impression. This is confirmed by other information in the late-Ming gazetteer. For example, Yang Jizong, a late-fifteenth-century official celebrated for his integrity and frugality, and who served on and off as the prefect of Jiaxing for nine years, is said to have stockpiled "several million *hu*" of grain. "In the great famine of 1467 and 1468, the people of the prefecture relied on this to preserve their lives." In a later famine, these reserves, depleted by being sent to other stricken areas, were even so insufficient.[113]

Superfauna

Other beings inhabited the Jiaxing landscape besides plants, birds, fish, insects, and animals. These were the creatures of the human mind: dragons, the spirits of the departed, and deities. They have to be remembered if we are to have a complete sense of how the environment was experienced by those who lived in it.

In the fall of 1283 magistrate Gu Yong wrote the following account of the Dragon Lord Shrine on Mount Chen in Haiyan county:[114]

It is the place where *one prays for rain* when there is a year of drought. It was first founded in the Song dynasty by county magistrate Li Zhiyang . . . and had long fallen in ruin. . . . It is in fact where a white dragon gives rise to rain. . . .

In the sixth moon of 1282 the Drought Demon was cruel. The farmers looked at each other and waited to die. On the first day of the tenth moon I went in urgency to Mount Chen and prayed as follows: "Today it is not only the farmers who have no hope. More than seventy-five thousand piculs of grain[115] are still due from us to the Court as the 'fall sprouts quota' rent for public lands."[116] I had barely spoken when ranks of clouds darkened the skies and a copious rain fell.

After a day had passed, the Milky Way shone gloriously bright and people's hearts became as fearful as on the day before. Consequently I led the officials and my friends among the scholars, together with Buddhists, Daoists, and elders, to pray a second time at the shrine. Now it should be said by way of explanation that on several days I had gone to Mount Chen to present my requests to the Dragon Pool [in which the Dragon lived], and had obtained clear manifestations in return for my salutations. Long previously I had obtained a True Seal[117] from the Daoist adept Feng. I therefore went to my private office and used it as *an additional technique to summon lightning and thunder, so as to assist the spiritual powers of the dragon,* and it actually rained! The common people were overjoyed, and there was enough moisture for the harvest that year to be a bumper crop.

In the fifth moon of 1283 there was still a drought. I went to the shrine as I had before and there prayed tirelessly with increased devotion. There was a downpour for two days. The common people still hoped for more and were not yet content. I prayed again and once more summoned lightning. The following night it rained as if a bowl had been turned upside down, and the people's hopes were comforted. . . .

On the twenty-second day of the seventh moon . . . I sent artisans to paint pictures of the Dragon Lord for him [in the partially restored temple]. In less than a moment there came a flash of lightning, with winds. The Great Dragon Lord appeared, and then a smaller dragon also appeared. It looked exactly as if a father and son were present. They rose and once they had risen there was a full foot of rain. At that time Shen Yu, who is a man of this county, the elder Sun Shimai, the Daoist master Ye Shichun, and others there, *all collectively saw them with countless eyes.* Every one of them was terrified. I have served the Dragon Lord to my utmost, and the Dragon Lord has rewarded me with no small recompense.

As is shown in chapter 11 it was common for groups of people to see dragons until at least the seventeenth century.

A different kind of spiritual force manifested itself at the Temple of the Lady of the Stalagmite.[118] The temple was first built between 1265 and 1274. It was rebuilt in 1520 by a holder of the metropolitan degree, so the faith was still sufficiently alive at this time to prompt financial support from a member of the official class. There is an account by a local called Zeng Bing which suggests that the process of the disenchantment of nature began by the middle of late-imperial times:[119]

> About 1265 CE, five kilometers to the southeast of the prefectural capital, a stone sprang up that was like a bamboo shoot. The people round about thought that it was uncanny, and hence they called the building housing it the 'Stalagmite Temple'. . . .
>
> In 1452 it was reconstructed, and for several hundred years down to the present, as if but a single day has passed, *it has created good fortune and brought down happiness*. Fathers and old men and boys, together with old village women and widows living in the back country, *pray to it* concerning bumper harvests and years of dearth; *they communicate with it* about floods and droughts, and they give it their requests about sicknesses. They are answered with the reliability of an echo. From far and near people vie with each other to hasten to it in a continuous line, as if it were a market.

But, Zeng asks, do natural objects really have magical properties, and if so, in what sense?

> For it to be able to be like this, and for a stone actually to possess magical properties, would be particularly uncanny! In people's opinions, things which are frequently seen in the world are called 'commonplace', while things but rarely seen are treated as uncanny, but they are not *intrinsically uncanny*. Nor are they intrinsically magical. It is simply that *people's minds make them uncanny* and so see them as magical. Thus what is weird is seen as magical and what is magical as the work of spirits.
>
> 'Spirits' are the minute germinal causal elements in matter–energy–vitality![120] The Transforming Force flows through them, contracting and extending, opening and closing, with a uniquely perfect and magical quality. When they are concentrated in human beings, even in married women or girls, they endow them with a nature that is unified and well-balanced. Thus these last-mentioned can maintain chastity and fidelity to a single husband.
>
> When these forces have accumulated pent-up for a long time between two points in space or time, the active essence becomes brilliantly apparent, lasting as long as famous mountains or great rivers. It is indeed what one calls 'existing without having been born, and disappearing without having died'. Who could maintain that a twisted stone that dribbles water does not

belong to the category of 'mountains and streams'?[121] This being so, this stalagmite's magical powers can increasingly awaken in our human minds the germinal causes of feelings of respect and reverence, whereby we can see the abundance of the virtuous powers of the shades and spirits. These are indeed *in* this stone, but also they are *not really* in it.

Thus some members of the educated minority tried to make rational philosophical sense of the seeming miracles that ordinary folk encountered in their daily lives. Others, however, like the author of a poem that follows the account just given, were quite certain that "the land does indeed possess feelings and so gave birth to the Lady of the Stalagmite, using the medium of the stone for her to become a spirit."[122]

The increased spread of the vision of a 'disenchanted' nature among the elite in the last centuries of the imperial age was thus both incomplete and not always clear-cut. If one reads through materials covering a long span of time, however, the evidence for this trend seems relatively persuasive. The most striking example known to me is the lives of virtuous women recorded in local gazetteers. For Song and Ming times, miracles associated with virtue are comparatively common. In accounts from the Qing they almost totally disappear. We will return to the complexities of this theme in chapter 12 on the interplay between virtue and the weather, and the multiplicity of different personal perspectives.

One way or another, nature sent messages. The line here between what we would classify as the 'natural' and the 'supernatural' was a fine one. Two short tales about Zhou Xin, who lived early in the fifteenth century, and was posthumously canonized as the City God, implicitly make this point:[123]

(1) He was appointed to be the provincial judge for Zhejiang. When he first reached the boundary of the province he saw swarms of gnats flying about his horse's head. He followed them to a thicket and there found the corpse of a man who had died a violent death. There were also a key and a small notebook recording transactions. "He was a cloth merchant," Xin declared. He took up the body and the other items. When he arrived at his post, he sent men into the markets, there to examine the lengths of cloth one by one. In all the cases where the cloth corresponded to that recorded in the notebook, he had the sellers detained, and found the robbers by means of interrogation. He then summoned the members of the family of the dead man and presented them with the cloth.

(2) Xin was sitting in his courtroom when a swirling gust of wind blew a leaf toward him. He marveled at this, and those in attendance on him said that the tree from which it came did not grow in the city. The only place that had

it was a temple a considerable distance away. "Have the monks of this temple then killed someone?" asked Xin. When he went there he found the corpse of a woman beneath the tree.

The first of these invokes only natural causes and Zhou's powers of observation and detection. But the second?

A belief in geomantic effects occasionally surfaces in the local histories. 'Geomancy' is the art or pseudo-science of manipulating the occult forces that are believed to run through a landscape, site, house, or even room. This is effected by altering the presence, position, alignment, or character of the objects in them, such as buildings, graves, and furnishings, in such a way that their impact on particular human lives and fortunes is altered. A Western partial parallel is the belief in the effects of ley-lines. Two comments made in the late-Ming gazetteer illustrate the theme:[124]

(1) Some time after 1573 people recklessly excavated a hole in the eastern wall of the prefectural capital, built a bridge, and altered the flow of the water in the moat. *In 1597 the prefecture did not have a single success in the imperial examinations.* In the winter of this year, Zheng Zhenxian, the county magistrate,[125] had the bridge demolished and the gap filled in. In 1600[126] *eight candidates were successful,* so that all at once we could be said to have been doing well.

(2) At that time[127] the school for Confucian scholars was located in an out-of-the-way spot. The 'aether–energies in the human and physical atmospheres' in the western part of the prefectural capital city [where it was presumably situated] were not concentrated, and so successes in the examinations for the second and third degrees were few and far between.[128]

An awareness of the Chinese sense of the intimate geomantic interconnections between what we would tend to think of as the material and the mental is what makes these two passages comprehensible.

Gentry representations

Our response to the landscape poetry of the middle and the late empire is altered by an awareness of the changes sketched in the preceding sections. The unremitting transformation of the natural world by generations of human intervention has left it no longer 'nature' but something else: a human–natural condominium. The lingering presence of local supernatural forces in the streams and mountains still gives them a magic; but in a tension with human activities. The remembered past conferred a resonance on particular localities, and a mournful but exalting psychological distance from the more prosaic present. Even under the later empire the remembrance of archaic times continued to haunt the landscape. Thus the Stateline Bridge that crossed the boundary between the preimperial states of Wu and Yue, once a battleground, inspired the Qing poet Mu Suiwu to write:[129]

> Scattered and bleak on either bank, the reed-tufts' heights are the same,
> As the sun's rays sink in the west, the wasteland weeds are a blur.
> As I cross the bridge in the wilds that once divided two states,
> Sorrowing still, in the wind from the north, the horses' cries can be heard.

The people of these two states, especially Yue, were known in the preimperial age for their ferocity in war. It is a curiosity of history that the populations who were their successors had the reputation in later times of being exceptionally lacking in military character. One biography of a local man engaged in organizing resistance to the so-called 'Japanese pirates' in the sixteenth century observed: "The men of Zhejiang are also soft and timid, being unaccustomed to fighting."[130]

The precarious, and not always successful, struggle of ordinary people to survive was in silent, ever-present, contrast with the momentary ease of the gentry writers and their partial emancipation from the world of necessity. Saying this is not to deny the sense of social obligation that often moved scholars and officials, but only to put their privileged position into context. Privilege brought its different pains: the stresses of official life, and the suave but merciless interpersonal warfare among the elite. These discomforts often underlie a yearning for escape into nature, either practical or metaphysical. Nature was a therapy for exposure to too much humanity. As Fan Yan wrote: "When one climbs to a high place, then public business is finished."[131] For, as Su Zai put it, more symbolically:[132]

> No cage-incarcerated bird forgets what it was to fly,
> The horse, though tethered, ever dreams that he is galloping wild.

There follows a mosaic of quotations that compose a picture of Jiaxing's countryside as seen through gentry and official eyes.

Here, to set the scene is a poem from the Yuan dynasty, "In a boat at Blackforest," by Sa Duci, a bureaucrat addicted to traveling through scenic places:[133]

> Wild duck, along the spring rills, are plump enough now to shoot,
> Hill partridge, in woods off the beaten track, chirp from the deep shade,
> Tourists, in their pleasure-craft, pass by in the third moon,
> Season when catkins dance on the willows, but apricot blossoms have
>   faded.

Forests, too, that rise to the clouds, and bamboos in repetitive rows,
While homesteads, then the shacks of monks, one after another pass by.
Though I hold a modest official post, my desire is still to go home,
But from where can I borrow the funds to buy a hill to retire to?

Sa's longing is for a *this-worldly* escape. "Going up with my friends to the Vāirōtchana Buddha Pavilion at the end of spring," written in Ming times by Xiang Yuanqi, a poet, calligrapher, and connoisseur of paintings,[134] is an evocation of the longing for a *spiritual* escape mediated through landscape:[135]

Climbing up to the sumptuous lookout kiosk, there spreads an unbroken
view;
We glance a thousand fathoms down, while unmoving mists glow like
cinnabar,
And, repeatedly, rich and varied scents greet us from different blooms,
Or, pure as a chiming stone, a sound — sometimes echoes across the
distance.

Round the city, its coiling moat-stream — looks like the belt on a garment;
Out on the sea, a mantle of sunshine turns all the islands to gold;
Our world-pity, stirred by this scene, has opened Lord Buddha's park;
Inspiration borrowed from spring blowing past, we talk of the Way a
moment.

The phrase 'Lord Buddha's park' refers to the park of the king of Śravasti in which legend has it that there stood the Jetavāna monastery, one of the favored resorts of Śākyamuni. The Chinese found a special inspiration in going up to a high point, and did this at certain times of the year, notably the ninth day of the ninth moon.

The second of the *Ten Songs on Jiaxing* by Shen Yaozhong, also in the Ming, mixes the real world and superfauna with no sense of incongruity:[136]

The transparent moat-stream winds its embrace round a bend in the city
wall.
What end do its whirling eddies serve, in their Five True Colors' beauty?
Wishing to peer with the magic Horn Torch into the depths of its waters,
But, fearing to startle the spirit beings, I remain irresolute.

The 'Five True Colors' of ancient times were blue-green, yellow-brown, red, white, and black, and regarded as primary as contrasted with intermediate. They were assigned to the Five Phases of Matter. The rhinoceros Horn Torch was a device said to have been lit by Wen Jiao, a general and official of the early fourth century CE, so he could see the uncanny denizens in the darkness of the Yangzi River.

In Ming and Qing times, these poems on local scenes—one could almost call them 'postcards in words'—seem often to incorporate a feeling for the economics, communications, hydraulics, and even the political power at work on a landscape. Shortly after the building of the Paceclouds Bridge in 1478, for example, the well-known Jiashan literary figure Zhou Ding wrote the following lines on it:[137]

> In the isolated hamlet that has now become a market,
> With two or three pavilions where wine is sold and quaffed,
> The bridge holds it all together, and stands in midstream adamant,
> While, on differing routes between the fields, the paths lead off aslant.
>
> Flowing through, unruffled, comes the broad sweep of the inlet,
> Where the Stone Well Embankment has stopped the deposited silt.
> Just as the sun is setting, the fishtail oar falls still,
> And looming high, when one looks west, rise the capital's walls in the
>   distance.

I have supplied the word 'fishtail' as this was the type of oar most commonly used. The person propelling the boat (in all likelihood not the poet) stood near the back, facing forward, and agitated the blade of the oar, whose long curving arm was held in a raised rowlock, in a back-and-forth feathering motion over the stern. This had an effect similar to that of a screw.

In the Qing dynasty many poets' sense of rural work became more and more deeply interfused with their aesthetic vision. Here, by way of illustration, are some lines by Cheng Ruiyue on "Anchoring at Wangjiang Creek":[138]

> The boat swings athwart the country inlet. The bright sands spread out level.
> Rising up through the cool, the jade-like moon makes the shadows more
>   sharply defined.
> The lantern reflects in the ripples; fireflies flit like random specks.
> Gulls and wild ducks on the opposite bank are soundless in nighttime
>   silence.
> People linger still to pluck the leaves in these numerous groves of
>   mulberries.
> Many acres of lakefields wait for the rain, before the plows score them
>   with furrows.

A 'lakefield' was a former lake that had been drained and turned into a rice-paddy. An awareness of labor—perhaps one should say more specifically, 'of other people's labor'—was now part of the appreciation of landscape. And the landscape itself was in large measure a human creation: dredged creeks, cultivated trees, diked and leveled fields.

On the edge

The life of the less fortunate was tough. Our evidence for this has of course been shaped by literary conventions, usually developed as a form of protest against inept or cruel official policies. Poems on poverty, on the suffering resulting from harsh weather, or excessive taxation, and on the sale of peasants' wives and children into whoredom and servitude, were in a sense genre pieces. Just as, in a different way, the verbal picture postcards were. But it was a repetition that also happened in fact. A cliché is not necessarily the less true for being familiar.

How then do we find a balance between texts that talk of horror and those that depict prosperity? The case will be made here that both are true. The first depicts extreme events. The second average events. In normal years peasants coped—indeed, even did moderately well at times—by means of ingenuity and extremely hard work. When things went wrong, though, there was virtually no longer any environmental resilience in the system. No wild foods, no forests in which to hunt or gather, no fish or other accessible resources not already put out of bounds by others' prior rights of private property. In addition to the bureaucratic buffer described earlier that was sometimes available there was also a useful if limited *economic* resilience in the system. This was the result of the increasingly well-developed marketing network. For all its effectiveness in shifting goods to where demand was most urgent, and hence sale the most likely to be profitable, it usually needed some stock of reserves to access it, both by buyers and sellers—credit, cash, collateral, or an inventory. In other words, most peasants and small traders were obliged to live 'on the edge'. A not inconsiderable number went over all the time. More in years of drought, flooding, or locusts.

"The Song of an Inspector of Fields" by Yuan Jie[139] belongs to a well-known genre of stories of misfortune: an encounter with an informant, who recounts his or her history to the poet in a retrospective panorama. This piece refers to Huating county, which was part of Xiuzhou (approximately Jiaxing) in the Song and part of the Yuan dynasty.[140] The 'Yellow Inlet' is the Huangpu, later famous as the river on which Shanghai was situated. The date of the drought is 1320. The reference to 'official fields' is a reminder that in this part of China, from late Song to well into the Ming dynasty, the state was the owner of large areas of farmland, where taxes were higher than elsewhere because they contained an added component of rent.

> An old gentleman made his appearance, like the onset of a disease,
> Wearing a shabby, tattered robe, and scrawny and thin as a devil.
> At daybreak he'd prop himself up, at the side of the principal street,
> Begging passers-by in piteous tones for rice or a handful of pennies.

At that time I'd received my commission — to leave for Jiangcheng in the
   south.
When I met with him unexpectedly, the sight at once made me feel sorry,
So, to give him five pints of my rice, I had my sack tipped upside down,
Then attempted to ask him the reason he was so afflicted with poverty.

After this the old man responded — to the question that I had given him:
"Li the Fifteenth is my name. My home's in the Eastern District.
Our family was poor. We'd no funds — to set ourselves up in business.
Five acres of official land was all we engaged in tilling.

"In the seventh year of the Yanyou reign, at the start of the third month,
We sold our clothes to buy a plow, and a hoe for cultivating.
Mornings we tilled, and evenings weeded. — Great bitterness we suffered
To pay back the private debts we owed, and the rent due to the
   government.

"Who *could* have foretold, in the sixth month, and the month following
   that,
Rain would be totally absent, with no movement in the tides?
If we'd had our wish for a single drop, even half a drop, to spatter
It would have been worth no less than the blood that reddened the farmers'
   eyes.

"The Yellow Inlet, once smoothly flowing, became like a ditch or gutter;
Peasants' families fought over water as though pearls were at stake in their
   struggle.
If several pumpings were tried in succession, the water would not be
   enough,
And overnight our paddy-fields turned — into sediments, and mud."

Catastrophe followed. The 'tribute grain' mentioned in the last verse but one
below was grain levied to be sent to the capital to provision the troops there
and meet other government needs.

"That year a difference in height determined good or bad luck.
Wasted lay all the upland fields, while those below grew grain.
County bureaucrats, blind to the fact that the higher fields were dried up,
Adjudged that fields at *both* levels should be treated just the same.

"Swift as flames to the countryside came down the claims for tax,
Coercing us to pay our dues before the other farmers.
Since we'd no desire to be first, they then worked off their anger
By treating every one of our fields as if it had had a full harvest.

"Their granaries opened in advance, as crops ripened in early fall,
But we, who'd to pay tax first, were too poverty-stricken to have it.
I had a son, then, named A-sun, and A-xi, who was my daughter.
They compelled me to sell her in marriage, to help meet the official
    exactions.

"A-sun I sold off to a family who transported the tribute grain.
I know of no place where, once again, he might be before my eyes.
It's sad, too, that A-xi, still not old enough even to be engaged,
Went off to the mountains near Huzhou, there to become a bride.

"Being this year, as it happens, more than seventy years old,
I have no food when hungry; nor have I clothes when cold.
I ask this way, then beg that, already beyond my last breath.
Before long, I shall make my way back — to the Yellow Springs of Death."

The Yellow Springs were the archaic Chinese underworld, where the shades of the dead lived, before the introduction of Buddhist and Daoist paradises and purgatories.

The point is not that the story this poem tells is heartbreaking, but that it is commonplace. There are too many poems about the need of the poor to sell their children in hard times for it to be possible to dismiss this as just a conventional literary exaggeration.[141]

The same theme is taken up in Yuan Huang's "Farmer's Song," probably written in the late sixteenth century.[142] The 'lily-like plants' he mentions were *Nymphoides peltata*, a waterweed that sometimes served as a famine food. In Ming times, 'serfs' were only meant to be in the service of officials, but this ban was often disregarded. The description of imperial favor as rich dew is an allusion to the *Scripture of Songs*.[143] The 'fallen leaves' are presumably lost children.

Outside the town in the springtime, where gray water runs in the river,
I pass by, under dull gray clouds, hearing tears in every doorway.
Each gate is chained shut in the daytime; smoke no longer plumes up from
    the kitchens,
And this way and that, in every valley, lie the skeletons as they have fallen.

In the year just passed, in the middle of summer, there were numerous
    rains and storms.
In place after place, the reed-thatched houses fell into the great whales'
    maws,
And it seemed as if the sky was floating, outside Suzhou's walls,
While lily-like plants and lotus-leaf buds are our 'grain' in the springtime
    shortage.

That family there had a girl, who was delicate in her beauty;
This family here had a son, whom they cherished like jade in importance;
But the seasons of Heaven and human doings were both of them in
    confusion.
The son now toils as a serf. Their daughter, they sold into whoredom.

Bondage violates human nature. So, too, does prostitution.
Deep runs the springtime hatred in the countless homes that are ruined.
Profound, and vast as the sea, is our present Dynasty's goodness,
But when will the favor of Its dew be moistening these woods?

In their grief for the fallen leaves, the countryfolk share their bitterness.
Their savings reduced to bits and pieces, they have trouble in making a
    living.
The plows are still not back on the job, although the rains have finished.
So they hack with hoes at the horse-fodder beans now clambering over
    their lintels.

Yuan then implies that the population has so diminished that "a cry or a foot-fall is as precious as gold." The looms are silent at night. He only hears owls hooting. His final lines warn the upper classes who are safely "lodged in the lofty heights," and "either folding their hands or drumming with their fingers," not to be indifferent. Reflect, he says, "what Azure Heaven might do to you."[144]

Joachim Radkau has referred to the image of China among geographers and environmental historians as "extremely contradictory." It has been both "a model and a horror story."[145] Both views have elements of truth. The one correction needed for the 'model' view is that most economic success was based on unrelentingly hard work, especially for women. Some time toward the end of the Yuan dynasty, or perhaps in the early Ming, Wang Mian wrote a poem on this theme. Later celebrated as a painter of plum trees, Wang came from a poor family. He had once run off to study rather than look after the cows with which his father had entrusted him. (It earned him a flogging.) One of his literary names was 'The Mountain Farmer Who Boils Stones'. He knew what he was talking about.

He begins by mentioning the women's torn skirts, bare feet, unkempt hair, and their "faces like the earth," and then goes on to note that:[146]

During the daytime they labor in the fields, following their husbands, and then, during the night, they spin hemp. They do not go to bed. The hemp they have spun is made into cloth which is used to meet that part of the official tax levied in cloth. The rice won by their toil in the fields goes into the official granaries. So long as payments to the officials have not been completed, they suffer from pent-up depression. Outside their doors they also hear people who have come to prompt them to pay private debts. Everyone borrows against pledges, and fresh grain may not be paid back in full even after ten years have passed. When an eldest son reaches five Chinese years of age,[147] they have to part with him, since his younger sister, aged three full years, cannot leave home in this way. When the community headman calls out the roster of names, he breaks up households, since two more persons will thus be added to the quota of official tax-grain due the next season.

Hemp's day was nearly over at this date, however. During the Ming dynasty there was a botanical revolution. Hemp, which produced a fabric much like linen, was largely replaced by cotton as a clothing fiber. Cotton was preferred because it was warmer, lighter, and better at absorbing moisture. It also grew about ten times as much fiber per hectare as hemp. The cotton plant's tolerance of the mildly salty conditions down the east coast of the area south of the mouth of the Yangzi gave rise to a seaside strip, from fifteen to sixty kilometers wide, where cotton growing was concentrated.[148] Although reliance on cotton does not seem to have been so extreme in Jiaxing as it was slightly further north, it probably gave rise to a similar dependence on the market network for the supply of food, and to the reduction in the need to maintain the irrigation system, since coastal cotton does not need substantial irrigation. When the late-Qing gazetteer speaks of the constant sound of looms in the prefecture,[149] unlike Wang Mian's poem, it is now largely referring to the weaving of cotton, and of course silk.

Two statistics bring home the underlying realities of life on the edge. Although they have to be presented in terms of numbers, their meaning is simple: life in Jiaxing was short, agriculture extremely productive. An interesting paradox.

The first figure gives the expectation of life at birth of women in Jiaxing. The expectation of life at birth can be thought of as the age that is the sum of the person–years lived by a particular group of a particular population (all born at one time), adjusted by the proportions surviving to each age. In other words, if we think in discrete and hence approximate terms, each component of this sum is, for each year of age from 1 up, the proportion still alive at that age. Graphically, one can represent this more precisely as the area under the curve of the life table that shows in continuous form the proportions of survivors at each age (taking the initial number at age 0 as 1). Two slightly different methods of calculating give slightly different results. The first method gives Jiaxing women 24.5 years, and the second method only 18.3 years.[150] The truth is probably nearer the higher value. But even this is low, and what is clear is that the women in Jiaxing in late-imperial times had a poor expectation of life at birth compared to those in the other two areas that will be studied in the following two chapters. It may be that we have here a proxy measure of the high stress under which they lived.

The second figure concerns the seed-to-yield ratios for rice, in other words the relationship between how much was sown and how much was harvested. This is one of several well-known measures of the productivity of agriculture.[151] For wheat in early modern Europe, for example, the average rarely exceeded 1:5.[152] In late-imperial Jiaxing, the seed-to-yield ratio for unhusked rice sown to unhusked rice reaped was, as a measure of volume, between 1:45 and 1:51 in good years for the better farmers.[153] For unhusked seeds to husked rice (the type that was eaten by most people), it was still between approximately 1:31 and 1:36. In other words, the productivity of cereal production per hectare was of a totally different order from that in Europe at the same time. This was due to a combination of factors, including the particular characteristics of the food plants concerned (rice rather than wheat and other dry-land grains), the natural conditions such as the mean annual temperature, the hours of sunshine, the soils and so on, and of course the farming technology.

Information on seed-to-yield ratios in China is fairly sparse. It is useful to translate the relevant passage from the Qing gazetteer in full. Note that I have intentionally mistranscribed *gé* as *he*, to avoid it being confused with *gè*, a different measure whose only difference is in the tone. The principal premodern Chinese capacity measures for grain came in multiples of 10: *he, sheng, dou,* and *shi,* in rising orders of magnitude. The exact modern equivalents are of no relevance in the present context. The *mou,* the usual measure of area, was about 0.07 hectare in Ming times, and 0.067 under the Qing. The *sheng,* the usual measure of capacity, was slightly more than 1 liter.

> [a] In general, for 1 *mou* one uses 7 or 8 *sheng* of seeds. [b] 6 *ke* make 1 *le*, and 8 *le* make 1 *ge*. [c] From 1 *mou* one harvests 360 *ge* of unhusked rice. [d] The best farmers in a good year can obtain 7 *he* of husked rice per *ge* [of unhusked], and 2 *shi* 5 *dou* per *mou*.[154]

(1) From [a] and [d] it is clear that 7 (or 8) *sheng* of unhusked rice seeds give 250 *sheng* (2.5 *shi*) of husked rice. The multiplier is 35.71 (or 31.25). (2) Note next that 250/360 is approximately 0.7 (more precisely, 0.694 . . .). This allows the conclusion via [d] that the *ge* was the equivalent for unhusked rice (and hence also, it would seem, for seeds) of the *sheng* for husked rice. (3) Hence, in volumetric terms, the multiplier for seeds (unhusked, needless to say) to unhusked rice was about 51 (or 45).

Slight uncertainties arise from the possible variation in the volume of seeds sown per *mou*, which can be either 7 or 8 *sheng*, and from the two possible ratios for husked to unhusked rice, which can be either 0.694 or 0.7. Table 5 displays the possible outcomes, using [*u*] for 'unhusked rice' and [*h*] for 'husked rice'.

Table 5 Seed-to-yield ratios for rice in late-imperial Jiaxing

	Seeds in	Grain out	Ratio	Units	Source
A.	7 *sheng* [*u*]	360 *ge* [*u*]	1:51.43	[*u*]/[*u*]	[a]+[c]
	7 *sheng* [*u*]	250 *sheng* [*h*]	1:35.71	[*u*]/[*h*]	[a]+[d]
	8 *sheng* [*u*]	360 *ge* [*u*]	1:45.00	[*u*]/[*u*]	[a]+[c]
	8 *sheng* [*u*]	250 *sheng* [*h*]	1:31.25	[*u*]/[*h*]	[a]+[d]
B.	4.858 *sheng* [*h*]	250 *sheng* [*b*]	1:51.46	[*h*]/[*h*]	250/360
	4.9 *sheng* [*h*]	250 *sheng* [*h*]	1:51.02	[*h*]/[*h*]	0.7
	5.552 *sheng* [*h*]	250 *sheng* [*h*]	1:45.03	[*h*]/[*h*]	250/360
	5.6 *sheng* [*h*]	250 *sheng* [*h*]	1:44.64	[*h*]/[*h*]	0.7

The point of section B is that it shows how much food-grain had to be foregone in order to sow enough seeds for a crop yielding a given quantity of food-grain.

The *ke* was a clump of 5 or 6 rice-plant seedlings,[155] in the condition in which it was ready for transplanting. As one *mou* was 0.07 hectare, it may be thought of as a square about 26.5 meters by 26.5 meters. One *mou*, we are told, held 6 times 8 times 360 *ke*, in other words 17,280 (or from 86,400 to 103,680 germinating seeds). The square root of 17,280 is close to 131. If 131 seedling-clumps are transplanted per 26.5 meters, this works out at about 5 per meter, or 20 centimeters apart. This seems reasonable. If farmers could have sustained a rate of 5 seedling-clumps a minute, it would have taken 6 people about 10 hours of work to transplant a *mou*.

These calculations show that, as regards farming, the population of Jiaxing rested on a productive system that was exceptionally effective even by early-modern European standards in seed-to-yield terms. There were two concomitants. First, keeping it going at the required level demanded very hard work. Second, any disruption by drought, flooding, pests, human diseases, or war, put the lives of an exceptionally large number of people at risk.

Economic pressure led to the partial degendering of farmwork. Hong Jinghao's "Peasants' song," written in Qing times shows how both men and women now regularly toiled in the fields. The 'well-sweeps' he refers to were bailing buckets mounted on one end of a long lever, with a counterbalancing weight on the other end. They were used for raising water. The 'lascivious worksongs' were the so-called 'mountain ditties',[156] and usually as much songs sung by workers as true chanties, though this is what seems to be referred to here. The 'rice-transplanting horses' were like miniature wooden boats with saddles on which the person doing the transplanting could sit astride, with his or her bare feet in the mud on either side. Throughout there is an emphasis on the economic need to endure discomfort—not only the mud and the insects, but also work in the hours of darkness—and on the prudence of keeping an eye on those who might be tempted to slack.[157]

> As the blossoms on plum trees open, the ears of the barley shine golden.
> In every village they take out their plows, to furrow the south-facing slopes.
> Confused, through the noise of the well-sweeps, drift lascivious worksongs'
>   notes.
> Tomorrow is good, the calendar tells them, for planting out rice-shoots to
>   grow.

> As the *women* insert them, fields are flecked green. In, at *men's* hands, water
>   trickles.
> *The lazy workers are put in front; some way further back, the diligent.*
> In their blue-green jackets and skirts, black pants, and tunics dyed with
>   indigo,
> They are unabashed, as each day breaks, if they splash themselves with silt.

> The moon sinks low, the roosters call, stars are few and far between.
> They make use of the cool, in dew-drenched clothes, to fossick out the
>   weeds.
> Trugs in their hands, or shouldering baskets, they straddle their rice-
>   planting 'steeds',
> And, vexed when their faces are battered at, slap dead the flies and
>   mosquitoes.

Qian Zai's "Transplanting Rice Seedlings" touches on the same themes.[158] Qian was a native of Jiaxing, from Xiushui county, and a holder of the highest examination degree. He served in the Board of Ritual during the second half of the eighteenth century, and was a poet, calligrapher, and painter. His biography describes him as having "slipped away across the fields to find his own independent style."[159] He wrote under the literary name of 'Stone Covered With Fallen Leaves'. His underlying message is the stoical endurance of pain by farmers.

> As she squats, the *wife* pulls up sprouts, from the bed that has served as
>   their nursery.
> Her *husband* stands in the field, pushing seedlings into the earth,

Her feet submerged in the water, she is sodden up to her skirts.
Under his rain-cape of straw, his shoulders are soaked as he works.

She has separated a thousand clumps, as neatly as one could wish.
He profits from this efficient help, and grips each between thumb and two
    fingers.
His back is stooped in a curve, but the square he has planted grows bigger,
Until, with perfect precision, the whole field of seedlings is filled.

In rectangular intersections — spread out a chessboard of verdure,
Densely textured and seamless, like the robes of the Buddhist clergy,
Multiple needle-like points are emerging, out of the flooded surface,
But the scars of their scratches still endure, upon the hands of the woman.

Mutual encouragement in adversity was also a feature of rural life:[160]

> Before and after the fifth of the fifth moon, when the transplanting of the
> rice seedlings is finished, people contribute money for a feast in honor of
> the God of Farmers. There is unstrained wine in earthenware jars, and those
> participating shout in drunken fashion *and mutually encourage each other to
> endure the bitter work.* It is called the 'Green Sprouts Gathering'.

One suspects—there is no proof one way or the other—that this was a festivity
for men only.

Why, then, was farm labor so demanding, both of wary attentiveness and of
hard grind? One reason was that a shortage of suitable land had pushed
premodern technology close to its limits. This made its regular performance at
the desired high level always somewhat problematic. Fine adjustments of
particular activities to time, and of varieties of crop to particular locations,
were critical. An example of the first of these is the application of supplementary fertilizer, that is, fertilizer applied to the plant while it is growing, not just
to the soil beforehand: timing and dosage are of the essence. The second was
most commonly relevant to differences in soil composition. Both points are
mentioned in the following description of Pinghu. The three awkward word-
doublets at the start reflect a real ambiguity in the Chinese terms.[161]

> Heaven–Weather has only one intrinsic energy–substance. Within a
> distance of fifty kilometers, the intrinsic energy–substance of the Earth–Soil
> will have variations. In our area, the fields are suitable for yellow rice. Both
> early-ripening and late-ripening yellow rice will yield harvests. Of the white
> rices, *only* early glutinous rice will yield a crop. If nonglutinous white rice
> meets with a flood, it dies. From north of Blackton and to west of Flow-
> market[162] the situation is different. Broadly speaking, this is because the soil

changes. As to techniques of plowing and sowing, *a rapid response to seasonal fluctuations is essential.* In addition to this, the work requires supplementary fertilizing, but *even a difference of a few days in timing will cause immense dissimilarities in harvest yields.* This is the difference between responding correctly and incorrectly to seasonal requirements.

Cautionary tales were told about timing. For example:[163]

> If farmers ever neglect to perform some task, or miss the right seasonal moment, it often happens that from some such small cause great harm results. On 1 July 1640, a flood drowned the fields. Those who had done their planting on or before 30 June had no disaster when the waters went down. Those who had planted on or after 1 July had a total write-off.

Sometimes these warnings were in the nature of fables, but the points they make are still valid. "There once was a man who did not have in readiness a straw rain-cape and a conical bamboo-leaf hat, so he could not plant his fields in the rain, which resulted in his family suffering from a lack of food." As the saying had it,

> For not spending ten cents,
> A family's wrecked.

More exactly, if more prosaically, "On account of a tenth of an ounce of silver, hunger can overturn an entire family."[164]

A second reason was the *time-intensification* of farmwork in the late-imperial age. Wheat and barley had been grown as winter crops in alternation with rice since Song times, but this was now done much more extensively, and they were joined by broad beans, peas, and colza.[165] These subsidiary crops, of which there were in fact far more numerous than the principal ones listed here,[166] were collectively called 'spring flowers'. There was a popular saying that if they did well that would provide enough for half a year.[167] Jiaxing seems to have been the focal point of this development, around the beginning of the seventeenth century, and the practice soon spread up the Yangzi valley.[168]

The passage on growing wheat and colza in *Mr Shen's Manual for Farmers*, a handbook current in the early seventeenth century, shows how concerned peasants had become with time as well as correct quantities:[169]

> Opening up the ridges for wheat: It is best for the fields [where rice has just been grown] to be dry. If they are soggy, it is necessary to open them up [by turning over the soil], *and to wait* until the backs of the ridges have dried out before putting in the seeds. *If the time for doing this has almost passed,* then steep the seeds [in water, and perhaps nutrients] in advance, so they

produce sprouts, *and it is possible to wait* until the ridges have dried out. It is impermissible to stamp down a firm area that is still surrounded by damp areas, as the colza and wheat will not be able to grow stalks, and are bound to wither when spring comes, or, even if they do not die, will not flourish for long.

When one is planting wheat, the covered reservoir [for liquid manure] must be full, and the distribution of the seeds must be uniform. *This work must not be skimped*; but one tells the women and the young serving-lads to take life easily. For wheat, one waters it [with liquid manure] once at the time of planting, and once again in the spring. If one puts on too much fertilizer, there will, on the contrary, be no harvest. . . . *If one sows the wheat seeds in advance* in the first ten days of the eighth moon, *one waits until winter* to prepare the fields to which to transplant them. Each transplanting clump contains five to six stalks. One applies liquid manure to them twice, as is the standard practice, and also banks them up with cattle manure, covering this over [with mud] shoveled out of the [adjacent small] ditch, after which the stalks are strong and the wheat heavy, yielding a doubled harvest.

Colza should be given twice as much liquid manure as wheat, and perhaps also household garbage or cattle manure. One digs mud from the adjacent ditch and once again applies liquid manure to force the blossoms.

The injunction that "one tells the women and the young serving-lads to take life easily,"[170] is in some ways more expressive of the pressure that everyone was under than the direct descriptions of unremitting toil.

The time-intensity of rearing silkworms is also often mentioned. As noted earlier, during the month or so, starting around the time of the spring festival, when the worms were feeding, both men and women neglected their toilette, and if the worms did not mount their trestles to turn into moths, "whole families would cry." If the silk harvest failed, the parents might have to sell their children.[171] Men would come home, even from far away, to assist with the collection of the essential mulberry leaves. Women would return, even if they had been visiting their parents, and "day and night they would be nervously preoccupied with the business of their cocoons."[172]

Sources both of fertilizers and of pasturage were also under pressure. It is not possible to date the following exactly, but it is probably from the Qing:[173]

Whether one is planting wet-land fields or dry-land fields, *supplementary fertilizer* is important. *Human manure* has a beneficial power, and *cattle manure* has a long-lasting effect. One should not use one and neglect to use the other. Making a contract with city residents to purchase their excrement is of fundamental importance.[174] Recently, however, the price of excrement has become dear. The cost of human labor is high, and fetching it from the city oneself wastes energy. Thieving is widespread. If it is not possible to rely entirely on such a contract for excrement, then *rearing sheep or pigs* is a convenient supplement. . . . For the food that a sheep eats in a year one obtains a sufficiency of wool and lambs, while the expenditure is merely the provision of grass [as fodder]. Without any effort one obtains a large quantity of supplementary fertilizer . . . . For sheep though, if one has to hire someone to chop the hay, then this can really waste one's reserves to provide this person's rations during the slack season in winter and spring. . . . These days sheep can eat nothing but withered leaves and dry grass. . . . Cattle manure is best applied to dry-land fields, and pig's manure to wet-land fields. . . . To purchase human excrement one has to go to Hangzhou. It is not possible to buy full loads [from the privies] along the levees.

The combination of arable farming and stock rearing in Jiaxing thus developed in part as a response to a shortage of fertilizers. In some areas of the prefecture at least, oxen were already present because they were used for plowing.[175] Pigs were of course scavengers and lived mostly off scraps. The sheep, though, were probably reared in a restricted area as they had to be hand-fed, since there was often no longer the space for them to graze.

Cotton had both positive and negative features from the point of view of the cultivator. Produced continuously in the same place, it drained the fertility away from the soil, so rotations were desirable. Cotton harvests were also apt to be highly variable. Against this, it required less water than did rice, and so reduced the labor needed for irrigation and for maintaining water-control systems. Jiaxing, as we have noted, was in fact less a producer of the raw material than a processor, developing a preindustrial industrialism of a kind found in Western Europe at much the same period, notably in parts of the Netherlands. This was emphasized by the late-Qing prefectural gazetteer in the case of Haiyan county:[176]

The land here produces very little raw cotton. Spinning it into yarn, however, and weaving it into cloth, are regular businesses to which families and households are accustomed. This is so not only in the rural villages but also in the county capital. Traveling merchants constantly come from the next-door prefectures to sell raw cotton, and set up their shops in lines on our land. The poor folk go to the market at the break of day with what they have spun or woven, exchange it for raw cotton, and return home. . . . They burn oil lamps to work in the hours of darkness. *Men and women sometimes do not sleep the whole night through.* When farming families have a harvest, once they have used it to pay off their obligations to the state, their dwellings are bare at the end of the year, so they rely entirely on this industry for their clothing and food.

There is no rule that determines that a preindustrial industrialism like this will necessarily turn into the real thing one day, even with a market system finely enough meshed, as this one was, to bypass any need for a system of putting-out. What we are seeing, though, is the beginning of something with which full-scale industrialization has made us more familiar: Haiyan was living in what was partly, so to speak, an 'invisible environment', that is, one many of whose determining conditions were no longer part of daily experience, or subject to direct observation, but mostly far away and linked to it only through a market mechanism and second-hand information.

The prefecture's population crashed to less than half its mid-nineteenth-century total as the result of the Taiping rebellion just after the midpoint of the nineteenth century.[177] A vivid reminder of the fragility of growth curves to more or less aleatoric fluctuations in political conditions. Nonetheless the people of Jiaxing had come a long way since wild rice once grew in the undiked wetlands of the delta. They had shown extraordinary ingenuity, and extraordinary powers of resilience and survival. But the final, sober, verdict on the value of this multimillennial journey remains ambiguous.

8

Chinese Colonialism: Guizhou and the Miao

Guizhou province was another world. Guiyang, the capital prefecture, perched at 1250 meters atop the headwaters of four river basins.[1] Its peach trees and plum trees were famous for a "beauty and fragrance that dazzled the eyes" when in blossom, and its climate was without extremes of hot or cold.[2] Around it spread a subtropical labyrinth of mountains and plunging river valleys. Snakes, monkeys, tigers, deer, and many other animals and birds flourished in its forests. Malaria lay in wait in some places, though not in others. Metallic ores like cinnabar, from which quicksilver is extracted, lured in Chinese merchants and entrepreneurs, as did its timber, which was floated out down its rivers.

Here was the ancient home of the Miao people, though not their original home. Miao songs, orally transmitted, suggest that they once lived along the eastern seaboard, but at some point made a long and difficult trek westward,[3] probably gradually driving back other tribes such as the Lolo as they moved. The songs refer to excessive population density as the problem that made them leave, but it is more likely to have been Chinese pressure. In the course of this journey they seem to have mastered the art of making axes to cut down trees, as well as other tools, all of this technical progress, including constructing boats and wooden houses, being remembered with delight in the chanted question-and-answer verses.[4]

In Guizhou, some of the Miao allied themselves with the incoming Chinese and became partially culturally assimilated; some of them were even led by the descendants of Chinese, often imperial appointees to local chieftaincies, who had 'gone native'. Others fought over many centuries for their liberty. Resistance seems to have started in Ming times, when a measure of direct Chinese government control was established and Han in-migration increased.[5] Their struggle for liberty was finally defeated only in the early 1870s.[6]

Although the Miao had both cannons and muskets by Qing times, possibly first acquired from the defeated remnants of Wu Sangui's anti-Manchu forces in the 1680s, imperial superiority in firearms probably played a part in keeping them in check.[7] Since the Miao "swarmed everywhere in the mountain valleys, skulking off in all directions into the jungle whenever they were attacked, only to regroup again a moment later,"[8] the government armies sought to destroy them by stripping them of their cover. They burned the Miao settlements, sometimes by shooting 'fire-arrows' at them,[9] and "cut down the mountain trees to open roads to put direct pressure on their forts."[10] To speed military transport along the rivers they "dredged the shallows and shoals, cleared away underwater rocks, cut down the great forests, and bored through the uncanny rocks."[11] The Miao protected themselves by felling huge trees to block the mountain roads, and building palisades with gaps to fire through.[12] Environmental conditions shaped the nature of warfare, and warfare reshaped the environment.

The social tensions caused by the Chinese conquest and occupation, which was always to some degree under threat, fostered the conditions for criminal activities. Thus in the early eighteenth century one group of Miao "from time to time would emerge to seize both Chinese and non-Chinese boys and girls, and sell them to Chinese renegades for resale in other provinces, which earned them huge profits."[13] The semi-assimilated Miao may have suffered the most, being caught between the two main warring forces:[14]

When there is no military business, they are conscripted for transport haulage. When there are military activities, they are driven in advance as guides. The soldiers and the commoner–civilians[15] treat them like slaves. The unassimilated Miao hate them like cruel foes. When the official forces triumph, the unassimilated Miao find an opening to slaughter the semi-assimilated Miao in order to give vent to their fury. When the unassimilated Miao triumph, the official troops move around at random butchering the semi-assimilated, so as to be able to make unjustified claims for military achievements.

On one occasion, when semi-assimilated Miao responded to attempts to conciliate them, the official troops killed the men and seized and sold their wives and daughters for profit. When news of this atrocity reached other Miao men, they "felt in their hearts that they were certain to die, and many of them killed their wives and daughters with their own hands" so as to steel themselves to resist to the end.[16] Whether at war or at peace, or in a state somewhere in between, it was a colonial territory where, as the late-nineteenth-century gazetteer noted, "since half the Miao do not understand our language or script, it is hard to unify attitudes and customs."[17] Besides the endemic warfare, there was continual danger from ordinary criminals and socially marginal groups of in-migrants, as well as the greedy and ill-disciplined troops of the government armies.

The region was beautiful, but in its own strange and frightening way. It was a place of economic profit for well-organized and wealthy outsiders, but one where the locals were dispossessed of their geographical inheritance. It was a refuge for Chinese adventurers, refugees, and malcontents from other provinces, but at times could terrify even them—climatically, medically, and militarily. For the Han people—officials, soldiers, merchants, and settlers— conquering it, and then bringing it under conceptual, environmental, economic, and administrative control was a difficult enterprise that was far from complete by the beginning of modern times.

Guizhou was Chinese colonialism in action. It may provide an approximate pattern for what happened in earlier ages in other regions when Han Chinese expansion was just beginning. The ideological justification was a civilizing mission, but administrators could be frank about the realities. Here is part of the prefect's preface to the 1850 Guiyang gazetteer.[18] It should be noted that he passes over in silence the long centuries in the first and early second millennia CE during which the region was ruled by independent, or semi-independent, states like Nanzhao and its successor Dali.

At the time of the transition from the Qin to the Han dynasty, the commandery[19] of Zangge had already been established in what is today Guizhou. The frontier was opened by Zhuang Qiao [a general from the state of Chu (in the Center), who set himself up as an independent ruler when faced with the appearance of the Qin empire late in the third century BCE]. When Tang Meng was sent [in the second century BCE] on his mission [to Nanyue in the Far South], the area forthwith fell under imperial jurisdiction, but it was only controlled on a light rein.

Coming down to the Mongol-Yuan and the Ming dynasties [from the thirteenth to the seventeenth centuries], there were innumerable battles before it was eventually subdued. Renewed revolts followed, and it came close to being abandoned. Such is the difficulty of controlling the imperial stronghold! In general it is only necessary to have feelings of scorn and indifference and these people will in their turn fearlessly and recklessly resist us.

At the present day registered households have been established everywhere in the poisonous gorges and the malaria-ridden mountain ranges. The natives, who clothe themselves with grasses, and talk with what sounds to us like the speech of birds, have all been enrolled in the official population registers. We have driven away the wolves and foxes, and opened up the rocky mountains and the weedy wastes for farming. Every year a harvest of grain is sickled and reaped, and no one dares to be a laggard in performing labor-services for the state.

The general explanation for this is the far-reaching range of the civilizing influence that treats strangers kindly. Men of talent have tacitly internalized the Court's intention of arousing people to exert themselves. Not wishing to be excluded, they collaborate with each other in making clear by explanation both moral principles and practical skills, and they hasten to pursue the 'carpenter's set-square and the plumb-line' of rectitude in conduct.

In 1854, not long after these complacent words were written, the last great uprising of the Miao broke out and was not put down for almost twenty years.

Two preliminary comments on this preface may be useful:

First, population. The earliest date for which approximately credible figures for Guiyang prefecture are available is "at the transition from the Qianlong to the Jiaqing reign," that is around 1800. At this time there were on the order of 152,000 households. The draft gazetteer prepared some time later but before 1850, recorded 173,000 households and about 904,000 individuals, a ratio of about 5.2 persons per household.[20] The prefect's comment about increased enrolment in the registers over time indicates that the difficulty in distinguishing between actual growth and statistical growth would make any estimate of population increase in the centuries or decades prior to this last date unreliable.

Second, the perpetual unrest. The crucial administrative crisis in this respect was the effort started by the Yongzheng Emperor in the 1720s and early 1730s to abolish or reduce the powers of the internally autonomous local chieftaincies through which most of the non-Chinese population had hitherto been governed by a system of indirect rule.[21] He expressed his view of the general situation in a decree issued in 1724 to the governors-general and governors of eight provinces:[22]

We have heard that few of the local chieftaincies in various places acknowledge the discipline of law. The annual levies on the local people under their jurisdiction are not merely twice to five times as much as the burden of the regular taxes, but may even go as far as the seizure of people's cattle and horses, the kidnapping of people's sons and daughters, and the butchering of people as they feel inclined. . . . The cause of the local chieftaincies daring to act in this depraved manner is, however, always Chinese renegades, who have either taken refuge with them to escape punishment on account of some affair or breach of the law, or who have piled one evil deed on top of another, relying on the power of the local chieftaincies to act outrageously.

In a decree the following year to senior officials engaged in suppressing unrest, the emperor described some of the ugly events reported to have been going on:[23]

> We have heard that the Miao people in Guizhou province are the most lawless. In the third and fourth lunar months last year, they dared to assemble like ants and loot the market towns. By the eighth lunar month, the provincial governor and commander-in-chief had mobilized two thousand soldiers who were given the task of advancing to exterminate the miscreants. In the ninth lunar month their travels brought them to the department of Dingfan in Guiyang prefecture. Here the soldiers forcibly purchased the goods of the commoner–civilians and created such an uproar that the market went on strike. That evening they reached Gulan, where fires did not stop all night. They further burnt five encampments of assimilated Miao tribespeople, so causing the Chinese commoner–civilians to join with the Miao in a joint defense during which they shot at and wounded the government soldiers.

Intermittent local warfare with multiple causes smoldered constantly, flaring up from time to time into major uprisings. During the Qing, the four main conflagrations occurred during the 1690s, 1730s (prompted by resistance to Yongzheng's reforms), 1790s, and 1854–73.[24]

Every document about Guiyang has to be understood against this background, no matter whether it is a decree, a preface, or a poem.

The Miao

What did this world look like from the non-Chinese side? There are only a handful of sources accessible at present that shed light on this, but an anthology of antiphonal wedding songs in the Miao language from the southeast of Guizhou gives us some vivid if unsystematic insights into their view of the environment in which they lived. These songs were collected in the last twenty or thirty years, in part because they were dying out. It is hard to know how far they have changed since late-imperial times, and to what extent they have been edited and possibly expurgated. The selection of translations that follow are based on the Chinese-language word-for-word versions of the Miao transcriptions.[25]

Here, to begin with, is a familiar storm:[26]

> Lightning flickering in the heavens
> Rumbles with the voice of thunder,

> Waters in the rivers swelling,
> Rills running off the hills and summits.

But in the hot summer weather "one takes off one's clothes as a snake sheds its skin, or the water scorpion its shell."[27] One is, though self-consciously, an animal too. Not a civilized Han sentiment.

Everything has a cause:[28]

> If there is a child, then there must have been a mother.
> If a river, then a trickling — from a cliff top above.

But, both to us and the Chinese, these causes could be strange. For the Miao, all living creatures, including deities and animals, were the outcome of *mixed marriages* made in mythical antiquity, and hence *kin*. That is why marriages were so important. Even rocks sought matrimony:[29]

> If these rocks do not get married,
> Then these rocks will all get angry!
> Necks swelling in rage to monstrous size,
> These rocks will swallow up our wives,
> Swallow each one of our affines!

Ordinary wildlife could be observed in straightforward fashion:[30]

> Yellow and gray, the sleeping locusts
> Upon the hillside's grassy slopes.

Or imagined in terms of marriage mythology:[31]

> The monkey family's seeing off the new bride's relatives
> To where the mountain's forest trees provide them all with shelter.
> Ah, how verdant are that mountain forest's depths!

Such woods are, more often than not, present in the actual or mental background, though at times only for rhetorical purposes, as in the following:[32]

> Thrusting their way through the villages, they go hunting for worthy
>   persons,
> Entering into the forest, it's dry firewood they are in search of.
> But even if they get their hands on a single half-dried stick,
> There's nowhere they encounter human beings of moral worth,
> For all that they meet up with a couple who *are* quick-witted.

Dry wood burns better than wet, but Guizhou is a rainy area. 'Looking for dry wood' was a common Miao way of symbolizing something difficult.

An agricultural landscape is, however, the one in which most people live, at least by this late period:[33]

Having passed the sinuous ditches that bring water to the paddies,
Channels for irrigation which wind this way, then wind that,
At last they make it to the place where the mighty bridge is standing.

Almost certainly, one suspects, not a bridge built by the Miao themselves. The folk songs have already incorporated the strange presence and constructions of the outsiders.

Further on, we are given some standard popular wisdom:[34]

A village's watercourse fully flowing
Means its harvests will be golden.
But, but little current in its river
Betokens harvests without fruition.

Stray phrases suggest that fishing and trapping could put pressure on resources as population swelled:[35]

Eight hundred homesteads in one hamlet:
Along one stream, eight hundred crab traps.

The traps were woven of bamboo and could also be made for catching fish. But the song may just be exulting in the richness of numbers: human and crustacean. And the fascination of one-to-one correspondences.

Nature was both metaphor and reality. In one song a father-in-law and mother-in-law, seeing silver piling up in the pan of the steelyard used to weigh it, are described as struggling over the money, tugging each other's hair, and their

Foreheads colliding, face to face,
Like sparrows stuck in sticky paste. [36]

In another, certain individuals are said to

Scoop up the tube-like webs of spiders,
As bait on hooks for fish on lines.[37]

A number of ground spiders do have sleeve-like webs of this sort.

Wild plants were gathered. Like the dry firewood mentioned above, they also served as parallels evoking aspects of human life. So one song poses the question: will the go-between

Discover an elder brother who can act as his sister's companion,
Or find wild, pungent, pepper as a side-dish for the garlic?[38]

Tasty spice, if you can get it.

The wild animals most commonly mentioned are small: wildcats, monkeys (eating the wild fruit), rats, water rats, and otters. Frogs are alluded to—as food. The references to tigers are all to antiquity, though they existed here in late-imperial times. There is also a poem about the search for marriage partners by the rhinoceroses, but this is wholly in mythical mode.

The dominant impression is of a society engaged in farming, both in fields and in hedged vegetable gardens, and in rearing stock—cattle, horses, mules, pigs, chickens, ducks, and geese—as well as domestic cats and dogs. But with a sense still alive of living closer to a wilder nature than the Chinese did.

The songs open with a ritual question. In the distant past, when this farming society was being created,

> Who was it sowed the cereal crops after opening up the land,
> And killed the ox to seal the bonds that constitute a marriage?[39]

The answer is two fabled ancestors of the Miao. Farming is linked to the emergence of a human society:[40]

> Deep lay the darkness on the sky
> And darkness on the earth below.
> There was thunder, there was lightning.
> Water from the floods rose high.
>
> Transforming it by weeding, hoeing,
> They cut the channels broad and wide,
> Built there a village, good and fine,
> Sending the waters downward flowing,
> A place where kinsmen could reside
> And affines too be domiciled.

Stubble was burnt to enrich the soil:[41]

> Land gains its fertility by feeding on the fires.
> As ducks grow plump by devouring husks of rice.

Acreage was a measure of wealth. Rainbow, acting as matchmaker for Dragon, tells the father of the prospective bride that the groom is exceedingly well-to-do:[42]

> A hundred thousand poles' extent is *his* family's property,
> And nine thousand hamlets in *one* single spot.

Simple hydraulic installations are constantly mentioned:[43]

In the deep, dammed-up, pool are thousand-year-old fish.

Water buffalo and ordinary cattle furnish the labor-power:[44]

> Off to harrowing the fields goes the gray water buffalo.
> It's by plowing up these clods that our senior folk are nourished.

And later:

> In the seventh lunar month, when the season's getting hot,
> The buffaloes will slosh about, deep in mud-filled wallows.[45]

Finally, the songs speak of a commercialized society, with markets in its settlements.[46] The Miao cast their own iron farm tools,[47] made boats,[48] and wove cloth.[49] The ridgebeams of their houses "curled up like a horse's saddle."[50] They had temples to local divinities,[51] and were familiar with law courts that used written plaints, one would guess in Chinese.[52] They also had their own system of symbolic recording, at least for marriage contracts, which were incised on wood. The description of one such contract praises its graphic precision, and speaking of what may be some sort of indigenous written characters says they were

> Either splayed apart, like a puppy's paws,
> Or curling, like a wether's horns.[53]

Some of these features of society, especially the familiarity with law courts, must have been due to Chinese rule and influence over the centuries, though it is unclear for each particular aspect how much. The core matter of the songs is likely to be very old, but more recent developments were easily embedded in them.

Miao sensory responses to nature were unusually empathetic. Lines such as "The soft murmuring of the countless leaves"[54] are evidence of this, but more distinctive are moments of wry empathy with other creatures. In the lines that follow, Xang is the person who is the main subject of the song. Looking for a wife, he is carrying a present:[55]

> Here is a flock of gray-hued drakes
> Standing along the paddy-field's bank.
> They watch Xang come to discuss engagement,
> With another drake dangling down from his back.

The comfortable living observing the uncomfortable and doomed.

It must be admitted that in many of these songs the sense is obscure. The quotations given above have not adequately conveyed the strangeness, from our perspective, of the Miao's conceptual world. But it should be clear that to think of them simply as 'barbarians' because they were not fully assimilated into the Chinese way of life is a misunderstanding based on the often less than generous Han perceptions. Equally it is evident that their simpler worldview could not forever resist the complex power of Chinese culture.

Warfare and development

Warfare was the driving force of the development of the southwestern frontier, and military success the prerequisite for full-scale economic and of course administrative penetration. There was no way in the Southwest of moving from conflict to a more or less stable peace based on the agreed fictions of 'tributary status' such as eventually proved possible with well-organized governments in Korea and Vietnam, which were also of course capable of mounting effective military resistance. Although the Song had had good relations with the highly sinized Nanzhao in Yunnan, there was no stable political structure here in late-imperial times with which the Chinese empire could establish an enduring and dependable understanding.

Nor could the area just be left in a condition of benign neglect. Frontier fighting between the Chinese and the Miao, Yao, Zhuang, and other tribesmen created what was, from the Chinese point of view, a perpetual problem of security. The main approach adopted under the middle empire was to offer imperial recognition to hereditary local chieftains, thus strengthening their positions against local rivals, in return for the acknowledgment by these chieftains of Chinese sovereignty and, often, the provision of tribute. This mostly continued on into the later empire, but with the introduction of a varying number of regular bureaucrats. Some of the old local families had however held positions of dominance in their own bailiwicks under varying titles for many centuries. Thus the forebears of Yang Yinglong, the pacification officer in charge of Bozhou on the border of Sichuan province with Guizhou, who rose in revolt in 1589, had held official positions here during the late Tang, the Song, and the Mongol dynasties, as well as under the Ming.

One of the best examples of the interaction between warfare and the environment is provided by the crushing of the rising of the Yao tribesmen of Great Vine Gorge in the later fifteenth century. This area is immediately south of Guizhou province, some thirty kilometers north of Guiping in Guangxi province. Though not identical in environment with southern Guizhou, having, for example, more persistent malaria, it is close enough to be a useful guide. The story below is taken from the unofficial compilation made by the Qing official Gu Yingtai in 1658, *The Main Themes and Details of Ming History*

Recounted. The perspective and the implicit evaluations are those of early Manchu times.[56]

> Countless mountains rise up in the region of Xunzhou[57] in Guangxi, winding this way and that. The Xun River runs through the middle. . . . The most evilly perilous place in the mountains flanking this river, and forming a lofty canyon, is the Great Vine Gorge. The reason for this name is that a single vine once grew across the gorge like a footbridge [and was used by the Yao for this purpose].
>
> Great Vine Gorge is the highest point in the region. If one climbs the mountains above it, every detail for more than a hundred kilometers round about lies spread before one's eyes. The gathering and dispersal of armies, and their movements, can all be observed. The tribesmen used it as their secret command post. . . .
>
> The Li mountains[58] lie within the Fu River of the Vine Gorge. These are twice as dangerous as the Vine Gorge. . . . Within the bend of the river are gloomy peaks, secluded valleys, multistepped cliffs, and walls of sheer rock. Those who venture in have to hold on and pull with their hands as they shift their foothold, changing direction with almost every step. If they lose their footing, their bodies plunge several hundreds of fathoms down. This is where the Yao people live . . . and also the Zhuang, skilled at applying poison to the arrows of their crossbows. Anyone struck by one of these dies there and then.

Gu goes on to describe the rising in 1450–6 of the Yao chieftain Big Dog Hou, whose forces "attacked and ruined prefectures and counties, appearing and then disappearing again among the mountains and valleys." By 1457–64, offering rewards for his capture had proved useless, and the president of the Ministry of War, Wang Hong, observed that dealing with Big Dog could be "compared to dealing with a spoiled child: the more indulgence was shown to him, the more he would howl. If he were not flogged until the blood flowed, he would not stop howling." In 1465 Han Yong led a suppression campaign aiming directly at the rebels' headquarters above Great Vine Gorge. After defeating some Miao 'bandits', and instilling fear into his own forces by ordering the beheading of four officers who had failed to observe discipline, he then used 160,000 soldiers drawn from local sources to destroy the outlying defenses. They took 1,200 prisoners alive and cut off more than 7,300 heads.

When he conferred with the local elders about how to proceed next they are said to have offered this advice:

> Great Vine Gorge is a natural fortress, with multiple peaks and dense thickets of bamboo. It is afflicted by malaria in spring, summer, and fall. We have grown up in this land, but even we have not been able to grasp its

essential features fully. What is more, the bandits have heard of the arrival of your great army, and have strengthened their preparations. The best plan for you would be to surround them by installing military colonists, who can both fight and mount guard over them. Thus the bandits will automatically perish without your meeting them in battle.

The elders were understandably anxious to avoid the carnage and destruction of all-out war in their homeland.

Han Yong disagreed. The terrain was too confused, and its area too extensive, for an effective blockade. He also had a poor opinion of the motivation of military colonists. He therefore ordered the passes out of the mountains to be blocked and launched an attack from all sides:

Having learned that the troops were coming, the 'bandits' put their womenfolk into encampments on the cliffs, . . . and set up palisades in the southern part of the Gorge area, sturdy and compactly built. They rolled tree trunks and boulders downhill, and their spears and poisoned arrows fell like drops of water. The government forces climbed the mountain, attacking uphill. . . . The commanders and subordinate officers advanced in file, using such devices as circular shields, climbing irons,[59] and alpenstocks,[60] all of them fighting to the death. . . . Han Yong ordered that the vegetation be set on fire. The smoke and flames from the fierce conflagration blotted out the light of the sun. Darkness came in the daytime, and the 'bandits' were scattered far and wide.

Numerous Yao were captured and the "goods accumulated in their houses were stained red with blood." Han had his forces pursue those who had gone to protect their women. To do this his men "cut down the trees on the mountains and drove roads through them." This destruction of the habitat was eco-war. Gu describes the woods and bamboo thickets on this second mountain as "hatefully dense, leaving no place for a human being." Han Yong enticed the Yao into making a sortie, and then mowed them down with cannon, which must have taken an immense effort to bring up the slopes. After "scaling trees and clambering up vines, . . . like gibbons chinning themselves or ants sticking to a surface," the imperial troops "burnt the palisades by shooting fire-arrows at them." This last term can also refer to small rockets. More than three thousand Yao heads were chopped off, after which Han had a patch of rock rubbed smooth and the year and the month of his victory inscribed on it. Last of all he had severed the huge vine that spanned the gorge, serving the Yao as a bridge on which they were said to have crossed "like ants," and renamed the place 'Cut Vine Gorge'.

The effects of this barbaric civilizing mission lasted somewhat more than twenty years. The reason for this was that Han Yong could suggest no plan for stabilizing the region other than a rejigging of the familiar quasi-feudalism. In practice, allocating fiefs to his subordinate officers. They were soon taking bribes from the 'bandits'. More generally,

> The 'bandits' ... blocked the river, and waylaid and robbed travelers. Censor-in-Chief Chen Jin declared that the tribesmen were only profiting from local trade, and made a pact with them: when merchant vessels entered the Gorge, they would give the bandits 'fish and salt' in an amount calculated according to the size of the boat. The bandits would go to the bank of the river to receive this protection money as if it were a customs levy on commerce. They would not, however, obstruct passage.
>
> At first the tribesmen took their profit and respected the terms of this agreement. The route became by and large passable. Censor-in-Chief Chen Jin further expressed the view that this system could prove an enduring one, and changed the name of the place to 'Gorge of Perpetual Thoroughfare'. Before long, however, the bandits had become increasingly shameless on this account, and robbed on a huge scale. If anyone was not happy with this, they would kill him forthwith.

In 1512, the philosopher–bureaucrat Wang Yangming took charge of the campaign to suppress the bandits, but the need to keep up the pressure continued long after his death in 1520. Gu Yingtai's comments show his sense of frustration at the difficulties of framing an effective policy. Mixing 'local' and 'circulating' officials did not lead to effective administration. Confucian education made a minimal impact on the ferocious Yao nature. Trade caused them to "snarl like dogs at the sight of profit." Pinning them down with strong-points gave rise to "a disruption that makes them panic like wild animals." They were useless as human material, but could not be "excluded from civilization." It was too costly to station a large number of troops permanently in the area, but a small number would not be able to do the job required. Military colonies did not stop pillaging.

A strategy for solving such problems by the transformation of the Guizhou environment through agricultural development eventually emerged in northwestern Guizhou from the program formulated by Zhu Xieyuan in 1629. Zhu had been put in charge with suppressing the linked uprisings of the Lolo leader She Chongming and of An Bangyan, a hereditary local official over the Miao in Shuixi, whose ancestors had sided with successive Chinese governments since the third century BCE.[61]

> Zhu convened a large meeting with his generals at which he said: "Shuixi has numerous dangerous places in its mountains, and dense thickets of bamboos. The smoke from the cooking fires of the tribesmen and the stinging rain together make it impossible to tell night from day. If one

goes in to any distance, it is hard to get out again. For this reason one can often be defeated. You and I must keep a firm grasp on the key positions, attack them repeatedly, and gradually cleanse the area of 'bandits'. *If we cause the 'bandits' to run short of food, this will in itself bring about that they perish.*"

They thereupon *burnt the places that shielded Shuixi.* They hacked open the caves that might have offered shelter. *They diverted the flow of the streams.* They sent out strong soldiers to move rapidly around over a range of more than fifty kilometers a day, either beheading woodcutters and herdsmen, or setting fire to their accumulated stocks of grain, returning each evening to their camps. The 'bandits' found it harder and harder to anticipate what was going to happen. In somewhat more than a hundred days the government troops had obtained over ten thousand decapitated heads, and several tens of thousands of live captives. Whenever they were guided by a local they would open up underground stores of grain and consume them, while the 'bandits' suffered severely from hunger.

When An surrendered, Zhu proposed to the emperor nine principles that he thought appropriate for maintaining peace:

(1) Normal bureaucratic prefectures and counties will *not* be established, but rather military Guard Areas. No change will be imposed on customs, so locals and Chinese will be at peace with each other.
(2) *More land will be opened up for farming.* Day by day *the settlements will become more densely populated.* Once the division of the land into fields has been correctly carried out, the local chieftains will not be able to make encroachments onto land not currently farmed by the commoner–civilians.
(3) Guizhou's soils are of poor quality, and the province depends for its supplies on the provinces outside. If it can now live off its own land, this will spare it the toil of transportation.
(4) Since the state's resources are close to the point of being exhausted, there is not enough money in the Treasury to reward the generals. If titles are used for rewards, they are of little substance, and it would be preferable to give them land, which does no damage to the state.
(5) Once they have been permitted to hold land on a hereditary basis, they can establish their families, and will constitute an enduring bulwark against enemies.
(6) Greater and lesser will be linked together, the weighty and the less weighty controlling each other. . . .
(7) Training will be given to farmers, and the soldiers kept in good order. . . .
(8) Soldiers and commoner–civilians shall be permitted to farm if they find it appropriate. By both farming and acting as frontier garrisons, the Guard

Areas and their constituent Company Areas will be self-sufficient, and there will be no difficulty in assembling an armed force.

(9) Farming by the soldiers will replace the provision of their rations. Farming by the commoner–civilians will make possible the payment of taxes. The military colony system will be used for taxing farming. They will not be obliged to be in the registers of population. Thus *farming will be the means by which the settled population will grow.* They will not be assigned to hereditary service [as in the early Ming], so that everyone may be contented with his occupation.

Bearing in mind that the Miao also practised farming, this may be seen as a program for the sinification of society by easy stages. A quasi-feudal military administrative structure would provide a framework for development, and cultural differences would be respected. He was soon able to report to the emperor that, "I have now divided up the territory of Shuixi and bestowed it on various tribal chieftains *and on meritorious Chinese,* so that all of them may maintain it through succeeding generations." He was homogenizing cultures. Although it is not stated, the implication seems to be that at some point well in the future, the transition to regular bureaucratic government could come about when there were the resources to support it, and enough social cohesion to avoid splits in society. It is also clear, both from the general tenor of the sources quoted in the preceding pages and some of the policies proposed, that there was plenty of cultivable land available here in the seventeenth century, even if not of a particularly good quality. There was a contrast here with late-imperial Jiaxing.

Thus the nature of the terrain in Guizhou and nearby areas had a decisive effect on the nature of warfare. It made prolonged guerrilla resistance to central authority possible, but it also made locally based success of a sustained, as opposed to a sporadic, kind almost impossible over the longer term. The province did not provide enough manpower or resources to match what the central government could put in the field. On the other hand, the cost of projecting power more than intermittently into such an environment was unacceptably heavy for the Chinese state. In the long run, as Zhu Xieyuan and a number of other Chinese leaders came to realize, the only solution was *to change the environment.*

Peng Ermi was the governor of Guizhou under the Manchus in the middle of the seventeenth century, a gung-ho conquistador who celebrated military subjugation, settlement, development, and the enslavement of the native population with enthusiastic relish. Here is his "Ballad of Shuixi," written just after the crushing of the An clan's rising in the region west of Guiyang.[62] The phrase 'plume-topped heavenly generals' is a rendering of a term with a double meaning: a group of stars in the constellation Aquarius, and the emperor's personal bodyguard. Wumeng and Dongchuan were just across Guizhou's western border in Yunnan.

Our Sage Ruler's sacred battalions — have engaged in long-lasting
    suppression
And holy strategic wars been waged by plume-topped heavenly generals,
Commanders especially despatched to transmit the Imperial Plans,
And ten myriad ironclad cavalry to be Shuixi city's garrison.

With leadership all that could be wished — beyond compare, in truth,
Amidst the tumult of angry menace, a tempestuous storm was brewing,
Their carven bows in carrying-cases, arrows tucked in at their waists,
Laughing, "*Such rats* don't make the grade, e'en for extermination!

"Miao forts are not fit battlefields for *real* military engagements,
And the underground boltholes of *those hardly human* don't merit
    consideration.
Not since the world emerged from chaos has one ever set eyes on the like
Of these forests, and thickets of bamboo, that extend beyond the
    horizon."

We have chiseled through hills, and flattened highways, drums rumbling to
    trumpets' music.
Helmeted on our chargers' backs, parched grain wrapped for travel food,
Ox carts carrying those of importance, while the lesser bear loads on their
    backs,
Every day, for our Imperial Court, *we've developed new arable lands.*

Across four prefectures, north and south, spread the fertile acres in plenty.
Wumeng, and Dongchuan, compete with us as to which shall enjoy
    supremacy.
Once the present generation has wed, we'll control what's before and what's
    after.
Farm settlements in the past southwest were once but no longer are
    marginal.

Our victory, yesterday proclaimed, has three outstanding triumphs:
We have lashed their hands behind their backs, or *swallowed their lands* like
    Leviathan,
And, with no more than a single blow, quelled or doomed to extermination,
These far-off wastelands and tribal domains yield us *menials and female
    slaves.*

> We've converted their spy posts along the frontiers to official providers of maps,
> And for hundreds of miles, both this way and that, have *abundance of rice from our paddies.*

Racial and cultural contempt, expropriation, and the imposition of a changed environment.

A delight in the new colonial settlements was expressed in the first half of the eighteenth century by Chang'an, a Manchu bannerman. Note that 'people' here means 'Chinese' (in the broad sense, including Manchus), and that the same holds true for 'homes'. 'Fogs' is a metaphor for the Miao presence and their culture. He says:[63]

> Below one's feet one dimly glimpses the crows winging home to roost.
> The back of one's ears is gently washed by the cumulus swiftly moving.
> There are roads going up the rockface. The boulders serve them as ladders.
> No walls protect the high-perched markets. The mountain mists are adequate.
>
> The villages are haphazardly placed. Their locations are irregular.
> People's characters are without affectation. Simplicity brings them contentment.
> *By sweeping away the barbarian fogs, the frontiers have been extended.*
> Countless homes delight in the proclamations that announce the army's successes.

The post-conquest reshaping of the aesthetic and cartographic landscape

Outsiders entering Guizhou for the first time were startled at what they found. When the same Chang'an rode in on horseback, he wrote these lines, probably referring to the karst limestone pinnacles:[64]

> Obliquely implanted, the tapering summits are strangely shaped and placed;
> Hanging in balance, the precipice walls form multiple fortress gates.
> Disordered pine trees hug the slopes, as the rain first clears away;
> Before the old postal relay doors, fogs make the hour seem late.
> Lightning strikes on the tops of the crags, pouring down hundreds of streams;

> The blue-green confusions of sunken depressions are filled with
> millennial trees.

Apart from the postal relay, which was part of the imperial courier service, the driving force behind the first reliable roads, it was an unfamiliar world.

Comparison with better-known parts of China was a common reaction. Zou Yigui, a high Court official of the mid-eighteenth century known for his paintings of flowers and landscapes, wrote about the way Guizhou streams played hide-and-seek.[65] 'Wu', in the translation that follows, is the old name for the lower Yangzi valley. A 'gill' is a northern English term for a small ravine or sinkhole, usually with a stream in it. It seems the most likely sense of a word meaning 'throat' in the original.

> My native Wu is rich in waters, Guizhou is rich in mountains,
> But mountains that have no waters are mountains that have no life.
> One feels nothing in the forests' depths but the weight of the mists about
>   one,
> There are many gills, but none wide enough for more than one hare to hide in.
>   So a trickle that flows some miles
>   A few miles further on runs dry,
> All of its bubbling ripples having plunged away underground.

Guizhou was in fact well supplied with rivers, but not with water in the quantities to which a native of the Yangzi delta was accustomed.

The most exuberant evocation of the Guizhou landscape is the rhapsody "Other Mountains" by the seventeenth-century monk Qian Bangqi. The title in one sense means exactly what it says: Guizhou's mountains are unlike those anywhere else. It is also a reference to a phrase in the *Scripture of Songs*:[66] "the stones of other mountains." In this sense it can also mean 'let others serve as grindstones', that is, be officials.[67] It is important to remember that Chinese descriptive prose-poems were, by the conventions of the genre, exhibitions of virtuoso verbal prowess, awash with onomatopoeia, and imaginative excess. It is necessary to allow for this when reading them as possible guides to reality. Guizhou was, however, uniquely suited to this sort of exaggeration.

Qian had his path and his views cleared for him, presumably by unmentioned servants using fire or equipped with axes, much as some early painters of the Australian landscape found it necessary to do a couple of hundred years later.[68] From the environmental point of view these lines testify to the density of the tree cover in the places he visited. Psychologically they provide insight into what Qian felt was the deeper significance of the wild mountainscape: the structure of cosmic forces was more nearly visible here than elsewhere.[69] But *whose* cosmic forces?

My eyes have looked upon the empire's vast extent,
Landscape's eccentricities having absorbed my heart.
But Guizhou, off the beaten path, a domain of wilderness,
Is the strangest in its excitement, and in its heights and depths,
With pinnacles uplifted clear, and precipitous descents,
Majestically scarped, yet tortuously bent.

And, for myself, forgetting the burden of sense and cognition,
I have chanced on a secluded spot where my footprints will be hidden.
To this uncanny domain heart and spirit are both committed:
I remove the vegetation up the winding mountain paths,
And burn off thorny brambles to clear the meandering hilltops.

Multitudinous altitudes are here revealed before me,
Assembled together, ahead and behind, elevated and awesome.
I make the ascent to the highest point, to gaze out into the distance,
Sensing how swiftly the serried summits sink down in subordination,
How clouds and mists open and close, assuming ten thousand forms,
Aether-wrought images of illusion, metamorphoses not to be caught.

The redoubled peaks in zigzag patterns are hard to travel across,
Almost too dark for investigation the repetitive caves and grottoes.
The unrestrained rush of the twisting brooks tosses up torrents of
    froth;
Sudden landslips in the huge ravines can love-crush living bodies.

Obscurely, I glimpse Earth's Axis, that binds the fabric together,
Far away, I intuit the support of the upright Pillar of Heaven.

Qian's feelings may be summed up in the words of Wang Xing, the author of
a prose-poem on a spring in Guizhou. Wang remarked of the scene before him
that "This is the mirror of the true message of the Transforming Force."[70] The
Transforming Force was an ancient Daoist concept, like that of an invisible but
omnipresent smith perpetually turning one thing in nature into another, but
not the creator of the universe. Contemplation of the landscape thus had a
religious character. But a new religion, a new metaphysics.

Qian was also describing what was in Chinese terms, though not those of
the Miao, a primal wilderness untouched by human hand. Scholarly opinion
tends to regard the Chinese as having found true 'wilderness' unattractive.
Qian, however, seems to have been comfortable with it. He goes on:

Thickets of pine trees and junipers, leaning against each other,
With the cypress and the Chinese firs, screen out the glare of the sun.

Bamboos in some spots are far apart, elsewhere they are densely huddled,
So, in complement, the flowering plants grow irregularly among them.

After talking about the streams, he goes on:

Lofty willows flourish in clumps by the water's wide expanses,
Their boughs and branches casting shadows over the flooding channels.
Tendrils trail on the surface from the lily-like floating plants,[71]
Unrolling their leaf blades, lettuce and celery stretch out their spikelets
    aslant.

The twittering birds are heard above, up in the forest twigs,
While, among the reeds and water-grain, duck and widgeon dive and nibble.
The line of peaks is reflected inverted, in the deeps below the ripples,
Where, implanting their roots in the lake's perspective, hang the
    suspended cliffs.[72]

Qian is at his ease in what seems to him an unspoiled paradise.

The bizarre shapes taken by the Guizhou rocks are intoxicating. The catalog-cadenza, with its accelerated rhythm, in which he describes them, is too long to be given in full. A few lines convey its exuberance:

Unique the weird boulders, here agglomerated,
From Earth wrenched out, and Heaven's vault impaling.
Some, plinths that can't be budged, are Atlas-solid,
Others, like inclined buns of hair, about to tumble off,
Some, not quite level, calender-rollers wobbling,
Some, vertical perversely, have bottoms above their tops.
Some appear coiled-up dragons, others tigers bursting forth,
Some seem a mounting roc, or else a phoenix soaring.

'Atlas' here is a Westernized equivalent of Beixi, a river god depicted as a tortoise and believed capable of bearing great weights on his back. The Chinese traditionally calendered cloth by rocking massive smoothed stones on it—this hardened the surface and improved its resistance to wear. The 'roc', found in *The Thousand and One Nights*, is a Western equivalent of the great *peng* bird of ancient Chinese fables.

Qian Bangqi is perceiving what is to him a new world through Chinese conceptions. He is also, though unaware of it, a cultural conquistador obliterating an earlier vision.

The mapmakers saw the same landscape differently again. This can be seen from the introduction to the 1850 gazetteer for Guiyang prefecture. By this date there was a growing taste for precision. The compilation is almost a Domesday Book: an inventory of topography, settlements, plants and animals, population, taxes, and so on, with tersely worded biographies of past officials and virtuous women, and only occasional flashes of color.

Grids had been known by Chinese mapmakers since at least Pei Xiu in the third century CE,[73] though little used in gazetteer maps, perhaps because of the demanding nature of the surveying required. These maps, however, are all constructed on grids, with thirty-kilometer spacing for the prefecture as a whole, and ten-by-ten squares for smaller spatial units. The tone of voice of the compilers is one of frustration at the difficulty of bringing so chaotic a place under cartographic conceptual control:[74]

Making maps is hard, but mapping Guizhou province especially so. . . .

Even if one is familiar with Mr Pei Xiu's six canons of cartography one will still find it impossible to finish the job of mapping southern Guizhou. The reason for this is that there are numerous deep gorges in southern Guizhou. Confronted with the way they go down and in, and the two sides seem to close together above one, if there are no others to help or inform one, how can one get down to enter them?

Southern Guizhou has numerous underground streams. If one is faced with determining where they are interrupted and where they run continuously, since it is difficult to ascertain where sources reappear repeatedly, if one does not have others to help or inform one how can one hasten quickly to survey the arterial pattern of the waterways? This is why the courses of the rivers that appear in past registers of inquiry sometimes have a source but no outlet, or an outlet but no source, or else have both a source and an outlet but no tributary streams flowing into them, or, alternatively, do have tributary streams but no proper sequence for them to make their entry into the river. . . .

The land in southern Guizhou has fragmented and confused boundaries. . . . A department or a county may be split into several subsections, in many instances separated by other departments or counties. A jurisdiction may sometimes jump half a kilometer, at other times five hundred,[75] before returning to what it was to begin with. There are also regions of no man's land where the Miao live intermixed with Chinese. This is even true outside some outer suburbs of cities or former barriers at passes. The villages and camps are no different. Their jurisdictions may be divided in as many as three or four different ways. . . .

Roads in southern Guizhou are as plentiful as thickets of bamboo, but of indeterminate lengths. They are blocked off by mountain cliffs, and in some cases may twist and turn five hundred times in the space of fifty kilometers. The official routes and imperial relay highways do have a degree of systematic pattern. One no longer has to pace out the distances through the close-pressing ravines and remote wastes. On them too, though, a distance of fifty kilometers on the road may only amount to half or a third of this in a direct line. . . .

Southern Guizhou has a multitude of mountain peaks. They are jumbled together, without any plains or marshes to space them out, or rivers or watercourses to put limits to them. They are vexingly numerous and ill-disciplined.[76] . . . Very few people dwell among them, and generally the peaks do not have names. Their configurations are difficult to discern clearly, ridges and summits seeming to be the same. Those who give an account of the arterial pattern of the mountains are thus obliged to speak at length. In some cases, to describe a few kilometers of ramifications needs a pile of documentation, and dealing with the main line of a day's march takes a sequence of chapters. . . .

As to the confusion of local patois, in the space of fifty kilometers a river may have fifty names, and an encampment covering a kilometer and a half may have three designations. Such is the unreliability of nomenclature!

Two different faces of the same quest for mastery.

The colonial administrator's perspective

What sort of a prefecture would a newly appointed local official, concerned with taxes, farm production and hence weather, and maintaining good order, have expected to encounter when he arrived? Consulting the section in the 1850 gazetteer on the place of the region in the universe—*fenye*, which signified relating it to the stars thought to rule its destiny—he would have found the following items of information:[77]

> The Southern Ridge winds its way between Guangshun, Guizhu, Guiyang, Dingfan, and Guiding [all cities in the central part of the prefecture], being the spine of the high mountains. For this reason the prefecture is cold, but since it is near the south it is also warm. Heat and cold are well accommodated to each other, and, contrary to expectation, the climate is equable. The winter cold is not intense, nor the heat in summer oppressive. *North of the Southern Ridge there is no malaria*. Luoxie county, which is the furthest south in the prefecture, being situated on the Hongshui River,[78]

does intermittently have malaria. Kaizhou and Xiuwen are the most northerly [in the northeast and northwest of the prefecture respectively], and suffer from 'cold epidemics' but not to any great extent.

The nature of the 'cold epidemics' is unclear. What is evident is that the Southern Ridge, which was the main watershed, divided Guiyang into two epidemiologically different halves.

The gazetteer then continues, at first in a practical mode and later in what we would call a metaphysical mode, but this distinction would have made little sense to a Chinese reader of premodern times. He or she would in most cases have seen all the comments as equally down-to-earth:

> This is a land where there is frequent rain in the mornings. The weather is constantly overcast on this account, and *rain suffices for the enrichment of the soil*. The mountains are lofty, and the streams deep, with extremely little horizontal ground. Hence the proverbial saying: "Never three days of clear skies, nowhere three feet of flat land." Because of the altitude the seasons come rather late.
>
> All of the main watercourses . . . run sunken far down, with precipitous banks on both sides. *Little benefit is had from man-made channels or dikes.* Enrichment of the soil by water relies entirely on rain from the skies. For this reason, if during the farming season no rain falls for five days, then people offer prayers . . . .
>
> In the valleys of the mountain torrents, the sun and moon are hidden from sight. Because of the concealed reserves of the Dark–Female Principle there is a lot of hail. The land is solely dominated by the Feminine–Chthonic Force in the form of high mountains, the 'cords of the earth'. Hence the great extent of docile accommodation in people's characters and the numbers of spirit mediums who call down supernatural beings. This is due to the abundance of the Dark–Female Principle.

The Dark–Female Principle is the *yin* of archaic Chinese metaphysics, and the Feminine–Chthonic is the *kun* hexagram from the ancient divining manual, the *Book of Changes*. There is a dual sense in the Chinese term *kunwei*. It can be taken either as 'the cords of the earth', that is, high mountains, or as 'the *kun* principle'.

The spirit mediums, who called down demons or the souls of the deceased, put on dramatic shows, with drums and gongs, and sent off 'yellow letters' to the world of the dead.[79] Zhu Gong, who served as a local official in nearby southwest Hu'nan province in the eighteenth century, wrote a poem on them entitled "The Miao Make Offerings to the Spirits: A Warning Against Improper Sacrifices."[80] His attitude of cultural, social, and racial disdain is evident, yet one side of him relishes the spectacle:

With whinnying clangor the gongs are booming,
As bronze drums beat out their repetitive rhythms,
They summon the mediums in pell-mell confusion,
Tricked out as tigers in odd, motley, mimicry,

Dangling red aprons are tied round their belts,
In pleats bound on their brows hang blue-green silk tassels,
Back-country serfs who leap with forked gestures,
Menials from caves who cavort with arms brandished.

They pretend to be generals, play-act ferocity,
Then bow to their elders, loose hair in disorder.
Girls from the village wear clasps of mixed blossoms,
Lads from the hills tie their clothes on with straw,

From masts of bamboo there droop paper pennants.
The clay pots on display contain betel peppers.
With rowdy guffaws they offer a pig's head,
And using a rope-hoist they roast roosters' feathers.

Purple clouds of sweet smoke gust denser and denser,
The white raindrops spraying as charmed water's sprinkled,
But the savages' babbling is incomprehensible
As they get drunk, and stuffed, for their spirit's epiphany.

I have heard that when teaching the vulgar behavior
One's model for ritual's that of the ancients:
A magnanimous face, and severe, sober vestments,
Obeisances courteous, and strict patterned steps.

One's words given weight by fasting and abstinence,
One spreads out dried meat, and wine, pure and fragrant,
Showing utmost respect, with no breath of blasphemy —
This it is brings good luck, *this* of reverence the basis.

Offerings otherwise offered delight not the spirits.
If the ritual is lost, they benefit nothing.
So one proffers *Hippuris* to monarch and ministers,
Greets the Farm God with clods, tapping on a clay drum.

How then can one cleanse these barbarians of their sooty moral grime,
And list them in the Zhou lineage so renowned in ancient rhyme?

The last line refers to the section in the *Scripture of Songs* that tells of the
founding of the Zhou state from which thirteen generations later the imperial

Zhou dynasty was to spring. Not all the details in the rest of the poem can be so easily explained—why, for example, burn chicken's feathers?—but it is worth recalling that the leaves of the betel pepper were chewed with the betel nut and lime as a recreational drug.[81] *Hippuris*, or mare's tail, is a water plant.

The shift of apparent attitude slightly after the halfway point is something one finds in a number of other poems of this age that touch on the demotic or unconventional. Here it is the concluding homage to Confucian rectitude that allows both poet and listener to enjoy with a good tourist conscience the colorful vigor of barbarism. But Zhu Gong's hauteur is not assumed. He is convinced that the Miao should be assimilated into the mainstream of proper Chinese culture.

Chinese officials' attitudes were at times more complex than this poem suggests. Some of them expressed admiration for the "generous virtue" of the Miao, and observed that while their "customs" were "savage and barbaric," their "character" was "honest and straightforward."[82] He Jingming wrote a set of poems on the villagers "in the south part of the Ping Barrage" in Ming times.[83] A phrase in the last line but one, which means 'outside the transforming influences of Chinese civilization', suggests they were most likely Miao. This is however a guess. In Ming times Ping Barrage was a garrison area in the western part of Guiyang, with a primarily non-Chinese population. He first describes the village turned in upon itself in the cold of the fall:

> Beside the forest in the fall, congealed under falling snow,
> A fine sprinkling of raindrops moistens the thatched huts.
> The village outskirts are now as far as they'll let the livestock go
> So that the cattle, and the sheep, remain in touch with each other.
>
> The flowers have long since fallen from the trees in their spacious orchards,
> And the leveled paddy-fields spread out, under a cloud-dark sky.
> Neither the adults, nor youngsters — now — will venture out of doors,
> But affectionately experience the delight of like in like.

There are philosophical echoes of northern Chinese antiquity in this seasonal familial seclusion. He then evokes the virtuous simplicity of their lives:

> Immense the depths of the water, held in the age-old reservoir.
> The chill of the sunset hour makes its green color more intense.
> Beyond the hillslope fields, we glimpse the people who dwell here,
> And the vines that grip the straw-roofed shacks under their twisting tendrils.
>
> They break off a few stalks of rice, for a meal to offer a visitor,
> And collect the wood for a fire by chopping a long-dead trunk,
> While wielding their poles of bamboo, the children

Run through the midst of the rain, driving the chickens and ducks.
In this realm of no significance, outside of civilized culture,
Natural living survives, still primal and unsullied.

The observed reality is interfused with the Daoist dream of a simple, anarchist-style, village society. Maybe, like Tacitus deriding Roman effete corruption by contrasting it with the straightforward vigor of the Germans, he was also implying criticism of his own Chinese world. But, as we know from other parts of the world, it is not uncommon for a colonial administrator both to admire and to condescend to those whom he governs.

Farming

Guizhou's Chinese-style premodern economic growth came late. The 1741 provincial gazetteer was still wistfully observing that[84]

> Guizhou has few local products, and the standard of living is meager. The people do not have reserves of grain to see them out to the end of the year. Thus if one calculates the population of the thirteen prefectures of Guizhou there are only 200,000 [households], and the soils are stony. . . .
>
> Nonetheless, a time comes when the aethers in the mountains and streams open. When the Huai-Hai region [Jiangsu province north of the Yangzi] was in 'Yangzhou' province in the time of the *Tribute Sent to Yu*, its land was then graded as the lowest of the low, . . . but since the Tang and the Song dynasties, its wealth has been foremost in the empire.[85] How can it not be the case that when population grows dense the land will then be developed, and that when this happens there will be an abundance of produce?

Brave optimism, given pressure from a difficult climate as well as resentful natives, a terrain cursed with rivers too swift to navigate and regarded at this date as unsuitable for supplying irrigation systems,[86] and with famines and major epidemics becoming more frequently recorded during the sixteenth century.[87] Nonetheless, it proved well-founded. By late Qing times, Guiyang at least had some developed irrigation systems. According to an earlier account quoted in the late-nineteenth-century gazetteer:[88]

> Those of Guiyang's paddy-fields whose springs of water overflow all year long without running dry are called 'overflow fields'. At places along the banks of rivers they weave bamboo into wheels and use them to lift the water; these are called 'water-pump fields'. Where the land is level they build dikes so that water can be retained or drained as needed, these being called

'diked fields'. Where land lies below cliffs over which streams cascade down and may be drawn off for irrigation, they call these 'cold-water fields'. Where water is stored in ponds, and may be released when there is dry weather these are called 'reservoir-pond fields'. Where mountain springs gush forth, and well water may be used for irrigation, these are called 'well-fields'. Where the mountains are high and water is lacking, so that they can only rely on moisture from the rain, they call them 'dry fields', or 'fields that look up to the heavens'. Where the fields rise up in successive levels, they call them 'ladder fields'. Where the fields extend obliquely, bending and winding, they call them 'waistband fields'.

The water pumps were norias, huge open-work wheels with pots mounted on their rims, emptying into a flume at the top of the rotation, and driven at the bottom by the current. They do not require an input of human energy such as was needed for treadle-pumps in Jiaxing. In some places, however, the precipitous banks of rivers made water-control installations impracticable, and "enrichment of the soil by water relies entirely on the rain from the skies."[89]

The farming calendar reveals a simpler system than Jiaxing's:[90]

In the first moon, during the Rain Water period in late February, the tong trees[91] and the chestnut oaks[92] all bear their nuts [used, respectively, to make an oil for waterproofing and a black dye]. In this moon they pull out the roots remaining from the previous year's wheat, and the broad beans compete with each other to blossom.

In the second moon, after the Spring Equinox, when it happens to rain, the irrigated fields are plowed, and water lifted into the ladder fields. As regards the handling of the dry fields, if there is a lot of rain, they store the water in ponds, so as to prevent the supply being exhausted. In this moon the wheat and barley fill out their seedheads, millet is planted, spring buckwheat dibbled in, and early grain [probably oats—see the ninth moon] sown broadcast.

In the third moon, during the Clear and Bright period in early April, they first sow the rice. After the Grain Rains period in late April they bank up the raised paths between the paddies to retain the water in readiness for transplanting. In this moon the wheats form their spikelets, and the broad beans and garden peas fill with seeds. Buckwheat sprouts appear above the ground. They plant the barnyard millets.[93]

In the fourth moon, during the Summer Begins period in early May, they transplant the rice. Barley is harvested in this moon, and buckwheat first forms kernels.

In the fifth moon, during the Grain In Ear period in early June all the planting of the cereals and vegetables is finished. They plant soybeans, lentils, and green lentils. They reap the buckwheat and harvest the wheat.

In the sixth moon the heat is intense. They wear clothes of fine or coarse linen. During this moon the barnyard millets grow at furious speed, while the rice begins to fill out.

In the seventh moon, the days are hot but the nights cool. If it rains, the daytime is also cool. The early rice is reaped in this moon, and the fall buckwheat dibbled in.

In the eighth moon, in the White Dew period of early September, the late rice develops full ears. All the rice is harvested in this moon, and the early barnyard millet reaped.

In the ninth moon, in the Cold Dew period during early October the harvesting of the rice is finished. The wild oats are yellow and hang their ears.[94] The beanstalks wither. The red variety and the *ti* variety of barnyard millet form kernels. The farmers at this point spade the fields in order to disperse the energy–vitality of the soil. In this moon they reap the wild oats, some of the beans, and the millet. They pick the barnyard millets, and plant the wheat and barley, and the winter vegetables.

In the tenth moon they put on their furs for the first time. In this moon they plant broad beans and garden peas.

In the eleventh moon, the farmers rest for the first time. In this moon the broad beans and the garden peas appear above the ground.

In the twelfth moon the cold is severe, though if the sky is clear there is some warmth. In this moon the snow melts and the wheats appear.

Scrutiny of these dates suggests that, unlike Jiaxing, two different crops would not generally have been grown at different seasons in the same field. (Buckwheat, growing from the second to fifth months, may have left time for a second crop, but the need for rotation makes this unlikely.) Apart from rice and wheat, they relied on tough but low-yielding cereals that are not particularly tasty, and on one, the barnyard millet, that can develop fast, seeding after a few weeks' growth in some cases, though here over four months'.[95]

Miao farming was sometimes simpler still. They prepared high-lying land for crops merely by setting it on fire. Jiang Yingke, in Ming times, recorded this in a poem, then added in another one:[96]

On the sheer cliffs, the scars of burning grow green once the rain has fallen,
And sweet the smell of last year's rice, husked by pounding in the mortar.

The Miao also had the environmental buffer provided by being able to supplement their food supply by hunting. Wu Guolun, an official and poet of the sixteenth century, made this point in an incidental way in the third line of the following quatrain:[97]

> First one then the next, atop steep banks, we pass doubly enclosed
>   barricades,
> With moats and with walls — so they seem — on their ramparts, of close-
>   set wooden palings.
> They use knives for plowing. Remaining energy's spent on *the shoot and*
>   *the chase.*
> They behead cocks for sacrifice, rat-a-tat drums, and take idols around
>   on parade.

It is not clear what they hunted. Wild pigs are quite often mentioned as being in Guizhou, but the most likely quarry was deer. Wang Yangming's[98] lines on "The Bamboo Thickets at Muge" suggest that these may have been quite numerous in the sixteenth century:[99]

> Once off on a path of his own, my tired horse — climbs up with unequaled
>   speed.
> The layers of cumulus gently cover the tops of the interlinked peaks.
> In the mountain hamlet the flock of crows is disturbed by the gloom in
>   the trees.
> In dense mists on the track along the ravine, *we meet with a herd of deer.*

In other words, the Miao could to some still extent feed themselves off nature, even if they had long become mainly farmers and herders.

One of the most momentous, yet all but invisible, psychological changes in human history has been the intensification of a sense of insecurity and alienation from the world around us that arose when we became no longer able easily to get food in a few hours just by gathering it, or hunting it, but had to organize ourselves in a purposeful fashion simply to survive. This change is undocumented, though occasional clues can be gained about it from the comments of the few still alive who have lived through a version of it, such as old Australian Aboriginals. Its essence is subjection to a pervasive but unacknowledged, indeed unnamed, fear.[100] It is the foundation of civilization.

Bitter treasures

Minerals were one of the prizes that drew Chinese workers and merchants into Guizhou. One product that was exclusive to the province, and nearby parts of Hu'nan and Sichuan, was cinnabar. Cinnabar is mercuric sulfide (HgS), and the only common source of quicksilver or mercury. Its main traditional uses were in medicine, traditional religious preparations (against nightmares, for example), and metallurgy. It was also important in Chinese alchemy, because the way in which cinnabar and mercury can apparently be turned back and forth into each other suggested that it held the secret of constancy in the midst of change.[101] The ore was also used to make a coloring material.

There were cinnabar mines in Guiyang, located in Kaizhou, also known as Kaiyang, in the north of the prefecture. Workings further north still are described in Tian Wen's *Book of Guizhou,* a series of short essays on the province in late-Ming and early-Qing times:[102]

> From the barrage to the Yang River and the Re River is more than twenty-five kilometers, and all along the route there are ore workings. The ore from the Yang and the Re takes the visual form of arrowheads and arrowshafts, while that of the Useful Ore Barrage takes the form of axes and the surfaces of mirrors. These are its commonplace forms.
>
> Those who select ores must examine the images that they present. If they seem to be like gourds or calabashes, or like the jointed segments of bamboo, they follow them in. Those shafts excavated downwards into the ground are termed 'wells'. Those that proceed in on the level are termed 'levels'. Those that rise straight upwards for some height are termed 'lights'.[103] Those that slope smoothly down are termed 'oxen sucking up water' [perhaps because of seepage]. In all of these there are wooden props and cover-boards overhead that make them into galleries. This done, it is possible to give protection to the work performed with the large carrying-baskets, crowbars, hammers, picks, and mattocks. Everyone prepares an oil-burning lamp for when they enter. They crawl like snakes, or like people chasing after a lost child. They tap gingerly with their hammers [like the fabled grave-robbing Confucian trying to tap the pearl out of the mouth of a dead man without damaging it].[104] Like deer, they turn the night into dawn with artificial light.[105] This is putting out of consideration any fearful oppression from thoughts of death and life.
>
> If they meet with rock, they hack it away. If it is too hard for this to be done, they heat it with coal [and then pour cold water on it, till it cracks]. They never stop until they have attained their objective. If there are semblances of lions, great elephants [symbols of the Buddha], tigers, or vermilion birds [phoenixes] in the shaft this signifies great good fortune. Failing these, semblances of wooden eating-bowls, baskets, or hairpins and earrings must likewise be paid attention to. Those that are plump and heavy are the jewels among the ore. One must not alarm any that are buried in the ground and making a clucking noise like a hen-bird sitting on eggs. If they

are startled, they will go off elsewhere. In general, when ores flee away, there is a sound like the wind in the pine trees, neither loud not soft.

Everyone considers the top grade of ore to have a crystalline luster. These are those called the 'color of hibiscus flowers'.

When they have carried the ore out of the workings on their backs, they throw it into water to be scoured and rinsed. They then agitate it on beds and toss it about in sieves. Once cleansed it is filtered through sackcloth. In due course they sublimate it in a dry retort[106] from which the liquid either accumulates in a pool or is drawn off through pipes. It 'passes over the ridges and ranges' of the rising and falling condensation pipes and drop by drop falls from the 'heaven above'.

How much is obtained depends on fate. The opening and closing of the earth depend on the season. Whether the ore is coarse or fine depends on its intrinsic substance.

The mineral was being hunted, as if it were alive.

Tian Wen's prose-poem on cinnabar puts the mining and refining into a historical, philosophical, alchemical, and social context.[107] It also shows how the substantial industrial and commercial system that produced and traded cinnabar was based on pseudo-science, fashion, and superstition. Many of our own commercial obsessions, and many useless or harmful products, will probably look equally bizarre in the course of time. The items referred to in the last line but one of the stanza are probably cosmetics.

> As to 'vermilion ore', the term first occurs
> In *The Tribute Sent to Yu* — the passage that refers
> To whetstones from Jingzhou, and to arrowheads of flint.
>
> Blended in scarlet lacquer, it confers on it its finish,
> An unvarying milky substance, yet one whose shapes are different,
> Composed of unalike purple florets whose every facet's similar,
> Refined, it yields us 'crimson snow', and also rouge-hued paste,
> Or else the magic pill of immortals' isles and caves.

After dwelling for a while on this Daoist search for physical immortality he describes the fever of the local cinnabar-rush. The cowry shell, used in archaic China as a form of currency, is a symbol of wealth.

> If one looks into the question of where it's mined, and treated,
> No one region stands out as unique.
> Ore issues from the slopes below the two You peaks,[108]
> Where, underneath the hot springs, it slumbers buried deep.

This is familiar news enough, but not until recently,
When I arrived in Guizhou, did I have the chance to *see* it.

By the Qian and Pan rivers, at Wuchuan, and Copper Cliffs,
Are places it can be obtained, if one only does the digging.
But these workings open suddenly, then shut down as abruptly.
Kaiyang, here, surpasses them in having an abundance.

That's why rascals who anticipate they can glean miraculous profits,
And those selling dear and buying cheap, that is — gentlemen and
scholars —
All race to be here first, set their hearts on mountain fogs,
And come with carts and horses, having driven hither headlong,
Then wheel and deal to hire their men through the guarantor-
contractors,
Delimit zones of operation, lay out shop-stalls to form markets,
— Like a line of worms and serpents who can follow but one track.

The many-layered sources of water are sought through the lonely
blackness.
Pit props, rising high above, give rooves to the hidden galleries.
To spy out the terrain ahead, they hold oil lamps in both hands.
Frustrated there's no way to tell whether it's dawn or dusk,
They no longer think it worth a thought — if they live, or they
succumb.

When on a sudden, sticking out, they see ore in pointed blades,
It's like stumbling across a cowry, where, with rocks and soil displaced,
It rests drowsily on its mineral bed, as if half inebriated.

> Some are like barbs of arrows,
> Others like choppers or axes,
> Else seeming a mirror flashing,
> Or intensely black, like lacquer,
> Orange red like sparkling fire.
> But every color's brighter.

The Daoist in cloud-patterned mantle, spirit focused, extracts the drops,
And stores them to separate the essence, where fire's potency's embodied.

He ends this section by observing

> And, since it banishes bad dreams, foul vapors, and all things vicious,
> Rich merchants, and famous families, gladly buy it in every city.

After sketching the work at the mines, with "ladders going up and well-ropes going down," Tian next points to the pollution caused by mercury production:

> Old countrymen, between villages, live alone by the torrents' banks,
> With baling-pans and inlet pipes straining tailings and gathering
>   fragments.
> But their toes are rotting away, though the water they stand in's
>   transparent;
> For all that their eyes are running with tears, even so their pupils are
>   damaged.
> The ripples are everywhere reddened, on account of these activities,
> And what they do stains their jacket sleeves the color of vermilion.
> If by chance they happen to obtain the minutest scruple of cinnabar,
> Even for something next to nothing, they forthwith become giddily
>   frivolous.

Mercury poisoning can cause the 'mad hatter' syndrome, whose principal symptoms are timidity, and loss of memory and concentration.[109] This seems to be what Tian is referring to here, though the wording of the text would also permit the interpretation that the old men, having acquired a little modest wealth, 'have the audacity to be impudent'.

The industry was growing in late Ming times:

> Stoves have been built just recently, and furnaces erected.
> Milling rollers have been installed; so, too, have pounding pestles.
> Our red dye, when it is pulverized, "is unalloyed and bright."[110]
> And sublimated, ore turns to rain, scattering sweat as it perspires.

The last line refers to the production of the quicksilver.

There is the usual change of tone at the end. Cinnabar, says Tian, "satisfies neither ears nor eyes with enjoyment." It has "perverted the transmission of the spirit of concern with daily necessities." It has also caused trouble for the government. He wants its production to be permanently banned, and asks, rhetorically, "How could this cause any distress to the mountains and the valleys?" A comment appended by Ding Wei, an official and poet who flourished in early Qing, adds a philosophical note:

> Things that are precious always exhaust people in their efforts to get hold of them. . . . Alas! Heaven and Earth give birth to materials basically for the purpose of profiting humankind, but when those collecting them have become worn out, those demanding them are not yet weary of them. At this point advantage gives rise to harm.

The section that follows[111] describes the techniques of distillation or sublimation, that is, producing a gas from a solid directly. It ends by alluding to the possible ill-effects on health of exposure to mercury vapor, observing that "those who open either the caldrons or the fired tiles always hold a leek in their mouths, or juice from meat pickled with its bones. If they do not do this, their teeth will drop out when they encounter the vaporous energy–matter." Man-made chemical hazards to health predated modern times. I will pass over the technical details except to note that the process has similarities to some of the German methods described in the *De Re Metallica* of Georg Bauer, or 'Agricola', published in 1555.[112]

Tian ends with a return to the alchemical theme:

If mercury that has already been made in finished form is distilled, it can once again be made into cinnabar [when it cools]. *It does not forget that which it fundamentally is.* Natural mercury also arises from inside cinnabar, and does not need to be heated and purified in order to form. This type is exceedingly difficult to obtain, *and is the material for elixirs for the transformation of mortals into immortals.*

Changelessness within change, hence the embodiment of the secret of immortality within mortality.

It was an illusion. Cinnabar, when heated, converts to mercuric oxide which then decomposes at about 500° Celsius, so yielding mercury. The reverse process, needing from between 300° to 350°, would have made not cinnabar again but red mercuric oxide, using oxygen from the atmosphere, as the sulfur needed would largely have been lost after the initial processing. This oxide could have then be turned back into mercury at 500°, apparently demonstrating changelessness within change, as, at the primitive level of chemical understanding described here, the oxygen drawn from the air was invisible to the mind's eye.[113]

Xie Zhaozhe, the late-Ming collector of *curiosa*, was blunt about the damage done by cinnabar-based longevity pills.[114] In his *Fivefold Miscellany* of 1608 he says that if taken for any great length of time they kill people, the effect being "like tossing lime into a fire." When a contemporary of his, who took them in his later years, died, "his skin and body were splitting apart like a grilled fish." Xie was puzzled by the "imperturbable stupidity" with which people consumed them and suggested that

Those who have made a fortune and acquired social distinction have reached the limits of their ambitions. The only goal they would still like to attain, but cannot, is the prolongation of their lives. For this reason criminal persons with vicious magic have a means to accommodate this desire. Their customers would rather perish than change their ways.

Another important mineral was lead. Zhao Leisheng, who flourished in the middle of the eighteenth century, has left us a description of a state-run lead and zinc mine in Qianyang, in Hu'nan, just across the border from Guizhou.[115] The poem is patently a polemic, though the problem he is addressing can now only be guessed at from the text itself. Turning to the details, it should be noted that zinc most commonly occurs in sphalerite (ZnS) which is often found together with galena (PbS), the principal ore of lead. The Chinese term *qian* in the first line can refer both to zinc and to lead, and so I have rendered it with the Latin *plumbum*, to convey something of the flavor of the original, though, strictly *plumbum candidum*, 'white lead', referred historically in the early modern West to tin.

> *Plumbum* has been produced in Qianyang since times that are now long past.
> It comes in *two* kinds — white-colored zinc, and the darker-hued true lead.
> These lie secreted out of sight beneath the deep-sunk valleys
> Above which mountain forests soar — to altitudes immense.
>
> If five miners toil to open a seam, they'll find the work hot and vexatious.
> Their cutting of holes into Chaos amounts — in effect — to a way of
> killing him.
> Their pickaxes grasped in both their hands, they attack the excavation,
> One foot, then the other, pushing aside a mess of disordered chippings.
>
> Between his upper and lower jaws, each one grips hold of his lamp,
> Whose flame flickers, and shifts about, as the faint air-currents tug it.
> Twisting *this* way, then turning *that*, they pierce their way deep into
> blackness
> To where, through the fissures in the rock, the water seeps out in
> abundance.
>
> They smash a hole in the rocky ceiling, to lower down a pump.
> The dribbles rise up in mid-air, like sleet's translucent pearls.
> When they've heat-dried the mud that's left behind, on the floor of the
> cave, as a slurry,
> It glitters like mercury globules that rest on a sandy surface.
>
> They separate metals out in a stove that they feed with charcoal sticks.
> And at times, quite unexpectedly, an auspicious ingot emerges.
> The best of these are transported off, to the capital at Beijing
> To be tokens of His Majesty's favor for those who have most deserved it.
>
> There's been a decline in recent years in the skill of merchants at
> commerce,

And contracts for taxes due to the State have not secured any takers.
In consequence, I regret to say, although the products are serviceable,
Like goods held back to raise the price, they've not entered circulation.

So how do we find officials who are competent in these matters,
And, in operations of this sort, will do a good job as managers?

The cutting of holes in 'Chaos' in the second stanza is an allusion to the fable at the end of the seventh chapter of the *Zhuangzi*, where the well-intentioned but ill-advised emperors of the Northern and Southern Seas attempt to repay the physically undifferentiated Chaos, Emperor of the Center, for his hospitality. They drill seven apertures in his body that they hope will let him breathe, see, hear, and taste like a human being. This kindness proves fatal, and Chaos dies on the seventh day. The implication of the phrase seems at first sight to be that there is something unnatural and deadly about piercing the earth in this way, but that does not seem to have been Zhao's actual view. Most likely it was no more than a literary flourish that he had failed to think through.

The colonial frontier was thus an important source of raw materials, the demand for which was driven, in classic fashion, by distant markets in more developed areas. Timber was another example. A poem by a sixteenth-century official[116] banished to the Southwest, who then became a historian of his adopted region,[117] tells of the pressure on remote areas by this time, from even as far away as Beijing, for trees large enough to serve as the structural members of buildings. The Red Viper River he refers to is probably a tributary of the present-day Liuhe River that empties into the Wujiang, which flows through northeast Guizhou into the Yangzi. Mangbu was the son of a ruler of the area in antiquity.[118]

> The source of Red Viper River rises — from what was once Mangbu's city.
> Its forests are full of tigers and leopards, highroads for monkeys and
>   gibbons.
> Since no route exists for traveling through — its layered ice and deep
>   snows,
> *Construction-quality towering trees* still prop up the skies in the cold.
>
> To secure the beams, and the rafters, for ritual halls and grand buildings,
> *Timber merchants*, and masters of works, find their way to where these are
>   hidden.
> Since the onward rush of the current is like that of a speeding arrow,
> They bundle the tree trunks into rafts and ride down to Sichuan *and the*
>   *Capital.*

On the order of at least 1500 kilometers in the second case, much more if one were to allow for the meanderings of the water-transport routes, and an illustration of the environmental impact of the market more than four hundred years ago. Colonialism, as almost always, was linked to the quest for raw materials.

Bridges

Bridges were less common in Guizhou than in the watery lands of the lower Yangzi, but more important. Crossing the vertiginous river gorges by fording them, or by boat, was often difficult, commonly dangerous, or even impossible. In the wild natural conditions, construction could be a heroic undertaking. Maintenance and renewal of the structures demanded more money and redoubled determination. As elsewhere in China, building a bridge was an act of local charity, and one of the few areas of public works where individual initiative had some degree of free play outside the constraints of official organization. Tian Wen's account of Ge Jing's Bridge illustrates many of these points.[119] The details of the rituals of folk-religion connected with Ge Jing's oath are unclear, but mentioning them is essential to the story: sincerity moves the spirits who control the natural world.

> Two-and-a-half kilometers east of Pingyue [northeast of Guiyang] two mountains form barriers, one on each side, being the elevated banks of a deep gorge. At the bottom flows the Maha River, its water as opaque as glue. Even when the winds are blowing, no ripples stir on its surface. People live and farm among these stony cliffs, holding hands with the gibbons and drinking the veiling mists. The mountains lie in gloom, such that one rarely glimpses the stars or the sun. Birds are rare, goblins numerous. People in ages past chiseled the rock away to open a road, *with ropes suspended to enable travelers to cross from one side to the other.* . . .
>
> Today[120] there is a bridge. The explanation for this is as follows. A local man, Ge Jing, lashed together a long, rainbow-shaped frame, placed it on foundation pillars that stood in the water, and thought the task done. Some time after it had been built in this way, it fell down. He erected it once more, and again it was overturned. When this happened he ate vegetarian food and observed taboos [perhaps on sex] for a hundred days. He then announced to the spirits of Mount Li in Yunnan and Mount E in Guangxi that he was moving to the abode of the supernatural monsters. He led his wife and children in making the sacrifice of an animal and sprinkling wine into the river. He swore an oath to the powers above in order to make his intentions clear: "That this bridge has not been completed is because the river has behaved like this!"

His words were stricken with grief. His eyes bulged with fury. He resembled Shen Baoxu [who wept for seven days in the Court of the state of Qin to persuade it to give him military help against the state of Wu that had attacked his own state of Chu] . . . . His clothes and footwear were worn out. His bodily frame became withered and wizened. Lu Ban and Chui [legendary artificers, now become spirits] were moved to tears by this. In such a fashion, after thirty years, the bridge was built.

Ge Jing's fame on this account became extraordinary. He had also to face difficulties in managing the structure. There were many defects and many weaknesses. He nonetheless vowed that, till the day of his death, he would not waver. He squandered the reserves accumulated by his family, and the entire region criticized him for not caring for them. Though what he undertook to do was hardly important enough to be mentioned, yet one can still describe him as a heroic gentleman. Was not his lifelong resolve outstanding!

Alas! To assist the people to press forward, and to live at Court far from home and with no thought of returning [that is, serving as an official] does not seem to equal one good deed done in the back-country like this one if an account of it is to be handed on down through the generations. Ge Jing's story thus also has its shaming side.

This sour conclusion is rebutted by the discussion that follows. It is observed that "Jing's abilities and his wisdom amounted to much more than his seeking to make a name for himself." Ding Wei's commentary reinforces this point, and stresses that Ge Jing's moral force made an impact on the numinous aspect of the natural world.

If an ordinary person [like Jing] *sets his mind on assisting natural objects, he will always be able to be helped by natural objects.* What is more, Jing bankrupted his family to establish his renown, never altering course when faced by manifold difficulties. Though his undertaking was of but little significance, it was still far better than fiercely holding on to his wealth for his sons and grandsons to waste on drinking and gambling. Gentleman that he was, he did good to others, and this leads to the opposite conclusion.

Let me describe the dangers in making that bridge: it was as if demons howled along the cloud-swathed escarpments, and gibbons screamed amid the snow-bound defiles. Let me tell you how his painful resolve guided his plans to fulfilment: it was like a widow who weeps alone at night firm in her resolve to stay faithful to her husband, or the anguished cries in the dawn of the loyal foreign counselors when told they were to be expelled from the state of Qin. He reached the subtle essence of the spirits, *and straightaway seized control of the operations of the Transforming Power.*

This is a literary tour de force, embellished with scenic descriptions and similes, and references to ancient history and the attitude of the appropriate dcities. What comes through is the impact that the building of this bridge must have made on the local population. Tian, a Confucian official and hence in the fame competition himself, is grudging about the way in which he and his colleagues were upstaged in the popular mind by Jing's achievement. It also brings home just how tough it must have been to bridge the Guizhou rivers in premodern times other than with ropes. Only possible, so the rhetoric implies, when the exceptional sincerity of a dedicated mind could gain an ascendancy over the responsive forces of nature.

A remarkable bridge built by government efforts was that on the main imperial road to Yunnan. This ran southwest from Guiyang and crossed the gorge cut by the Panjiang river in Guanling county. Its first version was the creation of Zhu Jiamin during the 1620s, when he was leading the campaign to suppress the uprising of the tribesmen led by An Bangyan. It was yet another case of development being driven by military necessity.[121]

> The Panjiang River . . . has to be crossed by those going into Yunnan. Two mountains flank it, standing erect, while the river cuts its way between them. Heaven placed these cliffs, a thousand feet in height, and these fiercely flowing currents, to mark the boundary between Yunnan and Guizhou. . . . *Those who traverse it by boat in many cases sink and are drowned.*
>
> In the Tianqi reign-period [1621–7], the provincial military intendant Zhu Jiamin decided to build a bridge, but found it impossible to do so in stone. He thereupon copied the method used for the Lancang River [the Mekong] in Yunnan, and had thirty-six cables forged of iron, each several thousand feet in length. These were threaded through rocks on each of the two banks, and so suspended. They were covered with planks to make a walkway like the gallery roads along the edges of cliffs in Sichuan. With this the road was opened. It was a great achievement.
>
> If cables are long, then they will not be strong. What is more, when people walk along them, with their feet alternately descending on the left and the right side, this causes the walkway to rise and fall. People's bodies also swayed on this account. If they looked down giddily, they could not maintain themselves. Those riding in palanquins or on horseback had to dismount. It was necessary for those in front to reach the opposite bank before those behind began their ascent. If people walked closely following one another, it was even more terrifying. The danger was indescribable.
>
> In recent times [that is, early Qing] it has therefore been redone in better fashion in wood. Several hundred enormous timbers were selected, and

arranged in serried rows lying horizontally [and projecting outward] at the landing-points on the two banks. They were held down by huge stones, and [the parts protruding beyond the banks] were propped up by sturdy struts. As each layer was added on it extended further out, being of a greater length than those beneath it. Rings were bound around them to ensure solidity. When the extremities of the timbers extending from each side were a mere thirty-four feet apart, they further selected trees of ten feet in girth, and crisscrossed them in trusses over this space. Once this had been done, it was possible for two palanquins to cross side by side or two riders to proceed with bridle-bits linked together, and in successive groups as tightly packed as a string of fish, without any cause for alarm. Handrails were fitted, and the walkway was covered over with a housing made of boards painted red. Buddhist shrines and monasteries were arrayed in rows to the left and right on the banks, so dazzling that one had to shade one's eyes from the light. It was like a painting by the renowned Tang-dynasty landscapist Li Zhaodao, and in due course became one of the scenic attractions of western Guizhou.

There seems no way to square the primitive method used for the wooden bridge, which might at best have spanned a hundred or two hundred feet, with the statement that the cables or chains of its predecessor were several thousand feet long, though it is possible that these latter were secured at a long distance back from the gorge. Until the site can be looked at with this problem in mind, we have to leave it unresolved for the moment, but can note two other points. The first is that large trees were evidently still plentiful here in the seventeenth century. The second is that the bridge was not simply an instrument of Chinese imperial political domination, facilitating safe passage along the route the imperial couriers traveled. It was also *a symbol of Chinese cultural domination*, with its elegant buildings housing a locally unfamiliar religion, and transforming the scene into one acceptable to Chinese sensibility, the simulacrum of a Tang picture. Ding Wei was explicit about the bridge's deeper function: it was to spread civilization. "How could what was accomplished only be seen as a bridge?" he asked rhetorically.[122] Cheng Feng, in the seventeenth century, was more pragmatic:[123]

> Our soldiers go across it in clouds, to parry barbarian attacks,
> And so, exhausting the region's resources, do military funds and rations.

Tian's poem on the river has a more sobering message: Guizhou was still foreign territory for Han Chinese. The invader had always to be vigilant, or, as in the case of the surprise attack by Yi tribesmen described here, risk paying for his negligence with his life:[124]

Four peaks rise up like screens, in hues of reddish ocher.
Between them crosses the river Pan, cutting a route below,
Terrified waters through its gorges rushing like thousands of cattle,
While the trussed deck hangs in the sky above — a path for a single
    stallion.

Old trees offer no forest shade, nor do precarious thickets,
And what traveler of the common sort would dare to peer over that
    brink?
When dawn is breaking, the Yao-tribe wives come out of their deep-sunk
    caverns;
Then, in broad daylight, mobs of tigers roam the woods that here are
    uninhabited.

West of the depths, where the river forms pools, lie many gigantic rocks.
Is a light boat, with its puny oars, equal to such a crossing?
Sunbeams pierce to the face of the cliff. Tribesmen's fires smoke yellowish
    gray.
The rain-mists steam, malaria-laden. Reddish buff run the river's waves.

A local, of Han descent, turned to me, saying — and weeping —
"This is the place where, some time past, an army of ours was defeated.
Those then enfeoffed to guard this land cared only for goods and profits,
While lust for easily gotten glory gripped leaders and lesser officers.

"When heroes prepare a strategy, they do it in proper wise,
But even *this* much still holds good for villains and runaway wives!
The drums and trumpets rang to the clouds out of that army's camp;
Their lines faced mountains to the front, with the water at their back.

"They were cooking up beef, and splashing out drink, intoxicated with
    pleasure,
Arrows scattered about and crossbows forgotten, and still carousing
    recklessly
When the war-horses, all of them, were turned — into dust at the foot of
    this mountain,
And the warriors on campaign, each one, driven into this river to drown.

"The only ones lording it after that were the foxes and the wild boars,
As, frontier folk slaughtered and stockades sacked, the Yi turned to civil
    war,
And countless homes, with their chickens and dogs, were to the last one
    massacred,

And half the county cities with walls emptied of their inhabitants."

Grieving, high over the course of the Pan, the evening sun is setting.
Yellowing wormwood is here and there. White skeletons lie about desiccated,
Their souls absorbed in each fall sky, congealed into clouds of
  resentment,
Their lifeblood staining each springtime expanse, with its tall weeds of
  enmity.

Only today is this alien land loyal once more to His Majesty,
High signal beacons and sunken moats are where wasteland creepers
  clamber.
The shepherd lad drives his flocks of sheep across the burial mounds,
While the farmer leads his oxen-team to furrow the battle grounds.

Only the wayfarer is left to utter a sigh of regret,
And, hearing tell of the river Pan, find tears have wet his breast.

The past lingered. The ghosts of the dead soldiers and horses inhabited the place where they had died, changing its character for those attuned to such presences. But the past was also fading. The practical preoccupations of the country people soon led them to forget what had once happened. Places of memory, no less than bridges, need maintenance.

Travel and tourism

Moving around remained difficult and dangerous. Ge Yilong's poem "On the Road to Zangge"—'Zangge' being an ancient name for the Guizhou region—opens with the following depressing lines:[125]

Chill blows the wind through the midst of the stinging rain,
Though resistant mists still linger, hanging low over putrid water.
The watchman's rattle startles us. From a fort and in the daytime.
— To protect our traveling after dark, we cut firewood, and truss it with
  cords.

They had to be prepared to build fires to help keep off wild animals. Shortly after this he tells us that the roads were a morass, which was probably often the case, given the amount of rainfall. At a ford,

Wading over, and going through water, is what makes the menials feel
  pleased,
At once washing all of the mud off that has mired them up to their knees.

The perpetual humidity of the atmosphere was part of the physical experience of being in Guizhou. The opening lines of Huang Ke's "Climbing East Mountain" evoke this well:[126]

> The flags along the battlements droop, being impregnated with rain.
> Through the trees, and grass, by the city wall's edge, rises a fresh morning
>   haze.
> As the mountains gleam with an aqueous tint some hundreds of miles
>   away,
> And chickens cheep on the river's bank, people pass the time of day.

Some of the attitudes of mind that we associate today with tourism seem already to be appearing. The tourist travels to look and to sample: unfamiliar scenery, new foods, exotic peoples, transient sex. He is not there for the day-to-day business of trading or government. He may also be a pilgrim, looking for some form of elusive enlightenment, something missing in the world at home. A few illustrations will reveal the gamut of attitudes.

Qi Shun was a Ming official who lived in the fifteenth century. He was famous for 'riding alone' to the reception given for a Ming embassy to Korea— in other words with no elaborate retinue—and for refusing the gifts offered to him. Gifts so sumptuous that they were later used to pay for the building of a 'Rejecting Gold Pavilion' in his honor. Nonetheless Qi seems to have visited Guizhou as a tourist, not an official, and he left a poem about it.[127]

> Since my heart has been set, from boyhood, on the life of war and
>   weapons,
> I have journeyed across the Chinese world to arrive here at Shiqian,
> Where they wear grass skirts, hair rolled in buns, on civilization's edge,
> And think putting oxen and calves to the sword represents a harvest of
>   plenty.
> Mountains open out, like a painted scroll, blue-green in the last of the rain.
> In the nighttime quiet, the voice of the water lets one lay aside strings and
>   pipes.
> *An ordinary outsider* — come to fill no official vacancy,
> I lean at the window, and often my soul feels as light as the clouds are
>   white.

The common Chinese term for tourism was 'rambling and diverting oneself', and those with a compulsive taste for scenery were labeled 'followers of the mists and clouds'. In Guizhou they frequented the caves in the limestone formations, an experience they likened to being transported to one of the mythical Chinese lands of the immortals, or the fabled rural utopia of the

'Peach [Blossom] Spring'. An example is Chen Derong's "Rambling around Snowcliff Grotto."[128] The natural features of this, and other, famous caverns were given names, some simply descriptive, but many of them drawn from Buddhist and Daoist scriptures. Visiting them was an act not unlike the mixture of tourism and pilgrimage, aesthetically revitalized piety, and casually curious rubbernecking, with which many Europeans still enter their own medieval churches and cathedrals.

> It's been said, so I've heard, that the River Zang's like the Islands of the
>   Immortals,
> A scenic trip for those addicted to loneliness pure and subtle.
> With rock crenellations on every side, the ranges run off to the north,
> While, under the twin-arched Lizard Bridges, the water flows toward the
>   sunrise.

> Do not open a road through the cloudbanks for the Bluebird to answer
>   your summons.
> Rest a while in the workings of *this* world. Delight in *these* white gulls.

The Bluebird was the immortals' messenger from Fairyland, and is usually described as an oriole. 'White gulls' are commonly mentioned in verses about Guizhou. Some lines on springtime in the province, for instance, say[129]

> These white gulls do not keep away from the presence of human beings,
> But alight, with their wings uplifted, at the mouth of the little stream.

In Chen's poem the implication is of course 'these *real* white gulls' are more than a match for the Bluebird of the imagination.

But one was only meant to spend 'a while' in the immediately visible world. He goes on to speak of the religious inspiration of the caves. It is useful at this point to provide a few explanations in advance. Vimalakīrti, a historical personage who was believed to have undergone the 'disease of existence' to help save all sentient beings, was the central figure in one of the scriptures most influential in China. He was also famous for using a moment of silence to express the nature of the Absolute.[130] Lanterns were a many-valued symbol: they often evoked transmission—one flame lighting another—whether of reincarnation or the communication of spiritual awakening. The phrase 'each life' relates to the unceasing cycle of death and rebirth undergone by the nonenlightened. 'Single Finger' meditation was a technique of inducing insight developed by the Song-dynasty monk Tianlong and his disciple Juzhi: the single uplifted finger expressed the idea that all *dharmas*, or morally correct ways of living, were ultimately identical. The 'West' here is India.

The gate towers by the Jade Void Palace are wreathed with clouds of
    all tints.
The small cave below is that of the Heaven which Vimalakīrti
    administers.
From the voices of bells, and chiming stones, a Buddhist purity issues,
While under the shadows of firs and pines, the nighttime lanterns are lit.

Hearing the chanting, I wish to confirm each life's progress toward its
    Enlightenment.
As I sink into Single Finger Reflection, my face wears a fleeting smile,
The limitless wisdom that comes from the West is — slowly —
    interiorized,
As, year after year, by Jasper Brooklet, the fragrant flowers revive.

It is unclear how much of this—the chanting and lanterns, for example—was
'real' and how much in the visitor's mind. Since, in the Buddhist view, all
composite entities were mind-created illusions, perhaps this mattered less
than we might think. Note, however, the gently ironic 'should be' at the end of
the next quatrain translated below.

Chen now introduces elements from older Chinese metaphysics and
Daoism. The 'shapes' are the hexagrams from the *Book of Changes*, the patterns
underlying the flux of the universe. The crane, a symbol of long life, was the
mount on which the immortals rode through the skies. Zhuang Zhou's
butterfly is the best-known story in Chinese philosophy: he dreamed he was a
butterfly, but, on awakening, wondered if he might not be a butterfly dreaming
he was Zhuang Zhou, the real point of the tale being not that it is hard to trust
the truthfulness of one's senses, but that things are constantly being changed
into one another.

The storeyed towers soar straight up. Clouds and rivers curve like bows.
The Dipper hanging, Orion's Belt crosswise, shapes beyond count unfold.
I half imagine, on Jasper Brooklet, salvation's raft downstream floating.
In the azure sky, a crane comes flying — or *should be*, I suppose.

The butterfly dreamed of by Zhuang Zhou was not illusion, but fact;
And, though one disdains them, compassion is owed to every mayfly
    and ant.
The committed Buddhist meets as an equal the Emperor's diplomats,
And how to find the Immortals' Isles none but the guile-free may ask.

Becoming a sage or an immortal requires "totally cleaning away the innumerable causal affinities" that tie us to this world. Those "outsiders who sleep on
the snow and feed on the clouds," that is, who, like him, endure the hardships

of travel, are those who "sing in the breezes and enjoy the moon," in other words are touched by the beauty of nature. Such people, he implies, become like "the empty room that receives the light." The room is a symbol of the mind, and the light the light of understanding. In other words, they have taken the first modest steps toward enlightenment. Travel was painful, like a penance. Like a penance, it could lead to exaltation.

In a more vulgar mode, Tian Wen's "Welcoming the Spring" expresses the mixture of fascination and condescension aroused in educated Chinese by the colorful exuberance of Miao festivals.[131] Catching the tone of this poem in translation is difficult. Mockery and excitement are both there, as are moments of racial and cultural prejudice.

> The ruddy brown hump-backed ox to be offered has a coat in decrepit condition.
> The Spring God of Growth sports raven black locks, and is cracking a lengthy whip.
> A thousand men hold a horned dragon aloft whose jaws are exhaling mists.
> — A variegated barbarian show, red seals stamped on their springtime inscriptions.

> Stirring music, and martial maneuvers, follow each other in sequence,
> Formations assembling, in array, with magnificent technique.
> A troupe that look like grandfatherly farmers inaugurates the proceedings,
> Shouldering hoes, or driving their calves, showing prowess at plowing and weeding.

> Banners stand high, and 'BUMPER HARVEST' enormous letters proclaim.
> Flat straw rain-hats covering their heads, pants as tattered as tails of quails,
> Their backwoods ballads and rice-planting ditties are incomprehensibly strange,
> Delightedly imitating each other, eyes goggling and gobs agape.

> Another troupe follows the one before. Each turn is a different act.
> Masts in the wind, or formations of cavalry, soar about with inspired élan.
> Only fourteen, or fifteen, years of age, the youthful barbarian lads
> Have red lead smeared on their foreheads, and embroidered waistcoats and pants.

> They strum many-stringed zithers, twang guitars, or tootle upon the pipes.
> In helmets, with armor on their backs, they flourish their spears and pikes,
> Some, in the Land of All Sentient Beings, ride on elephants and upon rhinos,
> Or else quest for pearls and cowry shells under distant Persian skies.

Their strong men are sturdy as ramparts, and much like our own county
  magistrates,
Their beautiful girls on a par with those held in the harem in our Palace,
But how can their turbulent motions equal *our* Heavenly Magical Dancers?
And a singsong lass from Chengdu would be sweeter — for charming one
  during a banquet.

The most extraordinary ensemble is the one that comes on at the close:
Like birds in the insubstantial air, with bodies weightlessly floating,
They uplift their rumps and, with tiptoed feet, take their place on each
  others' shoulders,
Where they strive to perfect the ancient sword dance with swirling
  banderoles.

Shortly after this

The old village gentlemen chatter their gibberish, like devils with multiple
  tails,
The unwed shake bells, and love-caper in moonlight, their minds topsy-
  turvily crazy.

After more description and comments, Tian notes that the barbarians' musical
theatricals to welcome the spring attracted numerous spectators and that
subordinate government officials were given the day off for the occasion.[132] He
concludes by observing, not very modestly, that he has written a book, *Folkways
of Guizhou*, to celebrate the region. The learned official was functioning like
that indispensable adjunct to tourism: the travel-writer. And pushing his wares.

Diseases

There was a downside: microfauna. In particular, malaria was a problem in the
southern half of the province. It was probably mostly one of the less lethal
varieties, in other words *not* that inflicted by *Plasmodium falciparum*. In spite
of careful collective observations of the environmental conditions under
which it was likely to occur, it is remarkable that no Han Chinese here seems
to have connected it with its vector, the *Anopheles* mosquito. The link was well-
known by the Bai people in Yunnan and, at least from early Ming times on, by
the Chinese in close touch with them.[133] This is what Tian Wen has to say about
it in the *Book of Guizhou*:[134]

The aethers of malaria[135] are, in general, to be found everywhere south of
Zhenning[136] and near the province of Guangxi. Malaria occurs whenever, as

spring passes into summer, a light fall of rain has just stopped, the setting sun is sending its rays aslant, with red light and blue shadows spreading everywhere like a painting, but without a rainbow or sunset clouds, and aethers like those rising off glutinous millet being cooked in a steamer.

When people encounter these conditions they hurriedly lie face-down on the ground, or chew betel nut, or else hold a piece of local sugar cane in their mouths, which gives them some chance of escaping. If this proves unsuccessful, they at once fall ill in a way that resembles two-day periodic fever. After some time they become jaundiced, and their stomachs grow distended, a condition for which there may be no help for from one to two to three years. The root of the 'yellowflower' is needed to cure it. The yellowflower grows by streams and marshes. It is rather more than a foot in height, with leaves like those of the water-pepper [*Polygonum hydropiper*, 'smartweed']. It opens a pair of petals. The root can be used to catch fish, and also to counter insects [or 'reptiles']. The local people have an extensive knowledge of it.

In all likelihood, malaria has its origin in mountain vapors, these being the noxious aethers of the mountains and the marshes.

Georges Métailié of the Laboratory of Ethnobotany in Paris identifies the 'yellowflower' as probably the *Euphorbia chrysocoma*, which seems to be found only in Guizhou. Its full name is the 'water yellowflower'.[137]

Malaria usually has a periodicity that occurs in multiples of twenty-four hours as the *Plasmodium* takes its timing from the temperature cycle in the human body, though this pattern is less clear for the *P. falciparum* form. Enlargement of the spleen and liver is common; a jaundiced appearance can also occur under some circumstances. So the identification seems reasonable.

It also appears that the geographical incidence of malaria changed at the margins with time. The same source continues by referring to an extraordinary practice that was believed to get rid of it, but also in passing records this sort of change:

> *In the past*, Huohong and Luojia, which come under the jurisdiction of Zhenning, habitually suffered from malaria. *In recent times* people have used *firearms* to startle it, and doing so have dispersed it. This practice has subsequently become the norm, and in like fashion the disease has gradually become unable to cause people distress. It is certain that the aethers of the Earth change with the changing of the times!

Descriptions of journeys often mention the presence or absence of malaria. An example is He Jingming's "On the Road to Anzhuang."[138] During Ming times Anzhuang was a Guard Area to the southwest of Guiyang.[139] He begins:

> Homes everywhere uninhabited, marsh-grass and wormwood spreading,
> How long will this desolation last that was caused by war's disruption?
> Going through mountains, I cross the White Stream, where the summits
>   rise up abruptly,
> And the road comes down to the Panjiang River, *where malaria is prevalent.*

Hang Huai, an official and poet who flourished at the turn of the fifteenth and sixteenth centuries, seems to have stressed the seasonal nature of safe travel in his poem on the Panjiang:[140]

> Crossing the ridges and climbing the ranges while ailing from multiple
>   sicknesses,
> As the year ended and spring arrived I no longer planned an itinerary,
> Being well aware *these malarial waters* had caused many travelers
>   bitterness,
> And the only place for journeying now was high in the barren hills.

Tian Wen was more philosophical:[141]

> One sighs at the green on the mountains: *now malaria's poison is coming.*
> Nonetheless one delights, when the snow melts, in the odor of blossoming
>   plums.

Du Zheng, in more verses on the Pan River, recorded that travelers carried prophylactics:[142]

> Boisterous spate on the Pan, on a day in the third month —
> One roof-mat fends off *malarial rains* in our boat from barbarian
>   country.
> The ferry crossing is overgrown, hanging clouds hold us down like
>   fetters,
> And we travelers, *betel nut in our sleeves,* commiserate with ourselves.

As Tian Wen had indicated, betel nut was thought to ward off the disease, but it was best if malaria was not present at all. Li Jing[143] wrote these lines in Mongol times on the Pass of Seven Stars:[144]

> Both cliff walls hacked out, as with an ax, soar till they join the sky.
> A stream, just brushing and shaking the flowers, surges forth from the vent
>   of a cave.
> I have heard it asserted *malaria's absent* — provided the weather is fine,
> And that wayfarers making the traverse here have no reason to feel
>   dismayed.

Malaria was present in neither Jiaxing nor Zunhua, the focus of the next chapter. In Guizhou its distribution defined when and where the outsider could move with safety.

Wild animals in imagination and reality

Wild animals were human beings in another form. Here are three stories that illustrate this theme, one each about gibbons, tigers, and an elephant. In each case their 'humanity' takes a different form.

A story placed in the Tang dynasty shows that the distinction between gibbons and human beings in people's minds was somewhat blurred, and that gibbons might on occasions also belong to the superfauna.[145]

> In the Yuanhe reign-period [806–20 CE] Cui Shang . . . entered the gorges and came to Guizhou. The fall floods had gone down and his boat proceeded extremely slowly. The stream, caverns, and woodlands along the banks formed unsurpassed scenery. Shang therefore disembarked and, leaning on his staff, walked slowly into a remote area. He had not gone in more than a kilometer or two when he suddenly came upon human habitations. There were stone bridges, bamboo gates, houses built of planking, and reed-thatched cottages set along a winding stream. They had quite a distinctive appearance.
>
> Shang therefore made his way forward and found himself welcomed as a guest by a crowd of more than ten nuns. They had a lovely appearance and their speech was full of laughter. They were certainly not mere persons from the mountain valleys. He at once made his way into their dwellings, where he observed that the courtyards and sheds contained a great deal of sun-dried fruit; and he also noticed that all the houses were piled full with it. A moment later a lot more arrived in clusters from outside, carried in on the people's shoulders.
>
> Shang remarked to himself that these remote mountains and lonely valleys were not places where one could reside permanently, and suspected the people were uncanny apparitions. He therefore abruptly reversed direction to return. The crowd of nuns held him back and spoke many words of entreaty. After Shang had reboarded his boat, he asked the boatmen about this experience. They answered:
>
> "They were only gibbons and monkeys. People have met them in different places at different times. Because of your enlightened understanding, you

left rapidly. If you had not done so, it is likely that you would have been destroyed by them."

Shang at once assembled his menservants; and, grasping their weapons, they went to search them out and seize them. But all trace of the nun–gibbons had vanished.

The appearance of the Buddhist nun, with her shaven head and brownish habit, may have prompted a visual identification with gibbons and monkeys. This story also refers to a period when Buddhism was becoming somewhat unpopular with at least a part of officialdom. The most important act of imperial repression and limitation of the religion was to occur a couple of decades later in 842–5 CE. So the possibility must be borne in mind that this tale may harbor an aspect of anti-Buddhism.

The story about tigers is set in Feizhou,[146] in the northeast of Guizhou province, and also in the Tang dynasty.[147]

All the families of the barbarians in Feizhou have the surname 'Fei'. The area in which the clan lives suffers numerous assaults by tigers. It is the custom for everyone to live in houses with upper storeys so as to escape them.

Some time in the Kaiyuan reign-period [713–41 CE] Di Guangsi was the prefect here, and his grandson Bowang was born in the official residence. The husband of Bowang's wet-nurse was Fei Zhong, a strong and courageous man who was skilled at shooting. On one occasion he was returning home from the prefectural capital, carrying rice on his shoulders. The road through the mountains was obstructed, and before he was aware of it, the sun was setting. More than fifteen kilometers of his journey remained ahead of him.

Zhong feared that he would not escape unharmed, so he took his sword blade in hand and cut several bundles of firewood. He obtained fire by striking stones together, and set the wood alight in order to protect himself. Before long he heard the voices of tigers setting the woods and the undergrowth shaking. He put his turban as a hat on top of the sack of rice, girdled the sack with his belt, and left it standing in the light of the fire. He then pulled himself up into a large tree.

A moment later four tigers arrived together, and noticed the sack of rice. The largest among them advanced and seized hold of it, but when they had realized that it was not a human being they looked at each other in silence. The second largest tiger led the two cubs away, and the largest tiger remained alone beside the fire.

Then, all at once, he took off his skin. He was an old *man!* After that he crooked his arm to serve as a pillow, and went to sleep. Zhong had always been endowed with strength and swift reactions, so he regarded him as easy enough to deal with. Slowly he descended the tree, grabbed him by the throat, and directed his sword at his neck. The old man begged for his life, so Zhong bound his hands together and questioned him.

"I am Old Fei from North Village," came the reply. "*I have been punished by becoming a tiger.* The underworld officials have a schedule commanding me to eat people. This evening I should have eaten Fei Zhong, and was therefore waiting for him to come along. In fact I met up with this sack of rice, which made me most disappointed and depressed, but I thought that if I remained here, he would be certain to come back. To my surprise, I have been taken hold of by you, sir. If you do not believe me, you can look at the schedule on my belt, after which you will understand."

Once Zhong had looked at the schedule, he asked how he could save himself.

"If there is someone who has the same surname and personal name as you have," came the answer, "he can substitute for you. If, at some later time, the matter comes to light, I will be punished but the punishment will only amount to going hungry for ten days."

"There's a Fei Zhong in South Village at present," said Fei Zhong. "Could he substitute for me, or not?"

The old man agreed that he could. Zhong then first took the skin and put it at the top of the tree. After this he came down again and unbound the old man.

"I am under constraint," said the old man. "My body is up in the tree, but once I re-enter that skin then I will no longer recognize you. If, when you hear me roar, you fall down onto the ground, you will assuredly be eaten. The pattern-principles that govern phenomena are of this nature. It will not be a breach of our agreement on my part."

Zhong bade him farewell, climbed the tree, and threw the skin down to him. When he had the skin, the old man entered it from the hind paws. Once he had resumed his previous form, he gave several dozen mighty roars, then departed.

Zhong was able to return home, but several days later, as Fei Zhong of South Village was hoeing his land, he was indeed devoured.

Folktales from many cultures are based on a belief that some animals are human beings under enchantment, and can for a time assume their human shape again by removing their skins, and be prevented from becoming animals once more if the skin is withheld from them. This old and widespread idea has been interwoven here with Chinese conceptions of a supernatural bureaucracy that disciplines the dead in accordance with a penal code and a tariff of penalties and, in this case, a schedule for homicides. It seems likely that the Chinese sense of the ambiguous nature of such animals, that they are both like and unlike human beings, may have diminished in late-imperial times.

Elephants were different. Tian Wen's *Book of Guizhou* tells the following story:[148]

In 1625, under the Ming dynasty, once the rebels An Bangyan from Shuixi and She Chongming from Lanzhou had . . . raised troops to attack Yunnan, . . . few had the willpower to struggle with them.

Martial law was proclaimed in the province of Guizhou, and the forces of local chieftain Tao were transferred to Malong to exterminate them. An elephant was lying here deeply submerged in a little ditch. He sucked a hundred to a hundred-and-fifty liters of its muddy water into his trunk and, when the 'bandits' were least expecting it, rushed out trumpeting, leaping several tens of feet at a time, and squirting out the muddy water from his trunk. This created a cloudy fog and directly blocked the enemy's front line. Men and horses dashed off in all directions, or turned in circles, beset by panic. The 'bandits' leapt and fell about, or else pawed the ground like deer. Once the 'bandits' had been scattered in this fashion, the local chieftain's forces took advantage of the opportunity to chase them off to the north. A total victory was secured.

As evening was falling and the commander was calling his soldiers back, the elephant was still bubbling over with more than enough courage to spare, but his trunk had been smitten by poisoned arrows. The day following he was critically ill, and they pressed on his body to extract the residues of three arrowheads. Not long after this he died.

The people of Yunnan and Guizhou *made him a burial mound in gratitude, and erected a stone memorial tablet* on the south-facing slope of the Southern Mountain. I contributed the words of a commemorative inscription for them:

"Here is only the image of an elephant, such as one may find in the *Scripture of the Changes.* His eyes were tiny, his form immense. His trunk was long, his tushes huge, his flesh that of all the beasts combined together. His courage followed the course of the seasons. He was born in the wilderness, and reared in workyards and markets. Moving, he was like a cloud going by. Standing still, he resembled an uplifted peak. He was like the Bed of Seven Jewels owned by the Emperor Wu of the Han dynasty, spread with a coverlet embroidered in fivefold patterning. He possessed a most intelligent nature, having besides a considerable understanding of fidelity and public-spirited service. . . .

"With your unyielding stare and refusal to capitulate, *in what way were you inferior to heroes and men of high worth?* Whether we were to be in peace or in peril hung upon this one battle. While all others stood by doing nothing, you alone 'bared your arms for combat'. The robbers were bereft of their souls; they spat out their vital force. . . . Your blood has been transformed into a flitting ghost-fire. Your bones, interred, have become jade. The remnants of your ardent bravery are still alive. The grasses grow verdant, and golden are the clouds. The sinuous dragons that support the sides of this stele have the curved shape of a dangling elephant's trunk."

This story was an addition to the Chinese myths and legends that celebrated righteous animals—the dog rolling himself in water and wetting his sleeping master to save him from fire, the horse kneeling at the side of a ravine into which his rider had fallen and letting his reins hang down to serve the latter as a means of escape, and many others. Unlike these tales, the core events recounted by Tian were probably true.

The assertion of the moral worth of a member of another species has to be understood within the context of values determined by the human hierarchy, not in, of, and for itself. The imagined geospiritual absorption of the departed elephant hero into the landscape, where he remained in some sense still present, was also true for his virtuous human counterparts. Beyond this, we may note that he was a tamed elephant, broken in to useful work, and at times richly caparisoned. A member of human society.

Descriptions of reactions to most real wild animals were also based on the sense that it was human nature to interact with them emotionally, and at times physically, as beings that were half alien but also half kin. Thus Chang'an could write:[149]

Hearing gibbons cry, and tigers scream, makes one's inner mood depressed.
Under bright stars and the chilly moon one hastens with fearful steps.

But more cheerful companionship was also possible. Jiang Yingke, an official who flourished in the late sixteenth century, wrote about the Temple at Huayan Grotto that[150]

Birds observe the monks by the stoves, engaged in steaming their rice.
Beside the gate to the cave, gibbons swing by their arms from the pines.

A fear of tigers, however, was never far from the back of people's minds.

Shadows, falling across the gorge, gave the rocks a thousand strange forms
That became transfigured in autumn light into patterns of textures and
    stippling.

Once we learnt that tigers were passing through, having chanced to hear
  people talk,
Color drained from our faces. Advancing further was placed under
  prohibition.

Thus Ge Yilong in his poem "Among the Mountains of Pingyue."[151] Even the
smell of the animals made people uneasy. An official in the second half of the
fifteenth century wrote in "The Road to Anzhuang":[152]

Day's curtain has closed. The colors have darkened. People head home
  from their shopping.
A frowsy stench gusts from mid-ravine: on the bridge, a tiger has crossed.
The night-alarm's beaten. The moon's not yet bright, so we tarry a little
  longer,
The whole sky still cerulean blue, and nighttime some hours off.

A ballad by Lu Can in the sixteenth century on the sufferings of the soldiers
and the army porters in the frontier areas of the province contains the lines:[153]

Feel compassion! This is the season of snows, and frosts, and tempests.
They are famished. They are frozen. Feeble, but driven forward by the
  unrelenting pressure.
Their hands clutch for wheat-ear scrapings, to sieve in the streams for
  dinner,
Scalps and faces are grimed with grease, where the lice and the leeches are
  clinging,
In these lofty peaks and massive ranges, where slopes turn round countless
  bends.
Shoulders protrude through tattered clothes. Their legs have lost their
  strength.
Every three strides they glance behind. Every five they sink in gloom.
For the bamboo thickets and deep-set woods are filled with tigers' spoor.

Many Guizhou travel poems, dull enough to be convincing, also mention the
author's apprehension that he may meet a tiger.[154] Humans could also be hunted.

Exaltation, terror, and depression

The landscape of Guizhou and the Southwest induced contrasting moods.
One of the most striking was a kind of mystical exaltation. An evocative
example is a poem by Zhang Pengchong, an official, traveler, poet, and painter
who flourished in the first half of the eighteenth century.[155] The subject of his

verses is the waterfall at Water Pavilion. It should be explained in advance that the Chinese believed that rainbows drank from streams, and that the 'Pearl of Illumination' refers to Buddhist doctrine, sometimes symbolized by a mythical pearl known as 'Mani' that was believed to shine in the darkness.

> On the high track through the desolate peaks, I reached the last vestige of green,
> Hearing at times the noise of rushing that spoke from the narrowing streams.
> Extending across an age-old torrent was a bridge that I chanced on, startled.
> The meanders on the upriver side were so sleek they seemed spread with carpets,
>
> But downstream the current plummeted, to the Ping, sheer a thousand feet,
> Through a cleft. Then suspended in empty space, it fell in a single leap.
> Its mistiness seemed like the oscillations of uncountable sheets of gold foil,
> As the air currents kept them aloft, alternately sinking and soaring.
>
> In an instant's simple astonishment they had been transformed to haze,
> Blown about like unsteady snowflakes that drift down on a cloudless day.
> Above us a rainbow, drunk to perfection, was made what it was by the light.
> *Of scant worth is the Pearl of Illumination when the sun shines forth in the sky.*
>
> Overlapping, and breaking, then joining once more, the patterns of shadows were multiple,
> While the cliffs crashed down and boulders split, with a roaring that rumbled like thunder.
> My spirit teetered. My eyes were blurred, my heart–mind and soul topsy-turvy.
> I have heard that, of old, wild rhinoceros — lay hid in that whirlpool's swirling.

Zhang ends by telling us that he recited "in a clear voice" two chapters from the *Master Zhuang*, the Daoist scripture, namely "Transcendental Roaming" and "Autumn Floods." Both of these touch on the relativity of size, and the place of human beings in a universe vaster than they can imagine. He ends by stating, "No doubt my body will become an immortal who wings through the void." At the heart of the poem is the assertion that it is the real world—"when the sun shines forth in the sky"—that takes one to this state, not the Buddhist doctrine of unreality underlying all phenomena.

The capacity of the landscape also to inspire fear is the leitmotif of some verses on the rapids of Wuman by Tian Rucheng.[156] These rapids are in Guangxi, well south of the Guizhou border, though described in the Guizhou gazetteer.[157] The river they are on is one of the main tributaries of the West River, and they are famous for dangerous rocks that have been given individual names such as 'The Three Demons', 'The Horse Trough', 'Thunderclap', and so on.

> Like a single leaf we are floating downstream, in the midst of the flowing
>   waters.
> A thousand peaks are opening out, on either side of the rapids.
> The aquatic lizards are blowing the waves till they eddy around in vortices,
> In repeating circles, the swallows soar, using the wind to carry them.
>
> From the river, the giant rocks emerge, in order to welcome our boat.
> We travelers listen as, close by, swells the mournful dirge of the gibbons.
> I have never before been burdened by terror when facing dangerous
>   moments,
> But, having once ventured on this course, helter-skelter my heartbeat's
>   rhythm.

The life of the place is expressed not only by the reptiles, primates, and birds, but also the threatening rocks that seem alive. Fear of this sort can inspire an irresistible excitement, an intensity of existence that comes from the sense of a more direct contact with reality.

But the shadow from history cast by colonial dispossession could never be wholly exorcised. Li Rui's poem "On the Road to Parrot Brook" reminds the reader of the revenge taken from time to time by the 'bandits', or freedom-fighters, who were the Miao, and how the life force of trees, dogs, waters, and birds contrasts with human criminality: [158]

> Beneath the full moon, here and there, some ruined walls remain,
> And the stone gate, under the shadows of the dark green of the willows.
> The inhabitants deserted this place before the bandits raided,
> But the dogs, though their masters have left, know *they* must defend the
>   village.
>
> Along the channel the water is flowing, and brimming over the spillway.
> At the edge of the trees, the orioles chirrup, till daylight has turned to dusk.
> What causes of war made this pastured land become the scene of killings?
> It has caused me to sob, repeatedly. And my throat has choked on my
>   supper.

A depression that haunted a land of spectacular beauty.

9

🐘 *The Riddle of Longevity:*
Why Zunhua?

People lived longer in the late-imperial department of Zunhua in the mountains along the old Ming northern frontier (on the border between the Northeast and Manchuria). The expectation of life at birth for a woman was in the high forties, twice as long as in Jiaxing.[1] Ferreting out possible reasons for these differences is the most important question underlying this chapter on an area that came by Qing times to flourish even though its development was limited by environmental restraints.

Was Zunhua somehow healthier? If so, why?

Let us begin with a negative. The latest local gazetteer from imperial times, published in 1886, has no record of epidemics of infectious disease, though there was a temple to the God of Medicine, and traditional rituals to prevent sickness. This was in marked contrast with the coastal province in which Jiaxing was located, namely Zhejiang. In Zhejiang people were gripped by a fear of epidemics, and the epidemics were real.[2] Zunhua's situation was also different from that of Guizhou in the Southwest, which, as we have seen, suffered from malaria south of the Southern Ridge line, and about which visitors wrote so bitterly.

Epidemics, of course, there were. This appears from a list of the causes of untimely death afflicting local people. The catalog is part of an imperial order to the local City God, instructing him to be sure, in the local other world over which he presided, to see to the sacrifices for the unhappy souls who had lost their lives in one of these ways, or who were without living descendants, and probably not receiving ritual offerings.[3]

Some will have suffered, without justification, under the swords of the soldiery. Some will have perished at the hands of bandits, either on the water or the land. Some will have expired from rage when others forcibly seized their wives and concubines. Some will have been compelled to die by those robbing them of their goods. Others will have been unjustly executed as official punishment. *Some will have succumbed to epidemics when natural disasters were spreading abroad.* Others will have been killed by fierce tigers or venomous snakes; others again by the combined pressure of starvation and cold. Some will have lost their lives in battles or affrays; others have strangled themselves because of anxiety in crises. Some will have been crushed to death when their walls or houses crashed down in ruins upon them. . . . Lonely souls of this sort have no one to depend on in death. Their spirits do not dissolve but congeal into dark shades that attach themselves to plants or trees, or else become ghosts that cry out in anguished voices beneath the moon and stars, and moan through the winds and rains.

These anguished dead were part of the local population, and good government required they be comforted. Epidemics are not treated here as anything more general and terrible than a misfortune that could kill an individual.

This apparent comparative freedom from epidemic disease and other infection may have been related to a relatively low density of population. The first approximately reliable figures for the department are for 1820 and give 702,316 persons, with a household size of 6.4. By 1910, there were 899,354 persons with a household size down to 5.4.[4] It is, however, hard to calculate a meaningful value for density in hilly terrain where only a small part of the surface is habitable.

It may also have been in part due to winters whose temperature fell below freezing, so reducing the activities of at least some potential micro-organisms and their carriers. (Only a few insects, for example, are active at zero temperatures, or below.) The persistence of the cold throughout much of the year is evident in some local doggerel.[5] The dates refer to the months and days of the old lunar calendar, which begins in most years in February:

> On the ninth of the first, and the ninth of the second,
> Our feet are frozen, our fingers gelid.
> On the ninth of the third, and the ninth of the fourth,
> The cold is deadly for dogs and boars.
> On the ninth of the fifth, and the ninth of the sixth,
> We walk by the rivers to view the willows.
> On the ninth of the seventh the streams are in spate.
> Wild geese arrive on the ninth of the eighth.
> On the ninth of the ninth there's no ice left to thaw,
> To the ninth of the ninth we add one nine more:
> Oxen everywhere tilling the soil.

Zunhua was cold until well into May.

The quality of the department's water was high. This could have helped limit stomach and intestinal ailments. The mountain environment caused rivers to flow swiftly, and the rapid currents and sandy and gravelly surfaces could have contributed to the microbial filtering and to cleansing the water. (Passage through sand will, for example, remove most *Giardia*.) The Chinese in this period everywhere routinely boiled water for drinking and making tea, but probably not for long enough to be completely secure, if modern experience can be taken as a guide. Initial quality could still therefore have been important.

Zunhua people knew water could transmit sickness. Hence their custom, in the small hours of the morning before each New Year's Day, of tossing red lentils into their wells, persuaded that, if they did so, "during the entire year, those who drink the water will not catch infections."[6]

Turning now to the postive factors, it is clear that their diet was unusually high in meat and fruit by late-imperial Chinese standards. The economy was based on a mixture of modes providing an exceptionally varied combination. Dry-land arable farming was the foundation. The basic crops were millets and wheats. The fields were backed up by vegetable gardens, but the people of Zunhua were also skilled at silviculture, the art of cultivating trees. The additional foods that these provided, apart from the products like construction timber, firewood, oils, and wax, were an *environmental buffer* against hard times.

There was still some hunting, ranging from bears, whose paws were a gourmet's delicacies, to foxes, who were disdained as almost not worth bothering with. Stock raising was extensive. There were large numbers of sheep and goats in addition to cattle, and also donkeys, who were sometimes eaten as meat or made into soup. Pigs were nourished on scraps. A little sheep's milk was also drunk, an unusual practice for late-imperial China Proper.

Zunhua had been famous since antiquity for its fruit trees, including peaches and plums, each of which had an immense number of varieties. In later times its apples were celebrated, and exported out of the department, carefully wrapped in leaves. In the seventh lunar moon, "when the fruits in the gardens have all been plucked, this is known as the 'fruit harvest,'" in explicit parallel with the "millet harvest." [7] Fruits were a distinctive part of local culture. On the eighth day of the last month of the year, for instance, it was customary to mix beans and fruits with rice, and cook them into a porridge. This was smeared onto the fruit trees, in the belief that it would cause them to have plentiful yields.[8]

The relationship of diet to health is well established as a general principle but the details are complicated and often problematic.[9] Diet has played a major and too-little-recognized part in history, as the work of Mark Cohen has shown for ancient times and that of Alan Macfarlane for England in the eighteenth century.[10] All we can do here is to speculate that this varied diet may have helped provide a more than usually reliable supply of animal proteins, and of necessary minerals and vitamins. This could have been especially true of vitamins B_{12} and D, which are respectively virtually impossible and difficult to obtain from a vegetarian diet. If so, this would have strengthened basic resistance to disease.

Looking at the problem from a different point of view, there are indications that seasonal rhythms of work provided a sustained period of relative rest during the winter, in contrast to the round-the-year activity of the center and south of China. People may have benefited from the chance to recuperate from overwork.

Abundant timber was available for fuel and for buildings, though the supply has diminished during the present century. Very few people would have had to be cold indoors during the winter. Thus:[11]

> Those mountain trees near the frontier that have not been converted into the property of village domains are, if of small size, gathered for *firewood*. Those of larger size are smoldered under a covering to form *charcoal*, and transported to other areas. The price is cheap, the quality solid. Those who peddle it gather north of the departmental capital by the bend in the large river.

A fuel surplus in late-traditional times!

Finally, the women were not subject to the same degree of stress that burdened them in the lower Yangzi region, where they had both to manage a household and children, on the one hand, and work at handicrafts and farming, on the other. This could also have made some contribution to better cared-for children and to female longevity.

These suggestions are grouped together here to provide a preliminary overview. They are illustrated, developed, and qualified in what follows. It needs to be stressed that, while the problem of longevity is a real one, the answers suggested are speculative. At this stage they need to be argued about rather than believed. But the general point holds: the nature of the environment is one of the crucial determinants of rates of human survival.

Landscape and geography

Zunhua is located in the mountains of the Northeast of China Proper.[12] In ancient times it was part of the domain of the Wuzhong, 'mountain barbarians', who later founded the state of Wuzhongzi. In the seventh century BCE it was subdued by Duke Huan of Qi, the Chinese state that then lay to its south; and he in turn handed it over to the state of Yan.

The Wuzhong were part of a complex of tribes that included the later Xianbi and the Qidan, both of whom ruled parts of China at times. Though once spread over a much larger area than just Zunhua, the Wuzhong disappeared from history quite soon. All that survived was their name in the names of various counties for more than a thousand years.[13] In the preimperial period the area was almost a purely forest economy, famous for having no fields but a wealth of Chinese date trees and chestnuts. Historical sources give us occasional glimpses of what life may have been like in the early-imperial age. For example, around the end of the second century CE, when the Later Han was collapsing in disorder, Tian Chou, who came from Wuzhong, led his kinsmen and followers "into the Xuwu Mountains, where he encamped on a plateau amid the depths of the defiles, living there for a number of years. The common people rallied to him, reaching more than five thousand families."[14] This suggests that relatively inaccessible but habitable land was abundant in Yutian, one of Zunhua's three constituent counties, at this time. This was probably because the Wuzhong, and the Xiongnu barbarians with whom they had become mixed after the latter's defeat by Emperor Wu of the Han, had still not to any great extent adopted farming.[15]

The general view of educated people in late-imperial times of Zunhua's remoter past was that it was primitive and all but unknowable. Here is part of an inscription composed in late-imperial times by a certain Shi Pu, of whom we only know that he came from the area, to commemorate one of the many rebuildings of the walls of the departmental capital. The 'Springs and Autumns' (see Table 1) refers to the second quarter of the first millennium BCE.[16]

> During the Springs and Autumns period Zunhua was the state of Wuzhongzi. In its origins it was an out-of-the-way location, secluded in the mountains, and *utterly primeval*. I have not heard that there were any [large-scale] building operations. Even if there were, this state left no historical records. . . .
>
> There is documentary evidence for *the great walls* that ran along the northern border of the commandery for sixty or so kilometers. That built by the state of Yan ran from Zaoyang to Xiangping; that built by the Qin dynasty from Lintao to Liaodong. Both of these passed through the territory of this department. *Large-scale building* first appears in the histories during the Han and Jin dynasties.[17] For the first time, a division was made between the two counties of Wuzhong and Junmi,[18] but they were later again combined into one, as Wuzhong. If we use the [distances in the] present-day jurisdiction to determine how far this other ancient county was from the

county capital at Wuzhong,[19] it was not more than fifty kilometers distant in all. This implies that it was merely a mean little frontier village. Those who dwelt there probably passed their entire lives without knowing what inner and outer city walls look like. If some of them did know, how could it have been more than a distant vision of lofty walls and towering observation-pavilions?

In the Wude reign-period of the Tang [618–26], *an Imperial Horse-Buying Agency* was set up within the jurisdiction falling under the present department. The old gazetteers say that in Tang times *the city walls* were made of rammed earth. Might this have been done at the time they set up the Agency? . . .

During the several hundred years [before the Ming, when the area was not under Chinese control], those who governed the people here were so habituated to their simple rustic ways that they did not venture to propose the undertaking [of rebuilding the crumbled walls]. I have learned from elderly people that the first system of [these later] walls was exceedingly constricted. What is today the Wenming River used then to be the city moat on the western side, and the present drum-tower was anciently the stopping-point outside the north gate. Its circumference did not amount to half of that of the present system of walls.

The 'first' system of walls spoken of here is actually likely to have been that of the Ming, but there is controversy about this. Let us look at the alternating periods of Chinese and non-Chinese rule in more detail.

During the period of political fragmentation from the third to the sixth centuries CE, Zunhua was on the edge of the small state of the Former Yan, and several of its successors, which also bore the name 'Yan' in some form, and then of the Xianbi empire created by the Toba Wei. This age saw the spread of a more settled and more agricultural way of life among non-Chinese in the Northeast. This must have been partly prompted by the flood of Chinese migrants into Former Yan, fleeing the disorders on the north China plain. Murong Guang, who came to the throne of Former Yan in 314, and died in 348, is reported as having abolished his hunting enclosures and grazing-parks to provide farmland and gifts of cattle for the poverty-stricken newcomers.[20] This influx of Chinese farmers must also have led to further ethnic mixing.[21] Nonetheless, it is obvious from the references in the histories to the seizures of gigantic quantities of livestock by the victors in the perpetual wars of this age—horses, cattle, and sheep—that the pastoral economy remained important.[22] A little later, Feng Ba, the founder of the Northern Yan in 409, and a promoter of farming, ordered that those farmers who slacked at it should be put to death.[23] This ferocity suggests an archaic level of difficulty in having the new mode of production accepted.

The climate was unusually cold in this age. There is a story about Murong Xi, one of the rulers of Later Yan, that touches on this. Xi's empress was besotted by hunting. On one occasion he followed her to White Deer Mountain, which is about 42° N, well north of Zunhua, and then east to a point now close to the Korean border. On the way, five thousand of his soldiers are said either to have been killed by tigers and wolves, or to have been frozen to death by the cold.[24] Agriculture up here would have become easier in the warmer climate that set in toward the end of the sixth century.

As we have noted, the shadowy Wuzhong, the original inhabitants of Zunhua, were related to the Xianbi, and there are hints in our sources as to the kind of life the latter led. In 415 CE, there was a famine in what was then the Xianbi heartland and is today northern Shanxi province. The statesman Cui Hao, for all that he was profoundly versed in Chinese philosophical culture, urged the ruler of the Toba Wei, a Xianbi dynasty, on no account to shift the capital south. He held out a traditional vision to the still undecided monarch: "When spring comes, the grass will grow, and milk curds be produced. If these are combined with vegetables and fruits, that will see us through to the fall. If we then have a middling harvest, the matter will be done with."[25] This sounds not unlike the mixed economy on which Zunhua throve in later times: a combination of herding, gathering, gardening, orchards, and agriculture. More than seventy years after Cui Hao's plea, however, in 487, a shortage of food and "no green grass on the plains," finally forced the Toba to move south to the ancient Chinese capital of Luoyang. The decisive reason was the need to be within reach of cheap transport for supplies. On this occasion, the harshness and variability of the weather dictated the destinies of history.

We can glimpse early Qidan ways of life around the middle of the first millennium CE from the description of the Qi people, a branch of the Qidan, in the *History of the Sui Dynasty:*[26]

> Some follow water and grazing as they care for their herds. They live in felt huts, and place their wagons in a circle to make a camp. . . . Others are scattered throughout the mountain valleys, have no taxes to pay, and hunt with their bows for their wealth. For the most part, they cultivate a coarse millet which, once they have gathered it, they store in cellars under the mountains. They cut wood to make mortars, and use earthenware three-legged pots for their thick and thin gruel, which they eat after mixing cold water with the pulverized grain.

Their early diet in fact seems to have been mostly meat and milk, with dung being burned as fuel.[27] Some elements of this Qidan economic technology seem to have passed directly into Zunhua's heritage, an example being this use of cellars for storing food over the winter.

Some Xianbi songs have been preserved in Chinese versions. Even in what may be a second translation, or else a rendering of Xianbi-style Chinese, they still evoke something of the environment in which these herdsmen and horsemen lived.[28] They mostly refer, however, to the steppe-like lands north of the forested Zunhua, and should be taken only as the roughest of indications, since we lack other sources. Related cultures, but different environments. Thus:

> The sky is a round-topped tent of felt,
> A lid on the plain from east to west.
> The sky is azure, deep and rich,
> The plain a vastness, where nothing's distinct.
> *Then, as the grasses bend down in the wind,*
> *Suddenly sheep and cows are visible.*

The excitement of seeing the animals on whom life depended.

What it meant, psychologically, to be a northern 'barbarian' can be glimpsed from other songs. They have at times a bleakness of heart, a directness about the imminence of death, and a celebration of physical sexuality that are un-Chinese. Here is a traveler away from home:[29]

> From the head of the slope, the water flows,
> And, flowing away, leaves the hill behind.
> I think of myself here, on my own,
> Like a changeable wind in the empty wilds.
>
> I start out at dawn with a heart that's light,
> And evenings I lodge at the top of the slope.
> The cold is beyond any words to describe.
> My tongue curls up inside my throat.
>
> From the head of the slope, the water flows,
> But the song of my voice, deep down, is choked.
> So remote Qin River, once my home,
> That my will to go on is forever broken.[30]

The second song is about masculinity, the frightened feelings behind the mask of courage, and the transience of the warrior's glory:

> A man must not waver in what he desires,
> Nor give pledges of friendship to many companions.
> The bird of prey wings on his way through the sky.
> Uncertainty reigns in a rabble of sparrows.

He lets loose his horse on the wide, watered, meadow.
His horse swells his stomach on fine-tasting grazing.
Plates of iron serve as bucklers across back and breast,
His sword curves like the plume on a hill-pheasant's tail.

The ranks standing in front eye those standing behind,
Then iron breastplates align in covered-off ranks.
Heads in the front glance along the rear line,
Then the points of iron blades become squared off exactly.

A man's but a crawling beast, fit for compassion.
He goes forth from his door, sick with anguish he'll perish.
His corpse lies there killed, in the narrow hill valley,
With none to pick up his bleached relics of skeleton.

One stanza will do to illustrate barbarian style in singing about making love. After four verses of amatory *double-entendres* on the subject of riding horses, such as whipping and saddling, a song concludes as follows:

A vigorous lad needs a frolicsome mount
As a frolicsome mount needs a vigorous lad.
Once hoofed under the dust, and heel-stamped down —
No more 'mares-and-stallions' after that!

The age-old message: Death is coming. Get on with it!

Life is almost always defined in terms of animals: the superiority of the determined raptor to the muddleheaded sparrows; the splendor of the young warrior on his well-fed steed, off to die; the image of the boundless vitality of love-making horses—propaganda for the sexual act.

During the later Chinese Middle Ages Zunhua was a zone in which the northern 'barbarians' clashed repeatedly with the Chinese. Su Che expressed a standard view of 'Yan', the ancient general name for this region, when he wrote in Song times that[31]

The hills, in the ranges of Yan, wind like a serpent extending
Over hundreds of leagues, to keep Chinese apart from barbarians.

The customs of the people, he noted, were different from those elsewhere in China. "From long ago they have been accustomed to both farming and fighting." And he added:

At the present, half, already, have it seems acquired the habits
— Heirs though they be to the Han and Tang, of — sad to say it — *savages*.

Why so? The area had passed into Qidan hands in 937, as part of a block of sixteen northeastern prefectures ceded by the Later Jin dynasty. It later came under the Jürchen in the twelfth century and the Mongols in the thirteenth, not reverting to Chinese sovereignty until the start of the Ming, four hundred years after it had first been surrendered.[32] Many Chinese had, however, fled of their own free will to the Qidan during the troubles at the end of the Tang, and just afterward, taking with them important technical skills, including iron-working. Since we do not have specific materials for Zunhua during the second half of the first millennium CE and the early second millenium, it is useful, to form some idea of the last, to look once again at more general accounts of Qidan life at this time, provided it is remembered that, as before, they mostly refer to areas north of Zunhua, and with a drier climate.

Those who were captured in war, or became part of subjugated populations after a military defeat, were treated as slaves. On occasion they might even be tied with cords to trees to stop them running away, but a better means of reducing the frequency of escapes was found to be furnishing them with wives.[33] Su Che, when on his mission to the Qidan, made the interesting observation about the Chinese laborers he found there obliged to toil at farming that "little by little their clothing changes, but they still keep their language."[34] Eventually, though, one suspects, even such slaves became assimilated.

When Su Song likewise went north on a mission he commented on the flocks of sheep "numbered in hundreds and thousands." He noted that the animals were allowed to find their own way to grass and water in the summer months, and not confined, "yet they multiply most abundantly." The Chinese style in animal management tended to favor tighter control—hence the slightly grudging 'yet'. He observed that the same held for horses. The Qidan neither trimmed their hooves nor clipped their manes. "They say that if horses can follow their own nature, they will multiply in greater numbers."[35] He was unhappy, however, to learn that the tenants he witnessed toiling at farming, all Chinese, were heavily burdened with exactions.[36]

> High and low, the balked fields spread away, like the lines on a board for chess.[37]
> Counted in valleys-full, horses, and cattle, crisscross in every direction.
> With hundreds of taxes and corvées, there are few days off for leisure.
> It calls for pity that people's lives should be so constantly vexed.

The term 'balked' is used for a Chinese term that means the end of or the boundary of a field, but what Su Song was seeing was probably ridges. This is explained in another account of the Qidan world from the eleventh century.[38] The key phrase is italicized:[39]

Once one has gone out through the Old North Pass one is in barbarian territory. The inhabitants here have straw huts or houses made of planking. They still engage in farming, but lack mulberry trees and silk-thorns [whose leaves were also eaten by silkworms]. Everything they plant is *on ridges,* because of their worry that the blowing sand will block their growth. Tall pines adorn the mountains, and many pursue the trade of charcoal-burning in the deep valleys. From time to time one sees animals being reared: cattle, horses, and camels, with black sheep and brown pigs being especially numerous.

The Chinese commentator's awe at the abundance of livestock comes through here, as in many accounts. When on one occasion the Qidan defeated the Jürchen, they are said to have appropriated over two hundred thousand horses.[40] Even discounting for historian's hyperbole, this must have been a staggering number. When, somewhat earlier, Liu Rengong had ruled in Youzhou at the end of the Tang dynasty he had used environmental warfare against the Qidan animals. Each year, as the frosts began to fall, he would have all the grass in their lands burned. This caused so many of their horses to perish from starvation that they had to bribe him to stop it. In part with a gift of horses.[41]

The glossary appended to the *History of the Liao Dynasty* expresses an appreciation of the intimate knowledge that Qidan hunters had of the habits and dispositions of wild animals.[42] In particular, "it is the nature of deer to hanker after salt, so they lure them by sprinkling salt on the ground, then shoot them." Hunters might also blow on a horn at night in such a way as to imitate the cry of a deer, and when the deer had gathered, dispatch them in the same manner.

A mix of farming, a little hunting, and a lot of stock raising, and tree cultivation can be glimpsed from the text of a stele composed under the Qidan-Liao dynasty that describes the restoration of the Buddhist Golden Cockerel Sighting Temple and its estate. Besides having to reopen the temple pawnshop to provide income from interest on loans, the estate had to be reorganized under an incorruptible manager lest "the elegance of the mountain workyards merely serves to bring in funds from firewood and stock raising." The farmland was therefore expanded to 3,000 *mou* and the "mountain forests" to over 10,000 *mou,* with more than 7,000 fruit trees.[43] As has been said earlier, the late-imperial Zunhua economy was to be a combination of elements from these three sources, with the different modes mutually supporting each other. Growing fruit trees and silviculture were ancient local skills. Intensive dry-field farming was a northern-plain component brought in by Han Chinese. Herding and hunting were the Wuzhong and Qidan contributions. The models for the agro-pastoral-silvicultural economy that we find in late-imperial times in Zunhua were thus already established by this period.

Knowledge of the centuries before the Chinese re-established themselves under the Ming was hazy even at the beginning of this dynasty. This gap in memory could haunt scholars of later times. Toward the end of the nineteenth century, Ding Wei, a holder of the metropolitan degree, wrote "An investigation into Back Lake," in the attempt to reconstruct the past of an area known as the 'Forest Off To One Side', about fifteen kilometers west of the county capital of Yutian.[44] It is one of the first attempts at environmental history in China, and so worth quoting at length,

During the reign of the Emperor Shizong of the Jin, from 1161 to 1189, the area had been the site of an imperial traveling lodge, and designated the 'Royal Forest'. But there was *no forest there* in Ding's day:

Granary South Of The Forest is one of the eight market towns of our county. To the north of it lie marshy thickets known as 'Back Lake'. . . . An old tradition has it that this was the hunting enclosure of the Qidan empress Xiao.[45] There is, though, no evidence that this was so.

The *History of the Jin* records a "Royal Forest for the Imperial Traveling Lodge at Yutian." It provides an extremely detailed account of the comings and goings involved in the emperors' tours there. For the most part, they went to hunt. . . . For the fall hunt they always went to Jizhou, but the springtime hunt was invariably held at Yutian, which must have had swamps and thickets where they could engage in fishing and the chase. My personal view is that Back Lake meets the requirements for this. Some may find fault with this as a forced interpretation, but it is one that I find I cannot avoid. Here is why:

I have reflected that though I was born and grew up in the town of Granary South Of The Forest, . . . I have never known from where the name 'South Of The *Forest*' was derived. Now, six kilometers east of the town is a village called 'East Of The Forest'. Four kilometers west of the town is another village, called 'West Of The Forest'. *Where, today, is this 'forest'?* Back Lake is directly to the north of South Of The Forest, and located exactly between East Of The Forest and West Of The Forest. It is spacious and open, yet secluded and hidden away. Water is abundant at all times of the year.

At the start of the Yongzheng reign-period [in 1723], several tens of hectares of wet-field rice-paddies were in operation here, with only the center of the lake left as a reservoir. Later on this latter was occupied by crafty folk, and farmed. . . .

Today, these wet-field paddies have become choked with rushes and weeds. When one passes through the area one thinks mournfully of *how swift is the change in landscapes in the course of time.* Lush vegetation stretches as far as the eye can see, the smoke rising from the hamlets blending with the bluish verdure of the hills. A place where, when the breeze is mild, the overflowing waters gentle, and the clouds low, the fish swim idly by and birds take their ease, while animals like foxes and badgers make their way unobtrusively up and down, appearing and disappearing in its midst. Whether one uses a hook or shoots with a bow and arrows, one always hits one's quarry.

It happens at times, when the grasses have withered and leaves fallen from the trees, and the height of the water is down so the sands extend out level, that brave men with eagles on their forearms, and brown hounds on leashes behind them, come out on excursions with fur-caparisoned horses and attendants following them. This is because its untenanted space serves as a hunting-ground, and why it is the most celebrated of the swampy thicketed areas in our county.

Imagine in addition the lavish arrangements of an enclosed park for hunting, embellished with palaces and residences, and it is not hard to reconstruct in one's mind a 'Weeping Willows' traveling lodge for an emperor or a 'Soaring Forest' enclosure for the chase.[46] *What other location, apart from this, fits so well with having been where long ago the Jin rulers hunted in Yutian?* So one may sigh: we need look no further for what was once called the 'Royal Forest'. What is more, the word 'forest' in the names of the villages and towns also derives from this. It is apparent that *what is today Back Lake was anciently a wood.* . . . That in times gone by it was the hunting-ground of emperors is hardly to be doubted.

How are we to be certain that the traces left by the Jin were not inherited by them from the Qidan? If this were so, it would not seem impossible that we can push back the place's use as a hunting enclosure to Empress Xiao. It is essential, though, to look for the site of the imperial traveling lodge. The departmental gazetteer records that there were broken bricks in the ground by the Decorated Pavilion of Empress Xiao, which served as witnesses. This was later enough to prompt His Honor Ji Jiguang to carry out *excavations* [in the sixteenth century]. . . . I have heard, moreover, that at the time when the wet-field paddies were in operation, and they were dredging the reservoir formed by the center of the lake, they found iron chains several tens of feet in length, as well as miscellaneous objects whose high value was consistent with their coming from the Decorated Pavilion. Much the same holds true for the mirrors and coins that are recorded as having been obtained, but if we do not have access to those who found them, how can we speak rashly? This does not apply to the finds by certain people in certain places of objects modeled in clay such as tiles in the form of bronze birds, or bricks shaped like quincunxes of phoenixes, things that one does not set eyes on in normal life. To sum up, a palace, a forest, and things pertaining to them, have not been found anywhere except Back Lake.

For recent times we must take into account that small groups of cow lads and aged woodcutters have sometimes glimpsed, half-hidden in the mists, city walls and the gate towers of palaces, which vanished when they approached them more closely, like mirages at sea. These uncanny wonders relating to Back Lake vie with each other to be passed on from one person to the next. I would not be so presumptuous as to doubt them. Were I to do so, I would be even more imposing my own interpretation, and doing no more than ridiculing them as the deluded tales of village folk. For the moment, let us appraise the matter on the basis of what is reliable in the histories and on what people have witnessed collectively, this being of more substance than what has only been seen often [by individuals], and so test the credibility of our conclusions.

What is interesting is the effort to reconstruct the memory, not so much of a people—since neither the Qidan nor the Jin were Chinese—as of a *place*. There was a powerful response to the appeal of archaeology, the emergence out of the soil of artifacts from a different world, eloquent and yet bafflingly mute. There was also a sense that the presence of an extraordinary past could linger in its old haunts, and show itself fleetingly to ordinary people.

When, toward the close of the Mongol dynasty in the mid fourteenth century, Pan Boxiu, who hailed from southern Zhejiang, wrote an attack in verse on foreign rule over China, he spoke as if he was in the Yan mountains.[47] Whether in fact or in imagination it is not possible to be certain—probably imagination—but the place was appropriate to his theme.

His reference-laden lines need a commentary in advance. The term 'Liao' indicates the Qidan people, whose Liao dynasty ruled Manchuria and the surrendered sixteen northeastern prefectures in Northern Song times. Many of the senior officials under the Mongols were drawn from lands to the west of China, and even spoke Persian, not Chinese or Mongol, as their lingua franca. The term 'fair lord', which normally has the singular sense of 'the ruler', is construed here in the plural to fit better with this western origin. The term 'gold' suggests the Jin or 'Gold' dynasty of the Jürchen people who ruled northern China for most of the twelfth century.[48] The phrase 'tussocked dunes' is an amplification of a reference to a sandy area in Shaanxi, near where the Luo River joins the Wei, not far from the great bend to the east taken by the Yellow River. This place[49] was a long way away from the Yan mountains, which reinforces our impression of a poem conceptualized rather than observed. It had long been famous as a grazing-ground for horses, who here symbolize the invaders. Cranes, on the other hand, were the mounts of Chinese 'immortals'. The brambles suggest the abandonment of farming, while the eagles may hint at Chinese heroes. The oddest feature is the use of the porcupine to represent Chinese resistance to foreign occupation, but he had the reputation of being a fierce beast, capable of fighting with tigers and shooting his quills into humans,[50] and the context seems to make this reading inescapable.

> The Liao sea, to the east, is an emptiness, whence no crane is now coming back.
> Sleet, falling, chills the horizons of these uplands cluttered with brambles.
> Heaven's vault does not move in the frost. The circling eagles have vanished.
> The fall sky's high aloft, above tussocked dunes, where the well-fed horses are pastured.
>
> Our fair lords, from the land where the sun sets, are singing of military discipline.
> In the wind from the west, the hunting horsemen grip the Gold bridle and bit.
> But the porcupine, fiercely facing forward, has taken his stand and now risen,
> Having broken clear by braving the onslaught of bows twanging and arrowshafts whistling.

The first four lines of Pan's poem show how landscape could at times be used as a political metaphor. But the political metaphor, by how it is chosen and formulated, also tells us something about the nature of the landscape.

After the Ming reconquest Zunhua county abutted on the rebuilt Great Wall, being home to many of the garrison troops. In 1513 the magistrate, Li Xinjian, after three years in the job, had a stone inscribed and set up in his office compound so that those who succeeded him could "understand the difficulties of this county, and the unending terrors of this official post." He noted that by his time there were only slightly more than two thousand registered households of commoner–civilians in a jurisdiction extending about a hundred and fifty kilometers in each direction. He ascribed this reduction in the population to the ravages committed by the soldiery, which had induced many civilians to return to their old homes elsewhere, and also to the vexations of taxes and compulsory labor-services. He was surprisingly frank about the way in which he was outranked by the local top brass:[51]

> At the most honorable of levels, the regional military authorities exercise their supervision here. At the most onerous of levels, the generals in charge of external military affairs exercise their commands from here. The soldiers under the Three Guards Camp are stationed here on frontier garrison duty. The hay and grain for nine battalions and thirty fortified camps at the barriers are supplied from here. In a more distant context, the tribute to the Court from the Duoyan Mongols[52] starts off on its journey to Beijing from here. Closer to hand, there has been a constant increase in the passage of imperial carriages, relatives of the imperial family by marriage, and meritorious officials through here.

This jeremiad suggests a crucial point. A century and a half later the Manchu–Qing conquest brought to an end the multimillennial war between farmland and steppe. By the middle of the seventeenth century the Wall was no longer a frontier zone, and most of this military superstructure vanished. What was left behind was an enclave of environmentally underexploited terrain.

Emotions associated with the Wall likewise changed once it was no longer a threatened line of defense. In Ming times, when it still was, Li Panlong wrote in a poem about it that "I do not know if any place, here, is not deserving of grief."[53] Under the Qing, however, Li Xijie took explicit delight in how the new dynasty had transcended the age-old conflict, and made obsolete the euphemistic names that Chinese governments had previously bestowed on their beleaguered border territories:[54]

> The snow on the hills is so hazy, that one's sunken eyes strain to see.
> Filing out through the Great Wall the horses are trembling and freezing.
> These days, to style it 'a frontier pass' is something that's almost ceased.
> — Who first called this ancient commandery by the name of 'Northern
>   Peace'?
>
> Those of strong and heroic temperament rise up to be seasoned generals.
> Those whose theories *follow* success or defeat are but contemptible
>   pedants.
> *This Great Work now takes its repose,* that was once Qin's especial splendor.
> — Do we know how long past the Mountains of Yan acquired their historic
>   celebrity?

The implied answer to the question with which each stanza ends is something like 'time out of mind'. 'Northern Peace' is of course 'Beiping'. A frontier that had seemed immutable had gone. Emotional responses had dissolved and recrystallized differently.

By the middle of the eighteenth century, educated people's experience of the Yan mountains had also changed again. Once synonymous with the clash of cultures across a frontier that had lasted, with shifting fortunes, for more than two thousand years, they had become transformed into a tourist attraction. One sign of this was a little guide, entitled *The Ten Scenes of Zunhua*, which is reproduced in the department gazetteer. Each entry consists of a topographical description followed by a poem from the brush of Fu Xiu, who served for a time as the department magistrate.[55]

> Omnipresent these outstretched ranges of Yan, where once lay the Yuyang domain.
> In unbroken succession, the overhung cliffs, stacked above with new growth in green layers.
> Their uplifted landforms seem empty of substance, as if cut adrift from their base.
> In touch with the skies, uprising, protruding — one might think they were soaring away. . . .
> I turn back my steed on the lofty ridge, my thoughts filling with history's residues,
> And examine the rock-walls — multitudinous — hazy, errant, with no fixed direction.

The dramatic millennial fault-line between cultures had become *scenery*.

The imperial tombs

Under the Qing, Zunhua became the location of the eastern group of imperial tombs. Seven preconquest Manchu rulers had been buried in Manchuria at three sites near Mukden. The first of those to be entombed here was the Shunzhi Emperor, who ruled from 1643 to 1661 (though the reign-period by which he is usually known did not start until 1644). The Zunhua group also included the great emperors Kangxi, who reigned from 1661 to 1722, and Qianlong who was on the throne from 1735 to 1796 (but died in 1799). Others there were the Xianfeng and Tongzhi emperors from the nineteenth century, and the famous—or infamous—Empress Dowager Cixi, who lived from 1835 to 1908. A third imperial burial site was inaugurated west of Beijing by the Yongzheng Emperor, who ruled from the end of 1722 to 1735. Others buried in the western tombs were the Jiaqing, Daoguang, and Guangxu emperors.

The tombs were sited just to the north of the Wall, and are now historical monuments. When they were still so to speak 'alive', the state maintained around them a ring of 'mountains out of bounds for geomantic reasons'. Geomancy, or 'winds and waters', is Chinese earth-magic. Since ordinary hunting was taboo here, the area turned into a nature park, and otherwise hunted animals like deer flourished. Today the area around the mausolea is one of the largest reserves in the People's Republic.[56]

Though there were always skeptics, most late-imperial Chinese believed to a greater or a lesser degree in sepulchral geomancy, that is, that the relationship of an ancestor's grave with the hidden forces coursing through the earth had an effect on the fortunes of his or her descendants. So it was that when, in the later nineteenth century, Li Hongzhang, the governor-general of the province that is today Hebei, wanted to open a railroad to service a new coal mine just to the south of Zunhua, his opponents accused him of menacing the geomantic well-being of the dynasty's tombs. Even if probably only a pretext covering other motives (especially since it only ran across the southeast corner of the department), it was an accusation not easily overcome.

The tomb complex lay in an enclosed valley north of the Wall, about seven kilometers from north to south, on the south-facing slopes of the Abundance Terrace Range of mountains (*fēngtái lǐng*) rather more than thirty kilometers west of the departmental capital. The more grandiose title of Phoenix Terrace Mountains (*fēngtái shan*) was bestowed on them for this purpose, a characteristic Chinese name-magic operation. In 1662 the designation of the principal peak was altered once again, this time to Gloriously Auspicious Mountain, which was even better nomenclatural wizardry. It was appointed an 'Altar to the Earth' where sacrifices were performed. The gazetteer for Zunhua tells us that the entire peak has the form of the tablet used by both an emperor and his officials to write on during sessions of the Imperial Court, and that "its shape resembles the Umbrella of State."[57] Choosing this spot was thus also configuration-magic, which we have already met in less exalted guise in the cinnabar mines of Guizhou.

The 'Pool of Heaven' in the following passage from the gazetteer is a literary name for the sea, and translations of place-names are given instead of mere transcriptions in order to convey the feeling of the piece. Topographical features acquired an evocative power deriving from names and semblances.

The Mist-Magic Mountains Of The Emperors To Come arrive here from the Great Line Mountains, winding this way and that down to the Pool of Heaven. The multitudes of pinnacles are arrayed in natural fashion like an enclosure wall. To the front rises Golden Star Hill, while behind runs the Watershed Range. To the east are Tallyfish Pass and Aster Gorge, while to the west lie Broadhunt Gorge Pass and Mount Yellowflower. All of these scenic points constitute *a surrounding entourage paying court to the imperial dead* just as the countless stars bow down before the Pole Star. Streams on their separate courses flow to either side, embracing the location, which they serve as outer halls and inner garments. They then join together in the Dragon And Tiger Gorge, to pay court to the Gulf of Bohai into which they discharge.

The position-power of the site is strong and its arteries [along which the earth-forces travel] are far-reaching. It is the multi-multimillennial foundation of our Qing dynasty from which this latter derives its solidity and durability.

The tombs were conceived of as a secret magical accumulator of forces from which the dynasty replenished its strength.

The beauty of the approach to the tombs moved several of the emperors to pen verses on their journeys to and fro. These may often have been polished by the scholars in their entourages—who knows?—but a handful are fine evocations of a countryside that was cool, rich, and healthy. An example is the Kangxi Emperor's "stanza improvised while in the imperial palanquin on the road through Plum Tree Gorge":[58]

As the single rivulet bends and unrolls, We behold the mountainside blooms,
Our bearers stepping on moss-covered stones, where the willows lean in from the vertical.
We look for those trees whose fruits in abundance are just *now* on the point of maturing,
Green hazelnut husks and excellent plums, both deserving of Our superlatives.

His somewhat baroque ballad on the hot spring at Lucky Spring Temple, to which an imperial travel lodge was attached, is perhaps more characteristic of imperial versifying. It is born of a mental state that moves back and forth between a sharply observed reality and a self-congratulatory fantasy distilled from history, myth, and metaphysics. Square Vase and Rounded Peak were two of the five island-mountains of the immortals. The Purple Fungus was an omen of good government. The Scarlet Herb was a food that bestowed eternal life. Emperor Wu of the Han dynasty, almost two thousand years before this poem was written, had built a Palace of Outflowing Fragrance, to which an allusion is made. Pills made from stalactites were reputed to convey longevity, and true Daoists were thought to be obliged to wear 'Metal Stalk Flowers' in their hair. Emperor Wu is also said to have left out a basin at night to catch dew, in the belief that drinking it would confer immortality. The Bright Force and Dark Force are of course the *yin* and *yang*. The Jasper Orchards were a part

of the domain of those who had achieved perpetual life. What follows is about
two-thirds of the original:

> The warm water, from the hot spring, is both transparent and bubbling:
> A source for immortals, trickling up from far off, out of the long-life
> cinnabar.
> On ritual bath-days, the magic-filled liquid brims over here in abundance,
> Its faint ripples, and imperceptible tremors, flowing past Us like jadestones
> tinkling.
>
> As it starts to run down the stone conduit's slabs, the overflow's sun-
> warmed and smooth,
> Filled, scalding, with power that can, unequivocally, challenge the
> sunbeams in ardor,
> And, while eddies, and jade-green rapids, give transient rest to dropped
> blooms,
> Under blue-green summits that darken the sun, the frostbound forests are
> sparkling.
>
> The stream meanders between the soft sand spits, then enters the railed-off
> precinct.
> Bricked about with its ornamented stones, how profound is its limpidity!
> Just as Mount Square Vase, and Rounded Peak, grow warm by themselves
> in season,
> So the Purple Fungus and Scarlet Herb still flourish throughout the
> winter.
>
> As the inner hall's opened, the fragrance diffuses, and precipitates stalactite
> marrow.
> The low basin collects enough dew of long life for the metal-stemmed
> flowers to float.
> Health's vigor is stored, as Bright Force and Dark Force come into a perfect
> balance.
> To recount how Fire's potency helps other beings is hard to find words to
> evoke. . . .
>
> We cannot be far from the Jasper Orchards, when here on Our seasonal
> visits.
> Our mind is composed, and at peace, when it contemplates all these
> perspectives.
> Clear, embroidered hills, in multiple colors, lie silently in the distance,
> While about Whale Rock, the wild duck, and wild geese, fly crisscross in all
> directions.

Why's this spring so unique in the way that it manifests numinous
   miracles?
Tens of thousands of years of valiant deeds gird round Our imperial citadel!

Dreams of the eternity of the self and of everlasting dynastic survival merge,
both of them elusive, problematic, and infinitely desirable. At the same time
Kangxi conveys the sense that the place was healthy. He may of course have
been inclined to say this because Shunzhi, the first Manchu emperor of China,
was entombed here; but it seems reasonable to assume that the location would
not have been chosen in the first place if it had not been so.

The Qianlong Emperor, a compulsive writer of mostly indifferent verses,
also left poems describing the Zunhua countryside. When escorting his
mother to visit the tombs of Shunzhi and Kangxi in October 1739, he noted the
severity of the cold:[59]

The sharp edge to the weather spurs forward Our cavalcade,
As the dazzle of hoarfrost crystals scatters round us at break of day.
The harvest has been gathered in. There's delight in the hamlet lanes,
And distended stomachs everywhere in Our outermost inner domain.

Ten years later, in the last days of April, on another trip to the mausolea, he
described the spring:[60]

On balks running between the fields, weeds flourish, a limitless green.
The kingfisher hue of the dike-top willows seems as if it wished to
   congeal.
As Our eyes encounter the fertile tilth, which is moist and glossy, and
   sleek,
Our dedication, and awe before Heaven, grow many times deeper and
   deeper.

Sentiments for public consumption, but not necessarily insincere. Qianlong
was a workaholic.

Inside the funerary complex itself a central axis ran in a straight line from
north to south. It began at the Gloriously Auspicious Mountain, passed
through the tomb of the Shunzhi Emperor, and continued down a long avenue
to a roofed ceremonial Dragon And Phoenix Gateway with five entrances.
South of this stood Shadow Wall Hill, presumably as a protective screen against
the intrusion of harmful influences. The avenue curved round this hill and then
resumed its original alignment until it reached the Great Red Portal, the main
entrance, outside of which stood another ceremonial gateway and yet another
protective hill. The other tombs mostly lay to either side of this central axis, and
were connected to it by lateral avenues in a design that had some similarities to

the layout of a genealogical chart, though also some differences. Thus the Shunzhi Emperor's mother's tomb was placed *outside* the main enclosure, perhaps because she was only attached to, but not of, the imperial line.

A basic rule seems to have been that each mausoleum had to have its own mountain presiding to the north at its back. The individual sites are also depicted as adorned with scattered stands of pines, trees that symbolized evergreen perpetuity. The burial chambers themselves were 'underground palaces' where incense was permanently burning, and food was prepared for the deceased in a 'spirit kitchen'. Above ground, along the 'spirit way' to the Shunzhi Emperor's tomb were stone carvings of animals, real and fabled, lying down and standing.

The main complex was ringed by a 'geomantic enclosing wall' wherever the mountains themselves were not an adequate barrier. Further outside lay the boundary of the forbidden zone, a circular avenue called The Fire Way Of The Emperors To Come. It was about 190 kilometers in circumference, and thus, on the assumption that it approximated a true circle, surrounded an area on the order of 60 kilometers across. It was protected by 352 guard stations, which would therefore have been rather more than 500 meters apart. The perimeter was also demarcated by 940 so-called Red Stakes, which would by the same logic have been about 200 meters from each other. There were also lines of White Stakes and Blue Stakes marking further zones outside this inner core.

Most economic activities by commoner–civilians that would have provided part of the resources of the local economy under the previous dynasty were banned inside these geomantically sensitive areas. According to the *Respectfully Determined Laws and Precedents of the Great Qing*:[61]

> There are boundaries indicating prohibitions both to the front and the rear of the mountains. If anyone, within the line of Red Stakes, thievishly cuts down the trunks of trees, removes soil or stones, opens kilns for charcoal [or possibly ceramics], or starts fires to burn the mountains for short-term farming, *he shall be beheaded* as if he had stolen imperial vessels used for sacrifices to the gods. A memorial is to be submitted requesting the final decision on such matters.
>
> As to the area outside the Red Stakes, but within the boundaries of the government-owned mountains, the restrained collection of branches and leaves for fuel is still to be allowed in accordance with the former regulations, and need not be banned. In parallel fashion, when commoner–civilians are repairing their houses or family graves, if they extract soil from pits dug not much more than ten feet deep, and gather and make use of loose stones on the mountainsides that are not more than ten feet in length, or cut down and take away privately owned trees that they have planted themselves, none of these activities is to be forbidden.

If, beyond these permitted activities, anyone thievishly cuts down officially owned trees, opens the mountains to quarry the rock, digs deep trenches in the earth, sets up kilns to burn charcoal [or fire ceramics], or lights fires to set the mountains ablaze for temporary farming, in the zone outside the Red Stakes but within the White Stakes, this shall be illegal as it would be within the Red Stakes. *The chief culprits shall be given a hundred blows with the heavy bamboo and banished to three years military service on the frontier* . . . If such acts are committed outside the line of the Blue Stakes but still within the officially owned mountains, the chief culprits will be given ninety blows with the heavy bamboo, and banished for two years frontier military service. . . .

If subordinate officers or soldiers accept bribes and deliberately allow the commoner–civilians to do as they please, they shall be deemed guilty of the same crimes. . . .

Those who privily enter within the line of the Red Stakes or the Fire Way, and steal livestock and stun them to death, shall for two months wear the punitive collar, with a label describing their misdeeds, in a place near to where the crime was committed. When they have done this time, *they shall be sent to serve as soldiers on the remotest frontier where malaria is prevalent. . . .*

Those who conceive the idea of making their livelihood illegally within the boundaries, and as a result in negligent fashion engage in fire-based farming, so causing the flames to burn through the vegetation and trees, shall wear a labeled punitive collar for two months at a place near the scene of their crime. When this period has expired, *they shall be sent to Xinjiang* [in the Far West], *where they will be allocated farmland and made to perform labor-services. . . .*

If any of the commoner–civilians in Zunhua, Jizhou, Miyun, or Pinggu, that is, in the departments and counties adjacent to the forbidden areas around the imperial tombs, thievishly cuts down any of the 'sea trees' [probably pines], illegally transports them out of the mountains, stores them in a hideout, or sells them, the department and county magistrates who have failed to detect these activities shall be demoted one rank and sent to serve elsewhere.

As so often in premodern China, and elsewhere, the conservation of nature was thus based on a preoccupation with the numinous and the supernatural. And, as so often, its most implacable opponent was economic self-interest, which here pitted the livelihood of the local poor against the punishments imposed by their masters. All of this conflict softened, of course, by the saving compromise of corruption.

The imperial tombs were a favored site for the appearance of superflora and superfauna.[62] It was a traditional Chinese belief that a preponderance of virtuous acts by humankind in particular places would evoke an auspicious response from Heaven, notably in the form of seasonal weather. Morally admirable government by the emperor was thought to attract certain further especial marks of approbation. Those at the eastern tombs included multicolored clouds, which were reported in 1677 and 1723. The most important were the appearance of the species of *Achillea*, akin to milfoil and sneezewort, used for casting oracles when consulting the *Book of Changes*, auspicious fungi, and the phoenix. All but one of these signs recorded in the Zunhua gazetteer date from the reign of the Emperor Yongzheng, that is, late 1722 to late 1735, a monarch who was notoriously addicted to them. He was in all likelihood a usurper, and may have felt the need for reaffirmations of celestial support and signs of approval from his deceased father, by whose mausoleum the auspicious mushrooms always grew, to bolster his claim to legitimacy and assuage his internal guilt. The fungi displayed "all five colors mixed together in bright splendor, with the beauty of gold and the substance of jade, in their uncanny strangeness far removed from the commonplace." They appeared three times, in 1728, 1729, and 1734, and were reverently preserved, carefully packed, in a pavilion near Kangxi's tomb. Species not identified.

The phoenix, sovereign of the birds, appeared in 1729 on the Celestial Terrace Mountain above the tombs. He was described as follows:

> He perched on the topmost summit, being five to six feet in height, with plumage resembling brocade. He possessed all five colors, interwoven in lustrous brilliance. The multitude of other birds encircled him where he stood, after which he flew off northward, singing.

The gazetteer compilers do not list any more such specific events after the Yongzheng reign, observing that while many were seen, they do not dare "to engage in excessive praise." One suspects they were steering a course between a necessary expression of respect for the capacity of later emperors to elicit favorable responses from Heaven, and a dislike of the excesses of some of Yongzheng's fawning officials. There is no overt expression of skepticism. This would have been politically disastrous. As regards their private opinions, one may legitimately wonder.

Economy, environment, demography

The department, as it became under the Qing, was expanded to contain three cities: the department capital north of the main watershed, and the county capitals of Fengrun and Yutian to the south of it. The climate in this period was probably very close to that prevailing at the present day, being markedly seasonal, with the mean monthly temperature, as recorded between the 1950s and 1980s, dropping below −7° Celsius in January but rising above 24° in July. Rainfall today is about 755 millimeters annually, more than three-quarters of it falling in the summer months from June through August. The historical staple foods such as millets, wheat, kaoliang (sorghum), and beans, with a little rice, were joined under the Qing by maize and sweet potatoes from the New World.

We also now have documentation for the local earthquakes. The worst on record was the one that almost totally destroyed the department capital walls in 1679. Their structure was rammed earth lined inside and out with large bricks, which must have been quite tough, but they had been battered intermittently during the previous seventeen years by floods. A lesser tremor in 1888 brought down the tower at the northeast corner and a section of the southeastern city wall.[63]

Under the Qing, most of the good farming land in Zunhua was allocated to members of the Eight Banners, the organizations that controlled the hereditary troops whose forebears had entered the service of the Manchus before the conquest. The bannermen then rented it to Han commoner–civilians. These tenants are said to have had little left over after paying Banner-land rents. "When they meet with disasters or dearth it is not easy for them to continue farming."[64] Some time between 1868 and 1871, when he was governor-general of the metropolitan province, Zeng Guofan remarked of the difficulty of raising money locally for the repair of the walls of the departmental capital that "Zunhua's territory is close to the imperial mausolea. Most of the commoner–civilians are tenant households. Wealthy commoners are rare. In addition to this, the afflictions of flood and drought in successive years have left them unable to respond any more."[65] Seen from the perspective of the ordinary people, Zunhua was not rich.

Many of them nonetheless enjoyed security of tenure:[66]

Households renting Banner land also pay a fee proportionate to the area of the land [when taking over]. . . . They also establish an undertaking about withdrawing or continuing in the lease. . . . Provided they do not accumulate defaults on the rental charges, *the landlord may not expel them from the land or raise the rent.* In cases where owners invite in tenants but do not take this fee . . . the raising or decreasing of the rent, and the expulsion or retention of the tenant may both be done as suits the landlord's convenience.

There also seems to have been an unusual stability of employment:[67]

Everyone has a job. The potters, the metalworkers, the tilers, the carpenters on down to those who hire themselves out for service as substitutes for others, all of them live by their own exertions. For this reason there are few vagabonds, and people's skills do not include misplaced and immoral ingenuity.

The abundance of timber also made a contrast with the shortage in most other parts of China by the late Qing. Pine forests were found all along the old frontier, and yellow pine was extensively used by the people of the department for building houses and making implements and utensils. Pines were also plentiful enough to support the extraction of resin:[68]

> Sometimes they do not cut the trunk completely, but only so that it will no longer produce shoots though it is not dead. The resin gathers at the base, and after a long time becomes transparent and easy to burn. They cut off pieces and bundle them up to serve as torches. . . . These are greatly superior to plaited bamboos.

Willow was used to make chairs and stools as it resisted well both humidity and heat. "The price is cheap and the workmanship needed is limited." Thin planks were used for measuring-boxes, baskets, and crates. Extremely thin splints were encrusted with sulfur to make matches.[69]

Active silviculture was practised. In the mountains along the old frontier the sprouts of horsetail pines that had generated naturally from seed were carefully transplanted, manured, watered, and banked up. Sometimes seeds were sown directly under the protection of small wooden cloches, which were later replaced as the saplings grew with small brush screens to break the wind.[70] By comparison with other areas, where timber was much more expensive, it can be deduced that naturally growing trees were still sufficiently abundant in Zunhua to reduce the anxieties about losses through theft, fires, and even lawsuits, that tended to restrict the long-term investment needed in silviculture in late-imperial China even when prices were high.

Environmental factors prevented the development of more than a small amount of intensive wet-field rice farming. Because of the sandy nature of the soil, water tended to soak away out of the fields.[71] While some hydraulic schemes were apparently durable,[72] many of those involving diversions gave rise to maintenance problems, tending to silt up.[73] It is, however, arguable that more intensive agriculture would have increased rather than reduced economic risk, and hence might have increased stress. A denser population might have been economically in a more precarious position; and the economy might have become locked in to the expenditure of the labor, time, resources, and administrative capacity needed for crucial hydraulic mainten-ance. Overall, especially given the easy availability of wood and water, late-imperial economic stability in Zunhua was probably good compared with most of the rest of China.

This is not to say that the farmers did not practise the most careful utilization of resources. The gazetteer says of millet that[74]

> The husks can be fed to livestock, and the bran to pigs. The stalks ... can repair the rooves of houses and serve as a covering for the tops of walls. They can also be a fuel. If one burns them for a long time the heat can melt the iron of a cooking pot. They can, further, be cut into short lengths to feed mules, horses, cows, and donkeys.

Stability is not the same as affluence.

Women's work and women's recreations are almost invisible in the late-Qing gazetteer for Zunhua. Two passages suggest a social and economic restraint that contrasts with Jiaxing:[75]

> The women do not have the custom of walking out in search of sexual encounters.[76] Those who are poor carry out food to the men toiling in the fields, hoe away weeds, or sew or spin. They do not shrink from hard work.

> *The women are not acquainted with farming.* They merely pluck cotton and pick beans, and at times tread the fields to harvest the wheat. In case of necessity they will take the grain up to the threshing-floor to winnow and flail it,[77] and they dehusk rice, contributing the woman's work of cooking, drawing water, and pounding in the mortar, year in year out. In poor families the women will also sometimes undertake other tasks such as carrying firewood and toting manure.

The biographies of virtuous women list only one case, from the Ming, where a faithful widow—who in this instance had two sons—"directed the farming" and, also in this instance, "taught them to read."[78]

An exception to the nearly total absence of any mention of handicraft production by women for the market is the observation that in Yutian county "the women plait wheat straw into braids and make hats from it ... that are sold everywhere."[79] Likewise:[80]

> In the villages near Granary South of the Forest in Yutian county numerous [women] weave rush mats, and some plait wheat stalks to make hats. Today they no longer make hats but plait braids to form *liu* [?skeins, pads, pockets] that are easy to put on the market. The diligent activities of their fingertips never cease. Old and young women alike in the villages delight in attending to such matters.

The stony hillslopes of Zunhua were also well suited to growing cotton but "profits from spinning thread and weaving cloth are slight, and many people have abandoned it. The inhabitants of the department were never accustomed to weaving; *they grow cotton but do nothing more with it.*"[81] The biographies of virtuous women list two cases, both from the Qing, in which a widow supported her family by "spinning *and weaving*,"[82] the fiber used not being identified. The section on customs modifies this over-simple picture, and also indicates in passing that the production of cotton textiles was probably thought of here by late Qing as work for males:[83]

> The people of the department were originally unversed in spinning and weaving. Merchants dealing in cloth went as far away as Deping [in Shandong province] and no nearer than Raoyang [in Hebei, near Baoding]. Their annual turnover was in tens of thousands of ounces of silver. In recent years foreign cloth has been cheaper than [local] yarn, and foreign yarn has been cheaper than [local] cotton. Those areas in the two counties of the department which previously produced cotton cloth have met with difficulties from reduced sales; those who spun and wove have made losses and abandoned their businesses. Lately they have petitioned that the Official Board for Encouraging Weaving that used to exist in the department capital should summon *sons and younger brothers* from the various rural districts to the Board to practise weaving, and that the pupils be provided with food and the loom-masters with bonuses. Those who have completed their training should receive looms, and weave and sell on their own account.

The few other scraps of information available on women's daily lives here are consonant with the general impression of a subdued, semisecluded, self-consciously hard-working existence in which manual dexterity was their most prized ability. These themes are illustrated by comments on events in the annual calendar of activities:

> Only on the sixth of the first month do married women return to their mother's family for a visit, and go to their affinal relations to convey the compliments of the New Year. The five days that precede this are called the 'Unlucky Five'.[84] *Married women may not go out of their doors during this period.*[85]
>
> At the beginning of spring many families stop doing women's handicraft work. They call this 'the day for tabooing the needle and filling the granary', stating that they fear pricking the eyes of the Granary Official.[86] On the second day of the second month they also say they are afraid of pricking the dragon's eye. . . . *They make fun of each other, moreover, in heedless fashion, saying that these are compacts for the women to be lazy.*[87]
>
> On the third day of the third month is the Purification Ceremony. Rope swings are erected and *the women play on them in the courtyards*, and *the men play on them in the streets.*[88]

The fifth day of the fifth month. . . . Snakes, frogs, scorpions, centipedes, and geckos are called the 'five poisonous creatures'. At noontime on this festival day people therefore always make them into a medicinal paste. *In the women's quarters* they copy the forms of these creatures in multicolored floss embroidery wound into a pendant clasp.[89]

On the seventh day of the seventh month *the girls sacrifice to the Weaving Lass* [the star Alpha Lyrae] *begging for manual dexterity*, while the *boys* put spiders in a little box and pray for *literary talent*. The preceding evening they screen off the courtyard and set out a melon cut into an indented shape like the petals of a flower, and place needles on top of these petals, offering them for augury. They bow to the Milky Way, make a prayer, and withdraw. After a while they look to see if there is a spider's web on top of the melon. If a web has been tied, they say *the girls will obtain dexterity*. On this day they use the flowers [or the patterns of the web?]—whether they are moving like clouds, are as delicate as threads, or coarse as pestles—to foretell a girl's manual dexterity.[90]

On the eighth day of the twelfth month they cook a congee of rice mixed with beans and fruits, called 'Eighth of the Last Month Congee'. . . . Sometimes it is playfully smeared onto the backs of the married women in order to pray that they give birth to sons.[91]

On the twenty-third day of the twelfth month [when the God of the Stove is sent off to report to Heaven on the family, his horse first being fed with hay]. . . *the boys' sacrifice is taboo to the women*, who are not allowed to see it. Young girls are forbidden to eat the sugared fruits left over from the ritual.[92]

The only time that men and women are reported by the gazetteer as appearing together in public is when they "filled the roads" going to graves at the Qingming festival, though there must have been other dates in the calendar when this regularly happened.[93]

Women's life in Zunhua was not without real stresses. Wolves, for example, still caught children in the mountain villages.[94] But there are grounds for at least cautiously suspecting that the demands of the economy on them, particularly as regards heavy physical labor in farming, may have been lighter than on their sisters in Jiaxing and Guiyang. This must have helped them live longer.

Health and water quality

Numerous poems and travel accounts attest the quality of Zunhua's water. Here are a few lines written by a department magistrate:[95]

Amid the clouds, among the mists, our city and suburbs loom grandly,
While encircling them, on every side, the viridian hills rise jagged.
The peach trees and willows, infused by spring, seem as one, on the facing
    banks.
With the coming of fall, the frost on the leaves will color them red as
    madder.

All day long the sounds of the springs are filling our ears with their clarity.
At every season a lush profusion of herbs and of jade-green grasses.

One local scholar wrote of water so pellucid that "one can count the fishes and
shrimps," and another of how, at night,

When, already, the silence has overtaken the farmers' and fishermen's
    songs,
The chorus of frogs on either bank incessantly goes on.[96]

There is a sense of vital energy everywhere.

When water was drinkable without boiling, this fact was sometimes singled
out for mention. Thus the gazetteer tells its readers that Stone-shed Mountain
"has Stone-shed Spring flowing out through a stone conduit. It is sweet and
cool and fit to drink."[97] This raises the obvious, and for the moment unanswerable, question of how far this was *not* true of other springs not given this seal
of approval.

The concern with the quality of water is evident in a poem written by Sun
Xianting, a local inhabitant.[98] It is on the simple well that was used for watering
trees near the top of Round Mountain:

There are no quaint stones on this mountain, and its well is without an
    enclosure.
Now the rope's repaired, though, the source can be reached, water drawn
    without running dry.
A reflection within it, vertically down, resembles a lonely pagoda,
In delight, to the east, corresponding, the circular mountain top rises.

On *min*-stone blue-green in the form of a stele, I'd wish to incise as a
    supplement:
"Tradesmen making white plaster are never to chisel these residue rubbles
    for limestone.
And here, along with transplanted bamboos, long may elegant saplings
    flourish!
Having more than enough irrigation water is something we *must* keep
    inviolate."[99]

Streams appear in probably the majority of poems about Zunhua. Thus Luo Jingqie, in Qing times, wrote as a preface to a second stanza on a literary drinking party at Mount Cuihua twelve or thirteen kilometers to the northeast of Fengrun city:[100]

> Grasses and leaves have faded away, leaving mosses the last bright green.
> The light is transparent. The guests, together, gaze thoughtfully about them.
> Straight up, the twigs on the hermitage trees try to touch the sky with their reaching.
> Cradled by slopes, the switchback stream zigzags toward us down the mountain.

Some small irrigation networks were built. The verses that Miu Siqi, a county magistrate of Yutian in late-Ming times, wrote on the Meng Family Spring seem to describe a simple hillside system by which water was deflected into contour channels and stepped fields, with pumps for the final stage of the distribution process. The square-trough pallet-pumps of the translation are actually called 'pumps that hold their tails in their mouths'. This is an allusion to the continuous chain of linked pallets that ran round and round, not unlike a rough wooden version of the chain on a bicycle. As it empties trough-full by trough-full, the discharge is periodic, hence it 'spurts'. The phrase about 'sweating out evil forces' presumably refers to the gradual improvement of the soil by the application of fertilizers and perhaps lime:[101]

> I went out through the eastern suburbs to investigate local customs
> As the spring light shone refulgent on the tree trunks of the forest.
> I looked back on this glorious vista with a sense of regretful reluctance,
> Then turned to my business of making good whatever was falling short.
>
> A river, in a single course, runs down rippling here, and clear,
> As though a dragon is curvetting, submerged beneath its depths.
> Its current deflected by a baffle, it is drawn off into the fields,
> And every drop is worth a jade, the water is so precious.
>
> In alternation, the light and shadow make apparent its flow,
> Nature's creation that human beings can use now to perfection.
> The square-trough pallet-pumps are machinery known to us from of old,
> Their green spurts tumbling out and over, to water the mountain's belly.
>
> Its loam, enriched with moisture, spreads out in a fertile expanse,
> But rice and millet each require the use of a different technique:
> The low dikes already constructed, to demarcate fields and paddies,

And the wet depressions and spaded-up ridges being respective key
    features.

We plow when a rain shower's fallen, to furnish us silt-free water,
So we're on the lookout for somber cumulus starting to cover us over.
Once these contiguous fertile acres have sweated out evil forces,
We'll have the use of every part of the lower mountain slopes.

That people should sometimes smilingly mock a raincoat of rough-spun
    fabric
Is an attitude that does not accord with a generous open mind.
I have my sedan chair turned about, and start to venture back,
While the herdsmen, under the setting sun, are descending home from
    the heights.

Very different from the sluggish creeks of the Yangzi delta, and its world of
levees and polders, and seawalls.

Zunhua was not, in any serious sense of the word, a 'hydraulic society'. Many
efforts to create irrigated farming proved impossible to maintain. Thus by the
later nineteenth century, the thousand or so hectares of irrigated fields under
state management in Yutian that had been supplied with water from the
Indigo Spring and the Ronghui River early in the eighteenth century had all
turned into dry-land fields because of silting up.[102]

At times supplies seem to have been deliberately underutilized. This was the
case with Bubbling Pearls Spring that emerged at the foot of a mountain
through gaps between heaps of boulders. "*In times of drought,* people draw
water from it to irrigate their fields."[103] In other words, although it could run
with so much water after a rainstorm that the noise set the valley shaking, no
attempt was made to store the runoff and exploit it on a regular basis. It was
treated as a climatic buffer.

The main obstacle to hydraulic development was that in many areas the soil
was too sandy to retain surface water easily. The Tenfold Stream that ran down
from the Great Wall, and then to the south of the department capital, turned
after this point into a "sandy river." "It dries up in spring but is in spate during
summer. Sometimes it is overflowing in the morning, but shallow by the evening,
lacking any consistency in its current, and having no fixed configuration." In the
1620s, a provincial governor wanted to open a transport canal here linking
Zunhua with Jizhou to its west, in order to supply the soldiers with grain more
economically. He was unable to carry out his plan and the gazetteer comments
that his failure "may also perhaps have been because the sand is deep and the
stones unstable,[104] so that it was not an easy matter to retain the water."[105] A transport canal was in fact later built, but in a different place some way to the south.

The fickleness of the hydrology is suggested by the case of Lake Louzi, six or seven kilometers south of the departmental capital, and so probably part of the unstable Tenfold Stream complex just mentioned.[106] The 'arrowhead' is the *Sagittaria sagittifolia*, a water plant whose roots are edible.

> It measures three to four kilometers both north-to-south and east-to-west, and produces lotuses and arrowheads. The site was once low-lying and swampy. In the Chenghua reign-period [1465–87] the marsh waters flowed together here to form a small lake, so it became deep and overflowing. *Today, it has little by little dried out,* and much of it has been developed into arable fields.

Shallow lakes are usually short-lived, and probably hundreds of them have either dried up or been drained in many parts of China over the last thousand years. What is interesting, and slightly out of the ordinary, about Lake Louzi is that, apparently without human intervention, it filled up with water before later disappearing.

Hydrological quirkiness put an environmental limit on the intensive late-traditional Chinese-style development of Zunhua. This may even have been to its advantage. The possibility is worth considering. Most premodern mountain hydraulic engineering had in any case to be on a small scale. Here, as an illustration, is a description of how the locals handled the Sage Stream:[107]

> When summer is passing into fall, and overcast, rainy weather is almost endlessly prolonged, the flow from the spring is greatly increased. It flashes with crystals of light, and pours down like a suspended curtain of pearls. In winter and springtime, the source is stopped up. Its ceaseless dripping resembles a string threaded with pearls. Both aspects can be beautiful.
>
> People have cut into the rock at the base of the cliff wall to make a channel to receive the water. *The depth is three feet, and the width about five.* They have opened a hidden underground conduit from the tank to drain it, and ground a receptacle out of the stone to receive it. From this it slowly descends by stages into two basins. The lower of these is about *a fifth of a hectare in extent,* and irrigates the gardens and groves of the local people, the water being transferred by counterbalanced baling-buckets.
>
> On the rocks above these basins the Pavilion of Secluded Cool spreads itself out. Mists and mountain vapors brush and press against each other. Warm greens and cool greens glitter interwoven. The character of this remote scenery is far away from the contamination of this world.

Scale matters. Such Lilliputian hydraulic systems cannot easily have had much effect on a social structure. And further expansion, within the same style of technology, was thwarted by a simple constraint: the seasonal volume of flow.

The quality of Zunhua water fascinated outsiders. One such was Song Quan, the governor of the metropolitan area in the first years of the Manchu dynasty. He himself came from the southern part of the north China plain, and he expressed his feelings in a poem on Black Dragon Stream, a couple of whose stanzas are translated below.[108] The occasion for this celebration may have been the construction, at his orders, of a brick-lined tank, eighty feet square and nine feet deep, to store the supply it provided. Regrettably, the flow of water was blocked up by an earthquake not long afterward, possibly the one that took place in 1679. It was running again by 1684.

> There's a spring in Zunhua department, sweet-tasting and unsullied,
> Whose fame hitherto in the capital region makes it the foremost and first.
> Gushing up amidst mists by the city's wall, and spraying out pearly
>   bubbles,
> It's the visage of this pure, still, place, the light swimming upon its surface.
>
> One glance can penetrate its depths, where fish seem to hang suspended.
> In the many-hued rays of the clouds at dawn, its tint resembles madder.
> As springtime opens, its ripples speed, and sing with movement's melody.
> In the winter's harshness, its duckweed leaves float in green, luxurious,
>   tangles.

To Song, Zunhua had an idyllic quality. He continues, putting on a pose of archaic simplicity, but inspired to do so by his surroundings:

> When I have multiple tasks to handle, I tell servants to launch my skiff,
> Where, comfortable, carried along by the breezes, I sit there taking my ease.
> The people are honest, subbureaucrats few; the administration is simple,
> While game from the mountains, and wilderness vegetables, make for a
>   governor's feast.

Note the local diet. Song goes on to describe the state of mind needed if one is to transcend the dusty world. He then ends:

> There is no fixed way through the Five Sacred Peaks for one's feet in their
>   sandals of straw,
> And the day may come when one doesn't disdain the gift of a cupful of water.

This poem became well known, and numerous successors replicated its rhyme-words, including versions by his son and one of his grandsons. One of these successor-poems, by a local resident, Shi Enpei, begins:[109]

East of the Dynasty's Eastern Tombs, and adjacent, lies Zunhua,
So in this, His Majesty's own domain, it's the scenery's crowning glory:
Northeast lie the sources of nine springs that pour through the mountains'
    arteries;
Southeast, the waters of ten rivers come together in swirling concourse.

The pre-eminence of the quality and abundance of Zunhua's water was generally recognized.

Water supported hydrotherapy and tourism. The famous hot springs of Zunhua were twenty kilometers to the northwest of the department capital. Even in the depths of winter the water here was close to boiling. The source came bubbling out of a mountainside and was then split into two streams. One of these supplied a water-lily pond. The other was directed into the bathhouses. "There are separate areas for officials and commoners, and separate domains for men and women." Channels and sluices let bathers have hot or cold water as they wished. Sitting in the water for half a day was thought instantly to cure any illness caused by "damp or cold or a swelling of the belly due to constipation."

Besides being a spa, it also attracted casual visitors:

Before one is within several tens of paces of the spring, the vapors rise up in muggy gusts, steaming like a caldron on the boil, such that one cannot approach it closely. When one does reach it, it is as clear and deep as a mirror, so pellucid that the bottom is visible. If one tosses in a copper coin, it will flutter like a small, yellow butterfly, going down by folding back and forth on itself, with supple front and back. Tourists make rather too much of this as a strange sight. If one tries the water with a finger, it is too hot for one to bear. If one draws out some water, it will cook raw foodstuff. It is also *of outstanding quality* when compared with that from wells and ordinary springs. The Great Transformer is in truth unfathomable!

A fascination with curious things, of course. But also a concern with, and interest in, good water.[110]

It was a healthy place.

Birds and animals

The Zunhua gazetteer has detailed descriptions of the normal local birds and animals. The entries generally begin by quoting a traditional account from a well-known source, such as Li Shizhen's *Herbal Arranged by Headings and Subheadings* of 1596, and then follow this with comments on the local situation.

Some of the descriptions cited are fanciful. An example, from this pharmacopeia, is that tigers eat the *top* half of victims they kill between the first and the
fifteenth days of each lunar month, but the *lower* half of those devoured from
the sixteenth through the thirtieth.[111] The local observations are colored at
times by superstitions, and certainly not always correct, but many of them are
plausible, and even occasionally note that knowledge on certain points is uncertain. The relationships between humans on the one hand and birds and beasts
on the other cover a wide range. They include symbiosis, mutual avoidance,
consumption as prey (in both directions), mutual companionship, observation, pets, and the exploitation of animals for medical materials.

We begin with eagles:[112]

There are *many of them* in the department. Their plumage is gray and black
in an alternating pattern. Their bodies are as large as that of a goose. Their
eyes are yellow and red; and the beak is sharply tapered and hooked. They can
catch both birds and rabbits. They do not eat any of the grains, but only meat.

One arranges for someone to watch over an eagle day and night, so that
he cannot sleep. The moment that he closes his eyelashes, the person watching
over him immediately shouts at the top of his voice to wake him up. This
goes on for a hundred days, and is called 'depriving the eagle of sleep'. After
this one of his feet is encircled with an iron ring, and more than a hundred
feet of light cord is attached to this ring. The other end of the cord is secured
to a perch-frame that can be carried through the fields.

When the handler sees a bird, he first points it out with his hand, in such
a way that the eagle can see what his hand is indicating. The eagle will then
follow his directions. Eagles do not miss, not even once in a hundred times.
If it should ever happen that an eagle fails to catch his prey, he feels that he
has lost face, and will be unwilling to come back.

Since he is attached to the cord, he is incapable of flying away. Not having
caught his prey, he is likewise unwilling to return. If one ventures to pull on
the cord, the eagle will frequently tuck in his thighs under his wingpits [and
refuse to move]. This is why those who rear and train them will always first
gauge that a strike is totally certain, and do not dare to fly them at a target
in a casual fashion.

These days four eagle-handlers have been established for each of the
imperial tombs. . . . This is so they can hunt game to be offered in sacrifice.

In other parts of China, however, training methods were used that were closer
to those of European falconry.[113]

The *tuqiu,* or 'bald *qiu*', was either a marabou (genus *Leptoptilus*) or a
similar large, stork-like, water bird.[114] It was reputed to be capable of fighting
with human beings and, the gazetteer tells us,

It delights in devouring ducklings, as well as worms, snakes, and other such creatures. Eating fish gives it particular pleasure and it is constantly stretching out its neck from the river bank. It will wait for them all day long and not stop until it has eaten its fill. . . . The mottled variety is the most common in our department.

Neither of these two birds is mentioned in a 1994 listing of the economically useful birds in Hebei; and 'use' includes being an interesting sight for tourists.[115] One can guess that the marabou lost its habitat with the disappearance of most natural wetlands, which have been drained or converted to reservoirs in recent times, while the water quality has been degraded by pollution.[116] Eagles, at the top of the food chain, are, for their part, well known to be sensitive to shifts in the environment.

Of domestic geese we learn that "They can submerge under water, and like eating meat and such beasts as snakes and worms; and can keep off venomous serpents."[117] The habits of the wild geese are noted next: their seasonal migrations, their formation in flight, and the way in which one bird will stay on the alert as a sentinel while the others sleep on the sandy islets at night. The only local observation is that "it has traditionally been said that if someone who has grown a tumor hears the cry of the wild geese, and lays his hand on it, it will at once fall off." A more reasonable popular conviction—whether it was true or not is another matter—was that if the storks who lived along the banks of Zunhua's rivers began to peck at each other while calling out, then rain was certain to fall.[118]

Magpies are credited with prowess as predictors of seasonal weather, and with complex cognitive processes, and something not unlike language, attributed to them.[119] Much the same is true for swallows.[120] Clearly, in the Chinese view of this time, birds had brains and emotions—like eagles who could lose face. House sparrows, incidentally, were also emotional: "They live under the eaves and are everywhere. They are temperamentally prone to rages. Sometimes, if they are captured, they will be peevish for a brief while; then their guts will swell up and they will perish."[121]

"Every family" reared domestic hens both for their eggs and flesh.[122] When fall had passed, people spread nets to catch the field sparrows, "and make use of them as a seasonal dainty."[123] The 'pine pheasant' was "the foremost mountain delicacy produced in the department."[124] The commoner 'mountain pheasants' were said "to fly up to roost in lofty trees once the snow has fallen, and are never willing to come down. Many of them starve to death, so people can get hold of them. Some can also be taken alive and reared."[125] Odd, and, if true, very unevolutionary.

A number of other birds are mentioned in the verses elsewhere in the gazetteer, probably including herons and/or egrets. They are not always easy to identify precisely.[126]

Bats lived in the cave on the Wuzhong Mountain where, in the third century CE, the hermit Bo Zhongli had had his residence. In Qing times, Wang Qingyuan mentions them in a poem called "Zhongli's Cavern."[127] The fleshy mushroom, here treated with a blend of visual fantasy and ironic mockery, was thought to confer long life or immortality.

> Attaining to immortality, the immortal's already ascended.
> His empty cave remains behind, inspiring our awe, and yet formless.
> When, now, will the cinnabar elixir ever be brought to perfection,
> Since the quest for Authentic Mercury is being pursued no more?

> His cinnabar-sublimating stove is nigh on a thousand years old.
> Draughts blow about clouds of dried-up dust with their intermittent
>   gusts.
> This is where, squirming and writhing, the bats have their abode.
> One half wonders, are these the twitchings of long-life flesh-pulp fungi?

> Our existence — an insect's cast-off coat — is not to be kept for ever.
> The home of the ever-moving spirits is the whole world's Immanent
>   Pattern.
> We must be heedful of the decrees that determine our lives and deaths.
> *The true immortal is someone freed of ignorance and madness.*

There is a self-conscious awareness that the landscape of this later age is no longer enchanted, though the memory of a past enchantment lingers.

Moving on to animals, we find that tigers were less a hazard to life here than an economic resource:[128]

> They are frequently seen in the department, in the mountains along its boundaries. The taste of their flesh is faintly salty and frowzy. The skin furnishes the best quality of bed-covering, which is not only of great price but also able to drive away the baneful beast-shaped demons born of the aethers of the mountains and forests. Their stomachs, kidneys, eyes, liver, fat, blood, fur, and bones are all ingredients of medicine. If the nose of a tiger is suspended in a doorway, and after a year boiled into a paste, and is given to a woman to drink, she will be able to give birth to a son who will achieve high rank. If the intestines of a tiger are bound round the waist of a pregnant woman, this will hasten the birth. Tiger's whiskers used as toothpicks can stop the teeth hurting.

Whether or not traditional Chinese medicines helped their patients, they were not good for the health of animals.

Li Wei, an eminent seventeenth-century official, wrote a poem on an excursion he made through Sandslope Gorge, which lies northwest of the departmental capital, and out to the now obsolete Great Wall.[129] His attitude toward tigers is relaxed compared to the anxiety found in Guizhou. Perhaps this is because he was on horseback, and someone of his importance would certainly have had some sort of escort, though not a word is said about it.

> The winding path loops back and forth, like rope round a block of
>   pulleys.
> Having gone, in my travels, above the clouds, I pause in the saddle a
>   moment.
> Down flutters a flock of pheasants, onto the hazelnut bushes.
> Deep sunk the pawprints of tigers, seen pressed in a recent snowfall.
> Sands and gravels sparkle like frost. I'm surrounded by blue-green bluffs.
> The Wall resembles a baldric, under wide violet mists.
> A miraculous trip, made on impulse! I throw back my cloak and exult,
> No longer remembering the tempest-blown dust, nor that the journey
>   was difficult.

Wolves, not tigers, were probably the main predators on human beings:[130]

> They are found everywhere in our department. Their fur varies according to the color of the vegetation. They hide in the grass and one never even has the time to draw one's sword. Those who encounter them must drop into a squatting posture and draw a circle on the ground if they are to escape death. They can also seize little children who are crying inside a village. Every time a small child has been eaten by wolves it is essential to whitewash the outside of the village wall to create a protective circle which the wolves will not dare to cross, or else offer prayers to the gods of the mountains.

More often the humans were the hunters:[131]

> *Deer*   These are to be found along the boundaries of our department. It is forbidden to hunt them, however, in the mountains around the imperial tombs that have been put off-limits for geomantic reasons. . . . After the antlers fall off, the bone can be used to decorate bows, or boiled into a paste that, when crystallized, can be used as an ingredient for medicines. The tail is a gastronomic delicacy. The venison likewise has a fragrant taste. If the fur is stripped from the skin it can make wadding for clothing. The leather serves for windbreakers.

There was also a pastoral sector.[132] Note that 'mountain sheep' is the term used for goats.

Sheep The department produces them *in very great numbers.* There are 'mountain sheep' and 'fleecy sheep'. The 'mountain sheep' have horns that are long and curved, and beards under their chins. There is a roll of meat on their tail but it has a very rank odor. . . . The 'fleecy sheep' have short horns and no beards under their chins. Their wool is all curly and will not stay stretched out. The flesh on their tails is as round in shape as a platter. . . . The meat is fresh and pleasant, and not frowzy. The color of the skin in most cases is white. A ewe's pregnancy lasts six months, and one lamb is born each year. Those born in the spring months are much the best. There are also cases of two births per year, but most of the lambs delivered in fall suffer from the staggers, and it would be better if they had never been born at all. . . . The fleecy skin can serve as a fur. The fat can be made into candles. . . . *Sheep's milk* is very delicious, but it is not easy to extract it. It is necessary to wait till the lambs are able to eat grass, and then to drive them away to another spot. Each pair of ewes should be bound facing each other, so they cannot move or see anything. The milk can then be obtained by taking it from behind their tails.

Dogs were mostly kept to ward off wolves and jackals, and to guard the homesteads at night. A few bitches were trained for hunting, and some dogs were eaten, under the shamefaced name of 'local mutton'. Decorative Pekinese were also bred, and esteemed for their intelligence and ability to learn tricks.[133] Likewise, because mice and rats were common in Zunhua, "many people in the department keep cats in order to catch mice."[134]

Several species served as pets, animals whose immediate function is solely to provide entertainment or company. Yellow orioles, common in the wooded regions, were kept in cages for their melodious singing.[135] Squirrels, we are told, two a penny where there were pine trees, "if fed for a long time and thoroughly trained, can be carried in the sleeves of one's clothing."[136] White mice were a speciality:[137]

They resemble field mice in shape, but are white in color, with red eyes. They nonetheless have an intelligent disposition, and are skilled at mounting on treadmills. The people of the department rear them, housing them in a box one side of which is adorned with a glass pane [to see them through]. Inside an inverted pillar is installed [fixed to the lid], on which there is placed a freely turning wheel. It looks like an umbrella hanging upside down.

When one taps the box with one's hand, the mouse will mount the wheel. The faster he climbs it, the more rapidly it rotates. The more one taps with one's hands, the more swiftly the mouse climbs. These wheels come in several forms, but they are all toys based on climbing to make them spin round.

One can only speculate why people have come to like pets. Perhaps those with an affinity for taming economically useful birds and animals have tended in the past to be successful over the generations, and pleasure in having pets and manipulating them, whether inherited or learnt, or something of both, is an extension of this affinity. Even if more likely to be an economic burden than a benefit. And some pets, of course, are skilled at manipulating their human 'owners'.

Animals thus had varying sorts of relationship with human society. A few were seen as morally unpleasant, like the marabou, or else as remote but beautiful, like the wild geese. Or as alien but sometimes evocative images, like bats. Some were predators, like wolves. Or a menace, like poisonous snakes. Many more were prey. Some, like tigers, both prey and predators. Eagles, cats, domestic geese, poultry, sheep, and dogs were servants and to some extent companions, controlled by measures that were often ingenious. Also, in the last four cases, food. Others again had a particular kind of intelligence, like the magpies with their believed gift for foretelling floods and drought, or the storks who knew when the rain was coming. White mice, squirrels, and orioles were pets. Interactions with both wild and domestic animals were thus woven into daily life practically, symbolically, recreationally, and imaginatively.

Plant foods

Vegetables and fruits represented a smaller proportion of the Zunhua diet than cereals, but one crucial for most essential vitamins and minerals.[138] The variety available was startling. In broad outline, and using the nearest English equivalents to the Chinese categories, the following groups of vegetables were found: celeries, mustards, Chinese cabbages, amaranths, aubergines, turtle-foot bracken, garlic, onions, lettuces, parsley, turnips and radishes, yams, lily, rape turnip, wild Chinese cabbage, day-lily, beetroot, tree pepper, chilli pepper, cucumbers, gourds, and melons, and beans, peas, and lentils. I have used the plural when there was more than one species.

Of these vegetables, the turtle-foot bracken was the only one that needed special preparation. It had to be boiled in an alkaline solution, probably lye, to get rid of its "oozing sap," and then dried in the sun. In the northern part of Zunhua it was "abundant along the frontier," and "the local people consider it to be a regular vegetable."

Fruits and nuts were among the glories of the region. The main groups were peaches, almonds, plums, persimmons, Chinese fruit hawthorn, Chinese dates, chestnuts, hazelnut, gingko, walnuts, yellowhorn, cherries, apples, crab apples, 'fragrant plum' (*Prunus japonica*), pears, grapes, peanut, water chestnut, and figs. People in Zunhua are unlikely to have been short of vitamin C, which is important in the diet for many reasons, such as the facilitation of the absorption of iron.

A special feature of local menus was the eating of the young buds of certain trees. Those of the 'small-leaved poplar' for example, were heated and then consumed. Early willow buds were soused in a mixture of oil and vinegar for eating. The buds of the tallow tree, and also the gingko, could likewise serve as food. Even the roots of bracken could be roasted in ashes and made into an edible dish.[139]

Some vegetables could be gathered from the wild rather than cultivated. Besides bracken, this was true for amaranth, both kinds of which "are found everywhere. One does not bother to plant them, since they grow of their own accord." *Lactuca denticulata*, a bitter-tasting lettuce, was sown by the wind and "much of it grows in fields lying uncultivated." The tastiest yams were said to be wild, though they were widely cultivated as well. Edible mushrooms were to be found "in the dense woods and on the wide lower slopes of the hills." 'Wild cabbage' (*Moricandia sonchifolia*) was found in the mountains. "In the summer its seeds fall on the ground, and grow again to provide fall vegetables. One does not expect to have to hoe, plant, fertilize, or irrigate it." Eating it regularly was believed to protect one from "seasonal epidemics." Some wild water chestnuts were available, as were wild grapes. Hazel trees "are very plentiful along the frontier. They all grow in the mountains, and few of them are cared for or planted." Finger-millet (*Eleusine coracana*) was found "everywhere," and "there is no need to sow it or plant it. Many poor families gather it as a means of facing up to the winter."[140] The day-lily, whose flowers could be dried or pickled for eating, was a plant that was originally picked wild, but had "recently" been grown in gardens as well. A transition probably made by a number of others in earlier days. There was thus still an *environmental buffer* offering some protection against a shortage of vegetables, nuts, and even cereals, at least in the summer months. And clearly some sort of 'common land' was still accessible to all for gathering.

It was usual for farmers to have vegetable gardens. Lettuces were grown there, as were *jiang* beans with their long, paired pods and slightly curved beans. But they were, first and foremost, the home of melons, gourds, and cucumbers. Great horticultural art was devoted to the care of these cucurbits, as is clear from the description of 'yellow melons', which may or may not have been cucumbers:

Many of the local people erect a hedge on the northern side of their gardens to serve as a windbreak. They dig a trench by it of rather more than a foot in depth. Prior to this, in the first month of the lunar year, they will have soaked the seeds in pottery basins, so that they have all put forth sprouts. During the second month they plant out these shoots in the trench and cover them with wooden boards or straw mats. When it is warm, they expose them to the sun, but when it is cold they cover them over again. In the solar period Summer Begins [in early May] they plant out the seedlings separately.

Gardens also played a role in the introduction of new plants. When maize came into Zunhua at the beginning of the nineteenth century, for example, it was grown in gardens before it became a field crop. "It is the regular food of poor families," says the gazetteer; and the cobs were used in winter as fuel in place of charcoal.

Grafting saplings onto existing rootstock of the same or a closely related species was the commonest method of producing new fruit and nut trees. Thus:

During the fall and the winter people spread peach stones in the ground. When these experience the freezing cold, they split open, and grow in the next springtime. Before the spring festival of the year following it is possible to graft them.

Persimmons were grafted onto the stock of the date plum persimmon (*Diospyros lotus*). Apples were grafted onto crab-apple stock, and pears onto 'birch-leaf pears' (*Pyrus betulaefolia*). In contrast, the yellowhorn (*Xanthocera sorbifolia*) was mostly reproduced either by the separation of roots or fresh sowing. But, we are told, "grafts will also survive."

Pruning was done regularly. Thus chestnut trees "must have their bark stripped every other year, and their branches cut back. The following year the nuts will be abundant. If this is done in alternate years, they will still be abundant over a period of several decades. Such are the efforts that human beings have to make!"

The gingko, or 'maidenhair tree', was manipulated in a subtler fashion:

It is essential that *a male and a female tree be planted together*, so that the two trees can look at each other. Only under such circumstances will [the female] bear fruit. Sometimes this will happen if a female is near water, and can see her own reflection. Failing this, a hole may be bored in her and a small amount of male wood inserted. Or she can be transplanted.

Gingkos do have male and female trees, and the first part of this prescription is in a sense reasonable enough. Then it slides into fantasy. Disentangling such combinations of useful knowledge and apparent nonsense is a characteristic problem with many premodern Chinese technical texts. It is important not just to pick out the impressive parts and neglect the others.

Another example of this is provided by the procedures prescribed for walnuts. Walnut trees (*Juglans regia*) do not have separate male and female trees. Each tree bears both staminate male and pistillate female flowers, which are distinct. Nor, obviously, are there 'male' and 'female' nuts. But note that, nonsense apart, the Zunhua orchard-men practised selective breeding:

> The people of the department aver that those nuts with sharp ends are *male*, and those without sharp ends *female*. If both male and female nuts are planted together, it is easier for them to grow. They wait for high-quality nuts on a tree to fall of their own accord. The greenish covering will naturally split open. *They select the largest,* with a shiny covering and shallow wrinkles, and a heavy body, and make a sowing trench two or three inches deep. They spread tile-sherds in this, and mix in manure. The nuts are inserted, covered with soil, and sprinkled with water. In the freezing cold of winter, the shell cracks, and the sapling will grow of its own accord in the coming spring. Since there are sherds of tiling beneath it, its roots cannot penetrate the soil vertically, which makes it easy to transplant.

Zunhua exported fruit. We are told of the flowering crab apple (*Malus spectabilis*) that "recently large quantities have been sent by sea to distant parts, the price being cheap and selling them a simple matter." Ordinary apples were also marketed beyond the departmental boundaries. "Once the fruit harvest has set, merchants from Tianjin will already have gathered to scrutinize the trees and discuss prices."

Given the severity of the winter, the storage and preservation of vegetables and fruits was of particular importance. Part of the crop of most vegetables was pickled. Vinegar controls the growth of bacteria and molds, and helps to conserve vitamin C. Some were salted, or immersed in brine, which also slows bacterial growth. A form of proto-canning was known. The leaves of the Chinese cabbage were sometimes boiled, covered with a layer of salt and pepper, and conserved in jars sealed tight by the weight of heavy stones. Vegetables might also be cut into slices and dried. This was done to turnips and aubergines, for example, and to Japanese pumpkins which were "regularly used to provide against the winter." 'Tree ear' mushrooms were dried. The pods of *jiang* beans were sometimes split and hung up in a shady spot to dry, after which they could be kept till the following spring. A whole range of methods were used on 'yellow beans', the type of soybean preferred for human consumption:

> The beans can be eaten [without processing], made into soy sauce, salted, pressed for their oil, or [ground into powder and] converted into beancurd.

> The residues from making beancurd can be fed to hogs. Human beings sometimes make use of them to still the pangs of famine.

Fruits and vegetables could be pickled, as was commonly done with the birch-leaf pear and yellow melons, aubergines, celery leaves, mustard roots, and amaranth flowers. Mostly, though, fruits and nuts were preserved in some sort of glacé form, using honey. This was done to peaches, fruit hawthorn, chestnuts, hazelnuts, walnuts, cherries, apples, crab apples, and the peel of water melons. No technical details are available, but the frequency with which honey is mentioned suggests that it was plentiful locally.

Storage in cellars was of crucial importance, and close attention was paid to whether particular species and varieties stored well or badly. Thus it was recorded of Chinese cabbage that "the variety that is planted in the spring and ripens in the summer neither has a good taste nor will it last for long," while cabbage sown in the late summer and planted out in the fall could be "put in cellars for storage, where it must not be permitted to freeze, nor be hurt by warmth." Varieties with blue-green leaves "can be stored for a long time," but "the white ones, when eaten, are tender and delightful, but easily spoil." The concluding lines of the section on turnips and radishes says that "all the above kinds ought to be put into a cellar for storage, in readiness for use during the winter and spring. If they freeze they become unfit for eating." As for the summer squashes "they are a common daily food, but once the fall has come they are totally unsuited to being preserved for long." Durability was a preoccupation.

Some vegetables were grown mainly to make feed for animals. The soybeans known as 'black beans' are the best example. They were roasted or boiled, then mixed with sorghum to be fed to horses, mules, donkeys, and cattle, or else ground into fragments for pigs "who produce fatter meat in consequence."

How a food is eaten also affects its nutritional value. There was quite a penchant in Zunhua for eating certain vegetables raw. An example is the root of the variety of toothed lettuce known as the 'bitter vegetable', and the leaves of some kinds of turnips. Also chilli peppers, possibly bean sprouts, and hazelnuts.

Was Zunhua's diet then better than those of Jiaxing and Guiyang?[141] The water was probably healthier. The pastoral and hunting components that complemented farming and gardening meant that meat was certainly more plentiful than in Jiaxing, and perhaps rather more than in Guiyang, though cattle were important here, too. A plus, therefore, for Zunhua as regards protein. This was heightened by the availability of soybeans, other beans and peas generally, peanuts, and wheat. All of these, especially the first, whose flour surpasses the average protein content in meat, have substantially more protein than rice which is the staple grain in the south. There were also hens' eggs seemingly commonly available, and a probably very small supply of sheep's milk.

There was a superabundance of fruits and nuts compared to Jiaxing, and clearly a richer supply than in Guiyang, though this latter was also known for its fruit trees. Hence some extra vitamin C. Vegetables were very varied, ensuring a supply of most necessary minerals and vitamins. Techniques for safeguarding them through the winter were well developed. There is no reason, though, to think that Zunhua was better off as regards vegetables than Jiaxing and Guiyang except, perhaps, for its access to wild vegetables and, in addition, wild nut trees.

As regards a supply of calcium, which has been a point of relative weakness in the Chinese diet in recent times, Zunhua had a good bulk source in soybean flour, and a very rich, if quantitatively limited, source in figs. Its cherries and plums would also have helped. Hence a probable relative advantage.

Retinol, or vitamin A, and substances from which the body can manufacture retinol, has been another problem in China. Here Zunhua's strength in melons would have helped. Melons can contain on the order of 175 micrograms of retinol equivalent in every 100 grams of edible weight. Peaches, plums, and cherries would have also been useful minor fruit sources. The main standby in all three areas, however, would have been the dark green leaves of vegetables. Lettuces, for example, can contain 290 micrograms of carotenes—precursors of vitamin A—per 100 grams of edible weight.

It is important not to be too confident when comparing one diet with another on the basis of the rough historical materials at our disposal. The 'same' foods can be significantly different depending on precisely where they come from, and how they are harvested and processed; and the human organism can to some extent adapt to the deficiencies of a specific local diet. Overall, though, the quality of the Zunhua diet seems likely to have been rather better than that in Jiaxing or Guiyang, and the substantial environmental buffer of wild foods and wild animals would have acted to stabilize supply.

We have the sketch of an explanation for the exceptional local longevity.

Perceptions

10

🐘 *Nature as Revelation*

Through more than three thousand years, the Chinese refashioned China. They cleared the forests and the original vegetation cover, terraced its hill-slopes, and partitioned its valley floors into fields. They diked, dammed, and diverted its rivers and lakes. They hunted or domesticated its animals and birds; or else destroyed their habitats as a by-product of the pursuit of economic improvements. By late-imperial times there was little that could be called 'natural' left untouched by this process of exploitation and adaptation.

At the same time there developed among the elite an artistic and philosophical attitude toward the landscape that saw it as the exemplification of the workings of the deepest forces in the cosmos. As, not a momentary, but a perpetually present and accessible revelation. The eye endowed with understanding could see in a landscape the self-realizing patterns of the Way, the ever-renewed cycles of the complementary impulses driving the world's changes. It could divine the geomantic fields of force in protective mountains and power-concentrating pools of water. It could perceive it as the serious playground, so to speak, of the Immortals who were also at the same time its constituents. Or as an embodiment of the Buddha whose spirit radiated, detectably, through all phenomena.[1]

This vision had crystallized by the middle of the fourth century CE. Didactically expressed, and hence perhaps deficient as poetry, its core components may be found in a suite of verses by Wang Xizhi (321–79 CE), the foremost of the circle associated with the Orchid Pavilion Mountain in what is today Zhejiang province (on the boundary between the East and Southeast).[2]

A few terms need preliminary explanation. The 'Great Patterns' are the hexagrams of the *Book of Changes*, the images whose sequences both define and reveal the tendencies in the world. The term *lǐ*, namely 'pattern-principle', occurs three times, and is rendered in a different way on each occasion as 'implicate logic', 'norms', and 'the deep lying structure', respectively. In this period it tended more often to be contrasted with *shì*, 'phenomena', rather than *qì* 'energy–substance–vitality', as was to become standard later. It indicated the pattern defining and controlling the distinctive way something functioned.

The image of the cosmic craftsman appears implicitly in the reference to the 'reshaping' of matter; the term used applied originally to the working of clay. It also appears explicitly as 'the demiurge Change'. This latter is the Chinese *zaohua*, who has already been mentioned in earlier chapters. He was a god-like transformer rather than a creator in the strict sense, and somewhat abstract in conception: more a force than a superhuman.

Note, too, how pattern-principles are said to be able to lodge for a moment in the eye of someone looking at a landscape, who can watch them 'unfold of themselves'. Contemplating an expanse of scenery provided an intimacy with the cosmos.

I

Gentle and numberless move the Great Patterns,
Revolving in cycles, unbounded, unceasing.
Such reshaping of matter's not part of *our* craft,
Nor can we command them to come. Or to leave.

Where *did* they originate? At whose command?
— Self-born their fulfilment, from implicate logic.
Those who have minds, but lack understanding
Stumble onward, entangled in losses and profits.

> *Best to let each encounter, then, occur just as it will.*
> *If one roams without fixed purpose, one's meetings are propitious.*

II

Spring first sees the multitudes burgeon diversely,
As each one swells stirred by its innermost being.
Eyes raised, the horizon's remotely discerned;
Eyes down, there's the bank, past which water flows green.

Vista silent and bright! Beyond limits of space.
Like guests lodged in my eyes, norms unfold of themselves.
Prodigious the deeds of the demiurge Change,
As dissimilar things blend in balanced effect.

> *Countless are the musical pipes, and though of varying lengths,*
> *We find them all to be akin, not one of them ill met.*[3] . . . .

V

Substance unceasingly gels, then dissolves.
No start *ever* occurred to perfecting–decaying.
Not one instant does making of new objects stop;
And — when once gone — they can't flourish again.

A miraculous gift: to exist in time present.
Two nights in one house — and we're like lees, or dust.
Unrealized hopes fill us all with regret.
— Break free by inferring the deep-lying structure.

> *And if one's words remain behind, what one is has not been broken.*
> *The river is only transparent so long as it lingers nowhere.*

People thus looked at landscape to achieve insight into the constant, internally driven, impermanence of a universe without beginning or end, and to attain the state of mind in which they could be carried along with it, unconcerned, holding fast to nothing, unstopping and hence uncontaminated.

A paradox thus lay at the heart of Chinese attitudes to the landscape. On the one hand it was seen, not as an image or reflection of some transcendent being, but as a part of the supreme numinous power itself. Wisdom required that one put oneself into its rhythms and be conscious of one's inability to reshape it. On the other hand the landscape was in fact tamed, transformed, and exploited to a degree that had few parallels in the premodern world. Certainly more than most of northwestern Europe, with the possible exception of those regions of the Netherlands that depended on hydraulic systems. Almost all European farming, for example, relied on rainfall, not irrigation, the basis of so much of Chinese agriculture; and long European transport canals, though briefly important, were more modest than those in China, and built much later, beginning in the sixteenth century.

This paradox shows that the relationship of a representation to a reality— so far as we can understand the first and reconstruct the second—may be complex. Even, as is the case here, at least superficially contradictory. What is portrayed can at times be the *opposite*, in a sense, of what is. Behind all such studies of perceptions of the environment there lurks a trap: that of assuming that people's actual *behavior* was on the whole necessarily in accord with the *ideas and feelings* expressed in our sources. This problem was first was established for ancient China in a combative, but brilliant, book by Heiner Roetz which has been unduly neglected.[4] Besides insisting on the existence of a wide spectrum of views on nature in China, even in ancient times, he argues that "a sympathetic feeling for nature, such as that in the *Zhuangzi*, was simply a *reaction* against the course being taken in an entirely opposite direction by reality as it developed."[5] He notes that "in its polemic against the destructive consequences of civilization the *Zhuangzi* passionately takes the side of the nonhuman world. One of the perpetually recurring motifs used to pick out the subjugation of nature for human purposes is *the tree*. The way in which it is processed into objects for human use is the characteristic illustration of the loss of our innate nature."[6] He also, however, reminds us that "grief at the destruction of nature is . . . never to be understood only as allegorical, but also in its direct sense."[7] Real forests were really destroyed.

There is no simple and definitive way of resolving the dilemma posed by Roetz: do our sources mainly reflect the dominant tendencies of an age, or are they more often *reactions*, by far-seeing and sensitive thinkers, *against* these dominant tendencies? And, if a mixture, where, and in what proportions? This unresolved doubt will haunt our attempts at understanding much of the translated material that follows in *Perceptions*.

Nature and the environment in Chinese poetry before early medieval times

The representation of nature in archaic and early-imperial Chinese poetry is a much-studied theme.[8] Here all that is needed is a sketch to create a context for what follows: poems touching on the environment down to early medieval times.

The oldest of the traditional anthologies is the *Scripture of Songs*.[9] The poems or songs it contains were mostly composed between the ninth and the seventh centuries BCE, and describe life in the north. 'Nature' usually comes on-stage as discrete objects, mostly birds, animals, insects, and plants. These usually parallel in some way the human situation: thus the wild geese flying evoke the spectacle of gentlemen setting off on an expedition.[10] More rarely they contrast with it, as in the case of the bustards who can rest when the singer cannot.[11] A simple illustration of a *parallel* is the girl nervously waiting to meet her husband-to-be:[12]

> The katydid chirps,
> The grasshopper jumps.
> Not having seen him,
> My anxious heart thuds.

Slightly more elaborate is the *contrast* effect in the song of the wife whose husband has gone away on campaign but has not come back. The animals and domestic birds return in the evening, but he does not:[13]

> My lord is gone away to war,
> Many a day now, many a moon.
> — Shall we two ever meet once more?
> Our fowls have nested on their roost,
>   The sun is down,
> Our sheep and cattle gathered in.
> My lord away to war is gone.
> Nor thirst nor hunger be on him!

These parallels are emotive but usually objective. Only occasionally is a moral lesson drawn from nature:[14]

> Chopped tree trunks resound to the axes.
> The birds echo back what they're hearing.
> They flee from the deep-hidden valleys
> And resort to the towering trees,
> Where they call and call — *we are here!*
> And search for the cries of companions.
> Those birds deserve our attention:
> If even *they* search for the voices of friends,
> How much more so then, surely, should *men!*

One method of building up to a climax is to vary one word in an otherwise identical line which is repeated in a sequence of stanzas. One song follows the making of cartwheels from the cutting of the wood, to the trimming of the spokes, to the shaping of the rims. As it does so, the flow of the nearby river changes its pattern, ending with rotating eddies.[15] A sort of sympathetic resonance. In another song, a girl waits for a faithless lover as millet grows from sprouts to awns to full ears, and her feelings alter from unease to an aching dullness to suffocation.[16] The plant acts as the clock of the seasons and the heart.

Weather can both mirror and create a mood. The song of the soldiers who have spent weary months far from home, on guard against the Xianyun barbarians, ends:[17]

> When we set off — now long ago,
> Green, with many leaves, were the willows.
> Today, when we are coming home,
> The flakes of snow are falling thickly.

> Slowly we travel along the road.
> Stomachs are empty, throats are parched.
> Our minds, too, wounded. No one knows
> The anguish that destroys our hearts.

There is no sense, though, of the natural environment being a naturally or morally coherent system except perhaps fleetingly in some of the poems on disasters. These convey the feeling that the power governing the world has turned against the people, causing epidemics, floods, famines, baleful portents, and droughts. The assumption is that this is, or should be, punishment for the misdeeds of the rulers but sometimes it is seen as indiscriminate:[18]

> Majestic Heaven is awesome, swift,
> It frames not Its plans nor carefully thinks. . . .
> Even those free of any guilt
> Fall everywhere in the abyss.

Bewilderment was sometimes the understandable response:[19]

> Drought overwhelms us.
> Stream beds and mountains, dry and lifeless.
> Under the Drought Fiend's fierce oppression
> All seems aflame, all seems on fire.
>
> Our minds flee the menace of the heat.
> Our hearts are burning with their fears.
> Our long-dead rulers pay no heed.
>
> O God Supreme, Majestic Heaven,
> Why do you make us cower in terror?

The second anthology of preimperial times is *The Songs of the South*, or, more literally, *The Compositions of Chu*, Chu being the great late-archaic state in the central Yangzi valley.[20] Its core works probably date from the fourth century BCE; some of the items are a number of centuries later. Several differences are at once noticeable in the way that nature is experienced and evoked.

The first is that the poets—Qu Yuan, and others, mostly anonymous[21]—have mastered the art of handling complex, integrated scenes, and use these as vehicles to convey emotion. The closing lines of "The Mountain Goddess" are an example.[22] Note that 'smirr' is a vernacular west-Scottish word for drizzling rain so fine that it is almost a mist. The 'lady' is the goddess herself.

> Smirring of rain. Drum-rolling thunder.
> Gibbons calling at night. The soft babbling of monkeys.

> The soughing of branches. Wind blown in gusts.
> My lone thoughts on my lady. How I grieve we are sundered.

The word rendered here by 'monkeys' would be more exactly translated as 'black gibbons'.

Specific landscapes are sometimes described. "Crossing the Yangzi" contains an account of traveling by a boat with a cabin up the Yuan River in what is today western Hu'nan.[23] Xupu is up a tributary of the Yuan. The area was inhabited by peoples who did not speak the poet's language.

> Turning in to Xupu — I hesitate, then pause,
> Confused and still unclear as to whither I am venturing.
> Darkness endlessly extends throughout the depths of forest.
> This is where black monkeys, and the gibbons, have their dwellings.

> So lofty are the mountain tops that the sun passes hidden,
> So filled with shadows the valley depths that squalls of rain are frequent,
> Sleet showers so chaotic that no boundaries are visible,
> Low clouds so thick amassed they seem to extend the eaves.

There is a first glimmering here of conscious environmental sensitivity in the intuition that darkness, and hence coolness, increases the likelihood of rain.

There is a new feature in many of these poems: magical journeys of the spirit in inspiration or trance. Often the poet seems to take to the air, and a panorama—a giddying mixture of the fantastic and the real—opens out below him. As an example we may look at a few lines from "Grief at the Eddying Wind."[24] This is a lament in which the writer finds relief from the frustrations and corruptions of the human world through his vision of the immensity and grandeur of the forces of nature. Kunlun was the magic world-mountain in the west. Sometimes it was described as 'the lower metropolis of God', and the home of the Queen Mother of the West. Those who ascended the Cold Wind Mountain above it were said to become deathless.[25] The Cavern of Winds, where the winds gathered, was also said to be here. Mount Min, a real mountain in what is today Sichuan province, was thought to be the source of the Yangzi.

> Ascending among the loftiest peaks, to gain the topmost escarpments,
> I dwell on the uttermost summit of the secondary rainbow's arch.
> My feet on the deep blue firmament, I mount up upon the main spectrum,
> And before the briefest instant's passed, my hand's laid hold on Heaven.

> I drink draughts of translucent dew, from the springs that go past me,
>   floating.

I rinse my throat with crystals of frost, congealed when the fogs have frozen.
I repose by the Cavern of Winds, to refill with the breath of vitality,
Then, on a sudden — awake again — feel the tug of the heart's
    attachments.

I walk high on the Kunlun Mountain, to gaze down over the mists.
I lean back against Mount Min, so the Yangzi is clearly visible.
I withdraw in terror — like boulders grinding is the noise of its torrent
    rushing.
I hear, too, the sound of its surges — like the clamor of quarrelsome
    drums.

Leaping away in chaos, with no ordained regularity,
Undisciplined and confused, spreading over a vast expanse,
Waves tumble and crush themselves in the spate, leaving no traces behind
    them,
Headlong as runaway horses, unstoppably weaving and winding.

The intoxication with both natural grandeur and the supernatural combined with the exuberant inventiveness of the Chu poets in a multiplicity of forms. They questioned the origins of the universe. They summoned forth visions of the inhuman but visually gripping worlds of the dragon-haunted ocean, the deadly jungles, the demon-infested deserts, and the ice-bound north. And they conjured up dramatic performances of real or simulated possession by spirits. An example of this last are the lines in a hymn spoken by the 'Sun God', in fact by his impersonator.[26] As he first rises above the dissolving darkness he declares:

> To my shafts I yoke dragons. I ride on the thunders.
> Bearing banners of cloud-wrack, shaking and fluttering.
> I sigh, I sigh deeply, as I start the path upward.
> I look back with longing, my heart so reluctant.

Then, at the end of the hymn, the Sun God sets. Note that the 'Wolf of the Sky' was a baleful star that had dominion over invasion and pillage. It was also a symbol for Chu's deadly enemy to the northwest, the state of Qin. The 'Bow' stands for the 'Bow and Arrow', a constellation of nine stars that ruled over defense against brigands.

> My robes are dark clouds, my skirts rainbows bright.
> My sunbeams I aim at the Wolf of the Sky.
> Then I loose the Bow back and, struck, he falls dying.
> So I lift up the Dipper, pour cinnamon wine!

Tightly grasping the reins, I haste home from the heights.
To return to the east, I plunge deep into night.

Nature was magical.

The styles of verse pioneered in Chu led to the development of the *fù*, a long, descriptive, and usually but not always unrhymed rhapsody with lines of varying length. Poems in this style were first written in Chu, and then flourished under the early empire. Subjects varied. They included such topics as the wind, the imperial hunting grounds, and the capital cities. Though they tend at times to become rhetorical catalogs, they can, at their best, achieve a cold, artificial magnificence. As an example, consider these lines written by Mei Sheng (or 'Cheng') in the middle of the second century BCE. They are from his *fù* "Qi fa" and describe a *tong* tree.[27] Though *tong* has several meanings, this is almost certainly a *wutong* or *Firmiana simplex* (formerly *Sterculia platanifolia*), a straight-trunked deciduous species producing edible nuts, normally from twenty to thirty feet in height, with long-stalked broad leaves, roughly palm-shaped, and with hairs on their backs. As mentioned earlier, myth held that it was the only tree on which a phoenix would alight. The Dragon Gate gorge referred to here is most likely to be that on the Yi River, just south of Luoyang in He'nan, but there were several others. The *handan* is said to be a bird that sings before sunrise; I have rendered it here by 'dawn-caller', since there is no scientific identification.

> Above Dragon Gate gorge, the *wutong* tree
> Rises unbranched to a hundred feet.
> Plate-fungi thick-clustered halfway up,
> Its roots subdivided, writhing, and multiple.
>
> Upward, thousands of fathoms, soar the peaks
> As it looks down to gorges a thousand beneath.
>
> The surging flows and the counter-currents
> Wind-agitated, swirl round and buffet it.
>
> In the wild gales of winter, and the spatter of hailstones,
> It is beaten upon by the flying snowflakes,
> While in summer the lightnings and thunders shake it.
>
> Mornings, orioles sing, and the dawn-callers chirp.
> At dusk it's a night-roost for off-course birds.
>
> Overhead, the lone goose greets the rising sun.
> At its foot, the quails chirrup, plaintively fluttering.

An illustration of the passion for parallelism that dominated so much of Chinese verse for so long.

Rhapsodic description of natural phenomena continued into the next millennium. In the third century CE, for example, Mu Hua produced a virtuoso *fu* on the sea.[28] Here are a few of its lines, freely rendered:

> Rage-swollen ocean!
> Waves foaming over, then rising, then floating
> Till the next clash and pummel
> When the breakers are lifting and spray scatters upward!
>
> ....
>
> Needling summits and ranges fly skyward
>   And then they collapse,
> As if, in wild dance, the Five Peaks
>   Were pounding each other like mallets,
>
> Chaotically spitting, or else sunk in gulfs, or amassing,
> Piling up against rocks to disintegrate, swelling, successively crashing!
>
> Whirlpools, hitting each other, are sucked down into cavernous maelstroms.
> Huge swells in collision erupt — into fantasmagorical wave-forms.

This is not without its element of realism. Freak waves do result from the encounter of two bodies of water moving in opposed directions, especially a wave-train meeting a current.[29] But it is a generalized, conceptual vision, and should be contrasted with the specificity of Xie Lingyun's description of Hangzhou Bay translated in the next section.

Finally, in the century following the end of the early empire, by some quantum jump in Chinese social mental processes, the totality of the actions that constitute the being of the universe came to be directly perceived and experienced as a whole. It would of course be reasonable to argue that the founders of philosophical Daoism, especially Zhuangzi, had reached this understanding half a millennium earlier. The counter-argument—which is more a qualification than a direct counter—is that this had achieved little or no expression in the poetry or art of these intervening centuries, and was for most people a fleeting intuition, not yet cognitively crystallized. Now it was becoming so.

One marker of the change is the weaving of an old philosophical term, 'being so of itself', the Chinese *ziran*, into the fabric of what *seemed* direct perception and its expression in poetry. Becoming generalized, 'being so of itself' became close to what we would call 'nature'. By 'direct perception' I mean only that the consciousness of conceptual preconditioning had vanished: one thought one just saw it.

'Nature' in this broad sense had a spectrum of meanings, as it does in English. Here are two couplets by Sun Chu (?233–93 CE), from two different works, that use it for that which bestows their *inherent character* on things and phenomena:[30]

I

Here grow the elegant grasses that, *by nature*, are their own selves,
Near the Magic Pool fed with the waters that sands and gravels have
    cleansed.

II

These flowers become the flowers they are — chrysanthemums sweetly
    scented —
By incorporating within themselves *nature's* pure, subtle, germinal
    elements.

The Magic Pool was the famous fish pond of King Wen of the Zhou dynasty and may have had overtones of fecundity and prosperity.

One implication of the use of 'nature' in this sense is that 'natural' processes are those with which human beings have not interfered. Guo Pu (276–324 CE) says:[31]

Using no farmer's art, I broadcast the bearded grains,
And pluck up the finest rice that *nature* has propagated.

The distinction between human beings and nature was only relative, of course. People were also a part of nature, and it could have lessons for them. In the fourth century, Su Yan wrote a rhapsody on the floating great duckweed (*Spirodela polyrhiza*) that contains the lines below.[32] The term I have rendered as 'Ultimate Logic' may also be translated as 'perfect pattern-principle'.

It always lets itself go, till it meets with some other thing,
Taking encounters as they come. It is not in its nature to cling.
A helpless weed. Yet one that, however unconscious,
Conjoins in the dark with itself the Ultimate Logic.

People should be duckweed.

Above all, nature was a source of *enlightenment*. This emerges from a careful reading of a travel poem written by Yinzhong Wen, who died in 407 CE.[33] It is full of allusions to Daoist and other metaphysical concepts.

Season follows after season, like the scales upon a fish,
The transformations of patterns that are all of them consistent,
But only the clarity of light from the sunshine in the fall
Inspires in us an elation exalted as well as flawless.

The force of life in the landscape is brilliant and yet remote,
The atmosphere, and beings in it, by their nature intense and cold.
A pipe of reeds sets resonating the hidden Tones of the Months.
The mournful gorge speaks, gently, of the Insubstantial Gulf.

The time of the year is chill, with no trace of its former lushness.
At dawn the leaves come drifting down, contentedly unreluctant.
What criterion will distinguish the tough from the easily crushed,
Here for a fleeting instant lodged in the pine tree and the mushroom?

In the early morning calm, the man of talent feels humbled,
And filled with respectful awe at this journey beyond the dust.

'Pattern' refers to 'pattern-principles', the shaping templates of the universe.
'Clarity', which also signifies 'purity', hints at the self-cleansing undertaken by
the adept. 'Life force' is *qi*, also variously translated as 'aether', 'pneuma', and
'energy–matter'. It is the term that was later used for the basic stuff of the
world. The 'Tones of the Months' are the twelve musically tuned breaths
thought to control the months and seasons; they were the focus of various
archaic rituals. The 'pipe of reeds' suggests Zhuangzi's description, through the
mouth of one of his fictional characters, of the workings of heaven and earth
as a sort of polyphonic pipe music. The 'Insubstantial Gulf' is the Daoist void,
paced by immortals, and perhaps also the Buddhist idea of the empty unreality of all composite things. The pine tree symbolizes the Daoist's quest for
immunity from physical deterioration, rather than see himself crumble away
like the fragile fungus. The 'dust' is the everyday world, whose contamination
the traveler has left behind, even if only momentarily.

Xie Lingyun slightly later sketched the outline of a philosophy based on the
idea that the 'delighting heart' or 'responsive mind'—alternative translations
of the same key term—interacting *aesthetically* with the natural world, was the
means of achieving Buddhist *enlightenment*. He wrote a didactic quatrain to
express this:[34]

Feelings work through responsive delight to make beauty.
Obscure are phenomena. Who can discern them?
When *this* has been seen, objects no more concern one.
One has, once enlightened, what one pursued!

The line of thought seems to be that the emotions that create a delighted
response to the sensory world lead eventually to an intuitive sense of beauty
that transcends the original intellectually unanalyzable phenomena, and
enables the person with this sense to understand that behind the phenomena
there lies nothing permanent or stable, hence no 'objects'. This is the path to

enlightenment. Elsewhere he says that "responsive mind alone is the source of innate insight."[35] And again, "delighting response once gone, who can see the pattern-principles?"[36]

Landscape was more than landscape.

The intuition that it possessed a meaning perpetually present, but perpetually elusive, was crystallized in a celebrated anthology piece by Tao Yuanming, an aristocratic hermit–poet who lived from 365 to 427 CE. This is the fifth in his twelve-part sequence "Quaffing Wine." I have incorporated in the translation glosses on some of the implications that are not spelled out in the original text. The southern mountains were, for example, a traditional symbol of immutability; here the reference may also suggest Mount Lu, the refuge of recluses and monks, and located not far south of Tao's property. Chrysanthemum wine was drunk to promote longevity, but drinking is not directly mentioned, only the flowers. The flower heads could also just be tossed into the wine. The phrase 'timeless, unmoving, conception' is a translation of *zhen yi,* more literally 'authentic intent', but which echoes both *zhen ren,* the Daoist immortal, and the Buddhist *zhen xin,* the mind that is undeluded, hence as unchanging as the calm sea. There may also be a hint that one reunites with the rest of the world only as life draws to its close.[37]

I have built myself a shack, within humankind's domain
Yet free of the rattle and clatter that horses and carriages make.
"How is it possible," you ask, "that you could have managed it so?"
When my heart is far away, this place — of itself — becomes remote.

Having picked, for tippling, chrysanthemums from beneath the eastern
    hedge,
I gaze wistfully at the southern hills, distant and changeless forever.
The aethers from off the mountains reach a perfect balance at sunset,
And, as they wing back toward their homes, the birds keep each other
    company.

A timeless, unmoving, conception lies hidden in these phenomena,
But just as one seeks to express it, the words are already forgotten.

He is conscious of something that can only be called, however contradictory it may sound, an immanent transcendence.

Tao's life represented several of the socio-literary patterns that lay behind this phase in the development of landscape poetry.[38] He was the ambitious descendant of a famous southern military family, and specialized in Confucian learning, holding various offices both civil and military until he was twenty-eight. Luckily for him, he was in mourning for his mother and thus out of the immediate political hurly-burly, when one of the power-holders on whom he was dependent launched a transitorily successful, but soon doomed, coup d'état. Another with whom he had had close relations committed suicide as a result of this coup. Tao at once withdrew to his estate at Xinyang in what is modern Jiangxi province, and remained out of office for the next thirteen years.

There was something of a fashion among the nobility at this time for a conspicuously visible withdrawal from the world, and even a degree of competition for the most distinguished modesty and anonymity. Tao was a superlative poet but also, like most of the others, a poseur. His mind, he said dwelt in "the heights and the wetlands":

> I amount to less than a high-flying bird, seen when gazing up at the
>   clouds.
> I am nothing compared to a swimming fish, seen when, by a stream, I
>   glance down.

Birds and fish had a freedom that he was denied, but envied. He wrote of his relief to be done with his life in the bureaucracy:

> Too long, too long, was I within that cage!
> But now, once more, have I returned to nature.

About a year later, he went back into the cage and accepted a post as a county magistrate. Eighty days later, though, he resigned, observing that "I am incapable of bending at the waist to a rural nobody simply on account of five pecks of rice." This last was a reference to his official salary. The 'rural nobody' was one of the local prefect's deputies who was on his way to see him. Resignation was motivated not by enlightenment, but by aristocratic snobbery.

During his retirement he constantly talked of his poverty. In so far as this had any reality it was relative to other members of the aristocracy, and the previous generations of his own family. On one occasion he described how, when he came back to his estate, "my serfs came to welcome me, while the children waited by the doorway," his farmers informed him about the fields, and he hesitated, deliciously, over whether to go out in his covered carriage or his "solitary boat." It was a sumptuous penury.

His uncle, Tao Dan, had earlier done much the same in an even more extravagant way. Dan had abstained from cereal foods, and striven to become an immortal, while living on a large slice of the family fortune and looked after by more than a hundred serfs. He may have felt that his chances in the official world were none too good, as his father had died young. The de luxe hermit's life, the pursuit of enlightenment, and the cultivation of a love of nature are perhaps best thought of as consolation prizes for members of the nobility who had come off second-best in the rat race of Court politics. Tao Yuanming's originality was to have made poetry out of it.

The first coherent conception of an environment

The conception of an environment first crystallized toward the end of the fourth century CE. The intellectual chemistry required was the work of Xie Lingyun, an aristocrat, estate owner, and poet who lived under the Liu Song dynasty. He was born in 385 and died in 433. Though he was the author of numerous beautiful lyric verses, his masterpiece—at least from the perspective of the environmental historian—is his long descriptive poem called "Living in the Hills."[39] This poem is the focus of the present section.

Why does it matter?

First, the poem is about a specific area, the edge of the mountains along the southern shoreline of Hangzhou Bay, at 30° N, in what is now Shangyu county. The descriptions should be recognizable from the accounts of Hangzhou Bay in chapter 6, though the coastal plain was unencumbered by most of the seawalls and water-control systems that have increasingly protected it since the Tang dynasty, and the forests were full of wild animals long since vanished. The climate was also colder then than now.

Second, though the language is intensified and enhanced, its content is in most places realistic. Xie is not, like some of his predecessors, describing a magic garden that symbolizes paradise. Nor is he letting himself go in a rhapsodic fantasy on a general theme, like Mu Hua in his prose-poem on the sea. He writes of Shangyu as it once was. A real place that is also part of, and an evocation of, the unbounded universe.

Experts having a familiarity with the tendency of most traditional Chinese poetry to refer to the memorized classics, or familiar literary formulas, as much as to the actual world, may be inclined to skepticism. I would offer three arguments in response. (1) The overall character of the location, and many details, is instantly recognizable to the environmental historian who knows the nonliterary sources as well as the location. (2) The geographer Chen Qiaoyi, who has studied the local forest history, regards the range of genera (where identifiable) of trees and mammals listed by Xie as broadly appropriate.[40] (3) Francis Westbrook, who has made a complete 'scholar's translation' of the rhapsody, is convinced that it "is inspired directly by the real landscape."[41] The most important place where he modifies this judgment is with regard to the sea: Xie, he says, "takes his sea-imagery into the realm of sheer hyperbole."[42] And this is due to a misunderstanding. As an expert in literature, he knows little about Hangzhou Bay, and mistakenly thinks that the Qiantang River is the Yangzi.[43] In this particular case, the reality *was* hyperbolic. Westbrook's support on the key issue is important, as in other analyses he has meticulously identified the presence of references to classics such the *Scripture of Songs,* the *Songs of the South,* and the *Book of Changes* almost everywhere in Xie's lyric verses. This said, one has still to be alert to the possibility of lines that are probably derived only from literature. There are a number, and I point out most of them where they occur.

Xie's poem makes it clear that he had quite a subtle concept of the 'environment' as an interrelated complex of different but mutually interdependent forms of life in varying habitats, even if he did not have a general term for it.

The reader today has difficulties because the poet's world of thought is embedded in an encyclopedia that is almost totally different from his or her own. In fact, Xie even appended his own notes to successive sections of his work, partly to explain his philosophy, and partly to clarify condensed allusions or unfamiliar local details. "Living in the Hills" was probably tough going even for educated readers at the time it was written. The translation is tentative to an exceptional degree.[44]

Third, the poem is a guide to understanding Chinese attitudes toward nature and the environment in later times, when they are often less explicitly formulated, being taken for granted after so many centuries. Most important of all, there was in Xie's mind no conflict between the excitement of what we now call 'development', that is, the practical mastering of nature, and the spiritual inspiration to be drawn from contemplating nature, that is, grasping that it is immeasurably greater than we are, and driven by processes that we can only partly intuit or discover. He delighted in having his serfs fell ancient trees and open new roadways through the wilderness. Anyone who has ever owned a substantial expanse of relatively untouched land—a disappearing minority, it is true—can probably feel a certain empathy with this inner urge. It would be unreasonable of us to think him unreasonable in this regard. Only in millennial hindsight has it become apparent with what imperceptible subtlety improvement can transform itself into its contrary: destruction.

Fourth, Xie's vision of the natural world in which his estates were located had multiple dimensions, all of which need to be understood to make sense of this vision's epiphany. He places himself in the context of history—'Chinese history' for us, just 'history' for him. The poem is in one respect propaganda for himself: his withdrawal to the country, in large measure because of the dangers of life at a Court where the factional balance of forces had turned against him, is implicitly compared to the real or alleged retirement from power of some of the greatest figures in Chinese history. Like him, they are said to have found politics lacking in personal fulfilment. He also contrasts his estates with other, earlier, celebrated estates and gardens, always in his own favor. He is continuing traditions, and, he hints, improving on them. The natural world he calls into life is set in a specific and identifiable local geography, echoing with the resonance of ancient, evocative names. But, in this terrain, everything is part of an interacting whole. This is why it may be called an 'environmental' poem. Everything is interlinked: the rivers, the shifting bars of offshore sand, the funnel-shaped estuary with its tidal bore, the human ameliorations of nature in the form of irrigated fields and ditches for drainage, the scattered lakes and islets, the water plants, medicinal herbs, bamboos and trees, the fish, birds, and mountain animals, as also such human activities as hunting, lopping timber, manufacturing paper, and cutting trackways and erecting buildings. Around this composite whole he weaves an encompassing dream of Buddhist enlightenment: the wisdom of the taboos on killing, the merit to be won from releasing living creatures back into freedom, the creation of places for preaching, and of monasteries and hermitages; also insights into the illusory character of our lives, and the workings of outer phenomena and inner pattern-principles, so often seemingly perverse and to our discomfiture. An environment in human perspective is not just biology, but also ideology.

At the same time we have to remember that he is, self-consciously, writing in a literary tradition. "Living in the Hills" is a *fu*, a form that carries with it the expectation of baroque exaggeration, contrasts and parallels, and celebratory catalogs. Even when he says that he is seeking simplicity, we are entitled to be respectfully skeptical.

The translation that follows presents about two-thirds of the poem, and portions of the original notes, with some explanatory comments before most of the sections. Details have in some places been moved from Xie's glosses into the main text for ease of reading. Only in a few places have I found it possible to match the varying lengths of the lines of successive blocks, which give a subtly shifting rhythm to the piece, and much of its acoustic vitality. Unlike most later *fu*, "Living in the Hills" has rhymes, though not universally nor, apparently, systematically. The use of vowel-rhymes in the translation is thus justifiable.

I have also subdivided the poem into larger parts, labeled with capital roman numerals, to give an idea of its overall structure. The first of these is a prelude in which Xie justifies his retirement, claims—by implication—an exalted place in history, and engages in a certain measure of aristocratic one-upmanship. Preceding this is a short prose introduction:

> In ancient times to be domiciled in a hollow place was called 'making one's bed in a cave'. To reside in the hills in a house [as I do] is termed 'living in the hills'. To be among the groves in the countryside is described as 'making

a garden in a village'. Dwelling in the suburbs is known as 'being beside the city wall'. The dissimilarities between these four modes can be inferred from underlying principles.

If we are speaking of the heart and mind, there is actually no difference between riding in the imperial carriage and living in retirement on the northern bank of the Fen River [like the sage–emperor Yao, according to the Daoist philosopher Zhuangzi]. If we turn to phenomena, though, then living in the hills is well and truly different from being in the bazaars. One's frantic feelings turn to leisured calm, and one effortlessly follows the inclinations of one's own character, having the courage to pursue what gives one pleasure.

I have composed a prose-poem on this matter. Yang Xiong [a lexicographer and poet who lived from 53 BCE to 18 CE] remarked that "Poets, when writing prose-poems, combine loveliness and observance of metrical rules. Decoration and structure should be conjoined for beauty to reach perfection." What I sing of on the present occasion is not capital cities, nor palaces and belvederes, nor hunting expeditions, splendid to ears and eyes alike. Rather *I tell of the phenomena of mountains and countrysides, of grasses and trees, of streams and boulders, and of cereals and husbandry.* I lack the talent of those in the past, but *my heart has been set free into what is beyond the everyday world.* If I sing as the rules of writing direct, I may with effort attain my aim. But the search for beauty is something far removed from my intent. You who are reading this should set aside the gorgeous phrases of Zhang Heng [who wrote the "Prose-Poem on the Two Capitals"] and Zuo Si [who wrote the "Prose-Poem on the Three Capitals"], and seek the deep meaning of Tai Tong [a cave-dwelling hermit of Later Han times] and Old Hoaryhead [a legendary recluse who is said to have lived in a fox's shape with foxes, but could shift back to his original form]. You must strip away the showy, and take hold of the unadorned. Only then may perchance it happen that you touch its heart. The idea is the substance of which words are the outer form; and in writing them one can never convey everything. In your search for the meaning in these traces that I have left behind me, put your confidence in that which inspires in you a delighted response.

The poem is as follows:

I

Master Xie lay resting, unwell, on top of the mountain's crest,
Reading his way through the documents the men of old had left,
And, since they corresponded with what he himself professed,
The thought set him gently laughing, and this is what he said:

So, then, it's the Way that matters.
Things are but insubstantial.

Since the patterns will always continue,
Events may fade in oblivion.

The present can not be altered. Neither can what is now gone.
Both stuff and surface appearance maintain their regular constancies.

His sacred thatched hut could never afford a true home for the Yellow
 Emperor,
Nor the crossroads palace give sage–king Yao what he found a congenial
 dwelling.
The former followed his deepest desires when he died beside Tripod Lake,
While the latter retired to the Fen's north shore in emotional exaltation.

Zhang Liang, once a warrior, changed his diet to grain-free macrobiotics,
Wishing to follow Immortal Red Pine, and range in the distant beyond.
I commend Fan Li who, revenged on Wu, let his oar-blades strike the
 waves,
Having vainly urged his comrade Wen Zhong to flee imminent death and
 escape.
He judged that his person and name's renown might exist in different
 domains:
Fame weighed less in the balance than everyday life, so he saw no cause to
 remain.

What's to do? Since few paths now exist on which my hounds can hunt
 hares.
And from where come the tracks whence, once more, I can hear the lament
 of the cranes?

Fan Li was a man of Wu in the age of the Springs and Autumns. Judging that
he had been insulted by its ruler, he fought for more than twenty years to help
the ruler of Yue destroy his own former country. Victory won, he left by the
inland waterways for Qi in the north, where he changed his name, but then,
without intending it, became famous again. He therefore departed once more,
and altered his name a further time. The last line but one refers to the Li Si, the
ruthless and innovative prime minister of the First Emperor. When, under
the Second Emperor, he was about to be executed as a result of the machina-
tions of his rival, the eunuch Zhao Gao, he observed to his second son that he
would have liked once more to go out with him, leading their brown dogs to
hunt "the crafty hares," but how, now, could this ever be possible? The last line

refers to a remark by Lu Ji, also from Wu, but who lived in the late third and early fourth centuries CE. He was defeated while leading an army in the service of the king of Chengdu. About to be put to death for alleged treachery, he asked, rhetorically, if he would ever again hear the cry of the cranes from his home in Huating by the mouth of the Yangzi. Xie makes the dark implications in these allusions explicit in his notes. Presumably he was thinking of his own political situation.

> When people were domiciled in hollows, gales and rains caused them
>   grief,
> A misfortune the sages abolished, by inventing rafters and eaves.
> When the luster of mansion and palace was created by glittering jades,
> The trend shifted. Unsullied hamlet gardens were the cynosures of their
>   age.
>
> Yet best of all is entrusting one's house to the hilly heights and the gullies,
> Where, with luck, the ancient and recent combine, and life is free of
>   obstructions.
> Though neither in marketplace, nor in Court, yet the chill and the hot are
>   in balance,
> And, even though artificially built, both the gaudy and drab are absent.

As Xie says in his notes, "the hilly heights and gullies have a deeper Way in them than the hamlet gardens, but [living there] is not being domiciled in hollows [as in primitive times]." He is advocating a *civilized wilderness*.

Nor was he above a little posthumous competition with others who had also in the past 'lived in the hills', and perhaps demonstrating his southerner's subtler sensitivity to geomancy. (Note, by the way, that, in the fourth line below, the 'uo' of 'Luo' has much the same sound as the 'o' in 'property'. 'Cwm', read 'coom', in the seventh line indicates a steep-sided valley closed off at one end.)

> Zhongchang Tong, in days gone by, had a taste for speaking his mind
> About the high mountains on his estate and the waters meandering by.
> Ying Qu, in a letter to Cheng Wenxin, described the site of his property
> As having Mount Mang on its northern edge, and southward the River
>   Luo.
> But the lines of force in their landscapes were lopsided and unbalanced,
> Lacking an all-round perfection, well-matched in every azimuth.
>
>   The secluded cwms in the Copper Hills
> Where the Zhuo clan went to the limit, digging ores and lopping down
>   timber,
>   And Golden Valley, amidst whose beauties

Master Shi roamed on sightseeing tours, while sating his ears with sweet
    music,
Were mere geomorphic formations, where the vegetation grew dense,
And, if I may say so, phenomena different from *my* spatial ensemble for a
    residence.

And as for the terrace where Mu's daughter's lover piped to the phoenix to
    come,
Or the Tower of Clusters that Zhao first built, and later Chu also
    constructed,
Or Clouds and Dreams Marshes, where King Ling gazed about him, at
    mountains, rivers, and lakes,
Or the fall at Viridian Hill in Huainan, where princes engaged in the chase,
Or the Zhang Canal that Count Wen had cut, in Wei, for irrigation,
Or the parkland of bamboos enfolded where the Qi winds round in a
    bight,
Or the Forest of Oranges in Sichuan, or Wu's garden upon the Long Island,
Though the prized glories of states whose forces were once reckoned a
    thousand chariots,
In which of these could a hermit find — a resting-place where he could
    vanish?

What is more, if these hills, and streams, were still not all he might wish,
What sort of sense would it be for him to seek to make additions?

The Zhuo clan were originally metalworkers from the state of Zhao who were
moved by the Qin imperial government to Linqiong in Sichuan, where they
openly appropriated the mountain forests and probably worked both copper
and iron. Master Shi was Shi Chong (249–300), a rich and unprincipled official
of the third century CE, who was also a poet. He built himself a country villa
at Golden Valley on the north side of the Yellow River, and organized a celebrated prolonged party there during which poems were written by the guests.[45]
He was later executed as the result of a false decree issued at the urging of a
rival, then in the political ascendant, to whom he had refused to present a
desirable singing-girl. There is a hint, in the reference to music, that what we
love can kill us.

'Mu' was Duke Mu of Qin, long before this western state gave birth to the
first imperial dynasty. His daughter and her lover are said to have vanished
when the phoenix finally responded to the latter's panpipes. 'Clusters' had two
different senses: in Zhao, bringing the separate together, and, in Chu, an abundance of auspicious crops. Ling was the king of Chu, and the great marshes,
now long since dried up, lay around the middle reaches of the Yangzi River (see

pages 50–2). On the last two lines, Xie observes in his notes that we have to accept the landscapes that the topography gives us.

The second part of the poem, which is relatively brief, describes the origin of the Xie family's country estate. The first section refers to Xie's grandfather, Xie Xuan, though we only know this from the poet's own notes.[46] Xuan had been a successful general but retired from Court politics to "avoid the disorderly behavior of those around the Throne."

II

I observed his far-reaching perception adapt — to the trends of the times,
    as they shifted,
In control, though the stirrings of change were shackled, and true
    principle-pattern invisible.
The twilight of life his apologia, he came home to rest in tranquillity.
Celebration of his distinguished deeds he bequeathed to the stone
    inscriptions.

Qu Yuan, he thought, showed his limitations when he drowned himself in
    the river,
Though Yue Yi who fled Yan, when maligned, aroused his pitying sympathy.
But it was *nature* — numinous, beautiful — for which he felt true affinity,
And in settling secure here, *above the world,* he attained to his ambition.

So in some measure Lingyun's response to the environment could be said to have been inherited, though it seems that he can have hardly known his grandfather directly.[47]

Qu Yuan of the state of Chu in the third century BCE was probably ancient China's most famous poet. He is traditionally believed to have drowned himself in despair that his ruler would not listen to his counsel. Yue Yi of Wei and then Yan was the commander who successfully led the allied armies of Yan, Zhao, Chu, Han, and Wei against the state of Qi. When the king of Yan who had appointed him passed away, his successor turned against Yue, who fled, in fear of his life, to the state of Zhao, though the breach was later mended.

In his note on the end of this section Xie comments that "the planning and starting of work on the hills and streams were in fact based on this," that is, on his grandfather's aims for his estate during his retirement. Intervention in nature was the family style.

In the final section of this part, Xie comments on his own psychology. The language is at times opaque, and what is said seems to reveal an idiosyncratic mixture of deference, hedonism, self-deprecation, despair, and a kind of optimistic and arrogant enlightenment. It is thus hard to be certain whether or not the translation has captured the appropriate sense of the original. By way of preliminary explanations, note that Ban Si, who lived in the Han dynasty, was a devotee of the Daoist masters Laozi and Zhuangzi. He believed, approvingly, that they had "cut themselves off from the sages and abandoned knowledge." Shang Fu was a long-lived minister who served the first three rulers of the Zhou dynasty. The two lines before the last seem to hint hazily at the famous saying of Laozi that "the greatest skill is like clumsiness," and at the chapter in the *Zhuangzi* called "Knowledge Travels North," describing Knowledge's futile pilgrimage in pursuit of understanding, since those who knew either couldn't, or wouldn't, tell him.

> I revere the guidance wise men have left, behind them, from times now
>   past,
> But I scrutinize, too, at a lower level, what suits my mood and my
>   character.
> We were endowed with our modest-sized bodies for savoring calm and
>   happiness,
> And must keep our inner selves prepared to snatch any opportune chance.

> It shames me Ban Si, unstained by this world, could become enlightened
>   so fast.
> That Shang Fu persevered to extreme old age makes me mortified I am
>   inadequate.
> Senility threatens me. So, too, does sickness. A pretty pair of companions!

> I'm resolved to make use of ineptitude, so that my life circles backward,
> Relinquishing ordinary existence and its quest for understanding,
> To live by the hillsides and the streams, immersed in an empty clarity.

After these prologs we move on to the geographical descriptions. The landscape some five or six thousand years before Xie's time had been a submerged coastline, in which hills emerged as islands from a shallow coastal sea perhaps four meters higher than it is today. As the sea receded it left behind a plain of sediments between these hills, dotted with shallow vestigial lakes, while the coast remained a tidal salt marsh. Efforts to build a seawall began before mid-Tang times, but it is not clear how long before, and it is likely that in Xie's day such a wall did not yet exist.[48] Xie was understandably preoccupied with water.

III

> As to my estate's location —
> Streams lie to its east. To the west are lacustrine basins.
> One journeys past islands here, then returns via sandy spits,
> One's shoulders turned on the heights behind, as one faces out to the hills,

With impasses blocking off the east, while the west slopes away in
   declivities.

In its bosom the inflowing–outflowing waters are all of them held fast.
The hills encircle us around, with a gently moving ambling.
Everywhere there are interconnected, and unpredictable, switchbacks.
Or else there are vertical flanks. Or flat and level expanses.

He then moves round the four points of the compass to survey the nearby
scenery. The names of the small-scale local features he mentions seem long
since to have been forgotten. Note that 'beck', in what follows, is an English
Lake District term for a small stream.

IV

Eastward, nearby, are fields high up. The lakes are lower down.
Gorges extend to the west. The vales lie off to the south.
There runs the Rockbound Trench, and the Spillway Through The
   Stones.
So, too, the Whetstone Of Grief, whose bamboos are the color of gold.

Down their unfathomable descents, the becks leap forth into flight,
And along the footslopes of countless hills where trellis-laced shrubs
   grow high
They pour out their sources into the river disappearing on the horizon,
Or distribute their water from deep-sunk springs into irrigation close by.

At this early epoch the majority of the fields were high up to exploit the hill-
foot alluvial fans laid down where the velocity of the water off the hills slowed
down, and then drained into the lakes below, such as Mirror Lake. In a later
age, as the coastal plain was diked and the soil cleaned of salt, the lakes were to
become reservoirs for newly opened fields now lying below them. In Xie's day,
though, these techniques were only in their infancy. They were, centuries later,
when exported north, to transform the Yangzi delta.

   Note that 'anastomotic' in the next section is a technical term from geomorphology and medicine for channels and tubes that have multiple intercom-
municating openings.

Southward, still close at hand, there lies the Twin Streams' confluence
Enfolding the Triple Islands composed of sediment deposits.
Inside then outside each other are the shifting courses they follow,
Mountain waters that part and join, endlessly anastomotic.

A crag that seems about to crash overhangs the steep east flank.
Huts serried, where once a city stood, cling beside the western path.

> The brook dashes against the blue-green woods, and waves from the
>   impact swash back,
> While ripples — response to the current's contact — reflect off shoals of
>   white sand.

The landscape was mobile and forever altering itself. In his notes, Xie remarks
that passers-by were terrified by the sight of this rock that looked on the point
of falling into the river below.

We omit the opening lines of the section on the nearby view to the west and
continue with its conclusion:

> Along the shore of the tidal inlet, bamboos cast their shadows of green.
> Reflections of rockwalls, in the torrent, flash with a reddish gleam.
> Darkness consolidates after the moon sinks hidden behind the peaks,
> And, their branches loud with singing, it seems — as if wind stirred in
>   the trees.

In his commentary, Xie says that "when birds gather on the branches singing,
then one refers to this as 'wind.'" The Chinese word for 'wind' (*feng*) can
also have the meanings of 'air' or 'tune' and of 'local atmosphere' or 'customs.'
There is thus something of a second sense hinted at: "as if folk music stirred
in the trees."

The following section contains a word (*li*) that appears in no dictionary.
It is most likely from a now-forgotten local dialect, and quite possibly, like
some place-names in the area, is of Yue, not Han Chinese, origin. Xie glosses it
as 'long stream', and I have rendered it here by the relatively unusual term
'flume' to flag this feature. The theme in the first quatrain is 'two-in-one and
one-in-two'.

> The pair of connected Shaman Lakes lies nearby to the north,
> Linked by the Inner and Outer Flumes to form one body of water,
> But Transverse Mountain and Everstone Hill have fully separate forms,
> And distinctive landmarks are Circular Peak and the Summit of Good
>   Fortune.

> Water is drawn, through circuitous channels, from the Renovated
>   Reservoir,
> Spewing forth, bubbling, as from a spring, agitated and plentiful.
> Checked under the mountains' salients, it eddies back, forming wetlands,
> But, rushing over the pebbled shallows, it cuts out a bed for itself.

Xie turns next to more distant prospects; and more familiar place names
come on stage. He opens with a roll call of mountains associated with Daoism.

Celestial Terrace is north of the city of Taizhou on the east coast. Sun Chuo (314–71 CE) wrote a famous prose-poem on its ascent, full of Daoist and Buddhist references. He mentions crossing the Oak Tree Stream or Oak Tree Gorge that also appears in Xie's poem, though in Xie's case it seems a more serious barrier. At the northern end of the Terrace was the Bridge of Rock, believed to be used by immortals to travel back and forth, but too difficult, like the gorge, according to Xie's notes on his own work, for ordinary human beings to use any more. Squarestone and Four Brightnesses, which is near Ningbo, both had natural stone 'windows' on all sides. The 'brightnesses' were the sun, moon, stars, and planets. Majestic Peace, on the border of Yuyao and Shangyu counties, was shaped like an umbrella, which also gave it an alternative name. The 'tong' tree referred to was probably a *Paulownia* or a *Firmiana simplex*, not the oil-bearing tong (*Aleurites fordii* or *montana*). The apocryphal scriptures Xie alludes to toward the end are the bogus additions made in the first centuries of the present era to the Confucian canon. Xie implies that nature itself was another, different, scripture.

V

Away in the distance, to the east,
Rise Celestial Terrace, and Tong-and-Cedar,
With Squarestone, and Majestic Peace,
The Four Brightnesses, the Twin Leeks,
The Garlic Flower, and Five Ao Peaks.

Exemplars of numinous powers, unrecorded in the apocrypha,
They attest that auspicious magic echoes back in our matching responses.
Those having their favor can travel across the Bridge of Rocks' lichens and
    mosses,
And leap clear above the Oak Tree Gorge's tortuous sinuosities.

In other words, they can become immortals.

A landscape like this was not mere prettiness, nor inspirational only in a general way. Even less was it solely an arena for predictable, or at least familiar, natural processes. It was magically alive, and this life had specific, identified, foci. We do not resonate to their names, being almost unaware of their history, but it is important to recognize that Xie's readers must have reacted. When the stories are not well known, he supplies details in his notes. Thus, of the Five Ao Peaks mentioned above, he says "each one of these *ao* [bay-like recesses] belonged respectively to the Daoist adept Tanji, and Messrs Cai, Chi, Xie, and Chen. They all gave each other mutual help, *and these too are wonderful places.*" He underlines the point with the phrase I have just put in italics: none of the mountains in the roll call is ordinary.

More mountains follow, again with evocative names. Then comes a realistic account of the difficulties of moving around in this swampy terrain, and through what he himself in his notes calls "the dense woods" that lined the river banks "in every place."

> Needles of Pine and Perching Rooster rise far away to the south,
> As do the Landslide of Stones, and the summit of sage–king Yao.
> Mounts Tu and Foursome confront each other across the county
> boundary.
> White Pinnacle stands in its own domain, separate from Meng
> Mountain.

> If I trace a tributary to its source, then turn around to come home,
> I grow bewildered, no longer discerning the way I ought to be going.
> Uphill, the heights are impassable. I am caged, and the cage covered
> over.
> Downstream I sink in a morass, as my struggles make me soaked.

In Xie's commentary he tells us that Daoist adept Tanji lived at Meng Mountain, where he had "fields cleared of weeds by burning for the growing of taro and yams." There were "limpid streams and an abundance of bamboos." Of course these remarks are designed to evoke a primitive Daoist simplicity: fire-farming, not irrigation; edible roots, not cereals. Even allowing for this, the land that appears in these descriptive phrases bears only little relation, its general location apart, to the stripped away, densely populated, feverishly industrializing, concreted and polluted countryside crisscrossed by overhead electric wires, and chugging or rushing vehicles, that one meets with today. Reflection suggests that it was also markedly different from its successor even a thousand years later, toward the end of the Chinese Middle Ages. The population then would have already become twenty or more times greater than in Xie's or Tanji's time, the sea excluded, the catchment rivers fully organized for productive purposes, and most of the original woods cut. If there is a common characteristic that lasted through all these years, it is probably that of the omnipresence of water, of the awareness of living at most a few meters above the level of the highest tides.

The text of the section that follows, on the distant prospect westward, has been lost. We therefore conclude this part of the poem by looking north, toward the Qiantang River emptying from west to east into Hangzhou Bay. This description is a recognizable portrayal of one of the world's great macrotidal estuaries, full of shifting sand banks, and famous for its tidal bore.[49] The distinctive rotation of the tides around the bay, coming in at the northeast and leaving by the southeast, observable today, seems from Xie's lines to have been broadly similar more than a millennium-and-a-half ago, even though the coastal geometry has considerably altered since then.

Far to the north the long river flows, seabound and homeward, forever,
Where the ocean, till it sinks from our sight, spreads out in its immensity,
While separate sediment-shoals pile up, as on filaments finely stretched,
And hummocked sandbanks interconnect in a loosely woven texture.

Mountains, haphazard in all directions, deploy their defensive shelter.
Water-gyres, plunging into the depths, clash in their circling complexities.
Sweeping away to the east — stretches uninterrupted emptiness.
To the horizon, the wind-swept waves join together and part irregularly.
 . . .

Where the coast is high, one can guess that, below, the water drops many
    fathoms,
And, by reading the patterns of islets, know the location of the shallows.
When the huge surges reach their full, they cover the Ceng Rocks over,
But when, dissipated, the swell sinks low, deep sandbars lie exposed.

If gales gust more fiercely than before, and the breakers' crests rear up,
Then the water gains position-power from its speed and its abundance.
At the new and the full moon, every year, in the springtime and the
    autumn,
The tides rise up to their maximum, and the waves froth tumultuously.

The terror-spreading billows are towering in their arrogance.
They shoot forth like spurts of lightning, or slump flat with a thunderous
    crashing.
Foam flows on the sea-surface, driven by wind, or leaps aloft flying and
    spattering.

Surmounting an abrupt embankment, the sea rushes up the escarpment.
When it meets the river current head on, it brings it under its mastery.
It starts by rapidly circling around, as it mounts to the skies above,
But ends by turning itself upside down, so one glimpses the bed of its
    gulf.

Intoxicated by this vision, Chu's heir-apparent was healed,
And the God of the Yellow River shamed when confronting the God of
    the Sea.

There are two literary references in the concluding lines. According to Xie's notes, an heir-apparent to the state of Chu, one Chu Er, was said by Mei Sheng (the Han-dynasty rhetorician who wrote the prose-poem on the tong tree quoted on page 329) to have been cured of a sickness by a visitor from the state of Wu. The cure was holding up to him a vision of the waves on the sea in the fall. The last line refers to the chapter "Autumn Floods" in the *Zhuangzi*. The God of the Yellow River is pleased with himself and his powers, until he reaches the sea, and discovers his relative insignificance in comparison with its inexhaustible immensity.

As to the science, it should be noted that I have supplied the word 'tides' on the basis of the reference to the phases of the moon. We can also be fascinated, so long as we are not too much impressed, by the poet's intuition that the 'position-power' of the water—or in modern, but of course historically misleading, parlance, its momentum and energy—is connected in some way to what we would now term its velocity and its mass.

We now turn to Xie's house and its estate. The descriptions evoke the half-sensed contrasts and fleeting paradoxes that the poet's mind intuits in the landscape.

VI

Not far away is the site of the place where they lived in times now past.
A manor house rose there once. Today, it's turned into a garden.
Hibiscus, still, lift themselves aloft, and the small-seeded elms with white
    bark.
The foundations, as ever, still exist. Likewise the well, with its shaft.

Along the frontage, and at its back, the winding tracks encircle it.
Straight field-paths, to its east and west, run upward and downward,
    vertically.
It not only overlooks a gorge, but has a round pool in its purlieus.
It both holds a summit in its embrace, and boasts hills outside as its girdle.

Inquiring into my grandfather's fief, and its magical bewitchment,
Reveals the truth that, beyond any doubt, this property is inimitable.
Pairs of rafters forming triplicate sections, the crag-foot hall's been rebuilt,
And a single roof-beam lodged in the cliff whose runoff below feeds the
    river.

I fling wide the doors, on the southern side, confronting the distant heights.
I open the window, facing east, to see fields of rice nearby.
These paddies, though adjacent to ridges, give me farmland in ample
    supply.
Through the hillslopes, pillowed upon the stream, runs a path to the
    burial site.

He is like any other owner of a new—or, in his case, renewed—house: recounting the details of the structure, and enjoying the views. The triple units of room-space are mentioned in his notes, and the "paired beams" may be thought of as placed across the ceiling like the horizontal equivalents of the two vertical folds in a triptych. He also comments that "what one can see, looking out from these two halls, is almost all of equally high quality." I have used the special sense of 'a path to a grave' for the word *qian*, as the placing of the hill above the water suggests a location suitable for tombs according to the earth-magic ruling luck-giving burial in south China.

In the next section the 'year-node divisions' referred to are the twenty-four solar periods into which the Chinese divided the calendar year.[50] Each one had approximately fifteen days. The Chinese term translated 'forecast' can be understood either as depending on some omen or presage about the weather in the coming period, or else simply on sharp observation. The description of farming that he gives suggests that sophisticated methods were already being used for growing rice in this area around the end of the fourth century: he mentions both an intricate irrigation system, and early- and late-ripening varieties of the grain.

> Dividing the fields, the pathways crisscross — in intersecting patterns;
> At right angles, dikes along contours meet the walls protecting the
>   channels.
> The current of water is led in flowing, along a feeder canal.
> Arteries spread it in random fashion. Rejoined ditches funnel it back.
>
> Abundant, our harvest stands as thick as vegetation is plentiful,
> Perfumed, nonglutinous, rice releasing the sweetness of its scent.
> We bid the early-ripening ears of the summertime farewell,
> To welcome the later autumnal crop as though coming to meet a guest.
>
> We have, in addition to our paddies, dry raised fields and ridges
> Where hemp-plants grow, and wheats, and beans and peas, and millets.
> Observing the seasonal changes, we forecast each year-node division,
> At some moments sowing the seeds, and, at others, gathering crops in.
>
> The food we serve's made of grain, combined with a rice-water drink.
> Herdsmen and wood wardens aren't required, nor those in crafts or business.
> For living our lives, why insist on acquiring a vast store of riches?
> Filling one's stomach's enough. — If one understands Pattern-Principle.

There is a hint here at the style of Chinese life in antiquity with the reference to 'rice-water'. The song "Da dong" in the *Scripture of Songs* contains the lines about elegant but useless and self-indulgent high officials:[51]

> Some of them will at times take wine,
> But not water that's an infusion of rice.

Xie's own notes draw attention to an allusion to the *Zhuangzi*: "Xu You said: 'The tapir drinks from the Yellow River, but only enough for a bellyful.'"[52] This quotation has also been used in our own times as an illustration of the Daoist ideal of ecological delicacy: of living so lightly off the world that one's presence in it is barely felt. Xie adds that if one can "reduces one's concern with oneself and diminish one's desires, then it suffices one just to exist," without needing craftsmen, merchants, wood wardens to look after game, or herdsmen to guard one's flocks. But, he adds, "without farmland there is no way one can establish oneself."

In commonsense terms, he is striking a philosophical pose. Pretending to beliefs that, as a wealthy aristocrat, he in no way puts into practice in his own life. Maybe one unstated purpose of proclaiming the attraction of an uncompromising archaic frugality was to imply the moral superiority of his precautionary self-imposed exile from active politics over the scheming and maneuvering of those still involved. But—it may sometimes be necessary to be skeptical of skepticism. My personal intuition is that he existed in at least a double mental state: in some sense believing deeply in these Daoist ideals, even at the same time as he constantly betrayed them. It is not an uncommon human condition.

A few preliminary comments are needed for the last section in this part, which describes the wetlands that lay almost on a level with the sea. *Zizania* was a plant that grew in shallow water, and whose seeds could be harvested and eaten not unlike those of grain. The 'pool-girt tower' is a reference to the soaring Jiantai tower built in the middle of the Taiyi Lake that lay to the northwest of Chang'an (in the Northwest) during the Han dynasty. This lake contained islands that were said to "resemble the mountains of the gods in the sea."[53] The reflection of the moon is a Buddhist image for the unreality of the sensory world.

> Leaving the gardens behind us, we descend to the fields growing grain.
> Then from the fields continue down, until we come to the lakes.
> Here rivers have flooded over their banks, causing spreading inundations,
> And all, as far as the eye can see, is a watery domain.

> I have dredged the pools and stream beds, yet they're quiet and
>   undisturbed,
> And cleared islets of the *Zizania* plants that created meandering curves.
> In the early months of the year, warm springs gushed boisterously forth.
> In the autumn, the chilly undulations speed swiftly by on their course.

Breezes arouse the ripples, besides islands covered with orchids.[54]
The upside-down sun is mirrored in mud, where pepper-fruits hang from
their stalks.
We fly in our minds to the pool-girt tower, among man-made isles of
immortals.
We seize the happiness of illusion, as though grasping the moon in the
water.

Solar light, at dawn, elongates shadows; yet objects show up distinct.
The setting sun puts to sleep perfumed flowers, yet their odors are still full
of vigor.
Looking back, I brood on ties of affection that, now, are forever broken.
For the future, I long for clouds of guests to call by for a passing moment.

His feelings shift back and forth. At one moment he feels an attachment to the
world of the senses and emotions, coupled with delight in an active involvement with it. Even improving on nature by dredging and tidying. At the next
he is aware of how easily we deceive ourselves with concocted fairylands, and
mistake perceptions—the sun seen shining upside-down in wet mud—for the
underlying realities. At the end he tacitly acknowledges that he, like all of us, is
a social animal that, however, enlightened, can never be wholly free of the need
for personal relations.

In the next part, we begin on the catalogs. These are sometimes felt to have
made the full text of "Living in the Hills" untranslatable as literature, and there
may be some truth in this opinion. At the same time they are a major part of
the justification for regarding it as the first environmental poem, and arguably
the greatest, in the Chinese tradition.

VII

As for the plants in the water's depths —
Duckweeds and algae are there, together with mare's-tail and sedges,
Reeds and rushes, and sweet-smelling *sun*-grass. So, too, are various
celeries,
Tall *jian*-reeds, *Zizania*, kernel-bearing, *Marsilea* with four-lobed foliage.
Likewise the white *Artemisia*.
Strainer-grasses and yellow, floating, *Nymphoides*, horned water chestnuts
and lilies.

Though the roll call of plants is complete, and each has its appropriate
elegance,
The lotus flower, when open, is unique in its dazzling freshness.

Its leaves lie seamlessly together, spreading further and further their green.
Its flowers, holding their scarlet enclosed, tremble like flags in a breeze.

It saddens me that the time is so brief during which that perfume's
distilled.
That those faces, once they've touched on perfection, so pitifully easily
wither.
As always, once prodigal gifts are given, they are afterwards snatched away.
How empty the wreckage of the blooms that, a few moments past, were
fragrant!

The last four lines of this section are omitted. They show how water plants had a long history as a topic in Chinese poetry. Xie was sensitive to the dual origin of a poem: both personal experience mediated through previous literature, *and* previous literature developed further on the basis of personal experience. And to its social acceptance or rejection being shaped by similar forces. He is engaging in these omitted lines, discreetly but unmistakably, in public relations for his own work.

He moves on to medicinal herbs. These remedies, real or imagined, were part of the character of a locality. In his notes Xie comments on the *Herbal of the Divine Husbandman*, a pharmacopeia edited in Later Han times, probably on the basis of earlier materials: "These days one no longer relies on its [list of] places where medicines are produced. They merely grow where the soil suits them." Observation could override authority. He adds that "this region produces a very great number of materials for medicines." There follow his own glosses on most of the allusions made in the poem's text. These include the legendary discoverers of curative drugs, and the spelling out of such sets as the Three Fruitstones, the Six Roots, the Five Flowers, and the Six Fruits. At the end he talks mostly about plants that "belong to the immortals," though all but one, the last, seem to have been real enough.

His theme in the closing lines of this medicinal subsection is the exceptional endurance that makes a long life, or even immortality, possible:

The hill *Eupatoria* bid fall farewell, showing forth in their shining colors.
Gardenia shrubs that grow beside snow are luxuriant, too, and supple.
Even after a myriad human lifetimes, the Tortuous Juniper flourishes,
And a thousand years pass before we're aware of the hidden fir-tree fungus.

The corolla, on its green-hued stem, reflects back a brilliant crimson.
Dense colorless stamens cluster together, up on the purple twig.
It both brings aging to a halt, and enhances one's mental quickness.
It can also expel a malevolent spirit, or provide the cure for a sickness.

The *Eupatorium chinensis* or *lan*-grass is one of the Compositae, which include daisies, and chrysanthemums. It is described as a sweet-smelling perennial, three or four feet high, that flourishes in wild places in the hills. Its pale purple tubular flowers open only at the end of the fall. The 'Tortuous Juniper' (a nonce translation) is *Selaginella involvens,* a tangled evergreen shrub rather more than a foot in height, and used to produce a dye and a medicine. The gardenia mentioned is *Gardenia florida.* The plant that is the subject of the last four lines is not named, but is clearly a herb of immortality. Stamens were sometimes eaten by Chinese hermits as a macrobiotic food.

The reference to *snow* is important. It is one of a number in the poem that confirm that the average annual temperature had fallen lower by the late fourth century than it is today. The four lines that follow immediately below as an illustration of this are taken out of sequence, and come from a part near the end of the poem that I have otherwise not translated:

> When grasses encounter the winter, their flowers close up tight.
> When the trees are shivering in frost, their green color withers and dies.
> By those on the south-facing slopes, though it's chill, the sunlight is still
>   absorbed;
> But *those on the northern flanks keep their snow*, even in times of warmth.

This seems to be referring to something that happens regularly, not momentary events. The mean temperature in Hangzhou for January, the coldest month, is about 4° Celsius at the present day; and the lowest recent recorded January has averaged 1° Celsius. Moments of snow and severe cold do occur, but are brief.[55]

The section on bamboos, which follows, attempts a rough-and-ready taxonomic approach. In addition to differentiating the shapes of the leaves, and the colors, of otherwise similar species, Xie also points to differences in the style of growth. Thus delicate 'streamside' bamboos did not form dense groves, whereas the heavier 'stony-ground' varieties did.

> One Arrow Bamboo has broader leaves. The other one's leaves are slender.
> The four Bitter Bamboos are distinguished by color: green, white, purple,
>   and yellow.
> One soil feeds the streamside variety, another the stony-ground species.
> The first, lightweight, we use for connecting ties. The second, heavy, for
>   beams.
>
> Elongated they rise, and trembling — graceful-armed girls dancing
>   merrily,
> Either growing in clustering thickets, or as multiple delicate stems.

Moistened by dew when the sun goes down, they grow chilled and sunk
    in the shadows.
When aroused by breezes at sunrise, they fill with a pure vitality.

They constantly brush against the clouds with their feather-duster tops.
Where they overlook a jade-blue lake, their kingfisher turquoise is
    prominent.
They disdain the Qin-Han Imperial Park, and Wei's garden within the
    Qi's bend,
And confirm the richness of bamboos that are our southeastern heritage.

This may also be read as referring to Mount Touchcloud (Shaoyun) in Wu,
and mentioned by the earlier poet Zuo Si, and to the Blue Ripples Lake
(Bilanghu), near Wuxing, to the northwest. Xie's regional chauvinism is
evident, though not offensive. He ends by naming places where one should
walk and stay, and alludes to some historical tales, such as that on the origin
of bamboo flutes.

Local trees form the coda to the survey of plants. Identifying them often
remains problematic, at times even at the level of the genus. 'Southernwood' is
Malachus nanmu. The *Cudrania* is *triloba,* a thorny tree whose leaves can be fed
to silkworms when mulberry leaves are in short supply. I have added a couple
of amplifications about the nature of two trees, the *Broussonetia* and *Ailanthus.*

As to its trees —
There are pines, cypresses, sandalwood, and oaks with chestnut leaves.
Also paulownias and elms, *pian* 'laurels' and southernwood 'cedars',
Dong, Cudrania, wild-growing mulberries, and the paper-source,
    Broussonetia,
Catalpa, tamarisks, and *Ailanthus,* whose leaves stink but whose nuts can
    be eaten.

Some are robust, and some soft. They have natures that greatly differ.
Their substances vary. Some are hardwoods. Others are fragile or brittle.
Some grow low down; some on heights. Some like loams; others soils of
    low productivity.
They seek their particular requirements, having their own specificities.

Trunks, of two arms'-lengths girth, block the sight of the mountain
    summits.
Perilous twigs rise a thousand fathoms, above the void of the gulfs.
They scale the mountainous ridges. They stand there, drawn up to full
    height,
Or shelter deep in the torrent gorges, their lush foliage branching widely.

Down the lines of the lengthy valleys, boughs balance the slope with their
    slant,
While clumps plunge their roots into boulder-heaps, and radiate twigs
    intertangling,
Where sun–dazzle's mirrored back from the streams, they seem to grow
    even brighter,
And their aethers congeal in an atmosphere closing round us on every side.

Confronting the harshness of the cold, the trees are a fresh-tinted green.
Then imbibing the gentle warmth, they wax fat, and their fragrances are
    sweet.
Next they bid farewell to their fallen leaves when autumn is nearly done,
And wait till the early days of spring with their stamens enclosed in their
    buds.

This passage conveys the relative environmental abundance of these early
medieval times, a theme of chapter 7, and, by implication, the relative environmental poverty of those that followed. It also shows that Xie had a clear
conception of specific habitats, as he likewise did in the case of animals.

VIII

The world of plants has been described,
But animals are in such variety
— Swimming and cantering, leaping and soaring —
There's no way to trace their complex origins.

One can only note what they look like, and consider their cries and calls,
To know if they belong in the hills, or by the flowing waters,
Where, during the chilly weather and warmth, obedient to the seasons,
But without encouragement, or taboos, they seek for what they need.

'Nature', understood here in the sense that contrasts it with the human world,
was not shaped by social constraints. Observe, too, the flicker of proto-
Darwinian insight. Xie says that the baffling multiplicity of species (*zhonglei*)
makes it impossible for him to "root or source them" (*gen-yuan*), to give his
words a literal translation. His instinct, though, is to suspect that they must have
come from somewhere, not that there was a single creation, once and for all.

Fish come first, with something of a confusion of names. Some of those he
mentions seem to correspond straightforwardly enough with fishes that exist
in Zhejiang province today. Among freshwater fishes living in lakes and local
networks of streams, we have the *Siniperca* spp. of which the broad-bellied
black-striped perch is representative, and *Cyprinus carpio*, the well-known
carp. Among fish that travel in fresh water, often spawning in the fast-flowing

upper reaches of the rivers, there is the toothless and laterally flattened *Hypophtha imichthys moritrix*. River-mouth fish provide the crucian carp, regarded in folklore as the epitome of faithfulness and mutual help, as they were always in pairs or groups. Hydraulic works seem recently to have disrupted their breeding and they are now said to be extinct.[56] Anadromous fish that live in the sea, but breed in spring or summer up the rivers, include the sea-perch (*Lateolabrax* spp.) and the *Coilia nasus*, a little fish only about three to nine inches long. Fish living in shallow seas where the salinity is less than that of the open ocean include the mullet (*Mugil cephalus*).

Some other identifications seem fairly reasonable. We can probably be confident about the snake-fish that eats other fish, the snouted sturgeon and the large sturgeon which is usually found near the sea. Slightly more problematic is the *Pseudobagrus aurantiacus*, a spiny, whiskered, and yellow-gilled fish, though there is no support for the traditional belief that it could fly. The same holds for the freshwater triangular bream (*Megalobrama terminalis*), and the *Elopichthys bambusa*, which is about three feet in length, and devours other fish with insatiable voracity. The term *zun* has been applied to a variety of fish, but my guess is that here it refers to another anadromous species, the *Oncorhynchus masou*, that leaves the sea in the summer and goes up a river to find sands and gravels where the water is swift-flowing and clear, and it can breed. In general, we would expect the environment on the south side of Hangzhou Bay in this period, saline tidal flats before major seawalls had been built, to have had a number of fish that either moved between saline and nonsaline water, or preferred semisaline surroundings. For this reason the *sha* is most probably the *Acanthogobius flavimanus*, a fish only six or seven inches long that likes semisaline water, rather than some sort of shark, which is the dictionary alternative. *Acanthogobius* was traditionally believed to spit sand, hence its name.[57]

Some species remain unidentifiable. These include the *you* and the *xun*. 'Perch', 'tench', and 'bream' in the translation that follows are merely approximate English equivalents.

As for the fishes here, there are —
You, and perch, and snake-fish, pairs of faithful crucian carps,
Tench, bream, and flattened *Hypophtha*, *zun* pursuing spawning urges,
Acanthogobius, fine-scaled bream, snouted sturgeon, black-striped perch,
Whiskered, yellow-gilled *Pseudobagrus*, mullet, carp, and the greater
  sturgeon.

Their colors associated together in a variegated medley,
Like multiple tapestries glittering, or bright-hued clouds in their freshness,

They nibble at the aquatic grasses, or disport themselves in the ripples,
Then drift, or float along — through deep pools and shallow riffles.

At times they agitate their gills, making the water quicken,
At others let their tails slap down, setting turbulent eddies spinning.
Sea-perch and *Coilia* both have their seasons when they swim up the tidal
inlets.
In the spate flowing over the shallows, *Elopichthys* and *xun* — can make
their escape from the springs.

Xie's catalog of birds lists wild geese, fish-hawks, herons, egrets, marabous, bustards, pheasants, ducks, and domestic fowl. All, presumably, personally observed. He expresses disdain in his notes for a Lu aristocrat in ancient times who, on one occasion, "did not know the bird concerned, and considered it to be a spirit." A couple of entries do however sound purely literary.[58] They might, of course, be local or archaic terms whose real-life meaning has since been lost. He continues:

Each sunrise, to pay respects at their court, the wild duck assemble.
When the season comes, the long-tailed pheasants meet on the mountain's
crest.

He comments that the wild ducks "regularly wait till dawn before they take to the air." The traditional Chinese Court was held in the early hours of the morning, when thinking was thought to be clearer. The line following refers to an obscure passage in the *Analects of Confucius*.[59] The idea underlying it is probably that, in the natural world, everything depends on the season.
Migrations come next:

Seeking to live in a different place, seabirds will battle the wind.
Wild geese fly south from the north, to be spared the winter's chill.
When spring shoots make their appearance, however, they wing their way
back north,
But return as guests to our warmer regions, as soon as the frost has fallen.

Their clamorous cries, each succeeding the next, reach up to the Milky Way.
Night by night they sleep, a skein of companions, beside some river or lake.
Making heard their unsullied voices to those far below who are listening,
They bear Wang Zi, the fairyland sojourner, aloft on his heavenly visit.

Soaring on high, with beating pinions, they treat thoughts of return with
contempt.
When a valley below them mirrors their plumage, they feel delight in
themselves.

Wang Zi, or Wang Zi Qiao, was the eldest son of King Ling of the Zhou dynasty. He roamed about, playing the bamboo mouth organ, and, after refining himself for several decades under the guidance of a Daoist master, rode off on a white crane. These verses are full of echoes from earlier literature, to a greater extent than I have explicitly indicated. What is interesting is Xie's sense that birds have a certain intelligence, and even a degree of spiritual insight and connection with the world of the numinous.

The mammals are more earthy:

> There are gibbons high in the hills, laughing gibbons and wildcats and
>   badgers,
> Wild dogs and wolves, and many-hued dogs, and bobcats marked yellow
>   and black.
> On the lower slopes, brown-and-white bears, black bears, jackals, and
>   tigers,
> Wild big-horned sheep, and timid muntjaks, plus *jing*-deer of massive
>   size.
>
> Along the skyline, on the escarpment, some set shaking the soaring
>   branches,
> Or cross the discontinuities that plunge down abruptly to canyons.
> Some crouch at the bottom of a valley, and roar without ever stopping.
> Others clamber up to the topmost boughs, where they cry with
>   heartbroken sorrow.

The 'black bear' is *Ursus torquatus*, and the 'brown-and-white bear' the larger *Ursus arctos*. The identifications of the 'wolf', 'jackal', and the 'many-hued dog' are approximations. Thus what I have rendered as the 'wolf' Xie says in his notes is "like the badger but larger, and belongs to the category of wolves." The 'muntjak' is a type of deer.

All of these species, without exception, seem to have vanished by modern times. The only wild animals that remain in the areas on each side of Hangzhou Bay are some insectivores and rodents, plus some small carnivores such as the yellow weasel, ferret–badger, leopard cat, and the small civet.[60] It would be a folly to overromanticize this fifth-century world. Tigers and wolves are dangerous. But human beings grew up for several hundreds of thousands of years with animals all around them. A strange silence has fallen. An emptiness. One cannot help wondering what the long-term implications of this are for the balance of our minds.

The economy was still in part based on hunting. Xie was unusual in wishing to have nothing to do with this activity, Buddhism providing him with another vision:[61]

Since I was young, I have not killed. Now my hair is white and I live in the hills but delight in hunting and fishing has vanished forever. Zhuangzi says: "The tiger and wolf are animals with empathetic feeling for others. How can it be that among them father and son are not mutually affectionate?"[62] That the world says that tigers and wolves are cruel is precisely because it thinks of them as beasts. Human beings, however, have not become aware of their own venomous harmfulness, yet talk of tigers and wolves as if they are hateful in the extreme. If humans follow their desires, how will they ever come to a limit?

Since I was of tender years, I have accepted the *dharma*. Thus I have been able to avoid actions involving the taking of life. So it is that to some slight degree I have understood the pattern-principle that the multitude of beings love life. . . . It is more or less by taking advantage of this that I have been able to enter onto the Way. Zhuangzi says:[63] "If those who live by the sea have contriving hearts, the seagulls will dance but not come down to land [sensing a snare]." Now that I have no desire to harm them, we can each of us [myself and the animals] take pleasure in the woods and pools.

The 'contriving heart' is the state of mind that one acquires, so Zhuangzi implies with one of his stories, when one becomes overly preoccupied with improving technology. The poem continues:

I have never upon these waters cast the angler's hooked and baited line.
Nor meshes spread for snaring rabbits. Nor nets to entangle birds when
    flying.
The sandstone arrow-barbs lie unused. Likewise untouched the tethered
    arrows.
Here, no webs are set for hares. No twigs interlaced for fish, as traps.

Empathy, and fellow-feeling, move even wolves' hearts, and tigers'.
I remember too how I was vexed, from chasing my endless desires,
As I took my first steps on the Way: my young strength was weak,
But enlightenment told me *love for their lives applied to all beings equally.*

Reach out to make contact with others. I have made this my guiding principle,
Since I am convinced that the Way can consist in nothing but this.
I take pleasure in caring for gulls and *tiao*, those white and slender fish,
And so by the tarns, and forest trees, *my contriving mind falls still.*

Some explanations of details are added in the notes.[64] From the historian's point of view, it is a paradoxical moment. Xie is living, not uncomfortably, at the end of a hunting culture when the expanded growing of cereals and vegetables has made hunting obsolescent. Soon, in this region, obsolete. The clever but murderous tools of the trapper, the archer, and the fisherman lie neglected—familiar but unused. This allows him a distinctively gentle and absorbed relationship with the wildlife around him, anchored in the new Buddhist doctrine of not taking their lives.

At the same time, the wild fish, wild birds, and wild animals—independent beings quite different from their domesticated agricultural counterparts—are on their long journey to becoming *merely* spiritual. *Merely* aesthetic. No longer relevant to the survival of everyday human life. Xie is attuned to them with what is still a socially inherited hunter's intensity, but without a hunter's unavoidable cruelties. Hence with an extraordinary and intoxicating purity. But intensity not rooted in necessity is hard to maintain over the longer run, except perhaps for a handful of scientists and artists.

Buddhism also stirred another impulse. Xie dreamed of transforming his estate into a latter-day incarnation of the holy parks and groves of the Buddhist scriptures. "These days," he wrote in his annotations, "we plant gardens and create parklands near to woods in imitation of the Buddha in times past." Faith inspired development.

IX

I have with reverence received the commandments of holy writings,
And scrutinized respectfully the scriptures of former times
That hold hills, and distant countryside, to be filled with space and light,
But say *cities and markets stink.* — Like live goats or rotting viands.

So the mighty Bodhisattva vow of all-encompassing pity
Draws up the multitude of beings from the gulf of their perdition.
How could he sojourn in this world and merely speak words that are
 empty?
He must lend others his excellence before he can reach perfection.

Thus we respect Gautama's deer park, flowered source of the Four Noble
 Truths,
Desire the famed Magic Vulture Summit where he spoke the Lotus Sūtra,
Longingly look for the unsullied grove where he passed at last into nirvāṇa,
And — the place where he preached the 'Vimalakīrti' — the sweet-scented
 Mango Garden.

He is far removed from us now, yet his face remains limpidly pure,
And it's said that the music of his compassion perpetually perdures.
So one hopes, when building lodgings for monks, on lonely, untroubled,
 peaks,
When their tin staves' reverberations stop, their shoulders will feel relief.

A 'bodhisattva' is a being who either will not, or perhaps even cannot, take the final step into nirvāṇa until all other beings are ready to do so, since all beings are interdependent.[65] He therefore remains in existence to help them. 'Nirvāna' may be thought of as the ending of the previously interminable cycles of reincarnation of a particular and distinctive individual 'soul' or 'self'. This occurs when the separate, personal soul dissolves as the result of its own awareness that, like all composite objects, it is itself an illusion, created by the mind. 'Gautama' is of course the Buddha. A 'sūtra' is a Buddhist scripture; it is rendered in Chinese by the same word as that for a Confucian or Daoist classic. The *Vimalakīrti-nirdeśa* was a set of dialogs on the beliefs of the Mahāyāna school, focused on the figure of Vimalakīrti, and popular in China during and after the fourth century.

This tradition had to be kept alive:

These were the reasons that when, at the outset, I made a survey and
    plans,
I tramped around on my own, with a staff supporting my balance,
Going down into the gorges, and fording my way through the depths,
Clambering into the ranges, then traversing the hills with my steps,
Scaling the mountain summits, but not pausing to catch my breath,
Following every spring to its source, but continuing on without
    stopping,
With only the breezes to comb my hair, and the falling rain to wash me,
And the dews at night to be confronted, and the turning stars to follow.

    I refined my superficial conceptions
    And removed any projects that were defective.
    Not divining by stalks or the turtle's shell
    I selected the best, picked out the exceptional.
    I hacked away brambles, I cleared open tracks,
    On the lookout for rocks and precipitous banks,
    Surrounded by mountains on all four sides
    And two rivers, with their circuitous winding.

      Its face toward the southern hills,
      I built a Pavilion for the Scriptures.
      Its back against the northern cliffs,
      I constructed a Hall for Exposition.
      Under the awe-inspiring fells
      I established meditation cells.
      Looking down to the plunging brooks below,
      I placed monks' dwellings in a row.

Face to face with towering trees, some hundreds of years in age,
I imbibe the sweetness of virtue grown rich through countless past generations.
Springs that date from remotest antiquity lie enfolded in my embrace,
I delight in their sleek-gleaming liquid, perpetually pouring unstained.

Gorgeous pagodas that rise in the suburbs, you have I bidden farewell,
To live a life different from the existence of those close to urban centers.
My pleasure is contemplating the simple, like the tree trunk ungouged by
    the blade,
And my fill of sweet dew — that favor bestowed — in a place where one
    grasps the Way.

The 'stalks' refer to the casting of a bundle of yarrow stalks to determine the appropriate hexagram when consulting the *Book of Changes*. The 'turtle's shell' indicates the undershell that in archaic times answered questions put to it about the supernatural causes of events and the future. This was done by interpreting the cracks that appeared when the shell was pierced with a sharp hot point (see chapter 5). The first method has continued to be used even until the present day, though tossing coins is much preferred; the second has long been obsolete. Perhaps the point of his lines is that neither would have been appropriate for a Buddhist enterprise.

According to Xie's notes, the followers of the Buddha "find no beauty in showiness," and hence leave the cities and suburbs behind. Rather, "it is where there are purity, emptiness, and silence that one obtains the Way." There were practical spiritual reasons for living deep in the countryside.

In the next section he describes two monks, Tanlong and Faliu, friends of his who seem to have lived for a time on his estate:

They have taken leave of the loving kindness of their parents, abandoned their wives and children, and, becoming weightless immortals, entered the mountains to live as hermits. All their links with the outside world have been severed. They consume neither flesh nor fish. This sweeping clean of impurities always affects the body: if one looks at them in appraisal, one's breath stops short in admiration, but the two masters of the *dharma* remain unaffectedly calm.

To make sense of his eulogy, it needs to be recalled that the 'Six Transitions', or means of reaching nirvāṇa, were charity, morality, patience, energy, contemplation, and wisdom. 'Phenomenal' here has its literal meaning: pertaining to outward phenomena. 'Noumenal' refers to the domain of the mind, where understanding comes through reason rather than the senses. 'Karmic response' indicates how all deeds (*karma*) are thought to carry with them inexorable consequences, good or bad depending on whether the deeds are moral or immoral.

> The monks' essential abstinence is, painstakingly, observed.
> They make clear, too, their cherished inner thoughts, so others may easily
>   learn them.
> In phenomenal life they interact with a multitude of persons,
> But in noumenal vision pierce beyond the human world's outer surface.

> They may make an excursion to one place, then elsewhere take their
>   repose,
> Or erect a thatched-roof shack, leaning angled against a boulder.
> Through the ever-moving seasons, as heat alternates with cold,
> Their wills, and their acts prompting karmic response, never need to be
>   remolded.

> *They look on past, present, and future as being but dreams in the night,*
> And put into practice the Six Transitions in order to reach enlightenment.
> They are borne along by their tranquil wisdom to reach the haven of
>   silence,
> To dwell in that dark remoteness where all patterns have combined.

> They designated the Eastern Peak for our other-worldly meeting,
> Which gave me an occult premonition of the Heavenly Western Region.
> Though this single, day-long, encounter seemed to *me* like a thousand
>   years,
> Yet I still felt dissatisfaction that we had never met previously.

The courtesies of the occasion, his appreciation of his friends and mentors, intertwine with the ultimate themes of existence.

The landscape has become an ever more complex conception. There are strata of literary references and history, mythology, philosophical polemics, geography, topography, landscape architecture, and botany and zoology. Now it is transformed into a deliberately created evocation of the scenes of the Buddha's life, as well as something ultimately unreal. An illusion. These dimensions coexist. Most of them, if a mathematical metaphor is not out of place, are orthogonal to each other. In other words, anything that exists in one dimension has no necessary implications for anything in a dimension at right angles to it, and vice versa. It is a misunderstanding of this style of thinking to be disturbed by what common sense, in one way quite reasonably, regards as contradictions.

Another of these appears in the pendant on Daoism. "Although those who study the immortals," he says, "have not reached the heights of the Buddhist Way, yet they have gone beyond the outer surface of the world." In spite of his earlier apparent fascination with herbs that may make it possible to attain physical immortality, he now presents it as a second best:

Other entities they dismiss as worthless, valuing only themselves.
Casting aside the everyday world, they treat magical power as precious,
> Appalled by the hastening of the years,
> *And regarding an endless life as dear.* . . .
They find the pine and the cassia sweet, though these both have a bitter
> taste.
They delight in skins and plebeian hemp as decrepit disguise for their
> shapes,
And long for the day when, like molting cicadas, *they toss their bodies*
> *away.* . . .
Although they have never trodden the steps to the ultimate stage of the
> Way,
They're detached from those hereditary frills that indicate social status.

Having described the superhuman inhabitants of the landscape, Xie turns to those who perform the daily labors on his estate. Note, though, that he does not mention them as individual human beings. They are present but anonymous. Subordinate. Implicitly interchangeable.

The identification of the less common plants once again presents problems. For example, the term that I think is used here for the Chinese gooseberry (*Actinidia chinensis*) is the normal Chinese name of the carambola, but this year-round tropical and subtropical tree is unlikely to have existed so far north, especially during a period of colder climate; nor would it have been described as a climbing shrub, fruiting late in the year. The *xian* is in all probability a lichen, maybe something like the *Evernia prunasti* that grows on plum trees and is used as a medicine, or the lung lichen (*Sticta pulmonaria*) that also grows on trees and is a substitute for Iceland moss. The names of plants even less easily identified have had simply to be transcribed.

Most of the additions to the original main text are easily justifiable on the basis of Xie's own notes, or simple clarification. Note, however, that I have translated 'chalky soil'—whereas the original just says 'mud'—in order to give some sense to the next line but one that talks about the extraction of 'lime'. Likewise I have written 'peat', rather than the dictionary translation 'coal', for the material that Xie says was taken out of the 'waterlogged' layer. That 'Pure Liquor From The Hills' is the name of their grape wine is a guess. It is worth noting, though, that the assertion that every entity follows its own 'laws' is a literal rendering. The key word is *lü*, which means several things: a standard pitch-pipe, for example, but also a law decreed by authority. The idea that nature had *laws*, as contrasted with patterns or principles, was thus within the conceptual range of early medieval Chinese culture, even if not common.

References to the *Scripture of Songs* are found in several places. The two lines on gathering grass and twisting it into cord are virtually a direct quotation.[66] As always this raises a shadow of uncertainty about the directness of all of the author's apparently personal observations.

X

Tasks have to be done in the hills, and obligatory work on the rivers,
But I need no herdsmen for guarding stock — not a single individual.
For the other jobs, I'm furnished with servants, people of every
    description,
Who, bestirring themselves as the seasons require, are competitively busy.

Making their way up the mountains, they fell the trees with their axes,
Cutting the stems of bamboos, rooting out thickets of brambles.
Pulling up edible bamboo shoots, where these burgeon in our plantations,
And scratching the earth, to bring to the surface the embedded sprouts in
    the vales.

The brown-haired gooseberries have the mastery over the plants that they
    grip,
But their fruits are harvested in full during the fall and the winter.
The creepers of recumbent grasses trail across the unfarmed places.
Like huntsmen who dash through the streams, my men search for the vines
    of wild grapes.

They ferment them into the vintage 'Pure Liquor From The Hills';
As the *Songs* record, when offered libations, the spirits "increase your
    felicity."[67]
Wine produced from glutinous millet possesses a bitter taste;
Per contra, that from well-matured *shen* has a much sweeter flavor.

They are fond of the lofty groves they demolish, to make logs that will
    grow *shen* fungus.
To get bark for paper, they scythe the *ji*, along the steep-pitched summits.
They dig out the purgative madder roots on the sunny south-face cliffs,

And from fallen trunks on dark north slopes scrape off lichens for herbal
  drinks.

In the hours of daylight one sees them out gathering grasses to serve as
  straw,
And during the evening glimpses them twisting it into new twine and cord.
They sickle the broad-leafed zizanias, or snip through the stalks of reeds,
And use them to manufacture matting, or as dried fodder for beasts.

One moment one meets with a chalky soil, the next with a waterlogged
  layer.
The products that each of these will yield are not at all the same:
The first supplies lime for mortar, the second gives peat for warmth:
All things perform in accordance with their own particular laws.

In the sixth lunar month they collect the combs that brim with wild bees'
  honey.
In the eighth they batter the chestnut trees, to set the chestnuts tumbling.
Commodities, ready for us to take, exist in such abundance
That I've only recorded a summary here, not listed every one.

This section is one of the foundations for the view that the 'environmental
richness', which chapter 7 on Jiaxing suggested existed in this region prior to
premodern economic growth, was a reality. Even so, this richness is under-
stated. Xie—the devout Buddhist vegetarian—says in his notes that "none of
the activities related to fishing and hunting has been recorded here." They
would have made a considerable difference to the livelihood of the non-
vegetarian majority.

The poem continues for several more pages after this. It includes local trav-
elogs, sections on his well-disciplined fruit orchards with their "lines of trees
laid out like spread netting," local longevity herbs, and comments on the
nature of life.

Perverse is the mismatch that exists between feelings and the
  phenomena:
Pattern-principles and external forms are forever clashing in conflict.

But there are only marginal gleanings to be had about environmental matters.

The problem formulated at the beginning of this chapter has been to some
extent solved. The apparent conflict between a mystical delight in nature, a
respect for it, and a religious and artistic sensitivity to it, on the one hand, and
a process of determined exploitation and development, on the other, is largely
an artifact of our modern perspective, at least for this early medieval period in

the eastern coastal region. The natural infrastructure was still robust enough, and natural resources still abundant enough, for it to be reasonable, in the context of those times, not to see any immediate contradiction. Six hundred years later this would be beginning to be doubtful. A thousand years later it would be untrue.

The case has also been made that more than a millennium-and-a-half ago, the concept of the environment had made its appearance, however fleetingly, in Chinese culture.

11

🐘 *Science and Superfauna*

The medieval Chinese poets' perceptions of their environment need to be compared with what was observed and imagined by those of a scientific cast of mind. In other words, their insights need to be complemented by an examination of the styles of *observation* and conceptions of *truth* as these affected the understanding of their environment by the Chinese in historical times. Since ideas and perceptions are subtly but indissolubly linked in two-way interaction, what did they *think* they saw? And why? How did they evaluate the *credibility* of their information and theoretical constructs?

The richest material for this inquiry comes from a millennium later than Xie Lingyun's poem. For this reason, after a brief survey of ancient and medieval Chinese proto-scientific attitudes to nature, the present chapter makes what I hope is not too disconcerting a leap forward in time to 1608 CE. This is the date when Xie Zhaozhe published his *Fivefold Miscellany* of some 1414 pages.[1] The logic behind this is the same as that which led to a detailed examination of "Living in the Hills." The *Miscellany* crystallizes a characteristic type of thinking that, once understood, can be used as a point of reference for looking at somewhat similar patterns, both contemporaneous, and earlier and later.

The reader will need to make an effort to readjust his or her time-frame after the preceding chapter. We are now in a world that has already long ago experienced the medieval economic revolution, undergone many centuries of the Chinese style of premodern economic growth, been familar with woodblock printing for over three-quarters of a millennium, is ruled by mandarins selected through competitive examinations rather than by aristocrats and warriors, and has acquired the habits of an increasingly systematic scholarship.

Xie's entertaining and ramshackle *Miscellany* is not a pinnacle of intellectual achievement. The justification for looking at it is that it reveals the strengths and weaknesses of most of the Chinese styles of proto-scientific thinking, and how they related to the environment. Above all, it obliges us to confront the problem of observation. In what ways did the Chinese at this time actually *see* a world that was different from the one we see, and tend, with an unreflective carelessness, to assume that everybody sees, and has always seen?

That this is not the bland inquiry it may seem can be shown by dramatizing it. Why did a lucid, sober, practical, and learned man like Xie Zhaozhe, who was also demonstrably a skilled observer, at times see dragons? *Dragons*. Even, on occasion, see them *in the company of others*, and agree with these others on what they were, all of them, witnessing? This sort of phenomenon is, of course, familiar from medieval Europe. Learned and lucid medieval Europeans were at times convinced they had observed miracles. And of course it also happens in some places even today.

Note that we are discussing *observation*, not belief. Because we tend, on the basis of an unjustified common sense, to assume that observation is the bedrock of belief, contemplating the possibility of influences sometimes running in the opposite direction can be unsettling. The dragon question needs to be taken seriously. Its restriction to China, and societies influenced by China, makes its culturally specific nature patent.[2]

Modern science has gone to historically unprecedented, and culturally unique, lengths to exorcise the problem of such false positives. Hence the importance of its emphasis on logical rigor and quantification, its largely formalized internal coherence of explanation across an astonishing range of phenomena, its public recording of information, its routinized experimental destruction-testing of its own hypotheses, and—when it is true to its own genius—its perpetual self-questioning. The probability that we are still, even today, somewhere, seeing 'dragons' of our own is lower, so far as we can tell, than it has ever been. This does not mean that this probability is, or can be, zero. Xie's curious compilation has a contemporary, as well as a historical, relevance.

The intellectual background

Just as early-modern science and quasi-science in the West had an intellectual pedigree, both ancient and medieval, so did Xie's. There were, for example, earlier Chinese thinkers such as Wang Chong in Han times,[3] and Shen Gua in the Song,[4] who touched on themes that Xie examines, and in a manner that sometimes has something in common with his. It may be useful to indicate some of the ways in which his work differs from theirs.

Wang wrote in a more structured argumentative form than Xie. He aimed at establishing certain a priori theoretical positions, notably that the universe was not teleologically directed, and that the Han theory of the Five Phases of Matter was untenable. A passage from his *Discourses* will illustrate his style:[5]

— Heaven and Earth are confluences of matter–energy–vitality. Human beings are *nonteleologically self-generated*, just as, after the confluence of the matter–energy–vitality of husband and wife, the child is self-generated. It was not the desire of the husband and wife when their matter–energy–vitality flowed together to give birth to a child; the confluence was driven by the force of emotional desire, the child being born once the confluence had occurred. It is from the fact that husband and wife do not give birth to a child by deliberate intent that we may know that Heaven and Earth do not of deliberate intent give birth to human beings. This being so, man lives in Heaven and Earth as a fish lives in a deep pool, *or a louse on a human body*.

If Heaven had of deliberate intent given birth to the ten thousand beings, it should have caused them to love each other as kin. It should not have caused them to prey upon each other. . . .

— Perhaps it will be said that it was for *functional reasons* that Heaven caused them to prey on each other, this preying being the way in which they fulfilled themselves. . . . If they did not prey on each other, they would not develop functional utility. If metal did not prey upon wood, the wood could not be fashioned into a state fit for use. If fire did not smelt metal, the metal could not become a tool or utensil. . . . All animals of flesh and blood conquer one another, biting and devouring each other, being caused to do so by the matter–energy–vitality of the Five Phases.

— I would answer this as follows: If it is the case that Heaven gives birth to the ten thousand beings, desiring that they be of mutual use to each other, and so have unavoidably to prey on each other, then, since Heaven has given birth to tigers, wolves, venomous snakes, all of which are harmful to human beings, does Heaven also want to make use of *humans* to be of service to *these* creatures? . . .

In general, the reason that the ten thousand beings hack each other, and despoil each other, and that creatures of flesh and blood go so far as to bite and eat one another, is that their teeth are sharp or blunt, their muscular strengths superior or feeble, their actions cunning or unimaginative, their matter–energy–vitality and their position-power[6] masterful or contemptible. . . . Human beings use sword blades to despoil each other, in the way that animals use teeth, horns, claws, and fangs. . . . Thus, when there is a victor and a

vanquished, the victor is not necessarily imbued with metallic matter–
energy–vitality, nor the vanquished necessarily possessed of the essence of
wood [as Five Phases theory might seem to imply, since metal, as in an ax, is
deemed to overcome wood].

This sustained polemical approach is motivated by a well-defined vision of the
amoral nature of the world. Xie's relatively unsystematic collector's approach
is quite different. He is open-minded, empirical, fragmented—questioning,
teasing, and entertaining—though he, too, does not like Five Phases theory
much more than Wang.

Shen Gua's *Jottings from the Garden of the Brook of Dreams* is closer to Xie's
Miscellany. It contains a similar potpourri of items on scholarship, history,
natural history, and literature besides *curiosa*[7] such as rainbows that drink
from streams[8] and tales of the supernatural.[9] Here and there it contains examples of modeling: he demonstrates that the shape of the moon is spherical by
covering half of a globule with powder and rotating it to show the phases. The
comparison is limited to the shape, however, since the moon is taken to be
aether-like and required to have no substance, although acknowledged to be a
reflector. This is necessary in order to avoid 'obstruction' when it meets the sun
in the sky.[10] Shen could also be an acute observer, capable of imagining the
mechanism and history that had shaped a landscape:[11]

> When I was on an official mission to Hebei, I journeyed north of the
> Taihang mountains [Northeast], where the shells of spiral and flat shellfish
> were frequently embedded in the cliffs, as well as stones like birds' eggs, lying
> horizontally in the rockface as if they were belts. *This area was thus once the
> sea coast,* though today it lies close to five hundred kilometers distant from
> the sea to the east. What we call the 'mainland' here is *entirely the deposition
> of sediments.* . . . In general, such streams as the Yellow River, the Hutuo, the
> Zhuo River, and the Sanggan are all laden with sediment. To the west of
> the passes [that is, modern Shaanxi], where the water runs through the
> land, it is at a depth of not less than a hundred feet. Every year the mud has
> been transported eastward, becoming the soil of the mainland, a pattern-
> principle that is inexorable.

He believed in the 'transformation of things', seeing as proof of certain aspects
of Five Phases theory the way in which water from a certain spring, if boiled,
left a precipitate of sulfate of copper, which if 'boiled up' again would yield
copper; or the way in which water dripping in limestone caves formed stalactites and stalagmites.[12] Hearing of the death of the disciple of a relative who had
swallowed an alchemical residue made from mercuric sulfide while preparing
an immortality elixir, he commented that "given the complementarity of

transformations, since it was able to turn into a major poison, how can it not be the case that it *could* turn into a great source of good? Having been able to kill a person after its transformation, it *ought* to possess the pattern-principle of giving life to someone. It is simply that we have not found the method for this, and therefore know that the formula for turning someone into an immortal cannot be said not to exist, but that extreme care is essential."[13]

He was also persuaded of the powers of a sorceress interrogated by one of his friends. He found it reasonable that she should know about people's affairs, "even five hundred kilometers distant," by putting her mind in contact with "the sprouts in their minds," but that, when put to the test, she did not have clairvoyant powers as regards matters that another mind did *not* know, such as the numbers of *go* counters "picked up at random" in a hand.[14]

It was the *moral implications* of what we should call 'scientific' phenomena that often interested him most.[15] Thus, at the conclusion of a discussion of the inversion of the image in a concave mirror, in which he hypothesized a "rowlock or drum with a waist" as "an obstacle" at the point where the reflected image disappeared before inverting, he observed:[16]

> How should this only be the case for material objects? *People are the same,* there being but few cases where concern with some material object is not an obstacle within them. If it is small, advantage and disadvantage are easily inverted, and right–true and wrong–false interchanged.

He was less interested than Xie in the problem of validating or invalidating evidence, but equally convinced of the key role of the mathematics and the interplay of numbers that lay at the heart of the workings of the universe, and of the difficulty, perhaps impossibility, of unraveling it. He was an expert in calendar-making and the construction of water clocks, but also an astrologer, who, in his own words, had spent many years "watching the Heaven for portents and looking for signs."[17] Nonetheless he thought that complete success was beyond human grasp:[18]

> Those in this world of ours who talk about [fate-determining] numbers have for the most part grasped their coarse vestiges, but some of these numbers are extremely subtle and not to be known by depending upon the calendar. They are, moreover, only vestiges. For those who can by sensitive apprehension make contact with the causes at work in the world, vestiges are not something with which they are involved. This is the reason why *spirits who have foreknowledge* cannot easily be sought out by means of such vestiges, let alone by the coarser aspects of the latter.
>
> Those in this world of ours who discuss the stars rely on the calendar to know what I have termed the extremely subtle vestiges, *but calendars are*

only the result of approximations. . . . When in the Yeping reign-period
[1064–7] Venus and Mars met in the stellar mansion Zhen . . . of the eleven
major calendars by which their courses were determined, none corresponded to the event, and in one case the discrepancy was thirty days. . . .
Their predictions all varied. . . .

Furthermore, the sky turns more than thirty degrees in a double hour,
this generally being called a 'palace'. But within that double hour there is a
beginning and an end. How can the Dark Force and the Bright Force be
identical across the space of thirty degrees, but then alter *abruptly* when a
heavenly body makes the transition into another palace? . . . They are not
aware at all that *within a month* there is waning and waxing, the orb
increasing with the Bright Force before the full moon, declining with the
Dark Force after the full moon, and during the first and last quarters being
in equilibrium. As to Wood dominating the spring, Fire summer, Metal fall,
and Water winter, there is the same phenomenon *within* a month. And not
only within a month. There is the same phenomenon within a day. . . . *How
can one be sure that the four seasons do not likewise occur within a double
hour? Or within half an hour, a minute, or a split second? . . .*

Furthermore, if spring is dominated by Wood, this latter must tirelessly
wane and wax during these ninety days. It is not possible for the world to
pertain to Wood up to the last double hour on the thirtieth of the third
month and then in the first hour of the next day *suddenly* pertain to Fire.
*Categories such as these cannot be fully known by the techniques that we have
in this world of ours.*

Shen seems to have been more firmly in the grip of the old Five Phases metaphysics than Xie, but both shared a sense of the ultimate unknowability of the
universe.

Both the loosely categorized scrapbook format and the title of the *Fivefold
Miscellany* were probably inspired by the *Miscellany from Youyang* compiled in
the Tang dynasty by Duan Chengshi.[19] The *Youyang Miscellany* is a mixture of
relatively credible historical anecdotes and observations, stories about the
uncanny feats of Buddhist monks and Daoist immortals, somewhat fanciful
'natural history', De Mandeville-style 'anthropology' of foreign countries, and
sober accounts of contemporary social customs. Brief examples are the
contempt of the Emperor Taizong for auspicious omens, which led him to
order the destruction of a white magpie's nest beside the imperial graves,[20] the
rainmaking by the monk Yixing with the help of an ancient mirror from the
palace treasury with a dragon on its handle-knob,[21] the winged heads of
certain people in the Far South that detached themselves at night from their
bodies and went flying away,[22] the practice by the cruel and jealous wives of

high-ranking officials of branding the faces of their servant-girls who in any way displeased them,[23] the ability of certain tigers to force a corpse to rise to its feet and *undress itself* before it was eaten,[24] and the lack of aesthetic interest in peonies before the Tang dynasty.[25] There is also an occasional concern with taxonomy, as in the classification of animals on the basis of their diet.[26]

What differentiates Duan Chengshi's book from Xie Zhaozhe's is that Duan almost never makes any attempt to appraise the truth or falsity of a report. One of the few examples comes at the end of a tale of how the monk Yixing saved the son of an old lady who had helped him in his poverty-stricken youth, after the young man had been convicted for murder. Yixing is said to have used his arts to make the stars of the Northern Dipper disappear, taking them captive in the form of seven pigs, after which he persuaded an alarmed emperor to issue a general amnesty, so that the stars reappeared at a rate of one per night. Duan says that he find this "exceedingly strange," but that "since the story was in every mouth, I have no option but to record it."[27]

Tales like this are a reminder that the sober realism and acute proto-scientific insight of many Chinese accounts of phenomena are to some extent misleading as a general guide to the culture of imperial times.

The man

Xie Zhaozhe was a Fujianese born in Hangzhou some time in the middle of the sixteenth century. He gained the highest degree in the civil-service examinations, held office as a vice-minister in the Ministry of Works, and wrote on hydraulics, the province of Yunnan, and other topics.[28] People have tended to regard the *Miscellany* as a catalog of oddities, regaling the reader with items like the bisexual who could make love both ways, the mule who kicked a tiger to death, famous gourmets who devoured children, or markets where living people did business with ghosts.[29] These were part of the book's appeal, and still make entertaining reading, but to think of Xie as merely the compiler of tidbits is to miss the seriousness of his concerns.[30] One of his motives was to prove that the universe was a more complicated place than the neo-Confucians allowed for with their simplistic invocation of 'pattern-principle',[31] or the traditional metaphysicians with their straitjacketed categories:[32]

> There are *cold flames* on the Mounds of Xiao [location unclear], and fire that pertains to the cold-dark principle on Lake Er [in the Southwest]. Furthermore, a temple in Jiangning county [in the East] has a perpetual lantern, dating from Jin times, the color of whose flame is blue-green and which gives off no heat. If there are hot springs in Heaven and Earth, then

there are certain to be cold fires. *We must not discuss these matters from the viewpoint of the summer insects* [who cannot believe in the ice of winter].

He was fascinated by the question of whether some assertion was true or not.

This concern was initially focused on history, which he read from the age of seven or eight on.[33] He was conscious from his own experience of how historical records had been distorted by the pressures of interested parties:[34]

> I once prepared the revision of a prefectural gazetteer. If the grandfather of a serving official was not included in the section on Illustrious Worthies, the latter would not stand for it. If the sons and grandsons of a serving official were not all of them recorded, their grandfather would not stand for it. As for those who had been lavish in their bribes, whose lands stretched in every direction, who carried a filthy reputation while alive and would meet with foul comments after their death, they even so pestered me unceasingly, or made indirect arrangements to prolong their fame, forcing their wives' relatives to make entreaties, or presuming on a power that I was obliged to comply with. . . . The strong interfered openly; the weak sabotaged my affairs in secret. On the day that the work was completed, less than ten to twenty per cent of the original contents were still in it. Alas! If this is the case for a prefectural document, what must it be like for the national histories?

Xie was not mesmerized by the written record. He was also aware of the problem of historiographical selectivity. This is shown by his discussion of the apparent 'verification' of dreams:[35]

> When the people of the present day read of the dreams recorded in the historical annals, most of these latter came true. . . . Now people dream every day. If these [few that were recorded] were the only ones to be so verified, the dreams that did *not* come true must have been innumerable.

Xie is frequently skeptical of recorded events and interpretations, though also on occasion bafflingly credulous. He also suspected that historians sometimes fabricated events. Thus he argues that "the statement that a 'guest star' [a nova] violated the constellation of the Emperor is *merely a literary artifice used by historians* [to convey their disapproval of the emperor's confidants]. *It is not necessarily an actual fact.*"[36] He saw the historiographical manipulations of portents in the same light:[37]

> After the [writing of the] monograph on the Five Phases of Matter in the *Han History*,[38] each event was categorized under a particular omen, and this has continued to the present. Historians speak *after* an event has happened, so that their words can be presented as having been fulfilled. Those charged

with watching the skies speak *before* an event has happened, and thus many of their utterances do not come true.

Finally, he thought that people could in good faith report illusions as true. The following anecdote is an illustration:[39]

> When my friend Sun Zichang was young, he was good-looking and clear-headed. On the night of the seventh of the seventh lunar month he was much moved by the story of the Cowherd and Spinning Damsel [the stars Beta and Gamma in Aquila and Alpha in Vega, traditionally believed to meet only on this date, crossing the Milky Way on a bridge of magpies]. He composed a prayer to them. . . . All at once, *as if in a dream,* he was summoned by the immortal damsel to the Jade Apartments in the Jade Watchtower, where he enjoyed the ultimate in human happiness. After seven days he regained consciousness. At that time we all laughed at him, and were of the opinion that he had been deceiving us. I would now say that it was not deceit but that *a demon* had possessed him. When people have improper thoughts, evil spirits can take charge of them, with the consequence that *what they think resembles a play on the stage* [in being illusory].

In counterbalance with this skeptical attitude toward written sources and human informants was an open-mindedness that was willing to consider, as he remarked of an account of a huge hailstone at the end of the Tang dynasty, that "although the words seem exaggerated, yet I suspect that there is nothing that does not exist [somewhere] in the universe." The lump of ice was said to have been as "high as the temple's first-floor rooms" and have taken a month to melt.[40] His underlying attitude is expressed by the following:[41]

> In most cases when people die and come to life again they depend on some physical object for this purpose. The Daoists have a technique of 'changing the womb'. The explanation of this is that those who have passed through their sojourn in this life purifying their bodily form can change the old so that it becomes new, or perhaps, as one does with a house that has become dilapidated, merely borrow the corporeal shell of some other person.
>
> This phenomenon occurred on numerous occasions in Jin and Tang times. It may be that those cases recorded in the *Taiping guangji*[42] are wild and fabulous, but as to what is said in the monographs on the Five Phases of Matter in the regular histories, *I suspect they are not all of them false.*
>
> The strangest of all of these concerns a tomb from the Zhou dynasty that was opened in the time of the Emperor Ming of the Wei [late in the fifth century CE], when a girl who had been buried alive there to accompany the deceased person was found still living. This period can be calculated to be

not less than five hundred or six hundred years. Could her bones and flesh not have rotted? When the rebels Wen Tao and Huang Chao opened graves throughout the empire [in the early tenth and the late ninth century respectively], no cases were heard of people coming back to life like this. *I likewise suspect that not all the cases recorded even in the regular histories are necessarily factually true.*

Xie valued his own observations of phenomena, as may be seen from the following two passages:[43]

> There are fire wells in Sichuan province.[44] Their springs are as though of oil, and when you heat them they burn. . . . There is also wood that yields no ash. If you light it, it burns; but when, after a long time, the fire goes out, the wood is just as it was before. These are all strange objects that can serve to extend our information about uncanny things. (Lu Konglin has heard about a wood that yields no ash and is used to make furnaces. When fire is placed within it, it goes a translucent red color. *I have not however seen it myself.*)
>
> There is a small hillock below Lotus Peak that lies north of Fuzhou, the color of whose soil is a dark red. It is popularly known as 'Rouge Hill'. The story goes that this is the place where the daughter of the King of Yue once dropped her rouge paint. None of the hills that encircle Fujian is red in color, and so [the natives of this province] are startled by its oddity. Later, *I myself traveled* to the Guixi and Yiyang hills in Jiangxi province, all of which are cinnabar red. . . . When I think now of the Red Cliffs in Chu . . . [and other such cases I have not personally seen], I now consider that they are indeed so, that is to say, red.

Xie implies that people tend to be startled only by, or skeptical about, that to which they are not accustomed:[45]

> I journeyed in 1579 with my paternal grandfather, . . . when he was in charge of the official travel arrangements [for the commissioner to the Liuqiu Islands]. We were halfway there when a typhoon arose. Thunder, lightning, rain, and hailstones all fell upon us at the same time. There were *three dragons* suspended upside down to the fore and the aft of the ship. Their whiskers were interwound with the waters of the sea and penetrated the clouds. All the horns on their heads were visible, but below their waists nothing could be seen. Those in the ship were in a state of agitation and without any plan of action, but an old man said: "This is no more than the dragons coming to pay court to the commissioner's document bearing the imperial seal." He made those attending on the envoy have the latter write a

document in his own hand bringing the court audience to an end. The dragons complied with the time so indicated and withdrew. That the authority of the Son of Heaven is effective over the manifold spirits is a principle about which there can assuredly be no doubt. *If I had not witnessed this event personally, it is unlikely that I would not have considered this principle to be false.*

Unless there is very clear evidence to the contrary we commonly see what we expect to see. In another account of the same experience, Xie says that the dragons were "suspended upside down from the edges of the clouds, and still more than a thousand feet above the water, which rose boiling like steam or smoke to conjoin with the clouds, the people seeing the dragons with minute particularity".[46] What is clear is the importance that he attached to direct observational validation.[47] Elsewhere he says:[48]

> The saying has been handed down that after the [winter] solstice snowflakes are *five*-pointed. But every year as the winter moves into spring, *I have gathered snowflakes and looked at them.* All are *six*-pointed. Not one or two out of ten is five-pointed. Thus one can learn that *old sayings are not all of them entirely valid.*

Impeccable.

The underlying metaphysics

The two concepts of *lǐ* or 'pattern-principle', and *qì* or 'matter–energy–vitality' underlay Xie's thinking, though with qualifications.

First of all he thought that every entity in the universe had *always* existed even if only as a potential:[49]

> I do not know where these entities [that we experience today] were lodged at the time *before* Heaven and Earth had come into existence. . . . Before Heaven and Earth existed, there was Chaos, something like a hen's egg. Although a hen's egg is a chaos, yet enwrapped within it is a conglomerate of vitality. Thus, even if years pass, it will come forth in its season, and be able to be transformed, and to take shape.
>
> If Heaven and Earth had *simply* been chaotic, having at no time this Way of Pattern-Principles enfolded within them, they would have been like foul and muddy water that remains unchanged for ten thousand years. How could they under such conditions have been changed in such a way that an immense number of beings and phenomena came forth?

He argues that, as we might put it, there was no creation out of nothing, since any void would have had to have contained, or been preceded by, the *potentials* for the entities that existed later.

He also discriminates between the concrete and the abstract:[50]

> Pattern-principle is the *controller* of Heaven–Nature. To declare that 'pattern-principle' is synonymous with 'Heaven–Nature' is, I fear, in the last analysis, mistaken. Pattern-principle is *insubstantial*, whereas Heaven–Nature has a definite *embodiment*. Heaven–Nature undergoes destruction, whereas pattern-principle is neither born nor extinguished.

Elsewhere he insists that "pattern-principle must have somewhere within which it can temporarily lodge, in the way that fire is transmitted by firewood. When the firewood is exhausted, the fire is extinguished." But then he goes on, perhaps ironically, "If one says that the fire is *not* the firewood, one might *also* say that the firewood *is* the fire. If, in comparable fashion, one says that when the firewood is exhausted the fire still remains, one might *equally* maintain that the fire and the firewood have both come to an end together. If this is so, there is no need to go on discussing the matter further."[51]

The *pattern* aspect of *lǐ* emerges from a discussion of the planting of trees around dwellings:[52]

> Northerners grow numerous trees like the *Sophora* and *Salix* both in front of their houses and at the back. Southerners do not. The people of Fujian province have a particularly strong taboo against doing so. According to Sang Daomao [an eighth-century expert on prognostication], when trees are thickly crowded around a human dwelling, people leave it. If the trees are dense the earth deteriorates; and when this happens human beings fall ill. People of the present day observe the taboo for this reason. But are these sayings of magic experts fit to be given credence? The earth has first to be rich and fertile before grasses and trees will become dense. *How could there ever be such a pattern-principle as 'trees being flourishing and earth deteriorating'?*

Xie dismisses the venerable theory of the Five Phases of Matter as having no general applicability. He argues that Liu Xiang and his son, in the later first century BCE, had forced the extension of what was originally a theory of portents onto "all of Heaven and Earth, the myriad entities, animals and plants, regardless of size". Further, [53]

> When they had sought for verification and correspondence and not obtained them, they further *forcibly imposed a match* on events with the theory of the Five Interactions;[54] and hierarchical position, high and low status, eating and resting, activity and repose, regardless of importance, were all allocated

to its categories, and assigned to one of the Five Interactions. Even the pattern-principles of the universe were made to appear to be no more than this, while *fudging and disregard of reason* were taken to an extreme. . . .

For dynasty after dynasty the national histories have continued to have monographs on the Five Phases of Matter. As to partial and total solar and lunar eclipses, and changes in the planets, as well as major calamities and uncanny events, these have *also* been assigned to the categories of astrology. How could the Dark and Bright Forces and the Five Phases of Matter simultaneously have *two different* pattern-principles?! What is more, how could winds, rain, thunder, and lightning not pertain to the categories of *astrology*? Their theory is infuriatingly wrong to an extreme degree, and does not reach to the essentials.

This rejection of forced categorizations was as perceptive as the insistence on distinct physical laws for the heavens and the earth was unfruitful.

Heaven–Nature was not, however, purely physical. It was something *conscious* that responded to moral concerns:[55]

The theory that Heaven is merely an accumulation of [relatively low-density] matter–energy–vitality has been current since ancient times without change. But if it really were just an accumulation of matter–energy–vitality, it would have to be inchoate and without understanding, confused and without any capacity to act. What then would exercise control over the four seasons and the multitude of beings? Who would preside over births and deaths, and over good political order and disorder? . . .

But Heaven's benevolent guiding and retribution for misdoing follow as swiftly as do the shadow and the echo. Good order and disorder, gains and losses—these are as dependable as metal or stone. The thunderbolt and the hailstorm, demons and monstrosities—none of these are accidents.

The moral dimension to causality will be looked at later. In practice, Xie more often than not ignores it when examining particular problems. When he does refer to it there are often implied paradoxes. An example is the entry on the *qiongqi*, "the most evil of all animals: it devours good people and will not eat the wicked."[56]

Xie also believed there were matters beyond any understanding based upon pattern-principle. These points emerge from his attack on Song neo-Confucianism:[57]

The sages did not do away with the study of the sun, the moon, and the planets, nor with numerological calculations. Sage–emperor Shun was concerned with farmers, potters, and fishermen. When, one morning, he took up the position of emperor, he fashioned astronomical instruments so as to master the orderly arrangement of these seven governors [the sun, etc.]. Thus the pattern-principles of the Transformative Force were indeed complete in their entirety in the world of the sages.

Among later generations, those such as Luoxia Hong [a calendrical expert of Han times], the monk Yixing [the Tang-dynasty surveyor and calculator of the size of the degree along a north–south meridian line], and Wang Pu [the calendrical expert of the mid tenth century] thought deeply about *the numbers that express what is of the essence.* They, too, were mentally able to encompass Heaven and Earth. The armillary sphere and the *yigai* revolved without error. The tubes used to divine the matter–energy–vitality originating in the earth from the movement of bulrush ashes, the sundials, and the water clocks, did not miss the mark, being also of an exceptional nature.

By the time of the discussions of the Song-dynasty [neo-]Confucians, however, they wanted to use the concept of pattern-principle to cover *everything.* Forsooth! There are many things under Heaven that cannot be fully exhausted by the pattern-principles of phenomena. How much more is this the case for Heaven itself!

Elsewhere Xie says: "As regards what we term as going to the ultimate limit, even the sage is ignorant."[58] The cosmos had an ultimately unknowable character.

Each phenomenon possessed a distinctive pattern-principle of its own, which was conceptually atomic. In other words, it was intuitively understandable *only as a whole* and not in terms of any constituent parts. It was also operationally monadic in the sense that it did not interlock structurally with other pattern-principles in any exact sense, even if there may have been, in some loose fashion, mutual harmony or discord among pattern-principles. These two properties of pattern-principle, namely *conceptual atomism* and *operational monadism,* were obstacles that prevented the scrutiny of pattern-principle from giving rise to a process of analysis with enough momentum to lead in the direction of modern styles of scientific thinking.

Two examples will anchor these observations. The first is on earthquakes:[59]

In Fujian and Guangdong the earth frequently moves. From Zhejiang northward, however, this is not regularly observed. Theorists aver that when there is much water along the coasts of the sea the earth floats. In Qin and Jin [in the Northwest] the land is high and dry, and without water.

At times however there are also trembling movements here, too. When these movements take place, the land splits for several hundred feet. Those who are unfortunate enough to encounter such an event fall into the crack together with their houses. When it closes up, there is no seam or fissure. Even if you dig very deeply, the people and the houses cannot be found. The Hanlin Academy Compiler Wang Weizhen actually met with this disaster. Thus, is it not a necessary reason for the fact that earthquakes in Fujian and Guangdong do not cause the land to split that they are near to water, which makes the land humid and not brittle? Even so, *it is still impossible to understand* whether or not the great earth is born as a single entity and has some strange pattern-principle that determines if it moves or not.

The second passage is about cloudbursts, freak floods, and landslides:[60]

When there are sudden rains out of season in Fujian, the mountain streams burst forth abruptly, and drown houses and huts. The locals refer to this as 'the flood-dragon (*jiao*) coming forth'. It is perhaps possible that *this* is the pattern-principle.

It is generally the case that flood-dragons and *shen*-dragons lie hidden in mountain caverns. When many long years have passed they are either transformed into *long*-dragons or enter the ocean. Some years ago the people who live near the offices of the Education Intendant below Mount Wudan in Fujian regularly observed a huge python several hundreds of feet in length either skulking on the lower slopes of the mountain or else coiled up by the corner of the office building. Its two eyes were like torches. One night in the eighth moon, in the fall of the year *siyou* [?1549], there was a great storm in which Mount Wudan collapsed. After this the python was never seen again.

Invoking a dragon as the event-shaping pattern-principle was apparently regarded as reasonable and adequate in such a context.

Sometimes, however, 'pattern-principle' comes close to indicating a secret technique. Xie pursued some of these with determination:[61]

There are *hu* monkeys in Hangzhou that can transform themselves into other entities. Most of them are in the examination halls and the old prefectural buildings. I lived alone in these places for several months with the idea that they would be certain to come, and that it might perhaps be possible for them to display the pattern-principle of transformation based on the two primary forces. But in all this long time I obtained nothing.

A pattern-principle that he did observe, but which baffled him, was that which underlay the building of a stork's nest:[62]

The technical cleverness of the avian tribes surpasses that of human beings. Building a nest only makes use of one beak and two claws, yet its interwoven structure is more secure than human handiwork. A great wind can uproot the tree but the nest to the end never falls.

When I was in Wuxing I observed a male and a female stork planning the construction of a nest on the statue of the mythical beast that guards against fire on the roof ridge of the prefectural hall. Since there were no side supports, and no branches or leaves, any wood inserted into it would have fallen. Everyone in my family laughed at the birds, but after ten days had passed, the nest was finished. A stork stands six or seven feet high, and for both the male and the female to lie hid within it meant, I would reckon, that it was more than ten feet across. I do not know how they crisscrossed random pieces of wood and withered branches in multiple layers to make it so cohesive and without weak points. This is a pattern-principle that is *impossible to comprehend.*

In these passages pattern-principle has become a 'black box', something with remarkable hidden internal properties whose workings cannot be examined. This is particularly striking since an old nest could easily have been taken down, inspected, and picked apart.

There may even have been a tendency to use the term 'pattern-principle' precisely on occasions when the explanation was obscure. Thus, after remarking (not quite accurately) that there were no locusts south of the Yangzi River, Xie adds: "This is a case of pattern-principle being incomprehensible."[63] When he thinks he does know the explanation, he is more inclined to use a term like *gù*, which may mean either 'reason' or 'therefore'. Hence he writes:[64]

Mosquitoes may be explained as the transformations of water creatures. *Therefore* they are numerous in all places near the water. In the region from Wu and Yue [the lower Yangzi delta area and Hangzhou Bay] to Jinling [Nanjing] and Huai'an, everywhere suffers from their poisonous effects. The worst afflicted are Wuxing and Gaoyou and Baimen. The *reason* for this is that these areas are affected by their interweaving creeks and innumerable waterways.

He had grasped the correlation, though not the cause.

The other key concept, *qì*, has been sometimes overtranslated in the foregoing pages as 'matter–energy–vitality'. It also retained its earliest sense of 'breath'. In a passage quoted above[65] it was seen to be, in and of itself, "inchoate, without understanding, confused, and without any capacity to act." *Qì* may be endowed with something like good or bad moral impulses, but it lacks consciousness. In general it carries the implication of being the force, or breath, of life. This is evident from Xie's discussion of what used to be called 'spontaneous generation':[66]

'Transformations of matter–energy–vitality' and 'transformations of configurations' each play an equal part in what happens between Heaven and Earth. Human beings, the six domesticated animals, and all that are born from the womb and from eggs, are cases of transformations of *configurations*. Others, such as fleas, lice, silverfish, grubs, tadpoles, and grain-borers are born without the use of ova.[67] After they have been born they enwrap themselves in a form and become complex, and when they are extinguished they vanish totally, without the means to come forth again. The explanation for this is that the matter–energy–vitality of the generative capacity of the Dark and the Bright Forces rules over their birth and parturition. Therefore, once they have undergone vaporization and fermentation they are capable by themselves of taking on a form.[68] This is to say that the Dark Force and Bright Force are their mother and father.

Later he records the popular belief that lice would desert someone who had been sick for a long time and was about to die, "because his matter–energy–vitality has become cold."[69] After discussing the difference between mules and hinnies, Xie extends his comments to human beings: "It is evident that in human beings the matter–energy–vitality with which one is naturally endowed comes from the father and not the mother."[70] (!) Sickness could also be conveyed by *qì*, moving as a sort of miasma.[71]

The matter–energy–vitality of the earth affected the growth of plants and trees.[72] It was in the clouds covering over the hills along the sea coast—under which dragons slept.[73] And it inspired the public-spirited righting of wrongs in the character of a famous worthy of ancient times.[74] Perhaps the most striking linking of *qì* with the force of life comes in a passage which opens with a discussion of whether or not the dead "have conscious awareness." He argues that both positions raise difficulties, and follows this with similar comments on the question of the existence or nonexistence of the shades of the dead and spirits. He then goes on: "Human beings obtain matter–energy–vitality from Heaven and Earth, and are thereby born. When they reach death, this matter–energy–vitality is exhausted."[75] The quality of their matter–energy–vitality determines the quality of their characters.

The concept of 'matter–energy–vitality' is thus protean. It can be the basic *substantia* of the universe, taking different forms by means of condensing and rarifying. It can be as it were the *vehicle* for other properties—public-spiritedness and disease, for example. In a discussion of the best kinds of water for making tea, Xie advocates "mountain water," but it is necessary to find it "near villages where people live," otherwise "in the depths of the mountains and empty valleys, it is to be feared that there are malarial mists and poisonous snakes that are not conducive to human benefit, and that even if they are not poisonous, will give people febrile diseases. The reason for this is that the flavor of the matter–energy–vitality and the five human viscera have not yet grown accustomed to each other."[76] And, finally, *qì* can be the direct source of life. In one form or another it is prevalent throughout the universe. It is a means of *linking* entities, whereas pattern-principles tend to be means of *dividing* and distinguishing them: "Between Heaven and Earth there is only a single matter–energy–vitality."[77]

The structure of *qì* also raises problems. Xie reports bizarre stories about the eating and drinking habits of rainbows, which drained wells dry and consumed banquets. He comments that "rainbows are the matter–energy–vitality of the Dark and Bright Forces. They are suddenly born and suddenly disappear. Though they have form, they have no substance, so it is strange that they can eat and drink."[78]

Neither of the two basic concepts outlined here was conducive to precise argument. They explained both too much and too little. Along with other ideas, like the Five Phases of Matter, they also helped shape the conceptions that lay at the back of perceptions. What is interesting about Xie is that he consciously felt the inadequacy of all of them, and at times for a moment broke free, though never decisively.

The collection of facts

One of the motives behind *The Fivefold Miscellany* was the collection of facts. Xie stresses the problems in making reliable observations. Thus, when discussing dragons, after noting that they are meant to have horns like a deer's, a head like a camel's, eyes like a demon's, a neck like a snake's, a belly like a sea-serpent's, scales like those of a fish, claws like those of an eagle, palms like a tiger's, and ears like those of a bull, he adds: "On all occasions when dragons appear, however, their bodies are guarded by thunder and lightning, and by clouds and mists. Times when their entire form can be seen are rare."[79] But there was some evidence:[80]

> In the summer of 1598, in Jurong,[81] there were two dragons mating with each other. One of them was in difficulties and fell to the earth, lying struck down amid the fields. People came from more than a hundred kilometers away in their eagerness to see it. After three days a storm picked it up and it rose into the air again.

He also mentions an official who, when working on the lower Yellow River, found the cast-off exuvia of a dragon some tens of feet long, "with scales, claws, mane, and horns all complete." The bones were "hard and white as jade."[82] A fossil dinosaur?

Other evidence was less direct. Early in the eighth century CE, for example, a phoenix was pursuing two dragons near Huaiyin, where they fell to the ground and were transformed into two streams. "One of them was wounded by the phoenix's claws to the point where its blood flowed, and the stream's color has ever since been red."[83]

Xie takes the existence of dragons for granted. "Although dragons are spirit-like beasts, they are nonetheless regularly to be found in the world. People see them but rarely. But it is because this one single species from the aqueous tribes controls all the clouds, rains, thunder, lightning, and hail that we designate them 'spirit-like'."[84] Since dragons were territorial beasts, certain areas might enjoy rain while those close by had none.[85] There was a large variety of types of dragon because they were so licentious that "there is nothing with which they will not copulate."[86] The result was a proliferation of hybrids. Their lust was also exploited in practical fashion by the rainmakers of southern China: "They suspend a young girl in the air, to compel the dragon to rise up. When the dragon sees the girl, he soars around her and desires to couple with her. The practitioners use their art to prevent him from coming closer to her, and before long the rain will have moistened people's feet."[87]

Xie had the same matter-of-fact attitude toward fox-spirits, assuring us that "these days sixty to seventy per cent of the residences in the capital have fox-spirits, but they do no harm to anyone. The northerners are as accustomed to them as those in the far south are used to sharing their dwellings with snakes."[88] When the cats of Jinhua in southern Zhejiang province are more than three years old, they are also capable of bewitching people, he tells us, observing that "it is not just foxes."[89]

Yet he was a seasoned observer who often pooh-poohed superstitions, such as the Fujianese belief that owls brought bad luck: "They say these birds are the envoys of the City God, gathering souls. If an owl hoots at night on a house in a city, the owner is destined to die. Those who live near the mountains, however, or deep in the woods, are accustomed to hearing them, but never witness this phenomenon."[90] If he had not seen something himself, he was apt to be skeptical: "The ancients say that the fish-hawk gives birth to its young by spitting them out. *This is by no means certain.* Furthermore, the fishing cormorant, which also gives birth from a womb, spits from its mouth. I frequently see assertions in books about phenomena that I have never observed personally."[91] He has himself played with stingless bees; so they are real.[92] Per contra he gives credence to stories about the human-faced snakes of the Far South: "They know people's family and personal names. In the mornings they covertly watch them walking in the mountain valleys, and call out their names. If the person answers, then that night they come to kill him."[93]

Here is the problem: Xie has no procedure that will systematically tend to establish facts and to discredit falsehoods. Hence it is possible for him to show a relatively high level of logic in his arguments, but to make no useful progress, because often what he takes to be facts are not.

The 'fact' was a complex European cultural invention that crystallized in the seventeenth century. It was not known in premodern China. By a 'fact' in this sense, I mean a publicly recorded and accessible statement about an *observable* aspect of the world, set in the context of a *systematic evaluation* of the evidence that yields an approximate probability of its being true, and subject to a *continuing public scrutiny* and re-evaluation, with the results and the evidence being *publicly recorded* and accessible. China came quite close; what was mainly lacking was the continuity of public scrutiny and the circulation of the results. In other words, the feedback process. In Western Europe the concept originally grew out of the practices of the law courts, before it spread into natural history and the laboratory. It depended upon the publication of reports through books and journals, and the exchange of ideas through learned societies, universities, museums, and other such institutions.[94] China had printed books, and some institutions such as the state university in the Tang and Song, as well as the local 'academies' founded in Song times and later, but the rest of the complex was largely missing.[95] We may even surmise that the 'fact' in this sense required a form of collective mental discipline that brings it into the 'civilizing process' described by Norbert Elias.[96] In terms of the partic-ular terminology used here, it is not unreasonable to say that late-imperial China was unacquainted with facts.

Something less obvious but equally important was also almost missing. This was the 'program', a plan of collective systematic work. The one exception by the seventeenth and eighteenth centuries was textual research.[97] It is strange that Xie, who had many friends and contacts, never thought to organize them to look, for example, at the details of the geographical and environmental distribution of goiter across the empire, which was a subject that interested him, and even to set up a continuing network of colleagues to elucidate the problem by communicating their results to each other. In Western Europe, in contrast, what Alistair Crombie calls the 'new style of effective scientific communication' was developed early in the seventeenth century, notably by Marin Mersenne. The idea of *the program*, of which there are hints in Francis Bacon, Mersenne, Robert Boyle, and others, had become a crystallized and self-conscious procedure by the later 1660s, as in Claude Perrault's plans for the collective work to be undertaken by the Académie royale des Sciences.[98]

Although there were intermittent collaborations and occasional communications, the Chinese, in science, seem to have been loners in comparison with the Europeans. Xie, like Wang Chong and Shen Gua in earlier times, seems never to have proposed any systematic and cumulative way, for himself or others, of setting out to learn *more* of the truth about something scientific in the future.

Experiments and thought-experiments

We may define 'experiment' as the use of man-made, controlled, and repeatable situations in order to establish the degree of the reproducible covariation between, ideally, one particular varying input and an output. Its roots are ancient and probably lie in the craftsman's ability to produce approximately consistent results, 'craftsmen' including horticulturists and cooks as well as ceramists, and in the physician's efforts to find consistency in the effects of medicines and other treatments on a given state of a patient's body.

The logic of experiment in this crude sense was evident to Xie, even if he never used it systematically. An example of the experimental style of thought is his use of it to dismiss the view that "all the hares in the world are female, and that only the hare in the moon is male, this being the reason that hares become pregnant at the time of the full moon." He argues that "if you were to place some hares in a darkened room, so that for a full year they were not allowed to see the moon, would there be none of them who were pregnant?" This thought-experiment, whose negative answer is assumed to be obvious, is strengthened by a reference to male hares in the *Scripture of Songs*, which thus serves as an authority, and by the theoretical argument that "the moon is the ancestral source of the multitude of dark-quiescent-female forces," which thus implies that the presence of a male hare on it is unlikely.[99]

A simple 'experiment' by which he thought the normally invisible matter–energy–vitality underlying phenomena could be made visible was the following:[100]

> It is commonly said that fish do not see water and that human beings do not see matter–energy–vitality. The reason for this is that people are moving in the midst of matter–energy–vitality all the day long, and so are never able to perceive it. In a room into which the sunlight leaks through a crack it is however possible to see the dust busily rising like [the convection currents in] boiling water. Even though one is inside a darkened room, it is as if there were swift winds driving them along. *In such circumstances one can apprehend how the universe works;* one can observe the world; one can make one's heart–mind be at peace in meditative contemplation of [Zhuangzi's

ancient] theory that all things are ultimately equal. If one brings out the underlying purport of this, it may be termed *the phenomenon of contact between Heaven–Nature and human beings.*

Xie's misunderstood motes of dust were not themselves matter–energy vitality, any more than iron filings held in a magnetic field are that field, or particles in Brownian motion the molecules that agitate them. They were its markers. A repeated religious sacrifice could be a type of experiment. Thus:[101]

> Liang Fu was an astronomical official. During a great drought he prayed for rain, but was not successful. He had firewood piled up in order to burn himself as a sacrifice. As the flames rose up, there was a heavy downpour [and he was spared]. Dai Feng had the same experience in Xihua. Zhang Xi of Linwu was the magistrate of Pingyu, and did likewise but immediately died in the fire. There have been registrars and other minor officials all of whom have followed the path of self-incineration, and for whom, once the flames have died away, an opportune rain has fallen. . . . The rain caused by the former two men was the means whereby Heaven showed that It listened to the wishes of the lowly. The burning to death of the last-mentioned was *the means whereby Heaven cut off any tendency toward insincere actions.* Heaven is indeed contriving!

This was in essence an experimental situation, even if the unreliability of covariation required an escape route. Xie also comments not long afterward that even numerous and sincere prayers for rain "are usually not answered," a clear negative correlation, speaking figuratively.[102] 'Coercing a god', as by putting a punitive neck-collar around the neck of his statue if he failed to bring rain, was also apt to be ineffective, and even dangerous;[103] yet coercing God is in a sense what consistently effective experiment is designed to do.

Horticulture was also a nursery for reliable proto-experimental practices:[104]

> These days flowers out of season are among the items regularly presented at Court. They are, moreover, all confined to semisubterranean cellars in the earth, where they are surrounded on all sides by fires so as to force their growth. Thus there are peonies even in the depths of winter. . . . In fact, such items out of their proper season are in conflict with the regular sequences of Heaven and Earth.

The tricks used by growers of fancy vegetables and fruit also had some affinity with proto-experiment:[105]

> Among the markets and theatrical performances these days one sees many bottle-gourds which have a square shape, and some embossed with characters

that form a poem. The explanation for this is that *they have been caused to be this way* by being held between boards while they were growing. There is nothing to marvel at.

Another example of conscious and controlled interference with the processes of plant growth is the following:[106]

> If bamboos grow too densely they need to be cut back. If this is not done they will flower and after a year has passed all of them will be dead. The same is true of epidemics among human beings [population density leading to the spread of infections]. . . . Generally speaking, if bamboos flower they should instantly be all cut down, leaving only their roots. They will re-emerge the following spring.

The famous poison made from insects and called *gŭ* needed, says Xie, to be "tested on a person" once it had been prepared:[107]

> If there is no stranger passing by then assure yourself of the poison's suitability on some member of your family. The person who has ingested this poison will experience a twisting pain in his guts and vomit. All his ten fingers will go black. When he chews beans they will have no savor, and if he puts alum in his mouth it will not taste bitter. This is the way the poison is experientially verified.

Mercifully, he adds that there were antidotes, like liquorice root, so long as they were taken reasonably swiftly.

Controlling ceramics fired in a kiln is notoriously tricky, dependent on a multitude of variables such as the sequence of temperatures over time, and the location of the piece in the kiln. It is not surprising that extreme means were sometimes taken to ensure desired effects:[108]

> At the town of Jingde there were [in the past] regularly 'transformations in the kiln'. It was said that pieces did not follow the standard pattern of manufacture but would suddenly change, showing on the surface either the form of live fish or a fruit that seemed to float. The story was handed down that when a kiln was inaugurated *it was necessary to sacrifice the blood of a boy and a girl*, so causing the congealed concentrate of their matter–energy–vitality to become these strange things. In recent times the use of humans for sacrifice has been prohibited, with the consequence that there are no longer any transformations in the kiln.

Ingredient X. Perfect negative correlation.

On a few occasions Xie did not check on an alleged property of an object that would not have seemed in the least difficult to examine. Thus he wrote of boxwood (*Buxus microphylla*) that "it has been said for generations to contain none of the element of fire, and that when it is put into a stream this latter will not flow. *This has not been put to the test*, but it is perhaps not entirely true."[109] Would it have been too much trouble to find out? And even to test the other popular belief about it, namely that it grew smaller during years that contained an intercalary month,[110] a view about which he also had doubts?[111] Finally, on at least one occasion he scoffed at the process of proto-experimental enquiry as lacking any practical point, not because the theory it might be seen as checking up on could be seen at the first glance to be ludicrous:[112]

> The *Record of Lost Things Picked Up* states that: "Those who are good at discriminating between horses split open the horses' brains after they die in order to scrutinize the color. If the color is bloody, the horse will *have been* capable of traveling ten thousand *li* a day [about 5000 kilometers]. In cases where the blood is yellow, the daily distance will have been a thousand *li*." Well now! *The horse is dead, so what is the point of grading it?* And is going to the point of slitting open the horse's brains still showing oneself good at discriminating between horses? This, too, is utterly ridiculous.

He is not interested in the reality, or otherwise, of any connection between the speed and stamina of a horse while alive and the color of its brains once dead. Nor does he comment on the absurdly inflated figures. His concern is only with the pointlessness, as he sees it, of *post-mortem* horse-grading.

We are left with a puzzle. Xie implicitly understands the basis of the experimental style of thinking, but he is not consciously aware of it as the foundation of a procedure that might lead to new insights.

Types of explanation

Xie's preferred type of explanation is what may be called the 'proto-epidemiological'. 'Proto-epidemiology' may be defined as the examination of *what covaries with what* spatially, temporally, or operationally, in the attempt to isolate probable causes. A simple example: why do some hills have clouds above them and others apparently not?[113]

> The *Record of Mount Lu* states that, when the heavens are about to rain, white clouds either cap the peaks or stretch along the central ranges. . . . In not more than three days it is certain to rain. But it is not only Mount Lu that is thus. For the most part, mountains *of great height and with caves in them* are all able to spew forth clouds and so cause rain. . . . In Anding prefecture there is Xianyang Peak, on top of which the clouds rise up when

it is about to rain, resembling an open umbrella. A local proverb has it that "Copious the downpour when Xian Peak opens its umbrella." In Fujian the principal summit of Drum Mountain towers over the sea and serves as a landmark to which everyone in the provincial capital looks up. When clouds shade its peak, it will be certain to rain on the morrow. . . . *But other mountains are not all like this.* The reason is that Drum Mountain has *caves*.

The key to the argument is the identification of a decisive differentiating factor. *Caves* are essential.

He uses much the same approach in his proto-epidemiology for the effects of drinking-water:[114]

People who drink 'light' water are most of them bald and suffering from goiter. Those who drink 'heavy' water mostly suffer from swellings and lameness. Most of those who drink sweet water are loving and beautiful, while those who drink bitter water are mostly afflicted with ulcers and tumors. Most of those who drink 'hard' water are puny and hunchbacked.

In my travels through the empire I have observed that most of those who drink water from streams are pure, and most of those who consume brackish water are stupid. Most of those who drink water from the mountain defiles have goiter, and those who drink hard water are constipated. Sweet-water people mostly live to a ripe old age. Those in Teng, Yi, Nanyang, and Yizhou who drink the water from the mountains all of them suffer from goiter, but those who themselves sink wells for drinking are not afflicted. The springs and wells in the departments and counties along the sea coast in Yanzhou in eastern Shandong are affected by the heavy salinity of the soil. If people drink from them for a long time they suffer from constipation. If, however, they do not eat foods made from flour and drink river water, then they are not affected. This last point needs to be known.

Another passage shows the same style of attempting to analyze what covaried with what:[115]

The teeth of those who live in Jin [modern Shanxi] are yellow, whereas those who live in the mountain defiles have necks affected by goiter. There are numerous jujube trees in the Jin area and those who are fond of the fruit have yellow teeth. *But there are also many jujube trees in Qi* [approximately modern Hebei], *so why should this apply only to Jin?* Although goiter is caused by the water of the mountain streams,[116] those who drink the water in many other northern places . . . are afflicted by it. *Why is this not the case for those who live among the countless peaks and valleys south of the Yangzi River?* I have never heard of any of them having neck disease.

As for the sedan-chair carriers in the north, whose backs and necks bear a heavy weight for many days on end, they get swellings *that resemble goiter in form but differ by being on their faces and backs.* The people of Lingnan [the Far South][117] love to chew betel and their teeth are mostly brownish black. Why should only Jin be thought to be so affected? As for the notions that a rich matter–energy–vitality in the environment causes the character of empathetic sympathy to be widespread, that a harsh matter–energy–vitality causes widespread greediness, that a cloudy matter–energy–vitality causes a lot of rheumatism, and that valley matter–energy–vitality is the cause of widespread longevity, I fear that these are not entirely the case.

People of the Tatar race never suffer from smallpox, because they never eat salt or vinegar. I have recently heard that those who trade with China, and have also copied the Chinese fashion of eating and drinking, all subsequently contract it.

Xie thus had an intuition of the environmental basis of a number of diseases, but his search to find patterns of covariation, and then to identify the exceptions, did not lead to an attempt to improve the analysis on a second round. There was no sense of a research program. Only a skeptical curiosity without stamina.

A somewhat different style of explanation is found in his efforts to elucidate physical phenomena. While still paying attention to what appear to him to be the key differentiating factors, he also attempts to identify the physical *processes* involved. A simple illustration is his description of a particular waterfall as "extremely strange" because it was silent but not projected over a concave cliff, the basic prerequisite, he thought, for other 'noiseless' waterfalls.[118] He is uneasy about the idea that the attraction of the moon is the cause of tides, or the only cause, because the timing does not fit exactly:[119]

As regards things that respond to the moon, the moon belongs to the dark-moist-female category, and is the ruler over water. When the moon is full, oysters grow; when the moon is covered over, camphor contracts. Each follows its category. Nonetheless, in the areas of Qi [in the Northeast], Zhejiang [in the East] and Min [in the Southeast], and Yue [the Far South] *the times of the high and low tides are not the same,* their arrival varying with distance.

This is empirically accurate so far as it goes. The timing of tidal maxima and minima is multicausal.

A more elaborate treatment is that of mirages at sea:[120]

When there is marine-monster matter–energy–vitality in the sea off Dengzhou,[121] it congeals to form multistoreyed buildings and towers, and is known as the 'sea market' [i.e., a 'mirage']. I would however describe this as *'marine* matter–energy–vitality' rather than just '*marine-monster* matter–energy–vitality'.

In general terms, when the essence of the seawater congeals in large quantities it forms a shape, and when it disperses it forms light. All the beings in the sea obtain possession of this matter–energy–vitality, and once this has continued for a long period they are all of them able to produce illusions. This is not merely the case for marine monsters.

My home is by the sea coast, and every fall the moon is extremely bright, with water and sky being of the same color, and no waves across a vast expanse. The largest of the oysters . . . are the size of a peck-measure dipper and emit a pearl whose rays reflect back the light of the moon until, all of a sudden, the emission forms [the illusion of] city walls, markets, many-storeyed buildings, and pavilions. If one intercepts the flux of light, the images will make the transition first to a state of obscurity and then vanish. People who live by the sea coast are so used to this that they think it commonplace, and are not aware how strange it is.

As for such creatures as crabs . . . and rock-oysters, they all have beneath their covering of accumulated shell the capacity to emit light in the darkness for more than a foot, appearing as a twinkling. There is no doubt but that this is the matter–energy–vitality of the seawater.

Preconditioned conceptualization.

From time to time Xie says that some phenomenon or other *cannot* be explained: "Some springs in the empire have a constant outflow, never running dry and never overflowing. Not running dry is easy to understand, but what is the reason for it never overflowing? This is *a pattern-principle that cannot be known*."[122] Why not? He was aware of ground water, or, as he called them, "the arteries of springs that are in the earth and invisible."[123] All he needed to imagine was some underground combination of sills, and a separate reservoir and overflow basin, not unlike the system used for the Ming Grand Canal where it went over the Shandong hills. Modeling would have been useful, but was not attempted.

He was at his best in proto-archaeology:[124]

The first emperor of Qin set up an *uninscribed stele* on Mount Tai. There are many confused explanations for this, none of them as yet established as correct. Some people consider it to be a stele-type receptacle; some a guardian-stone; some a surface for an inscription that was never cut; and some a monument. All of these are notions without foundations. *I have made a personal visit to the site*, and gone on a tour of inspection around the vicinity. The view that I have come to is that the theory closest to the truth is that it was a monument.

The explanation is that although the stone is high and of a size large enough to make it comparable to an ordinary stele, it is certainly not a container. The type of stone is not to be found locally on the mountain, nor is it the kind of stone ordinarily used for inscribing characters. There is a cover on its top and a pediment at its base, which appear to constitute a completed whole. Thus it is not an as-yet uninscribed stone.

If one examines the *Records of the Grand Historian*, the First Emperor went up Mount Tai and set up a stone on which to offer sacrifices. During his descent the violence of a storm led him to shelter under a tree, on which he bestowed the rank of 'Wudafu'. He also sacrificed to Mount Liangfu [a subsidiary summit]. The stone he set up there *was* inscribed. . . . Thus a stone on Mount Tai was inscribed, and at present there is still preserved in the side-office of the shrine of the Lady Immortal Yuan-jun a broken stele bearing twenty-nine characters, which I suspect was this *inscribed* stone.

This being so, it becomes clear that the piece of [uninscribed] stone under discussion here was that erected on the summit as *a monument* to the sacrifice.

Where, as in this last passage, Xie is in possession of a reasonable assemblage of facts, including a personal inspection of the evidence, he is capable of presenting a well-argued case. Whether he was right or wrong is another matter, but not immediately relevant to the question of his style of thought.

He also had an embryonic conception of the capacity of the skilled artisan to mimic or *model* the operations of nature. Thus he said of some archaic astronomical instruments, military devices, and other mechanical contrivances that: "Such extreme ingenuity as this surpasses the proper norms for human beings *and resembles the transformations of nature*, being artisanal skill that approaches the excessive. It is also, however, the intelligent apprehension of the free course of Heaven–Nature, and not something that may be attained by the forcible application of wisdom."[125] The craftsman's intuition could be uncanny in its ability to capture aspects of the working of the world in models, instruments, or mechanisms but was often beyond the reach of a solely intellectual understanding. Elsewhere he speaks about wooden automata that could, for example, bake bread for a housewife, and a boat that could go by itself without the help of wind or currents.[126] The only example that probably worked as described was an automated toilette cabinet for an empress, with figurines that came in and out of doors, or so it appeared, of their own accord.

The concept of modeling a natural process also appears explicitly, if briefly, in one of his comments on the astronomical instruments at Beijing: "There is also a bronze sphere one rotation of which from left to right is a means of *imitating* the structure of the heavens."[127]

The idea of invoking a *historical process* to explain a present-day situation in the natural world was likewise familiar to Xie:[128]

> There are many rocks in the Yi hills[129] of a bluish black color. Looked at from below they seem crowded together like bamboo shoots. All the mountain paths run along by the edge of these rocks, or look out from beneath them. Underneath all of them there is sand, on which the rocks depend for a stable footing.
>
> *Over a long course of time*, the sand has gradually been stripped completely away by the winds and the rains, and holes and cavities have opened up as it were in competition each one with the others. The rocks have likewise lost the ability to stand steady, and it regularly happens that some of them will fall down from the mountain crests and into the middle of the farmers' fields.

Geomorphology!

The closest parallel in China to the historical logic developed in Europe for the filiated development of languages would, however, have been the analysis of the slowly changing pronunciation of the Chinese characters over the centuries, a study that became highly refined during the following Qing dynasty,[130] but is hardly present in the *Fivefold Miscellany*.

Xie's limited concern with taxonomy and classification is surprising, given the existence of numerous pharmacopeias and herbals in China, of which the latest at the time he was writing was that of Li Shizhen, published in 1596.[131] He seems mainly interested in discussing why the written characters for certain animals were composed with an inappropriate radical, like the graph for the long-tailed proboscis monkey (*wei*, i.e., *Cercopithecus aethiops*) which incorporated the 'insect' radical,[132] or why the names for certain plants assigned them to the wrong category. Thus the aspen was the 'white willow', and the 'water-pine' was a type of alga (*Codium fragile* or *macronatum*).[133] He did, however, have a rudimentary idea of the problems involved:[134]

> [The ancients] did not know what to make of the Siberian jerboa [also written with the 'insect' radical], which is a rodent in front and a hare behind. . . . When Shen Gua was on an embassy to the Qidan in Song times, there was a jumping hare in the great desert. It had the shape of a hare but its forelegs were little more than an inch long, while its hindlegs were more than a foot in length. It progressed by bounding, and when it stopped it dropped level with the ground. This was the Siberian jerboa. *Such is the difficulty for classifiers when they are trying to treat animals comprehensively.*

At the price of admitting extremely elementary examples, the foregoing account leaves only two of the principal styles of scientific thinking without representation in Xie's work. These are the probabilistic and the postulational. In general we can conclude that here was a distinct, if underdeveloped and unquantified, scientific component to the understanding of the environment in late-imperial China.

Moral versus material causation

Xie was concerned in a variety of ways with whether or not morality was a causative force. Do we live in a natural environment interfused with morality, or is it morally neutral? A simple case of this is the problem, Why does lightning strike where it does?

He first explores the nature of 'thunder', which is taken as the basic phenomenon:[135]

> During the Tang dynasty, in the western part of the prefecture of Daizhou[136] there was a large *Sophora japonica* tree which was split by a thunderbolt[137] for a length of several tens of feet. The God of Thunder was entrapped in the grip of the tree and shouted wildly all day long. Everyone scattered and no one dared to approach him. Di Renjie, who was the military governor, came up and questioned the god, who answered: "There is a crafty dragon in the tree who has caused this, having made me pursue him, and so fall into this unbearable situation where I am in the grip of the tree. Were you to help me, I would amply repay your kindness." Di forthwith told a sawyer to demolish the tree, whereupon the god made his escape. Now it is already strange enough for the God of Thunder to be held fast in a tree, but that he should speak with human beings is odder still.

He goes on to note that "usually in cases *where people have seen the shape of the God of Thunder,* he has by and large resembled a rooster with fleshy wings, the sound he makes being the energetic striking of these wings."[138] This enables him to argue that the Song-dynasty neo-Confucians' explanation of thunder and lightning in terms of the pattern-principles of the Dark Force and Bright Force is "truly ridiculous" since thunder has "a form and a sound" and therefore belongs to "the category of things."[139]

He then comes to the problem of whether or not a lightning strike is morally accidental when seen from a human point of view:[140]

> It often happens that when a thunderbolt strikes someone this has been caused by a dragon rising up, or because the thunderbolt has risen from the

ground *and smitten them accidentally*,[141] to their misfortune. One opinion is that when a wilful dragon is shirking his duty of making rain, he will more often than not escape into the wall of someone's house, or into someone's ear or nose, or possibly between the horns of an ox. The God of Thunder is thus obliged to arrest him, and this often causes a clap of thunder.

There would also appear to be cases in which the strike is made *with conscious intent* and is not just abandoned recklessness. . . . When I was young and living with my grandfather, . . . the maidservant carried me in her arms into the garden, where a thunderbolt came down and struck her. When she fled, it pursued her into the house, where it rested on top of my cot. The maidservant was struck dead but I, the child, came to no harm.[142]

Xie then confronts the basic problem:[143]

When a thunderbolt strikes a human being, may we say that it has a heart–mind? [That is, does it have a morally aware conscious intent?] If we do, then how can rotten trees and livestock, which are also smitten by thunderbolts, be thought to have been guilty of a sin? If, to the contrary, we maintain that it does *not* have a heart–mind, then how do we account for the fact that those who have been recorded, both in ancient and in modern times, as having been struck by it were all of them evildoers and unrestrained robbers? *I have never yet heard of an upright man or a superior man dying from a thunderclap.*[144] . . .

Only a major cause is sufficient to move Heaven to wrath; but, granting this, why should it be that not all the evildoers and unrestrained robbers in the world have been struck down? I would answer that this is the means whereby Heaven is Heaven. If the God of Thunder were to spend all day booming about, searching out people and striking them down, Heaven's majesty would be defiled.

This sequence of passages provides an example of 'rationality without facts'. However oddly they may strike the modern reader, the logic, if not flawless, is not negligible. The factual foundations on which it rests are rubbish.

Xie, having ascribed a sort of bureaucratic causation to thunder, was however also alert to the possibility of what we would think of as natural patterns:[145]

Long ago I used to live at the foot of the Nine Immortals Hills. There was a tallow tree[146] outside the kitchen, and *every year at the beginning of spring* the thunderbolts [i.e., lightning] would rise up from the side of this tree. Its roots and branches were half burned away, and the color resembled that of charcoal. It is said that over a period of four years thunderbolts rose up from here four times. Thus it would also seem that the thunder lies hibernating in specific places.

He distinguished explicitly between material and moral causation:[147]

> Since the conjunctions and the eclipses of the sun and the moon depend on their regular orbits, and they can be foreseen in numerical detail several tens of years in advance, it is not possible to escape them. . . . Is it not erroneous to point to them as portents from Heaven?

He further argued that the poor historical correlation between periods of bad government and the occurrence of solar eclipses implied that believing eclipses to be portents was equivalent to regarding Heaven as perverse, "like a father flogging and scolding a well-behaved son, and indulging a worthless one."[148] Predictability had, he said, altered people's attitudes.[149] Per contra, planetary motions and comets *did* have moral significance:[150]

> Venus is a 'star' associated with war. If one examines the patterns of Heaven through successive dynasties, one finds that when Venus has dominated Heaven, wars have arisen on a great scale, and that when comets have dominated Heaven, there have been conflicts over the succession to the throne.

In the early sixteenth century, after a comet had swept across the constellation of the God of Literature, there had been a rebellion, and "disaster fell on every high official." Likewise, after a "strange star" had been seen in the southwest late in 1577, "the imperial court was entirely emptied of upright men." He concludes that "celestial portents do not appear for no reason; they are as they are because of causes."[151] Moralism just wins out over agnosticism:[152]

> I have never seen an epoch of a Sage in which there were many disasters, nor an age of disorder in which there were many auspicious events. Are we to maintain then that Heaven has a conscious intent? There are also occasions when people meet with disasters that subsequently turn to good fortune, and with auspicious events that then become baleful.
>
> There are cases, too, where the responses of events to disasters and good fortune that were otherwise identical have been totally dissimilar. When people look for the reasons for this, there is always forced interpretation, yet if they do not look for the reasons, and assign these events entirely to chance, this is where the [morally disruptive] theory that . . . the portents of Heaven do not require one to fear them has its starting point. How can this be permissible?

We will return to this theme in the next chapter which looks at the religion of the weather sponsored for a time by the Qing state.

Companionship, tourism, and connoisseurship

What motivations drove Xie? At the risk of oversimplifying, we may describe him as seeking *companionship with nature*, as being an intellectual tourist forever in search of novelty, and one who relished the appraisal of the ideas and experiences he had collected, and their placing in an appropriate literary context. The first aspect emerges from a discussion of happiness. After observing that poverty and low status are not as pleasant as vulgar wisdom had claimed them to be, he goes on: "A rough sufficiency of farmland and gardens is needed for hills and vales to afford one pleasure, and for one to be the companion of fish and shrimps by the streams, and the friend of the deer among the mountains, to 'plow the clouds and cast one's fish-hook among the snows', and to intone songs to the moon and hum poems to the flowers."[153]

He is open about his taste for the new and unexpected: "To read books that one has not seen before, *to pass through scenery that one has not before encountered*, these resemble obtaining extremely precious objects or tasting unusual flavors, being strange pleasures that are hard to convey by speech to others."[154] He liked to meditate on what he had seen and to moralize. The following passage, which arouses thoughts of the fables of La Fontaine in the Western reader's mind, may suggest something of this aspect:[155]

> The dung-beetle rolls up a pellet in which to hide its body, never failing to laugh at the dry straws of the cicada's bed. The spider drops her silken threads in order to seek her prey, never failing to laugh at the silkworm being boiled [in the vat of the silk-reeler]. Thus things being so, the pure and the filthy have different patterns of causation, and the empathetically concerned and the cruelly violent belong to different categories.
>
> The superior man would therefore prefer to go hungry in order to remain pure, rather than to stuff his stomach and become morally filthy. He would rather bring to perfection his empathetic concern for others, even if this means killing his own person, than give way to cruel violence in order to live on by ignoble means.

Although most of Xie's observations of arthropods are objective in spirit (for example those on the *Sphex* wasp[156] and the dragonfly[157]), he thus also had a side that enjoyed drawing a moral from a natural spectacle. Even when he did not do this overtly, it is hard not to suspect that his primary motive was usually a connoisseur's enjoyment rather than the deepening of his understanding.

Humankind and habitat

Xie had a multifaceted interest in the relationship of human beings with their environment. Traveling around had sharpened his sense of variations in space, and of the differences in climate, quality of drinking-water, and people's health. He was aware of population pressure in some of the country's regions and cities, and how higher densities of population increased the spread of epidemic disease. Also of shortages of labor in other areas. He had witnessed reductions in accessible resources in some of China's provinces, and the loss of fertility in some soils. Wide reading had conferred on him a sense of changes over long periods of time: an example is the shift he noted in the aesthetic attitude toward cultivated flowers during the middle empire, which moved from one of indifference to one of intoxication. He was aware how the built environment affected human safety and health: different urban housing materials had different risks of fire, and different sanitation arrangements different probabilities of disease. He was intrigued by people's reactions to the environment: their religious fascination with mountains, for instance, but also their fear of heights. Contemplating the variety of natural conditions with which humans had to contend, including the sea, had impressed on him that adaptation was often the price of survival.

These themes interlock. Though the passages that illustrate them approximately follow the order given above, this means that they are too entangled with each other for the sequence to be sharply defined. Incidental empirical information abounds but some of it is of doubtful validity. The focus is on Xie's thinking.

We begin with population.

Xie saw the Ming dynasty as one of exceptional population growth. This view is to some degree at variance with the current scholarly consensus,[158] but the divergence is probably to some extent due to Xie's focusing on particular areas, as will become clear. His overall view, though, was as follows:[159]

> For the last two hundred and forty years the people have been at their ease and rearing children, being unacquainted with war. *The population is abundant,* the result of a situation that has not existed since antiquity. For this reason, those who do not make redoubled efforts to contrive their preparations, and who are not concerned with timing their actions aright, cannot avoid having their plans go awry.

He is flattering the dynasty, of course, and his ancient history is off target. What is convincing, though, is his dismay at the psychological effects on people of the intensified competition between them. A little later he says:[160]

In Xin'an in Wu, and in Futang[161] in Fujian, the land is constricted and the population numerous. The properties of the common people have reached everywhere, no matter how remote, and are regularly found in barren, out-of-the-way corners where human feet have [previously] left no traces. There is really something inexplicable in this. The land is so limited that the people cannot feed themselves from it, but the population is numerous. This is because the ways in which they are aiming to make a profit extend across an ever-broadening range.

When I was in Xin'an I saw many cases in which a further storey had been added on top of the upper storey of people's houses. Instances of houses without an upper storey were rare. I estimated that the accommodation in one of these houses could match that of two or three one-storey houses, and there would still not be a foot or an inch of vacant space [so dense is the population].

In Fujian province all the land, from the high hills down to the plains, has been cut into fields. Seen from far off they look like ladders. . . . Even so, the people roam about in small bands to pursue a living away from home. If the land were to be allocated in accordance with the 'well-field' system of antiquity,[162] seventy per cent of them would be without land.

But population pressure was not universal:[163]

Only in Fujian and Guangdong and Guangxi is it possible to accumulate a surplus by farming. Recently, though, the soil in Fujian has also become badly degraded. The region south of the ranges, Guangdong and Guangxi [the Far South], is unique in having abundant resources and a sparse population, with arable land plentiful, and rice cheap. If it were not afflicted by malaria and poisonous animals, it would indeed be heaven on earth.

The normal dictionary translation of the first sentence would be 'accumulate a surplus of farmland'. This leads to such obvious contradictions, both internal and with the preceding passage, that I have emended it. Xie did, however, also note that in much of the *central* Yangzi valley "rice is cheap and farmland abundant, with not enough people to farm it." It was to this that he attributed the relatively egalitarian income distribution in these provinces.[164] In the Northeast he noted salinization: "As far as one can see along the coastal lands of Shandong there are tidal salt flats. They are unfarmable, and nothing remains of the fields but the name." The people were poverty-stricken.[165] The overall picture that emerges from his pages of the relationship between population and resources is thus that it was patchy and variable.

We have already seen in passing, in the course of his discussion of bamboos, how Xie ascribed epidemics among human beings to a high population density.[166] A particular illustration of this was the temporary concentration of a workforce to dredge a stretch of the Yellow River in the fall and winter of 1603. The facilitating cause of the illness was the insanitary conditions:[167]

> Neither firewood, hay, rice, nor wheat was available along the banks of the river. The laborers all of them brought their own clothing and food, forming encampments on both banks. It was estimated that there were more than three hundred thousand men. *Filthy vapors rose up like steam.* The dead lay pillowed one on top of the other. Every worker who died had to be replaced by a substitute from the same county. When spring arrived, the vapors of the epidemic burst forth once more. From beginning to end, more than a hundred thousand perished.

Inadequate provision for sanitation was probably one reason why such crowded conditions were so dangerous in the cities:[168]

> Dwellings in the Capital press closely together without any space to spare. There is also *a lot of excrement and muck* in the markets. People from every region live together in a rowdy hubbub. Flies and gnats are likewise numerous. When the hottest season of the year comes round, it is almost impossible to survive. If rain falls for any great length of time, flooding causes disasters. For these reasons periodic fevers, dysentery, and epidemics follow one another constantly. The only way of safeguarding one's health is to sit calmly and venture out of doors as little as one can, and deal with it thus.

The 'periodic fevers' were most likely malaria. The *vivax* species of the plasmodium only needs a temperature of 16° Celsius in which to operate.[169]

Disposal of human feces was a problem in Beijing. In what follows, the term 'privy' refers to a storage pit, usually covered, with a crossbar or seat, for defecating, not anything like a modern water closet:[170]

> Although privies are foul and filthy places, the people of ancient times attached importance to them. These days *they no longer build privies north of the Yangzi River....* South of the Yangzi privies are all constructed to sell their contents to farmers. There are no wet-fields for rice north of the Yangzi, and thus no use for feces in liquid form. They leave it on the ground till it has dried, then mix it with soil and blend it into the fields. In the capital it remains in trenches until the springtime, when they take it out to dry it in the sunshine. The vapors coming off it are so foul that one cannot go near it. *Anyone who suffers invasive contact from them falls sick.*

Elsewhere he comments, when discussing the making of tea, that "north of the Yangzi it is not appropriate to use rainwater, as the tiles on the rooves of the houses are mostly made of clay mixed with shit."[171]

Xie's depiction of the filthy condition of the cities of his day contrasts markedly with the laudatory account given by the Jesuits a century-and-a-half later, and presented in the "Concluding Remarks" (p. 468). We will find ourselves faced with a puzzle at this point: had conditions changed, or were the standards of judgment different?

Xie believed that people in remote areas tended to live longer than in those more economically developed (and chapter 9 on Zunhua confirms this insight). In the course of his discussion of ginseng he comments:[172]

At the present time, commoners who dwell deep in the hills or in desolate valleys, eat herbs and coarse vegetables, having no knowledge of what a medical drug might be, enjoy long lives with robust bodies, and are unacquainted with acute illnesses. Only in the families of those who are well-to-do or of high status, where the everyday behavior of the sons, younger brothers, and women lacks restraint, and their times of eating and resting are not well harmonized, do they rely on the effects of treatment with ginseng.

Wild plants were healthier than their domesticated counterparts for similar reasons:[173]

Mei-plums, cassia, and orchids cultivated by human beings with great effort are, in the last analysis, inferior to those that grow of their own accord in the mountains. The reason that this is so is that these latter receive the seminal essences of the sun and moon, and the vitality of the winds and frosts, and also are not in the vicinity of smoke or cities. They bestow their fragrances of their own accord, with an unstressed demeanor in a setting that suits them. This is why the sinews and bones of people brought up in rich and distinguished families are commonly more fragile than those of the poor and humble.

Human beings were affected by climate:[174]

There are places afflicted by cold at the frontier passes where, if one spits, one's spittle at once freezes. In some of the swelteringly hot areas in the far south if one does not dry one's clothing in the sunshine and the wind, it goes moldy with the damp. The climatic aethers of Heaven and Earth are thus not uniform.

It is better for southerners to go north than the reverse, since when northerners come south, if they don't suffer from malaria they will from dysentery. Cold is bearable, but not heat. When I was in the north, I did not suffer from the cold but from the dust. In the south I do not suffer from the heat but from the humidity. Dust makes things filthy—white garments turning black as a result. Humidity affects human beings: powerful bodies become rheumatic.

Adaptation to local variations in climate was normal. Speaking of the wind-blown dust that obscured vision in the Northeast, he says "when people from the lower Yangzi valley first arrive, they find it vexing, but the locals are not in the least put out by it."[175] The most dramatic illustration of the difference between those adapted and those not adapted was seasickness. He had witnessed this when accompanying his paternal grandfather to the Liuqiu islands:[176]

Even those who live on the water, and are also used to being submerged in it, if they are not accustomed to crossing the sea, become dizzy and vomit when they go aboard a ship, and sprawl about this way and that. All the envoys had hammocks in their quarters which permitted the ship to roll while the bed remained level. Even so they were still dizzy and disturbed, unable either to eat or drink This was because on the boundless waste there is no day when the wind does not blow, and no moment when there are not waves.

The built environment also varied:[177]

Disasters from fires are uniquely frequent in Fujian province, but the places worst affected are Jianning and my own home prefecture of Fuzhou. One reason for this is that the people's houses converge like spokes on a hub, and they work at night without resting [so the oil lamps are a hazard]. A second reason is that their construction is based on a unified wooden framework. Bricks and masonry are no longer used. If ever anyone is careless [and knocks over a lamp], there is nothing to stop the power of the conflagration. . . . North of the Yangzi River, the walls of people's houses are made of earth or glazed tiles. They hold their thatch together with mud. Even if a fire breaks out, it will not burn, or, if it does break out, will not spread. This does not only apply to north of the Yangzi. Even in the Fujianese prefectures of Xinghua and Quanzhou extensive use is made of bricks, and fires are infrequent.

It is worth noting that there was still enough wood in some places along the southeast coast for houses to be routinely built of it. Building in wood had other drawbacks, however. Xie says of the Far South: "After time has passed a house will be bored through [by termites], and commodities will rot. There are no houses a hundred years old, nor any books that are fifty years old, nor again any clothes that are twenty years old."[178] At times, typhoons could flatten houses. He says of the severe storms that ravaged the coast of the Far South once every three to five years:[179]

When one erupts, the roof tiles of the village dwellings, and the trees in the groves, over a distance of more than a hundred kilometers will be as if washed away. Boats and their oars are tossed about, pounded totally into fragments. Several days before the storm arrives, the locals will be aware of it and take precautions to avoid its effects. All the large mansions install tree trunks edged with iron as pillars, and bronze or iron plates as tiles, as a defense against damage.

I have myself, in a typhoon that hit Hong Kong in 1965, seen massive billets of wood blown off housetops like matchsticks, quite enough to despatch anyone foolish enough to venture outside and unlucky enough to be hit by one.

Xie was interested in other people's responses to the environment. One facet was *fear*. He comments that "in a lifetime of roaming around the mountains, I would regard Mountain Goat Gorge on Fangguang Peak[180] as the most perilous point." He continues:[181]

When one looks upward, one finds oneself up against a sheer cliff-wall. When one gazes down, it is bottomless. No creepers afford a handhold on which to haul oneself up. The track is only a little over a foot in width and, what is more, slopes outward and is splattered by the waterfall. The uneven footholds are slippery with moss. The moment one reaches it and gives a sideways glance, one's courage has already disappeared. I once went in a party of some six or seven people composed of friends and serfs, but only one of the young serfs went across. He was barely able to make his way back, and his face was drained of any human coloring.[182]

Another emotion that intrigued him was the popular passion for pilgrimages up mountains. He gives the following acerbic account of that up Taishan, the Great Mountain, in Shandong:[183]

All the commoners north of the Yangzi River, from the northeast, northwest, and the southern part of this region, go to the Great Mountain to offer incense. Their adherence to a vegetarian diet and other taboos, their correctly adjusted clothing, feelings of reverence, and singleminded determination appear spontaneously identical. Even married women from the villages and rustics from the hills abstain from meat and recite the name of the Buddha, as if He were watching over them from above. "Any lack of purity," they declare, "will occasion acute illness, and the disaster of tumbling down head over heels."

Once the prayers and worship have been concluded, however, and they are descending from the mountain lodges on the return journey, they will stop somewhere with their relatives and friends, and every one of them abandon their vegetarian diet and butcher animals in large numbers. They will dance drunkenly about and make a noisy clamor. Effeminate boys will sing them songs in which no indecency is spared. Now! Since they are incapable of leading a morally proper everyday life or showing a respectful restraint once the ceremonies are over, their observance of taboos and repetition of the Buddha's name are no more than deceptions toward the numinous powers.

But, one wonders, was there not—even so—some profound impulse drawing these folk up the mountain in the first place? Whatever may have happened once the tension was released.... The contrast with Xie's own self-conscious savvy governing-class connoisseurship is not necessarily entirely to his advantage:[184]

If one goes touring in the mountains and does not make use of one's official underlings, there is no way to pay for cooks or palanquin carriers. However, if these underlings come on tour in the mountains with one, this is also exceedingly discommoding. One reason for this is that, if one has a large number of attendants, one cannot be one's natural self. A second is that the complexities of the commissariat will occasion this, that, and the other anxiety. A third reason is that the yelling of those clearing the way in front and bringing up the rear ruin the scenery, and it is doubly difficult when one is rigged out in one's formal clothing to strip off garments or go barefoot.

Palanquin carriers and attendants shrink from traveling anywhere remote. The Daoist priests and Buddhist monks are solely concerned with having done as quickly as possible with roads through dangerous places. It is a cause of worry that the porters will grumble at unusual and perilous scenery, and, fearing to get into difficulties, will only lead each other down paths that they are already accustomed to. One will not manage to visit even ten or twenty per cent of the subtler scenic delights.

This is why those who go touring in the mountains should depend on landowners who share their tastes, or superior monks who live in seclusion.... Go where you feel inclined! If a place is off to one side, nothing is gained by failing to visit it.... Take your time. Don't hurry. Prefer difficulties to taking it easy. Prefer to do things thoroughly, but don't feel obliged to do so. Don't become bored halfway through. Don't bring along too many friends. If there are a lot of them, they will be interested in different things. Don't be too stingy with food and supplies. If you are, then enthusiasm, after being aroused, will falter midway. Regularly encourage the enterprising spirit of your capable and experienced serfs.... Don't take a drunkard along. Don't have someone in an enfeebled condition as a companion. Whenever you come to a point of scenic transition where it is necessary to engage in its appreciation, set out your writing-brush and inkstone to prepare notes that will stop you forgetting it.

These are the broad essentials of touring in the mountains.

Eminently reasonable. And depressingly uninspired. The contrast with Xie Lingyun's feeling for the landscape a millennium earlier, or the intense philosophic and competitive enthusiasm of the early European conquerors of the Alps, sums up one aspect of the shift from the aristocratic to the bureaucratic soul.

The response to flowers underwent a long-term change of a different kind. In Xie's view, "the people of ancient times seem not to have paid attention to flowering plants. The poets then sang only of such things as plantains, the common mouse-ear, *Marsilia quadrifolia*, and white artemisia."[185] He further comments that:[186]

> From time to time they touched on peaches, *li*-plums, cherries, peonies, and lotus buds. As for *mei*-plums and cassia, they only considered them useful as culinary flavorings, for titivating the taste buds. Initially they did not allude to their fragrances. It can hardly have been the case that at this time these latter two trees were not to be found in the northwest or the north China plain, seeing they used both of them as dried or fresh fruits!

Chrysanthemums were only referred to in the poem "Encountering Sorrow" in *The Compositions of Chu* as something to be *eaten*, not as a source of visual pleasure. The author was "not yet an intimate friend of chrysanthemums." As for peonies, "the people of ancient times likewise thought of them as seasoning for food. If someone were to act in this way today, he would greatly damage the scenery!"[187]

This situation had changed around the middle of the first millennium CE:[188]

> Peonies were not exalted with praise before the Tang dynasty. Only in the works of Xie Lingyun do we find a line like: "Among bamboos, by the river's bank, grow peonies in throngs." He was the first close friend of this sovereign among flowers. . . .
>
> When [a century-and-a-half later] Emperor Yang of the Sui had a site cleared for his Western Park, the department of Yizhou presented him with twenty-four species of peony. These included the 'Brownish Earth-Red', the 'Blushing Red', and the 'Fly Hither Red'. How foolishly besotted he was! . . . By the Kaiyuan reign-period [713–41 CE] the peony had little by little come to be highly prized.

Symbolic flowers proliferate in "Encountering Sorrow," which was written long before this time, toward the end of the preimperial era, and include species described as planted, tended, and raised. If there really was, then, a long-term historic change such as Xie asserts, it was a subtler one than he intimates. Perhaps it could be more precisely formulated as the intensifying aestheticization of cultivated flowers.

In later times, he says of *mei*-plums:[189]

> Men of superior attainments and littérateurs have sung their praises one after the other without stopping. Their viewpoint, which finds pleasure in the blossoms but forgets the fruit, is exactly the opposite of that of people of ancient times.

There is an implication here of the aristocratic or mandarinal superiority of being able to afford to admire what is, in any direct sense, useless. Xie goes on:

> There are places in Fujian, Zhejiang, and the lower Yangzi region where the blossoms of the *mei*-plums can be seen stretching without a break for five or six kilometers. They are all however grown by uncultivated rustics and *merely for the purpose of selling the fruit.* In the season when they are in blossom, people suffer from the cold and shiver in the wind. There is snow in the hill valleys. How could commonplace people endure this? Those who grow the *mei*-plums are not necessarily those who delight in them. Those who delight in them are not always those who grow them. *Mei*-plums differ in this respect from other flowering plants.

Some flowers did indeed generate popular enthusiasm. An example was the magnolia, of the species *denudata* or *conspicua*:[190]

> In Nanjing they are to be found at the Bounds of Heaven Temple, and in Suzhou at Tiger Mound Hill. Every year, when they open, they are considered a delight quite out of the ordinary. The matrons who frequent the pagodas in monastery grounds choke up the thoroughfares. One looks all round one but sees *no end to these people*, one's head growing dizzy from the ferocious stench they emit.

Some wild flowers were, however, at least in his view, universally neglected. He says of the *Daphne odora*, a shrub with pale purple blossoms that open early in the year: "I would describe it as a rare plant of the mountain valleys that is not restricted to being unknown in the cities. Even those who live in the mountains neither know of it nor take delight in it."[191]

Environment was critical for the well-being of flowers:[192]

> North of Fujian province, peonies are to be found everywhere, but are most plentiful in Shandong and He'nan. . . . When I passed along the road through Puzhou and Caonan, their fragrance assaulted my nostrils for fifty

kilometers. This was because everyone there grows them in garden plots, like vegetables.

The reason that peonies could not be successfully transferred to Fujian was in a sense the mirror-image of the reason why lichee trees and long'an trees could not go north of Zhejiang.[193] Climatic preference.

Why then did the self-conscious appreciation of cultivated flowers begin to increase so rapidly in China around the middle of the first millennium CE, and remain so strong for so long afterward? Xie offers some fleeting clues.[194] He begins by asking:

> On how many occasions in human life, in the course of a hundred years of looking at flowers, are one's feelings and the scenery in a joyful concord, and one's senses extended to the utmost?

For himself, he answers, only twice. He describes the first of these moments as follows. Caonan was a hilly area in the southwest of Shandong. Peony country.

> At the home of a first-degree holder in Caonan I saw a garden of peonies that may have been more than three-and-a-half hectares in extent, entirely covered with these flowers. Apart from the pavilions and kiosks, there was hardly a foot or an inch of ground to spare. A cloud-like brocade of every color made an arresting sight as far as the eye could see. Our host sang in a refined style, played [the ancient game of] pitchpot with arrows, and let his guests go where they felt inclined, not shaming us with the commonplace rituals of host and guest. That night was brilliant with a pure white moon, as bright as the daytime. We exclaimed out loud with pleasure, and our humorous badinage flowed without cease. Not till dawn did we go home. The scents lingered on my clothing for several days without disappearing.

Cultivated flowers had become participants in social life.

The second episode goes deeper. It suggests that the psychology of flower-viewing involved a tension. Xie was a guest at a party in what he styles 'Chang'an', the old name for Xi'an when the city had been the imperial capital under the Han and the Tang. His hosts were an unnamed official family of high status. The focus was a display of several hundred bowls of chrysanthemums, regimented with exceptional discipline into patterns of constant height and alternating colors. There was singing and dancing, with "effeminate boys moving easily and elegantly among them," as well as the chance to admire paintings, ancient vessels—presumably bronzes and ceramics—and musical instruments and books. At the same time, he comments, "we did not talk of commonplace matters," and "although we were among decorated balustrades and vermilion archways, there was, without a word being spoken, the effect of 'the hedge to the east and the southern hills.'"[195] They evoked the profound but perpetually elusive meaning hidden in the nature before our eyes.

The flowers were a *horticultural zoo*. Their deepest appeal was to an instinctive remembrance of the lost world of human interaction with an untransformed and almost independent nature. At the same time they exemplified and celebrated the taming and reshaping of this nature by humankind. Their beauty was a triumph of refined artificiality under affectionate but uncompromising control. From our perspective the long-term rise of the love of cultivated flowers is indirect evidence of the domestication of the natural world in China with which it ran parallel in time, a sophisticated substitute for daily contact with, if one dares use the phrase, 'the real thing'.

12

🐘 *Imperial Dogma and Personal Perspectives*

There was no one view of nature that can be called *the* 'Chinese' view. There was not even a spectrum. Rather a kaleidoscope of fragments most of which reflected something of most of the other fragments. The demonstration of this for the final centuries of the empire is the task of the present chapter. It falls into two contrasting parts: the imperial ideology and the multiple personal perspectives of poetry. Considerable investments in prestige and publicity in official circles went for about a century into maintaining the state orthodoxy, but it seems to have had a surprisingly limited impact. The poets, most of whom were either officials themselves or from the official classes, seem to have been barely if at all touched by it in their personal writings.

The first part of what follows is a sketch of the dogmas of moral meteorology enthusiastically espoused by the Manchu–Qing rulers until around the middle of the eighteenth century, though much less so thereafter. That is, the doctrine that people were responsible for their weather. Rainfall and sunshine were deemed to be seasonable or unseasonable, appropriate or excessive, according to whether human behavior was moral or immoral. The effects were statistical. Bad individuals in a community could benefit from the goodness of the majority; good individuals could suffer if the majority were evil. Some counted for more than others. The emperor's conduct was of pre-eminent importance; bureaucrats came in second place; and the common people ranked last. But all, or any, of these could be decisive in a particular case. Further, since weather was mostly regional there was a corresponding regionality of rewarded or sanctioned behavior; and the weather around the capital was thought to have particular relevance to what Heaven thought of the emperor's conduct. The ideology was a political tool, distinctive for its structured rationality interwoven with a rationalized political opportunism on the part of the ruler, who could utilize the modesty of self-reproach implicitly to highlight his own awe-inspiring ethical qualities, or else cast blame on others either to damn them or discipline them. Also remarkable for its at least intermittent efforts to discover an empirically *observable* correlation between morals and rainfall.

The second part surveys an *ad hoc* anthology of poems touching on the environment put together from *The Qing Bell of Poesy*. This collection of verses was edited by Zhang Yingchang, an official who served in the Grand Secretariat, and published in 1869, originally as *The Bell of Poesy of the Present Dynasty*. It contains over 2,000 poems, the work of 911 poets, mostly on topics that relate to everyday life. They are of uneven quality. Some are profoundly beautiful; many are doggerel. But they illustrate a medley of conflicting themes. The romance of economic development. The disaster of economic exploitation. The limitless stores of the earth's bounty. The exhaustion of natural resources. Uncompromising war on nature. Dexterous cooperation with nature. Respect for nature. Mystical absorption into it. Landscape as a human body, fecund but vulnerable. Landscape as a playground for the deities of the seas, rivers, storms, and earthquakes. Environment as the molder of the human character. The aethers dominating a landscape as a legacy created by people's past behavior in it. Nature as the mirror and symbol of mankind and its activities. The indifference of nature, living its own story. . . . And so on.

Perhaps the only thing all these beliefs had in common was that in some sense everything in the environment was felt to be *alive*, whether with a natural or a supernatural life.

Moral meteorology

The roots of meteorological ideology in China were archaic. The ode *Yun Han* declared of a drought: "The king says, 'Alas! what guilt rests on the present men? Heaven sends down death and disorder, famine comes repeatedly.'"[1] The section called 'The various confirmations' in the 'Great Plan' chapter of the *Scripture of Documents* lists rain, fine weather, warmth, cold, winds, and their timeliness, or lack of it, as 'confirmations' caused by the good or bad conduct of the ruler.[2] Under the Later Han dynasty, a natural disaster like drought could also be explained in terms of a lack of *yin*, and measures taken to increase the power of this principle, as by sacrificing to mountains and rivers, and freeing innocent prisoners.[3] Xiang Kai could write at this time of "repeated frosts and hail, and . . . heavy rains and thunderstorms" as being "*caused* by subjects who flaunt their personal power, and by punishments that are excessively cruel."[4]

The main sources used for the analysis presented here are the sections on 'Reverence for Heaven' in the so-called 'Sacred Instructions' of the Manchu emperors from Kangxi to Daoguang.[5] These pose several problems. Different rulers had different personalities, hence different preferences and practices. During a long reign there could also be changes of importance within the reign itself. An example is the Qianlong Emperor's sponsorship of public ceremonies for rain by Daoists and Buddhists in the 1780s and 1790s, something that he had not done before.[6] Some emperors probably engaged in moral posturing.[7] We have also to bear in mind the caveat formulated by Rafe de Crespigny for an earlier age: "Portents recorded in the histories do not reflect the disorders of nature so well as they do the discontents and political disagreements of man."[8] The hypermoralizing and omen-besotted Yongzheng may have been uneasy at the continuing belief that his succession was not legitimate, and sought to emphasize both the closeness of his relationship with Heaven and his trembling humility before It.[9] The selection of the materials included is also presumably biased: thus occasions when rain resulted from an emperor's prayers are probably overrepresented as compared to the occasions when it did not.

Clearly, though, the publicly announced beliefs that the documents describe would not have been set forth in imperial decrees, where the prestige of the emperor was both the guarantor of their authenticity and a hostage to their plausibility, had they not commanded a substantial measure of assent, however formalistic in nature. Even seemingly trivial violations of ritual could have unfortunate consequences: In 1747 an official sacrificing at the Altar of Heaven had a headache and squatted down. For this irreverence he was at once impeached.[10] These doctrines were an ideological exoskeleton that helped hold the political system in place. But probably not an endoskeleton.[11]

Seen in the perspective of environmental history, perhaps only in an area such as northern China could a belief in moral meteorology have maintained a hold on people's convictions. The reason is that the weather here in late-imperial times, if the modern record may be taken as an approximate guide,[12] was very variable over the short term. Probably only high short-term variability can provide enough short-term coincidences—such as apparent responses to prayers—to sustain belief in the moral-meteorological mechanism. The weather in central and south China was stabler.[13]

At least two Qing emperors, Kangxi and Yongzheng, adopted a quasi-scientific attitude to the verification by observation of moral-meteorological causality. Kangxi declared in an edict of 1678 that, "If human affairs go amiss down here below, then the response of Heaven Above will be as swift as [that of] a shadow or an echo. How can one say that this has not been checked by examination?"[14] On another occasion, when there had been an earthquake, he said, "We pondered hard *within the palace* on the causes of the disaster, and strenuously sought some way to dispel them."[15]

Two types of problem thus arose. First, how were the moral causes of meteorological phenomena to be identified, especially as some celestial phenomena, notably eclipses, were predictable in advance? Kangxi, for example, maintained that, as a result of the rapacity of the officials, "The grieved and resentful matter–energy–vitality of the humble folk rises up to Heaven, and thereby causes floods, droughts, changes in sun, moon, stars, and planets, and uncanny events such as earthquakes and springs running dry."[16]

Second, how was religious or philosophical sense to be made of Heaven's behavior? To us it would seem that obvious questions were usually avoided. Why, in the circumstances just described by Kangxi, should Heaven have responded to the people's woes by making them *worse?* Sometimes, however, the questions were at least raised, if not answered. Qianlong wrote a prayer in which he declared, "The fault is not with the officials, or with the common people, but with your minister [the emperor himself being the 'minister' of Heaven], and grows worse daily." He followed this by asking, rhetorically no doubt, "How can Heaven Above, on account of the person of this one minister [that is, himself] cause the multitudes of common people to be afflicted by disaster?"[17]

There was tension between the spiritual approach to the world of suprahuman powers and what may be called 'religious technology', especially folk technology when it escaped from imperial control. This is evident from a decree issued by the Yongzheng emperor in 1725 about the worship of a proscribed deity, Liu Meng:[18]

> Li Weijun, the governor-general of Zhili, memorialized last year: "There have been disasters from locusts everywhere in the metropolitan area. The locals who have prayed devoutly in the temples of General Liu Meng[19] have not suffered harm from them." We were acutely pained at this. The practice of all matters that are of benefit to the livelihood of the people should be widely disseminated. The *recognized spirits* who ward off disasters are, moreover, listed in the sacrificial rituals. . . . The people of old likewise did not refrain from making use of the powers of spirits to drive away disaster caused by locusts.[20] Chabina, the governor-general of the Liang-Jiang, has now stated in a memorial: "Those localities in Jiangnan that have erected temples to General Liu Meng have no disasters due to locusts, whereas in places that have not yet erected such temples they are not able to be free of

locusts." This shows the warped narrowness of Chabina's views. He suspects that We rely exclusively on *prayers* as a method of dispelling catastrophes. Many of the other governors-general and governors have also said in their memorials that they have established ways to pray for rain or sunshine.

Now . . . disasters arising from floods, droughts, or locusts are due either to a defect in the government at Court, . . . or to the chief officials in the area being unable to serve the state in a fair and correct fashion, . . . or else again the low moral quality of customs in some particular prefecture or county, where people's heart–minds are false and treacherous, thereby causing the Dark Force and Bright Force to be thrown into confusion, so that disasters are numerous and repeated. . . .

When We heard that . . . rain and fine weather were occurring out of season, We were obliged deeply to reform Ourselves and reflect on the correction of Our faults, being attentive and fearful morning and evening, in the hope of regaining Heaven's [benevolent] attention. You senior provincial officials and local officials, as well as common folk, should in like fashion be fearful, and examine your moral character. . . . As for praying to the daemonic beings[21] and spirits, this is only a means whereby one attains a single-mindedly devoted heart–mind. If one relies exclusively on prayer as a method of dispelling disasters, and pays no attention to fearfulness and moral self-examination, this is inevitably like 'dredging a watercourse but neglecting the spring'. . . . We are in no wise deluded by the vulgar custom of shamanistic prayers to daemonic beings and spirits.

The emperor accepts religious technology at a vulgar level in principle, provided that it is within imperially prescribed bounds, but tries to give it a higher meaning. It is not currying favor with a lesser deity that brings results, but having a heart whose moral qualities find favor with Heaven.

The earliest decrees of Nurhaci, the founder of the Qing, were designed to establish that he was the Son of Heaven and aided by Heaven in his 'great enterprise'. In 1626 he hinted at the tenets of moral meteorology.[22] Huangtaiji, his successor, who was uneasy at the sinification and softening of the Manchus, only spoke about the weather and natural disasters in practical terms. In 1637, faced with the possibility of more poor harvests due to a second cold spring in succession, he simply told the Board of Finance to mobilize the base-level military leaders since "if plowing and weeding are done in good time, the crops will not be harmed by disasters."[23] In 1644, inveighing against addiction to alcohol among lower-level officers, which had in turn led to poverty among their rank and file, he asked if these latter were not just as much the subjects of the dynasty as their commanders, adding,

"Does Heaven send down the ill-omened disasters of frost, hail, drought, and floods only on *them*?"[24]

Doctrinal moral meteorology only appeared in Qing decrees in 1653 with the Shunzhi emperor. Faced with floods in the capital, where houses had been destroyed, and food and firewood had become expensive for poor people, he declared that this "has been caused by Our lack of virtue," and promised to reform himself. In 1656, he issued a longer edict which combined ritual self-accusation with shifting the blame onto his regent predecessor:[25]

> Since We assumed personal rule . . . there has been thunder in winter, snow in the spring, meteorites, and rainfalls of earth. One can see such communication everywhere, for untoward events do not occur for no reason. *They have all been caused by Our lack of virtue.* . . . There have now been successive years of floods and droughts, and the common people are having difficulty in making a living. This is because We have failed the expectations of Heaven Above of one who acts as a ruler. . . .
>
> When Prince Rui [Dorgon] was regent,[26] those who surrendered were massacred, rewards were distributed without restraint, the loyal and the good were driven from office, the greedy and the treacherous employed, and the wealth of the State recklessly wasted, so causing the common people to sigh with resentment. Everyone looked forward to the day when We assumed personal rule and would swiftly afford them succor. Six years have now passed, and although We have made every effort to pursue a renovation . . . disasters and ill omens are frequently seen. In this case We have failed the common people's hopes for good government.

By implication, the weather here is still solely a matter between Heaven and the ruler.

A wider-ranging theory of causation was formulated in the Kangxi reign that followed. There were two somewhat distinct modes. (1) The sincerity of the spiritual attitude with which Heaven was approached was critical for "reaching upward, and by affect attaining the heart–mind of Heaven." A bad attitude could 'summon' disasters from on high. (2) Cruel, ill-judged, or ill-motivated actions by the government and its officials generated resentful matter–energy–vitality among the ruled, and this acted as a material force that "upward did violence to the harmony of Heaven." These two modes may be illustrated by passages from three decrees:

(1) 1678
If human affairs go awry in this world below, there will be corresponding changes in Heaven above. . . . It is now the height of summer; the weather is hot and dry; rain-fed moisture is not easy to come by. . . . The sprouts of

grain are hanging down dried out. . . . We have on this account directed. Our efforts toward reflecting upon the reformation of Our character, practicing abstinence, and devoutly praying for sweet and prolonged rain, Our hope being that Our quintessential single-mindedness will reach upwards, and affect the heart–mind of Heaven. . . . [27]

(2) 1679

There has now occurred a large and sudden earthquake. *The general explanation for this is that We are lacking in virtue . . . and that many of those whom We have employed to administer the government are not sincere or helpful.* Central and provincial officials, you are unable to purify your heart–minds, . . . you deceive your superiors, act in your personal interests . . . or behave wantonly and oppress the people, turning right and wrong upside down, . . . *disrupting the harmony of Heaven above, and calling down this disaster.*[28]

(3) 1679

The difficulties faced by the common people in making a living have become extreme. . . . Families without food or clothing have been coming into the Capital in uncountable numbers to sell their children at cheap prices. . . . *This is all because the local officials have toadied to the higher officials, and imposed unauthorized levies on the common people.* The governors-general, provincial governors, and intendants pass on [these pickings] in the form of presents to those in the Capital. The great officials thus transfer the limited material output to which Heaven can give birth, and the easily exhausted wealth of the people, into the private pockets of greedy bureaucrats. *The aggrieved and resentful matter–energy–vitality of the people of modest means reaches up to Heaven, thereby causing the summoning forth of such untoward events as floods, droughts, changes in the heavenly bodies, earthquakes, and the drying up of springs.*[29]

The precarious credibility of the first mode (sincerity) was well appreciated by the Kangxi emperor. Thus in 1708 he said that he had formerly prayed to the Supreme God[30] for relief from drought. On the day that he went to the Altar of Heaven "it was immediately apparent that Our feelings had touched Him, for timely rain fell copiously, and We then knew that Our deep and lonely single-minded sincerity had found its reflection in Heaven Above." When later there was another drought, his officials pressed him to pray again for rain, but he refused, saying: "The empire is now prosperous. We fear that Our single-minded sincerity is not what it was on the previous occasion. . . . One ought not to engage in prayer light-heartedly."[31]

Morality-based theories lost plausibility when a phenomenon could be predicted by calculation, as was the case for eclipses of the sun and moon, something that some Chinese thinkers had realized for at least a century.[32] For Kangxi it was, however, axiomatic that "the Way of Heaven is related to human affairs." In 1682 he observed that "If a comet is seen above, there are *always* deficiencies in political matters."[33] He was aware, though, of the problem regarding eclipses, since in 1697 he responded to a prediction from the Board of Astronomy[34] as follows:[35]

> Although human beings can predict solar eclipses in advance, yet, from ancient times, sovereigns have all regarded them as warnings to be fearful. The general explanation for this is that reforming human affairs is how one shows reverence for portents from Heaven. Only commonplace rulers ascribe them to matter–energy–vitality and numerical parameters. Last year there were floods and earthquakes. Now there is going to be an eclipse of the sun. The significance of this is undoubtedly that it will be caused by a preponderance of *yin*. How can it be maintained that it is not connected with the doings of humankind?

He later tried to consolidate his position by arguing that the historical record showed that rulers who had treated celestial phenomena as warnings had "long enjoyed Great Peace," while those who had treated them as "accidental" had fallen into decline.

The Yongzheng emperor reiterated the formulae promulgated by his father, but refined the philosophy behind them. He also introduced two novelties. The first was the concept of the *statistical* nature of moral-meteorological phenomena; the second a rough-and-ready *decision procedure* for determining whether their causation was at a local or a national level. We shall deal with this second innovation later, and turn now to look at the first.

His central position is expressed in his response to a report in 1724 from the provincial authorities of Jiangsu and Zhejiang on irruptions by the sea at the mouth of the Yangzi River and in Hangzhou Bay:[36]

> It is Our opinion that within Heaven and Earth there are *only* the pattern-principles of the Five Phases of Matter. It is by these means that human beings are born, and all beings grow and are nourished. The controllers of the Five Phases are none other than the Dark Force and the Bright Force. The 'Dark Force' and 'Bright Force' are other names for the daemonic beings and the spirits. . . .
>
> How does the Way of the Spirits establish correct doctrine? The general explanation is that the activities of *daemonic beings and spirits* are, precisely, the *pattern-principles* of Heaven and Earth. It is not possible that they should act in arbitrary fashion. *Everything*, be it as small as a hillock or a

mound, or immense as a river or great mountain, contains *a spirit* in it, which is its master. All of them must therefore be reverently believed in and honored with service.

The sea is the destination to which the four great rivers flow. If it is thought to be unworthy of reverence, why did the [ancient] sovereigns Yao and Shun sacrifice to mountains and streams? ... The common people of today are, in their ignorance, unaware of this pattern-principle. They often believe in sacrifices for which there is no justification, and have no faith in the Spirits Bright. They lack respect and blaspheme, so provoking a reprimand from Heaven.

Now, *if good people are numerous, and bad people few in number, then Heaven will send down good fortune upon them.* Even if there are a certain number who are not good, they too will receive Its protection. *If bad people are in the majority and good people in the minority, then Heaven will send down punishments upon them.* Even those who are good will be affected by Its calamities.

The authorities in Jiangnan have recently reported that the sea has flooded in everywhere in Shanghai and Chongming. The Zhejiang authorities have also reported that ... the sea has broken through the defensive dikes, damaging the crops in the fields. ... Although disasters from water pertain to Heaven-determined parameters, some cases may result from people living close to the sea, and enjoying a peaceful prosperity, failing to remember the efforts of the Spirits Bright to protect them, and so being insolent and blasphemous.

Now, reverence for the spirits is appropriate in principle; and it is moreover the way in which good fortune is to be pursued and disaster avoided. ...

The state of mind of *human beings* is the state of mind of the *spirits*. The moving effect of a single thought is enough in itself to bring about good fortune. How could it only be that a single rural district, or a single family, receives its benefit? If every member of the common people can maintain his or her heart–mind in a state of reverent fear, it is certain they will obtain perpetual good luck and peaceful waves [on their sea].

And he ordered that the coastal population be made acquainted with this decree.

Human beings and spiritual beings were conceived of as interacting in a mind-field whose components determined the actions of the corresponding material components of every entity in the universe. The nonhuman part of this mind-field was constrained in certain ways by its own inherent character, and obliged to react in a specific fashion to a specific stimulus. Human beings, though subordinate, and required to be reverent and fearful, were the independent variable, possessing a free will. Thus in 1729 Yongzheng said that "the rewards and retributions for good and for evil are all to be seen in the choices that a person makes for him- or herself.[37] It is like sowing seeds. If one sows panicled millet, panicled millet will grow. It is also like striking an instrument: if one hits metal, there will be a metallic sound, and if a stone, then a stony sound."[38]

In a decree of 1731 the emperor touched on the other side of this position, namely that there were some things that it was impossible for Heaven to do:[39]

> Since the middle of the summer of this year, the fertilizing rains have not come to the Capital at the right season. . . . Heaven Above has a loving heart–mind. It is in no way the case that there is some pattern-principle whereby It sends down disasters on humankind [undeservedly]. *The people of the empire bring floods, droughts, and famines on themselves.* . . . If any of them should chance to develop feelings of resentment, their offense is greater still. . . . If they have the audacity to feel resentment and hatred against Heaven [for Its just punishments and warnings], then a perverse matter–energy–vitality will take form from the outside. Even if Heaven Above wishes to be lenient, this will be impossible.

Conversely, if the common people were without sins, they would never be placed in circumstances from which they could not escape.

The statistical nature of moral-meteorological effects, which apply only to groups of people, and not to individuals,[40] becomes intelligible in terms of the collective nature of the mind-field. It also solves an ancient religious problem, why the virtuous often suffer and the wicked often prosper in a world thought to be ruled by a supernatural justice.[41]

The collectivity notwithstanding, the Yongzheng emperor had no doubt but that he himself was special:[42]

> The Lord of Men receives from Heaven a mandate of especial affection. . . . The affective contact that he makes is especially swift. . . . For example, on the sixteenth of the third month of this year [1725] We perused a memorial from Yi Duli, the governor of the province of Shandong, informing Us that there had been little rain during the three months of spring. . . . We reverently informed the Spirits Bright, then devoutly prayed with a purified heart. We subsequently received a memorial from Yi Duli reporting that on the eighteenth, nineteenth, and twentieth they had received a sufficiency of moisture from rain.

Q.E.D. He then quoted another case of his effective intervention, and told the provincial officials to be sure to memorialize him about local floods and droughts. Otherwise, he said, "We may have no means of using self-examination and abstinence to bring back the heart of Heaven, so allowing these droughts and floods to become disasters." He then modestly added that "This decree of Ours is in no respect Our styling Ourselves skilled at awakening the understanding [of Heaven], or a wish to vaunt Ourselves before the masses." He was, he insisted, trying to make the point that "between Heaven and humankind, affect and response working in unfailing fashion, and the inhalation and exhalation [of matter–energy–vitality in the form of aethers], form a channel of communication."[43]

The doctrine that the weather and portents constituted a celestial–terrestrial system of communications led to difficulties once a systematic attempt was made to relate them to human behavior actually observed. The category of 'accident', elsewhere denied, had to be invoked in order to sidestep the contradictions. Early in 1730 the Yongzheng emperor was told by the Board of Astronomy that on the first day of the sixth month there would be an eclipse of the sun lasting 9 minutes and 22 seconds. He reacted by saying that he was "deeply fearful," that the "feelings of the people" were perhaps still discontented, and that this was probably a warning from Heaven.[44] After the event had happened he issued the following decree:[45]

Sui Hede, Superintendent of the Imperial Manufactories at Nanjing has stated in a memorial: "At the time of the solar eclipse . . . , the weather in the Jiangning region was at first overcast and rainy. By the afternoon the appearance of Heaven had become clear and bright. Everything was visible. *There was no blemish on the light of the sun. Everyone in the area took this to be an auspicious omen.* I have especially sent in this memorial as congratulations." We especially censured Sui Hede at this time in a rescript, saying: "This is in no way a matter for one in your position to memorialize about. . . . " The governor of Shanxi, Jueluoshilin, has also memorialized: "In Taiyuan and other places there were dense clouds and heavy rain. *The solar eclipse was invisible.*" We have likewise sent down a decree issuing a sharp rebuke. . . .

It may happen that those whom Heaven assists in auspicious fashion become proud, boastful, reckless, or indolent, whereupon their previous moral self-cultivation turns good fortune into disaster. . . . The solar eclipse . . . of 1730 was a sign from Heaven, to warn us as to what was right, to feel forever respectful fear. . . . How can it be right, because it was *accidentally* not seen clearly, to engage in exaggerated talk in order to praise Us? That the Shanxi region *accidentally* met with overcast and rainy weather cannot be generalized over the whole empire. As to Sui Hede's statement that in

Jiangnan there was no blemish on the light of the sun, We may infer the reason. This occurred because, when the sun shone out after midday, it had already gradually regained its circular shape. The portion missing was only twenty or thirty per cent. It was for this reason that the portent of its incompleteness was not apparent.

In years gone by when We experienced a solar eclipse of forty or fifty per cent, the light was so bright that it was hard to look up at it. Our Late Father [the Emperor Kangxi] led Us and Our brothers to the Qianqing palace, where we used *a telescope, with doubled paper on all sides to block out the sun's light.* After this we were able to look out and examine the missing portion. This We experienced in person. If the eclipsed portion had not reached the proportion [forecast], then [this would have been because] the Bureau of Astronomy had made *a mistake in its calculations.* How is it possible on this account to disregard the warning from Heaven? . . .

In 1719 there was a solar eclipse on the first of the first month. . . . On this day it was overcast and cloudy, with a light amount of snow. *The eclipse never clearly appeared.* Our Late Father said in a decree to the officials of the Court: "Although the Capital has not seen it, in cloud-free places in the other provinces there will certainly be some who have witnessed it. . . . " We now see that there are some officials in the provinces away from the Capital who, on account of this year's solar eclipse not being visible there, have become overjoyed and written memorials of congratulation. This is a gross violation of proper pattern-principle.

The introduction of a modest proto-scientific component into the system opened up contradictions that the Emperor could only wish away by the force of authority. His successors understandably kept off such issues.

If the weather and other celestial and terrestrial phenomena were a response by Heaven to the moral behavior of local officials or local populations, it followed that there should be variations detectable at a local level. Thus in 1732 the Yongzheng emperor commented that floods, droughts, and famines in a particular locality could have many reasons: bad government at the center, errors by local officials, "vexatious commands by the authorities," or "degenerate customs among the local population." He went on:[46]

We have to take into consideration that the population of the empire is numerous, and that some are good but others perverse. *There may even be some so stupid and ignorant that they feel grief and resentment at famine and hardship.* Now there is nothing worse than people turning their backs on Heaven and pattern-principle by having a false heart–mind in normal times, and perverse habits, and then—when Heaven sends them signs as a warning—forgetting why Heaven Above bestows such chastisement, and regarding themselves as guiltless recipients of a reprimand.

Even if We reform Ourselves and offer prayers, We will not always be able, though acting on their behalves, to avert calamity from them or to render their punishment lenient. This is something that is quite evident whenever We see, *in departments and counties that are not far distant from each other, that the quantities of moisture provided by the rainfall are different,* and that some have good harvests and others dearth.

He reiterated this in 1733: "When Heaven Above sends down disasters, *It often demarcates localities* and distinguishes boundaries, sometimes of wide extent and sometimes narrow. . . . There are cases when an entire province has a harvest, but a single prefecture, or a single county, or even a single rural district or a single canton is alone afflicted by disaster. How could Heaven Above be generous or stingy as between them? . . . There has always to be a reason for the calling down [of a disaster]."[47]

Yongzheng was explicit about the responsibilities of local officials: "If governors-general and governors are actually able loyally to embody the dynasty–state, and love the people with a sincere heart, they will always be able to summon the response of Heavenly harmony which will bestow auspicious omens on the territories under their command."[48] Likewise he declared with ferocious specificity: "With provincial governors like *you,* We are aware of the pattern-principle that localities you rule will never have good harvests. Heaven has sent down icy hailstones only on the areas under Mang Guli, Chen Shixia, and Wei Tingzhen, which is most uncanny and fearful."[49] As he saw it, "the level of the harvest will correspond to the level of the governor-general and the governor," and mentioned that when Mang Guli first went to Hu'nan there were floods, and, when he was transferred to Jiangxi, drought. When Bulantai ruled over Gansu there were repeated reports of icy hailstones. "Such have been the responses," he said. "Remarkable!"[50]

A once-good official could also fade with age:[51]

Consider Tian Wenjing: when he was governor of He'nan, the strength of his heart–mind was amply sufficient, . . . and no one in the empire could match him. When later he was ordered at the same time to be governor-general of Shandong in addition to these other duties, the effects of age and illness had caused his spiritual power to decline . . . and errors and disasters subsequently appeared with great frequency in both provinces. Was not this a relatively clear proof [of the link between a state of mind and actual events]?

Yongzheng was developing moral meteorology into a weapon for psychologically terrorizing both local populations and officials.

The case of Xuanhua prefecture shows how the population at large could be condemned for having an adverse effect on the weather through its bad behavior. In 1729, Yongzheng issued this decree to the Grand Secretariat:[52]

> We have already determined that the differences between the various localities in seasonality, and in rainfall and sunshine, are due either to defects in the government at Court, or to local officials failing in their duties, *or else to the customs of the people being corrupt,* and their heart–minds false and ungenerous. . . .
>
> There were abundant harvests everywhere last year throughout the province of Zhili. Only three administrative subdivisions, Xuanhua, Huailai, and Baoan, missed being fertilized by the rains. *We thereupon entertained suspicions toward the officials and commoners of these localities, fearing there might be causes for them to have called this down upon themselves.* In the fall, Wang Tang, intendant of Koubei circuit, came to the Capital and We . . . have now received a memorial from him:
>
>> During the summer and fall last year there was a drought in Xuanhua, Huailai, and Baoan. In spring this year *every other place received auspicious snow,* but there was uniquely little of it in these localities. I left my area on official business during the second month, and observed that between the Jiming relay station and Xin Baoan there runs the old Huimin Channel which irrigates several hundred *qing* of farmland. The bannermen and civilian–commoners have been engaged in a lawsuit over it for more than thirty years without it being settled. I examined in detail the route taken by the channel, and first of all made clear the rights and wrongs of the matter. I then repeatedly proclaimed the imperial decree that was received last year, and urged the parties to repent. In an instant the bannermen and the commoner–civilians lauded the imperial compassion, coming to their senses at once. They shared out the channel and used it for irrigation jointly, putting an end forever to the grounds for their dispute.
>>
>> On the first and second days of the third month there were actually *successive falls of auspicious snow,* covering the land to the depth of more than a foot on the level. . . .

If in some particular district the people are suspicious of one another, and quarrel and start lawsuits, *the disrupted matter–energy–vitality in people's breasts will cut through the matter–energy–vitality of Heaven and Earth.* It will also become blocked up in this particular place, unable to flow freely or be at ease, so how can there not be cases when rainfall and sunshine do not come at the proper time?

Having proved his case, the emperor then insisted, as usual, that he was not trying to push the blame onto the officials and the common people, since "rulers and people, superiors and inferiors, are basically a single entity."

Later in the same year, when the situation had deteriorated again, he was not so magnanimous.[53] He called for strenuous local self-rectification by both the local officials and populace. But the prefecture was still not off the hook of imperial displeasure. Early in the fall of 1734 Yongzheng recapitulated the past weather history of the place and then continued: "In the winter months [of 1723] everywhere else had auspicious snow, but this area had uniquely little, which was certainly caused by either the local civilian and military officials being unable to cooperate with each other, or by ignorant commoners disrupting the harmony of the [local] matter–energy–vitality."[54] He noted that there had now been a drought in Xuanhua followed by damage to the crops from icy hailstones, "the biggest of which were the size of a fist or a chicken's egg." This was followed by more moral-meteorological analysis:[55]

> We are of the opinion that although icy hail commonly occurs in the northern regions, yet the disasters suffered by the villages of Xuanhua seem *uniquely severe,* and rarely seen in recent times. *It is evident that Heaven Above has been sending signs again and again to warn Xuanhua.* If by any chance the local officials or common peoples regard these as *accidents* due to *natural* causation then they are inferior people who do not know how to tremble in fear and reflect on their transgressions.

He ordered copies of his decree to be issued far and wide, so that the officials and people of Xuanhua would "every one of them reflect on their misdoings" so as to enjoy seasonable weather and good harvests in the future.

The Qianlong emperor who succeeded Yongzheng may have had reservations about the attitudes among officials induced by these obsessions of his predecessor. In 1735, the year of his accession, he issued[56] a decree noting that even certain of the sage–emperors of antiquity had not been able to avoid droughts and floods, and continued:[57]

> Governors-general and governors have the weighty charge of provincial government laid upon them, and *report on the percentile levels of the harvest.* This is related to the fate of the people of the region concerned. It must be accurate and without falsification, so that one may discuss tax remissions and relief measures. . . . We . . . have observed that in the reports of the harvest percentiles from the various provinces it sometimes happens that

these are determined only on the basis of *an abundant harvest in a single place,* or that in areas with an excess of rainfall *the harvest in high-lying places has been taken as the standard,* while in years of drought the standard is *what has been reaped in low-lying areas.* . . . The sole purpose is to paint a deceptively pretty picture, so as to attract the reputation of summoning forth harmonious matter–energy–vitality. . . .

You governors-general and governors, . . . how can you, because the harvest has been abundant, greedily treat the achievements of Heaven as your own? If a bumper crop is to be adduced as your own achievement, then, necessarily, We fear, a dearth must be accounted your fault. To fabricate the report of a good harvest is to lack pity for the people's difficulties.

Meteorological religion intensified statistical malpractice.[58]

Qianlong maintained the assumption of local responsibility.[59] He was even willing to blame his own lack of virtue when all of the metropolitan province received spring rain, *except* for the area immediately around the capital.[60] In 1740, when the governor of Shanxi reported at mid-year that all of his province had received satisfactory rain except for the two prefectures where the provincial capital was located, he received the rebuke that "since only the areas in which your prefectural capital lies have not been able to be sufficiently moistened, it is abundantly clear that this was caused by [*your*] slack government." Nonetheless it seems that, as his reign progressed, this question of localized responsibility only intermittently interested Qianlong.

The topic regained a momentary importance in 1758 with a prolonged drought in Gansu. The governor and other officials were told to go on offering their prayers, and also to clear off the backlog of outstanding legal cases. They were to exercise discretion in this regard, however, for "if in all cases criminals are forgiven, this is, on the contrary, not the way to summon down omens of good fortune, and to look up for fertilizing rain." Additionally, "they are to pay attention to *searching out every manner of person who is well-versed in praying for rain,* and find means to set them praying."[61] This partial substitution of virtuous behavior by religious technology reappeared in 1784 with the case of Weihui, a prefecture in He'nan that remained rainless after the rest of the province had been rained on during the eighth month. The emperor sent officials to clarify by investigation why this place had repeatedly suffered from droughts. He told them to procure an "established Muslim prayermaker for rain," and have him ride via the relay service to He'nan province where he was to "reverently offer prayers in the hope that this will swiftly spread about a sweet fertilization."[62] These two cases contrast with earlier moralism, and were part of a trend in the Qianlong reign toward a morally empty ritualism.

Qianlong's successor Jiaqing only once became explicitly concerned with the question of localization. This was in 1817, near the end of his reign. Late in the summer of that year he decreed to the Grand Council:[63]

> Fertilization from rain has been deficient this year throughout Zhili, but the areas under the jurisdiction of Shuntian [around the Capital] have been the most severely affected. . . . We have now especially composed *Some Words on Our Hope for Rain and Reflections upon Our Transgressions to Recount Our Anxious Concern.* Let it be issued to [Governor-general] Fang Shouchou, Provincial Treasurer Yao Zutong, Provincial Judge Changbi, and the various intendants and prefects for them to read. Each of them ought to examine himself with his hand on his heart.
>
> Heretofore the pattern-principle of [human] affect and [Heavenly] response has been unfailing time and again. If the said provincial officials had managed affairs diligently and in a completely public-spirited manner, all cooperating with each other, there would not have been a case such as this in which every neighboring province has a rich harvest, and only in this province is there drought as a portent of warning.[64] The wheat harvest has already proved deficient. If the great fields are not sown broadcast in good time, there will be no supply of food for the humble folk.

He ordered them to take practical measures, such as destroying locust larvae, and observed that "Whenever a locality suffers from the disaster of dearth, worthless people harbor thoughts of taking advantage of this occasion to fan confusion," a prospect that required preventive measures. He concluded that it was to be hoped that diligent fulfilment of duty by everyone might "regain the [kindly] intentions of Heaven," but that if they continued to neglect the people's livelihood and disregard his instructions, "good conscience would be destroyed" and Heaven's help prove unattainable.

By the beginning of the winter he had found a different explanation that exonerated the provincial officials:[65]

> The quality of the harvest in the metropolitan area and the other provinces is of the acutest relevance to the people's livelihood. That across the width of the four seas [that is, in China] there can be *immense disparities between harvests,* and that rainfall and sunshine are not alike, is because the pattern-principle of affect and response between human activities and the weather from Heaven is assuredly one that is manifestly unfailing. Whenever one sees provincial officials putting government in good order, and the people's customs being of a good and pure nature, again and again the sunshine and the rain are seasonally appropriate, and the harvests full. But if it so happens that the officials are greedy and corrupt, and the temper of the people

abrasive, then perverse matter–energy–vitality will form itself into portents, which is enough to cause disasters. If one reflects and examines, this can be substantiated in case after case.

In the summer of this year the area near the Capital suffered from drought. After repeated prayers had been offered, there were still no copious rains. We gave this matter anxious thought from dawn till dusk, but were unable to determine the reason. Subsequently, in the seventh and eight months, the serious *treason* of Haikang and Qingyao came to light, while Xiao Zhen's greedy and filthy pursuit of his own personal interests, which had given him an evil reputation, was destroyed by being discovered. All of these have been judged and punished. *In the ninth month there were repeated downpours of sweet enrichment.* The entire area around the Capital has had excellent moistening.

The explanation for this is that Haikang and Qingyao were using the descendants of the Imperial House to liaise with rebels, and that Xiao Zhen was using his position as an official in charge of morals to throw the legal framework into disorder. Both of these were cases of the major destruction of the constant pattern [of good government]. It may perhaps have been on this account that the Azure Above sent warnings. Now that subversion has been extirpated and harmonious sweetness been forthwith summoned down, one has a deep insight into the pattern-principle of affect and response between humankind and Heaven. Should we not all be warned and affrighted?!

Weather that had earlier seemed a rebuke to the established order could be dexterously spin-doctored to serve as a proof of its legitimacy.

The localized character of moral-meteorological effects vanishes as a major theme after this time, though there were brief reappearances.

It may be asked to what extent the emperors of the middle Qing period *believed* in the meteorological religion described here. In the case of the Yongzheng emperor at least[66] extended affirmations of his convictions are to be found scattered through the *Sacred Instructions* in various contexts. They are not confined to the chapters on showing respect for Heaven. Thus they occur in decrees on 'sage-like virtue', 'loving the people', 'giving instruction to officials', 'extending the avenues of communication [to the emperor]', 'being cautious about punishments', 'emphasizing farming and sericulture', 'consolidating customs', 'tax exemptions and relief', and so on. Certain comments hint at the depth of the emperor's concern with the weather. "In the middle of the night," he says, "We repeatedly get up to look out at the appearance of the clouds, so as to divine fine weather or rainfall."[67] In the first year of his reign he ordered several hundred people awaiting trial to be released, and observed afterwards that "in not more than three or four days there were heavy falls of welcome rain," adding that "no one says that this was a contingent conjuncture of events, or that it happened as the result of accident."[68]

Underlying this was his doctrine of universal intersensitivity:[69]

The emptiness that is before our faces is indeed August Heaven. That upon which we walk, and whose soil we shovel, is indeed the Great Earth. Just as for a human being's body of seven [Chinese] feet, if one pulls on a single tiny hair, then the whole frame will feel pain and irritation, how can a person placed between Heaven and Earth give rise to a single thought, or effect a single action, without Heaven and Earth being in mutual contact with him or her, just as breath passes in and out of us?

He wanted local officials to engage every year in ritual plowing, as he did, "so they know how hard husbandry is, and understand the bitter lot of farmers."[70] When the minor miracle occurred of rice *regrowing* shoots after being cut, that was because local officials and people had touched the sensibilities of Heaven.[71] Everything was sensitive to everything else. Yet, often enough, obvious connections were not made. The customs of Fujian were notoriously violent,[72] yet no mention was made of this in 1726 when the province had excessive rains and rice prices soared.[73]

Virtue was, on exceptional occasions, rewarded. In 1729, the emperor decreed:[74]

We have also received a memorial from the governor-general, governor, provincial treasurer, and provincial judge of Guangdong, in which they state that the rains this year have been well distributed, that the various kinds of grain are coming smoothly to maturity, and that they calculate that the price of rice throughout the province has come down from eight *qian* [tenths of an ounce of silver] to five or six *qian* per picul, which is something that happens rarely in the province. We were delighted at this news. *This has come about because the people of the province concerned have heart–minds that are pure, good, loyal, and stripped of any levity.* This has caused Heaven Above to send down Its help, bestowing rich crops. For the year 1730 Shandong [discussed earlier in the decree] and Guangdong are to be excused 400,000 ounces of silver of land and capitation tax to reward the goodness of the local officials and people.

Imperial brownie-points. This section of the decree is also interesting in being one of the few in which moral meteorology was applied to south China with its less variable climate, typhoons apart.

The brownie-point approach could bring its difficulties. In 1729 the emperor noted how the able rule of Tian Wenjing in He'nan province had for a number of years been attended by excellent harvests. Now, per contra, there had been a bad one. Concerned not to cast doubt on the qualities of one of his most capable officials, the best the emperor could do was to comment, "Now, Our excusing the people the payment of the principal tax on account of the dearth is to be taken in the sense of providing relief for the poor and showing of pity for those in difficulties." He felt obliged to sidestep as best he could the evident ideological trap.

The majority of the decrees in the *Sacred Instructions* are in fact practical. Thus seawalls should be rebuilt in stone so as to prevent any further worries.[75] So what determined why, on any particular occasion, the emperor responded in the language of meteorological religion or in the language of straightforward administrative response?

The same event could evoke *both* responses on different occasions. On 5 and 6 September 1724 a typhoon smashed the seawalls in a number of places along the coast of southern Jiangsu and northern Zhejiang. On 1 October[76] the emperor issued the decree translated earlier, suggesting that the sufferers might have been in some measure responsible for their own misfortune, because of their moral defects. Ten days later[77] he noted that he had already ordered relief in a secret decree, as the matter was urgent.[78] A further twenty-seven days later, on 6 November,[79] he promulgated an unideological decree on this event, followed by another the day after. The sequence seems surprising, but the contents of the first of these last two documents confirm that there had indeed been earlier decrees of a practical nature:[80]

> The fields and cottages of the common people have been inundated. Our thoughts are with them in the keenest compassion. *We have already issued decrees* to the local officials of Jiangsu and Zhejiang *to undertake relief measures* as a matter of urgency, and to comfort them, so that those smitten by disaster do not become displaced persons. If the breached seawalls are not quickly repaired, it is to be feared that the salt water will enter the inland waterways, which will make difficulties for farming. You governors-general and governors ought to inspect the damage in each place, estimate the cost of the labor and material for the dikes, mobilize the principal tax funds,[81] and quickly set the work in motion so that the coastal people who have lost their lands can survive these difficulties with food supplied by the daily wages from this task.

The decree issued the following day provided for the importation of rice from other provinces at official expense.[82] It is clear from the first of these two documents that the compendium does not always have the complete set of official responses available, since the decrees to local officials referred to are not included in the *Sacred Instructions*. The seemingly odd sequence—moralizing first, help afterwards—was thus not necessarily what actually happened. But the basic point is that both responses could exist in parallel, and on occasion in different documents, with respect to one and the same event.

Moral-meteorological language was most commonly resorted to on two sorts of occasion, of rather different natures. The first was a shortage of rain, since drought seems to have been felt to be Heaven's distinctive way of showing Its displeasure, and rainfall the distinctive mark of Its response to sincerity. The second was when there was no easy direct way of sanctioning undesirable attitudes and behavior, especially if this behavior was diffuse and collective, hence elusive.

Examples of the first type are too numerous to be worth listing, but a somewhat curious instance may be found combined with the second type in a decree of 22 July 1730, where the unhappy consequences of badly targeted imperial praying and an immodest collective psychological attitude are offered as complementary possibilities for the causes of flooding:[83]

> We have heard that in Jiangsu and Zhejiang the rains have been somewhat heavy, and that the grain in the fields has been inundated to a disastrous degree. We have bent Our thoughts to deducing the cause for this, and it has occurred to Us that as spring moved into summer this year the fertilization by rain in the Capital did not take place in the proper season. We offered prayers for the metropolitan area, and Our anxious solicitude reached out to the areas of Jiangsu and Zhejiang. Once the Capital had received rain Our heart–mind concentrated on requests on behalf of *Jiangsu and Zhejiang, causing the situation where the south has had a large quantity of precipitation.* We were not informed of this, but were still apprehensive that the rain there was but little. . . . Now, when you officials are aware of a certain degree of flooding or drought you must immediately submit a memorial to Us about it, precisely for this reason. The south had already had extensive rains at a time when Our heart–mind was still continuing to pray for rain there. Might it have been that it was this attitude of mind of Ours that caused Heaven Above to bestow *an excessive quantity of rain,* and Zhejiang province to have places that were flooded?

The power of imperial prayer was not to be underestimated. He then however switched to a second hypothesis, that excessive rain was well known as a rebuke from Heaven for arrogance, and Zhejiang had been doing perhaps too well in the imperial examinations lately. Perhaps the people there were getting above themselves? He did not adjudicate between these possibilities.

The second especial use of moral meteorology was to put corrective pressure on a psychological attitude that the emperor felt to be undesirable. An example may be found in a decree of 1732. Yongzheng starts by observing that "The ancients used to say that harmonious matter–energy–vitality caused good fortune whereas perverse matter–energy–vitality caused untoward events. This is the ultimate pattern-principle of mutual influences between Heaven and humankind." He then comes to the specific problem, quite transparently exploiting the meteorological leverage once the actual problem had in fact passed:[84]

In summer last year and in spring this year there was drought at the Capital. Slight earthquakes still continued. . . . We have concentrated Our thoughts on examining the bannermen. In one or two matters *there seems to be matter–energy–vitality that has been repressed and is not comfortable, so in upward fashion causing Heaven to be angry.* We cannot be lenient with Ourselves, and each of the many concerned ought likewise to reflect upon himself.

When armed force was used against the Zunghars,[85] generals and soldiers from the Eight Banners were sent on distant duty to an area outside the empire. Their fathers and mothers, wives and children, either looked at each other in grief within their families or else thought that the Court had no compassion for its servicemen. Do they not realize that, as regards this unavoidable undertaking, the Zunghar bandit-barbarians are cunning and cruel, . . . that they molest the Mongols who have become our feudatories, and cast eyes on our northwestern frontiers? . . . In no way are We fighting [unreasonably] to the bitter end or prolonging hostilities in the desire to expand Our territory, exhausting Our soldiers in the Gobi and the wastelands. . . .

The men of Our eight Manchu banners have constantly in the past had heart–minds that were loyal and public-spirited, and a heroic and daring matter–energy–vitality. When your grandfathers and fathers followed the imperial founder in through the frontier passes, they all considered the sacrifice of their lives to be glorious, and death of old age beneath the window to be shameful. You now enjoy peace and have long become habituated to banquets and taking your ease, and merely on account of a few years of campaigning have given vent to grief and resentment. . . . Even [your] fathers and mothers, wives and children, ought to be conscious of great public obligation, suppress personal and selfish feelings, setting their minds on what is far-reaching and of major importance. Then will single-minded sincerity in loyalty to the ruler and repayment of favors to the dynasty–state certainly receive the regard of Heaven Above, and Its silent granting of good fortune and assistance.

It should be recalled that in 1731, the previous year, the imperial forces under Fudan had been severely defeated by the Zunghars.[86] It is not surprising that banner morale was low. The second part of the decree continues in the same vein to inveigh against the financial malpractices and extortions of the bannermen's leaders. It is thus likely that the supernatural was felt to be a useful weapon in combatting deeply rooted bad attitudes as well as abuses that may have related to the power-struggle between the Yongzheng emperor and three of the banner leaders.[87]

In formulating a provisional assessment we have to balance an evident opportunism in the use of moral meteorology on the part of the emperor with the acknowledgment that it would not have been a useful weapon in his armory of political tactics had it not been able to appeal to a stratum of real belief both in the elite and in the populace. It is also hard to imagine that, with at least with a part of his mind, Yongzheng did not also give some credence to it. His officials were aware of his fascination with auspicious portents, and served him up a steady diet of reports of multiheaded stalks of corn,[88] lucky mushrooms,[89] sightings of 'phoenixes'—one of them allegedly seen by a thousand people,[90] and 'unicorns', the last one of which came complete with its own portrait.[91]

He was also aware that they were aware, and so he remained generally skeptical of these reports. A Shandong 'unicorn' was rejected because the northern weather had been too bad for it to be credible, and because he had had to use the army in the northwest.[92] An 'auspicious' piece of silk woven directly by the silkworms themselves—or so it was said, the emperor remaining doubtful—was dismissed with the remark that the occasional favorable omen like this was not enough to protect people from hunger.[93] The only omen that mattered for him, he declared of the unicorn with the portrait, was the well-being of the people, caused by the quality of the polity attracting the harmonious accord of Heaven. One suspects he enjoyed the ideological luxury both of having these omens and then—with ostentatious virtue—rejecting most of them.

The fascination is palpable in his reaction to a report in 1727 that the Yellow River had flowed clear. This was an omen he accepted, though stressing both that it owed much to the help of his late imperial father, and that it must have been collectively merited.[94] A stele was set up with an inscription on it to commemorate the event, every detail being listed:[95]

[Various officials] have memorialized that, following the breaking up of the ice, *the Yellow River ran clear* from Fugu county in Shaanxi province, passing through Shanxi, He'nan, and Shandong provinces to Taoyuan in Jiangnan, being limpidly translucent. It was first observed in Shaanxi and Shanxi on 30 December 1726 (*yichou*),[96] and continued until 3 February, 1727 (*gengzi*).[97] All in all it lasted thirty-six days. In He'nan and Shandong it first appeared on 31 December 1726 and lasted until 31 January in the following year, a total of thirty-one days [*sic*]. In Danxian in Shandong it was likewise clear from 1 January to 8 January,[98] and on 9 January it was so lucid that one could see the bottom. On the twelfth day of this same month, however, it gradually returned to its old [muddy] condition. This was fourteen days [*sic*] in all. In Jiangnan it began on 7 January[99] and lasted until 14 January, seven days in all. The general conclusion is that *the clarity came from above* [i.e., upstream] and moved down, and that *the return to its old former condition came from below* [i.e., downstream] and moved upwards. This was the pattern in time and space.

The emperor's own comment on this flattering phenomenon (especially because the movement of the clear area 'from above' suggested his own primacy in the matter) was, after ordering the promotion of the officials concerned by one rank, as follows:

> Now, once Heaven has produced rainwater, the matter–energy–vitality of Heaven and Earth flows through it. The Yellow River is moreover designated the ancestor of the four great rivers, and corresponds to the Milky Way above. For its clear and peaceful flow to constitute an auspicious portent, a cooperative reaction to the harmony of Heaven must come from somewhere. The *Scripture of Songs* says: "King Wen ascends and descends [in Heaven], assisting at the left and the right hand of God."[100] What this says is that King Wen and Heaven shared the same virtue, and that his sons and grandsons received good fortune from him. *Our Late Imperial Father has accompanied the magical efficacy of Heaven in being manifest on high. His affectionate concern and guidance are deep and substantial.* We have received this auspicious omen with awe.

Decoded, the message is simple: the Yongzheng emperor, still haunted by the accusation that he was a usurper, was seizing on this unusual behavior by the Yellow River to prove his legitimacy by maintaining that his late father, the Kangxi emperor, was showing his approval from the other world. We are back with opportunism, but—as I have said already—Yongzheng must have believed that many people would be persuaded by this tortuous nonsense. Without an audience that can be convinced, there is no sense in making such pronouncements. Indeed there is a risk of mockery.

His real thoughts on the matter remain a mystery.[101]

The Bell of Poesy

Poems are dangerous sources for the historian. They are written—for the most part—to arouse the emotions rather than to convey information. The only immediate political, legal, or organizational purpose they serve, when they serve it, is that of persuasion. In other words, they can be propaganda. They are also imaginative creations, even when written in explicit response to particular real events, as many Chinese poems of the late-imperial period were. But in the present context these arguments can be turned round. If many of the poems in *The Bell of Poesy* were written to persuade, the attitude they embodied toward nature must have been felt by the writer to be persuasive to his readers. That they were chosen by Zhang Yingchang for his anthology also argues in favor of their being in some measure representative. What is significant is that they show remarkably diverse attitudes toward nature and the environment.

More than a few Chinese were allured by the romance of large-scale development. An example is given by some lines written by Zhang Yongquan after he had seen flooding from the Yellow River, then on a southern course, impair the functioning of the Grand Canal.[102] He was aware—as were all Chinese concerned with water control—of the way in which trouble was caused by the Yellow River blocking the natural exit of the Huai River (discussed in chapter 6), and the need for constant hydraulic work to enable the imperial grain-transport to cross the Yellow River safely near this point:

> This year we build the dike secure,
> Yet next year it has fallen breached.
> This bank has just been made complete,
> When that bank's falling down in ruins.
> Each year a million cash disbursed,
> Like filling the sea — to little use.

He then asserted that the reason the Yellow River did not flow peacefully was because the ditches and channels, used for irrigation and draining, were "silted up." He followed this wrongheaded hydrology with a paean of praise to regional self-sufficiency in ancient times. The reference to the Qin altering the 'boundary strips' comes from a tradition that this was part of the new empire's destruction of the so-called 'well-field system' of land tenure that allegedly reigned in antiquity.

> When, long ago, they founded states,
> Their lands produced the food they ate.

One never heard of Yan and Zhao
Relying on taxes *from the South!*

When Qin redrew the boundary strips,[103]
The once rich land fell derelict.
Earth's storehouse yielded no more crops.
Hard to maintain were millet stocks,

And scarce was grain in the Northwest
Because hydraulics were neglected,
The Southeast awash with rushing waters,
A menace caused by the selfsame fault.

Putting bad hydrology and dubious history together, Zhang was inspired by an engineer's vision of a fully irrigated, bureaucratically controlled, north China plain, producing enough food to make the imperial grain-transport system unnecessary, and presenting an obstacle to mounted brigands with its dense network of water channels:

Forth comes the Yellow River, out from its Dragon Gates,
And endless, endless, are the miles it flows with furious waves!
Now — to train its traveling surges not to overspill their course,
The current of the waters must be weakened near their source.
Once split apart in branch streams along the upper reaches,
The distributaries that lie downstream will then spread out in peace.

. . .

In the lands of the north, and the central plains,
Officials will govern the adits and the drains.
For the pattern of conduits they'll lay down the rules,
So the land's watered as water runs through!

. . .

We'll use water's *own* requirements to fix the varying depths,
And follow the topography for the straight parts and the bends.

And when ten years have run their course, we shall proclaim the fruits:
How all along the River there are multiple branch loops,[104]
Such that the terrain there has been turned to fertile acres,
And every last locality has abundant ears of grain.

The supplies of tax rice sent to Court, and cargoes, too, of millet,
Will have cut the costs of shipping grain down close to nonexistent.
So dense a channel network will make riding horses difficult,
And malfeasance won't be simple for brigands or for miscreants.

Here, before the modern age, is the passion for misconceived grandiose projects that today continues to inspire constructions such as the Three Gorges Dam.

Counterbalancing this was an awareness of the disastrous results of some of the development that had actually been put into effect. Zhou Xipu, who was for a time the magistrate of a county in Gansu (on the border between the Northwest and the Far West) during the eighteenth century, gave a description of the salinization of farmlands opened in an inappropriately arid region. He begins with a prose preface:[105]

I was deputed to inspect a disaster caused by hail at Xiangshan, . . . and to reach it I had to traverse a terrain of fractured rocks. I was unable here to exchange my money for grain and fodder. On asking the reason for this I learned that the people who live in these mountains eat *peng* grasses. They showed me three kinds, namely 'sandy *peng*', 'watery *peng*', and 'flossy *peng*'. The way in which they were eaten was to boil them first in water, take them out, strain them, and then put them into water again and cook them into a broth. . . . When there was a surplus, they were dried in readiness against the winter. . . . I ordered some to be boiled and served to me. Their taste was rank, and so astringent that I could hardly get them down my throat; yet the frontier people eat them from one year's end to the next. . . . It is my view that raining hailstones is a common disruption of Heaven, but that humans eating grasses is a strangely desperate circumstance.

One kind resembles a feathery screen, and has a head that droops.
So it is known as the 'sandy *peng*'. It grows on the edge of dunes.
Another kind is a sprout, and is found in swamp-like dips.
It bears the name of 'watery *peng*'. It's a type of artemisia.
There is besides a 'flossy *peng*', with many-lobed, blue-green, leaves.
As summer commences it gently puts forth a fleecy white appearance.

The young wives in their dark blue dress melted the last of the ice,
And, to give me something to choose from, boiled together all three kinds.
Bitter and rank is the soil's vitality. Their taste was bitter and harsh. . . .
I asked the people, For how many years had they been eating these plants?
How was it they did not break the clods, in the fields, for the five main
　　crops?

"From the River at Ningxia — they said — our access is blocked off.
These lofty crags with knife-like edges are far beyond its course. . . .

It has so happened that humans here dwell mingled with mountain
　　goblins,

Dried up in heat, a-shiver in frosts. The Dark Force vitality's lost,
With many-fold mists, close-pressing dews, and the Bright Force likewise
  closed off. . . .

Springtime we know, but not the twigs upon the willows swelling.
To refresh the dryness of our lungs, we long for unsullied wells.
After the snowmelt, mud in the sands is all we have to drink,
Yet, in times gone by, our forebears here managed both plowing and
  ridging.
Countless hoes chopped at the hills. — *Then the hills' arteries changed,*
And, as the first sprouts opened, so too did saline flakes.
They tell tales as well of mosquito larvae, huge as caterpillars' pupae.
The state-given hoes were tossed away, as trifles no longer useful.

We sons, and grandsons, eat *peng* grass now, in order to stay alive.
One meal a day, for people are many, but grasses in short supply.
In hunger, our guts turn round and round, like silk-reeling wheels a-
  crying.

Not long ago we sought pasturage on the west hills' lower slopes
To graze our sheep and cattle there, and good returns were hoped for:
Meat for consumption and oxen's hides to serve as clothing cover,
And surplus resources for famine congee boiled up out of the husks.
Once the disastrous hailstones struck, in a moment this turned to nothing.
The bones of dead stock, in the pastures, are a glut of rotting flesh,[106]
And the old crows and the loathsome kites fatten upon the wreckage. . . .

We have had to look to the *peng* grass again. Alas! It is all that is left.
Heaven we thank, and bow to It twice, beseeching Its compassion.
Yet all we should want for a regular crop would be *Polygonatum*.[107] . . .

This piece was written, as was often the case, to appeal to the local officials for
their pity and help. We have therefore to consider the possibility that the
tragedy was drawn too starkly. The justice and mercy of Heaven, or
Heaven–Nature, are also implicitly questioned—once again a not infrequent
feature of such poems, and a contrast to the pieties of imperial decrees and
most philosophers. While it describes only one small tessera in the vast mosaic
of pressures on the environment in late-imperial China, it is clear that the
author understood that what had happened was the consequence of what we
today see as inappropriate development.

Optimists, as always, maintained that further resources could be found, given
the effort. Here are some lines written on Dunhuang in the far Northwest by
Xu Naigu, who served as its magistrate some time around 1831:[108]

Dunhuang commandery, under the Han, once had its hour of glory.
And commoners who migrated there forgot their past exhaustion.

They selected metallic ores to offer, as tribute, to the Treasury;
The region was rich, but those it supported declined and lost their energy.
The mountains are void, and the veins of ore, today, are totally empty,
Like pelts that now are all that's left of what once were living leopards.

Off to the west the farmland stretches, grown desiccated and waste.
What means are there of chasing after the farmers who have absconded?
The soils are covered over with sand, and heavily salinated,
Where the sprouts that sprout today will tomorrow have no tomorrow.

I wanted to excavate down deep, to the springs where the waters flow.
The masses gathered in response, their spades upon their shoulders.
Nothing is wrong with these riches of Earth still being further sought for.
It may be that in the empty bag remain some last resources.

It is not clear from the poem how successful he was in reaching ground water.
The theme of endless resources was, though, something of a cliché. Thus Xie
Yuanhuai's verses on the salt monopoly contain the lines:[109]

> The treasuries of Heaven and Earth, now *they* are rich indeed.
> How could it ever be that *they* were appropriated completely?

The opposite view was also powerfully expressed. Concern with the depletion of mineral resources, notably metal ores and coal, surfaces in many
poems. Some dramatic verses by Yao Chun on the dangers of coal mining,
including the deaths of miners from subsidence, and from drowning when
underground waters were released by mistake, note that "after long excavations, the bones of the mountains are empty."[110] A representative statement of
this theme of resource exhaustion may be found in some lines by Wang Taiyue
in a long and famous poem on the official Yunnan copper mines (in the
Southwest), probably written around the middle or late eighteenth century:[111]

> They gather at dawn, by the mouth of the shaft,
> Standing there naked, their garments stripped off,
> Lamps strapped to their heads in carrying-baskets
> To probe in the darkness the fathomless bottom.
>
> Grazed by the stones' teeth, by sharp-edged projections,
> They grope down sheer cliffs, and across mossy patches.
> The hot months torment them with harsh epidemics,
> When poisonous vapors mix with hot gases.

In the chill of the winter, their bodies will tremble,
Hands blister with chilblains. Their feet will be chapped.
Down the mine, for this reason, they huddle together,
But hardly revive, their life's force at a standstill. . . .

As the underground ways to the ores pierce new depths,
They fear, as they cut and they drill, to hit marble.
What took, in times past, a mere morning's efforts
Now needs ten days of their work to be garnered.

The wood they must have is no longer available,
The forests shaved bald, like a convict's head. Blighted.
Only now they regret — felling day after day
Has left them no way to provide for their firewood.

Problems therefore threaten them, in mining and in smelting,
And risks that soon they may provoke the bureaucrats' ill temper.

Resource exhaustion led to increased danger. Wang went on:

Worse still, as the mountainsides' bellies were hollowed,
The subsidence this caused demolished the rocks,
And smashed them to fragments, like scattering pebbles,
As, in one death, a few hundreds perished. . . .

Their spirits were heard, in the depths of night, wailing,
As their ghost-fires were flickering, chilled in the gale.
How worthless, alas! is a human's existence,
Its price even less than a chicken's or piglet's.

Even multitudinous riches, spread about them on all sides,
Could still not give a guarantee that even one survived.
So fecund are the hills and seas, it seems to deserve no answer
To ask, Do they only flourish when they're guarded by disasters?

— The Dark Force and Bright Force contract, then dilate,
Like busy artificers, shaping and shaping.
Yet, if used up entirely, and restraint not observed,
Human effort's enough to void Heaven and Earth.

Or as Wei Yuan prosaically observed, "When the population is full up and the land is full up, these two causes are enough to engender catastrophe."[112] Zhu Zhang, writing, either late in the seventeenth or early in the eighteenth century, about a boatload of refugees from Hu'nan (in the Center), with their dogs and fowls on board, moving into Sichuan (in the West), likewise bluntly remarked that "the land of Sichuan is full, and the fertile spots are on the point of all being occupied."[113]

The most horrific moments of the environmental crisis of late-traditional China were summed up in gruesome fashion by Qiao Xu in one of his doggerel poems on famine:[114]

We gather and gather the elms off the fells,
   Till the elm bark is stripped away utterly,
Gather, gather the grass by the cemetery entrance,
   Till the grass roots are not fit for sucking.

To get two pints of grain costs a thousand cash, copper.
   A hundred in cash buys us two pints of husks.
We sell clothes, and buy husks, to nourish our offspring,
   Sell our ox to buy grain to feed father and mother.

But without an ox, how can we plow?
   How keep ourselves warm without clothes?
— *Don't ask us how we will plow,*
   Nor how we'll keep from the cold.

Though the season is neither the winter nor fall,
Our family can, all of us, still stay indoors.

   One can't bear to butcher a man still alive.
   But there's no need to cover the dead, even naked.
   From my carrying-bag I extract a sharp knife,
   And, from his carcass, carve me a steak.

With withered stalks warming the stoneware container,
   He is boiled till half done, but likewise half raw.
He lacks blubber, is scrawny, his body is wasting,
   Needing seasoning with herbs picked beside the hill torrent.

   If those still alive can thereby be rescued,
   The dead should be pleased when they are ingested.

These two they were once a mother and child,
   But with one mouthful taken and just one cry uttered,
Before that cry's echo had died into silence,
   Their limbs all grew chilled, then shriveled up suddenly.

   And when, moments later, their life-force was cut,
   They also served to bloat the other folks' guts.

Elm bark was a common famine food, and one poem on the theme of hungry people stripping it says: "Once the elms are finished we shall come to die together beneath the trees."[115] The tone of Qiao's verses just quoted seems savage to Western ears, but the Chinese view may often have been, as Qin Ying put it in a poem on the victims of a flood in Zhedong, that:[116]

> For the dead it's finished,
> To live on is bitterer still.

Those who took up their brushes to record such events were only too aware that, as Shen Shuben said,[117] even as he excused Heaven for a disaster by blaming it on "the numbers," that is, on fate:

> Writing this verse is no more than a dirge,
> As, even though freezing, an insect still chirps.

In real life, as opposed to philosophy, Heaven–Nature was not so easily loved.

The question of Heaven–Nature's justice was often raised, but then, almost equally often, shied away from to avoid the all-too-apparent negative answer. The commonest view of human relationships with nature was, however, more confident and assertive. By preparation, determination, and skill, human beings could handle most of the problems with which nature confronted them. Thus, in a poem on drought, Liu Shufang declared:[118]

> Disharmony, and disasters, do not need to cause us hurt,
> Since human efforts *always may* contest what Heaven determines.

Zhu Jinzong spoke from this point of view in his poem advocating the sinking of wells:[119]

> It is Earth gives birth to the sources of underground springs and of wells,
> But the water in a reservoir pond always owes its existence to Heaven,
> And Heaven, from time to time, puts a temporary end to Its rains.
> The arteries deep in the Earth are not so subject to change.

> Since the water drawn up from a spring can never be used to exhaustion
> The Drought Demon then, so it follows, has no longer the power to
>   torture us.

Wang Ruyang's poem on the creative skills of fashionable flower-growers declared that "Their ingenuity surpasses the Transforming Force, and inverts the workmanship of Heaven."[120] In Li Zhan's poem on the merchant Li Benzhong, who spent the years 1805 to 1840 organizing, at his own expense, the leveling and clearing of forty-eight dangerous passages on the towing-ways to Guizhou in Hubei and Kuizhou in Sichuan, there are these heroic lines:[121]

By heating them with fiery coals he split stubborn rocks to clasts,
Flame-lights flashing downward to the River God's palaces,
While the ringing of his hammers filled the precipice-walled valleys.
. . .
He cleared away the hazards on both routes, step by step.
Once the human will is fixed, then Heaven has no effect!

A similar attitude was explicitly taken towards deities such as the River God Feng Yi. In Qin Lian's poem on the rebuilding of the seawall along the southern coast of Jiangsu, he celebrates it as[122]

Rising upward for a hundred feet, toward the towers of Heaven!
So if Feng Yi is angry, he will still not dare transgress,
And uncanny beasts beneath the sea will, in terror, hold their breath.

There was a sense that human life was a constant struggle against an ever-changing environmental situation. The inherent instability of hydraulic systems was the most striking example of this. As Lu Kuixun observed in a poem on building dikes: "That which men can maintain is that which Heaven destroys."[123] Zhang Jingcang, writing with immediate reference to central Jiangxi (in the inland Southeast), but speaking generally, expressed the same idea:[124]

A hundred-year-old levee will be broken open and gapped,
With water flooding through it over swathes of fertile land.
Although our forebears built it, if it is not kept maintained.
Even spending a peck of gold a day will not see it long unchanged.

The hope was often expressed that the benefits of each new project would, as Zhang put it, "be imperishable throughout a thousand falls," but it was for the most part understood both that a major cause of this instability was human intervention, and that *a battle against nature* was often practically unavoidable. Zhou Kai described an all-too-familiar situation in his stanzas on "The Dikes of the Yangzi":[125]

Down from the ancient land of Shu descends the Mighty River,
Headlong along a hundred leagues, till it reaches Jiangling city,
An oceanic flood, that roars like boulders crashing —
How could this be something that a single dike can vanquish?

The local peasants in defense of homesteads and of farms
Willingly commit themselves to contending with the waters:
From west to east, and east to west, along both river margins,
Dikes are constructed, strand by strand, the way they reweave hawsers.

Higher, and each day higher, mounts the current of the River,
And each day higher, too, the levees' masses ascend.
Below one, spread about, one surveys the countless villages,
While *above* one, like a roof-beam, the water flows suspended.

The language of warfare. The idea that the Chinese did not strive for an active mastery of nature, which has been advocated by some scholars since at least the time of Max Weber,[126] is—as a simple generalization—ludicrously wrong.

On the other hand there was unquestionably an adaptationist tendency as well, often interwoven with that of direct confrontation. This combination may be seen in Chen Wenshu's verses on flood control:[127]

> Controlling inundations is like controlling sickness:
>   One must trace the etiology right back to its beginnings.
> Controlling inundations is like managing the military:
>   One must take consideration of every possibility.
>
> . . .
>
> But those who are in charge of handling floods today
>   Are not in any mood to see their task this way,
> Unwilling to adapt themselves to patterns in terrain,
>   Or to adjust their interventions to the timing of the rains.

Faults that he much deplored.

Yuan Mei's radical proposal to abandon altogether the tight control of the lower reaches of the south-course Yellow River was an example of an adaptationist attitude taken toward a specific problem.[128] The 'cancers' in the fourth line probably refer to problems discussed in chapter 6: the accumulation of alluvium that choked the sea mouth, and the deposits of sediment dropped by the Yellow River across the confluence where the Huai joined it, so partially blocking the weaker river.

> My personal conception of the Yellow River at present
> Is that its current's position-power is swelled by the Huai and Bian
> Simply to support the grain going north by canal-borne transport,
> Which constricts the River so tightly it makes it swell with cancers.
>
> As humans have seized possession of what is the River's territory,
> Is it not that men and River have become each other's enemy?
>
> The body of the River's bed keeps on piling up incessantly
> So defenses, counterbalancing, must become more comprehensive.
> The disaster of one morning, should our vigilance be weakened,
> May easily cause us anguish, even to the year's end.

So why not open breaches up in the conducting channels
And magnanimously abandon one, or even more, departments,[129]
Then redirect the funds used now to pay for River management
To subsidize the cost of resettling the inhabitants?

We should see to the establishment of some transshipment
    granaries,
And move the tribute grain along in a smaller size of craft
Which draw so little water that they skim the shallows with ease,
And our conflict with the River Huai from that moment on will
    cease.
The Great River, on a roadway vast, will hasten to the sea,
And its inundation-sickness immediately be healed.

The idea behind these proposals, which Yuan admitted would "startle most people," seems to have been to restore an extensive flood plain on which the course of the lower Yellow River could move about easily, constantly abandoning channels in which deposited sediment had accumulated and occupying new ones. It showed a profound intuitive sense of the natural condition of the Yellow River, but it is inconceivable that an already overpopulated Chinese society could have left so much fertile alluvium forever untouched by agriculture.

A minor, but beautiful, voice was that advocating complete absorption into the environment. Huang Heqing's poem, "The Girl who Gathered the Flowers of the Leek" is an evocation of this deep-ecological world-view:[130]

When the leek-flower-gathering girl meets the elderly neighborhood
    women,
With pitying faces they ask her, how, so young, she can bear such suffering?
"Wouldn't you rather sit by the window and set the loom a-singing?
Why prefer you the untilled lands where the wastes are bright with dew,
Where the sun burns and the wind blows, giving such unspeakable pain?
Large leek-flowers are everywhere, and one collects *them* ungrudgingly,
But, the livelong day, the finer flowers will not fill a trug of bamboo.

If you sell to well-to-do households, the price is as cheap as dirt,
And the girls of these well-to-do households will disdain to give you good
    day. . . .
When *we* do an exchange with you, *our* rice is mixed with husks.
When, ever, did the flowers of leeks fill up a hungry stomach?
We sigh for you most deeply, and the way you do yourself hurt."

She thanks the aged women and says: "My fate is of no concern.
Human life is like a flower, blown about and never still.

The slime-mold, exuding its trail of muck, does as ordained at its birth,
And the skirt a weaver wears herself will not cover over her shins,
Nor the plowman's rice, though roughly hulled, reach to his steamer's brim.
Wealth, and social position, have no hold over my heart.
The insects on smartweed are used to pain, and delight to be as they are."
Bowing her head, she goes off to her picking. The day is already dark.

More commonplace is the conventional enlightenment evoked in Shao Changheng's poem on a fisherman, adrift in the fall rains among the white-tufted reeds. He sits there unconcerned as to whether or not he catches a fish. Or, if he catches one, whether or not he sells it.[131]

The educated Chinese mind looked on a landscape with a mixture of attitudes. In first place was an awareness of Heaven and the gods contriving its events, and of the dragons and spirits concealed in its depths. This could be a half-symbolic rather than a fully literal belief. Second was a historical consciousness of the human past that had both been shaped by a particular place and contributed to its shaping. The third was a combination of natural history—relating to the flora, fauna, and geography—with metaphysical notions, often laden with moralizing implications, relating to its physical and geomantic structure and the forces running in its veins. In the final section of this chapter, I sketch something of these representational and interpretative filters.

Some writers saw the landscape as a body. Thus Zhu Shifa wrote a poem for a friend of his who was a county magistrate, advocating the prohibition of quarrying, presumably in the county under his friend's jurisdiction:[132]

When a quarry's opened up
The chisels' and the axes' clamor startles the Heavens above.

. . .

On the south side of the county a mountain range extends
That could be made to furnish your whole area's protection,
But villains, hunting profit, give the bureaucrats their bribes,
Who, once they've been corrupted, do whatever is required.

Every morning they're extracting rock,
Deep in the wilderness.
Every evening they're hacking rock,
Climbing a cliff face.

There are aspects of this process not unlike a *human's* body
Being cut, till gouging's penetrated deep inside its vital organs,
And the life force that sustains it is everywhere exhausted.

> Masons dangle hanging
>   From ropes of monstrous length,
> Lashing bastinados
>   On the rock walls of a precipice.

The injunctions of Our Emperor have repeatedly adjured:
The mountains' magic must be kept — forever — free of hurt.
While these magic powers rest unharmed, your folk are in good spirits,
And Your Honor's virtue rises up as lofty as their pinnacles.

Even the rocks are thought of as alive, and their well-being, assured by the ability to function properly and a healthy constitution, is linked with the well-being of the human population. This sense of an almost magical ecology can also be found in a poem by Tang Sunhua, who flourished at the end of the seventeenth century, on three outstanding officials, all of whom had been governors of the poet's own province of Jiangsu. Yuzhou in the first line is, roughly speaking, what is now He'nan province. It begins:[133]

> The ancient heartland of Yuzhou holds the central region fast.
> The Two Forces come together here. Its vitality's in harmony.
> Here, too, the Yellow River, and Luo, once presented mystic charts.
> The powers enfolded in its peaks are uncanny, and their magic
> Has engendered multitudes of men of superior moral caliber.

The 'mystic charts' were reputed to have been supernaturally revealed in archaic times. The 'Yellow River chart' was a numerological diagram that is thought to have inspired the Eight Trigrams, components of the structure of the universe and of divination. It allegedly emerged from the Yellow River on the back of a 'dragon-horse'. The 'Luo Text', also numerological, came out from the Luo, carried, so it was said, by a turtle, and was reputed to have inspired the nine divisions of the 'Great Plan' in the *Scripture of History*.

This venerable hocus-pocus about the environment is used to explain the high qualities of character possessed by the first of these governors, Tang Bin, who was born in the Yuzhou region. This was what prompted him to clear up the superstitious miasma that reigned there. Tang Sunhua describes it as if it was as much as a physical contamination as a religious one, spread through the cult of deities not sanctioned by the state as orthodox:

> Once into oblivion he'd swept temples vowed to filthy worship,
> The demons living in the hills were rejected as monstrosities.
> The aethers of orthodox belief cleansed the fogs of foul perversion.
> True faith put public duty back among the folk in honor.

The health of a countryside required spiritual good housekeeping.

Just as landscape shaped history, so history also left its impress on the landscape. A poem by Fang Huan from a set of nine that he wrote on China's ancient frontiers contains these lines on what is today part of northern Hebei province:[134]

> Shanggu, now millennia ago, was where the Han camp was pitched.
> In the defiles, where warriors' banners waved, the aethers of killing linger.

In this view landscape and humankind intermingled through the mediation of matter–energy–vitality.

The world was also full of daemonic beings. —I again use the old alternative form 'daemonic' to characterize supernatural beings that were not necessarily evil, even if some of them were on occasion hostile. The poem by Wang Lianying on a break in the Yellow River dike conveys something of the multitude of these powers and their violence. It also suggests that to some extent they might have been seen as having a symbolic character. How far Wang fully believed in Feng Yi, the River God, or He Bo, the Earl of the Yellow River, or Feng Long, the Lord of the Thunderbolts, is difficult to say; but the references to them, echoing ancient literature, must have been powerfully evocative. After all, until near the end of the fifth century BCE, He Bo had received the annual sacrifice of a human being. The place where Wang lived when young, and referred to here, was Yongcheng in He'nan province. The words are put into the mouth of an old man, remembering:[135]

> "A whirlwind in the seventh month swept across three hundred miles.
> Waves turned somersaults, sandbanks shifted, scattered clouds raced
>   along.
> In the midst of the darkness the Yellow River rose equal to Heaven's
>   height.
> I was fourteen then. 1664. This was the day that dawned:

> From in front of my bed came the roaring of the Yellow River's
>   turbulence.
> The lightnings flashed, huge fish plunged forward, and winds bellowed
>   loud in fury.
> Feng Yi rattled rolls on his timpani, and He Bo was venting his anger,
> As Feng Long, Lord of the Thunderbolts, split open the gaping caverns.

> First I beheld the whirlpools, as they drowned the shrubs and the
>   grasses,
> Then slowly perceived Inundation Dragons, who had come to the
>   Ninefold Marshes.

> Sunk deep were mounts Huanyuan and Song, in the Water Treasury's
> depths. . . .
> As the Candle Dragon blazed his light, the dragon hosts ascended."

The hidden forces in the world made visible.

In another poem on floods and storms in the lake Tai region, by Zhu Heling, the same kind of images are summoned up.[136] The 'tide wall' refers to the tidal bore in the nearby estuary of the Qiantang River.

> The typhoon burst forth in its fury. The spirits and shades felt afflicted.
> The Fire Dragon javelined his flames, coercing the tide wall upriver.
> As the sands swirled and boulders tumbled, the boundary banks had
> vanished,
> While houses were tossed and trees uprooted by the writhing water-
> dragons.

Often the poets were puzzled. Why had Heaven permitted, or caused, a particular natural disaster? There was always an underlying assumption that the punishment was deserved, and that Heaven was basically well-disposed towards humankind; but they questioned the appropriateness of Its having picked out this place, rather than that, for chastisement. Two lines of a poem by Zhu Zhu encapsulate the respectful but interrogatory tone:[137]

> If it's the will of Heaven's Lord to give amnesty to this region,
> Why doesn't He lash the dragons, force floods' withdrawal, and fashion us
> fertile fields?

Zhang Yanyi put the problem in a different perspective.[138] The term translated 'God' is the 'Lord' in Chinese, implying 'Lord Above':

> God's heart has ever, from times long past, been loving and compassionate.
> So why does He let the countless beings be thwarted or driven
> backward?
> Evil forces work at cross-purposes, and harmful aethers abound.
> Time and again we're in dire straits. Too many to be recounted.

Theodicy was also a problem for the Chinese. Chen Weisong, in a poem on an earthquake that had caused numerous deaths, spoke of the deities Tianwu and Zifeng "competing to see which of them could be foremost in sporting with human beings".[139]

The picture is complicated further by the need to take into account an element of quasi-scientific analysis. The poem "A Record of Uncanny Events" by Yang Xiheng shows the poet trying to develop a hydrological theory of earthquakes in the context of various traditional metaphysical suppositions.[140]

His candidate for the troublemaker was Xuanming, a water-god connected with the winter season. The Ai River mentioned later has proved impossible to identify unambiguously. A plausible candidate is the hot spring rising on Mount Ai, or Milfoil Mountain, in Shandong, which is appropriately surrounded by other mountains. An alternative, but less likely, option is the Aigun River in Manchuria, another name for the Amur.

> The Earth is the Consort of Heaven,
>   Her Way should be peaceful and trustworthy,
>   Yet in this place, all of a sudden,
> She trembled, and never stopped trembling.
>   As when a typhoon has struck — abrupt! —
>   But then, like the Thunder Chariot, rumbling.
>
>   . . .

I learned from investigation, looking through the histories and annals,
These changes are 'manifestations of the Five Phases of Matter'.
Only superannuated pedants who hold fast to scriptural texts
Could think in such over-simple terms, and only in polemics.

No! The present era of our world is ruled by a Sage Intelligence,
So how from any *moral* cause could such disasters emanate?
Seeing this pattern-principle as being hard to penetrate,
I weighed the question carefully, when seated at my leisure.

> *On each of these occasions, after there's been a quake,*
> *The omens have pointed to Xuanming as the responsible deity.*

Around the axis of the earth there circles Dark Force energy,
Though always eager to emerge, barred from rapidly ascending.

When there's a minor earthquake, a little water percolates,
While a major one resembles a basin overturning.
When tested out repeatedly, *this theory never fails.*
I've long believed there's evidence to give it a sound basis.

Thus the streams on Milfoil Mountain run sunk in a depression,
And east-to-west and north-to-south crisscross in all directions.
When accumulated runoff has caused an inundation,
Its position-power strives to make the mountain translocate.

The theories that an observer holds can influence his or her perceptions—whether of stars or rock strata by the sea shore—and his or her feelings about these perceptions. We may imagine that it was the same for Yang. Seismic events were the stirrings of a hidden god.

Many interesting aspects have been left untouched by the preceding remarks. To give but one illustration, there are a number of poems in *The Bell of Poesy* that deal with animals. The predation of tigers on rural populations is documented,[141] and so is the spectacle of villagers setting off on a tiger hunt, gongs sounding, unarmed, but determined to overwhelm the predator by force of numbers.[142] There are lines on the peasants' use of biological controls: wild duck must not be netted, for example, whatever damage they do to crops, because they keep the locust larvae in check.[143] There are mentions of whales peacefully spouting in the Yangzi estuary, in the remembered golden past of the Yuan dynasty.[144] There are evocations of the affection felt by peasants for their plow oxen.[145] Also a tribute to 'Black Servant' the cat, who was as resolute as a tiger with rats, but a perfect gentleman—unlike the average pet—when it came to sharing his food with a famished neighborhood moggy.[146] All of these are strands to be woven into the tapestry of environmental history.

Animals could also be used as symbolic vehicles for moralizing, as in some lines by Zhu Yizun, that reveal a somber view of both the natural and human worlds:[147]

The insect that lifts its wings to soar
Will soon be trapped in the spider's orb.
The white deer, roaming through the wood,
Will be fortunate not to be shot and cooked.

The wise man is cautious what quarry to choose,
Lest greed make him victim of his own pursuit.
Above, unattainable, wings the wild goose.
May the bowman not himself be pierced by the shaft that he has loosed?

Most of the poems on nature in *The Bell of Poesy* evoke the struggle against nature, as well as of that of humanity against human predators. Life had its happy moments, but they were hard won. An example is Xu Rong's long and evocative farmer's calendar on Leizhou in the Far South.[148] The uncommonest attitude of all, though it also exists, is that nature does not care about humankind one way or the other. Here are a few such lines from Chen Yin's "Singing my Feelings."[149] They stand out from a poem of otherwise conventional melancholy. 'Frith', by the way, is a useful north Welsh word meaning the gentler lower slopes of a mountain immediately above the floor of a valley. 'Kine' are cattle.

By the forest's margins the small birds fly,
On the frith of the hills lie the kine and sheep.
All things in themselves delight.
Man alone has many griefs.

🐘 *Concluding Remarks*

It is clear from the foregoing pages that by late-imperial times, and in some cases much earlier, the Chinese environment was under significant 'pressure' from human economic activities. But was this 'pressure' any more intense than that on Europe's environment around 1800? Or was it even conceivably *less* intense, as Ken Pomeranz, focusing above all on England and the Netherlands, has suggested?[1] If an answer could be given to this question it would help us to make an intelligent guess as to at least one aspect of the role played by environmental factors in Europe's pioneering breakthrough into early modern economic growth, and in China's failure to do so independently.

The inverted commas are needed around 'pressure'. As it stands, the notion embodied in this word is fuzzy. More exactly, it is metaphorical. To be useful, it has to be made operational in terms of a range of questions that at least in theory can have precise answers. These questions also have to be thought of as being addressed to a range of different areas or regions, with possibly different answers. As we have seen, Zunhua was very different from Jiaxing, for example, or from Guizhou. And the same was presumably true in premodern Western Europe for, say, Sicily, the Netherlands, and Norway.

In these final pages I offer some speculations as to how this comparative issue might be approached. But it needs to be stressed that they are exactly that—speculations, points for future discussion—not theses nailed to a church door.

Let us begin by setting aside for the time being two of the important aspects of an ecological system, namely, the complex *interconnectedness* of almost everything with almost everything else, and *nonlinear* phenomena where the proportions that hold between an input and an output do not stay constant regardless of the size of the input. Let us also begin by considering only *renewable* resources. For premodern economies this sector is the predominant one by far. We will bring in nonrenewables later, as they need slightly different handling.

Let us, then, with these restrictions, just look at how one might approach a single simple question: Over a short cycle of a year or several years, how much recurring environmental 'trouble' does an economy create for itself, given a particular technology at a particular time, and a particular region in which it operates? 'Trouble' is defined as the cost, over the short to medium run, of *restoring* the productivity of the local environment to the same level of economically useful output for a given input of work and investment as it had at the start of this period. For purposes of making comparisons possible between two or more systems we then convert this to the *proportion* $p_{renewables}$ of total product that would be required *if* full restoration is to be effected, which in practice it may not be.

Formally we could write this as

$$p_{renewables,\,(t)} = \frac{R_{renewables,\,(t)}}{O_{(t)}} \tag{1},$$

where $R_{renewables,\,(t)}$ is the cost of restoring the renewable resources used in the period of time t, and $O_{(t)}$ is the value of output in the same period.

To illustrate: if you cut down trees for fuel or construction, what does it take to regrow what has been removed? (Talking in this way of course bypasses issues such as the difficulty of restoring habitats, of crucial importance for activities like hunting and so on. Note also that it may exclude some of the effects of cutting for clearance only.—For clearance the relevant restoration cost per cycle may be that of *keeping* the fields clear.) If you construct an irrigation system, how much does it take each year, or each cycle of years, to clear out the accumulated sediments in the ditches and repair the dikes, so that it functions at least as well as it did during the year or cycle before? How much does it take each year to restore the fertility of soils depleted by growing crops—with an output equivalent to that from the original soil depth and acreage, and level of application of fertilizer? And so on.

Often this restoration process will be partially neglected; in other cases the cost will be too high to be paid, even if the participants would like to be able to do so. 'Nonsustainability' occurs when the cost of restoration plus subsistence exceeds total income. In symbols,

$$R_{renewables\,(t)} + S_{(t)} > O_{(t)}$$

Insuperable technical problems are deemed to have indefinitely large costs. Thus the early-imperial Zheng-Bai irrigation system in what is today Shaanxi quite soon became impossible to restore in full, because of hydrological problems seemingly insoluble with premodern techniques, though great efforts were intermittently made.[2] Some late-imperial attempts to introduce irrigated farming into the arid Northwest likewise rapidly became impractical because what little ground water there was was drawn to the surface by capillary action and there evaporated leaving heavily salinated and unfarmable soil, the former farmers on occasion being reduced to stock rearing or even gathering wild plants to survive. (See pages 439–40 above.)

Many side-effects of the exploitation of nonrenewable resources can also be included in the required process of restoration. If the use of coal is partially substituted for that of wood for fuel, as happened both in early modern Western Europe and in a few parts of late-imperial China,[3] preventing, or at least so far as possible compensating for, the ill-health to miners and members of the population inhaling air laden with coal particles is a far from trivial cost. People, considered as producers, are also part of the productive system that may need a form of 'restoration'.

'Pressure' is thus calculated in terms of the cost of the *human* component of a restoration that is complete in economic terms, supplementing as needed any restoration effected by *nature*. (An interesting example of the combination is fallowing. All that is needed for the fallow field to recover is human abstention, but this may in fact have a cost in income foregone.) 'Relative pressure' is the proportion that this represents (or would, if effected, represent) of an economy's total income. These measures apply over a span of time short enough to avoid the need to consider technological changes. At a given level of income per person, relative pressure is expressed by p, an approximate indicator of the relative ease of sustainability, but it seems likely that a rich society would find it easier to pay a given percentage of its income for restoration than a poor one. The *rate of change* of relative pressure per cycle is also a significant, and different, measurable quantity. It may obviously be decreasing, stable, or increasing, depending on circumstances. Over one discrete interval of time this rate of change can be measured as

$$\frac{p_{(t)} - p_{(t-1)}}{p_{(t-1)}}$$

The basic definition just given is not without its ambiguities. For example, if a peasant grows legumes for part of the year in his rice fields these will help to replace lost organically accessible nitrogen but also yield an edible crop. Is this a part of the cost of remedying the environmental trouble caused by rice-growing? Clearly in some sense, yes, because it is close to unavoidable in an intensive system not practicing fallowing, but also, equally obviously, not entirely. For the moment we note the presence of this sort of problem but leave it to one side as not affecting the core issue.

The mental model that lies behind this way of looking at the issue can be illustrated from Zhou Xipu's account of the salinization of farmlands in a part of Gansu that was too arid to be suited to the Chinese style of cultivation.[4] This was cited in the preceding chapter, but is worth repeating in briefer form as the context is quite different:

> I was deputed to inspect a disaster caused by hail at Xiangshan. . . . To reach it I had to traverse a terrain of fractured rocks. I was unable here to exchange my money for grain and fodder. On asking the reason for this, I learned that the people who live in these mountains eat *peng* grasses. . . . I ordered some to be boiled and served to me. Their taste was rank, and so astringent that I could hardly get them down my throat; yet the frontier people eat them from one year's end to the next. . . . Humans eating grasses is a strangely desperate circumstance.

He followed these observations with a poem, some of whose lines show what had happened. In the words he put into the mouth of one of the locals:

> "After the snowmelt, mud in the sands is all that we have to drink,
> Yet, in times gone by, our forebears here managed both plowing and
>   ridging.
> Countless hoes chopped at the hill. — Then the hills' arteries changed,
> And, as the first sprouts opened, so too did saline flakes.
> They tell tales as well of mosquito larvae, huge as caterpillars' pupae.
> The state-given hoes were tossed away, as trifles no longer useful.
>
> We sons, and grandsons, eat *peng* grass now, in order to stay alive.
> One meal a day, for people are many, but grasses in short supply.
> In hunger our guts turn round and round, like silk-reeling wheels a-crying.
>
> Not long ago we sought pasturage on the west hills' lower slopes
> To graze our sheep and cattle there, and good returns were hoped for:
> Meat for consumption and oxen's hides to serve as clothing cover,
> And surplus resources for famine congee boiled up out of the husks.
> Once the disastrous hailstones struck, in a moment this turned to nothing.
> . . .
>
> We have had to look to the *peng* grass again. Alas! It is all that is left."[5]

Excessive pressure on the local environment, and its consequent reaction, which turned out to be too violent for any affordable restoration, forced them to try a shift in technology, to a more nearly exclusive reliance on stock rearing;

but climatic unpredictability in turn made this at least temporarily unviable. This is an extreme example. Normally the problems made themselves felt much more slowly, and were mostly manageable at the cost of a payable proportion of income.

Nonrenewable resources, such as iron, copper, and coal, cannot—by definition—be looked at in the same way. The cyclical restoration of the actual productive capacity (including its potential) at the start of a cycle is not possible, even in theory. Assuming a constant level of technology, the pressure on the environment can be approximated over a short period of time by the rate of change per cycle in the cost needed to produce the same output as in the preceding cycle. This can of course be zero, or, if new and easily used supplies are found, even negative. The commonest pattern in the absence of technical change, namely increasing cost over time, was summed up in a few lines from Wang Taiyue's poem on the eighteenth-century copper mines in Yunnan, also quoted earlier but translated here with a slightly different emphasis:[6]

> Deeper each day, and deeper down, they sink galleries to the ore,
> Concerned, even as they chip it free, they'll hit rock too hard to break.
> The output that, in earlier times, took *no more than a morning*
> Requires *now* nothing less from them than *ten full days of labor*.

In a rough-and-ready way we can regard any increase per cycle in the cost needed to extract a nonrenewable resource in the same quantity at the same functional quality (energy output in the case of coal, for example) as in the previous cycle as a measure of the 'trouble' being caused by the 'resistance', so to speak, of the environment to human economic activities. We represent this *change* in actual (not relative) cost by $C_{nonrenewables}$ or C_n for short.

Aggregating the *restoration* cost per cycle of the system of *renewable* resources (farming, forestry, livestock rearing, and so on) with the sum of the *increases* (or decreases) in costs for a comparable mix of output per cycle for all the various types of *nonrenewable* resources (such as metal ores, coal, and quarried stone), and determining the *percentage* this represents of total output per cycle, gives a first approximation to a single quantitative measure of the 'environmental pressure' exerted by an economy during a short period of time in which other factors, like technology and organizational structure, can be taken as given. 'Short' may in fact be usefully defined in terms of the absence of significant change in these other components of the productive system. The measure thus created for comparison between systems may be called 'the aggregate pressure proportion' to distinguish it from the various other types that are mostly amounts of money or else rates of change and, in all cases, either partial and/or nonrelative in character.

Equation (1) (on p. 455) now becomes

$$P_{r+n,\,(t)} = \frac{(R_{r,\,(t)} + C_{n,\,(t)})}{O_{(t)}} \tag{2}.$$

The formulae defining the point of nonsustainability and the rate of change in environmental resistance can now be rewritten in the obvious way to give the complete measure. Some of the implications of this way of thinking need to be sketched in briefly.

Increasing population, with no change in technology, will normally require additional costs in the form of accessing new resources and the use of additional 'natural services' (such as the neutralization or removal of increased wastes), if resource usage *per person* is to stay at least constant. Besides land, water, and fuels, these include resources underpinning the additional investment needed in tools, overheads, education, and training. Under some circumstances additional labor power can make a disproportionately large positive economic contribution, and in such circumstances this can decrease the proportionate pressure on the environment. There is no reason to think that this applied to late-imperial China.

For a given spatial unit, *cross-boundary movements* of goods and people (in other words, cross-boundary trade and migration) will also usually tend to alter the proportionate pressure on the environment.[7] But here there is no necessary single pattern.

Once the short run is left behind, *changes in the technology* being used can either reduce or increase the proportionate pressure on the environment. Innovation can make the use of a resource more efficient, as with the production of more usable work per unit of energy input for example, which will cause total product to rise to a greater degree than input of the resource, so reducing the pressure proportion, other things being equal. New techniques can also open up whole new areas of the environment to exploitation that were previously all but untouched. Deep-sea fishing and whaling are examples. This will, other things being equal, also tend to reduce the pressure proportion, at least initially, because it is characteristic of new resource areas to yield relatively high returns for effort expended. Today, the restoration of the earlier productivity of either of these activities, which have come to be based on seriously depleted renewable resources, would require above all the loss of income from *abstention* in order to allow natural forces to promote recovery to the extent possible.

In dealing with nonrenewables the inclination to think in terms of the long-term running down of stocks of a given size has to be resisted. Market demand may over a long period, step by step, make it commercially viable to extract a resource of a quality so low that previously it was not commercially viable to do so. A stock of a resource is thus not a simple given physical quantity, approached asymptotically as the rate of successful exploration for fresh reserves falls toward zero. Technological change can both alter the relationship between the quality of a resource and its commercial viability, and also make an old resource economically irrelevant by finding a much cheaper functional substitute. These are some of the reasons the measures suggested here are virtually 'point' measures, to be determined for short periods of time as far as possible from information relating to these short periods.

The real-life problem is, however, that other things are often far from equal. And also that the middle or even long run can be needed to establish what the costs actually are. Technical progress often brings a larger absolute proportion of an environment into contact of some sort with productive processes, and, especially in modern times, often conjures up side-effects that are hard to detect at first, as well as important new nonlinear effects that require time for the crucial thresholds of a causal input to be crossed. This increasingly complicates proper measurement and the calculation of the impact of causal linkages. In economic terms, the bottom line is that it becomes harder and harder to know what the *real* price is that is being paid.

And, we might also add, by *whom*, and *where*, and *when?*

Bearing these analytical ideas in mind, what then can be suggested, in a preliminary way, about China and Europe, given that the quantitative research needed for a quantitative assessment in these terms has not so far been attempted?

In summary, provided we restrict ourselves to the agricultural cores of the two economies, it seems likely that in late-imperial China the pressure on the environment as defined above was much higher than in Western Europe overall around the end of the eighteenth century, and fairly probably somewhat higher than in England and the Netherlands, though less unarguably so.

Why?

First, some general considerations. The extent of unavoidable *hydraulic maintenance work*, including not only irrigation with its multiple channels, barrages, reservoirs, and sluices, but also the huge flood-protection levees and seawalls, plus canals for transport, was much greater in China than in the West. (There was only a limited amount of irrigated farming in most of early-modern Europe, notably in a few special parts of Italy and Spain, and only a handful of modest-length canals, originally mainly in Italy and France, then later also in England. The Netherlands, a large part of which was built on water control, was a special and important exception.) Water-control systems almost always have maintenance costs that seem high in absolute terms, though evaluating these costs as a proportion of output, which is the crucial analytical step, is work still to be undertaken. Qualitative evidence, a fraction of which has been presented here in chapter 6 on water, suggests that this expenditure could on occasion hurt seriously, even if the extreme cases that tended to be preferentially recorded are not a sure guide to average values.

Likewise most Chinese farming was more, or much more, *intensive* in its use of land than most European farming. Maintaining the 'power of the soil', as it was called, was a constant concern of lowland farmers, and the collection, creation, and application of fertilizers and river mud virtually universal. Lowland seed-to-yield ratios, at least for rice (barely grown in Europe) and under different climatic conditions, were however probably several times higher than for wheat in Europe, as shown in chapter 7 on Jiaxing. If this was so, it would have made an investment of time and effort in restoration that was at least several times greater no more than comparable in relative terms.

For upland farmers, many of whom practiced a shifting cultivation of a lesser intensity, the equivalent cost was that of every few years gaining access to, and preparing, new land for temporary use that would replace the exhausted land that was for the time being no longer viable. Over the short term, such land approximated to a nonrenewable resource, and the probable relative cost is for the moment once again opaque. My guess though is that, outside this shifting upland agriculture, the relative burden (system restoration as a proportion of income) was heavier in China, even though it is important to note the present opacity of the proportions of income used for it. This is above all because, both in the irrigated and in the rainfall-farming parts of China, there was virtually *no fallowing*, and this meant that human effort had to do here a part of what nature did in the West in restoring vitality to the fields.

Do such geographically aggregated answers make any environmental sense at all? Can we, one way or another, meaningfully 'add', say, the lower Yangzi valley to Gansu to Yunnan, or the Netherlands to Sicily to Norway? My inclination on this last point is to be skeptical, and to suspect that environmental comparisons are best limited to comparing approximate like with like. Thus the Netherlands and the lower Yangzi valley might, perhaps, be at least considered as reasonable candidates, but not the bigger aggregates. This is yet another caveat.

Second, such general probabilities aside, is there any contemporary comparative evidence?

Surprisingly, the answer is 'yes'. The Jesuit missionaries who were based in Beijing through the greater part of the seventeenth and eighteenth centuries were personally familiar both with at least some parts of China and at least some parts of Europe. Collectively they were present in the capital for a substantial length of time, though their most important observations on the environment relate mainly to the middle of the eighteenth century. They also had a good knowledge of the Chinese language, and of Chinese history and culture.

How reliable was Jesuit information?

The notes and essays on China they published in Europe were intended to advertise the Jesuit cause, and probably, by implication, the success of their culturally adaptive methods in gaining access to the political power ruling the most populous nation in the world. In many respects they also unabashedly used China as a model whose thrift, diligence, propriety, lack of conspicuous consumption and waste, relatively humane treatment of servants, and general good sense could be used to criticize Europe, besides being a source of useful practical techniques and interestingly different ways of seeing the world.

For example, they held up to admiration the avoidance by Chinese artists of the infatuation of European painters with the nude, just as they found becomingly modest the limited presence of the better class of Chinese women in public places and their seclusion in the home. In a more radical mode, they contrasted favorably the appointments made to high office in China on the basis of merit (the imperial family excepted) with the practice of doing so on the basis of heredity in most of Europe. Some comments were by implication revolutionary. Noting how large a proportion of Chinese peasants owned their own lands, one author felt prompted to write that "the great misery of our France is that the farmers do not own any of their lands in freehold, while those to whom these guarantee a certain revenue think of nothing but their enjoyment of it."[8] As self-conscious aesthetic iconoclasts, they also extolled the Chinese art of the 'natural' garden in contrast to the stiff symmetries of its continental European counterpart, brought to life, so far as it was, by statues rather than by the subtle use, Chinese style, of flowing water. The fathers, as one might expect, thus had certain ideological orientations, but their views were by no means always conservative or conventional, and certainly not mechanically predictable.

In reading what they wrote about what they saw, it is necessary to be aware of these inclinations, but there does not seem to have been any particular ideological prejudice distorting their views on the economy and the environment. At most, the prospect from Beijing may have at times inclined them to mistake imperial intentions for Chinese social reality, or local for general practices. Thus one memoir asserts that:[9]

> The Chinese have an excellent understanding of the economic policing of the woods. One may not cut anything down without planting [a replacement]; and in the capital the owner does not have the right to decide what is to be done with the old construction timbers of a house. If they can still

serve for building they must continue to be used for this purpose. There is no option to cut them into pieces.

The first part of the second sentence, that in general no wood could be cut without planting its replacement, was certainly not universally the case.

It is thus probably safer to be guided by the general impressions that emerge from their pages rather than take particular assertions as necessarily dependable. Suitable caution observed, though, scattered passages in the sixteen volumes of their *Mémoires concernant les Chinois* (to give the collection its usual abbreviated title) are an almost unique source for our quest for comparisons. The juxtaposition of China with Europe was explicitly part of the project from the beginning.[10] China, opined the notice at the start of the first volume, "has not been less rich than we are, nor less happy, but maybe even more so."[11] That introducing the fifth volume likewise noted that readers would wish "to judge Europe by China, and China by Europe."[12]

The most important single text is probably an excursus embedded in a memoir on interest rates in the Chinese economy:[13]

In France, the land rests every other year. In many places there are vast tracts under fallow. The countryside is broken up by woods, meadows, vineyards, parks, and lodges for recreation,[14] etc. Nothing of this sort could exist here. . . . Even if the land is exhausted by thirty-five centuries of harvests, it has to provide a new one every year to supply the urgent needs of a countless population. This excess of population . . . here increases the need for farming to the point of forcing the Chinese to do without the help of cattle and herds, because the land that would feed these latter is needed for feeding people. This is a great inconvenience as it deprives them of fertilizer for the soil, meat for the table, horses, and almost all the advantages that can be gained from herds. Were it not for the mountains and the wetlands China would be absolutely without the benefit of woods, and without venison and game. Let us add that it is the strength and application of human beings that meets all the costs of farming [here]. More labor and more people are needed to obtain the same quantity of grain than are required elsewhere. The total quantity surpasses the imagination, but even so it is no more than sufficient. . . .

Pigs and poultry provide almost the only meat in China, which means that the consumption per person is not great. . . . We have said 'almost' because we are talking of the empire as a whole. . . . Some districts are, as it happens, better provided for in this respect, and support numerous herds. In some, people even plow with cattle, water buffalo, or horses. Overall, though, proportionate to the size [of the two countries] there are at least ten head of cattle in France for every one in China. . . .

Let us note, nonetheless, that every year Manchuria provides Beijing and the entire metropolitan province with a prodigious amount of cattle, sheep, and deer. . . . And that necessity . . . has taught our Chinese to take advantage of many vegetables, herbs, plants, and roots that grow of their own accord in the countryside and need no cultivation. . . . Although not much land can be used for orchards or gardens, the enclosures around houses, the avenues of the villages, and the hillslopes provide a supplement. The majority of the provinces would be at the level of the best-endowed provinces of France but for the fact that the extreme size of the population swings the balance in France's favor.

The author (who is not identified) goes on to note that the Chinese wore fewer clothes than the French when the weather was warm enough to permit this. Timber, too, he says, "would be more than sufficient but for its heavy consumption for the building of the boats with which the major rivers are covered." And, "as regards heating, the coal mines and skill in the handling of fire make the shortage of wood in places far removed from the mountains almost impossible to detect."[15]

The burden of maintenance, which lies at the heart of the definition of pressure on the environment proposed here, is the focus of another passage, probably from the hand of another author:[16]

The Chinese are too much farmers, and too rich in experience, not to have observed that there are improvements, renovations, and, as they put it, remoldings of the terrain that change its nature, giving it an unreal and artificial fertility from which great benefits can be derived. In their view, however, first, these sorts of undertakings only succeed to the degree that they are appropriate to the nature of the soil and the lie of the land; second, they are extremely expensive, requiring much careful attention; and, third, no matter how well they have been done, and whatever the success with which they have been crowned, they should never be expected to last for ever. Sooner or later everything has to be started over again. The foregoing does not refer [only] to [projects like] the draining dry of marshes. It applies to nothing other than lands, fields, gardens, and orchards that are [already] under full cultivation.

Population pressure and population size are both recurrent themes in the *Mémoires*. Another writer, probably different from the preceding, says:[17]

A hundred and twenty years of peace have so increased the population that the pressing need for survival has caused the plow to enter all those lands where there has been the slightest hope of a harvest. Hard work has outdone itself and gone so far as to create amphitheaters of harvests on the slopes of the mountains, to convert sunken marshes into rice-paddies, and to gather harvests even from the midst of the waters by means of inventions of which Europe has as yet not an inkling.

In some areas the density of the use of the land was astonishing. Thus a Chinese official is cited with approval as saying:[18]

"Has anyone who has traveled in certain parts of Zhejiang province failed to observe that the ditches and canals yield a harvest of very useful aquatic roots? That the edges of all the roads are planted with various trees? That the hedges have been made of wild bushes whose small fruits have many uses? That the paths through the fields are trimmed, as far as the eye can see, with cotton shrubs, maize, or other useful plants, depending on the time of year? That villages that look from afar off like thickets are well protected from the spells of fierce summer heat by the fruit trees set about the houses and their enclosed yards? That the wildest hills, and the most precipitously banked rivers, have become decorative on account of the trees and bushes with which they are covered? That there are mulberry trees for silkworms everywhere they can grow? And that those marshes that no one knows how to drain dry provide the choicest reeds, and large-leafed plants that are extremely helpful. . . . Why is our France not in a similar condition, at least in her more beautiful provinces?"

The final rhetorical question of course implies that this was not the case in France.

Of course such an intense usage of the land was not found everywhere in China. A letter from a missionary just arrived from Europe to a colleague about his journey from Canton to Beijing contains the remark, with strong overtones of disillusionment, that on the way north to the border of Jiangxi province, "in a country that people would like to think the equal of France, I saw neither forests, not fountains, nor gardens, nor fruit trees, nor vines, nor lodges for recreation."[19] When he had crossed over into Jiangxi, he said,[20]

I saw arid mountains reaching to the horizon, and, lower down, almost no cultivable land. I expressed my surprise at this to my interpreter and to the official who was leading us. I remarked that, judging from the accounts I had read of China, I had envisaged that it resembled a vast garden cultivated with much art and devotion; that the mountains were cut into terraces and laden with rice or wheat from the base to the summit, constituting one of its finest ornaments and its principal wealth.

His Chinese companions laughed at him when he said this and assured him there were mountains like these in most parts of China. The prospects that he had anticipated only appeared at the start of the section of the Grand Canal going north from the Yangzi River:[21]

> Here we are at last in the good part of China. This is the land that lies between the two great rivers, the Yangzi and the Yellow. It is fifty leagues from south to north, and there is no question of mountains. This landscape is as level as a mirror all the way to the horizon. The soil has several crops a year, and all the fields have them *at the same time,* a striking sight that we do not have in Europe, where some portion of the land is always resting under fallow. For this reason all the land is exceptionally densely populated.

These large numbers had their uses. According to the writer cited earlier on the increase in the population:[22]

> The public works that exist in the form of dikes, levees, canals, locks, and jetties along the banks of the Yellow River, the Yangzi, the Wei, etc., are so numerous, so unending, and so difficult to maintain, that they both presuppose and prove the existence of an immense population. The Europe with which we are acquainted has nothing [to show] that might shed doubt on this conception.

In a certain tension with this was the prevalence of rural underemployment emphasized by the author of the memoir on interest rates:[23]

> The large population, something so much desired elsewhere, is here a scourge, and the foremost cause of all revolutions. Whether the farmers cultivate their own lands, as most do [at least in north China], or those owned by others, they barely have enough on which to live pleasantly, even when the land responds in the optimal fashion to their care for it and hard work. This care and hard work are not enough to keep most of them busy around the whole year, especially in the southern provinces. This has caused the extension of the crafts of necessity and of painstaking toil into the countryside. As for those who farm the fields of others, they keep a larger share for themselves than do their counterparts in other countries.

The implication of this last remark seems to be that the amount produced from a family's rented lands was so low in terms of the family's needs that they had to keep a larger proportionate share if they were to survive.

Hence, too, the famous garden-style agriculture:[24]

> It may be of some use to observe that the little efforts and knacks, inventions, and discoveries, resources and combinations, that have created what

seem like miracles in gardens have here been transported on an increased scale into the countryside, and done wonders there . . . as witness manures, which have become so varied, so multiplied, so abundant, so easy to use, so effective, and so well combined.

In general, these time-consuming refinements can also be seen as part of the process of offsetting the cyclical environmental losses caused by economic production. But we have to be careful not to apply this finding too automatically. There were probable exceptions:[25]

Our France is prodigiously fertile in water plants of all species. Why does she then not profit from these gifts that Nature has lavished on her? What is the reason that this Chinese taste, which is so sensible, does not take hold among us, and does not lead us to find, as they do, a decoration for our gardens and an annual harvest that *needs no work* for our farmers?

It would seem from this that, where agriculture was concerned, early modern northwestern Europe may have exploited a more restricted *range* of possible resources than did China. If, however, we keep to the definition of pressure adopted here, a harvest like this needing little or no labor to alter a natural system would seem, because it increased total output by making use of an ecosystem that caused essentially no reactive 'trouble', probably to represent a *reduction* in the aggregate proportionate pressure on China's ecosystem.

If there was one theme that inspired the fathers to rhetoric about the Chinese handling of the environment like no other it was that the changes wrought by humans in the landscape were always in conformity with Nature:[26]

[I]f people here have drained the marshes dry, and led water into fields, carried the soil from below up to the hills above and that from the hills down to the plains, flooded some districts for a time while removing all their waters from others, even to the point that they are scorched by the sun in the dog days of summer, if they have made openings in ranges of hills to let the air circulate more immediately, or blocked up small gorges to stop torrents that cause people misery, if they have felled all the large trees on one side to allow the rays of the sun to penetrate to depths too deeply sunk [to receive them before], and broken up with [tree-lined] avenues plains that are too bare, so as to bring them shade and freshness, if extended hillsides have been shaped into amphitheaters, the better to handle harvests on them, and if valleys have been furrowed with levees and level beds, the better to handle the rivers in them, if people have dreamed up so many ways of joining together or splitting apart, forcing to rise or to fall, to repel or to beckon, to contain or to distribute all kinds of waters, and if, finally, they have taken gardens and orchards out to the midst of [grain] harvests, pastures to the midst of forests, fields to the midst of ponds, and lines of rocks to the midst of motionless waters, with clumps of reeds along their shores, this has been only to *supplement* or to *imitate* Nature, as the men of ancient times did, and, like them, to *match* what she has done.

The verses quoted in the second half of the preceding chapter showed that this was, as a generalization, at best an overly simple view of the multifaceted late-imperial Chinese conceptions of Nature. At worst it was unwarranted romanticism. It remains evidence, though, for the exceptional extent of the transformation of the landscape, as seen through Western European eyes, but we would probably want to interpret it differently. Bearing in mind that there are always local variations and exceptions in environmental matters, the likelihood is that, in general, the late-imperial tendency to try to extend farming into places where it was inherently difficult, and sustain it there, increased the costs of restoring the original levels of productivity and hence the proportionate pressure. And the astonishment of the Jesuit observers at what they saw implies that this tendency was probably more pronounced in China than in Western Europe. And that, as one of them wrote, "since mountainous and arid areas are little suited to farming, only an extreme need would drive people to seek for harvests from them."[27]

The authors of the *Mémoires* also enthused about the widespread use of human excrement for manure, in part because its rapid removal to the farms (where it was usually matured before use) left Chinese cities cleaner than their Western counterparts at this time.[28] The demand for this material meant that "in all the quarters of Beijing, and almost all the cities in China, there are public conveniences that save the streets from the filthy habits of those who come and go, and that [the cities] are not infected by the latrines." Europe's record was less good:

> Our medicine has had to be concerned in our cities with many illnesses that are unknown in the countryside. . . . [I]t is our view that the more people study the nature of the air and its instantaneous action on our bodies, the more they will become persuaded that streets that are narrow, constricted, and bordered by extremely high houses that are almost always dirty and stinking, must change it and corrupt it. . . , and that [our rarely emptied] public conveniences, so numerous and so infected, are the means of introducing into it these germs of sickness and death. . . . Our Europeans, who have noticed that illnesses and epidemics are very rare in China . . . have not observed that the manner in which the cities are constructed must contribute much to this state of affairs.

This dovetails with another often enunciated theme, that "the population of the Empire is today so great that the pressing interest of the common need requires that people extract from the fertility of the land and the hard work of human beings all that can be extracted from them."[29]

It also fits with the later observations of the German agronomist Wilhelm Wagner in the early twentieth century that the avoidance of the exhaustion of the Chinese soil was due above all to the painstaking collection and use of waste of all kinds. Although the relative paucity of large farm animals required the use of human excrement as a manure, it was also true that:[30]

> The Chinese use the greatest care in the gathering of animal dung as much as for human. To this end the peasant goes off on the roads in the winter, or at other times in the year when he is idle, with a basket on his shoulder and a spade in his hand, and looks for manures.

In contrast to the practice in Europe, manure was also applied in China to every crop, not just to the more important ones. Although the major input was at the time of sowing, further dressings were normally applied during growth, and up to as many as four times, which Wagner seems to imply was also distinctive.[31] He regarded as revealing the observation of the earlier geographer Von Richtofen that even thirteen years of fallow had not allowed the areas in Zhejiang province laid waste and depopulated by the Taiping rebels in the mid nineteenth century to recover their productivity, and that the re-establishment of farming had been achieved in proportion to the availability of human manure from the reviving population.[32]

More generally, Wagner stressed with regard to the flood-plain lands that were, and are, the heartland of Chinese farming that preserving their fertility necessitated "the gigantic burdens of labor that are inherent in the arable land thus reclaimed and that are bestowed on it afresh every year."[33] He added to the items that have already been touched on above the important but wearisome need to rebuild the level surface of the fields each year, commonly after river mud rich in nutrients had been spread across them, because such a horizontal surface reduced the runoff during the violent summer rains, so in turn limiting the loss of topsoil, and of course also made irrigation possible where rice was grown.[34] Without water-control systems to facilitate drainage, many of the most productive parts of China would in his view revert to being "fever-ridden and uninhabitable swamps," and here and there neglect of the maintenance of drainage had actually caused this to happen.[35]

There is a need in the future for a more precise and detailed study of the facts relating to these these questions. Overall, though, the Jesuit evidence, buttressed by Wagner's later observations, makes a persuasive prima facie case that the 'pressure' of the late-imperial Chinese productive system on the natural environment, as defined above in terms of the 'aggregate pressure proportion', was significantly heavier than that at least of France around the beginning of the modern era. This can probably be extended, though with less certainty, to other parts of northwestern Europe.

Patterns of economic causation can be counterintuitive at times, but it would seem reasonable to believe something like the following, if only in a tentative way. First, when compared with the situation in early-modern Western Europe, the relative cost of environmental restoration after each cycle of production was significantly greater in late-imperial China. This was combined with the need in China *actually largely to effect* this restoration in a region where the resources relevant to traditional technology were already close to being fully exploited, and there were no new imperial overseas resources, such as some European countries possessed, and that could be drawn on like an environmental overdraft without any immediate need for full restoration. Likewise China had reached a moment in time at which the potential for further improvements within the old technology without recourse to an external modern science was virtually exhausted.[36] This complex of causes tended greatly to slow down the Chinese speed of response to the challenge of modernizing of the rural economy when it became critical in and after the later nineteenth century as the Western–Japanese political and economic challenge became ever more pressing. And, apart from special enclaves like Shanghai that were able follow with some success a partially independent path because of their access to foreign know-how and capital, the brake on the immense rural sector slowed the advance toward modernity of the economy as a whole.

Such seems to have been the uncomfortable legacy of the empirical aspects of the thrice-millennial environmental history reconstructed in these pages.

Finally, the history of values and ideas as outlined here presents a problem. A problem not just for our understanding of China's past but for environmental history generally. The religious, philosophical, literary, and historical texts surveyed and translated in the foregoing pages have been rich sources of description, insight, and even, perhaps, inspiration. But the dominant ideas and ideologies, which were often to some degree in contradiction with each other, appear to have little explanatory power in determining why what seems actually to have happened to the Chinese environment happened the way it did. Occasionally, yes. Buddhism helped to safeguard trees around monasteries. The law-enforced mystique shrouding Qing imperial tombs kept their surroundings untouched by more than minimal economic exploitation. But in general, no. There seems no case for thinking that, some details apart, the Chinese anthropogenic environment was developed and maintained in the way it was over the long run of more than three millennia because of particular characteristically Chinese beliefs or perceptions. Or, at least, not in comparison with the massive effects of the pursuit of power and profit in the arena provided by the possibilities and limitations of the Chinese natural world, and the technologies that grew from interactions with them.

So, if such a view survives further scrutiny, the question arises: Was China, among the great developed premodern civilizations of the world, unique in this? And if not, what does this imply for the realism, or otherwise, of the hope that we can escape from our present environmental difficulties by means of a transformation of consciousness?

 *Notes*

Primary sources are identified by initials in italic capitals, and may be found in the first section of the Bibliography.

Introductory Remarks

1. For a brief but deeply informed sketch of the earliest historical period see D. Keightley, "The environment of ancient China," in M. Loewe and E. Shaughnessy, eds., *The Cambridge History of Ancient China* (Cambridge University Press: Cambridge, 1999).
2. See, for example, J. Lee and Wang Feng, "Malthusian models and Chinese realities: The Chinese demographic system 1700–2000," *Population and Development Review* 25 (1) 1999; J. Lee and Wang Feng, *One Quarter of Humanity: Malthusian Mythology and Chinese Realities, 1700–2000* (Harvard University Press: Cambridge, Mass., 1999); T.-J. Liu, *et al.*, eds., *Asian Population History* (Oxford: Oxford University Press, 2001); and M. Elvin, "Blood and statistics: Reconstructing the population dynamics of late imperial China from the biographies of virtuous women in local gazetteers," in H. Zurndorfer, ed., *Chinese Women in the Imperial Past: New Perspectives* (Brill: Leiden, 1999).
3. 'Nature' is capitalized when it is considered as a cosmic entity in its own right.
4. For example, those mapped and discussed in M. Elvin, *The Pattern of the Chinese Past* (Stanford University Press: Stanford, Calif., 1973), 310–11, and in H. Dunstan, "The Late Ming epidemics: A preliminary survey," *Ch'ing-shih wen-t'i* 3.3 (1975).
5. See for example the chapters on cholera by K. M. MacPherson and by Zhang and Elvin on tuberculosis in M. Elvin and T.-J. Liu, eds., *Sediments of Time: Environment and Society in Chinese History* (Cambridge University Press: New York, 1998). C. Benedict, *Bubonic Plague in Nineteenth-Century China* (Stanford University Press: Stanford, Calif., 1996) is also an important study, with a strong environmental component, though the identification of the disease-entities in the epidemics discussed may in some cases need further testing.
6. For example, R. Grove, V. Damodaran, and S. Sangwan, eds., *Nature and the Orient: The Environmental History of South and Southeast Asia* (Oxford University Press: New Delhi, 1998).

7. On the West, see Nicolas Giudici, *La Philosophie du Mont Blanc: De l'alpinisme à l'économie immatérielle* (Grasset: Paris, 2000). There is comparison with China on 276–80. On China more broadly see Xie Qiyi, "Wudai ci-zhong-de 'shan' yixiang yanjiu" [The conceptional representation of the 'mountain' in the lyric songs of the Five Dynasties] (Master's thesis, National Taiwan Normal University, 2000), whose range is much wider than its title suggests. I am grateful to Professor Liu Ts'ui-jung for a copy of this work.

8. Quoted in Xie Qiyi, "Conceptional representation of the 'mountain,'" 68. Lines have been omitted between the first quatrain and what follows.

9. Chou Zhao'ao, ed. *Du Shaoling ji xiangzhu* [Du Fu's collected works with detailed notes] (4 vols., Wenxue guji kanxingshe: Beijing, 1955), I:2:2–3.

10. Chinese *zaohua.*

11. Giudici, *La Philosophie du Mont Blanc,* 189–91.

12. Giudici, *La Philosophie du Mont Blanc,* 249.

13. C. J. Glacken, *Traces on the Rhodian Shore: Nature and Culture in Western Thought from Ancient Times to the End of the Eighteenth Century* (University of California Press: Berkeley, Calif., 1967).

14. *Shangdi* (of which there are many translations, including 'Lord Above'), and *Tian,* 'Heaven', which could have anthropic qualities including moral judgment and communication. On hypatotheism see M. Elvin, "Was there a transcendental break-through in China?" in S. N. Eisenstadt, ed., *The Axial Age and its Diversity* (State University of New York: Albany, N.Y., 1986).

15. The *zaohua* mentioned above. See also note 10.

16. *Li.*

17. The *xiàng* expressed as the sixty-four hexagrams (*guà*) of the *Book of Changes.*

18. 'Premodern' can be defined as that existing prior to the routine incorporation of science into productive and destructive technologies.

19. See M. Elvin, D. Crook, Shen Ji, R. Jones, and J. Dearing, "The impact of clearance and irrigation on the environment in the Lake Erhai catchment from the ninth to the nineteenth century," *East Asian History* 23 (June 2002).

20. M. Elvin, *Changing Stories in the Chinese World* (Stanford University Press: Stanford, Calif., 1997).

21. M. Elvin and N. Su, "Man against the sea: Natural and anthropogenic factors in the changing morphology of Harngzhou Bay, circa 1000–1800," *Environment and History* 1.1 (Feb. 1995). Note: post-vocalic 'r' in 'Harng' shows a rising tone in tonalized pinyin.

22. Elvin, "Blood and statistics."

23. A. Leopold, *A Sand County Almanac and Sketches Here and There* (Oxford University Press: New York, 1949), vii.

24. P. Bak, *How Nature Works: The Science of Self-Organized Criticality* (Oxford University Press: Oxford, 1997).

25. The word 'logistic' comes from a type of mathematical curve. Where $N(t)$ is the number of units after a time t, and the other letters stand for constants, it has the formula $N(t) = a / [1 + b \exp(-ct)]$ where 'exp' is the exponential function. Its shape is close to that of an inclined '∫'.

26. *QSD*: Zhang Yingchang, ed., *Qing shi duo* [The Qing bell of poesy]. (Originally *Guochao shi duo,* 1869, reprinted, Xinhua shudian: Beijing, 1960), 155.

27. Qiu Guangming, *Zhongguo lidai du-liang-heng kao* [Researches on measures of length, capacity, and weight in the successive Chinese dynasties] (Kexue chubanshe: Beijing, 1992).

1 Landmarks and Time-marks

1. C. Blunden and M. Elvin, *A Cultural Atlas of China*, rev. edn (Facts on File: New York, 1998).
2. The term 'Han' is hard to define rigorously. The general sense is that of a 'mainstream' Chinese as characterized by the combination of a perceived ethnicity, the use of the Chinese language, certain key aspects of culture such as the avoidance of the levirate and cross-generation marriage, and acceptance by others as being Chinese. This identity was gradually constructed through the course of time. See Nicola Di Cosmo, *Ancient China and Its Enemies: The Rise of Nomadic Power in East Asian History* (Cambridge University Press: Cambridge, 2002), esp. 'Introduction'.
3. CE stands for 'common era', that is AD. It corresponds to the Chinese term *gongyuan* or 'common origin', and is useful as a nondenominational indicator. BCE likewise is 'before the common era'.
4. BP means 'before present'. The 'present' is commonly taken as being 1950 CE. BP will only be used here, however, where broad approximations are used.
5. J.-Q. Fang and G. Liu, "Relationship between climatic change and the nomadic southward migrations in East Asia during historical times," *Climatic Change* 22 (1992).
6. I define the 'modern era' as having begun in China around 1850, a deliberately round figure. The criterion is simply that after this time the influence of the West was an essential component in determining the broad course of events within China. The term 'early modern' as usually applied to Europe refers to a considerably earlier period, and raises conceptual difficulties. 'Early modern' in China can, however, be taken simply to mean between 1850 and the First World War.
7. For descriptions of the sale of children both during famines, and to ease the pressures on the budget of poverty-stricken families, see the poems in Zhang Yingchang, ed., *Qing shi duo* [The Qing bell of poesy] hereafter *QSD*, (originally *Guochao shi duo*, 1869, reprinted, Xinhua shudian: Beijing, 1960), 564–74.
8. *QSD*, 444.

2 Humans v. Elephants: The Three Thousand Years War

1. Wen Huanran *et al.*, *Zhongguo lishi shiqi zhiwu yu dongwu bianqian yanjiu* [Studies on changes in plants and animals in China during historical times] (Chongqing chubanshe: Chongqing, 1995). See also H. T. Chang, "On the question of the existence of elephants and the rhinoceros in northern China in historical times," *Bulletin of the Geological Society of China* 5 (1926).
2. For a picture of one of the finds of tusks at Sanxingdui, in the Shu kingdom that existed in part of Sichuan contemporaneously with the later Shang, see Liu Yang and E. Capon, *Masks of Mystery: Ancient Chinese Bronzes from Sanxingdui* (Art Gallery of New South Wales: Sydney, 2000), 47, also 23–4.
3. The stomach shells of turtles or shoulder blades of oxen on which the replies to oracular inquiries were recorded in Shang times.
4. Fan Chuo, cited in Wen Huanran, *Plants and Animals*, 196.
5. J. Legge, *The Works of Mencius*, vol. 2 in *The Chinese Classics, with a Translation, Critical and Exegetical Notes, Prolegomena, and Copious Indexes* (7 vols., Trübner: London, 1861), III.2.ix (156–7). Translation slightly altered, and emphasis added.
6. *Qì*, 'aethers', also has the senses of 'matter', 'energy', and 'vitality'. *Yang*, 'bright–positive', has the further implications of warmth, masculinity, taking the initiative, and so on.

7. *HNZ: Huainanzi* [The book of the Prince of Huainan] (2nd century BCE; reprinted, Zhongguo zixue mingzhu jicheng bianyin jijinhui: Taibei, 1978), 'Zhuixing xun', 143–4. Cp. ibid., 137.

8. Song Queming, cited in Wen Huanran, *Plants and Animals*, 192.

9. Ye Tinggui, cited in Wen Huanran, *Plants and Animals*, 191.

10. Wen Huanran, *Plants and Animals*, 191.

11. Li Wenfeng, cited in Wen Huanran, *Plants and Animals*, 195.

12. Wen Huanran, *Plants and Animals*, 188.

13. Wen Huanran, *Plants and Animals*, 192.

14. Liu Ts'ui-jung, "Zhongguo lishi-shang guanyu shanlinchuanze-de guannian he zhidu" [The concepts and institutional forms relating to mountains, forests, rivers, and marshes in Chinese history], in Cao Tianwang, Lai Jingchang, and Yang Jiancheng, eds., *Zhongyang yanjiuyuan Zhongshan renwen shehui kexue yanjiusuo juanshu* 46 (Academia Sinica: Taibei, 1999), 14. The phrase used, namely "[if] the common people can obtain their teeth," tends to suggest that this was intermittent, not a regular pursuit.

15. Wen Huanran, *Plants and Animals*, 192.

16. Song Zhenhao, *Xia-Shang shehui shenghuo shi* [Social life under the Xia and Shang] (Zhongguo shehui kexue chubanshe: Beijing, 1994), 244–6; Xu Jinxiong, *Zhongguo gudai shehui* [Ancient Chinese society] (Taiwan shangwu yinshuguan: Taibei, 1988), 42.

17. S. Couvreur, *Tch'ouen Ts'iou et Tso Tchouan: La Chronique de la principauté de Lou* (1914; reprinted, 3 vols., Cathasia: Paris, 1951), bilingual text, I:346.

18. Couvreur, *Tso Tchouan*, III:512.

19. Couvreur, *Tso Tchouan*, II:411.

20. Wen Huanran, *Plants and Animals*, 189.

21. Wen Huanran, *Plants and Animals*, 193.

22. Liu Xun, cited in Wen Huanran, *Plants and Animals*, 191 and 193.

23. M. Elvin, *The Pattern of the Chinese Past* (Stanford University Press: Stanford, Calif., 1973), 93.

24. In the translations of premodern Chinese texts in this book the word 'month' (or 'moon') always indicates the Chinese lunar calendar month. In 1388, the 'third month' indicates the period from 7 April to 6 May in the Western Julian calendar, but the pattern of correspondences with the Julian, and after 1582 the Gregorian, calendar varied from year to year.

25. Wen Huanran, *Plants and Animals*, 198.

26. *WZZ*: Xie Zhaozhe, *Wu zazu* [Fivefold miscellany] (1608; reprinted under the supervision of Li Weizhen, Xinxing shuju: Taibei, 1971), 706–8.

27. The Qing made ceremonial use of elephants. See H. S. Brunnert and V. V. Hagelstrom, *Present Day Political Organization of China*, translated A. Beltchenko and E. E. Moran (Kelly and Walsh: Shanghai, 1912; reprinted, Taibei, 1960), 37–8. They were obtained as tribute from countries like Burma, where they had been given personal names, which they seem to have kept in China. Yunnan and Guizhou provinces sent tusks as tribute. See Wu Zhenyu, *Yangjizhai conglu* [Collected records from the Yangjizhai Studio] (printed from the nineteenth-century MS by the Zhejiang guji chubanshe: Hangzhou, 1985), 291 and 268. I am grateful to Professor Mark Elliott-Smith for providing this reference.

28. Evidence of a general sort for this intuitive feeling may be found in S. R. Kellert and E. O. Wilson, eds., *The Biophilia Hypothesis* (Island Press: Washington D.C., 1993), S. R. Kellert, "The Biophilia hypothesis: Aristotelian echoes of the 'Good Life'," in Itō Suntarō and Yoshida Yoshinori, eds., *Nature and Humankind in the Age of Environmental Crisis*

(International Research Center for Japanese Studies: Kyoto, 1995), and S. R. Kellert, *Kinship to Mastery: Biophilia in Human Evolution and Development* (Island Press/Shearwater Books: Washington D.C., 1997).

29. Dali-zhou wenlian [Literary Association of Dali], *Dali gu yishu chao* [Transcriptions of ancient lost books from Dali] (Yunnan Renmin chubanshe: Kunming, 2001), 68–71, and also 18, 128, 144, and 167. On the use of fire to drive out rhinoceroses, tigers, and leopards see 270.

3 The Great Deforestation: An Overview

1. Liu Zongyuan, *Liu Zongyuan ji* [Collected works of Liu Zongyuan] (Tang: Zhonghua shuju: Taibei, 1978), 43:1240–1, "Xing nan lu."

2. Chen Qiaoyi, "Gudai Shaoxing diqu tianran senlin-de pohuai ji qi dui nongye-de yingxiang" [The destruction in ancient times of the natural forests of Shaoxing and its impact on agriculture], *Dili xuebao* 31.2 (June 1965), 130.

3. S. D. Richardson, *Forests and Forestry in China* (Island Press: Washington D.C., 1990), 115.

4. He Baochuan, *China on the Edge: The Crisis of Ecology and Development* (China Books: San Francisco, Calif., 1991), 29.

5. Wang Shuizhao, ed., *Su Shi xuanji* [An anthology from Su Shi (Dongpo)] (Shanghai guji chubanshe: Shanghai, 1984), 118. The location of Peng, the place referred to in the poem, was about 34° N and 117° E. Note that I read *feng* = 'wind' as *fen* = 'divide'.

6. N. K. Menzies, *Forestry*, vol. VI.3 of J. Needham, ed., *Science and Civilisation in China* (Cambridge University Press: Cambridge, 1996).

7. N. K. Menzies, "The villagers' view of environmental history in Yunnan province," in M. Elvin and T.-J. Liu, eds., *Sediments of Time: Environment and Society in Chinese History* (Cambridge University Press: New York, 1998).

8. At 35° 10′ N and 113° 5′ E.

9. Cited in Wen Huanran *et al.*, *Zhongguo lishi shiqi zhiwu yu dongwu bianqian yanjiu* [Studies on changes in plants and animals in China during historical times] (Chongqing chubanshe: Chongqing, 1995), 120.

10. I use 'county' for the Chinese *xian*, the lowest level of formal bureaucratic government under the later empire, and 'district' for *xiang*, which was often the next level down. 'Canton' is the Chinese *li*.

11. Deng Gang [Kent], *Development versus Stagnation: Technological Continuity and Agricultural Progess in Pre-Modern China* (Greenwood: Westport, Conn., 1993), xxv.

12. Cited in Wen Huanran, *Plants and Animals*, 119. Pages 117–22 give the background.

13. R. H. Waring and S. W. Running, *Forest Ecosystems: Analysis at Multiple Scales*, 2nd edn (Academic Press: San Diego, Calif., 1998), 217–18.

14. Mei Zengliang [Boyan], *Bojian shanfang wenji* [Collected works from the Bojian Studio], in *Zhonghua wenshi congshu* no. 12 (Qing; reprinted, Jinghua shuju: Taibei, 1968), 'Ji pengmin shi' [A record of matters relating to the shed people]. Also cited in Chen Rong, *Zhongguo senlin shiliao* [Historical materials on China's forests] (Xinhua: Beijing, 1983), 52, and discussed in A. Osborne, "Barren mountains, raging rivers: The ecological and social effects of changing land-use on the Lower Yangzi periphery in late-imperial China," (Ph.D. thesis, Columbia University, 1989), 18–19.

15. That is, theories about the effects on human beings of occult forces running through the earth.

16. The location of a grave was thought to affect the fortunes of the buried person's descendants.
17. Between 1957 and 1980 present-day Xuanzhou (Qing-dynasty Xuancheng) had a mean annual rainfall of 1289 mm. The minimum was 777 mm, the maximum 1328 mm. See *ZGZRZYCS: Zhongguo ziran ziyuan congshu* [Series on the natural resources of China] (42 vols., Zhongguo huanjiing kexu chubanshe: Beijing, 1995), 23:249 (Anhui). About seventy per cent of this fell during the six months from April through September. Xuancheng is thus likely to have abundant rainfall in most years. Removing trees would most probably have slightly increased total annual local runoff, as trees absorb and then transpire water, that is, 'breathe' it out into the atmosphere. Waring and Running, *Forest Ecosystems*, 110, note that the "return of nutrients in litterfall" is the "major route of recycling from vegetation to soil."
18. R. B. Marks, *Tigers, Rice, Silk, and Silt* (Cambridge University Press: New York, 1998), 66–70, 76–9, and also 35–7, 319–22, and 327–30.
19. Xu Hailiang, "Huanghe xiayou-de duiji lishi fazhan qushi" [The history and trend of development of the sedimentary deposits in the lower reaches of the Yellow River]," *Zhongguo shuili xuebao* 7 (1990); and Ye Qingchao, "Shilun Subei fei-Huanghe sanjiaozhou-de fayu" [On the development of the abandoned Yellow River delta], *Dili xuebao* 41.2 (June 1986).
20. M. Elvin and Su Ninghu, 'Action at a distance: The influence of the Yellow River on Hangzhou Bay since AD 1000', in Elvin and Liu, eds., *Sediments of Time*.
21. A summary of Japanese and Chinese studies on the growth of the Yangzi delta region may be found in M. Elvin and N. Su, "Engineering the sea: Hydraulic systems and premodern technological lock-in in the Harngzhou Bay area circa 1000–1800," in Itō Suntarō and Yoshida Yoshinori, eds., *Nature and Humankind in the Age of Environmental Crisis* (International Research Center for Japanese Studies: Kyoto 1995).
22. Fujita Katsuhisa,"Kandai no Kōka shisui kikō" [Flood control measures on the Yellow River], *Chūgoku sui rishi kenkyū* 16 (1986), 14.
23. Elvin and Su, "Action at a distance," 364–5.
24. Zhongguo Kexue-yuan *Zhongguo ziran dili* bianji Weiguanhui, ed., *Zhongguo ziran dili: Lishi ziran dili* [The natural geography of China: Historical natural geography] (Kexue chubanshe: Beijing, 1982), hereafter *ZZD*, 33.
25. Fujita Katsuhisa, "Flood control measures on the Yellow River," 12–13.
26. Cited in Fujita Katsuhisa, "Flood control measures on the Yellow River," 13–14.
27. Calculated from Fujita Katsuhisa, "Flood control measures on the Yellow River," table facing p. 10. I have omitted the floods of 107 CE as they were due to rains.
28. Fujita Katsuhisa, "Flood control measures on the Yellow River," 7 and 11.
29. Yuan Qinglin, *Zhongguo huanjing baohu shihua* [Historical discussions on the conservation of nature in China (Zhongguo huanjing kexue chubanshe: Beijing, 1990), 72, gives the lower figure of one breach in every 125 years between 69 CE and the Sui dynasty at the end of the sixth century CE.
30. In the southern Northwest, modern Xi'an.
31. *ZZD*, 33, and Yuan Qinglin, *Conservation of Nature in China*, 30 and 90–1.
32. Li Yuanliang's restoration of Liangyuan. Yuan Qinglin, *Conservation of Nature in China*, 91.
33. A *li* was roughly half a kilometer in length, but the *hu* was a variable measure of capacity that had two ranges of values in late-imperial times. Surviving vessels either containing 28 to 29 liters or from 50 to 56 liters (Qiu Guangming, *Zhongguo lidai du-liang-heng kao* [Researches on measures of length, capacity, and weight in the successive Chinese

dynasties] (Kexue chubanshe: Beijing, 1992), 277). A *hu* surviving from the Wei of the Three Dynasties (third century CE) has a capacity of somewhat over 20 liters (Qiu Guangming, *Measures*, 254–5). It is not possible to be confident about the present values of this premodern capacity measure.

34. Yuan Qinglin, *Conservation of Nature in China*, 72.

35. Calculated from data in Itō Hashiko, "Sōdai no Kōka shisui kikō" [The structure of flood control on the Yellow River under the Song dynasty], *Chūgoku suiri shi kenkyū* 16 (1986), tables following p. 16.

36. Tuotuo, *et al.*, (eds.), Yuan, *Songshi* [History of the Song] (Reprinted, Zhonghua shuju: Beijing, 1977).

37. Summarized in Elvin and Su, "Action at a distance," 393–406.

38. Loess is rock in powder form, usually laid down by the wind. The top layer can develop into a fertile so-called 'loessial soil'.

39. Matsuda Yoshirō, "Shindai no Kōka shisui kikō" [The structure of flood control on the Yellow River under the Qing dynasty], *Chūgoku suiri shi kenkyū* 16 (1986), 34–40.

40. J. Jeník, *Pictorial Encyclopedia of Forests* (Hamlyn: London, 1979), 152, 154, 156–7, 169, and 210.

41. Manchu and Mongol names of persons are, by convention, written as single words to distinguish them from those of Han Chinese.

42. Cited in Wen Huanran, *Plants and Animals*, 48.

43. At about 39° N and 100° E, being the upper reaches of the historic Ruo. The system is one of inland drainage.

44. Waring and Running, *Forest Ecosystems*, 46, and 49–50, note that if warm, moist, turbulent air condenses on the snow surface, it adds heat to it, and this can lead to melting. Pines are more effective in delaying snowmelt than deciduous trees. An important variable is the density of the stand, or, approximately equivalently, the area covered by foliage. See also Jeník, *Forests*, 148 for a picture of snowmelt in a forest and the point that the temperature of the trunks is a critical variable.

45. By Tao Baolian, cited in Wen Huanran, *Plants and Animals*, 48.

46. At present the annual precipitation in Ganzhou is about 150 mm, and the total annual hours of sunshine about 3,000. See *ZGZRZYCS*, 38: maps facing 268 and 274 (Gansu). The two-phase snowmelt awaits explanation.

47. Tulishen, *Yiyu lu* [An account of unfamiliar lands] in Imanishi Shunjū, ed., *Jiaozhu yiyu lu* (Tenri: n.p., 1964), 146, 201, and 349.

48. At about 105° E.

49. When reflecting the light?

50. Wen Huanran, *Plants and Animals*, 29.

51. The general need for such caution emerges clearly from A. Grove and O. Rackham, *The Nature of Mediterranean Europe: An Ecological History* (Yale University Press: New Haven, Conn., 2001), albeit in another context.

52. They can inhibit storms, for example. See Waring and Running, *Forest Ecosystems*, 275. They also reduce the intensity of the light reaching the ground, the percentage depending on the dominant species. See Jeník, *Forests*, 155, 159–60.

53. In boreal regions, forest cover can increase the temperature, while the reverse is true in temperate climates. See Waring and Running, *Forest Ecosystems*, 304–6.

54. For a general outline of the issues, see R. G. Barry and R. J. Chorley, *Atmosphere, Weather and Climate*, 5th edn (Methuen: London, 1987), 338–48. H. H. Lamb, *Climate, History and the Modern World* (Routledge: London, 1995), 329, stresses the probable distinctive nature of the low-latitude zones. There is also a useful summary in M. Mann, "Ecological change

in North India: Deforestation and agrarian distress in the Ganga–Yamuna Doab 1800–1850," in R. Grove, V. Damodaran, and S. Sangwan, eds., *Nature and the Orient: The Environmental History of South and Southeast Asia* (Oxford University Press: New Delhi, 1998), esp. 400–2.

55. Or 'Hepu'.

56. At roughly 22° N and 109° E.

57. Wen Huanran, *Plants and Animals*, 81. The square-pallet chain-pump mentioned here was colloquially known as the 'dragon's backbone pump', as the circulating wooden chain of linked square pallets that hauled the water up a sloping trough looked like a line of huge vertebrae.

58. Early nineteenth-century gazetteer for Lianzhou quoted in Wen Huanran, *Plants and Animals*, 81.

59. The *qi*, that is the matter–energy–vitality.

60. *Yin* and *yang*.

61. Vietnam.

62. Liu Ts'ui-jung, "Han migration and the settlement of Taiwan: The onset of envrionmental change," in Elvin and Liu, eds., *Sediments of Time*, 197.

63. M. Berenbaum, *Bugs in the System: Insects and their Impact on Human Affairs* (Addison-Wesley: Reading, Mass., 1994), 230–7.

64. H. Morin, *Entretiens sur le paludisme et sa prévention en Indochine* (Imprimerie d'Extrême-Orient: Hanoi, 1935) lists the various species of *Anopheles*. Cited in Hardy, "Migration in 20th century Vietnam," see the following note.

65. I owe this suggestion to Dr Andrew Hardy, author of a remarkable Ph.D. thesis for the Australian National University, "A history of migration to upland areas in 20th century Vietnam." See Intro.5, iii.19, iv.6–9. Chapter 9 quotes an informant as saying of his home area that "there was a period when malaria was rife, the time when the forest was still thick" (and pp. 263–8 generally).

66. Hardy, "Migration in 20th century Vietnam," chapter 9 footnote 11, quotes an informant as saying of one area that "only people just arrived got it."

67. Jeník, *Forests*, 'The animals of the forest', 367–425.

68. *YL: Yueling* [Ordinances for the months] (pre-Qin), in Chen Hao, ed., *Liji jishuo* [*The Record of the Rites*] (Shijie shuju: Taibei, 1969), *passim*.

69. Li Ge scolding Duke Xuan who ruled the state of Lu (Northeast) from 607 to 589 BCE.

70. *GY: Guoyu* [The tales of the various states] (pre-Qin; Shanghai guji chubanshe: Shanghai, 1978), 178–80.

71. Xu Jinxiong, *Zhongguo gudai shehui* [Ancient Chinese society] (Taiwan shangwu yinshuguan: Taibei, 1988), 40–1.

72. Xu Jinxiong, *Ancient Chinese Society*, 45.

73. Xu Jinxiong, *Ancient Chinese Society*, 42–4.

74. Wen Huanran, *Plants and Animals*, 226.

75. Wen Huanran, *Plants and Animals*, 220–8.

76. In the Northwest, north of the loop of the Yellow River.

77. Wen Huanran, *Plants and Animals*, 25.

78. Liu Ts'ui-jung, "The Settlement of Taiwan," 172–3.

79. Wu Zhen. Not to be confused with the Yuan-dynasty painter of the same name.

80. Wen Huanran, *Plants and Animals*, 175.

81. Li Xinheng.

82. At about 102° E, west of Chengdu. Wen Huanran, *Plants and Animals*, 178.

83. Ji Han, *Nanfang caomu zhuang* [The forms of the plants and trees of the South],

translated Hui-lin Li, *A Fourth Century Flora of Southeast Asia* (Chinese University Press: Hong Kong, 1979), 131–2, 146.

84. Wen Huanran, *Plants and Animals*, 177, 179, 181.
85. Lu Zuofan.
86. Wen Huanran, *Plants and Animals*, 168.
87. In modern Liuzhou.
88. Modern Guiping.
89. On Lianzhou (Far South) see Wen Huanran, *Plants and Animals*, 81.
90. Present-day Enshi in Hubei at 30° 20′ N and 109° 30′ E on the western edge of the Center. The town was Nanjiao.
91. Chen Rong, *China's Forests*, 52–3.
92. By Shao Changheng, who was born in nearby Wujin. In Zhang Yingchang, ed., *Qing shi duo* [The Qing bell of poesy] (originally *Guochao shi duo*, 1869; reprinted, Xinhua shudian: Beijing, 1960), hereafter *QSD*, 444.
93. By Qian Yikai. *QSD* 7–8.
94. *QSD*, 446.
95. *QSD*, 562. The poem is by Zhu Shou.
96. Wu Nongxiang. In *QSD*, 246.
97. Respectively, (south) Zhejiang (Southeast), southwest Shanxi (Northwest), and Shaanxi and Gansu (Northwest).
98. *QSD*, 928.
99. *QSD*, 932–3.
100. They run from about 110° E to about 108° E. Taibai is at about 107° 30′ E.
101. There is a description of some of the technology used in E. Vermeer, "Population and ecology along the frontier in Qing China," in Elvin and Liu, eds., *Sediments of Time*, 250. Pictures of modern forestry cableways may be found in Jeník, *Forests*, 436 and 456.
102. For a picture of a western Eurasian *Castanea*, to gain an approximate idea of the *Castanea* mentioned in the second verse, see Jeník, *Forests*, 53 (*Castanea sativa*, Spanish chestnut).

4 *The Great Deforestation: Regions and Species*

1. Wang Chi-wu, *The Forests of China, with a Survey of Grassland and Desert Vegetation* (Harvard University Press: Cambridge, Mass., 1961), 10–11; Hou Xueyu, *Zhongguo ziran dili* [The natural geography of China], vol. 2, *Zhiwu dili* [Vegetation geography] (Kexue chubanshe: Beijing, 1988), enclosed color map and 112–13; N. K. Menzies, *Forestry*, vol. VI.3 of J. Needham, ed., *Science and Civilisation in China* (Cambridge University Press: Cambridge, 1996), 550–4; Ueda Makoto, *Mori to midori no Chūgoku-shi: Ekorojikaru-hisutorii no kokoromi* [Chinese history in terms of its forests and vege-tation: A tentative essay in ecological history] (Iwanami shoten: Tokyo, 1999).
2. Pictures of comparable European larches can be found in J. Jeník, *Pictorial Encyclo-pedia of Forests* (Hamlyn: London, 1979), 21 and 167.
3. Pictures of the first two of these may be found in Jeník, *Forests*, 12 (holm oak), 249, 341, 274, 286 (oaks); 24, 26–7, 63, 65, 105, 128, 131, 132, 179, 181, 194, 290 (pines). The range of the Scots pine (*Pinus sylvestris*), shown on 34, goes from the north of Scotland to northern Manchuria.
4. *Cihai* [Sea of Phrases] (Zhonghua shuju: Shanghai, 1947), hereafter *CH*, 791.
5. B. Karlgren, *The Book of Odes: Chinese Text, Transcription and Translation* (Museum of Far Eastern Antiquities: Stockholm, 1950), #241. Alternative readings of the second half

of the second line of the last verse would be 'and the thorns with white flowers', or just 'oaks'. The interpretation adopted is a guess that depends on S. Couvreur, *Dictionnaire classique de la langue chinoise* (Imprimerie de la Mission Catholique: Hejian fu, 1911), 459: 'yeuse' for the *yu* in *zuo yu*, and the sense of the context: the song is describing massive trees, not shrubs. This, and other translations, are mine.

6. Karlgren, *Odes*, #245.

7. Karlgren, *Odes*, #290.

8. Karlgren, *Odes*, #237. The Gunyi referred to here are usually identified as the 'dog barbarians' who lived in what is now the western part of Shaanxi province. Furthermore, like the anthem at the opening of this section, the text only says *zuo yu*, usually rendered just 'oaks', as by the great Swedish sinologist Karlgren. My reading of *yu* as 'evergreen oaks' is, again, a guess. Its only bases are, as before, Couvreur's dictionary, and an instinct that the terse style of the *Songs*, and their authors' distaste for mere reduplication, make simple redundancy unlikely. Menzies, *Forestry*, 601, regards *yu* as a synonym for *zuo*, and takes *zuo* as *Quercus mongolica*, or else, by inference, *Q. acutissima*, both deciduous. However this may be, the climate was warmer in the second millennium BCE, so the presence so far north of evergreen oaks or acorn-bearing oak-like trees, such as *Lithocarpus*, would not have been impossible at this time.

9. S. Couvreur, *Tch'ouen Ts'iou et Tso Tchouan: La Chronique de la principauté de Lou*, (1914; reprinted, 3 vols., Cathasia: Paris, 1951), bilingual text, I:292.

10. Zhang Juncheng, "Shang-Yin lin kao" [A study of forests under the Shang-Yin dynasty], *Nongye kaogu* 1 (1985), 182.

11. J. Legge, *The Works of Mencius*, vol. 2 in *The Chinese Classics with a Translation, Critical and Exegetical Notes, Prolegomena, and Copious Indexes* (Trübner: London, 1861), III:1.iv.7, 126. Shun is traditionally said to have become emperor in 2255 BCE.

12. Examples in Couvreur, *Tso Tchouan*, e.g., I:18, 27, 36, 47, 66, 85, 115, 138, 140, 153, 322, etc.

13. H. Roetz, *Mensch und Natur im alten China: Zum Subjekt-Objekt-Gegensatz in der klassischen chinesischen Philosophie* (Lang: Frankfurt am Main, 1984), 81.

14. Couvreur, *Tso Tchouan*, I:630.

15. Couvreur, *Tso Tchouan*, II:13.

16. Couvreur, *Tso Tchouan*, II:392.

17. E.g., Karlgren, *Odes*, ##163, 180, and 237.

18. Couvreur, *Tso Tchouan*, I:143–4.

19. It is near modern Fei county. See Couvreur, *Tso Tchouan*, III:355–6.

20. Couvreur, *Tso Tchouan*, III:56.

21. Couvreur, *Tso Tchouan*, III:323.

22. *Zhouli zhushu* [The Rituals of Zhou], in Ruan Yuan, ed., *Shisan jing zhushu* [The thirteen classics with notes and explanations] (Qing; reprinted, Zhonghua shuju: Beijing, 1980), hereafter *ZL*, 747. The duties of the *shanyu* listed here are mostly ensuring that trees are not cut at a time of year not allowed by the imperial laws. I am grateful to Ulrike Mittendorf of the University of Heidelberg for drawing this passage to my attention.

23. *LJ: Liji* [Records of ritual behavior] (later Han), in vol. 4 of *Shisan jing zhushu* [The thirteen scriptures] (reprinted, 7 vols., Chūbun shuppansha: Tokyo, 1971), "Yue ling," 2935. First month.

24. I take the words *shanlin* in his job description as 'mountain forests' rather than 'mountains *and* forests' because, as indicated in note 4.22, his duties predominantly related to controlling the felling of trees at the permitted times.

25. *ZL*, 747.

26. Song Zhenhao, *Xia-Shang shehui shenghuo Shi* [Social life under the Xia and Shang] (Zhongguo shehui kexue chubanshe: Beijing, 1994), ch. 8.
27. Couvreur, *Tso Tchouan*, III:33.
28. Couvreur, *Tso Tchouan*, I:576.
29. Couvreur, *Tso Tchouan*, I:55.
30. Karlgren, *Odes*, #300.
31. Karlgren, *Odes*, #238.
32. Karlgren, *Odes*, #229.
33. Karlgren, Odes, ##172 and 176.
34. For example, Couvreur, *Tso Tchouan*, I:478.
35. Karlgren, *Odes*, #192.
36. Karlgren, *Odes*, #204.
37. For example, Karlgren, *Odes*, ## 60, 76, 100 and 109.
38. Couvreur, *Tso Tchouan*, III:123.
39. Couvreur, *Tso Tchouan*, III:673. Note also I:426, though the species is not given.
40. Couvreur, *Tso Tchouan*, II:54–6.
41. Possibly dropsy, beriberi, or a related condition.
42. This sketch is based on Hou Xueyu, *Vegetation Geography*, and J. Thorp, 'Soils', in J. L. Buck, ed., *Land Utilization in China* (1937; reprinted, Paragon: New York, 1964).
43. 'Neutral' is defined as a pH of 7.3 to 6.4 and 'acid' from 6.4 to 4.0.
44. *Catalpa ovata*.
45. Couvreur, *Tso Tchouan*, II:462–3.
46. For examples, see D. Hawkes, *Ch'u Tz'u: The Songs of the South* (Clarendon Press: Oxford, 1959), 43 and 64.
47. There is a not very wonderful translation into German by E. Von Zach, *Die chinesische Anthologie: Übersetzungen aus dem Wen hsüan* (Harvard University Press: Cambridge, Mass., 1958), 103–7. The Chinese texts I have used are from *SJ: Shiji* [Records of the Grand Historian] (Han; reprinted, Zhonghua shuju: Beijing, 1959), "Sima Xiangru zhuan" [Biography of Sima Xiangru], 57:3002–4, and *Wenxuan* [The Chinese anthology] (6th century CE, 1181 edn; reprinted, 4 cases, Zhonghua shuju: Beijing, 1974), hereafter *WX*, 7:17a–24b.
48. *Xin yu* [New discourses] xia, "Zizhi." Cited from Sugimoto Kenji, "Chūgoku kodai no mokuzai ni tsuite" [Timber in ancient China], *Tōhō gakuhō* (Mar. 1974), 83–4.
49. Both in the Northwest.
50. Sugimoto Kenji, "Timber in ancient China," 86–7; Wang Chi-wu, *Forests of China*, 31, 32, and 65; and *CH*, entry on *bianbo* (*Chamaecyparis obtusa*).
51. Wang Fu in his *Qianfu lun* [Discourses of the Hidden Master], *Fuchi pian*, cited in Sugimoto Kenji, "Timber in ancient China," 96 and 118.
52. Liu Ts'ui-jung, "Zhongguo lishi-shang guanyu shanlinchuanze-de guannian he zhidu" [The concepts and institutional forms relating to mountains, forests, rivers, and marshes in Chinese history], in Cao Tianwang, Lai Jingchang, and Yang Jiancheng, eds., *Zhongyang yanjiuyuan Zhongshan renwen shehui kexue yanjiusuo juanshu 46* (Academia Sinica: Taibei, 1999), 12. The original is in Fan Ye, *Hou Han shu* [History of the Later Han] (Reprinted, Zhonghua shuju: Beijing, 1965), 1278. By the time this work was compiled in the fifth century, Buddhism had become solidly established in China, and it is legitimate at least to wonder if this may have helped to motivate the selection and 'angling' of this anecdote, notwithstanding the impeccably Confucian vocabulary.
53. Shen Yue, *Song shu* [The history of the Song] (Reprinted, Zhonghua shuju: Beijing, 1974), 54:1536–7 ('Kong Jigong'). Note that this is not the famous Song dynasty at the

turn of the first and second millennia CE, but an earlier and relatively short-lived southern dynasty (420–478).

54. Nakahara Teruo, "Shindai sōsen ni yoru shōhin ryūtsū ni tsuite" [The flow of commodities on grain-transport ships during the Qing dynasty], *Shigaku kenkyū* 72 (1959), 69.

55. See the map of the Grand Canal in C. Blunden and M. Elvin, *Cultural Atlas of China*, rev. edn (Facts on File: New York, 1998), 104–5.

56. At 26° 10′ N, 109° 45′ E.

57. Yuan Qinglin, *Zhongguo huanjing baohu shihua* [Historical discussions on the conservation of nature in China (Zhongguo huanjing kexue chubanshe: Beijing, 1990), 267.

58. For these questions see N. Menzies, "Trees, fields, and people: The forests of China from the seventeenth to the nineteenth centuries" (Ph.D. thesis, University of California, Berkeley, Calif., 1991), 67–85.

59. See Blunden and Elvin, *Cultural Atlas of China*, 123, map on 'Tripartite divisions: the Three Kingdoms period and Northern Song marketing regions'.

60. Data on present-day Sichuan is taken from *Zhongguo ziran ziyuan congshu* [Series on the natural resources of China] (42 vols., Zhongguo huanjing kexue chubanshe: Beijing, 1995), hereafter *ZGZRZYCS*, 33 (Sichuan).

61. Lin Hongrong, "Sichuan gudai senlin-de bianqian" [Changes in the ancient forests of Sichuan], *Nongye kaogu* 9.1 (1985), 162–7, and "Lishi shiqi Sichuan senlin-de bianqian" [Changes in the forests of Sichuan during the historical period], *Nongye kaogu* 10.2 (1985), 215–40. Information in the present section about Sichuan's forests in historical times is drawn from these two linked articles, unless noted otherwise.

62. Lin Hongrong, "Historical forests of Sichuan," 218–19.

63. Lin Hongrong, "Ancient forests of Sichuan," 63.

64. See the photograph of the decorated brick picture of this in Menzies, *Forestry*, 642.

65. Reading *cuo* 'trim' for *zuo* 'sit'.

66. Cited in Lin Hongrong, "Ancient forests of Sichuan," 168. Emphasis added.

67. I have used *WX*, 4:13b–27a, and also Qu Tuiyan, *Han Wei Liuchao fu xuan* [Selected rhapsodies from the Han, Wei, and Six Dynasties period] (1964; reprinted, Shanghai Guji chubanshe: Shanghai, 1979), for its notes. The translation is tentative in places, but there are grounds, if not always decisive ones, for the readings adopted.

68. Qu Tuiyuan, *Rhapsodies*, 140–1.

69. Qu Tuiyuan, *Rhapsodies*, 140–1.

70. Named for Robert Fortune, a nineteenth-century agricultural and botanical spy who secured the tea plants from China on which the Indian tea industry was later based.

71. Lin Hongrong, "Ancient forests of Sichuan," 162.

72. *CH*, 673.

73. The star-zone Bi was one of the twenty-eight divisions of the night sky according to the Chinese astronomical system. (It contained the first-magnitude star Aldebaran.) Archaic superstition thought that when the moon was in this zone, there would be heavy rain. But note that, even if the meteorology was mythical, the engineering was real. See Karlgren, *Odes*, #232.

74. Strictly, the 'grapefruits' should be 'pomelos'.

75. Ji Han, *Nanfang caomu zhuang* [The forms of the plants and trees of the South], translated Hui-lin Li, *A Fourth Century Flora of Southeast Asia* (Chinese University Press: Hong Kong, 1979), 90–2.

76. Song Qi, quoted by Lin Hongrong, "Historical forests of Sichuan," 217. Song was an official and historian who lived in the Northern Song period.

77. Chou Zhao'ao, ed., *Du Shaoling ji xiangzhu* [Du Fu's collected works with detailed notes] (4 vols., Wenxue guji kanxingshe: Beijing, 1955), II.iv.9 and 107, "Ping He Shiyi shaofu Yong mi qimu." I have put the translation in the past tense since in the next poem quoted here it seems that they have already grown, and both poems were probably written at about the same time.

78. Chou Zhao'ao, *Works of Du Fu*, II.iv.9 and 108.

79. Su Dongpo, *Su Dongpo quanji* [Complete works of Su Dongpo] (13 vols., Hanguo wenhua kanhanghui: Seoul, 1983), II:137, "Tengxian-shi tongnian xiyuan."

80. Lin Hongrong, "Historical forests of Sichuan," 218.

81. Su Dongpo, *Complete Works*, II:199.

82. 'Contrary' here is pronounced to rhyme with 'Mary'.

83. Su Dongpo, *Complete Works*, II:199–200.

84. Guo Zhengzhong, *Songdai yanye jingji shi* [An economic history of the salt industry during the Song dynasty] (Renmin chubanshe: Beijing, 1990), 57. 'Jiang' is approximately present-day Chongqing.

85. Just possibly the sense is 'drawing it off' down piping.

86. Referred to by Guo Zhengzhong, *Economic History of the Salt Industry*, 62. Full text in Su Dongpo, *Dongpo Zhilin* [Su Dongpo's miscellany] (1097–1101; reprinted, Zhonghua shuju: Beijing, 1981), 76–7.

87. Illustrated in J. Needham and Wang Ling, *Science and Civilisation in China*, vol. 4.II, *Mechanical Engineering* (Cambridge University Press: Cambridge, 1965), 371. This passage is discussed on 142–3, not altogether convincingly in that it is suggested that what was involved here was a 'piston-bellows' rather than what I have called a 'flap-bellows', as shown on 371.

88. Qiu Guangming, *Zhongguo lidai du-liang-heng kao* [Researches on measures of length, capacity, and weight in the successive Chinese dynasties] (Kexue chubanshe: Beijing, 1992), 162–3.

89. Sung Ying-hsing, *T'ien-kung k'ai-wu: Chinese Technology in the Seventeenth Century*, translated E-tu Zen Sun and Shiou-chuan Sun (Pennsylvania State University Press: University Park, Penn., 1966), 116–23.

90. Li Yuan, *Shu shuijing* [The classic of the waterways of Sichuan] (1794; reprinted, 2 vols., Ba-Shu shushe: Chengdu, 1985) I:4:15a–16a. I am most grateful to Dr Warren Wan-kuo Sun for the gift of this book.

91. The translated place-names in this passage are, in order of occurrence, Shizi Qiao, Siwang Qi, Daning, Xianshui, Zidong, Yun'an, Wentang, Jianwei, Fushun, and Chuanbei.

92. Sung Ying-hsing, *T'ien-kung k'ai-wu*, 120, shows the animals rotating a turntable.

93. Li Yuan, *The Classic of the Waterways of Sichuan*, I:27a–28b. The numbering has been added.

94. The idea that the text means 'drying away from the sunlight' is a guess in as much as 'drying' has to be supplied.

95. Background information is taken from *ZGZRZYCS*, 30 (Guangdong), mainly chapter 7, 'Climatic resources'.

96. Ji Han, *Flora of Southeast Asia*, 32.

97. *Ipomoea aquatica*.

98. Ji Han, *Flora of Southeast Asia*, 15–17.

99. *Areca catechu*.

100. *Piper betle*.

101. Su Dongpo, *Complete Works*, XI:79–80.

102. Qu Dajun, *Guangdong xinyu* [New comments on Guangdong] (1700; reprinted, Zhonghua shuju: Hong Kong, 1974), especially 609–68.

103. Qu Dajun, *New Comments on Guangdong,* 616–18.
104. There are a photograph and a drawing in Jeník, *Forests,* 67, 263.
105. Qu Dajun, *New Comments on Guangdong,* 615–16.
106. *Firmiana* may be a misidentification here. Possibly some other species with a samara (winged seed) is indicated.
107. *Arenga pinnata.*
108. *Livistona chinensis.*
109. *Tilia miquelana.* Mistakenly identified as the Bo tree under which the Buddha attained enlightenment.
110. *Glyptostrobus pensilis.*
111. Qu Dajun, *New Comments on Guangdong,* 631.
112. By Sheng Hongzhi.
113. Cited in Sugimoto Kenji, "Timber in ancient China," 102–3.
114. This 'Guiyang' was probably only slightly to the north of Yangshan, near Lian county in the north of modern Guangdong.
115. *Aquilaria agallocha.*
116. Qu Dajun, *New Comments on Guangdong,* 669–72.
117. The text says "ants," but termites are more plausibly associated with decomposing wood and substantial mounds.
118. *Yousu:* a kind of perfume.
119. The passage in parentheses has been interpolated here from p. 671 to clarify the nature of the technique.
120. Or, perhaps, "in which the perfume and the wood have not separated clearly." The sense is problematic.
121. Following a common convention, the terms 'in-migrants' and 'out-migrants' are used for people who move *within* a political unit, in contrast with 'immigrants' and 'emigrants' who move from one state to another.
122. Qu Dajun, *New Comments on Guangdong,* 609.
123. *Ursa major.*
124. Over the pass between the two provinces.
125. Of phloem and xylem.
126. Qu Dajun, *New Comments on Guangdong,* 612.
127. The translation of the second sentence is a conjecture, though the only one that seems to fit the context.
128. R. B. Marks, *Tigers, Rice, Silk, and Silt* (Cambridge University Press: New York, 1998), 326.
129. Qu Dajun, *New Comments on Guangdong,* 624.
130. See, for example, J. Gonda, *Les Religions de l'Inde,* vol. 1, *Védisme et hindouisme ancien* (translated from the German; Payot: Paris, 1979), 378–80.
131. S. Guha, *Environment and Ethnicity in India, 1200–1991* (Cambridge University Press: Cambridge, 1999), 153–4. For the last few hundred years and the British Raj, see also 49–53 and 136–7.
132. Later called Huangyuan county under the Republic.
133. Note the 'Huang' here was not the Yellow River. The Chinese character is a homophone but not a homograph.
134. Domesday Book was a detailed nationwide survey of the resources of England made in 1085–6 at the orders of William the Conqueror.
135. Li Qing, ed., *Qinghai difang jiu zhi wu-zhong* [Five old gazetteers from Qinghai] (Qing; reprinted, Qinghai Renmin chubanshe: Xining, 1989), hereafter *QHDFJZWZ,* 237–40.

136. *QHDFJZWZ*, 235–7.

137. Chinese 'feet' and 'inches'. Conversion ratios varied locally, but were near enough to allow the terms to be left unadjusted here, since no guide to an exact local equivalent is available.

138. See, for example, *QHDFJZWZ*, 351, and for background, 287–8.

139. Because the rate of increase in a logistic starts slowing down after a certain point and the curve heads asymptotically toward a maximum value. The exponential, in contrast, explodes off the top of the graph at a rate that increases for ever (in the world of the mind, at least).

5 War and the Logic of Short-term Advantage

1. Xiaoneng Yang, *Reflections of Early China: Decor, Pictographs, and Pictorial Inscriptions* (Nelson-Atkins Museum of Art with the University of Washington Press: Seattle, Wash., 2000), 175.

2. J. Baechler, *Esquisse d'une histoire universelle* (Fayard: Paris, 2002), 63.

3. J. Golson, "From horticulture to agriculture in the New Guinea highlands: A case study of people and their environments," in P. Kirch and T. Hunt, eds., *Historical Ecology in the Pacific Islands* (Yale University Press: New Haven, Conn., 1997). Under certain circumstances the degradation of forest soils after they had been subjected to a shifting horticultural system of multiple crops in each unit of area led to the development of a more stable but tilled agricultural system with a single crop per plot, located within regular ditches and later on raised beds.

4. M. Cohen, *Health and the Rise of Civilization* (Yale University Press: New Haven, Conn., 1989), generally and 119 and 214 on the tendency for average body size to fall in the Neolithic.

5. L. H. Greenwood, *Epidemics and Crowd Diseases* (Macmillan: New York, 1935); F. McFarlane Burnet, *Natural History of Infectious Diseases*, rev. edn (Cambridge University Press: Cambridge, 1972).

6. J. Swabe, *Animals, Disease and Human Society: Human–Animal Relations and the Rise of Veterinary Medicine* (Routledge: London, 1999), esp. chapters 1, 2, and 3.

7. C. K. Maisels, *Early Civilizations of the Old World: The Formative Histories of Egypt, The Levant, Mesopotamia, India and China* (Routledge: London, 1999), 344.

8. There is an excellent summary of the process as described in Western scholarship in Maisels, *Early Civilizations*, chapter 5. Chapter 6 puts China into a comparative Old-World perspective.

9. J. Gledhill, B. Bender, and M. Larsen, eds., *State and Society: The Emergence and Development of Social Hierarchy and Political Centralization* (1988; reprinted, Routledge: London, 1995).

10. Gledhill *et al.*, *State and Society*, 62–3, 65, 68, 110, 149, 151–2, and 205.

11. Gledhill *et al.*, *State and Society*, 68.

12. Gledhill *et al.*, *State and Society*, 71.

13. Gledhill *et al.*, *State and Society*, 23, 94, and 98.

14. Gledhill *et al.*, *State and Society*, 78 and 93.

15. Gledhill *et al.*, *State and Society*, 92 and 97.

16. Gledhill *et al.*, *State and Society*, 63 and 201.

17. Gledhill *et al.*, *State and Society*, 67.

18. Gledhill *et al.*, *State and Society*, 157.

19. Gledhill *et al.*, *State and Society*, 113, 149, and 152–3.
20. Gledhill *et al.*, *State and Society*, 149.
21. Gledhill *et al.*, *State and Society*, 149, 152–3, chapter 11, 193, 195–6, and 202.
22. For sketches of patterns close to the opposite end of the range of sizes, see L. Mitchell and P. Rhodes, eds., *The Development of the Polis in Archaic Greece* (Routledge: London, 1997).
23. Primarily in J. Baechler, *Démocraties* (Calmann-Lévy: Paris, 1985), but also in J. Baechler, *Nature et histoire* (Presses Universitaires de France: Paris, 2000).
24. Baechler, *Nature et histoire*, 152 and 246–7.
25. Baechler, *Démocraties*, 658 and 660.
26. Baechler, *Démocraties*, 659.
27. Baechler, *Démocraties*, 662.
28. Baechler, *Démocraties*, 620, 623, and 665, and Baechler, *Nature et histoire*, 449.
29. Baechler, *Démocraties*, 616.
30. Baechler, *Démocraties*, 666.
31. Baechler, *Démocraties*, 667.
32. Baechler, *Démocraties*, 629.
33. Baechler, *Démocraties*, 613.
34. Baechler, *Démocraties*, 629.
35. Baechler, *Démocraties*, 625.
36. Baechler, *Démocraties*, 641.
37. Baechler, *Démocraties*, 663.
38. Baechler, *Démocraties*, 667.
39. Or, exceptionally, in what is now Zhejiang province, massive platforms raised on hill tops. See Xiaoneng Yang, *Reflections of Early China*, 174.
40. Two books by Mark Lewis offer a background to several of these themes, even though they are written from a different perspective. These are M. E. Lewis, *Sanctioned Violence in Early China* (State University of New York Press: Albany, N.Y. 1990) and *Writing and Authority in Early China* (State University of New York Press: Albany, N.Y., 1999). On early pictograms, see Kaizuka Shigeki, *Chūgoku kodai sai hakken* [Further discoveries about Chinese antiquity] (Iwanami: Tokyo, 1979), 70.
41. Song Zhenhao, *Xia-Shang shehui shenghuo shi* [Social life under the Xia and Shang] (Zhongguo shehui kexue chubanshe: Beijing, 1994), 515–22.
42. B. Karlgren, *The Book of Odes: Chinese Text, Transcription, and Translation* (Museum of Far Eastern Antiquities: Stockholm, 1950), #305. The translation given here varies at points from the accepted version. The only item about which the reader needs to be warned is the term rendered 'enfeoffment'. This is logical in terms of the usual dictionary meanings and overall context, but not supported by commentators. The usual rendering is by the adjective 'great' (in the sense that the subordinate states were told they enjoyed 'great good fortune'). Since Shirakawa Shizuka, *Kōkotsubun no sekai* [The world of the oracle bone script] (Heibonsha: Tokyo, 1972), 142 and 148, talks of a sort of royal 'familial feudalism' in Shang times, this makes the translation at least arguable. For a similar view as regards late Shang, see Yabuuchi Kiyoshi, *Chūgoku bummei no keisei* [The formation of Chinese Civilization] (Iwanami: Tokyo, 1974), 37, 42, and 45. Tang was the founder of the Shang-Yin. Yu was the last of the sage–emperors, and famed for his hydraulic achievements. Jing and Chu were states in the middle Yangzi region.
43. Assigning precise dates before the mid ninth century BCE is a well-known problem in archaic Chinese history. Here I follow D. Keightley, *Sources of Shang History: The Oracle-*

Bone Inscriptions of Bronze Age China (University of California Press: Berkeley, Calif., 1978), 174–6 and Table 38 on 228. Alternative views put the date considerably earlier.

44. Karlgren, *Odes*, #241. Chinese societies at this period still retained some of the characteristics of the social structure based on age-groups, hence the explicit addition of 'cousins' to 'brothers' and the gloss 'kin of one generation'.

45. Drawings may be found in Song Zhenhao, *Social life under the Xia and Shang*, plate 56 (at the end of the volume). Liu Yang and E. Capon, *Masks of Mystery: Ancient Chinese Bronzes from Sanxingdui* (Art Gallery of New South Wales: Sydney, 2000), provide stunning color photographs.

46. Kaizuka Shigeki, *Further Discoveries*, 71, 101–2, and 107. Xiaoneng Yang, *Reflections of Early China*, 47–82.

47. Song Zhenhao, *Social Life under the Xia and Shang*, 107.

48. Xu Jinxiong, *Zhongguo gudai shehui* [Ancient Chinese society] (Taiwan shangwu yinshuguan: Taibei, 1988), 408–11.

49. Kaizuka Shigeki, *Further Discoveries*, 83–7. Photographs and map in K.-C. Chang, *Shang Civilization* (Yale University Press: New Haven, Conn., 1980), 274–5.

50. Yabuuchi Kiyoshi, *Formation of Chinese Civilization*, 39.

51. Satō Taketoshi, *Chūgoku kodai kogyō-shi no kenkyū* [Researches on industries in ancient China] (Yoshikawa kōbunkan: Tokyo, 1962), 1–20 and 116–20. See also Kaizuka Shigeki, *Further Discoveries*, 88.

52. K.-C. Chang, *Shang Civilization*, 153–5. This only applies to one of the two species, *Cypraea annulus*.

53. K. Polanyi, *Primitive, Archaic and Modern Economies* (Doubleday: New York, 1968), 280–305, stresses the links that cowry money had to the initial creation of states, notably in west Africa.

54. Xu Jinxiong, *Ancient Chinese Society*, 361.

55. Chao Lin, *The Socio-Political System of the Shang Dynasty* (Academia Sinica: Taibei, 1982), 61, 68, and 103. For a royal grave at Anyang with about 7,000 shells see 3.

56. Xu Jinxiong, *Ancient Chinese Society*, 361–2.

57. Xu Jinxiong, *Ancient Chinese Society*, 358.

58. Song Zhenhao, *Social Life under the Xia and Shang*, 236–7. The evidence relating to Wang Hai is interesting but not conclusive.

59. Kaizuka Shigeki, *Further Discoveries*, 101.

60. Kaizuka Shigeki, *Further Discoveries*, 145. On the distribution of the sources of copper and tin in Shang times, see K.-C. Chang, *Shang Civilization*, 131–3.

61. R. Fletcher, *The Limits of Settlement Growth: A Theoretical Outline* (Cambridge University Press: Cambridge, 1995). On Shang urban drainage, see Song Zhenhao, *Social Life under the Xia and Shang*, 26.

62. J. D. Hughes, *Pan's Travail: Environmental Problems of the Ancient Greeks and Romans* (Johns Hopkins University Press: Baltimore, Md., 1994), 33. Ancient Egypt was less confrontational.

63. Hughes, *Pan's Travail*, 168.

64. Yang Kuan, *Zhongguo gudai ducheng zhidu shi yanjiu* [Researches in the history of the systems of the capital cities of Chinese antiquity] (Shanghai guji chubanshe: Shanghai, 1993), 10, 13, and 16–17.

65. *LJ*: *Liji* [Records of ritual behavior] (later Han), in vol. 4 of *Shisan jing zhushu* [The thirteen scriptures] (reprinted, 7 vols., Chūbun shuppansha: Toyko, 1971), "Li yun," 3059.

66. Yang Kuan, *Capital Cities of Chinese Antiquity*, 19, 20, 23–5, and 31–9. See also K.-C. Chang, *Shang Civilization*, 134, 158–61, and 268.

67. Karlgren, *Odes*, #250.
68. Karlgren, *Odes*, #237.
69. Karlgren, *Odes*, #237.
70. See the introduction to W. A. Rickett, *Guanzi: Political, Economic, and Philosophical Essays from Early China* (2 vols., Princeton University Press: Princeton, N.J., vol. I, 1985, vol. II, 1998). My translations were drafted before I consulted this painstaking and valuable work. I have made many emendations after reading Rickett's version, and owe it a debt that should be acknowledged, even if at times I differ significantly in my interpretations. References to his translation are marked with an 'R'.
71. Huang Jie and Lin Boxhou, eds., *Guanzi jiping* [The *Master Guan* with collected appraisals] (late fourth century BCE; Zhongguo zixue mingzhu jicheng bianyin jijinhui: Taibei, 1978), hereafter GZ, 191–2 / R I:227.
72. GZ, 79 / R I:104.
73. Cited in Yang Kuan, *Capital Cities of Chinese Antiquity*, 242, footnote 2.
74. The translation of *zhi qiao* in the last sentence is highly speculative.
75. Yang Kuan, *Capital Cities of Chinese Antiquity*, 209–11, 219, 224–6, and 232.
76. The reference is to the old German tag 'Stadtluft macht frei'.
77. Cheng Te-k'un, *Archaeology in China*, vol. 2, *Shang* (Heffer and Sons: Cambridge, 1960), 200; Xu Jinxiong, *Ancient Chinese Society*, 361–2.
78. Xiaoneng Yang, *Reflections of Early China*, 200–3.
79. The final speculations apart, this picture is based on Shirakawa Shizuka, *Oracle Bone World*, 40–183; Xu Jinxiong, *Ancient Chinese Society*, 438–57; Song Zhenhao, *Social Life under the Xia and Shang*, 452–532; Xiaoneng Yang, *Reflections of Early China*, 36, 43, 63, 116–17, 197, 200–3, and 211; K.-C. Chang, *Shang Civilization, passim*; and Cheng Te-k'un, *Archaeology in China*, vol. 2, *Shang*, 134, 136 (unit of length), 200 (shells per string), and 225 (musical scales).
80. P. Clastres, *Society against the State: Essays in Political Anthropology* (1974; English translation; Zone Books: New York, 1987).
81. *Ling.*
82. *Shangdi* or *di.*
83. *Di.*
84. Shima Kunio, *Inkyo bokuji kenkyū* [Researches on the divination texts from the ruins of Yin] (Kyūko shoin: Tokyo, 1958), 198, 191–2, and 199.
85. Shima Kunio, *Divination Texts*, 206.
86. Shima Kunio, *Divination Texts*, 211.
87. Shima Kunio, *Divination Texts*, 416, 485–6, 493–4, and 502.
88. Shirakawa Shizuka, *Oracle Bone World*, 204 and 207–9. Also Yabuuchi Kiyoshi, *Formation of Chinese Civilization*, 37–8.
89. Shima Kunio, *Divination Texts*, 410–12.
90. Shirakawa Shizuka, *Oracle Bone World*, 188, 194, 199, 204–5, 209, and 211.
91. Shirakawa Shizuka, *Oracle Bone World*, 199 and 201.
92. Shirakawa Shizuka, *Oracle Bone World*, 189 and 192.
93. Shirakawa Shizuka, *Oracle Bone World*, 203.
94. S. Couvreur, *Tch'ouen Ts'iou et Tso Tchouan: La Chronique de la principauté de Lou* (1914; reprinted, bilingual text, 3 vols., Cathasia: Paris, 1951), III:501–2, Ding 4.
95. Yabuuchi Kiyoshi, *Formation of Chinese Civilization*, 37.
96. Shirakawa Shizuka, *Bronze Inscriptions*, 60, 68, 78 158–61, 185, 249–50, 257, and 259.
97. Clastres, *Society against the State*, 202.
98. Clastres, *Society against the State*, 206.

99. Clastres, *Society against the State*, 208.
100. Clastres, *Society against the State*, 214–18.
101. Discussed in M. Elvin, "Three thousand years of unsustainable growth: China's environment from archaic times to the present," *East Asian History* 6 (Nov. 1993), 17–18.
102. 'War economy', the term given during the First World War to the command system of production developed in Germany by Walther Rathenau.
103. As noted earlier, the use of the plural here is unusual in works of English, though normal in French, while the Chinese term permits either translation. For a brief discussion and a reference please see Table 1 on page 6 above.
104. Hughes, *Pan's Travail*, 198–9.
105. *GZ*, 108–9 / R I:131.
106. *GZ*, 152 / R I:195.
107. *GZ*, 152–3 / R I:195.
108. *GZ*, 198 / R I:230. R renders "if the ruler . . . is unrestrained in the area of resources, . . . the people will have no rest in their expenditure of energy."
109. *GZ*, 202 / R I:233. R renders 'armed forces' as 'state'.
110. *GZ*, 350–1 / R I:370.
111. *GZ*, 183 / R I:220. R reads 'the nations's knights' for 'state's territory'.
112. *GZ*, 192–3 / RI:227.
113. The term *ye* refers to the cleared space beyond the permanently farmed core but before the surrounding woods. In later times *ye* has tended to acquire the sense of 'wild', 'the wilds', or 'wilderness'.
114. R renders 'do not collect their harvests' rather than 'cannot be retained'.
115. *GZ*, 198 / R I:230.
116. S*JS*: *Shangjun shu jiegu dingben* [The book of the Lord of Shang, definitive edition with explanations] (pre-Qin; Guji chubanshe: Beijing, 1956), 7, 'Kenling'. This passage is also cited by Yoshinami Takashi, "Chūgoku kodai santaku-ron no saikentō" [A re-examination of the theories about 'mountains and marshes' in ancient China], in Chūgoku Suiri Shi Kenkyūkai, ed., *Chūgoku suiri shi ronshu* [A collection of essays on the history of water control in China] (Kokusho kanōkai: Tokyo, 1981), 11.
117. *GZ*, 296 / R I:325.
118. The 'seasonal rains' were traditionally assigned to the late spring of the lunar calendar. The main rains in north China today fall from mid June till late August, and so the term fairly certainly does not apply to these but to the return of some limited rainfall after the dry winter. Rainfall patterns more than two thousand years ago may have been different, but there is a faint bimodal pattern at present, north of about 30°, with a first, and very small, peak in April. See Ding Yihui, *Monsoons over China* (Kluwer: Dordrecht, 1994), 29. See also J. Chapman, "Climate," in J. L. Buck, ed., *Land Utilization in China* (1937; reprinted, Paragon: New York, 1964), 111.
119. *GZ*, 297 / R I:325–6. R puts the passage in the past tense, which is one legitimate way of reading it.
120. *GZ*, 321–2 / R I:346.
121. *GZ*, 83–4 / R I:107–8.
122. Derk Bodde has noted that *ze*, which is normally translated 'marshes', and which I often render as 'wetlands', is sometimes used in contexts where a watery environment does not seem very likely. This includes references to their being burnt. 'Meadows', or, in my view, 'open bushland' may therefore at times be a better reading. See D. Bodde, "Marshes in *Mencius* and elsewhere: A lexicographical note," in D. Roy and T. Tsien, eds., *Ancient China: Studies in Early Civilization* (Chinese University Press: Hong Kong, 1978).

123. *GZ*, 605–8 / R II:247–50.

124. This last is a guess, based on taking *cai* as having the meaning of *sui*, 'years of age', and seeing a plausible parallel in Hoshi Ayao, *Chūgoku shakai-keizai-shi go-i* [Glossary of terms in China's social and economic history] (Kindai Chūgoku kenkyūsentā: Tokyo, 1966), 164, entry *caiguan*.

125. Literally a 'bag', that is, an enclosure.

126. *GZ*, 304 / R I:330–1.

127. For example, *GZ* 109, 111, and 149.

128. *HNZ:Huainanzi* [The book of the Prince of Huainan] (Second century BCE; reprinted, Zhongguo zixue mingzhu jicheng bianyin jijinhui: Taibei, 1978), 8: 257–61. My attention was first drawn to this passage by H. Roetz's essay, "On nature and culture in Zhou China," unpublished paper presented to the conference on "Understanding Nature in China and Europe until the eighteenth century," Rheine, March 2000.

129. 'Vital aethers' are *qì*, which I often translate as 'matter–energy–vitality'. The underlying sense is 'breath' conceived of as an attenuated form of animate matter.

130. Cp. H. Roetz, *Mensch und Natur im alten China: Zum Subjekt-Objekt-Gegensatz in der klassischen chinesischen Philosophie* (Lang: Frankfurt am Main, 1984), 128–35.

131. *SGZ: Sanguo zhi* [Record of the Three Kingdoms] (Jin; reprinted, Zhonghua shuju: Beijing, 1969), "Wei shu," 28: 775–6. This passage is also discussed in Sakuma Kichiya, *Gi Shin Nanboku-chō suiri-shi kenkyū* [A study of the history of water control under the Wei, Jin and Northern and Southern Dynasties] (Kaimei shoin: n.p., 1980), 13–14, and in Elvin, "Three Thousand Years," 24.

132. Li Qing, ed., *Qinghai difang jiu zhi wu-zhong* [Five old local gazetteers from Qinghai] (Qing; reprinted, Qinghui Renmin chubanshe: Xining, 1989), hereafter *QHDFJZWZ*, 627–8. The subordinate was Deputy Military Commissioner Liu Minkuan, stationed at Xining.

133. The catty or *jin* was about 590 grams. See Qiu Guangming, *Zhongguo lidai du-liang-heng kao* [Researches on measures of length, capacity, and weight in the successive Chinese dynasties] (Kexue chubanshe: Beijing, 1992), 491.

134. Hematite, the principal source of iron, when well crystallized, has "glittering mirror-like surfaces." See A. Hallam, ed., *Planet Earth* (Phaidon: Oxford, 1977), 130 (and photograph).

135. Coke, or 'charcoal coal', was also sometimes used for smelting iron ore in the Northwest. See *QHDFJZWZ*, 581.

136. The stele text has a gap of a character at this point.

137. Hoshi Ayao, *The Tribute Grain Transport under the Ming Dynasty*, translated M. Elvin (Center for Chinese Studies: Ann Arbor, Mich., 1969).

6 *Water and the Costs of System Sustainability*

1. See the comments of J. Radkau, *Natur und Macht: Eine Weltgeschichte der Umwelt* (Beck: München, 2000), esp. chapter 3 "Wasser, Wald und Macht."

2. Shiba Yoshinobu, *Sōdai Kōnan keizai-shi no kenkyū* [Researches on the economic history of Jiangnan under the Song] (Tōyō Daigaku Tōyō Bunka Kenkyūjo: Tokyo, 1988), 403–22. Yuanzhou in early Song times had 20,000 to 25,000 inhabitants.

3. J. Needham with Wang Ling and Liu Gwei-djen, *Science and Civilisation in China*, vol. 4.III, *Civil Engineering and Nautics* (Cambridge University Press: Cambridge, 1971), 350–60.

4. Morita Akira, *Shindai suirishi kenkyū* [Researches on the history of water control under the Qing dynasty] (Aki shobō: Tokyo, 1974), 118–34.

5. Yu Yue, ed., *Tongzhi Shanghai xianzhi* [Gazetteer of Shanghai county for the Tongzhi reign] (Shanghai, 1871), 4:43a.

6. A 'polder' may be defined as an area that for at least some part of the year lies below the mean level of the water outside it, and from which it is protected by a dike.

7. M. Elvin, "Market towns and waterways: The county of Shang-hai from 1480 to 1910," in G. W. Skinner, ed., *The City in Late Imperial China* (Stanford University Press: Stanford, Calif., 1977), 466–7. 'Public selection' indicates a form of informal election, that is, without quantified balloting.

8. Morita Akira, *Qing Water Control*, 161.

9. Morita Akira, *Qing Water Control*, 364.

10. M. Elvin, "On water control and management during the Ming and Ch'ing periods: A review article," in *Ch'ing-shih wen-t'i* 3.3 (Nov. 1975), 89.

11. See K. A. Wittfogel, *Oriental Despotism* (Yale University Press: New Haven, Conn., 1957) for the extreme version. The same author's *Wirtschaft und Gesellschaft Chinas* (Harrassowitz: Leipzig, 1931) is more measured.

12. M. Elvin and N. Su, "Man against the sea: Natural and anthropogenic factors in the changing morphology of Harngzhou Bay, circa 1000–1800," *Environment and History* 1.1 (Feb. 1995), 47–8.

13. Morita Akira, *Qing Water Control*, 289.

14. See K. MacPherson, "Cholera in China 1820–1930: An aspect of the internationalization of infectious disease," in M. Elvin and T.-J. Liu, eds., *Sediments of Time: Environment and Society in Chinese History* (Cambridge University Press: New York, 1998), esp. 497–8.

15. D. Perkins, *Agricultural Development in China 1368–1968* (Edinburgh University Press: Edinburgh, 1969), 60–5 and 333–44.

16. Shuili shuidian kexue yanjiu-yuan and Wuhan shuili dianli xueyuan, eds., *Zhongguo shuili-shi gao* [Draft history of water control in China], *xia*, 2–12.

17. Tsuruma Kazuyuki, "Shōsuikyo Tokōen Teikokukyo wo tazunete: Shin teikoku no keisei to Sensokuki no san daisuiri jigyō" [A visit to the Zhang river canal, the Du river dike, and the Zheng Guo canal: On the formation of the Qin empire and the three great hydraulic schemes of the Warring States period], *Chūgoku suiri shi kenkyū* 17 (1987), 40–1. The numerical data are all taken from this source.

18. Li Yuan, *Shu shuijing* [The classic of the waterways of Sichuan] (1794; reprinted, 2 vols., Ba-Shu shushe: Chengdu, 1985), 2:11b. See also Needham, *Science and Civilisation in China*, 4.III, 293.

19. H. Chamley, *Sédimentologie* (Dunod: Paris, 1987), 142.

20. Shuili shuidian kexue yanjiu-yuan, *Draft History of Water Control*, *shang*, 66–70.

21. Needham, *Science and Civilisation in China*, 4.III, 285–7; Tsuruma, "Great hydraulic schemes of the Warring States," 44; Shuili shuidian kexue yanjiu-yuan, *Draft History of Water Control*, *shang*, 118–32.

22. P.-E. Will, "Clear waters versus muddy waters The Zheng-bai irrigation system of Shaanxi province in the late-imperial period," in Elvin and Liu, eds., *Sediments of Time*, 283–343.

23. W. B. Arthur, "Positive feedbacks in the economy," *Scientific American* 262.2 (Feb. 1990), 84–5.

24. Examples are the VHS video system, the Fortran programing language (now fading), the QWERTY layout of the standard typewriter keyboard, and English spelling.

25. M. Elvin, D. Crook, Shen Ji, R. Jones, and J. Dearing, "The impact of clearance and irrigation on the environment in the Lake Erhai catchment from the ninth to the nineteenth century," *East Asian History* 23 (June 2002).

26. Li Zhiyang, ed., *Jiajing Dali fuzhi* [Jiajing reign-period Dali prefectural gazetteer]. (1563 (incomplete), microfilm 1055 in the Menzies Library), Australian National University, 1:56b. On 'commoner–civilians' see footnote 8.15.

27. *Dali Prefectural Gazetteer*, 1:57a.

28. *Dali Prefectural Gazetteer*, 1:57a.

29. This presumably refers to timber already cut and stacked for use, and so a particularly tempting target.

30. *Dali Prefectural Gazetteer*, 1:57b.

31. Hou Yunqin, comp. and rev., *Dengchuan zhouzhi* [Dengchuan department gazetteer] (1854/1855; reprinted, Chengwen chubanshe: Taibei, 1968), 82.

32. *Dengchuan Department Gazetteer*, 79 and 82.

33. *Dengchuan Department Gazetteer*, 90–103.

34. Cited in Li Yuanfang, "Fei-Huanghe sanjiaozhou-de yanbian" [Changes in the deltas of the abandoned Yellow River], *Dili xuebao* 10.4 (1991), 38, footnote 39.

35. Tani Mitsutaka, *Mindai Kakō-shi kenkyū* [Studies on the hydraulics of the Yellow River in the Ming dynasty] (Dōhōsha: Kyōto, 1991), 20.

36. Tani Mitsutaka, *Yellow River*, 17.

37. Tani Mitsutaka, *Yellow River*, 165. His name was Shu Yinglong.

38. On this theme see R. Dodgen, *Controlling the Dragon: Confucian Engineers and the Yellow River in Late Imperial China* (Hawaii University Press: Honolulu, 2001). When I say "dirtied his hands," this has probably to be interpreted metaphorically.

39. Tani Mitsutaka, *Yellow River*, 271.

40. This account is based mainly on Tani Mitsutaka, *Yellow River*. I am most grateful to Professor Tani for the gift of his book.

41. Tuotuo, *et al.*, eds. *Jin shi* [History of the Jin] (Reprinted, Zhonghua shuju: Beijing, 1975), "Hequ zhi," 27:670.

42. Tuotuo, *History of the Jin*, 27:674. It was usual, as already noted, to distinguish 'position-power' from 'strength'. Wang Chong, for example, noted that while cattle and horses had greater strength (*li*) than the mosquitoes and gnats who pestered them, they had less position-power (*shi*). See Huang Hui, ed., *Lun heng jiaoshi* [Wang Chong's 'Discourses weighed in the balance', corrected and explained] (Han; 4 vols. Shangwu yinshuguan: Taibei, 1964), hereafter *LHJS*, 145.

43. For a channel of given roughness and slope, the speed of the water varies as the two-thirds power of *R*, the cross-sectional flow area divided by the length of the wetted perimeter. The capacity to carry sediment is proportional to the fourth power of this speed.

44. Tuotuo, *History of the Jin*, 27:678.

45. At 33° 30′ N, 114° 50′ E.

46. At 32° 30′ N, 116° 45′ E.

47. Tani Mitsutaka, *Yellow River*, citing the *Baoying tujing*: introduction, 20, footnote 24 and main text, 5–6.

48. Cited in Wu Qihua [Wu Chi-hua], "Huanghe zai Mingdai gaidao qianxi hejue Zhangqiu-de niandai" [On the date of the breach at Zhangqiu just prior to the change of course of the Yellow River in the Ming dynasty], in Wu Qihua, ed., *Mingdai shehui jingji shiluncong* [Collected historical essays on the society and economy of the Ming dynasty] (Taiwan xuesheng shuju: Taibei, 1970), 368.

49. I.e., the Qin He in Handan in northern Zhili.
50. Wu Qihua, "On the date of the breach at Zhangqiu," 375.
51. Li Yuanfang, "Abandoned Yellow River delta," 30.
52. Tani Mitsutaka, *Yellow River*, 54.
53. Zhu Shang.
54. Fu Zehong, ed., *Xingshui jinjian* [The golden mirror of the passing streams] (c. 1725; reprinted, Wenhai: Taibei, 1969, in Shen Yunlong, ed., *Zhongguo shuiliyaoji congbian*), 23:958.
55. Gu Zuyu, ed., *Dushi fangyu jiyao* [Essential geography for the reading of history] (1667; reprinted, Xinxing: Taibei 1972), *chuandu* 3, "Da He" *xia*, 126:6b. Also cited in Tani Mitsutaka, *Yellow River*, 12.
56. Tani Mitsutaka, *Yellow River*, 53.
57. Tani Mitsutaka, *Yellow River*, 24, footnote 29.
58. Tani Mitsutaka, *Yellow River*, 64.
59. Li Yuanfang, "Abandoned Yellow River delta," 30.
60. A traditional phrase for the total transformation of a situation.
61. Gu Yanwu, comp., *Tianxia junguo libing shu* [Documents on the advantageous and disadvantageous aspects of the principates and commanderies of the empire] (1639–62; reprinted, Shangwu yinshuguan: Shanghai, 1936), 'Huai', *ce* 10, [13], 56ab.
62. Gu Yanwu, *Advantages and Disadvantages*, 'Huai', *ce* 10 [13], 44b.
63. Gu Yanwu, *Advantages and Disadvantages*, 'Huai', *ce* 10 [13], 44b.
64. For an excellent introduction to Pan's work, see E. Vermeer, "P'an Chi-hsün's solutions for the Yellow River problems of the late sixteenth century," *T'oung Pao* LXXIII (1987).
65. Tani Mitsutaka, *Yellow River*, 373.
66. Tani Mitsutaka, *Yellow River*, 374.
67. Tani Mitsutaka, *Yellow River*, 374.
68. Tani Mitsutaka, *Yellow River*, 392. On the name '*menxian* sediments' see Zhang Tingyu, ed., *Ming shi* [History of the Ming dynasty] (Qing; reprinted, Zhonghua shuju: Beijing, 1974), "Hequ zhi er," "Huanghe xia," 84:2059.
69. Zhang Tingyu, *Ming History*, 84:2052.
70. Zhang Tingyu, *Ming History*, 84:2051.
71. *Natura non vincitur nisi parendo.*
72. Zhang Tingyu, *Ming History*, 84:2056.
73. Zhang Zhenguan.
74. Zhang Tingyu, *Ming History*, 84:2056.
75. Zhang Tingyu, *Ming History*, 84:2056.
76. Zhang Tingyu, *Ming History*, 84:2057.
77. Zhang Tingyu, *Ming History*, 84:2060–2.
78. Zhang Tingyu, *Ming History*, 84:2062.
79. See the life of Jin Fu in A. Hummel, ed., *Eminent Chinese of the Ch'ing Period* (2 vols, U.S. Government Printing Office: Washington, D.C., 1943), 161–3.
80. Fu Zehong, *Golden Mirror of the Passing Streams*, 47: 1718–19. See also 51:1836–7.
81. Converting at 1 Chinese foot = 0·35814 meters, following Naval Intelligence Division, *China Proper* (His Majesty's Stationery Office: Edinburgh, 1945), III:610. This was presumably the length of waterway diked, not the total length of dike, which ran on both sides. The distance from Yunti-guan to the sea was taken at this time as approximately 100 li (Fu Zehong, *Golden Mirror of the Passing Streams*, 48:1730), about 50 kilometers, or 57.6 according to the *China Proper* table. In other words, not greatly different from 64.5 km.
82. Fu Zehong, *Golden Mirror of the Passing Streams*, 52:1875.

83. Fu Zehong, *Golden Mirror of the Passing Streams*, 50:1818–19.

84. Jin Fu was of the opinion that the river mouth was still large enough to carry the peak discharge in the middle of the century. See Fu Zehong, *Golden Mirror of the Passing Streams*, 48:1749–50, and also Jin's comment in 1677 that the lowest section of the main course had "all silted up and become land" for "more than ten years," *in eodem*, 48:1725.

85. Fu Zehong, *Golden Mirror of the Passing Streams*, 49:1783.

86. Wang Zhibin, "Huanghe wenti-de jidian kanfa—dui Wei.Jin.Nanbeichao" [Some understanding of the issue of the Yellow River during the Wei, the Jin, and the Northern and Southern dynasties], *Renmin Huanghe* 5 (1980), and "Kaifeng Huanghe jueyi mantan" [A general discussion of the breaking of the Yellow River dikes at Kaifeng], *Renmin Huanghe* 4 (1984).

87. Fu Zehong, *Golden Mirror of the Passing Streams*, 47:1721.

88. Fu Zehong, *Golden Mirror of the Passing Streams*, 48:1751 and 49:1767.

89. Fu Zehong, *Golden Mirror of the Passing Streams*, 48:1725–6.

90. Fu Zehong, *Golden Mirror of the Passing Streams*, 49:1768–9.

91. Fu Zehong, *Golden Mirror of the Passing Streams*, 48:1726.

92. Fu Zehong, *Golden Mirror of the Passing Streams*, 49:1775.

93. J. Leonard, *Controlling from Afar: The Daoguang Emperor's Management of the Grand Canal Crisis, 1824–1826* (Center for Chinese Studies, University of Michigan: Ann Arbor, Mich., 1996).

94. I. Amelung, "Der Gelbe Fluss in Shandong (1851–1911): Überschwemmungskatastrophen und ihre Bewältigungen im spät-kaiserlichen China" (Ph.D. thesis, Institut für Philosophie, Wissenschaftstheorie, Wissenschafts- und Technikgeschichte, Technische Universität Berlin, 1999).

95. On the canal, which also had irrigation functions, see Sheng Hongyuan and Qiu Zhirong, "Woguo zuizao-de rengong yunhe zhi yi: Shanyin gu shuidao" [One of the oldest man-made waterways in our land: The old Shanyin canal], and Yao Hanyuan, "Zhedong yunhe-shi kaolüe" [A summary of a historical investigation into the Zhedong Canal], both in Sheng Honglang, ed., *Jianhu yu Shaoxing shuili* [Mirror Lake and water control in Shaoxing] (Zhongguo shudian: Beijing, 1991). The oldest section of this composite waterway, partly constructed and partly adapted from natural streams, goes back to the fifth century BCE. As a continuous system across the Shaoxing plain it probably dates from between the early fourth and the fifth century CE.

96. Lin Chengkun, "Changjiang-kou nisha-de laiyuan fenxi yu shiliang jisuan-de yanjiu" [Analysis of the sources and quantitities of sediments at the estuary of the Yangzi River], *Dili xuebao* 44.1 (1989), and "Changjiang yu Hangzhou-wan-de nisha yu hechuang yanbian dui Shanghai ji qi tonghai hangdao jianshe-de yingxiang" [The influence of the sediment in the Yangzi River estuary and Hangzhou Bay, and changes in the river bed, on the port of Shanghai and the construction of shipping channels giving access to the sea], *Dili xuebao* 45.1 (1990), 80; and also Cao Peikui, Gu Guochuan, Dong Yongfa, and Hu Fangxi, "Hangzhou-wan nisha yundong-de jiben tezheng" [The basic characteristics of sediment transport in Hangzhou Bay], *Huadong Shifan Daxue xuebao* 3 (1985), 75.

97. Zhou Sheng, Ni Haoqing, Zhao Yongming, Yang Yongchun, Wang Yifan, Lü Wende, and Liang Baoxiang, "Qiantangjiang shuixia fanghu gongcheng-de yanjiu yu shijian" [Research and practice relating to the protective underwater engineering on the Qiantang River], *Shuilixuebao* 1 (1992), 23.

98. Cheng Mingjiu (Hezhu), comp., *Sanjiangzha-wu quanshu* [Complete documents relating to the affairs of the lock at Three Rivers' Mouth] (prefaces of 1684, 1685, and 1687; published in 1702, republished with a continuation in 1854 (by Ping Heng),

Sanjiangzha-wu quanshu xuke [Supplement to the *Complete Documents Relating to the Affairs of the Lock at Three Rivers' Mouth*] (prefaces of 1835 and 1836)), *shang*, 2:2a. I am very grateful to Professor Shiba Yoshinobu for the gift of a copy of this book.

99. Within the imperial period at least the major southern cleft, or 'sea gate', seems to have been the regular mouth until the seventeenth century.

100. Su Shi, *Su Dongpoji* [Collected works of Su Dongpo] (Song: Shangwu yinshu-guan: Shanghai, 1939), *ce* 5, 9:53.

101. Cited in Chen Jiyu, Luo Zude, Chen Dechang, Xu Haigen, and Qiao Pengnian, "Qiantang-jiang hekou shakan-de xingcheng ji qi lishi yanbian" [The formation of and the historical changes in the sandbar at the mouth of the Qiantang River], *Dili xuebao* 30.2 (June 1964), 121.

102. At this date between Mount Kan and Mount Zhe, not the present mouth.

103. Chinese Academy of Sciences, *Zhongguo ziran dili* [Natural geography of China] (Kexue chubanshe: Beijing, 1982), 238–42. 'Wangpan' is also written 'Huangpan'.

104. Morita Akira, "Kōetsu ni okeru kaitō no suiri soshiki" [The hydraulic organization for seawalls in Jiangsu and Zhejiang provinces] (1965; reprinted in Morita Akira, *Researches on the History of Water Control under the Qing dynasty,* 1974).

105. F. Pearce, "Tidal warming," *New Scientist* 1.iv (2000), 12, summarizing the research of Charles Keeling. Tides are said to have reached their maximum strength around 1425 as part of an 1,800–year cycle contributing to driving climatic change. Tidal maxima in this cycle are associated with cold conditions.

106. Gu Zuyu, *Essential Geography,* 3760.

107. *RHXZ: Renhe xianzhi* [Renhe county gazetteer] (reprinted, Chengwen: Taibei, 1975); *Zhonghua fangzhi congshu* #179, Huazhong), 390.

108. Gu Yanwu, *Advantages and Disadvantages,* 'Zhejiang' *xia*: 3b–4a.

109. *Haining xianzhi* [Gazetteer of Haining county] (1765; reprinted, Chengwen: Taibei, 1983), *Zhongguo fangzhi congshu* #516, Huazhong, hereafter *HNXZ*, 461 and 463.

110. *HNXZ,* 1663.

111. Gu Yanwu, *Advantages and Disadvantages,* Zhejiang *xia*: 42ab.

112. Compare *HNXZ,* 463: "The 20 kilometers south of the county capital have turned entirely into sea."

113. Liu Hou.

114. Gu Yanwu, *Advantages and Disadvantages,* Zhejiang *xia*: 42b–43a. Compare *HNXZ,* 463.

115. In Gu Yanwu, *Advantages and Disadvantages,* Zhejiang *xia*: 47ab.

116. The discoloration of the coastal water due to its load of sediment is strikingly visible from satellite photographs.

117. Converting at 1 *qing* = 100 *mou* = approximately 7 hectares.

118. The passage within braces only appears in the *HNXZ,* 471.

119. Gu Yanwu, *Advantages and Disadvantages,* Zhejiang *xia*: 46b.

120. Di Junlian, ed., *Haitang-lu* [A record of the seawall], in *Qinding siku quanshu,* Shi-bu, *ce* 583 (compiled between 1764 and 1781; reprinted, Wenyuan-ge edn., Taiwan shangwu yinshu-guan: Taibei, 1986, hereafter *HTL,* 667. His name was Zhang Cizhong.

121. Probably the *xia ba shan* off Zhapu.

122. At this period in the southwest corner of Xiaoshan county.

123. Probably at the Lower Yan Family Bay on the right bank obliquely opposite Mount Wentang. See *Hangzhou fuzhi* [Hangzhou prefectural gazetteer] (1898, prefaces of 1888, 1894, and 1898; reprinted, Chengwen: Taibei, 1974), *Zhongguo fangzhi congshu* #199, Huazhong, hereafter *HZFZ /Q,* map, 256.

124. *HNXZ*, 474–5.
125. Zhu Shi.
126. *HNXZ*, 477.
127. *HTL*, 323–4.
128. *HTL*, 331.
129. *HNXZ*, 342, and compare 351.
130. Such scars were thought to indicate the imminent removal of the sediment in which they appeared.
131. Located east of Mount Chanji and on the northeast extremity of the south bank of the Central Cleft. See *HNXZ*, 70–1.
132. *HTL*, 353.
133. Sun Xiangping, *et al.*, *Zhongguo yan'an haiyang shuiwen qixiang gaikuang* [An outline of the hydrological patterns and weather of China's coastal seas] (Kexue chubanshe: Beijing, 1981), 13.
134. Chen Jiaqi, "Nan Song yilai Taihu liuyu dalao-dahan ji jinqi qushi guji" [Major floods and droughts in the Lake Tai basin since the Southern Song, and an estimation of the trend in the near future], *Dili yanjiu* 6.1 (Mar. 1987).
135. Gu Yanwu, *Advantages and Disadvantages*, Zhejiang *xia*: 50a. The term taken to indicate facing is *zou/zhou*, which means 'a well', and 'to repair a well'.
136. Gu Yanwu, *Advantages and Disadvantages*, Zhejiang *xia*: 41b. There are similar comments in Gu Zuyu, *Essential Geography*, 3833–4.
137. Zhou Xucai, comp., and Yu Qing, rev., *Shaoxing fu zhi* [Gazetteer for Shaoxing prefecture] (1719; reprinted, Chengwen: Taibei, 1983), *Zhongguo fangzhi congkan*, #537, Huazhong, hereafter *SXFZ*, 591.
138. The quotation from Ma Yaoxiang below describes this lock as lying to "the north." Cheng Mingjiu's *Three Rivers' Lock* (*Xia, xia*: 34a [from the sequence, the given pagination being faulty here]) says that it is 45 *li* (≈ 22.5 km) northwest of Shanyin county capital, that is Shaoxing, at the foot of Baima, that is, White Horse, Mountain.
139. Gu Yanwu, *Advantages and Disadvantages*, Zhejiang *xia*: 48a.
140. Chen Jiyu, Luo Zude, Chen Dechang, Xu Haigen, and Qiao Pengnian, "The sandbar at the mouth of the Qiantang River."
141. *HNXZ*, 469.
142. The character in the text is unclear. *Zhu qi* ('all the streams') may be *Zhe qi* ('[Mount] Zhe's streams'), but Mount Zhe is too small to have any major stream, so the reading given seems best.
143. In Gu Yanwu, *Advantages and Disadvantages*, Zhejiang *xia*: 43a–44b.
144. Present-day Pujiang.
145. Present-day Zhuji.
146. In the middle of the first millennium CE, the Puyang River entered a lake, the Linpu, north of where Linpu town stands today, but which has long since vanished, and then passed through a narrow channel into Fisherman's Inlet (Yupu), also now disappeared, which in turn emptied into the Qiantang some way upstream of Hangzhou city. See Chen Qiaoyi, "Lun lishi shiqi Puyang-jiang xiayou-de hedao bianqian" [Changes in the lower course of the Puyang River in historical times], *Lishi dili* 1 (1981), and Shiba Yoshinobu, *Economic History of Jiangnan*, 554–5 and 64.
147. Gu Yanwu, *Advantages and Disadvantages*, Zhejiang *xia*: 47a.
148. Gu Yanwu, *Advantages and Disadvantages*, Zhejiang *xia*: 47ab.
149. Cited in Gu Yanwu, *Advantages and Disadvantages*, Zhejiang *xia*: 48b.
150. Taking 4 square *li* as 1 square kilometer.

151. Gu Yanwu, *Advantages and Disadvantages*, Zhejiang *xia*: 47b–48a.

152. Located a short way upstream of the point where the Puyang River had been rerouted.

153. Gu Yanwu, *Advantages and Disadvantages*, Zhejiang *ce*: 50; *fuzhu* [appended notes]: 60a, note 9. The stones of the piers were tapered where they met the impact of the water, "so that they did not fight with it."

154. Gu Yanwu, *Advantages and Disadvantages*, Zhejiang *xia*: 49a.

155. Cheng Mingjiu, *Three Rivers' Lock, Shang, shang*, 'Tang-shen shishi lu', 12b.

156. Cheng Mingjiu, *Three Rivers' Lock, Xia, xia*: 3a.

157. Cheng Mingjiu, *Three Rivers' Lock, Xia, xia*: 36ab.

158. Cheng Mingjiu, *Three Rivers' Lock, Xia, xia*: 38a.

159. Cheng Mingjiu, *Three Rivers' Lock, Xia, xia*: 39a.

160. Cheng Mingjiu, *Three Rivers' Lock, Shang, shang*: 45b also speaks of removing fishing screens "so that the current of the river would flow swiftly to the sea."

161. Cheng Mingjiu, *Three Rivers' Lock, Xia, xia*: 39b–41a.

162. This term seems originally to have referred in Song times to uncultivated official land sold off for farming. See Sutō Yoshiyuki, *Chūgoku tochi-seido-shi kenkyū* [Studies of land tenure systems in China] (Tokyo University Press: Tokyo, 1954), 194, note 11. Later it could simply mean 'untaxed land', with an implication of its being heavily saline soil. See Hoshi Ayao, comp., *Chūgoku shakai keizai shi go-i zokuhen* [Supplement to 'A glossary of Chinese social and economic history'] (Kōbundō: Yamagata, 1975), 132.

163. *HTL*, 319.

164. *HTL*, 384.

165. *HTL*, 384.

166. *HTL*, 381–2.

167. *HTL*, 381. The term 'glacis' here indicates a sloping stone apron on the outside of the sea-wall.

168. For the justification of this translation, see *shansun* in E-tu Zen Sun, *Ch'ing Administrative Terms: A Translation of the Terminology of the Six Boards with Explanatory Notes* (Harvard University Press: Cambridge, Mass., 1961), #2428, 354.

169. Qiu Guangming, *Zhongguo lidai du-liang-heng kao* [Researches on measures of length, capacity, and weight in the successive Chinese dynasties] (Kexue chubanshe: Beijing, 1992), 513, gives around 596 grams to the Qing-dynasty *jin*. The Chinese 10-'inch' 'foot' at this time was about 35.24 cm. Ibid., 118–19.

170. *HTL*, 383.

171. Meaning unclear. Perhaps the 'roots' were obstructions?

172. *HTL*, 365.

173. Cheng Mingjiu, *Three Rivers' Lock, Shang*, Lu preface: 2a.

174. Cheng Mingjiu, *Three Rivers' Lock, Shang, shang*: 35b.

175. Ping Heng, *Sanjiangzha-wu quanshu xuke* [Supplement to the *Complete Documents Relating to the Affairs of the Lock at Three Rivers' Mouth*] (no publisher indicated: n.p., 1854), Prefaces of 1835 and 1836.

176. Cheng Mingjiu, *Three Rivers' Lock, Shang*, Luo preface: 1b.

177. Cheng Mingjiu, *Three Rivers' Lock, Shang, shang*: 14ab.

178. *Huishu* on its own was used, presumably as a mortar, to "stick stones together." See Cheng Mingjiu, *Three Rivers' Lock, Shang, shang*: 16a.

179. Compare the account in Cheng Mingjiu, *Three Rivers' lock, Shang, shang*: 16ab.

180. Cheng Mingjiu, *Three Rivers' Lock, Shang, shang*: 20b–21a.

181. Liu Guangdou.

182. Ping Heng, *Three Rivers' Lock, Supplement*, 1: 15a–16a.

183. Unidentified place name, possibly related to the alternative name for Hangzhou Bay, namely 'Houhai', and perhaps with a sense of 'the defensive perimeter of the Hou Sea'.

7 Richness to Riches: The Story of Jiaxing

1. There are hints of an early environmental richness similar to Jiaxing's in parts of the north almost a thousand years earlier. But only hints. Thus, probably speaking of the state of Han that around 800 BCE lay in the Northeast, south of modern Beijing (and not the better-known one in southeastern Shaanxi province), the *Scripture of Songs* says:

> Far-spreading its wetlands and streams,
> Plump and teeming its perch and its bream,
> Stags and does thronging — the herds of its deer!
> Bears, too, both the black, and bears brown-and-white.
> All were there. And likewise its wildcats and tigers.

This was where the ruler then "made walls of rammed earth, dug moats, laid out fields, and compiled registers of population." See B. Karlgren, *The Book of Odes: Chinese Text, Transcription and Translation* (Museum of Far Eastern Antiquities: Stockholm, 1950), #261.

2. Xu Yaoguang *et al.*, eds., *Jiaxing fuzhi* [Jiaxing prefectural gazetteer] (1879; 5 vols., revision of Wu Yangxian *et al.*, comp., reprinted in *Zhongguo fangzhi congshu* as Huazhong #53, Chengwen: Taibei, 1970), hereafter *JXFZ/Q*, 783.

3. The nature of this technology is a source of controversy among scholars. See Watabe Tadayo and Sakurai Yumio, eds., *Chūgoku Kōnan no inasaka bunka* [The rice culture of Jiangnan in China] (Nihon shōsō shuppan kyōkai: Tokyo, 1984), 1–54.

4. Shan Qing, *Zhiyuan Jiàhe zhi* [Gazeteer for Jiahe {≈ Jiaxing} in the Zhiyuan reign-period (1264–94)] (Yuan; revision of Xu Shi, comp., reprinted in Zhonghua shuju bianzhibu, ed., *Song-Yuan fangzhi congkan*, 8 vols., Zhonghua shuju: Beijing, 1990), hereafter *ZYJHZ*, 4500.

5. *ZYJHZ*, 4422.

6. *ZYJHZ*, 4441–2.

7. *ZYJHZ*, 4442.

8. *ZYJHZ*, 4444, 4450, 4452, etc.

9. *ZYJHZ*, 4597.

10. *ZYJHZ*, 4451–2.

11. *ZYJHZ*, 4453, 4455.

12. *JXFZ/Q*, 523, and Cao Shuji, *Qing shiqi* [The Qing period], vol. 5 of Ge Jianxiong, ed., *Zhongguo renkou shi* [History of China's population series] (Fudan daxue chubanshe: Shanghai, 2001), 472.

13. *JXFZ/Q*, 521 notes that there were 223,038 households in Guiji commandery in 'Han' times (a very long period, without specifying the date more precisely) and 1,032,604 inhabitants (a mean of 4.6 persons per household). There were 26 *xian* units in Guiji, 2 of which were in the Jiaxing area. Dividing by 13 gives 79,431 persons as a crude approximation.

14. *JXFZ/Q*, 524 and 528.

15. Shiba Yoshinobu, *Sōdai Kōnan keizai-shi no kenkyū* [Researches on the economic history of Jiangnan under the Song] (Tōyō Daigaku Tōyō Bunka Kenkyūjo: Tokyo, 1988), 146. I have omitted the much lower figure of 116,850 for 980 CE as probably a reflection of poor data collection in the early years of the dynasty.

16. It now seems to be agreed that from 1776 to 1850 the official figures became reasonably reliable. See Cao Shuji, *Qing Period*, 3.
17. *JXFZ/Q*, 523.
18. The precise Song rate was 0.57% a year, the later Qing one (1769 to 1838) was 0.26%.
19. Most of the mid- and late-Ming official population figures are unconvincing as they hardly vary. From the 1420s through the 1520s they fluctuate slightly within the range between 833,000 and 735,000, and from the 1570s through the 1630s between 563,000 and 565,000. Qualitative evidence tends to suggest that for most of this period the real trend is likely to have been upward rather than downward or steady. The official late Ming figures could have been as low as a third of the true value. See Yim Shu-yuen, "Famine relief statistics as a guide to the population of sixteenth-century-China: A case-study of Honan province," *Ch'ing-shih wen-t'i* 3.9 (Nov 1978).
20. It was they who sacrificed to the goddess of sericulture. See *JXFZ/Q*, 803.
21. *JXFZ/Q*, 793.
22. *JXFZ/Q*, 793.
23. M. Elvin and N. Su, "Man against the sea: Natural and anthropogenic factors in the changing morphology of Harngzhou Bay, circa 1000–1800," *Environment and History* 1.1 (Feb. 1995) 42–4.
24. *JXFZ/Q*, 789.
25. *JXFZ/Q*, 789.
26. *JXFZ/Q*, 783.
27. *JXFZ/Q*, 784–5 and 788.
28. P. R. Katz, *Demon Hordes and Burning Boats: The Cult of Marshal Wen in Late Imperial Chekiang* (State University of New York Press: Albany, N.Y., 1995).
29. *JXFZ/Q*, 291.
30. Modern usage labels these the 'plum rains', as *mei* ('plum') is a homophone of *mei* ('mildew'). This is prettier but confusing as they do not have anything obvious to do with plums. Plum blossoms appear from late March to early April in the Jiaxing region. See C. Blunden and M. Elvin, *Cultural Atlas of China*, rev. edn (Facts on File: New York, 1998), 29. This is somewhat too early for the rains, which are due to the summer monsoon meeting cold air from the north above the lower Yangzi valley in mid June to mid July. On the timing of the 'plum rains' see Ding Yihui, *Monsoons over China* (Kluwer: Dordrecht, 1994), 19–22, 128, 134, and 195 *et seq.*
31. This passage cannot be dated for the time being.
32. Liu Yingke and Shen Shaozhong, eds., *Jiaxing fuzhi* [Jiaxing prefectural gazetteer] (1600; reprinted as Huazhong #505, Chengwen: Taibei, 1983), hereafter *JXFZ/M*, 1842–3.
33. Zhang Yingchang, ed., *Qing shi duo* [The Qing Bell of poesy] (originally *Guochao shiduo*, 1869; reprinted, Xinhua shudian: Beijing, 1960), hereafter, *QSD* 473. In the last line, 'made one sick at heart' might be a more accurate translation, but the term in the Chinese can also indicate heartburn, which is not far from the idea of throwing up.
34. *JXFZ/M*, 1969–70.
35. There is an illegible character in the gazetteer text here. I have supplied what I hope is an appropriate meaning.
36. The word 'splashing' is added to make sense of this line.
37. See A. Corbin, *Le Territoire du vide: L'Occident et le désir du rivage, 1750–1840* (Aubier: Paris, 1988).
38. *ZYJHZ*, 4514.
39. See Yoshida Teigo, "Umi no kosumorojii" [The cosmology of the sea], in Gotō Akira *et al.*, eds., *Rekishi ni okeru shizen* [Nature in history] (Iwanami: Tokyo, 1989).

40. *JXFZ/M*, 1969.

41. Discussed in Elvin and Su, "Man against the sea."

42. *JXFZ/M*, 509–13.

43. An unidentified place.

44. At this time on the south and north shores of old Hangzhou Bay.

45. The south side of the lower Yangzi delta.

46. M. Elvin and N. Su, "Action at a distance: The influence of the Yellow River on Hangzhou Bay since AD 1000," in M. Elvin and T.-J. Liu, eds., *Sediments of Time: Environment and Society in Chinese History* (Cambridge University Press: New York, 1998), esp. 352.

47. *JXFZ/M*, 491–2.

48. This notion was archaizing fantasy.

49. The translation of this technical term is tentative.

50. The name of the locks here sounds the same but is not written with the same characters as the earlier reference to them.

51. Just as 'dike' in traditional English usage can refer either to the raised embankment or the ditch running alongside it, so the Chinese term used here (*tang*) has a comparable ambiguity.

52. Here, as earlier, where minor names with a clear sense are concerned, and identification on a map is not an important issue, I have often taken the liberty of translating the meaning, in order to convey something of the flavor of old Chinese place-names.

53. *JXFZ/M*, 493.

54. I.e. 907–60 CE.

55. Chang Tang and Luo Shuhao, eds., *Ganshui zhi* [Gazetteer for Ganshui] (Song), reprinted in Zhonghua shuju bianzhibu, ed., *Song-Yuan fangzhi: congkan* (Zhonghua shuju: Beijing, 1990), hereafter *GSZ* 5:4662.

56. That is, a dike across a waterway, blocking it, rather than a levee running parallel with one of its banks.

57. About four to five meters. The 'fathom' was an archaic unit of height or depth, said to represent the height of a human being. It was seven (or sometimes perhaps eight) archaic 'feet'. The foot (*chi*) was around 23.1 centimeters in Warring States times. See Qiu Guangming, *Zhongguo lidai du-liang-heng kao* [Researches on measures of length, capacity, and weight in the successive Chinese dynasties] (Kexue chubanshe: Beijing, 1992), 11.

58. This translation of *che suo*, whose literal sense is something like 'machinery rope', is a guess based on context.

59. Wine made from rice, not grapes.

60. *JXFZ/M*, 494–5.

61. Li Bozhong, *Tangdai Jiangnan nongye-de fazhan* [The development of agriculture in Jiangnan under the Tang dynasty] (Nongye chubanshe: Beijing, 1990), 30, 86, and cp. 106 (on fallowing under the Song).

62. Li Bozhong, *Agriculture in Tang Jiangnan*, 41.

63. Li Bozhong, *Agriculture in Tang Jiangnan*, 51.

64. Li Bozhong, *Agriculture in Tang Jiangnan*, 89–95, 106–29, 149, and 190 *et seq.*

65. Shiba Yoshinobu, *Economic History of Jiangnan*, 146.

66. *ZYJHZ*, 4494.

67. *JXFZ/Q*, 196.

68. His surname was Yuan, but he is not otherwise identified. Possible candidates include Yuan Jie and Yuan Zai.

69. *JXFZ/Q*, 196.
70. The text says "more than 1000 *li*." Jiaxing prefecture in Song times was 7790 km², which is roughly equivalent to 88 km by 88 km, so trying to fit a *length* of about 500 km into it, even a twisting and turning length, makes little sense. If *li* is taken as meaning a 'square *li*' then it is roughly on the order of one quarter of a square kilometer (0·5 × 0·5 km). Hence "more than 1000 square *li*" probably indicates an area of the order of 250 km², just under a fifth of the total area. In Li Bozhong, *Agriculture in Tang Jiangnan*, 86, the figure is given as "twisting and turning over an *area* of over a hundred *li*." If this means an area of 100 square *li* it is probably too small at about 25 km². If, on the contrary, it indicates 100 × 100 linear *li*, then at 2500 km², it is almost a third of the entire area of the prefecture. Though this is not impossible, the figure of 1000 seems more likely.
71. That referring to *sui*, areas more than 100 *li* from a capital city. The reference is to the quasi-classical work the *Zhouli* [*The Rituals of Zhou*] in Ruan Yuan, ed., *Shisan jing zhushu* [The thirteen classics with notes and explanations] (Qing; reprinted, Zhonghua shuju: Beijing, 1980), hereafter *ZL*], 'diguan', 'xianglao' section.
72. Once again an official designation from *The Rituals of Zhou* is used here.
73. *JXFZ/Q*, 196, account of the achievements of Zhu Gong.
74. *JXFZ/Q*, 196.
75. *ZYJHZ* 4532–3.
76. 406 *mou*. This was 0.285 of a square kilometer.
77. The term 'mortgage' is strictly inaccurate. It was not a loan on the security of landed property but a purchase with a right of repurchase at the sale price by the vendors or their heirs over an indefinitely extended period of time.
78. Which 'ministry' was involved is not clear.
79. Xi Tianxi.
80. *JXFZ/M*, 853.
81. *JXFZ/M*, 498.
82. For example, the poem by Zhou Binhe in *JXFZ/Q*, 190.
83. *GSZ*, 5:4661.
84. *GSZ*, 5:4660 and 4671.
85. *JXFZ/Q*, 290.
86. That is, the 'Japanese', coastal raiders who were in fact mostly Chinese at this time.
87. Just to the south of Ganpu.
88. *JXFZ/Q*, 161.
89. Karlgren, *Odes*, #34. "The gourds have their bitter leaves, / The ford has a deep crossing." Another possible translation, given the reference, is 'for a ford so deep that one crosses it with one's clothes on, a gourd is essential', which employs an archaic sense, namely 'to ford fully dressed', of the word rendered here in its normal later meaning as 'risky'. Finally, the words 'for support' have had to be supplied. This accords with the archaic practice of attaching a gourd at one's belt when crossing water and otherwise the lines make little sense.
90. *JXFZ/Q*, 161.
91. For example, *JXFZ/Q*, 160 and 166.
92. *JXFZ/Q*, 148.
93. *JXFZ/Q*, 160.
94. *JXFZ/Q*, 154.
95. *JXFZ/Q*, 149.
96. *JXFZ/Q*, 158–9.

97. *JXFZ/Q*, 159. The term 'position-power' used here was applied, as noted earlier, to mosquitoes pestering livestock. The animals are 'stronger' in a crude sense, but the mosquitoes, who can maneuver better, enjoy superior position-power.

98. The text says 'fall and summer', but (1) this is in the wrong order, and (2) heavy rain in the fall was not usual in Jiaxing, which does not fit well with the phrase 'every year' at the beginning. I have therefore changed 'fall' to 'spring' here.

99. *JXFZ/Q*, 159.

100. *JXFZ/Q*, 144.

101. *JXFZ/Q*, 146.

102. *JXFZ/Q*, 146.

103. *JXFZ/Q*, 161.

104. *JXFZ/Q*, 122–3.

105. *JXFZ/Q*, 127.

106. In early-imperial times the *zhong* ranged from over 6 liters to 37.5 liters, with 20 liters as a frequent value. See Qiu Guangming, *Measures*, 248–53.

107. R. B. Marks, "'It never used to snow': Climatic variability and harvest yields in late-imperial South China, 1650–1850," in Elvin and Liu, eds., *Sediments of Time*, esp. 435–44.

108. *JXFZ/M*, 1812–14.

109. Qiu Guangming, *Measures*, 105.

110. *JXFZ/M*, 887.

111. *JXFZ/M*, 807.

112. The Song *hu* was fixed at 5 *dou* or half a *shi*, and so held about 29.25 liters; see Qiu Guangming, *Measures*, 262–3. The additional ration per person from the tribute grain thus worked out at about 12.3 liters of rice per person. Such a quantity might have lasted for close to a month.

113. *JXFZ/M*, 831–2.

114. *JXFZ/Q*, 287.

115. The Yuan-dynasty picul was about 83 liters, and about 1.43 times as large as the Song picul. See Qiu Guangming, *Measures*, 263.

116. On this tax in the Southern Song and the system of public lands, see Shiba Yoshinobu, *Economic History of Jiangnan*, 72, 90, 152–9, and 254.

117. A device used in Chinese astrology.

118. The term 'stalagmite' is strictly speaking inappropriate here, since there was no cave involved, but we will keep to the term as it is in the Chinese text.

119. *JXFZ/Q*, 266.

120. 'Matter–energy–vitality' is the basic substance of the universe. For a more extended discussion of the fine 'germinal causes' in seventeenth-century thinking, see M. Elvin, *Pattern of the Chinese Past* (Stanford University Press: Stanford, Calif., 1973), 229–32.

121. The usual term for 'landscape'.

122. *JXFZ/Q*, 266.

123. *JXFZ/Q*, 266.

124. *JXFZ/M*, 859.

125. Probably of Xiushui.

126. The year of the next triennial examinations.

127. Probably some point in the sixteenth century.

128. *JXFZ/M*, 859, biography of Huang Xianke. The term 'aether–energies in the human and physical atmospheres', literally 'atmospheric aethers', most commonly refers to the human environment in later texts such as this, but its original meanings are physical: aethers moving through the world to create winds, and climate, for example.

129. *JXFZ/Q,* 149.

130. *JXFZ/M,* 791, life of Wang Yu.

131. *JXFZ/M,* 1560.

132. *JXFZ/M,* 1554.

133. *JXFZ/Q,* 141. Note that, as elsewhere in this book, 'moon' is used for a month in the old Chinese lunar calendar. The third moon was most often April and early May. Occasionally, for the sake of vowel-rhyme in the poems, I have broken this convention and used 'month'.

134. The standard short biography of Xiang describes him as "timid, having few companions, and without a family life or business." Fang He, *et al.,* eds., *Zhongguo renming da cidian* [Large Chinese biographical dictionary] (Taixing shuju: Hong Kong, 1931), hereafter *ZGRMDCD,* 1314.

135. *JXFZ/M,* 1559–60.

136. *JXFZ/M,* 1563.

137. *JXFZ/Q,* 155. For Song poems on country markets, see Shiba Yoshinobu, *Commerce and Society in Sung China,* translated M. Elvin (Michigan University Center for Chinese Studies: Ann Arbor, Mich., 1970), 144–5, 147, 149, 151, 152, and 154.

138. *JXFZ/Q,* 136.

139. *JXFZ/M,* 2192–4.

140. In Ming times it was assigned to Jiangsu province.

141. See M. Elvin, *Changing Stories in the Chinese World* (Stanford University Press: Stanford, Calif., 1997), 50, 62, 68–9, 81–2, and 86 for examples. These are mostly translated from the section in *QSD,* 564–70 on this subject.

142. *JXFZ/M,* 1852–3. The unusual rhyme-scheme is approximately that in the original.

143. Karlgren, *Odes,* #174.

144. *JXFZ/M,* 1853.

145. J. Radkau, *Natur und Macht: Eine Weltgeschichte der Umwelt* (Beck: München, 2000), 126.

146. *JXFZ/M,* 2188. The exact mechanism referred to in the last sentence of this passage is not entirely clear.

147. Recall that, on average, a Chinese year of age (*sui*) indicates an exact age one less than the age in *sui.*

148. M. Elvin, *Another History: Essays on China from a European Perspective* (Wild Peony/Hawaii University Press: Sydney, 1996), 106–8.

149. *JXFZ/Q,* 783.

150. M. Elvin, "Blood and statistics: Reconstructing the population dynamics of late imperial China from the biographies of virtuous women in local gazetteers," in H. Zurndorfer, ed., *Chinese Women in the Imperial Past: New Perspectives* (Brill: Leiden, 1999). In principle it might be better to use the 'adult' expectation of life, that is after some age like 15, as the data all relate to women above 48.5 years of age, and the adjustment of a model life table is used (quasi-linearized by means of logits) to extrapolate the values for the earlier ages by optimizing the match of its corresponding section with the values of this truncated data distribution.

151. Others include the yield per unit of area, yield per time-unit of work, and the ratio of energy in to energy out (excluding sunshine), as well as economic measures based on the relationship of costs and financial returns.

152. A. Maddalena, "Rural Europe 1500–1750," vol. II.4 in C. M. Cipolla, ed., *The Fontana Economic History of Europe* (1970; reprinted, Collins: Glasgow, 1974), 334–43. The highest ratio given here for the period before 1750 is 8.7 for Holland and England in 1500–49.

153. Rice grains have a bran casing which, though nutritious, was commonly removed by the Chinese by the process of 'husking' or 'hulling' which was thought to improve the flavor, and made storage easier.
154. *JXFZ/Q,* 783–9.
155. *JXFZ/Q,* 790.
156. See Oki Yasushi, "Feng Menglong 'Shan'ge' no kenkyū" [Studies on the 'Mountain Ditties' of Feng Menglong], *Tōyō bunka kenkyūjo kiyō* 105 (1988).
157. *JXFZ/Q,* 784. The first character of this poem is too defaced to read. I have supplied 'plum' as the name of the tree.
158. *JXFZ/Q,* 789.
159. *ZGRMDCD,* 1618.
160. *JXFZ/Q,* 783.
161. *JXFZ/Q,* 788. Cp. ibid. 784–5. For a detailed analysis of these questions, see Li Bozhong, "Changes in climate, land, and human efforts: The production of wet-field rice in Jiangnan during the Ming and Qing dynasties," in Elvin and Liu, eds., *Sediments of Time.*
162. Wuzhen and Lianshi.
163. *JXFZ/Q,* 785.
164. *JXFZ/Q,* 785.
165. Colza is otherwise known as 'rape' and its seeds are pressed for oil.
166. Kawakatsu Mamoru, *Min-Shin Kōnan nōgyō keizai-shi kenkyū* [Researches on the farm economy of Ming and Qing Jiangnan] (Tōkyō Daigaku shuppankai: Tokyo, 1992), 121.
167. *JXFZ/Q,* 788.
168. See Kawakatsu Mamoru, *Farm Economy of Ming and Qing Jiangnan,* 111.
169. Kawakatsu Mamoru, *Farm Economy of Ming and Qing Jiangnan,* 114.
170. Cited from Shen's manual in the gazetteer: *JXFZ/Q,* 790.
171. *JXFZ/Q,* 793. Also discussed on pp. 169–70.
172. *JXFZ/Q,* 798–803.
173. *JXFZ/Q,* 791.
174. For the justification of this translation, see Hoshi Ayao, *Chūgoku shakai-keizei-shi go-i* [Glossary of terms in China's social and economic history] (Kindai Chūgoku kenkyūsentā: Tokyo, 1966), 253.
175. E.g., Pinghu. See *JXFZ/Q,* 784.
176. *JXFZ/Q,* 807.
177. Cao Shuji, *Qing Period,* 102–3 and 470.

8 Chinese Colonialism: Guizhou and the Miao

1. *Zhongguo ziran ziyuan congshu* [Series on the natural resources of China] (Zhongguo ziran ziyuan congshu bianzhuan weiyuanhui, ed. 42 vols., Zhongguo huanjing kexue chubanshe: Beijing, 1995), hereafter *ZZZC* (Guizhou volume), 34:408.
2. Jing Daomo, *et al.,* comp., *Guizhou tongzhi* [Comprehensive gazetteer of Guizhou] (1741; reprinted, Huawen shuju: Taibei, 1968) hereafter *GZTZ,* 1:1b; 15:1b.
3. Yan Bao, arra. and annot., *Hxak Lul Hxak Ghot: Miaozu guge* [Hxak Lul Hxak Ghot: Ancient songs of the Miao race] (Guizhou minzu chubanshe: Guiyang, 1993), translator's preface, 1, and the chapter "Yanhe xiqian" [Moving west along the rivers], 651–786. For the background to the process of collection and transcription from which this book emerged, see the remarks later in the text at the start of the section 'The Miao'.
4. *Ancient Songs of the Miao,* 740–3 and 774.

5. As indicated on p. 485, n. 121, the term 'in-migrants' refers to persons changing residence within a political unit. 'Immigrants', in contrast, refers to those who cross a political boundary.

6. There is an overview of these events in H. J. Wiens, *Han Chinese Expansion in South China* [originally published as *China's March to the Tropics*, 1954; 2nd edn., Shoe String Press: Hamden, Conn., 1967), esp. 70–93, 187–91, and 234–6.

7. See, for example, *GZTZ*, 24:14b; 24:23a–27b, etc., on the Yongzheng reign campaigns. On Miao firearms, including cannon, see *GZTZ*, 24:25a; 24:27b, etc.

8. *GZTZ*, 24:14b.

9. *GZTZ*, 24:27b.

10. *GZTZ*, 24:26a.

11. *GZTZ*, 24:29b.

12. *GZTZ*, 24:24b, 26b, and 27b.

13. Zhou Zuoji, comp. and rev., *Guiyang fuzhi* [Guiyang prefectural gazetteer] (Guiyang-fu xueshu: Guiyang (?), 1850), hereafter *GYFZ*, 64:1b.

14. *GYFZ*, 64:2b.

15. The Chinese term *min* is defined both as 'commoners' in contrast with 'officials' (*guan*) and as 'civilians ' in contrast with 'soldiers' (*bing*). Hence the two-component translation is sometimes appropriate.

16. *GYFZ*, 64:3a.

17. *GYFZ*, 50:20ab.

18. *GYFZ*, 1:4b–5a. His name was Wang Chenglu.

19. A commandery was approximately a prefecture.

20. *GYFZ*, 44:2b–11a.

21. See Feng Erkang, *Yongzheng zhuan* [A life of the Yongzheng Emperor] (Taiwan shangwu: Taibei, 1992), 382–99.

22. *GYFZ*, 1:1b.

23. *GYFZ*, 1:2b–3a. To Gao Qizhuo and others.

24. See the map in C. Blunden and M. Elvin, *Cultural Atlas of China*, rev. edn (Facts on File: New York, 1998), 36.

25. See Yang Tongsheng, *et al.*, eds., *Hxat Khat: Kaiqin ge* [Hxat Khat: Songs on the occasion of the formation of alliances through marriage] (Guizhou-sheng minzu yanjiu-suo: Guizhou, 1985), introductory remarks.

26. Yang Tongsheng, *Songs on Marriage*, 34.

27. Yang Tongsheng, *Songs on Marriage*, 385.

28. Yang Tongsheng, *Songs on Marriage*, 19.

29. Yang Tongsheng, *Songs on Marriage*, 12.

30. Yang Tongsheng, *Songs on Marriage*, 85.

31. Yang Tongsheng, *Songs on Marriage*, 89.

32. Yang Tongsheng, *Songs on Marriage*, 344–5.

33. Yang Tongsheng, *Songs on Marriage*, 315.

34. Yang Tongsheng, *Songs on Marriage*, 362.

35. Yang Tongsheng, *Songs on Marriage*, 672.

36. Yang Tongsheng, *Songs on Marriage*, 640.

37. Yang Tongsheng, *Songs on Marriage*, 6.

38. Yang Tongsheng, *Songs on Marriage*, 43.

39. Yang Tongsheng, *Songs on Marriage*, 1.

40. Yang Tongsheng, *Songs on Marriage*, 23.

41. Yang Tongsheng, *Songs on Marriage*, 35.

42. Yang Tongsheng, *Songs on Marriage*, 48.
43. Yang Tongsheng, *Songs on Marriage*, 71.
44. Yang Tongsheng, *Songs on Marriage*, 328.
45. Yang Tongsheng, *Songs on Marriage*, 322.
46. Yang Tongsheng, *Songs on Marriage*, 369–70.
47. Yang Tongsheng, *Songs on Marriage*, 636.
48. Yang Tongsheng, *Songs on Marriage*, 32.
49. Yang Tongsheng, *Songs on Marriage*, 36.
50. Yang Tongsheng, *Songs on Marriage*, 79.
51. Yang Tongsheng, *Songs on Marriage*, 388.
52. Yang Tongsheng, *Songs on Marriage*, 635.
53. Yang Tongsheng, *Songs on Marriage*, 62.
54. Yang Tongsheng, *Songs on Marriage*, 79.
55. Yang Tongsheng, *Songs on Marriage*, 387.
56. Gu Yingtai, *Mingshi jishi benmo* [Main themes and details of Ming history recounted] (1658; reprinted, 4 vols., Shangwu: Taibei, 1956), 2:157–66.
57. Guiping.
58. Fifteen kilometers west of Mengshan.
59. Literally 'tigers that climb mountains'. This is commonly used for a two-person sedan chair that can go up hills, but this sense seems inappropriate here.
60. This a guess at the meaning of *ya er ba*, the idea being that it is a type of stick, rake, or handle that gives the climber a *second* foothold or grip.
61. Gu Yingtai, *Ming History Recounted*, 4:60–72. Fang He, *et al.*, eds., *Zhongguo renming da cidian* [Large Chinese biographical dictionary] (Taixing shuju: Hong Kong, 1931), hereafter *ZGRMDCD*, 242, describes his father An Jiangchen as from a family that had "lived for generations in Shuixi, and had the direction of the Miao tribes." See also Tian Wen, *Qian shu* [The book of Guizhou], in Yan Ping, ed., *Yueya-tang congshu*, case 36 in *Baibu congshu jicheng* [Collection of collections on all topics] (Qing. Reprinted, Yiwen yinshuguan: Taibei, 1965–8), 3::10a–12a.
62. Around what is today Qianxi county. *GZTZ*, 45:51b–52a.
63. *GZTZ*, 45:58a.
64. *GZTZ*, 910.
65. *GZTZ*, 911.
66. B. Karlgren, *The Book of Odes: Chinese Text, Transcription and Translation* (Museum of Far Eastern Antiquities: Stockholm, 1950), #184.
67. Since Qian's pen name was 'Great Grindstone' it may also indicate that he saw himself as the one who corrected others.
68. T. Bonyhady, "Artists with axes," *Environment and History* 1.2 (1995).
69. *GZTZ* (Siku quanshu edn.), 572–493, 44:9ab.
70. *GZTZ* (Siku quanshu edn.), 572–491, 44:4a.
71. Probably *Nymphoides* and *Myriophyllum*.
72. *GZTZ* (Siku quanshu edn.), 572–493, 44:9ab. The identification of 'water-grain' is uncertain.
73. J. Needham, with Wang Ling, *Science and Civilisation in China*, vol. 3, *Mathematics and the Sciences of the Heavens and the Earth* (Cambridge University Press: Cambridge, 1959), 538–41.
74. *GYFZ*, 24:1a–2a.
75. Rhetorical exaggeration. The entire prefecture of Guiyang was only about three hundred kilometers from north to south.

76. *Sic.*
77. *GYFZ*, 40.13a–15b.
78. The text reads 'Chishui', but it is explained on the preceding page that the river referred to is not the river that usually bears this name (which lies to the northwest) but the Panjiang or Hongshui River.
79. The Chinese term used in the gazetteer is *wugui.* For a poem describing what this implied in eastern China, see the fourth of the "Laments on epidemics in the fall" by Guo Yixiao in Zhang Yingchang, ed., *Qing shi duo* [The Qing bell of poesy] (originally *Guochao shiduo*, 1869; reprinted, Xinhua shudian: Beijing, 1960), hereafter *QSD*, 871.
80. *QSD*, 883, and "Catalog of the poets' names, ranks, and writings," 32. The 'mediums' referred to are 'spirit mediums'. Practitioners of this art, in a wide variety of forms, were found in most parts of south China, not only among the Miao.
81. See Ji Han, *Nanfang caomu zhuang* [The forms of the plants and trees of the South] translated Hui-lin Li, *A Fourth Century Flora of Southeast Asia* (Chinese University Press: Hong Kong, 1979), 46–53. Also chapter 4 of the present book, section on 'The Far South'.
82. From an eighteenth-century document cited in Wiens, *Han Chinese Expansion*, 235.
83. *GZTZ*, 44:28a, 572–503.
84. *GZTZ*, 11:1a.
85. A misjudgment, perhaps based on the renowned wealth of the Yangzhou salt-merchants?
86. *GZTZ*, 2:4a.
87. *GZTZ*, 1:1a–5a.
88. *GYFZ*, 40:15a.
89. *GYFZ*, 40:13ab.
90. *GYFZ*, 40:15ab.
91. *Aleurites* spp.
92. *Quercus acutissima*, formerly *sinensis.*
93. Varieties of *Echinochloa crus-galli*, a variable plant, often treated as a weed.
94. This is one reason why the 'early grain' of the second moon is probably wild oats. The other is that wild-type oats are known to have been grown in Guizhou, but are not separately mentioned in this calendar. See *GZTZ*, 1:1ab.
95. C. A. Lamp, S. J. Forbes, and J. W. Cade, *Grasses of Temperate Australia* (Inkata Press: Melbourne, 1990), 144 and 146.
96. *GZTZ*, 45:38ab.
97. *GZTZ*, 44:48a.
98. The philosopher–bureaucrat, recorded here by his personal name Wang Shouren. See p. 228.
99. *GZTZ*, 45:32a.
100. See R. Lawlor, *Voices of the First Day: Awakening in the Aboriginal Dreamtime* (Inner Traditions International: Rochester, Vt, 1991), 373.
101. Yamada Keiji, "Sōdai no shizen tetsugaku: Sōgaku ni okeru no ichi ni tsuite" [The Song philosophy of nature: Its place in Song learning], in Yabuuchi Kiyoshi, ed., *Sō-Gen jidai kagaku gijutsu* [Science and technology in the Song and Yuan period] (Jimbun kagaku kenkyūjo (Kyoto, 1967), 47–8. The interchange is actually illusory, as explained later.
102. Tian Wen, *Book of Guizhou*, 64, 4::2:2a–3a. The text is not easy to translate, and my suggested reading differs in places from that made earlier by Claudine Lombard-Salmon of parts of it. See Claudine Lombard-Salmon, *Un Exemple d'acculturation chinoise: La province de Guizhou* (École française d'Extrême-Orient: Paris, 1972), 190.
103. Literally, 'skies' or 'daylight'.

104. This is a reference to the 'Wai wu' chapter of the *Zhuangzi*, which talks of "using a metal hammer to tap on his chin." See Guo Qingfan, ed., *Zhuangzi jishi* [The Zhuangzi, with collected explanations] (Zhonghua shuju: Beijing, 1961), hereafter *ZZJS*, 928.

105. This rendering is a guess. Deer tended to be associated with the dawn. Thus in the first of Du Fu's poems to Hermit Zhang, he says "You feel no need for the nightly knowledge of aethers of silver and gold. / All thoughts of killing set aside, you watch the deer roam in the dawn." See Chou Zhao'ao, ed., *Du Shaoling ji xiangzhu* [Du Fu's collected works with detailed notes] (4 vols., Wenxue guji kanxingshe: Beijing, 1955), 2:1:5, "Ti Zhang-shi yinju er shou."

106. Literally, 'a dry mouth'. This and the other technical terms that follow are plausible guesses that fit the context.

107. *GYTZ*, 44:11b–13b.

108. The first of the two You mountains is in Hu'nan (the lesser of the two) and the second in Sichuan (the greater).

109. J. V. Roddricks, *Calculated Risks. The Toxicity and Human Health Risks of Chemicals in our Environment* (Cambridge University Press: Cambridge, 1992), 98.

110. A quotation from the *Scripture of Songs*. See Karlgren, *Odes*, #154.

111. Tian Wen, *Book of Guizhou*, 4::4:5ab.

112. Georgius Agricola [G. Bauer], *De Re Metallica* (1556, translated and edited by H. C. and L. H. Hoover, 1912; reprinted, Dover: New York, 1950), notably the methods described on 430–2.

113. I owe these explanations to Dr Ian Williams of the Research School of Earth Sciences, Australian National University, and would like to express my thanks for his help.

114. Xie Zhaozhe, *Wu zazu* [Fivefold miscellany] (1608; reprinted under the supervision of Li Weizhen, Xinxing shuju: Taibei, 1971), hereafter *WZZ*, 952–3.

115. *QSD*, 929.

116. Yang Shen.

117. *GZTZ*, 44:44ab.

118. He gave his name to a town near modern Zhenxiong, just across the Guizhou border in Yunnan.

119. Tian Wen, *Book of Guizhou*, 11:12a–13b.

120. In the seventeenth century.

121. Tian Wen, *Book of Guizhou*, 11:13b–14b.

122. Tian Wen, *Book of Guizhou*, 11:15b.

123. *GZTZ*, 45:51a.

124. Tian Wen *Book of Guizhou*, 11:15ab. The date of the attack is unclear.

125. *GZTZ*, 45:11b.

126. *GZTZ*, 45:46b.

127. *GZTZ*, 45:32a. Note that in the pinyin system of transcription the place-name 'Shiqian' is pronounced something like 'Shurr-chyenn', with the stress on the last syllable.

128. *GZTZ*, 45:54b–55a.

129. By Xie Sanxiu. *GZTZ*, 44:32b.

130. E. Zürcher, *The Buddhist Conquest of China* (Brill: Leiden, 1959), 131–2.

131. *GZTZ*, 44:58a–59b. Cp. p. 239 above.

132. The 'hump-backed ox' was a zebu (*Bos indicus*), also found in India and parts of east Africa. It has spectacular high curling horns. The 'red seals' may perhaps have indicated that the slogans had official permission, but this suggestion is only a guess. The 'Heavenly Magical Dancers' were a troupe formed at Court toward the close of the Mongol dynasty in the middle of the fourteenth century. Their inspiration was reputedly a histor-

ical record of Tang-dynasty dance music of the same name. The 'love-capers in moonlight' refer to the dances held on moonlit nights during the springtime by young unmarried Miao men and women, after which marriages were arranged. The Chinese were intrigued by this custom and left numerous accounts of what was believed to go on.

133. Dali-zhou Wenlian [Literary Association of Dali {Yunnan}], *Dali gu yishu chao* [Transcriptions of ancient lost books from Dali] (Yunnan Renmin Chubanshe: Kunming, 2001), 162 and 437.

134. Tian Wen, *Book of Guizhou*, 4::4:24b–25a.

135. *Zhang.*

136. At 26° N, 100° 45´ E, and southwest of Guiyang.

137. In full, *Euphorbia chrysocoma* Levl. and Vant. Personal communication of 7 January 1999, from the Musée National d'Histoire Naturelle, Paris.

138. *GZTZ*, 45:35b–36a.

139. In what is today Zhenning county.

140. *GZTZ*, 45:34ab. Note that I have supplied the 'now'.

141. *GZTZ*, 44:59ab.

142. *GZTZ*, 45:36b–37a.

143. Li Jingshan.

144. *GZTZ*, 45:30b–31a.

145. *GZTZ*, 46:4b–5a.

146. Near the modern Dejiang county.

147. *GZTZ*, 46:6a–7a.

148. Tian Wen, *Book of Guizhou*, 2:27b–28b.

149. *GZTZ*, 44:59b–60a.

150. *GZTZ*, 45:12b.

151. *GZTZ*, 45:12a.

152. Ding Yanghao. *GZTZ*, 45:44b.

153. A line not translated in the text specifies that the piece refers to Guizhou.

154. See for example Zhang Yigu's "Going from Slantbridge to Zhenyuan," the latter place being rather more than thirty kilometers downriver to the east. The author was an official, skilled in painting and composing verses, who flourished in the second half of the seventeenth century. *GZTZ*, 44:44ab.

155. *GZTZ*, 44:60a–61a.

156. *GZTZ*, 45:8b–9a.

157. At about 22° 45´ N, 109° 15´ E, in Heng county.

158. *GZTZ*, 45:41b.

9 The Riddle of Longevity: Why Zunhua?

1. M. Elvin, "Blood and statistics: Reconstructing the population dynamics of late imperial China from the biographies of virtuous women in local gazetteers," in H. Zurndorfer, ed., *Chinese Women in the Imperial Past: New Perspectives* (Brill: Leiden, 1999).

2. P. R. Katz, *Demon Hordes and Burning Boats: The Cult of Marshal Wen in Late Imperial Chekiang* (State University of New York Press: Albany, N.Y., 1995).

3. He Songtai *et al.*, eds., *Zunhua tongzhi* [Zunhua department comprehensive gazetteer] (no publisher stated) hereafter *ZHTZ*, 25: sidian 3ab. Microfilm courtesy of Columbia University Library, to whom I would like to express my thanks. For another reference to 'epidemics' see page 314 below.

4. Cao Shuji, *Qing shiqi* [The Qing period], vol. 5 of Ge Jianxiong, ed., *Zhongguo renkou shi* [History of China's population series], (Fudan daxue chubanshe: Shanghai, 2001), 335–6. This yields a growth rate of 0.28 per cent per year in the nineteenth century.

5. *ZHTZ*, 15: yudi, fengsu 14a.

6. *ZHTZ*, 15: yudi, fengsu 15a.

7. *ZHTZ*, 15: yudi, fengsu 13a.

8. *ZHTZ*, 15: yudi, fengsu 14b.

9. See J. Chen, T. C. Campbell, J. Li, and R. Peto, *Diet, Life-style and Mortality in China: A Study of the Characteristics of 65 Chinese Counties* (Oxford University Press, Cornell University Press, and People's Medical Publishing House: Oxford, 1990).

10. M. Cohen, *Health and the Rise of Civilization* (Yale University Press: New Haven, Conn., 1989), and A. Macfarlane, *The Savage Wars of Peace* (Blackwell: Oxford, 1997).

11. *ZHTZ*, 15: yudi, huobu 40b.

12. The information on modern Zunhua in the pages that follow is mainly taken from Zunhua xianzhi bianzuan weiyuanhui, ed., *Zunhua xianzhi* [Zunhua county gazetteer] (Hebei renming chubanshe: Shijiazhuang, 1990), hereafter *ZHXZ*.

13. *ZHTZ*, 43:2b.

14. *ZHTZ*, 13: yudi, shanchuan 21a.

15. Lin Lüzhi, *Xianbi shi* [A history of the Xianbi] (Bowen shuju: Hong Kong, 1973), 13–14.

16. *ZHTZ*, 16: chengchi 2ab.

17. From the third century BCE to the early fifth CE.

18. In the northwest of modern Zunhua.

19. Present Yutian.

20. Lin Lüzhi, *Xianbi*, 35–6.

21. Lin Lüzhi, *Xianbi*, 332.

22. Examples in Lin Lüzhi, *Xianbi*, 77, 145, 161, etc.

23. Lin Lüzhi, *Xianbi*, 87.

24. Lin Lüzhi, *Xianbi*, 80–1.

25. Lin Lüzhi, *Xianbi*, 201–2.

26. Quoted in Chen Shu, *Qidan shehui jingji shigao* [Draft history of the society and economy of the Qidan] (Sanlian: Beijing, 1963), 7.

27. Jin Weixian, *Qidan-de Dongbei zhengce* [The administrative policies of the Qidan in Manchuria] (Huashi chubanshe: Taibei, 1981), 9.

28. Lin Lüzhi, *Xianbi*, 361–4.

29. To make sense out of the first line of the second verse, I have had to emend *chéng* = 'city' to *chéng* = 'complete', but there is no certainty that this is right. It is also not entirely consistent with the tone of the rest of the song to have a moment of exhilaration such as this seems to be.

30. Qin River (Qinchuan) is a part of the Qingshui River in northwestern Shaanxi. It empties into the upper Wei.

31. *ZHTZ*, 13: yudi, shanchuan 4a.

32. The account that follows is based mostly on Chen Shu, *Society and Economy of the Qidan*, with additional information from Jin Weixian, *Administrative Policies of the Qidan*.

33. Chen Shu, *Society and Economy of the Qidan*, 17–20.

34. Chen Shu, *Society and Economy of the Qidan*, 70.

35. Chen Shu, *Society and Economy of the Qidan*, 30–1.

36. Chen Shu, *Society and Economy of the Qidan*, 70.

37. The chessboard referred to here refers to *weiqi*, 'surrounding chess' or *go*, which is played on the 361 *intersections* of the lines, not in the squares between them.

38. From Wang Ceng.
39. Chen Shu, *Society and Economy of the Qidan*, 106.
40. Jin Weixian, *Administrative Policies of the Qidan*, 68.
41. Jin Weixian, *Administrative Policies of the Qidan*, 11.
42. Chen Shu, *Society and Economy of the Qidan*, 36.
43. *ZHTZ*, 47: jinshi, beike 2a–3a, and Chen Shu, *Society and Economy of the Qidan*, 73–4.
44. *ZHTZ*, 43: guji, gongyuan 4ab.
45. Most likely the consort of Emperor Shengzong, who ruled from 983 to 1030. The carriage in which she was conveyed was famous for having a dragon's head and a kite's tail. It was decorated with gold, and when she traveled through the mountain valleys during the summer and fall, the carriage hangings seemed to be interwoven with the tapestry-like flowers and trees, so that, it was said, those who descried her in the distance thought she must be a goddess. There were, however, two other Qidan empresses who had this name. See Fang He, *et al.*, eds., *Zhongguo renming da cidian* [Large Chinese biographical dictionary] (Taixing shuju: Hong Kong, 1931), hereafter *ZGRMDCD*, 1645.
46. Both of these were historical places in northwestern China famous in Qin and Han times.
47. *ZHTZ*, 13: yudi, shanchuan 4b.
48. Or possibly, according to one theory, 'metal', since metal cuts wood, the dominant element adopted by the Qidan. Jin Weixian, *Administrative Policies of the Qidan*, 137. There might be a covert war of symbols here.
49. The *shayuan*.
50. Xie Zhaozhe, *Wu zazu* [Fivefold miscellany] (1608; reprinted, Xinxing shuju: Taibei, 1971), hereafter *WZZ*, 716.
51. *ZHTZ*, 16: jianzhi, shijie 9a.
52. North of the Wall.
53. *ZHTZ*, 43:1a.
54. *ZHTZ*, 43:1a.
55. *ZHTZ*, 43: guiji, Zunhua shijing 22a.
56. Zhongguo ziran ziyuan congshu bianzhuan weiyuanhui, ed., *Zhongguo ziran ziyuan congshu* [Series on the natural resources of China] (Zhongguo huanjing kexue chubanshe: Beijing, 1995), hereafter *ZGZRZYCS*, 14: Hebei volume, 348.
57. For these points and what follows, see *ZHTZ*, 1:1a–12b.
58. *ZHTZ*, 5: lingqin, chenhan 3ab.
59. *ZHTZ*, 6: lingqin, chenhan 1a.
60. *ZHTZ*, 6: lingqin, chenhan 2b.
61. *ZHTZ*, 7: qinling, jinling 13a–14b.
62. *ZHTZ*, 2: qinling, xiangrui 4a–7b.
63. *ZHTZ*, 16: chengchi 1ab and 2b.
64. *ZHTZ*, 15: yudi, fengsu 1b–2a.
65. *ZHTZ*, 16: shujie 3a.
66. *ZHTZ*, 15: yudi, fengsu 1b.
67. *ZHTZ*, 15: yudi, fengsu 2a.
68. *ZHTZ*, 15: yudi, wuchan, mupu 25a.
69. *ZHTZ*, 15: yudi, wuchan, mupu 27a.
70. *ZHTZ*, 15: yudi, wuchan, mupu 25a.
71. *ZHTZ*, 15: yudi, wuchan, gushu 1b.
72. *ZHTZ*, 13: yudi, shanchuan 16b.

73. *ZHTZ*, 13: yudi, shanchuan 23b (Shuangcheng he) and 24b (Lanquan).
74. *ZHTZ*, 15: yudi, wuchan, gushu 1b.
75. *ZHTZ* 15, yudi, fengsu 3a.
76. By late-imperial times the term *ye you* used here normally meant 'to frequent brothels', which is clearly inappropriate in this context, so I have gone back to its ancient meaning of an amatory ramble by a girl.
77. The term *ji-zhou* used here normally means 'dustpan and broom', and more generally 'a wife'. It makes no sense in the present context, so I have based my speculative reading here on the original sense of *ji*, a 'winnowing basket'.
78. *ZHTZ*, 55: lienü zhuan 8a (Zhang-shi).
79. *ZHTZ*, 15: yudi wuchan 3b.
80. *ZHTZ*, 15: yudi fengsu 3a.
81. *ZHTZ*, 15: yudi wuchan 14a.
82. *ZHTZ*, 55, lienü zhuan 2a, 12b and 56.
83. *ZHTZ*, 15: yudi, fengsu 2ab.
84. Not the usual sense for *po wu*. H. Giles, *A Chinese–English Dictionary*, 2nd edn (1912; reprinted, Jingwen shuju: Tabei, 1964), 1143, gives "the 5th of the 1st moon—the end of the holidays" for *po wu ri/er*. The analogy on which my translation rests is *po ri*, an unlucky day.
85. *ZHTZ*, 15: yudi, fengsu 9b.
86. From context, probably a deity.
87. *ZHTZ*, 15: yudi, fengsu 11a.
88. *ZHTZ*, 15: yudi, fengsu 11a.
89. *ZHTZ*, 15: yudi, fengsu 12ab.
90. *ZHTZ*, 15: yudi, fengsu 12b–13a.
91. *ZHTZ*, 15: yudi, fengsu 14a.
92. *ZHTZ*, 15: yudi, fengsu 14a.
93. *ZHTZ*, 15: yudi, fengsu 11b.
94. *ZHTZ*, 15: shoushu, no pagination.
95. *ZHTZ*, 13: yudi, shanchuan 13a.
96. *ZHTZ*, 13, yudi, shanchuan 13a and 14a. The first of these two poems comments that in years past the water in the Myriad Measures Spring had dried up, but was now flowing again. Not every source was perennial.
97. *ZHTZ*, 13: yudi, shanchuan 21b.
98. *ZHTZ*, 13: yudi, shanchuan 18b.
99. I have glossed 'limestone' for 'stone', because that is what would have been needed for plaster or whitewash. *Min* is often translated as 'alabaster' and this compact form of gypsum is well suited to carving, but the color is usually close to white, which does not fit with the 'blue-green' in the text of the poem.
100. *ZHTZ*, 13: shanchuan, Fengrun, page number illegible.
101. *ZHTZ*, 13: shanchuan, Yutian 23ab.
102. *ZHTZ*, 13: yudi, shanchuan 23b–24b.
103. *ZHTZ*, 13: yudi, shanchuan 18a.
104. Literally, 'lively'.
105. *ZHTZ*, 13: yudi, shanchuan 14b.
106. *ZHTZ*, 13: yudi, shanchuan 15a.
107. *ZHTZ*, 43: guiji, Zunhua shijing 24b.
108. *ZHTZ*, 13: yudi, shanchuan 12b.
109. *ZHTZ*, 13: yudi, shanchuan 14a.

110. *ZHTZ*, 13: yudi, shanchuan 16ab, and 43: guiji, Zunhua shijing 24b–25a.
111. *ZHTZ*, 15: yudi, wuchan, qinshou 1a. Li Shizhen in fact gave his source as "it is also said that," indicating hearsay. The wording is somewhat different and the observation is not specifically linked to the eating of humans as it is in the gazetteer. See Li Shizhen, *Bencao gangmu* [Pharmacopeia arranged by headings and subheadings] (1596: reprinted, Shangwu yinshuguan: Shanghai, 1930), vol. 5, 51:3.
112. *ZHTZ*, 15: yudi, wuchan, qinshou 1a. It is possible that the birds referred to here were falcons, but their large size suggests eagles.
113. In the *WZZ* of 1608, 736–7, we find the following: "Those who train falcons [or 'eagles'] first seel the bird's eyes by sewing them up, and then hood it with a bag. They next shut it in an empty room with a man made of straw to provide it with a forearm. To begin with the bird leaps about in a rage, striking out in frenzy, and is unwilling to perch here. Only after some time, when it is exhausted, will it alight on the forearm. Once the trainer reckons that it is extremely hungry, he will lure it with a morsel of meat, but not at first let it eat its fill. After some tens of days the seeled eyes will open, and he will then tie its wings together and remove the hood. When the hood is taken off, the bird strikes out in anger just as before, but once again becomes exhausted and docile. At this point a man will provide it with a forearm in place of [the straw dummy]. This takes about forty-nine days. The door is then opened and the bird is released to soar aloft for a while. The other birds will all be in hiding and it will secure nothing to eat. At this point the trainer makes an imitation pheasant out of bamboo, puts some meat in it, and places it half-hidden and half-exposed in the grass. When the falcon sees the bamboo pheasant it seizes it violently. The trainer then slowly draws in its braided silk leash. After accustoming it to this for a long time, the trainer can go out hunting with the bird, which will capture prey and release it exactly as he wishes."
114. *ZHTZ*, 15: yudi, wuchan, qinshou 1a.
115. *ZGZRZYCS*, 14: Hebei, 10.
116. *ZGZRZYCS*, 14: Hebei 67–8, 69, 71–2, 127, 147, etc.
117. *ZHTZ*, 15: yudi, wuchan, qinshou 1b.
118. *ZHTZ*, 15: yudi, wuchan, qinshou 1b.
119. *ZHTZ*, 15: yudi, wuchan, qinshou 2a.
120. *ZHTZ*, 15: yudi, wuchan, qinshou 2a.
121. *ZHTZ*, 15 yudi, wuchan, qinshou, no pagination.
122. *ZHTZ*, 15: yudi, wuchan, qinshou, no pagination.
123. *ZHTZ*, 15: yudi, wuchan, qinshou, no pagination.
124. *ZHTZ*, 15: yudi, wuchan, qinshou, no pagination.
125. *ZHTZ*, 15: yudi, wuchan, qinshou, no pagination, but on the page following that for the preceding reference.
126. *ZHTZ*, 13: yudi, shanchuan Fengrun 27a.
127. *ZHTZ*, 13: yudi, jiangyu 7b. I have used 'Immanent Pattern' for the Dao or 'Way'.
128. *ZHTZ*, 15: wuchan, shoubu 1a.
129. *ZHTZ*, 14: yudi, guanyi 3a. I have replaced the phrase 'lift up my skirts' in the original with 'throw back my cloak', because the former is a conventional phrase inherited from archaic times before Chinese men rode on horses and had to change to wearing trousers to do so. The underlying sense is to ready one's dress in a determined fashion for wading across water or striding forward on a journey.
130. *ZHTZ*, 15: yudi, wuchan, shoubu, pagination illegible.
131. *ZHTZ*, 15: yudi, wuchan, shoubu 1ab.

132. *ZHTZ*, 15: yudi, wuchan, shoubu, pagination illegible.
133. *ZHTZ*, 15: yudi, wuchan, shoubu, pagination illegible.
134. *ZHTZ*, 15: yudi, wuchan, shoubu, no pagination.
135. *ZHTZ*, 15: yudi, wuchan, qinshou, no pagination.
136. *ZHTZ*, 15: yudi, wuchan, shoubu, no pagination.
137. *ZHTZ*, 15: yudi, wuchan, shoubu, no pagination.
138. The items in this section are all taken from *ZHTZ*, 15: yudi, wuchan 7b–11b; luobu 11b–13b; and guobu 29b–34a, unless otherwise indicated.
139. *ZHTZ*, 15: yudi, wuchan, mubu 27a, 28b, and 29b.
140. *ZHTZ*, 15: yudi, wuchan 6a.
141. Specific data on the nutritional values of foods in the paragraphs that follow are taken from B. Fox and A. Cameron, *Food Science, Nutrition and Health*, 6th edn. (Arnold: London, 1997), and J. Garrow and W. James, eds., *Human Nutrition and Dietetics*, 9th edn. (Churchill Livingstone: Edinburgh, 1998). General points on nutrition in China are based on Campbell in Chen, Campbell, Li, and Peto, *Diet, Life-style and Mortality in China*, 47, 55, 59, and 62.

10 Nature as Revelation

1. H. Delahaye, *Les Premières Peintures de paysage en Chine: Aspects religieux* (École française d'Extrême-Orient: Paris, 1981), 81.
2. Obi Kōichi, *Chūgoku bungaku ni aratawareta shizen to shizenkan* [Nature and the concept of nature in Chinese literature] (Iwanami shoten: Tokyo, 1963), 205–6.
3. Reading *qin* 'akin' for *xin* 'new'.
4. H. Roetz, *Mensch und Natur im alten China: Zum Subjekt–Objekt–Gegensatz in der klassischen chinesischen Philosophie: Zugleich eine Kritik des Klischees vom chinesischen Universismus* (Lang: Frankfurt am Main, 1984).
5. Roetz, *Mensch und Natur im alten China*, 85. My italics.
6. Roetz, *Mensch und Natur im alten China*, 82.
7. Roetz, *Mensch und Natur im alten China*, 83.
8. As by Obi, *Concepts of Nature in Chinese Literature*.
9. Convenient translations are A. Waley, *The Book of Songs* (Allen and Unwin: London, 1937), and B. Karlgren, *The Book of Odes: Chinese Text, Transcription, and Translation* (Museum of Far Eastern Antiquities: Stockholm, 1950). The latter has the Chinese text as well. References below are to the Karlgren, with his numbering of the pieces.
10. Karlgren, *Odes*, #181.
11. Karlgren, *Odes*, #121.
12. Karlgren, *Odes*, #14.
13. Karlgren, *Odes*, #66.
14. Karglren, *Odes*, #165.
15. Karlgren, *Odes*, #112.
16. Karlgren, *Odes*, #65.
17. Karlgren, *Odes*, #167.
18. Karlgren, *Odes*, #194.
19. Karlgren, *Odes*, #258.
20. An eloquent translation is D. Hawkes, *Ch'u Tz'u: The Songs of the South* (Clarendon Press: Oxford, 1959; revised edition, Penguin: London, 1985).
21. The question of authorship being a vexed one but irrelevant for our purposes.

22. Ma Maoyuan, ed., *Chuci xuanzhu* [*The Songs of the South*, with selected notes] (Xinyue chubanshe: Hong Kong, 1962), hereafter *CCXZ*, 105.

23. *CCXZ*, 128.

24. *CCXZ*, 177. I follow Obi, *Concepts of Nature in Chinese Literature*, 18, in reading *fuyuan* in the first line of the second quatrain, rather than Ma's *fuliang*.

25. Shirakawa Tadahisa, *Tō Enmei to sono jidai* [Tao Yuanming and his age] (Kembun shuppan: Tokyo, 1994), 325–7.

26. *CCXZ*, 95.

27. Obi, *Concepts of Nature in Chinese Literature*, 34–5; Xiao Tong, comp., Li Shan, annot., *Wenxuan* [The Chinese anthology] (sixth century, 1181 edn.; reprinted, 4 cases, Zhonghua shuju: Beijing, 1974), hereafter *WX*, j. 34.

28. *WX*, 12:1a–8b, and Obi, *Concepts of Nature in Chinese Literature*, 241–2.

29. J. Brown, *et al.*, *Waves, Tides and Shallow-Water Processes*, (rev. edn. (Pergamon: Oxford, 1991), 32–4.

30. Obi, *Concepts of Nature in Chinese Literature*, 50.

31. Obi, *Concepts of Nature in Chinese Literature*, 50.

32. Obi, *Concepts of Nature in Chinese Literature*, 247.

33. Obi, *Concepts of Nature in Chinese Literature*, 188.

34. Obi, *Concepts of Nature in Chinese Literature*, 294.

35. Obi, *Concepts of Nature in Chinese Literature*, 291.

36. Obi, *Concepts of Nature in Chinese Literature*, 293.

37. For detailed analyses of these and related questions, see Shirakawa Tadahisa, *Tao Yuanming*, 150–64.

38. The following paragraphs are based on Shirakawa Tadahisa, *Tao Yuanming*, *naihen* section.

39. I have used the text in the anthology *Quan shanggu sandai Qin-Han liuchao wen* [Complete literature from high antiquity, the Three Dynasties, the Qin and Han, and the Six Dynasties] (Zhonghua shuju: Beijing, 1965), hereafter *QW*, Song, "Xie Kangle jixuan," *fu*, 1a–11b. Variant readings from Gu Shaobo and Wang Honglu, *Xie Lingyun-ji jiaozhu* [The works of Xie Lingyun with variant readings and notes] (Zhongzhou guji chubanshe: n.p. [He'nan], 1987), 318–76, have also been consulted. A number of references have also been identified from the invaluable J. D. Frodsham, *The Murmuring Stream: The Life and Works of the Chinese Nature Poet Hsieh Ling-yün (385–433), Duke of K'ang-Lo* (2 vols., University of Malaya Press: Kuala Lumpur, 1967).

40. Chen Qiaoyi, "Gudai Shaoxing diqu tianran senlin-de pohuai ji qi dui nongye-de yingxiang" [The destruction in ancient times of the natural forests of Shaoxing and its impact on agriculture], *Dili xuebao* 31.2 (June 1965), 130 and 135.

41. F. A. Westbrook, "Landscape description in the lyric poetry and 'Fuh on Dwelling on the Mountains' of Shieh Ling-yunn" (Ph.D. thesis, Yale University, 1972), 222.

42. Westbrook, "Landscape description", 236.

43. Westbrook, "Landscape description", 235.

44. I should like to express my thanks to Chiang Yang-ming (Sam Rivers) of Canberra for his scholarly care in checking doubtful points. Where, from time to time, I have differed from his interpretations, I am doubly conscious of the risk that I have taken.

45. Shirakawa Tadahisa, *Tao Yuanming*, 268–75.

46. Shirakawa Tadahisa, *Tao Yuanming*, 506–7, gives an extensive genealogy of the Xie family, which included several other poets besides Lingyun, both in earlier and later generations.

47. Frodsham, *The Murmuring Stream*, II:103.

48. On the geographical history of this area, see M. Elvin and N. Su, "Man against the sea: Natural and anthropogenic factors in the changing morphology of Harngzhou Bay, circa 1000–1800," *Environment and History* 1.1 (Feb. 1995).

49. M. Elvin and Su Ninghu, "Engineering the sea: Hydraulic systems and pre-modern technological lock-in in the Harngzhou Bay area circa 1000–1800," in Itō Suntarō and Yoshida Yoshinori, eds., *Nature and Humankind in the Age of Environmental Crisis* (International Research Center for Japanese Studies: Kyoto, 1995).

50. Following the spirit of the suggestion of Professor Nathan Sivin that the term *jieqi* be rendered '*qi*-nodes' or 'nodes of the year'.

51. Karlgren, Odes, #203. Karlgren renders *jiang* 'rice-water' as 'congee' here, which is rice-porridge. S. Couvreur, *Dictionnaire classique de la langue chinoise* (Imprimerie de la Mission catholique: Hejian fu, 1911), 536, has "eau de riz," and B. Karlgren, *Grammata Serica Recensa* (Museum of Far Eastern Antiquities: Stockholm, 1957), 192, "rice-water, drink." These fit better with Xie's explicit categorization of it as a drink.

52. Guo Qingfan, ed., *Zhuangzi jishi* [The Zhuangzi, with collected explanations] (Zhonghua shuju: Beijing, 1961), hereafter *ZZJS*, "Xiaoyao you," 24.

53. Fang He, *et al.*, eds., *Zhongguo renming da cidian* [Large Chinese biographical dictionary] (Taxing shuju: Hong Kong, 1931), hereafter *ZGRMDCD*, 143.

54. Translating as 'orchids' the term *lan* is misleading. *Lan* include the *Orchidaceae*, in modern Chinese the *lanke*, and most especially the *Cymbidium* group, but also all sorts of other flowers that are not true orchids at all. Roughly, proper orchids have flowers with three sepals and three petals, one of these latter usually being larger than the others, and also a distinctive bisexual reproductive organ, the 'column'. Given the waterside location, the *lan* referred to here are probably bog-orchids of the genus *Arethusa*.

55. Zhongguo ziran ziyuan congshu bianzhuan weiyuanhui, ed., *Zhongguo ziran ziyuan congshu* [Series on the natural resources of China] (Zhongguo huanjing kexue chubanshe: Beijing, 1995), hereafter *ZGZRZYCS*, *Zhejiang juan*, 229, 232, and 246.

56. *ZGZRZYCS, Zhejiang juan*, 305.

57. *Sha* sounds the same as the word for 'sand'.

58. Those for the *kun* and *xiang*.

59. S. Leys [P. Ryckmans], *The Analects of Confucius* (Norton: New York, 1997), 48 and 168.

60. *ZGZRZYCS, Zhejiang juan*, 324.

61. Xie's own note to the text.

62. The wording given by Xie is not quite exact. See *ZZJS*, 14, "Tian yun."

63. Actually the *Liezi*. See *Liezi xuanji sanzhong* [Three selected versions of the Liezi] in Xiao Tianshi, gen. ed., *Zhongguo zixue mingzhu jicheng* 64 (Zhongguo zixue mingzhu jicheng bianyin jijinhui: Taibei, 1978), hereafter *LZXJSZ*, 2:Huangdi 61, 327, and 609. My thanks to Dr Steve Bogenkamp for pointing this out. It should also be noted that the fable in the *Liezi* is in the past tense, about a man who lived beside the sea and "loved seagulls." The reference to 'contriving' appears *only* in the *notes* to one edition of the three I have looked at, *LZXJSZ*, 327. If the sage is without conscious intent, the birds and animals regard him as a companion.

64. I have added 'sandstone' to 'arrow-barbs' on the base of a roughly contemporary source (*Cihai* [encyclopedia] (Zhonghua shuju: Shanghai, 1947), 974: 'pan'). The 'tethered arrows' were shafts with a long thread attached to them so they could be recovered after they had been shot. This ancient usage may or may not have still been current in Xie's day. No inference should therefore be made about hunting technology at this time. The *tiao* is a literary fish, referred to in the *Scripture of Songs* (Karlgren, *Odes*, #281), and without an identifiable modern equivalent. The reading of 'what is

not distant' in the second line of the last verse as 'the Way' is inferred from the cliché 'the Way is not distant from human beings' in the scriptural *Doctrine of the Mean*.

65. See F. Cook, *Hua-yen Buddhism* (Pennsylvania State University Press: University Park, Penn., 1977), 110–22.

66. Karlgren, *Odes*, #153.

67. Karlgren, *Odes*, #207.

11 Science and Superfauna

1. Xie Zhaozhe, *Wu zazu* [Fivefold miscellany] (1608: reprinted under the supervision of Li Weizhen, Xinxing shuju: Taibei, 1971), hereafter *WZZ*. References are to this facsimile reprint of the original 1608 edition, using the modern page numbers.

2. This refers to the Chinese aquatic species, whose particular power is to bring or to withhold rain, not the Western species of dragon, who is associated with fire, and whose habitat is usually a mountain cave rather than the deep pool or the depths of the ocean frequented by his Chinese counterpart.

3. Wang Chong, *Lun heng jiaoshi* [Wang Chong's 'Discourses weighed in the balance', corrected and explained] (Han dynasty: 4 vols., Huang Hui, ed., Shangwu yinshuguan: Taibei, 1964), hereafter *LHJS*.

4. Shen Gua, ed., *Mengqi bitan* [Jottings from {the garden of} the brook of dreams] (Song dynasty; Hu Daojing, ed., as *Xinjiaozheng 'Mengqi bitan'*, (Zhonghua shuju: Hong Kong, 1975), cited as *MQBT*, with modern page numbers. J. F. Billeter, *et al.*, "Florilège des *Notes du Ruisseau des Rêves* (Mengqi bitan) de Shen Gua (1031–1095)," *Études Asiatiques* XLVII.3 (1993), offer the most balanced exegesis of Shen's style of thought presently available.

5. *LHJS*, 136–43.

6. As noted on p. 493, n. 42, 'position-power' *(shì)* is contrasted with 'strength' *(lì)* on page 145 of *LHJS*. Wang Chong notes that cattle and horses have greater 'strength' but inferior 'position-power' as compared to the mosquitoes that pester them.

7. J. C., Brenier, J. P. Diény, J.-C. Martzloff, and W. de Wieclawik, "Shen Gua (1031–1095) et les sciences," *Revue d'histoire des sciences* XLII.4 (1989), 339–40, ask, of recent scholarship on Shen, "how is it that such a work, which by its style, its structure, and its eclecticism evidently seems to be allied to general literature, has been associated with the sciences?"

8. *MQBT*, 209.

9. *MQBT*, 197 *et seq.*

10. *MQBT*, 83. M. Kalinowski, "Le Calcul du rayon céleste dans la cosmographie chinoise," *Revue d'histoire des sciences* XLIII.1 (1990), 32, suggests that "the Chinese cosmographers built their theories on the basis of an image of the world that they drew from their instrumental models. Sky charts, celestial globes, and armillary sphere seemed to them to be miniaturized reproductions of the cosmos."

11. *MQBT*, 237.

12. *MQBT*, 249.

13. *MQBT*, 238.

14. *MQBT*, 198. The word translated as 'random' here is *màn*, which has the sense of 'at will', 'in uncontrolled fashion'. Recall that *go* is 'Chinese surrounding chess', played with black and white counters on a board 19 by 19 in size.

15. Brenier, *et al.*, "Shen Gua et les sciences," 347–8 and 350, argue that Shen's "science" is

"wholly directed toward effective action," and is "indifferent to the search for truth in and of itself."

16. *MQBT*, 38.

17. *MQBT*, 81.

18. *MQBT*, 78–9.

19. Duan Chengshi, *Youyang zazu* [Miscellany from Youyang] (Tang dynasty; reprinted in the Wenyuan edition of the *Qinding Siku quanshu*, vol. 1047, Shangwu yinshu-guan: Taibei, 1983), 637–768 and 769–835.

20. Duan Chengshi, *Miscellany from Youyang*, 639.

21. Duan Chengshi, *Miscellany from Youyang*, 666.

22. Duan Chengshi, *Miscellany from Youyang*, 669.

23. Duan Chengshi, *Miscellany from Youyang*, 688.

24. Duan Chengshi, *Miscellany from Youyang*, 742.

25. Duan Chengshi, *Miscellany from Youyang*, 760. On this see also the last part of the section 'Humankind' in the present chapter.

26. Duan Chengshi, *Miscellany from Youyang*, 737.

27. Duan Chengshi, *Miscellany from Youyang*, 643–4.

28. Fang He, *et al.*, eds., *Zhongguo renming da cidian* [Large Chinese biographical dictionary] (Taixing shuju: Hong Kong, 1931), hereafter *ZGRMDCD*, 1056.

29. *WZZ*, 389, 766, 381, and 258–9, respectively.

30. The book has sometimes been drawn on as a source for social and economic history, as by the Fujian historian Fu Yiling. See his *Ming-Qing nongcun shehui jingji* [The social economy of villages in Ming and Qing times] (Sanlian: Beijing, 1961), 155–6, or his *Mingdai Jiangnan shimin jingji shitan* [Essay on the urban economy of Jiangnan in Ming times] (Shanghai renmin: Shanghai, 1963), 44, footnote 94.

31. *WZZ*, 14–15.

32. *WZZ*, 160–1. Even in the mid-eighteenth century certain English scientists were intrigued by such phenomena as 'fire set alight by water or ice'. See G. Bachelard, *La Formation de l'esprit scientifique*, 3rd edn (Vrin: Paris, 1957), 35.

33. *WZZ*, 1116–17.

34. *WZZ*, 1103–4.

35. *WZZ*, 1080–1.

36. *WZZ*, 21.

37. *WZZ*, 30.

38. Compiled in the first century CE.

39. *WZZ*, 51.

40. *WZZ*, 74.

41. *WZZ*, 397.

42. Compiled late in the tenth century by Li Fang and his collaborators.

43. *WZZ*, 317–18.

44. See chapter 4, pages 66 and 68–9.

45. *WZZ*, 360–1.

46. *WZZ*, 272.

47. Francis Bacon testified from *his personal experience* that warts could be cured by an application of bacon fat which was then removed, *and allowed to rot*, a process that took about seven months. See Bachelard, *L'Esprit scientifique*, 146.

48. *WZZ*, 127.

49. *WZZ*, 11–12.

50. *WZZ*, 13.

51. *WZZ*, 1059–60.
52. *WZZ*, 810–11.
53. *WZZ*, 155–6.
54. Facial expression, words, vision, hearing, and thought.
55. *WZZ*, 14.
56. *WZZ*, 709.
57. *WZZ*, 14–15.
58. *WZZ*, 13.
59. *WZZ*, 301–2.
60. *WZZ*, 304–5.
61. *WZZ*, 719.
62. *WZZ*, 741–2.
63. *WZZ*, 769.
64. *WZZ*, 773.
65. *WZZ*, 14.
66. *WZZ*, 780.
67. Literally, 'seeds'.
68. Elsewhere (*WZZ*, 161–2) Xie talks about the different fixities with which the different phases of matter 'received a form', water having the 'subtlest form' and losing it most swiftly, earth being the 'heaviest' and its form 'never gnawed away'. He gives no general discussion of forms or configurations.
69. *WZZ*, 783. Gaston Bachelard quotes the view expressed in an eighteenth-century letter that 'electricity' would be better called 'vivacity'. The writer went on: "We generally see that youth has much more of what we call *fire* and *vivacity* than old age . . . . Now, if animal life is to be ascribed to the same cause as electric fire, it will no longer be difficult to imagine the reason for the danger in having old people sleep together with children: since an old body contains much less of this fire than a young one, it is not surprising that it attracts some of this from the latter toward itself, the young body thereby losing its natural force and falling into a state of languor, as experience has always proven to be the case with infants." Retranslated from Bachelard, *L'Esprit scientifique*, 154.
70. *WZZ*, 714.
71. *WZZ*, 515.
72. *WZZ*, 801 and 820.
73. *WZZ*, 874.
74. *WZZ*, 859.
75. *WZZ*, 666–7.
76. *WZZ*, 226–7. Acquired immunity to micro-organisms?
77. *WZZ*, 297–8.
78. *WZZ*, 56.
79. *WZZ*, 692–3.
80. *WZZ*, 694.
81. Near Ningbo in the Southeast.
82. *WZZ*, 694.
83. *WZZ*, 696.
84. *WZZ*, 697.
85. *WZZ*, 693. A quite different view is discussed in the next chapter.
86. *WZZ*, 696.
87. *WZZ*, 692.
88. *WZZ*, 716.
89. *WZZ*, 719.

90. *WZZ*, 732–3.
91. *WZZ*, 735. *Phalacrocorax capillatus* is not vivaparous.
92. *WZZ*, 776.
93. *WZZ*, 788.
94. B. Shapiro, *Probability and Certainty in Seventeenth-Century England: A Study of the Relationships between Natural Science, Religion, History, Law, and Literature* (Princeton University Press: Princeton, N.J., 1983).
95. Nakayama Shigeru, *Academic and Scientific Traditions in China, Japan, and the West* (1974), translated J. Dusenbury (University of Tokyo Press: Tokyo, 1984), esp. chapter 4.
96. N. Elias, *The Civilizing Process: The History of Manners* (1939), translated E. Jephcott (Blackwell: Oxford, 1978, rev. edn 1994, 2 vols.), I, esp. chapter 2.
97. B. A. Elman, *From Philosophy to Philology: Intellectual and Social Aspects of Change in Late Imperial China* (Harvard University Press: Cambridge, Mass., 1984).
98. A. C. Crombie, *Styles of Scientific Thinking in the European Tradition* (3 vols., Duckworth: London, 1994), II:811, 829, 851, 948–9, 956, and 988–9.
99. *WZZ*, 68–9.
100. *WZZ*, 76–7.
101. *WZZ*, 65.
102. *WZZ*, 66.
103. See *WZZ*, 67 for an example.
104. *WZZ*, 857.
105. *WZZ*, 837.
106. *WZZ*, 818–19.
107. *WZZ*, 940.
108. *WZZ*, 1013.
109. *WZZ*, 848.
110. In the Chinese imperially promulgated lunar calendar.
111. *WZZ*, 849.
112. *WZZ*, 714–15.
113. *WZZ*, 83.
114. *WZZ*, 222–3.
115. *WZZ*, 386–7.
116. In fact by an insufficiency of iodine.
117. Modern Guangdong and Guangxi.
118. *WZZ*, 287.
119. *WZZ*, 297–8.
120. *WZZ*, 234–5.
121. In Shandong province.
122. *WZZ*, 230.
123. *WZZ*, 230.
124. *WZZ*, 277–8.
125. *WZZ*, 415–16.
126. *WZZ*, 421–2.
127. *WZZ*, 146.
128. *WZZ*, 277.
129. In Shandong.
130. See Elman, *Philosophy to Philology*, 212–21.
131. The *Bencao gangmu*. Georges Métailié, "Histoire naturelle et humanisme en Chine et en Europe au XVIe siècle: Li Shizhen et Jaques Dalechamp," *Revue d'histoire des sciences* XLIII.1 (1990), 353–74, describes the use of various classificatory criteria by Li, such as

size, type of stem, and the part eaten. He concludes that the *Bencao gangmu* was "a practical system whose end-purpose was not so much to allow the unambiguous identification of an unknown plant met with in nature, as an ordering . . . designed to give access to information that would facilitate a correct curative or preventative usage."

132. *WZZ,* 712.
133. *WZZ,* 813.
134. *WZZ,* 712–13.
135. *WZZ,* 57–8.
136. In modern Shanxi.
137. In other words, lightning.
138. *WZZ,* 60.
139. *WZZ,* 60–1.
140. *WZZ,* 58–9.
141. That is, without deliberate purpose.
142. This was probably ball lighting.
143. *WZZ,* 61–2.
144. No explanation is given of the maidservant's sin, if such there was.
145. *WZZ,* 62–3.
146. *Sapinum sebiferum.*
147. *WZZ,* 39.
148. *WZZ,* 39.
149. *WZZ,* 41.
150. *WZZ,* 25.
151. *WZZ,* 25–6.
152. *WZZ,* 29.
153. *WZZ,* 1061.
154. *WZZ,* 1064.
155. *WZZ,* 778.
156. *WZZ,* 781.
157. *WZZ,* 789.
158. Though see the pioneering work of Yim Shu-yuen, "Famine relief statistics as a guide to the population of sixteenth-century China: A case-study of Honan province," *Ch'ing-shih wen-t'i* 3.9 (Nov. 1978), which shows, for one province at least, that the official figures in late Ming may have only been a third of the correct total.
159. *WZZ,* 330.
160. *WZZ,* 331–2.
161. Modern Fuqing, south of Fuzhou.
162. The semilegendary 'well-field' system was an arrangement of the fields in a three-by-three grid (like that for ticktacktoe). Eight families farmed the eight outer fields for their own use, and cultivated the center one collectively to provide a tax for their lord. The Chinese character for 'well' looks like a three-by-three grid. Hence the name.
163. *WZZ,* 308–9.
164. *WZZ,* 334.
165. *WZZ,* 336.
166. *WZZ,* 818. See page 391 above for his earlier comment.
167. *WZZ,* 195–6. The date, given only by the sexagenary Chinese cycle, might have been 1543. If so, Xie would not have seen it personally.
168. *WZZ,* 113.

169. See F. L. Dunn, "Malaria," in K. F. Kiple, ed., *The Cambridge World History of Human Disease* (Cambridge University Press: Cambridge, 1993), esp. 856.

170. *WZZ*, 249–50.

171. *WZZ*, 227.

172. *WZZ*, 949–50.

173. *WZZ*, 818.

174. *WZZ*, 315–16.

175. *WZZ*, 48.

176. *WZZ*, 293.

177. *WZZ*, 307.

178. *WZZ*, 336.

179. *WZZ*, 80.

180. In Yongtai county in Fujian.

181. *WZZ*, 264.

182. It is worth noting that the translation of *nupu* by 'serfs' here can be justified by passages such as that on page 259 about markets in Shandong where "mules, horses, cattle, sheep, male and female serfs [*nu-bei*], and wives and children" were on sale. It may be that one should even say 'slaves'. Certainly 'servants' implies a degree of liberty that is not justified.

183. *WZZ*, 281–2.

184. *WZZ*, 285–6.

185. *WZZ*, 824. These are, respectively, *Plantago* spp., *Cerastium vulgatum*, *Marsilia quadrifolia*, and *Artemisia stellerana*. The first, third, and fourth of these can be found in B. Karlgren, *The Book of Odes: Chinese Text, Transcription, and Translation* (Museum of Far Eastern Antiquities: Stockholm, 1950), ##8, 15, and 13.

186. *WZZ*, 825. *Li*-plums are 'plums' generally, but probably mainly *Prunus salcina* and *P. communis*. *Mei*-plums are *P. mume*, the 'Japanese apricot'. Lotus buds are mentioned in Karlgren, *Odes*, #145.

187. *WZZ*, 826–7.

188. *WZZ*, 838.

189. *WZZ*, 826.

190. *WZZ*, 846.

191. *WZZ*, 845–6. *D. odora* has a sweet scent, but is toxic.

192. *WZZ*, 840.

193. *WZZ*, 842.

194. *WZZ*, 853–4.

195. *WZZ*, 854. This last phrase is a reference to the lines of Tao Yuanming, "Having picked, for tippling, chrysanthemums from beneath the eastern hedge, / I gaze wistfully at the southern hills, distant and changeless forever" translated on page 333 above.

12 *Imperial Dogma and Personal Perspectives*

1. B. Karlgren, *The Book of Odes: Chinese Text, Transcription, and Translation* (Museum of Far Eastern Antiquities: Stockholm, 1950), #258.

2. *Shangshu* [The scripture of documents] (Pre-Qin: reprinted in Ruan Yuan, ed., *Shisan jing zhushu* [The thirteen scriptures with notes and explanations] (Chūbun shuppansha: Kyōto, 1971), hereafter *ShSh*, I:406–7.

3. B. J. Mansvelt Beck, *The Treatises of Later Han: Their Authors, Sources, Contents and Place in Chinese Historiography* (Brill: Leiden, 1990), 163.

4. R. De Crespigny, *Portents of Protest in the Later Han Dynasty* (Faculty of Asian Studies with the Australian National University Press: Canberra, 1976), 23.

5. The entire collection is called the *Da Qing Shichao shengxun* [The sacred instructions of ten reigns of the Great Qing dynasty] (99 vols, n.p. and n.d. but evidently an official publication). The years covered are 1616 to 1874. Most references below are to the initials of the emperor's reign-period and the subsection-number for the relevant 'Jing Tian' section. These initials are: KX (Kangxi), YZ (Yongzheng) [1741], QL (Qianlong) [1799], JQ (Jiaqing) [1829], and DG (Daoguang) [c. 1856]. See *SCSX* in the Bibliography for more details.

6. E.g., *SCSX*, QL 29:2a, 5a, and 7a. Private imperial enthusiasm for Buddhism and Daoism was of course of long standing. On Yongzheng and Chan Buddhism, see A. Hummel, ed., *Eminent Chinese of the Ch'ing Period* (U.S. Government Printing Office: Washington D.C., 1943), 918.

7. Yang Qiqiao, Y*ongzheng-di ji qi mizhe zhidu yanjiu* [The Yongzheng emperor and his system of secret memorials] (Sanlian shuju: Hong Kong, 1981), 26.

8. De Crespigny, *Portents of Protest*, 11. De Crespigny also draws attention to the possible use of portents as a "means of conducting debate at one remove" in Court circles; see *Portents of Protest*, 15.

9. On the succession question, see Hummel, *Eminent Chinese*, 916–17, and also H. Kahn, *Monarchy in the Emperor's Eyes: Image and Reality in the Ch'ien-lung Reign* (Harvard University Press: Cambridge, Mass., 1971), 232 and 239, and Yang, *Yongzheng Secret Memorials*, 37–70.

10. *SCSX*, QL 2:1a.

11. For some background remarks as to why one has to be skeptical about how deeply entrenched they were see M. Elvin, "How did the cracks open? The origins of the subversion of China's late-traditional culture by the West," *Thesis Eleven* 57, 'East Asian Perspectives' (May 1999).

12. J. Chapman, "Climate," in J. L. Buck, ed., *Land Utilization in China* (1937; reprinted, Paragon: New York, 1964), 112: "percentage deviation about the annual mean precipitation [is] . . . about 30 per cent for the Wheat Region and become[s] higher as the mean annual precipitation decreases."

13. See R. B. Marks, "'It never used to snow': Climatic variability and harvest yields in late-imperial South China, 1650–1850," in M. Elvin and T.-J. Liu, eds., *Sediments of Time: Environment and Society in Chinese History* (Cambridge University Press: New York, 1998).

14. *SCSX*, KX 10:2a.

15. *SCSX*, KX 10:2b.

16. *SCSX*, KX 10:2b.

17. *SCSX*, QL 28:4b.

18. *SCSX*, YZ 8:2a

19. A real general, although stories about him differ, who became a god. See *Cihai* [Sea of phrases] (Zhonghua shuju: Shanghai, 1947), hereafter *CH*, 190, and E. T. C. Werner, *Dictionary of Chinese Mythology* (1932; reprinted, Julian Press: New York, 1961), 257–8. Kangxi had prohibited official sacrifices to Liu Meng.

20. An indirect reminder that Liu Meng was not an authorized deity.

21. Note that 'daemonic' does not carry the implication of 'demonic' that these beings are evil.

22. *Da Qing Taizu . . . Gao-huangdi shengxun* [Sacred instructions of Taizu of the Great Qing] (Qing; first preface 1686), hereafter *DQTZ GHD SX*, in *SCSX* 1:1b.

23. *Da Qing Taizong . . . Wen-huangdi shengxun* [Sacred instructions of Taizong of the Great Qing] (Qing), hereafter *DQTZ WHD SX*, in *SCSX*, 4:4ab.

24. *DQTZ WHD SX*, in *SCSX*, 1:3b.

25. *Da Qing Shizu Zhang-huangdi shengxun* [Sacred instructions of Shizu], hereafter *DQSZ ZHD SX*, in *SCSX*, 1:4b.

26. See A. Lui, *Two Rulers, One Reign: Dorgon and Shun-chih 1644–1660* (Faculty of Asian Studies, Australian National University: Canberra, 1989).

27. *SCSX*, KX 10:2a.

28. *SCSX*, KX 10:2a.

29. *SCSX*, KX 10:2b.

30. On Chinese hypatotheism (the belief in a 'top' god who is not, however, a unique god), see Elvin, "Transcendental breakthrough," in M. Elvin, *Another History: Essays on China from a European Perspective* (Wild Peony/Hawaii University Press: Sydney, 1996), 263–4.

31. *SCSX*, KX 10:4a.

32. Such as Xie Zhaozhe discussed in the previous chapter. See page 400 above.

33. *SCSX*, KX 10:3b.

34. Perhaps more appropriately, 'Board of Astrology'.

35. *SCSX*, KX 10:3b.

36. *SCSX*, YZ 1:1ab.

37. For another use of this phrase, see *SCSX*, YZ 1:6b.

38. *SCSX*, YZ 1:4b.

39. *SCSX*, YZ 1:6b.

40. Apart from lightning. See M. Elvin, "The man who saw dragons: Science and styles of thinking in Xie Zhaozhe's *Fivefold Miscellany*," *Journal of the Oriental Society of Australia* 25 and 26 (1993–4), 32–4.

41. V. Reichert, ed., *Job* (Soncino Press: London, 1946), chapter 21.

42. *SCSX*, YZ 1:1b.

43. *SCSX*, YZ 1:1b. See also 1:5a for another comparison with breathing.

44. *SCSX*, YZ 1:5a.

45. *SCSX*, YZ 1:5ab.

46. *SCSX*, YZ 1:7a.

47. *SCSX*, YZ 1:7b.

48. Yang, *Yongzheng Secret Memorials*, 27.

49. Yang, *Yongzheng Secret Memorials*, 28.

50. Yang, *Yongzheng Secret Memorials*, 28.

51. Yang, *Yongzheng Secret Memorials*, 28.

52. *SCSX*, YZ 8:3b.

53. *SCSX*, YZ 8:4a.

54. *SCSX*, YZ 8:7b.

55. *SCSX*, YZ 8:7ab.

56. One conventionally says 'he issued' but this avoids the question of how far he was advised to do so by his senior Court officials, and why.

57. *SCSX*, QL 27:1a.

58. On harvest percentile reports, see Marks, "'It never used to snow,'" 422–35.

59. *SCSX*, QL 27:4b.

60. *SCSX*, QL 27:4b. A similar case is listed in QL 28:7b.

61. *SCSX*, QL 28:4a.

62. *SCSX*, QL 29:1b–2a.

63. *SCSX*, JQ 14:8a.
64. It may be of interest to specialists that this sentence is contextually established as a counterfactual conditional, a grammatical form sometimes thought not to exist in Chinese. The structure here is *Ruo . . . , wei you . . . zhe.*
65. *SCSX*, JQ 14:8ab.
66. The major reigns of the mid-Qing were each in certain ways distinctive, and care should be taken not to generalize on the basis of the Yongzheng patterns presented here.
67. *Shizong shengxun* [Sacred instructions of the Shizong Emperor {= Yongzheng}], here-after *SZSX* (in *SCSX*), 22:2a.
68. *SZSX*, 24:1b.
69. *SZSX*, 12:5a.
70. *SZSX*, 25:1b.
71. *SZSX*, 25:4a.
72. *SZSX*, 26:5b–6a.
73. *SZSX*, 28:3a.
74. *SZSX*, 29:1b.
75. *SZSX*, 26:4b.
76. *Jiashen* in terms of the sixty-day cycle.
77. *Jiawu.*
78. *SZSX*, 28:2a.
79. *Xinyou.*
80. *SZSX*, 15:2a.
81. See E-tu Zen Sun, *Ch'ing Administrative Terms: A Translation of the Terminology of the Six Boards with Explanatory Notes* (Harvard University Press: Cambridge, Mass., 1961), #417.
82. *SZSX*, 15:2b.
83. *SZSX*, 2:3b.
84. *SZSX*, 20:4b.
85. Often also written 'Sungars', as in Hummel, *Eminent Chinese*, 9–10, etc.
86. Hummel, *Eminent Chinese*, 264. The Eleuths, Fudan's opponents, constituted the dominant tribes in Zungharia.
87. Hummel, *Eminent Chinese*, 916–17.
88. E.g., *SZSX* 1:3b and 6a.
89. *SZSX*, 2:4b–5a.
90. *SZSX*, 2:2a.
91. *SZSX*, 2:5a.
92. *SZSX*, 2:4ab.
93. *SZSX*, 2:1a.
94. The report is noted in *SZSX* 20:1b, for 8 January 1727.
95. *SZSX* 1:5a–6a.
96. There is a mismatch of one day here according to the *Liangqian-nian Zhong-Xi li duizhao biao* [A Sino-Western calendar for two thousand years, 1–2000 AD] (Shangwu yinshu-guan: Hong Kong, 1961) hereafter *ZXDB*. The cyclical character indicates 31 December. Note that here, exceptionally, I have converted the Chinese lunar-calendar dates into Western dates to make the pattern easier to follow.
97. There is the same one-day mismatch. The cyclical character indicates 4 February.
98. According to cyclical character dates, which may therefore be one day misaligned, as indicated above.
99. The day cycle again indicates a day later.
100. Karlgren, *Odes*, #235, "Wen Wang."

101. I would like to pay tribute here to Professor Wolfgang Kubin, of Bonn University, whose original idea for a conference on the feelings of 'ease' and 'unease' in Chinese culture inspired me to look at the topic treated in this first section, though the conference theme was later changed.

102. Zhang Yingchang, ed., *Qing shi duo* [The Qing bell of poesy] (originally *Guochao shiduo*, 1869; reprinted, Xinhua shudian: Beijing, 1960), hereafter *QSD*, 113–14.

103. *Qianmo.* See Sima Qian, *Shi ji* [Records of the Grand Historian] (Han; reprinted, Zhonghua shuju: Beijing, 1959), hereafter *SJ*, 'Qin benji', 5:203, and 'Shang-jun liezhuan', 2232.

104. *Fenhui.* A tentative rendering inspired by the fact that a *hui* could be an oxbow bend left behind where a river had previously meandered. See Morita Akira, "Water Control in Zhehdong during the later Ming" translated M. Elvin and K. Tamura, *East Asian History* 2 (Dec. 1991), 61, footnote 90.

105. *QSD*, 174–5.

106. The translation of the last few words of this line is tentative.

107. *Weirui*, or *Polygonatum officinale.*

108. *QSD*, 12.

109. *QSD*, 86.

110. *QSD*, 935.

111. *QSD*, 927–8.

112. *QSD* 579.

113. *QSD*, 554.

114. *QSD*, 454.

115. *QSD*, 440.

116. *QSD*, 479.

117. *QSD*, 473.

118. *QSD*, 142.

119. *QSD*, 143.

120. *QSD*, 175.

121. *QSD*, 13. 'Clasts' are sedimentary fragments of rock ranging in size from pebbles to boulders.

122. *QSD*, 107.

123. *QSD*, 132.

124. *QSD*, 131.

125. *QSD*, 123–4.

126. M. Elvin, "Why China failed to create an endogenous industrial capitalism: A critique of Max Weber's explanation," *Theory and Society* 13.3 (May 1984), 382.

127. *QSD* 122.

128. *QSD*, 117.

129. *Zhou*, that is one of the lowest-level administrative units, roughly on a level with a 'county' (*xian*).

130. *QSD*, 654.

131. *QSD*, 751.

132. *QSD*, 30.

133. *QSD*, 585.

134. *QSD*, 9.

135. *QSD*, 111. M. Loewe, "He Bo Count of the River, Feng Yi and Li Bing," in R. May and J. Minford, eds., *A Birthday Book for Brother Stone* (Chinese University Press: Hong Kong, 2003), 197–201.

136. *QSD*, 471.
137. *QSD*, 500.
138. *QSD*, 504.
139. *QSD*, 506.
140. *QSD*, 508.
141. For example, *QSD*, 248 and 706.
142. *QSD*, 527.
143. *QSD*, 515.
144. *QSD*, 75.
145. *QSD*, 166 and 169.
146. *QSD*, 749.
147. *QSD*, 758.
148. *QSD*, 150–2. Translated in M. Elvin, "Unseen lives: The emotions of everyday existence mirrored in Chinese popular poetry of the mid-seventeenth to the mid-nineteenth century," in R. T. Ames, R. Kasulis, and W. Dissanayake, eds., *Self as Image in Asian Theory and Practice* (State University of New York Press: Albany, N.Y., 1998), 118–26.
149. *QSD*, 756.

13 Concluding Remarks

1. K. Pomeranz, *The Great Divergence: China, Europe, and the Making of the Modern World Economy* (Princeton University Press: Princeton, N.J., 2002), esp. 239 and 283.
2. P. E. Will, "Clear waters versus muddy waters: The Zheng-Bai irrigation system of Shaanxi province in the late-imperial period," in M. Elvin and T.-J. Liu, eds., *Sediments of Time: Environment and Society in Chinese History* (Cambridge University Press: New York, 1998).
3. Missionaires de Pékin, *Mémoires concernant l'histoire, les sciences, les arts, les moeurs, les usages, &c. des Chinois*, vols. 1, 2, 4, 5, 8, and 11 (Nyon: Paris, 1776, 1777, 1779, 1780, 1782, and 1786), hereafter *MCC*, 11.334–42 describes the use of coal for domestic heating and some handicrafts, like smithy work, in eighteenth-century Beijing. It was sold by numerous shops, mostly in the form of briquettes in which the coal dust brought by carts to the capital was mixed with ashes, and a little earth and water, and then shaped in a mold. A small quantity of charcoal was usually needed to start these briquettes burning. It took about a thousand pounds ('livres') of this coal to heat a medium-sized room through the four months of winter.
4. Zhang Yingchang, ed., *Qing shi duo* [The Qing bell of poesy] (originally *Guochao shi duo*, 1869; reprinted, Xinhua shudian: Beijing, 1960), hereafter *QSD*, 174–5.
5. Full version on pages 439–40 above.
6. *QSD*, 927–8. Compare the version on page 442 above.
7. We need to use the term 'cross-boundary' rather than 'international' or 'interregional' here in order to leave open the decision as to what the most useful geographical units of comparison are in any given instance.
8. *MCC*, 11.267.
9. *MCC*, 11.268.
10. *MCC*, 1.ii.
11. *MCC*, 1.xiii.
12. *MCC*, 5, 'avertissement'.
13. *MCC*, 4.320–3.

14. Maisons de plaisance.
15. All from *MCC*, 4.323.
16. *MCC*, 11.187.
17. *MCC*, 2.407.
18. *MCC*, 11.196. The quotation marks are designed to pick up the fact that the entire passage in the original is in italics.
19. *MCC*, 8.293.
20. *MCC*, 8.295.
21. *MCC*, 8.298.
22. *MCC*, 2.414.
23. *MCC*, 4.318.
24. *MCC*, 11.226.
25. *MCC*, 11.218.
26. *MCC*, 11.225. The italics are in the original.
27. *MCC*, 2.402.
28. *MCC*, 11.227–8. Compare Xie Zhaozhe's views on pages 404–5.
29. *MCC*, 4.343.
30. W. Wagner, *Die chinesische Landwirtschaft* (Verlag Paul Parey: Berlin, 1926), 212.
31. Wagner, *Die chinesische Landwirtschaft*, 211.
32. Wagner, *Die chinesische Landwirtschaft*, 238.
33. Wagner, *Die chinesische Landwirtschaft*, 181.
34. Wagner, *Die chinesische Landwirtschaft*, 181.
35. Wagner, *Die chinesische Landwirtschaft*, 179.
36. Note, for example, the comment by Wagner, *Die chinesische Landwirtschaft*, 239, that "I will only stress that any progress through the present system of compensating for [consumed] plant nutrients is not possible. Only if new sources of plant nutrients are made available to the land, can the Chinese farm economy be capable of meeting the increased demands of a self-developing national economy. It is in the nature of things that synthetic fertilizers here become the unique issue. . . ." This theme is developed at length in the last part of M. Elvin, *The Pattern of the Chinese Past* (Stanford University Press: Stanford, Calif., 1973).

Bibliography

Abbreviations for primary sources

CCXZ *Chuci xuanzhu* [The Songs of the South, with selected notes], Ma Maoyuan, ed. Xinyue chubanshe: Hong Kong, 1962.

CH *Cihai* [Sea of phrases]. One-vol. edn.: Zhonghua shuju: Shanghai, 1947.

DQSZ ZHD SX *Da Qing Shizu Zhang-huangdi shengxun* [Sacred instructions of Shizu]. In *SCSX*.

DQTZ GHD SX *Da Qing Taizu . . . Gao-huangdi shengxun* [Sacred instructions of Taizu of the Great Qing]. Qing; first preface 1686. In *SCSX*.

DQTZ WHD SX *Da Qing Taizong . . . Wen-huangdi shengxun* [Sacred instructions of Taizong of the Great Qing]. Qing. In *SCSX*.

GSZ *Ganshui zhi* [Gazetteer for Ganshui]. Song. Chang Tang and Luo Shuhao, eds. Reprinted in Zhonghua shuju bianzhibu, ed., *Song-Yuan fangzhi congkan*. Zhonghua shuju: Beijing, 1990.

GY *Guoyu* [The tales of the various states]. Pre-Qin. Shanghai guji chubanshe: Shanghai, 1978.

GYFZ *Guiyang fuzhi* [Guiyang prefectural gazetteer]. Zhou Zuoji, comp. and rev. Guiyang-fu xueshu: Guiyang(?), 1850. Microfilm courtesy of Harvard-Yenching Library.

GZ *Guanzi jiping* [The *Master Guan* with collected appraisals]. Late fourth century BCE. Huang Jie and Lin Boxhou, eds., in Xiao Tianshi, gen. ed., *Zhongguo zixue mingzhu jicheng* #69. Zhongguo zixue mingzhu jicheng bianyin jijinhui: Taibei, 1978.

GZTZ *Guizhou tongzhi* [Comprehensive gazetteer of Guizhou]. 1741. Jing Daomo, *et al.*, comp. Reprinted, Huawen shuju: Taibei, 1968. Some passages are cited from the Siku quanshu edn., vol. 572, which is noted where applicable.

HNXZ *Haining xianzhi* [Gazetteer of Haining county]. 1765. Reprinted as *Zhongguo fangzhi congshu* #516, Huazhong. Chengwen: Taibei, 1983.

HNZ Huainanzi [The book of the Prince of Huainan]. 2nd century BCE. Reprinted, with Han-dynasty notes, from the 1804 edn., in Xiao Tianshi, gen. ed., *Zhongguo zixue mingzhu jicheng* #85. Zhongguo zixue mingzhu jicheng bianyin jijinhui: Taibei, 1978.

HTL Haitang-lu [A record of the seawall]. Di Junlian, ed., in *Qinding siku quanshu*, Shi-bu, *ce* 583. Compiled between 1764 and 1781. Reprinted, Taiwan shangwu yinshu-guan (Wenyuan-ge edn.): Taibei, 1986.

HZFZ /Q Hangzhou fuzhi [Hangzhou prefectural gazetteer]. 1898. Prefaces of 1888, 1894, and 1898. Reprinted in *Zhongguo fangzhi congshu* #199, Huazhong. Chengwen: Taibei, 1974.

JXFZ/M Jiaxing fuzhi [Jiaxing prefectural gazetteer]. 1600. Liu Yingke and Shen Shaozhong, eds. Reprinted in *Zhongguo fangzhi congshu* #505, Huazhong. Chengwen: Taibei, 1983.

JXFZ/Q Jiaxing fuzhi [Jiaxing prefectural gazetteer]. 1879. Xu Yaoguang *et al.*, rev., Wu Yangxian, *et al.*, comp. Reprinted in *Zhongguo fangzhi congshu* #53, Huazhong. 5 vols., Chengwen: Taibei, 1970.

LHJS Lun heng jiaoshi [Wang Chong's 'Discourses weighed in the balance', corrected and explained]. Han. Huang Hui, ed. 4 vols., Shangwu yinshuguan: Taibei, 1964.

LJ Liji [Records of ritual behavior]. Later Han [of earlier materials]. Reprinted in vol. 4 of *Jūsan kei chūso = Shisan jing zhushu* [The thirteen scriptures annotated and explained]. 7 vols., Chūbun shuppansha: Tokyo, 1971.

LZXJSZ Liezi xuanji sanzhong [Three selected versions of the *Liezi*]. Han? In Xiao Tianshi, gen. ed., *Zhongguo zixue mingzhu jicheng* 64. Zhongguo zixue mingzhu jicheng bianyin jijinhui: Taibei, 1978.

MCC Mémoires concernant l'histoire, les sciences, les arts, les moeurs, les usages &c des Chinois, par les Missionaires de Pékin, Vols. 1, 2, 4, 5, 8, and 11. Nyon: Paris, 1776–86.

MQBT Mengqi bitan [Jottings from {the garden of} the brook of dreams], by Shen Gua. Song. Hu Daojing, ed., as *Xinjiaozheng 'Mengqi bitan'*. Zhonghua shuju: Hong Kong, 1975.

QHDFJZWZ Qinghai difang jiu zhi wu-zhong [Five old local gazetteers from Qinghai]. Qing. Li Qing, ed. Reprinted, Qinghai Renmin chubanshe: Xining, 1989.

QSD Qing shi duo [The Qing bell of poesy] (originally *Guochao shiduo*). 1869. Zhang Yingchang, ed. Reprinted, Xinhua shudian: Beijing, 1960.

QW Quan shanggu sandai Qin-Han liuchao wen [Complete literature from high antiquity, the Three Dynasties, the Qin and Han, and the Six Dynasties]. Zhonghua shuju: Beijing, 1965.

RHXZ Renhe xianzhi [Renhe county gazetteer]. Reprinted in *Zhonghua fangzhi congshu* #179, Huazhong. Chengwen: Taibei, 1975.

SCSX [Da Qing] Shichao shengxun [The sacred instructions of ten reigns of the Great Qing dynasty [1616–1874], 99 vols. The first preface is from 1666, the last from 1880. There are no publication details, but dates of first printing of reign-period sections, where known, are appended in brackets to the list of abbreviations below. Each of these reigns has a full title in the general form 'Da Qing X zong (...) Y huangdi shengxun', where the dots in parentheses stand for the emperor's full formal title. 'Jing Tian' sections of these are referred to by the initials of the emperor's reign-period and the subsection number. These initials are: XH (Kangxi), YZ (Yongzheng) [1741], QL (Qianlong) [1799], JQ (Jiaqing) [1829], and DG (Daoguang) [*c.* 1856]. References to other parts of the *Instructions* are given by *juan* and double-page in the usual way. See also *DQSZ ZHD SX, DQTZ GHD SX,* and *DQTZ WHD SX.*

SGZ Sanguo zhi [Record of the Three Kingdoms]. Jin. Chen Shou, comp. Reprinted, Zhonghua shuju: Beijing, 1969.

ShSh Shangshu [The scripture of documents]. Pre-Qin. Reprinted in Ruan Yuan, ed., *Shisan jing zhushu* [The thirteen scriptures with notes and explanations]. Chūbun shuppansha: Kyōto, 1971.

SJ Shiji [Records of the Grand Historian], by Sima Qian, Han. Reprinted, Zhonghua shuju: Beijing, 1959.

SJS Shangjun shu jiegu dingben [The book of the Lord of Shang, definitive edition with explanations]. Pre-Qin. Zhu Shiche, ed. Guji chubanshe: Beijing, 1956.

SXFZ Shaoxing fu zhi [Gazetteer for Shaoxing prefecture]. 1719. Zhou Xucai, comp., and Yu Qing, rev. Reprinted in *Zhongguo fangzhi congkan,* #537, Huazhong. Chengwen: Taibei, 1983.

SZSX Shizong shengxun [Sacred instructions of the Shizong Emperor {= Yongzheng}]. In *SCSX.*

WX Wenxuan [The Chinese anthology]. Sixth century. Xiao Tong, comp., and Li Shan, annot., 1181 edn. Reprinted, 4 cases, Zhonghua shuju: Beijing, 1974.

WZZ Wu zazu [Fivefold miscellany], by Xie Zhaozhe. 1608. Reprinted under the supervision of Li Weizhen. Xinxing shuju: Taibei, 1971.

YL Yueling [Ordinances for the months]. Pre-Qin. In Chen Hao, ed., *Liji jishuo* [The Record of the Rites, with collected explanations]. Shijie shuju: Taibei, 1969.

ZGRMDCD Zhongguo renming da cidian [Large Chinese biographical dictionary]. Fang He, *et al.,* eds. Taixing shuju: Hong Kong, 1931.

ZGZRZYCS Zhongguo ziran ziyuan congshu [Series on the natural resources of China]. Zhongguo ziran ziyuan congshu bianzhuan weiyuanhui, ed. 42 vols., Zhongguo huanjing kexue chubanshe: Beijing, 1995. Volumes are mainly by province, some by topic.

ZHTZ Zunhua tongzhi [Zunhua department comprehensive gazetteer]. He Songtai, *et al.,* eds. Zunhua, ?1886. Microfilm courtesy of Columbia University Library. In some *juan* the pagination restarts in each subsection. Where necessary for clarity, the subsection heading is therefore included.

ZHXZ Zunhua xianzhi [Zunhua county gazetteer]. Zunhua xianzhi bianzuan weiyuanhui, ed. Hebei renmin chubanshe: Shijiazhuang, 1990.

ZL Zhouli zhushu [The Rituals of Zhou, with notes and explanations]. Late first millennium BCE. Ruan Yuan (Qing), ed., in *Shisan jing zhushu* [The thirteen classics with notes and explanations]. Reprinted, Zhonghua shuju: Beijing, 1980.

ZXDB Liangqian-nian Zhong-Xi li duizhao biao [A Sino-Western calendar for two thousand years, 1–2000 AD]. Shangwu yinshu-guan: Hong Kong, 1961.

ZYJHZ *Zhiyuan Jiahe zhi* [Gazetteer for Jiahe {≈ Jiaxing} in the Zhiyuan reign-period (1264–94)]. Yuan. Xu Shi, comp., Shan Qing, rev. Reprinted in Zhonghua shuju bianzhibu, ed., *Song-Yuan fangzhi congkan.* 8 vols., Zhonghua shuju: Beijing, 1990.

ZZD *Zhongguo ziran dili: Lishi ziran dili* [The natural geography of China: Historical natural geography]. Zhongguo kexue-yuan Zhongguo ziran dili bianji Weiyuanhui, ed. Zhongguo huanjing kexue chubanshe: Beijing, 1982.

ZZJS *Zhuangzi jishi* [The Zhuangzi, with collected explanations]. Guo Qingfan, ed. Zhonghua shuju: Beijing, 1961.

ZZZC *Zhongguo ziran ziyuan congshu* [Series on the natural resources of China]. Zhongguo ziran ziyuan congshu bianzhuan weiyuanhui, ed. 42 vols., Zhongguo huanjing kexue chubanshe: Beijing, 1995.

Books and articles

Agricola, Georgius [G. Bauer]. 1556. *De Re Metallica.* H. C. and L. H. Hoover, transl. and ed. 1912. Reprinted, Dover: New York, 1950.

Amelung, I. 1999. "Der Gelbe Fluss in Shandong (1851–1911): Überschwemmungskatastrophen und ihre Bewältigungen im spät-kaiserlichen China." Ph.D. thesis, Institut für Philosophie, Wissenschaftstheorie, Wissenschafts-und Technikgeschichte, Technische Universität Berlin.

Arthur, W. Brian. 1990. "Positive feedbacks in the economy," *Scientific American* 262.2 (Feb.).

Bachelard, G. 1957. *La Formation de l'esprit scientifique,* 3rd edn. Vrin: Paris.

Baechler, J. 1985. *Démocraties.* Calmann-Lévy: Paris.

Baechler, J. 2000. *Nature et histoire.* Presses Universitaires de France: Paris.

Baechler, J. 2002. *Esquisse d'une histoire universelle.* Fayard: Paris.

Bak, P. 1997. *How Nature Works: The Science of Self-Organized Criticality.* Oxford University Press: Oxford.

Barry, R. G. and R. J. Chorley. 1987. *Atmosphere, Weather and Climate,* 5th edn. Methuen: London.

Beck, B. J. Mansvelt. 1990. *The Treatises of Later Han: Their Authors, Sources, Contents and Place in Chinese Historiography.* Brill: Leiden.

Benedict, C. 1996. *Bubonic Plague in Nineteenth-Century China.* Stanford University Press: Stanford, Calif.

Berenbaum, M. 1994. *Bugs in the System: Insects and their Impact on Human Affairs.* Addison-Wesley: Reading, Mass.

Billeter, J. F., *et al.* 1993. "Florilège des *Notes du Ruisseau des Rêves* (Mengqi bitan) de Shen Gua (1031–1095)," *Études Asiatiques* XLVII.3.

Blunden, C. and M. Elvin. 1983. *Cultural Atlas of China.* Facts on File. New York. Rev. edn, Checkmark: New York, 1998.

Bodde, D. 1978. "Marshes in *Mencius* and elsewhere: A lexicographical note." In D. Roy and T. Tsien, eds., *Ancient China: Studies in Early Civilization.* Chinese University Press: Hong Kong.

Bonyhady, T. 1995. "Artists with axes." *Environment and History* 1.2.

Brenier, J. C., J. P. Diény, J.-C. Martzloff, and W. de Wieclawik. 1989. "Shen Gua (1031–1095) et les sciences." *Revue d'histoire des sciences* XLII.4.

Brown, J., A. Collings, D. Park, J. Philips, D. Rothery, and J. Wright. 1991. *Waves, Tides and Shallow-Water Processes*, rev. edn. Pergamon: Oxford.

Brunnert, H. S. and V. V. Hagelstrom. 1912. *Present Day Political Organization of China*, transl. A. Beltchenko and E. E. Moran. Kelly and Walsh: Shanghai. Anonymous reprint: Taibei, 1960.

Buck, J. L. (ed.). 1937. *Land Utilization in China*. University of Nanking: Nanking, 1937. Reprinted, Paragon: New York, 1964.

Burnet, F. McF. 1972. *Natural History of Infectious Diseases*, rev. edn. Cambridge University Press: Cambridge.

Cao Peikui, Gu Guochuan, Dong Yongfa, and Hu Fangxi. 1985. "Hangzhou-wan nisha yundong-de jiben tezheng" [The basic characteristics of sediment transport in Hangzhou Bay]. *Huadong Shifan Daxue xuebao* 3.

Cao Shuji. 2001. *Qing shiqi* [The Qing period]. In Ge Jianxiong, ed., *Zhongguo renkou shi* [History of China's population series], vol. 5, *Qing period*. Fudan daxue chubanshe: Shanghai.

Chamley, H. 1987. *Sédimentologie*. Dunod: Paris.

Chang, H. T. [Zhang Hongzhao]. 1926. "On the question of the existence of elephants and the rhinoceros in northern China in historical times." *Bulletin of the Geological Society of China* 5.

Chang, K.-C. 1980. *Shang Civilization*. Yale University Press: New Haven, Conn.

Chao Lin. 1982. *The Socio-Political System of the Shang Dynasty*. Academia Sinica: Taibei.

Chapman, J. 1937. "Climate." In J. L. Buck, ed., *Land Utilization in China*.

Chen, J., T. C. Campbell, J. Li, and R. Peto. 1990. *Diet, Life-style and Mortality in China: A Study of the Characteristics of 65 Chinese Counties*. Oxford University Press, Cornell University Press, and People's Medical Publishing House: Oxford.

Chen Jiaqi. 1987. "Nan Song yilai Taihu liuyu dalao-dahan ji jinqi qushi guji" [Major floods and droughts in the Lake Tai basin since the Southern Song, and an estimation of the trend in the near future]. *Dili yanjiu* 6.1 (Mar.).

Chen Jiyu, Luo Zude, Chen Dechang, Xu Haigen, and Qiao Pengnian. 1964. "Qiantang-jiang hekou shakan-de xingcheng ji qi lishi yanbian" [The formation of and the historical changes in the sandbar at the mouth of the Qiantang River]. *Dili xuebao* 30.2 (June).

Chen Qiaoyi. 1965. "Gudai Shaoxing diqu tianran senlin-de pohuai ji qi dui nongye-de yingxiang" [The destruction in ancient times of the natural forests of Shaoxing and its impact on agriculture]. *Dili xuebao* 31.2 (June).

Chen Qiaoyi. 1981. "Lun lishi shiqi Puyang-jiang xiayou-de hedao bianqian" [Changes in the lower course of the Puyang River in historical times]. *Lishi dili* 1.

Chen Rong. 1983. *Zhongguo senlin shiliao* [Historical materials on China's forests]. Xinhua: Beijing.

Chen Shu. 1963. *Qidan shehui jingji shigao* [Draft history of the society and economy of the Qidan]. Sanlian: Beijing.

Cheng Mingjiu (Hezhu). (comp.) 1702. *Sanjiangzha-wu quanshu* [Complete documents relating to the affairs of the lock at Three Rivers' Mouth]. Prefaces of 1684, 1685, and 1687. Republished with a continuation in 1854 (see Ping Heng).

Cheng Te-k'un [Zheng Dekun]. 1960. *Archaeology in China*, vol. 2, *Shang*. Heffer and Sons: Cambridge.

Chinese Academy of Sciences. 1982. *Zhongguo ziran dili* [Natural geography of China]. Kexue chubanshe: Beijing.

Chou Zhao'ao. (ed.) 1955. *Du Shaoling ji xiangzhu* [Du Fu's collected works with detailed notes]. 4 vols., Wenxue guji kanxingshe: Beijing.

Clastres, P. 1974. *Society against the State: Essays in Political Anthropology*. English translation, Zone Books: New York, 1987.

Cohen, M. 1989. *Health and the Rise of Civilization*. Yale University Press: New Haven, Conn.

Cook, F. 1977. *Hua-yen Buddhism*. Pennsylvania State University Press: University Park, Penn.

Corbin, A. 1988. *Le Territoire du vide: L'Occident et le désir du rivage, 1750–1840.* Aubier: Paris.

Couvreur, S. 1914. *Tch'ouen Ts'iou et Tso Tchouan: La Chronique de la principauté de Lou*. Reprinted, bilingual text, 3 vols., Cathasia: Paris, 1951.

Couvreur, S. 1911. *Dictionnaire classique de la langue chinoise*. Imprimerie de la Mission Catholique: Hejian fu.

Crombie, A. C. 1994. *Styles of Scientific Thinking in the European Tradition*. 3 vols., Duckworth: London.

Dali-zhou Wenlian [Literary Association of Dali {Yunnan}]. 2001. *Dali gu yishu chao* [Transcriptions of ancient lost books from Dali]. Yunnan Renmin chubanshe: Kunming.

De Crespigny, R. 1976. *Portents of Protest in the Later Han Dynasty*. Faculty of Asian Studies with the Australian National University Press: Canberra.

Delahaye, H. 1981. *Les Premières Peintures de paysage en Chine: Aspects religieux*. École française d'Extrême-Orient: Paris.

Deng Gang [Kent]. 1993. *Development versus Stagnation: Technological Continuity and Agricultural Progress in Pre-Modern China*. Greenwood: Westport, Conn.

Di Cosmo, N. 2002. *Ancient China and Its Enemies: The Rise of Nomadic Power in East Asian History*. Cambridge University Press: Cambridge.

Ding Yihui. 1994. *Monsoons over China*. Kluwer: Dordrecht.

Dodgen, R. 2001. *Controlling the Dragon: Confucian Engineers and the Yellow River in Late Imperial China*. University of Hawaii Press: Honolulu.

Duan Chengshi. Tang. *Youyang zazu* [Miscellany from Youyang]. Reprinted in Wenyuan edn of the *Qinding Siku quanshu*, vol. 1047. Shangwu yinshu-guan: Taibei, 1983.

Dunn, F. L. 1993. "Malaria." In K. F. Kiple, ed., *History of Human Disease*.

Dunstan, H. 1975. "The Late Ming epidemics: A preliminary survey." *Ch'ing-shih wen-t'i* 3.3.

Elias, N. 1994 (orig. 1939). *The Civilizing Process: The History of Manners*. Transl. E. Jephcott, Blackwell: Oxford. Rev. edn., 2 vols. Vol. 1 first published 1978.

Elman, B. A. 1984. *From Philosophy to Philology: Intellectual and Social Aspects of Change in Late Imperial China*. Harvard University Press: Cambridge, Mass.

Elvin, M. 1973. *The Pattern of the Chinese Past*. Stanford University Press: Stanford, Calif.

Elvin, M. 1975. "On water control and management during the Ming and Ch'ing periods," [a review article of Morita Akira, *Shindai suirishi kenkyū* {Studies on water control in the Qing dynasty} (Aki shobō: Tokyo, 1974)], *Ch'ing-shih wen-t'i* 3.3 (Nov.).

Elvin, M. 1977. "Market towns and waterways: The county of Shang-hai from 1480 to 1910." In G. W. Skinner, ed., *The City in Late Imperial China*. Stanford University Press: Stanford, Calif.

Elvin, M. 1984. "Why China failed to create an endogenous industrial capitalism: A critique of Max Weber's explanation." *Theory and Society* 13.3 (May).

Elvin, M. 1986. "Was there a transcendental breakthrough in China?" In S. N. Eisenstadt, ed., *The Axial Age and its Diversity*. State University of New York Press: Albany, N.Y. Reprinted in Elvin, ed., *Another History*.

Elvin, M. 1993. "Three thousand years of unsustainable growth: China's environment from archaic times to the present." *East Asian History* 6 (Nov.).

Elvin, M. 1993–4. "The man who saw dragons: Science and styles of thinking in Xie Zhaozhe's *Fivefold Miscellany*." *Journal of the Oriental Society of Australia* 25 and 26.

Elvin, M. and N. Su. 1995a. "Man against the sea: Natural and anthropogenic factors in the changing morphology of Harngzhou Bay, circa 1000–1800." *Environment and History* 1.1. (Feb.).

Elvin, M. and N. Su. 1995b. "Engineering the sea: Hydraulic systems and premodern technological lock-in in the Harngzhou Bay area circa 1000–1800." In Itō Suntarō and Yoshida Yoshinori, eds., *Age of Environmental Crisis*.

Elvin, M. (ed.) 1996. *Another History: Essays on China from a European Perspective*. Wild Peony/Hawaii University Press: Sydney.

Elvin, M. 1997. *Changing Stories in the Chinese World*. Stanford University Press: Stanford, Calif.

Elvin, M. 1998. "Unseen lives: The emotions of everyday existence mirrored in Chinese popular poetry of the mid-seventeenth to the mid-nineteenth century." In R. T. Ames, R. Kasulis, and W. Dissanayake, eds., *Self as Image in Asian Theory and Practice*. State University of New York Press: Albany, N.Y.

Elvin, M. and T.-J. Liu (eds.) 1998. *Sediments of Time: Environment and Society in Chinese History*. Cambridge University Press: New York.

Elvin, M. and N. Su. 1998. "Action at a distance: The influence of the Yellow River on Hangzhou Bay since AD 1000." In Elvin and Liu, eds., *Sediments of Time*.

Elvin, M. 1999a. "Blood and statistics: Reconstructing the population dynamics of late imperial China from the biographies of virtuous women in local gazetteers." In H. Zurndorfer, ed., *Chinese Women in the Imperial Past: New Perspectives*. Brill: Leiden.

Elvin, M. 1999b. "How did the cracks open? The origins of the subversion of China's late-traditional culture by the West." *Thesis Eleven* 57, 'East Asian Perspectives'.

Elvin, M., D. Crook, Shen Ji, R. Jones, and J. Dearing. 2002. "The impact of clearance and irrigation on the environment in the Lake Erhai catchment from the ninth to the nineteenth century." *East Asian History* 23 (June).

Fan Ye. c. 445. *Hou Han shu* [History of the Later Han]. Reprinted, Zhonghua shuju: Beijing, 1965.

Fang, J.-Q. and G. Liu. 1992. "Relationship between climatic change and the nomadic southward migrations in East Asia during historical times." *Climatic Change* 22.

Feng Erkang. 1992. *Yongzheng zhuan* [A life of the Yongzheng Emperor]. Taiwan shangwu: Taibei.

Fletcher, R. 1995. *The Limits of Settlement Growth: A Theoretical Outline.* Cambridge University Press: Cambridge.

Fox, B. and A. Cameron. 1997. *Food Science, Nutrition and Health*, 6th edn. Arnold: London.

Frodsham, J. D. 1967. *The Murmuring Stream: The Life and Works of the Chinese Nature Poet Hsieh Ling-yün (385–433), Duke of K'ang-Lo.* 2 vols., University of Malaya Press: Kuala Lumpur.

Fu Yiling. 1961. *Ming-Qing nongcun shehui jingji* [The social economy of villages in Ming and Qing times]. Sanlian: Beijing.

Fu Yiling. 1963. *Mingdai Jiangnan shimin jingji shitan* [Essay on the urban economy of Jiangnan in Ming times]. Shanghai renmin: Shanghai.

Fu Zehong (ed.). c. 1725. *Xingshui jinjian* [The golden mirror of the passing streams]. Reprinted, in Shen Yunlong, ed., *Zhongguo shuiliyaoji congbian,* Wenhai: Taibei, 1969.

Fujita Katsuhisa. 1986. "Kandai no Kōka shisui kikō" [Flood control measures on the Yellow River under the Han dynasty]. *Chūgoku suiri shi kenkyū* 16.

Garrow, J. and W. James (eds.). 1998. *Human Nutrition and Dietetics*, 9th edn. Churchill Livingstone: Edinburgh.

Gernet, J. 1972. *Le Monde chinois.* Colin: Paris.

Giles, H. 1912. *A Chinese–English Dictionary*, 2nd edn. Kelly and Walsh: Shanghai. Reprinted, Jingwen shuju: Taibei, 1964.

Giudici, N. 2000. *La Philosophie du Mont Blanc: De l'alpinisme à l'économie immatérielle.* Grasset: Paris.

Glacken, C. J. 1967. *Traces on the Rhodian Shore: Nature and Culture in Western Thought from Ancient Times to the End of the Eighteenth Century.* University of California Press: Berkeley, Calif.

Gledhill, J., B. Bender, and M. Larsen (eds.). 1988. *State and Society: The Emergence and Development of Social Hierarchy and Political Centralization.* Reprinted, London: Routledge, 1995.

Golson, J. 1997. "From horticulture to agriculture in the New Guinea Highlands: A case study of people and their environments." In P. Kirch and T. Hunt, eds., *Historical Ecology in the Pacific Islands.* Yale University Press: New Haven, Conn.

Gonda, J. 1979. *Les Religions de l'Inde,* vol. 1, *Védisme et hindouisme ancien.* Translated from the German; Payot: Paris.

Greenwood, L. H. 1935. *Epidemics and Crowd Diseases.* Macmillan: New York.

Grove, A. and O. Rackham. 2001. *The Nature of Mediterranean Europe: An Ecological History.* Yale University Press: New Haven, Conn.

Grove, R., V. Damodaran, and S. Sangwan (eds.). 1998. *Nature and the Orient: The Environmental History of South and Southeast Asia.* Oxford University Press: New Delhi.

Gu Shaobo and Wang Honglu. 1987. *Xie Lingyun-ji jiaozhu* [The works of Xie Lingyun with variant readings and notes]. Zhongzhou guji chubanshe: n.p. [He'nan].

Gu Yanwu (comp.). 1639–62. *Tianxia junguo libing shu* [Documents on the advantageous and disadvantageous aspects of the principates and commanderies of the empire]. Reprinted, Shangwu yinshuguan: Shanghai, 1936. Siku shanben facsimile reprint, reissued Taibei: n.d.

Gu Yingtai. 1658. *Mingshi jishi benmo* [Main themes and details of Ming history recounted]. Reprinted, 4 vols., Shangwu: Taibei, 1956.

Gu Zuyu (ed.). 1667. *Dushi fangyu jiyao* [Essential geography for the reading of history]. Reprinted, Xinxing: Taibei, 1972.

Guha, Sumit. 1999. *Environment and Ethnicity in India, 1200–1991.* Cambridge University Press: Cambridge.

Guo Zhengzhong. 1990. *Songdai yanye jingji shi* [An economic history of the salt industry during the Song dynasty]. Renmin chubanshe: Beijing.

Hallam, A. (ed.). 1977. *Planet Earth.* Phaidon: Oxford.

Hardy, A. 1998. "A history of migration to upland areas in 20th century Vietnam." Ph.D. thesis, Australian National University.

Hawkes, D. 1959. *Ch'u Tz'u: The Songs of the South.* Clarendon Press: Oxford. Revised edn, Penguin: London, 1985.

He Baochuan. 1991. *China on the Edge: The Crisis of Ecology and Development.* China Books: San Francisco, Calif.

Hoshi Ayao. 1966. *Chūgoku shakai-keizei-shi go-i* [Glossary of terms in China's social and economic history]. Kindai Chūgoku kenkyūsentā: Tokyo.

Hoshi Ayao. 1969. *The Tribute Grain Transport under the Ming Dynasty.* Transl. M. Elvin, Center for Chinese Studies: Ann Arbor, Mich.

Hoshi Ayao (comp.). 1975. *Chu⁻goku shakai keizai shi go-i zokuhen* [Supplement to 'A glossary of terms in Chinese social and economic history']. Ko⁻bundo⁻: Yamagata.

Hou Xueyu. 1988. *Zhongguo ziran dili* [The natural geography of China], vol. 2, *Zhiwu dili* [Vegetation geography]. Kexue chubanshe: Beijing.

Hou Yunqin (Comp. and rev.) 1854/55. *Dengchuan zhouzhi* [Dengchuan department gazetteer]. Reprinted, Chengwen chubanshe: Taibei, 1968.

Hughes, J. D. 1994. *Pan's Travail: Environmental Problems of the Ancient Greeks and Romans.* Johns Hopkins University Press: Baltimore, Md.

Hummel, A. (ed.). 1943. *Eminent Chinese of the Ch'ing Period.* 2 vols., U.S. Government Printing Office: Washington D.C.

Itō Hashiko. 1986. "Sōdai no Kōka shisui kikō" [The structure of flood control on the Yellow River under the Song dynasty]. *Chūgoku suiri shi kenkyū* 16.

Itō Suntarō and Yoshida Yoshinori (eds.). 1995. *Nature and Humankind in the Age of Environmental Crisis.* International Research Center for Japanese Studies: Kyoto.

Jeník, J. 1979. *Pictorial Encyclopedia of Forests.* Hamlyn: London.

Ji Han. Fourth century CE. *Nanfang caomu zhuang* [The forms of the plants and trees of the South]. Transl. Hui-lin Li, *A Fourth Century Flora of Southeast Asia,* Chinese University Press: Hong Kong, 1979.

Jin Weixian. 1981. *Qidan-de Dongbei zhengce* [The administrative policies of the Qidan in Manchuria]. Huashi chubanshe: Taibei.

Kahn, H. 1971. *Monarchy in the Emperor's Eyes: Image and Reality in the Ch'ien-lung Reign.* Harvard University Press: Cambridge, Mass.

Kaizuka Shigeki. 1979. *Chūgoku kodai sai hakken* [Further discoveries about Chinese antiquity]. Iwanami: Tokyo.

Kalinowski, M. 1990. "Le Calcul du rayon céleste dans la cosmographie chinoise." *Revue d'histoire des sciences* XLIII.1.

Karlgren, B. 1950. *The Book of Odes: Chinese Text, Transcription, and Translation.* Museum of Far Eastern Antiquities: Stockholm.

Karlgren, B. 1957. *Grammata Serica Recensa.* Museum of Far Eastern Antiquities: Stockholm.

Katz, P. R. 1995. *Demon Hordes and Burning Boats: The Cult of Marshal Wen in Late Imperial Chekiang.* State University of New York Press: Albany, NY.

Kawakatsu Mamoru. 1992. *Min-Shin Kōnan nōgyō keizai-shi kenkyū* [Researches on the farm economy of Ming and Qing Jiangnan]. Tōkyō Daigaku shuppankai: Tokyo.

Keightley, D. 1978. *Sources of Shang History: The Oracle-Bone Inscriptions of Bronze Age China.* University of California Press: Berkeley, Calif.

Keightley, D. 1999. "The environment of ancient China." In M. Loewe and E. Shaughnessy, eds., *The Cambridge History of Ancient China.* Cambridge University Press: Cambridge. Now greatly expanded as *The Ancestral Landscape: Time, Space, and Community in Late Shang China.* Institute of East Asian Studies, University of California: Berkeley, 2000.

Kellert, S. R., and E. O. Wilson (eds.). 1993. *The Biophilia Hypothesis,* Island Press: Washington D.C.

Kellert, S. R. 1995. "The Biophilia Hypothesis: Aristotelian echoes of the 'Good Life.'" In Itō and Yoshida, *The Age of Environmental Crisis.*

Kellert, S. R. 1997. *Kinship to Mastery: Biophilia in Human Evolution and Development.* Island Press/Shearwater Books: Washington D.C.

Kiple, K. F. (ed.). 1993. *The Cambridge World History of Human Disease.* Cambridge University Press: New York.

Lamb, H. H. 1995. *Climate, History and the Modern World.* Routledge: London.

Lamp, C. A., S. J. Forbes, and J. W. Cade. 1990. *Grasses of Temperate Australia.* Inkata Press: Melbourne.

Lawlor, R. 1991. *Voices of the First Day: Awakening in the Aboriginal Dreamtime.* Inner Traditions International: Rochester, Vt.

Lee, J. and Wang Feng. 1999a. "Malthusian models and Chinese realities: The

Chinese demographic system 1700–2000." *Population and Development Review* 25 (1).

Lee, J. and Wang Feng. 1999b. *One Quarter of Humanity: Malthusian Mythology and Chinese Realities, 1700–2000.* Harvard University Press: Cambridge, Mass.

Legge, J. 1861. *The Works of Mencius,* volume 2 in *The Chinese Classics with a Translation, Critical and Exegetical Notes, Prolegomena, and Copious Indexes.* 7 vols., Trübner: London.

Leonard, J. 1996. *Controlling from Afar: The Daoguang Emperor's Management of the Grand Canal Crisis, 1824–1826.* Center for Chinese Studies, University of Michigan: Ann Arbor, Mich.

Leopold, A. 1949. *A Sand County Almanac and Sketches Here and There.* Oxford University Press: New York.

Lewis, M. E. 1990. *Sanctioned Violence in Early China.* State University of New York Press: Albany, N.Y.

Lewis, M. E. 1999. *Writing and Authority in Early China.* State University of New York Press: Albany, N.Y.

Leys, S. [P. Ryckmans]. 1997. *The Analects of Confucius.* Norton: New York.

Li Bozhong. 1990. *Tangdai Jiangnan nongye-de fazhan* [The development of agriculture in Jiangnan under the Tang dynasty]. Nongye chubanshe: Beijing.

Li Bozhong. 1998. "Changes in climate, land, and human efforts: The production of wet-field rice in Jiangnan during the Ming and Qing dynasties". In Elvin and Liu, eds., *Sediments of Time.*

Li Shizhen. 1596. *Bencao gangmu* [Pharmacopeia arranged by headings and subheadings]. Reprinted, 5 vols. and index, Shangwu yinshuguan: Shanghai, 1930.

Li Yuan. 1794. *Shu shuijing* [The classic of the waterways of Sichuan]. Reprinted, 2 vols., Ba-Shu shushe: Chengdu, 1985.

Li Yuanfang. 1991. "Fei-Huanghe sanjiaozhou-de yanbian" [Changes in the deltas of the abandoned Yellow River]. *Dili xuebao* 10.4.

Li Zhiyang (ed.). 1563. *Jiajing Dali fuzhi* [Jiajing reign-period Dali prefectural gazetteer]. Incomplete. Microfilm 1055 in the Menzies Library, Australian National University.

Lin Chengkun. 1989. "Changjiang-kou nisha-de laiyuan fenxi yu shiliang jisuan-de yanjiu" [Analysis of the sources and quantities of sediments at the estuary of the Yangzi River]. *Dili xuebao* 44.1.

Lin Chengkun. 1990. "Changjiang yu Hangzhou-wan-de nisha yu hechuang yanbian dui Shanghai ji qi tonghai hangdao jianshe-de yingxiang" [The influence of the sediment in the Yangzi River estuary and Hangzhou Bay, and changes in the river bed, on the port of Shanghai and the construction of shipping channels giving access to the sea]. *Dili xuebao* 45.1.

Lin Hongrong. 1985. "Sichuan gudai senlin-de bianqian" [Changes in the ancient forests of Sichuan] and "Lishi shiqi Sichuan senlin-de bianqian" [Changes in the forests of Sichuan during the historical period], in four continuous parts. *Nongye kaogu* 9.1 and 10.2.

Lin Lüzhi. 1973. *Xianbi shi* [A history of the Xianbi]. Bowen shuju: Hong Kong.

Liu Ts'ui-Jung. 1998. "Han migration and the settlement of Taiwan: The onset of environmental change." In Elvin and Liu, eds., *Sediments of Time.*

Liu Ts'ui-Jung. 1999. "Zhongguo lishi-shang guanyu shanlinchuanze-de guannian he zhidu" [The concepts and institutional forms relating to mountains, forests, rivers, and marshes in Chinese history]. In Cao Tianwang, Lai Jingchang, and Yang Jiancheng, eds., *Zhongyang yanjiuyuan Zhongshan renwen shehui kexue yanjiusuo juanshu* 46. Academia Sinica: Taibei.

Liu, T.-J., J. Lee, and A. Morita (eds.). 2001. *Asian Population History.* Oxford University Press: Oxford.

Liu Yang and E. Capon. 2000. *Masks of Mystery: Ancient Chinese Bronzes from Sanxingdui.* Art Gallery of New South Wales: Sydney.

Liu Zongyuan. Tang. *Liu Zongyuan ji* [Collected works of Liu Zongyuan]. Zhonghua shuju: Taibei, 1978.

Loewe, M. 2003. "He Bo Count of the River, Feng Yi and Li Bing." In R. May and J. Minford, eds., *A Birthday Book for Brother Stone.* Chinese University Press: Hong Kong.

Lombard-Salmon, C. 1972. *Un Exemple d'acculturation chinoise: La province de Guizhou.* École française d'Extrême-Orient: Paris.

Lui, A. 1989. *Two Rulers, One Reign: Dorgon and Shun-chih 1644–1660.* Faculty of Asian Studies, Australian National University: Canberra.

Macfarlane, A. 1997. *The Savage Wars of Peace.* Blackwell: Oxford.

MacPherson, K. 1998. "Cholera in China, 1820–1930: An aspect of the internationalization of infectious disease." In Elvin and Liu, eds., *Sediments of Time.*

Maddalena, A. 1970. "Rural Europe 1500–1750." In C. M. Cipolla, ed., *The Fontana Economic History of Europe.* Collins: Glasgow. Reprinted, Collins: Glasgow, 1974.

Maisels, C. K. 1999. *Early Civilizations of the Old World: The Formative Histories of Egypt, The Levant, Mesopotamia, India and China.* Routledge: London.

Mann, M. 1998. "Ecological change in North India: Deforestation and agrarian distress in the Ganga–Yamuna Doab 1800–1850." In Grove, *et al.,* eds., *Nature and the Orient.*

Marks, R. B. 1998a. *Tigers, Rice, Silk, and Silt.* Cambridge University Press: New York.

Marks, R. B. 1998b. "'It never used to snow': Climatic variability and harvest yields in late-imperial South China, 1650–1850". In Elvin and Liu, eds., *Sediments of Time.*

Matsuda Yoshirō. 1986. "Shindai no Kōka shisui kikō" [The structure of flood control on the Yellow River under the Qing dynasty]. *Chūgoku suiri shi kenkyū* 16.

Mei Zengliang [Boyan]. Qing. *Bojian shanfang wenji* [Collected works from the Bojian Studio]. In *Zhonghua wenshi congshu* 12. Jinghua shuju: Taibei, 1968.

Menzies, N. 1988. "Trees, fields, and people: The forests of China from the seventeenth to the nineteenth centuries". Ph.D. thesis, University of California, Berkeley, Calif. Microfilm volume 8916794, U.M.I.: Ann Arbor, Mich., 1991.

Menzies, N. K. 1996. *Forestry,* vol. VI.3 of J. Needham, ed., *Science and Civilisation in China.* Cambridge University Press: Cambridge.

Menzies, N. K. 1998. "The villagers' view of environmental history in Yunnan province." In Elvin and Liu, eds., *Sediments of Time.*

Métailié, G. 1990. "Histoire naturelle et humanisme en Chine et en Europe au XVIe siècle: Li Shizhen et Jacques Dalechamp." *Revue d'histoire des sciences* XLIII.1.

Mitchell, L. and P. Rhodes (eds.). 1997. *The Development of the Polis in Archaic Greece*. Routledge: London.

Morin, H. 1935. *Entretiens sur le paludisme et sa prévention en Indochine*. Imprimerie d'Extrême-Orient: Hanoi.

Morita Akira. 1965. "Kōetsu ni okeru kaitō no suiri soshiki" [The hydraulic organization for sea-walls in Jiangsu and Zhejiang provinces]. Reprinted in Morita, *Researches on the History of Water Control under the Qing Dynasty*.

Morita Akira. 1974. *Shindai suirishi kenkyū* [Researches on the history of water control under the Qing dynasty]. Aki shobō: Tokyo.

Morita Akira. 1991. "Water control in Zhehdong during the later Ming." Transl. M. Elvin and K. Tamura, *East Asian History* 2 (Dec.).

Nakahara Teruo. 1959. "Shindai sōsen ni yoru shōhin ryūtsū ni tsuite" [The flow of commodities on grain-transport ships during the Qing dynasty]. *Shigaku kenkyū* 72.

Nakayama Shigeru. 1974. *Academic and Scientific Traditions in China, Japan, and the West*. Transl. J. Dusenbury, University of Tokyo Press: Tokyo, 1984.

[British] Naval Intelligence Division. 1945. *China Proper*, vol. 3. HMSO: Edinburgh.

Needham, J. with Wang Ling. 1959. *Science and Civilisation in China*, vol. 3, *Mathematics and the Sciences of the Heavens and the Earth*. Cambridge University Press: Cambridge.

Needham, J. with Wang Ling. 1965. *Science and Civilisation in China*, vol. 4.II, *Mechanical engineering*. Cambridge University Press: Cambridge.

Needham, J. with Wang Ling and Lu Gwei-djen. 1971. *Science and Civilisation in China*, vol. 4.III, *Civil Engineering and Nautics*. Cambridge University Press: Cambridge.

Obi Kōichi. 1963. *Chūgoku bungaku ni aratawareta shizen to shizenkan* [Nature and the concept of nature in Chinese literature]. Iwanami shoten: Tokyo.

Ōki Yasushi. 1988. "Feng Menglong 'Shan'ge' no kenkyū" [Studies on the 'Mountain Ditties' of Feng Menglong]. *Tōyō bunka kenkyūjo kiyō* 105.

Osborne, A. 1989. "Barren mountains, raging rivers: The ecological and social effects of changing land-use on the Lower Yangzi periphery in late-imperial China." Ph.D. thesis, Columbia University, New York. Microfilm volume #9020586, U.M.I: Ann Arbor, Mich., 1991.

Pearce, F. 2000. "Tidal warming." *New Scientist* 1.iv.

Perkins, D. 1969. *Agricultural Development in China 1368–1968*. Edinburgh University Press: Edinburgh.

Ping Heng. 1854. *Sanjiangzha-wu quanshu xuke* [Supplement to the *Complete Documents Relating to the Affairs of the Lock at Three Rivers' Mouth*]. Prefaces of 1835 and 1836. See Cheng Mingjiu.

Polanyi, K. 1968. *Primitive, Archaic and Modern Economies*. G. Dalton, ed. Doubleday: New York.

Pomeranz, K. 2002. *The Great Divergence: China, Europe, and the Making of the Modern World Economy*. Princeton University Press: Princeton, N.J.

Qian Ning, Xie Hanxiang, Zhou Zhide, and Li Guangbing. 1964. "Qiantang-jiang hekou shakan-de jindai guocheng" [Fluvial processes in recent times of the sandbar at the mouth of the Qiantang River {authors' own translation}]. *Dili xuebao* 30.2 (June).

Qiu Guangming. 1992. *Zhongguo lidai du-liang-heng kao* [Researches on measures of length, capacity, and weight in the successive Chinese dynasties]. Kexue chubanshe: Beijing.

Qu Dajun. 1700. *Guangdong xinyu* [New comments on Guangdong]. Reprinted, Zhonghua shuju: Hong Kong, 1974.

Qu Tuiyan. 1964. *Han Wei Liuchao fu xuan* [Selected rhapsodies from the Han, Wei, and Six Dynasties period]. Reprinted, Shanghai Guji chubanshe: Shanghai, 1979.

Radkau, J. 2000. *Natur und Macht: Eine Weltgeschichte der Umwelt*. Beck: München.

Reichert, V (ed.). 1946. *Job*. Bilingual text, Soncino Press: London.

Richardson, S. D. 1990. *Forests and Forestry in China*. Island Press: Washington D.C.

Rickett, W. A. 1985. *Guanzi: Political, Economic, and Philosophical Essays from Early China*. Vol. 1. Princeton University Press: Princeton, N.J.

Rickett, W. A. 1998. *Guanzi: Political, Economic, and Philosophical Essays from Early China*. Vol. 2. Princeton University Press: Princeton, N.J.

Roddricks, J. V. 1992. *Calculated Risks: The Toxicity and Human Health Risks of Chemicals in our Environment*. Cambridge University Press: Cambridge.

Roetz, H. 1984. *Mensch und Natur im alten China: Zum Subjekt-Objekt-Gegensatz in der klassischen chinesischen Philosophie: Zugleich eine Kritik des Klischees vom chinesischen Universismus*. Lang: Frankfurt am Main.

Roetz, H. 2000. "On nature and culture in Zhou China." Paper presented to the conference at Rheine, March 2000, on "Understanding Nature in China and Europe until the Eighteenth Century." Unpublished.

Sakuma Kichiya. 1980. *Gi Shin Nanboku-chō suiri-shi kenkyū* [A study of the history of water control under the Wei, the Jin and the Northern and Southern Dynasties]. Kaimei shoin: n.p.

Satō Taketoshi. 1962. *Chūgoku kodai kogyō-shi no kenkyū* [Researches on industries in ancient China]. Yoshikawa kōbunkan: Tokyo.

Shapiro, B. 1983. *Probability and Certainty in Seventeenth-Century England: A Study of the Relationships between Natural Science, Religion, History, Law, and Literature*. Princeton University Press: Princeton, N.J.

Shen Yue. 492–3. *Song shu* [The history of the Song]. Reprinted, Zhonghua shuju: Beijing, 1974.

Sheng Honglang (ed.). 1991. *Jianhu yu Shaoxing shuili* [Mirror Lake and water control in Shaoxing]. Zhongguo shudian: Beijing.

Sheng Hongyuan and Qiu Zhirong. 1991. "Woguo zuizao-de rengong yunhe zhi yi: Shanyin gu shuidao" [One of the oldest man-made waterways in our land: The old Shanyin canal]. In Sheng, ed., *Mirror Lake and Water Control*.

Shiba Yoshinobu. 1970. *Commerce and Society in Sung China*. Transl. M. Elvin, Michigan University Center for Chinese Studies: Ann Arbor, Mich.

Shiba Yoshinobu. 1988. *Sōdai Kōnan keizai-shi no kenkyū* [Researches on the economic history of Jiangnan under the Song]. Tōyō Daigaku Tōyō Bunka Kenkyūjo: Tokyo.

Shima Kunio. 1958. *Inkyo bokuji kenkyū* [Researches on the divination texts from the ruins of Yin]. Kyūko shoin: Tokyo.

Shirakawa Shizuka. 1972. *Kōkotsubun no sekai* [The world of the oracle bone script]. Heibonsha: Tokyo.

Shirakawa Tadahisa. 1994. *Tō Enmei to sono jidai* [Tao Yuanming and his age]. Kembun shuppan: Tokyo.

Shuili shuidian kexue yanjiu-yuan and Wuhan shuili dianli xueyuan (eds.). 1979. *Zhongguo shuili-shi gao* [Draft history of water control in China]. *Shang* and *xia* only.

Skinner, G. W. 1977. "Regional urbanization in nineteenth-century China." In G. W. Skinner, ed., *The City in Late Imperial China*, Stanford University Press: Stanford, Calif.

Song Zhenhao. 1994. *Xia-Shang shehui shenghuo shi* [Social life under the Xia and Shang]. Zhongguo shehui kexue chubanshe: Beijing.

Su Dongpo [Su Shi]. Song. *Su Dongpo quanji* [Complete works of Su Dongpo]. Seven collections in 13 vols., Hanguo wenhua kanhanghui: Seoul, 1983.

Su Dongpo. 1097–1101. *Dongpo Zhilin* [Su Dongpo's miscellany]. Reprinted in a topical ordering, Zhonghua shuju: Beijing, 1981.

Su Shi. Song. *Su Dongpoji* [Collected works of Su Dongpo]. Shangwu yinshu-guan: Shanghai, 1939.

Sugimoto Kenji. 1974. "Chūgoku kodai no mokuzai ni tsuite" [Timber in ancient China]. *Tōhō gakuhō* (Mar.).

Sun, E-tu Zen. 1961. *Ch'ing Administrative Terms: A Translation of the Terminology of the Six Boards with Explanatory Notes.* Harvard University Press: Cambridge, Mass.

Sun Xiangping, *et al.* 1981. *Zhongguo yan'an haiyang shuiwen qixiang gaikuang* [An outline of the hydrological patterns and weather of China's coastal seas]. Kexue chubanshe: Beijing.

Sung Ying-hsing [Song Yingxing]. Ming. *T'ien-kung k'ai-wu. Chinese Technology in the Seventeenth Century*. Transl. E-tu Zen Sun and Shiou-chuan Sun, Pennsylvania State University Press: University Park, Penn., 1966.

Sutō Yoshiyuki. 1954. *Chūgoku tochi-seido-shi kenkyū* [Studies of land tenure systems in China]. Tokyo University Press: Tokyo.

Swabe, J. 1999. *Animals, Disease and Human Society: Human–Animal Relations and the Rise of Veterinary Medicine*. Routledge: London.

Tani Mitsutaka. 1991. *Mindai Kakō-shi kenkyū* [Studies on the hydraulics of the Yellow River in the Ming dynasty]. Dōhōsha: Kyōto.

Thorp, J. 1937. 'Soils'. In Buck, ed., *Land Utilization in China*.

Tian Wen. Qing. *Qian shu* [The book of Guizhou]. In Yan Yiping (Qing), ed., *Yueya-tang congshu*, case 36 in *Baibu congshu jicheng* [Collection of collections on all topics], reprinted by Yiwen Yinshu-guan: Taibei, 1965–8, in 4145 vols., 830 cases. The ':::' in citations indicates the number preceding is that of the 'case'.

Tsuruma Kazuyuki. 1987. "Shōsuikyo Tokōen Teikokukyo wo tazunete: Shin teikoku no keisei to Senkokuki no san daisuiri jigyō" [A visit to the Zhang river canal, the Du river dike, and the Zheng Guo canal: On the formation of the Qin empire and the three great hydraulic schemes of the Warring States period]. *Chūgoku suiri shi kenkyū* 17.

Tulishen. 1723. *Yiyu lu* [An account of unfamiliar lands]. Manchu/Chinese texts in Imanishi Shunjū, ed., *Jiaozhu yiyu lu*, Tenri: n.p., 1964.

Tuotuo, *et al.* (eds.). Yuan. *Jin shi* [History of the Jin]. Reprinted, Zhonghua shuju: Beijing, 1975.

Tuotuo, *et al.* (eds.). Yuan. *Song shi* [History of the Song]. Reprinted, Zhonghua shuju: Beijing, 1977.

Ueda Makoto. 1999. *Mori to midori no Chūgoku-shi: Ekorojikaru-hisutorii no kokoromi* [Chinese history in terms of its forests and vegetation: A tentative essay in ecological history]. Iwanami shoten: Tokyo.

Vermeer, E. 1987. "P'an Chi-hsün's solutions for the Yellow River problems of the late sixteenth century." *T'oung Pao* LXXIII.

Vermeer, E. 1998. "Population and ecology along the frontier in Qing China." In Elvin and Liu, eds., *Sediments of Time.*

Von Zach, E. 1958. *Die chinesische Anthologie: Übersetzungen aus dem Wen hsüan.* Harvard University Press: Cambridge, Mass.

Wagner, W. 1926. *Die chinesische Landwirtschaft.* Verlag Paul Parey: Berlin.

Waley, A. 1937. *The Book of Songs.* Allen and Unwin: London.

Wan Yansen. 1989. "Subei gu Huanghe sanjiaozhou-de yanbian" [Changes in the old delta of the Yellow River in northern Jiangsu]. *Haiyang yu huzhao* 20.1.

Wang Chi-wu. 1961. *The Forests of China, with a Survey of Grassland and Desert Vegetation.* Harvard University Press: Cambridge, Mass.

Wang Shuizhao (ed.). 1984. *Su Shi xuanji* [An anthology from Su Shi (Dongpo)]. Shanghai guji chubanshe: Shanghai.

Wang Zhibin. 1980. "Huanghe wenti-de jidian kanfa—dui Wei.Jin.Nanbeichao" [Some understanding of the issue of the Yellow River during the Wei, the Jin, and the Northern and Southern Dynasties]. *Renmin Huanghe* 5.

Wang Zhibin. 1984. "Kaifeng Huanghe jueyi mantan" [A general discussion of the breaking of the Yellow River dikes at Kaifeng]. *Renmin Huanghe* 4.

Waring, R. H. and S. W. Running. 1998. *Forest Ecosystems: Analysis at Multiple Scales.* 2nd edn., Academic Press: San Diego, Calif.

Watabe Tadayo and Sakurai Yumio (eds.). 1984. *Chūgoku Kōnan no inasaka bunka* [The rice culture of Jiangnan in China]. Nihon shōsō shuppan kyōkai: Tokyo.

Wen Huanran, *et al.* 1995. *Zhongguo lishi shiqi zhiwu yu dongwu bianqian yanjiu* [Studies on changes in plants and animals in China during historical times]. Chongqing chubanshe: Chongqing.

Werner, E. T. C. 1932. *Dictionary of Chinese Mythology.* Reprinted, Julian Press: New York, 1961.

Westbrook, F. A. 1972. "Landscape description in the lyric poetry and 'Fuh on Dwelling on the Mountains' of Shieh Ling-yunn". Ph.D. thesis, Yale University, New Haven, Conn. Microfilm volume #7316410, U.M.I.: Ann Arbor, Mich., 1973.

Wiens, H. J. 1967. *Han Chinese Expansion in South China,* 2nd edn. [Originally published as *China's March to the Tropics,* 1954). Shoe String Press: Hamden, Conn.

Will, P. E. 1998. "Clear waters versus muddy waters: The Zheng-Bai irrigation system of Shaanxi province in the late-imperial period." In Elvin and Liu, eds., *Sediments of Time.*

Wittfogel, K. A. 1931. *Wirtschaft und Gesellschaft Chinas.* Harrassowitz: Leipzig.

Wittfogel, K. A. 1957. *Oriental Despotism.* Yale University Press: New Haven, Conn.

Wu Qihua [Wu Chi-hua]. 1970. "Huanghe zai Mingdai gaidao qianxi hejue Zhangqiu-de niandai" [On the date of the breach at Zhangqiu just prior to the change of course of the Yellow River in the Ming dynasty]. In Wu Qihua, ed., *Mingdai shehui jingji shiluncong* [Collected historical essays on the society and economy of the Ming dynasty]. Taiwan xuesheng shuju: Taibei.

Wu Zhenyu. Nineteenth century. *Yangjizhai conglu* [Collected records from the Yangjizhai Studio]. Printed from the MS, Zhejiang guji chubanshe: Hangzhou, 1985.

Xie Qiyi. 2000. "Wudai ci-zhong-de 'shan' yixiang yanjiu" [The conceptional representation of the 'mountain' in the lyric songs of the Five Dynasties]. Master's thesis, National Taiwan Normal University: Taibei.

Xu Hailiang. 1990. "Huanghe xiayou-de duiji lishi fazhan qushi" [The history and trend of development of the sedimentary deposits in the lower reaches of the Yellow River]. *Zhongguo shuili xuebao* 7.

Xu Jinxiong. 1988. *Zhongguo gudai shehui* [Ancient Chinese society]. Taiwan shangwu yinshuguan: Taibei.

Yabuuchi Kiyoshi (ed.). 1967. *Sō-Gen jidai kagaku gijutsu* [Science and technology in the Song and Yuan period]. Jimbun kagaku kenkyūjo: Kyoto.

Yabuuchi Kiyoshi. 1974. *Chūgoku bummei no keisei* [The formation of Chinese civilization]. Tokyo: Iwanami.

Yamada Keiji. 1967. "Sōdai no shizen tetsugaku: Sōgaku ni okeru no ichi ni tsuite" [The Song philosophy of nature: Its place in Song learning]. In Yabuuchi, ed., *Science and Technology in the Song and Yuan Period.*

Yan Bao (arra. and annot.). 1993. *Hxak Lul Hxak Ghot: Miaozu guge* [Hxak Lul Hxak Ghot. Ancient songs of the Miao race]. Guizhou minzu chubanshe: Guiyang.

Yang Kuan. 1993. *Zhongguo gudai ducheng zhidu shi yanjiu* [Researches in the history of the systems of the capital cities of Chinese antiquity]. Shanghai guji chubanshe: Shanghai.

Yang Qiqiao. 1981. *Yongzheng-di ji qi mizhe zhidu yanjiu* [The Yongzheng emperor and his system of secret memorials]. Sanlian shuju: Hong Kong.

Yang Tongsheng, *et al.* (eds.). 1985. *Hxat Khat: Kaiqin ge* [Hxat Khat: Songs on the occasion of the formation of alliances through marriage]. Guizhou-sheng minzu yanjiu-suo: Guizhou.

Yang Xiaoneng. 2000. *Reflections of Early China: Decor, Pictographs, and Pictorial Inscriptions.* Nelson-Atkins Museum of Art with the University of Washington Press: Seattle, Wash.

Yao Hanyuan. 1991. "Zhedong yunhe-shi kaolüe" [A summary of a historical investigation into the Zhedong Canal]. In Sheng, ed., *Mirror Lake and Water Control.*

Ye Qingchao. 1986. "Shilun Subei fei-Huanghe sanjiaozhou-de fayu" [On the development of the abandoned Yellow River delta]. *Dili xuebao* 41.2 (June).

Yim Shu-yuen. 1978. "Famine relief statistics as a guide to the population of sixteenth-century China: A case-study of Honan province." *Ch'ing-shih wen-t'i* 3.9 (Nov.).

Yoshida Teigo. 1989. "Umi no kosumorojii" [The cosmology of the sea]. In Akira Gotô, *et al.*, eds., *Rekishi ni okeru shizen* [Nature in history]. Iwanami: Tokyo.

Yoshinami Takashi. 1981. "Chūgoku kodai santaku-ron no saikentō" [A re-examination of the theories about 'mountains and marshes' in ancient China]. In Chūgoku Suiri Shi Kenkyūkai, ed., *Chūgoku suiri shi ronshū* [A collection of essays on the history of water control in China]. Kokusho kanōkai: Tokyo.

Yu Yue (ed.). 1872. *Tongzhi Shanghai xianzhi* [Gazetteer of Shanghai county for the Tongzhi reign]. Shanghai.

Yuan Qinglin. 1990. *Zhongguo huanjing baohu shihua* [Historical discussions on the conservation of nature in China]. Zhongguo huanjing kexue chubanshe: Beijing.

Zhang Yixia and M. Elvin. 1998. "Environment and Tuberculosis in Modern China." In Elvin and Liu, eds., *Sediments of Time*.

Zhang Juncheng. 1985. "Shang-Yin lin kao" [A study of forests under the Shang-Yin dynasty]. *Nongye kaogu* 1.

Zhang Tingyu (ed.). Qing. *Ming shi* [History of the Ming dynasty]. Reprinted, Zhonghua shuju: Beijing, 1974.

Zhou Sheng, Ni Haoqing, Zhao Yongming, Yang Yongchun, Wang Yifan, Lü Wende, and Liang Baoxiang. 1992. "Qiantangjiang shuixia fanghu gongcheng-de yanjiu yu shijian" [Research and practice relating to the protective underwater engineering on the Qiantang River]. *Shuilixuebao* 1.

Zürcher, E. 1959. *The Buddhist Conquest of China*. Brill: Leiden.

Index

administration, terms for divisions of, 476 n. 10
aggregate pressure proportion, 458, 467
agriculture *see* cultivated trees; farming; garden-farming
alchemy, cinnabar and, 245, 249; *see also* Daoist quest for physical immortality
alders, cultivation of for fuel, 64
An Bangyan, and Miao uprisings, 228, 229, 254
ancestors, Zhou religion and, 98
animals, disappearance of species, 359; and morality, 269; in *The Qing Bell of Poesy*, 453; relationship of humans to, 308, 313; as symbolic vehicles for moralizing, 453; Xianbi and, 280, 281; in Xie Lingyun's "Living in the Hills", 356, 359; in Zunhua, 307–8, 310–12; *see also* pets; wild animals
Anopheles mosquito, 262; forests and, 29, 29–30; *see also* malaria
arboriculture *see* cultivated trees
art, and nature, xx
assimilation to Han Chinese culture, of Guizhou landscape, 235; of Miao, 216, 225, 240
assimilation to Qidan culture, of Han Chinese laborers, 282

Baechler, Jean (*Esquisse d'une histoire universelle*), on war and development, 87, 88
Bai Canal, 122–3
bamboo, and book production, 59; cultivation of, 21–2; and engineering, 59; natural forests of, 40; and tubing for brine wells, 66–9; and tubing for natural gas, 66, 67–9; in Xie Lingyun's "Living in the Hills", 354
banyan, 72
bats, 309
Bauer, Georg (*De Re Metallica*), 249
Bell of Poesy see Qing Bell of Poesy, The
betel nut, 71, 264
birds, and the numinous, 359; relationship of humans to, 308, 313; in Xie Lingyun's "Living in the Hills", 358, 359; in Zunhua, 307–9; *see also* pets

births, spacing of, and fertility, xix
Boai, cultivation of bamboo in, 21
bodhisattva ideal, 362
Book of Changes, 76, 238, 260, 321, 363
Book of Guizhou see Tian Wen
Book of the Lord of Shang, on regulation of exploitation of forests and marshes, 104
Book of the Prince of Huainan, on Daoist critique of the state and development, 108–10; on elephants and rhinoceroses, 12
books, use of trees for production of, 59
botanical revolution of Ming dynasty, 207
bridges, 187–90, 200, 202; in Guizhou, 252–7; over Pan River, 254–5; as symbols of Han Chinese cultural domination in Guizhou, 255; warfare and, 254
brine wells, use of bamboo in, 66–9
bronze inscriptions, on Zhou quasi-feudal landed economy, 100–1
Buddhism and Buddhist monks and monasteries, 259, 260, 271; and bridges, 189; and caves, 259; and the environment, 470; farmland for support of, 183–4; and forests, 78, 79; and holy parks and groves, 361; and hunting, 359, 361; landscape and, 321; trees associated with, 73; in Xie Lingyun's "Living in the Hills", 332, 337, 362, 363, 363–4, 364; *see also* bodhisattva ideal; enlightenment
buffers *see* bureaucratic buffer against inadequate harvests; climatic buffer in times of drought; environmental buffer against inadequate harvests
buildings and architecture, and Chinese colonialism and imperialism, 255
bureaucracy, 102; supernatural, 267–8
bureaucratic buffer against inadequate harvests, 193–4, 203; *see also* climatic buffer in times of drought; environmental buffer against inadequate harvests
bureaucratized maintenance of water-control systems, 124

cable bridges, use of wood and bamboo in, 69–70